See what others have said about Peter A Hubbard's 'Tears' trilogy

The US Review of Books *"The result is a masterclass of investigative acumen, psychological insight, and global coordination."*

HOLLYWOOD Book Reviews *"The writing style has a literary structure that crafts poignant visuals drawing you into the intensity of the moment, such as a mushroom cloud described with sooty grey contrails against the blue sky and compared to a canvas from Dante's Inferno."*

Pacific Book Review *"The action and intensity of the plot balanced out the depth of relationship building that occurred with this cast of characters, from the protagonist's own traumatic past that brought her into the field and into a life of government and military service, to the tragedies which befell the children who would become the faces behind the movement which these terrorists fuel their campaign with."*

Christina Avina-Professional Book Reviewer *"As a fan of this genre, I was enthralled with the author's writing and was even more moved by the rich themes developed in this book, including the heavy look at the morality behind those who are radicalized or brainwashed into committing such heinous actions after having witnessed or experiencing their own brand of injustice early on in life. The cycle of violence and destruction plays a major role in this thriller."*

http://peterahubbardbooks.com/

the tears of wonder

BOOK TWO OF THE TRILOGY

PETER A. HUBBARD

ISBN: 979-8-88945-191-4 (paperback)
ISBN: 979-8-88945-193-8 (hardback)
eISBN: 979-8-88945-192-1

Brilliant Books Literary
137 Forest Park Lane Thomasville
North Carolina 27360 USA

Mollydookers
ADVERTISING I DESIGN I DIGITAL I PRINT

Look for the psychological thrillers by Peter A Hubbard

The Tears of Hope
The Tears of Wonder
The Tears of Joy
The Island of Tears

https://peterahubbardbooks.com/

This book is dedicated to Lyla Brooks, Agent extraordinaire, without whom this would not have been possible.

Flashback

The Boss stood; everyone else in the conference room ringed outside by Israeli soldiers in full combat gear sat, mostly uncomfortable on the small metal chairs. They formed a circle, so everyone could see everyone else without turning their heads, and for once, there wasn't a single presence of electronic equipment in evidence. On the contrary, a massive sign on one wall said, "אזהרה! איןמכשירימאלקטרונייםמורשים, זהומתקןואטומומאאובטח. עוש." I wondered how many years of jail time I would serve if I breached the no electronics rule, then forgot about it as the Boss started to talk.

"Firstly, thank you, Colonel, for your excellent performance in bringing down Shetani and his mercenaries and for your support in getting Mohammad bin Azaria and his henchmen." The Israeli Sgen Aluf, head of the Shayete 104 commando troop, looked anything else but happy, the stoic look on his face giving nothing away. "Colonel, Tom, I'm asking you both to leave at this point and pass our thanks to your men and women for excellent work." Tom, who Pete had forewarned that this would happen, stood, smiled, looked directly at the Boss, and saluted. He walked out behind the Israeli commando, whose body language was anything but compliant.

"We now enter a difficult phase of our investigation, and I'm going to hand over to Captain Riley to summarize where we are and what we will do next." And he sat down in the seat vacated by Tom and looked expectantly at me. I looked around the faces I was now so familiar with, Indigo with his little smile, as if all was right with the world; Anna, a little grim-faced, probably still lagged from her flight

9

back across the Atlantic; Pete, relaxed, although anyone who knew him would easily spot his eyes casually scanning every inch of the room. Arie, looking all his years, the past weeks had taken a heavy toll on him, yet the sparkle in his grey eyes was encouragement in itself. General Bridget Saunders, now dressed in mufti, looking like someone's mother but not able to disguise her military bearing. She had flown over with Anna, an afterthought by the president, who was feeling distinctly not in control of her country or the events that were unraveling at such a frantic rate.

The room we were in had been organized by the local Interpol office in Tel Aviv, and in recognition of this, Senior Agent Beth Arezzo was also sitting in. As I had had the pleasure of briefing her just an hour ago, I was again impressed by the caliber of agents Interpol attracted.

At just thirty-two, she ran one of the busiest offices in the area and worked under the same duress as every other Israeli citizen from the constant rocket attacks on the city.

She was married, had a child, and dressed like a fashion model, currently wearing a tight red sheath with a purple-and-gold scarf dropping between her arms. A lightweight cotton jacket in peach completed the ensemble, no doubt concealing her weapon and credentials. She also spoke five languages like a native. I stood up, breathed in deeply, held my hands loosely in front, and relaxed as far as possible. "We have Mohammad bin Azaria and his lawyer secured and under guard; we have left the Jesuit priest to his own devices, but we have asked him to remain to be debriefed sometime tomorrow. The electronics and intelligence we recovered from both successful attacks are now being examined, and we expect the first summary within the next hour. This meeting aims to determine exactly what we will do from here on and who will be responsible for each activity.

"While we have used paramilitary tactics against the terrorists and the mercenaries, this is, still, essentially a police action. Interpol has been commissioned by several countries as well as those represented here to discover and bring to justice the persons responsible for the attacks that were initiated last month in Italy, Jerusalem, Abu Dhabi, the United States, and, more recently, the international consortia that controlled the International Space Station.

"Our investigations uncovered the mercenaries led by Shetani, who was responsible for at least two mass bombings, the destruction of the Arabia oil field, and the destruction of some three hundred and fifty oil and gas pipelines and fracking sites. Needless to say, every country impacted by these attacks has requested us to add their support to our mandate, which we have accepted on the condition that all political interference be withheld until a satisfactory outcome has been achieved."

"And what, exactly, do you think a 'satisfactory outcome' looks like?" asked the general in a tone more suited to the parade ground than a meeting of the minds. I turned slightly to look at her and sensed the Boss flexing his shoulders, a sure sign he was going to jump in, so I paused in my reply to let him do so.

He didn't.

I continued.

"For some days, we have been working closely with one of the refugees who was groomed to participate in developing the technology weapons used in the attacks. She quit and ran, years before the attacks were launched.

"Apart from helping us to uncover the internet destruction, she had records of her time with some of the other participants, who we are now identifying and tracking.

"When you look at the possibility of combining what the Jesuit priest can tell us, what your secretary of state can tell us, the intelligence we are now unraveling, we may well get a better understanding of how to find the refugees who did participate in the attacks."

"You'll have to go through the president to get to the Secretary," the General barked, "and you'll have to go through me to get to the president."

"We understand the circumstances. We have been briefed by both Roger and Julius." The general seemed to be thinking about something; she nodded to herself and tilted her head to one side. She looked directly at me with an intensity I felt in my bones. She held up one manicured hand, her perfect nails showing just a hint of clear polish, and ticked off her fingers, one by one.

"So, firstly, you have identified and taken out of play a mercenary terrorist crew in Canada responsible for shutting off the oil and gas pipelines as well as destroying the fracking sites across northern America and Canada. Secondly," as another finger flicked up, "you seemed to have solved the UAV attacks on the sports arenas, at least in the US." I held her eyes, determined to hear everything she had to say before I acknowledged anything.

"Then you have masterminded an attack on Arabia, forcing the third regime change in two weeks, destroying the mercenary terrorist leader Shetani in the process." She watched me for any reaction and saw none; I played poker with people so hard to read you had to actually rely on the cards you were dealt! A wan smile crossed her eyes, her thin lips struggling to follow.

"Fourthly, you have identified, located, and captured the banker and prime suspect in the organization of all the attacks and currently have him here somewhere under guard." I held her eyes as hard as I could, not giving any sign of acknowledgment. The silence in the room was deafening; I could almost hear everyone breathing. She wasn't exactly attacking us, but her tonality suggested she was after something, but I wasn't sure what it might be. I nodded, just once, to see what she would say next. Her hand opened up so all fingers could be seen as she ticked off the last on her list.

"The problem I'm having is seeing exactly where a military action starts and stops, and a police one takes over." The tension in the room ratcheted up a notch, and I saw Pete stiffen out of the corner of my eye and Indigo visibly lean forward as if to pounce on the general. Before I could answer, the Boss stood up again, rolled his shoulders as if preparing for a physical fight, and motioned for me to take my seat.

"General, as you would know, my unit within Interpol is authorized to engage and utilize military forces as and when we see fit. As you know, our standing guard is made up of US Special Forces on loan to us from the Pentagon.

"The two attacks in the desert were led by an Israeli Colonel supported by Israeli commandos, whom you have been introduced to, and Interpol simply provided an observer in each of those two attacks. And before you point it out, yes, we had more boots on the ground when we took down bin Azaria; the situation was judged to warrant it. And don't forget the Canadians and all the other countries who have used lethal force in attacking the various arms of Shetani's net-work of mercenaries, including your very own, on several occasions, all without any Interpol presence." The look she gave the Boss was anything but contrite; the edges of her face would have cut glass. If there was one thing the Boss hated, it was Monday morning quarter-backing. The general, to her credit, immediately sat back as far as her little metal chair would allow and shook her head.

"Colonel, I apologize if it seemed I was attacking your tactics. I fully realize we would not be as far down the comeback road as we are without the excellent efforts of Interpol and your team. I was just trying to see where the line in the sand was; please put it down to bad manners and bloody-mindedness." The Boss visibly relaxed, and with one simple gesture, the tension drifted out of the room. Pete sat back, Indigo relaxed, and even I felt some existential crisis had been avoided. But I still did not know what was behind her verbal attack.

"General, we're all a little wound up, and I suspect if you have had as little sleep as my people, more than just a little tired. The fact remains, and I freely admit it, we have used national troops for vari-ous parts of our investigation, with the overt approval and under the direct control of each country involved. In the case of the mercenaries, we provided intelligence to some sixteen countries, and each country then dealt with them as they saw fit—the US is one of those coun-tries. All within our mandate. And I took the measure of checking in with the director of your FBI, NSA, and CIA, and even yourself and the president, as warranted before we initiated any direct action." He flexed his shoulders again, looked down at his scuffed boots, raised his eyes in surprise, then looked up back at the group. Maybe he had meant to clean them?

"So as for a satisfactory outcome, while we have involved the politicians at every step so far, what we do next will be determined by what evidence and data we can analyze and which direction it suggests we move in. And to answer your unasked question, no, we may not collaborate with anyone nation-state at that point. The next moves will be an Interpol police action, full stop."

"You suspect a nation-state of masterminding the attacks, or at least covert support of the banker?" she asked.

"We have from the very start. The fact that the earliest attack on the computer systems in the US and Europe took place on the back of the Y2K debacle, now over twenty-five years ago, which would make the women we are chasing just out of nappies at that time, means that someone was setting all this up well before the use of the refugees was even thought of. Or, at the very least, concurrently. We have a statement from the Jesuit priest that the discussion regarding taking the children occurred around twenty years ago; we can't be definite, but we might get closer to the actual date once we chat with him tomorrow.

"Whatever that outcome, someone paid a lot of talented people for decades setting all this up. Look at the chronology—backdoors were set up in secure systems; tactical munitions were stolen from secured storage and transshipped around the world; aircraft and UAVs are either stolen or purchased outright and secreted in—we think, but can't prove yet—Turkey; a decommissioned nuclear missile base is taken over, refurbished, extended, all under the noses of both state and federal authorities; state-of-the-art technology weapons are developed out in the open initially at least two world-class universities we know of, then moved underground and perfected. In fact, we have evidence that an early version of the nanomachines that took out the world's oil pipelines were trialed off the coast of Nova Scotia in full public view! The resources needed to support all this were more than just a handful of talented women. No doubt they played a part, but someone else played a much bigger one for nearly thirty years."

"How many women from the refugee camps do you think were involved?"

"Good question. In fact, a great question. Indigo?" The Boss turned, then yielded the floor to our Italian head-of-station in Italy. His thickset body was in direct contrast to the Boss's, but you couldn't miss his natural swagger or, for a change, his perfect English. Must be wanting to impress the general!

"General, Colonel, good people, our computer experts, with the help of Anna and the FBI, have run simulations working backward from the ground zeros of the attacks, based on the real-time mirror-attacks, both the Colonel and the Captain ran. Allowing for the Hercules and the UAV to have been housed in Turkey, adjacent to the terrorist base we discovered there, we estimate one woman pilot, one engineer, and or one technology specialist. There would have to have been a support crew at some point to keep the aircraft in flyable condition, and the bombs and missiles maintained, but they could have been locally hired from the airport. That is being ascertained as we speak by local authorities."

"Two to three women for the attack on the Vatican and the Dome of the Rock!" the general exclaimed, her tonality dripping with disbelief and sarcasm.

"Yes, at a minimum, but easily doable with the right equipment and training."

"The Grand Mosque? Lloyds of London? The nuclear attack on the Arabian oil field? The bombings in Avion? The UAV attacks in England and Germany?" Deftly, the general had held up her fingers again, counting off the attacks. She stopped at five, looking very hard at Indigo. He wasn't ruffled one bit by the intensity or harsh tone, choosing to smile and bow ever so slightly towards her.

"General, I know this is on the very edge of believable, but then, I would suggest if we had come to you a month ago with an outline that these attacks were even possible, I believe you would have laughed us out of the room as conspiracy theorists." The general latched her fingers together, shut her eyes for a minute, obviously getting herself under control. There was something behind her continued aggression; I wished I could divine it.

"Colonel, I apologize; I am letting all this get to me when I should be listening to your reports and helping you move forward. Please forgive me." Indigo bowed slightly again, a huge smile causing his whole face to light up.

"*Generale, per favore, capisco il tuo dolore, questo ha causato a tutti noi un po 'di dolore, e noicomprendiamo il tuo.*"

"*Colonnello, lei è troppo gentile. Per favore, continuate. Dovreicongratularmi con lei per isuoieccellentisforzi, non appendendo il mio dolore personale al collo.*" We all smiled, Italian being a second language for all of us except Indigo, and were warmed by the general's words.

"So, General, to answer your questions, we believe that the order of battle was-the Grand Mosque, mercenaries; Lloyd's was the women, the nuclear attack on the Arabian oil fields was the mercenaries using a weapon developed by the women; Avion was the mercenaries, and lastly, the UAV attacks were mercenaries using weapons designed by the women." She nodded, the list obviously lining up with one she had in her head.

"Just humor me for a minute. What makes you so sure Avion was the mercenaries?"

"The investigators found no bodies in the burnt-out trucks. Mercenaries are not known for self-sacrifice or becoming suicide bombers." She nodded again, then seemed to relax a little. She played the finger game again.

"How about the attack on West Point, the Alaskan pipeline, the Australian gas terminal, and the Russian/Chinese pipeline attacks?"

"West Point was the women, as was the space station. The pipelines, gas terminals, and fracking sites were mercenaries using weapons provided by the women."

"You see a distinct difference in the roles and responsibilities here?"

"Yes, we do. The women provided the weapons, the hardware, and possibly the tactical plan, although, to be frank, we can't prove that, and our best strategists have summarized that our nation-state player might eventually get the credit for that. We do not believe the women played any physical role in any bombings, truck-based UAV attacks, or oil and gas system attacks other than, and not yet proven, the design, manufacture, and fitting of the UAV bombs in the trucks and possibly communication—as in giving the 'go' order. In a sense, you have them as the planners, designers, inventors, creators, and possibly the manufacturers, although we have yet to track that down. The mercenaries were the hired hands that did all the on-the-ground dirty work.

"And at a stretch, if the women were using artificial intelligence or remote control for the aircraft attacks and never physically present, it could be tough to convict them." I started to see what might be lingering behind her animosity towards how we had developed our case so far. I looked at the Boss; he saw me out of the corner of his eye, nodded minutely, then gestured to Indigo. Indigo nodded and sat down. I stood up. My next words would be critical if we were to keep the Americans behind us and onside.

"General, let's take the case of the Hog pilot. We have her on video doing an engineering pre-flight in the hangar, gearing up, entering the cockpit, starting the Hog, and taxiing out to the holding area. From that point on, it could be argued that she left the aircraft—maybe or maybe not under her own auspices—on the ground and had no notion of the intended attack. She could claim that she was paid to get the Hog to the holding point and nothing more—or that she was coerced out of the cockpit and taken prisoner. When she left the aircraft, as far as we are able to prove at this time, the armaments were not live; the safety pins had not been pulled; the inflatable was not in use; all she had done to that point was get the aircraft into position as per her filed flight plan." The general looked gob-smacked, this alternative narrative on the actions of the Hog pilot who had caused so much death and destruction at West Point obviously never having occurred to her or anyone in her orbit. But we were Interpol—and we worked to policing mandates that required absolute proof to support a conviction in the world court, or the court of any civilized country on whose behalf we were operating, not a military organization that could shoot first and ask questions later. I wasn't going to let her off the hook.

"Take the case of the refugee child who was established in a home in Israel twenty-three years ago. Yes, she later developed the nanotechnology that would be used by the terrorists to take out our oil and gas reserves. At the time she left the program, she had successfully demonstrated a genuine ecological solution to oil spills. She developed a system that was supposedly for environmental reasons. She left years before the final development of the nano weapons, played no part in it, and freely admits that she was a refugee who was taken out of the camps and placed in a normal home when she was but a child. It is the intel that she acquired during her time at various universities that we are now plumbing for information on some of the other players. But what, exactly, would you hold her guilty of?" The general looked like she had swallowed an apple whole; her whole body showed extreme stress, and I was afraid she would start to hyperventilate. Then the crisis passed, and she shook her head violently from side to side. Military training had its advantages.

"You cannot tell me that the woman that set up the Hog to attack West Point, killing thousands, not to mention the joint chief of staff, can get off scot-free?" She rose to her full height, an impressive one-meter eighty-eight, the look on her face enough to make a lesser person cringe.

"No, General, I'm not. I'm just putting it out there that we have a lot to do to prove beyond a shadow of a doubt the complicity and guilt of anyone involved in the attacks. And I'd like to add to what Colonel Kashasini said to us earlier. If you look at the attacks in the US critically, you really don't see a role for more than three women." I remained standing, held her icy stare, and braced myself for whatever might come. She seemed to be considering her options, but what was going on behind those icy eyes was hard to fathom.

"Captain, you graduated from our NCIS academy?" she asked, her voice frosty and hard-edged.

"Yes, General."

"And at that academy, were you exposed to the nightmare of what is now regarded as the 'Terrorist Laws'?"

"Yes, General. In fact, I helped write some of them after the attacks in Egypt on our Air Force base. If you remember, we had a medical facility there that specialized in burns and reconstruction. It was destroyed, killing all sixty of the doctors, nurses, and scientists there. The fact that it was someone else's sovereign soil, the base was not listed as a US military establishment, and the terrorists escaped initially over the border into Libya made it all the more difficult to prosecute a case."

"But you did get them and prosecute them?" she asked, knowing fully that I could not answer the question. Two reasons: I had signed a non-disclosure agreement issued by the Justice Department, the downside of that being thirty years in the stockade, no parole. The second reason was that NCIS had tracked them down using Special Forces on an illegal, unsanctioned mission that had resulted in a one hundred percent kill rate, with the small sample of proof recovered after the attack enough to justify prosecution but not lethal force. The whole sorry episode had thrown the military lawyers into turmoil, and to prevent anyone from ever uncovering anything about the retribution, it had been buried deep in the Pentagon files.

"General, as you well know, that prosecution caused a lot of debate in legal circles, and that was why we wrote the 'Terrorist Laws.' Cross border jurisdiction, arrest, and detention versus weapons-free, nation-state permissions, you know the content. And you also know I cannot answer your question." The general smiled for the first time, not much of one, but enough to crease her face somewhat.

"Well, as you know, under the 'Terrorist Laws,' it is perfectly legal to arrest someone on suspicion of aiding and abetting a terrorist act, providing comfort to identified terrorists, being suspected of arranging or planning a terrorist act, and the kicker, as far as I am concerned, physically or substantially providing materials or substances that were or could be used in a terrorist act. Now, if I am not wrong, Interpol operates under these laws, is that correct?" I looked at the Boss to see if he wanted to take this; he just stared blankly at the general, leaving me to my own devices.

"General, the laws under which we operate are those struck by the world court. And we are allowed to also act under those laws mandated by the countries who support us, providing such laws do not contravene any law of the world court. What's your point?" I asked, this time letting my voice have just a little edge. I was getting a little tired of all the legal mumbo jumbo. The Boss, Indigo, Anna, and I had discussed all the rules of engagement we would operate underway back at the start of this horror show; it should be no surprise to the Americans, or anyone else for that matter. At least she had the good graces to sit back in her chair and hold her hands out as a sign of acquiescence.

"Captain, again, my apologies. The idea of the Hog pilot getting off on a technicality riled me somewhat. Let's get back to the main conversation. If I have heard you correctly, you are saying the total number of women used in these attacks is five or six?" she couldn't disguise her lack of belief, but there was no longer a bite in her tonality.

"Yes, we are. At least in minimum terms. Your own special forces reported on their clean-up of the silo and the discovery of the helicopter in the underground hangar. The documents of the local municipality show that the restoration was done in plain view; only one woman was identified on the applications; she no longer exists, of course, but the local workers whom your FBI questioned said they only ever saw the one woman, and that the work was completed over a year and a half ago. The physical records exist, but the electronic ones are gone."

"And we have no satellite footage of the data cable channel being dug or the underground hangar." I nodded; this was the real sticking point. The terrorists had used their black hole technology on the entire site and one hundred miles from the site to hide everything that had happened for over two-plus years from any intelligence agency. Maybe.

"No, General, not at this time." And I left it at that, happy to have an ace up my sleeve. In this case, Amira believed that she could reverse engineer the code she had been sent from Michele and reveal the actions of the terrorists.

"This 'satisfactory outcome'—what exactly is it?" she asked, folding her arms.

"We view the capturing and disbandment of the mercenary terrorists and the banker as a significant phase in this case. Our next objective is to interrogate those captured and ascertain their roles in the attacks. At the same time, we will analyze all the captured data and mine all the intelligence opportunities we have now within our grasp. Then we will sit down and determine what to do and how to do it. It's that simple."

"And that would be your 'satisfactory outcome.'"

"For this phase, yes. We may have to rejig our approach to what we do next, depending on the intelligence we might have. We might require different resources and engage with different technologies. We are not forgetting anything, just thinking through what we might need to finish the job." The general remained still, her head bowed slightly, a neutral expression on her face.

"How long before you decide on this future action?" she asked. I looked at the Boss, and he nodded.

"We will take an official break of twenty-four hours to rest our people and let things settle, then we expect to have the intelligence sorted within three days and a comprehensive plan in another two." The general nodded twice, stood up, looked around the room, and probably saw the same tiredness in everyone's face that I saw—at least, I hoped so. Arie stood up, nodded to the Boss, smiled at me, making me feel warm inside.

"General," he said, "why don't you and I have a chat and let these good people do what they have to do?" he gently took the general's arm and walked her out of the room. The bright shaft of sunlight that suddenly flooded through the open door caused me to shield my eyes with one hand. I had forgotten the time, the day, and, for that matter, the month.

Time to calm things down a little.

Chapter 1

On the day that Amira (no last name at this time) was taken out of the refugee camp at Baalbek, Lebon, sometime around or just after the turn of the century, one hundred and six children under the age of nine died, to be added to the pile of dead bodies in the fire pit reserved for this gruesome daily task. The average was one hundred and forty dead bodies every day, so, in many ways, this was a good day for the camp.

It was a perfect day for Amira, around five or six years old, orphaned by a senseless war, and still alive only due to happenstance in that she had been collected up while still essentially a baby with a hoard of other distressed and abandoned children and taken to the camp by nurses from the Red Crescent.

With no one to claim her, she was literally dumped in a large tent that already held some two hundred children and just two adults—women who had taken on the task of trying to keep their young and mostly compliant changes alive for another day. They did their best, replaced by other loving women from time to time when the task proved too much, and despite the odds, kept many of their charges alive. As fast as some died, their beds were filled with the next collection of abandoned children.

The fact that these conditions existed, that the UNHCR and other Aid Agencies visited these camps at least annually, and that the death rate was so high and so consistent, yet the continual wars and skirmishes forced more and more desperate people into these camps, was a global tragedy that the whole of the modern world should have taken responsibility for.

It didn't, and as the crisis in the camps got worse throughout the Middle East, Europe, and Northern Africa—if you can imagine worse—an imam who was teaching in the campsite next to a Jesuit priest in a cobbled-together school decided to take matters into his own hands and rescue the smartest and the brightest of the starving children and have them fostered by caring families around the world.

I opened the transcript of our interrogation of Amira just a short week ago, and shook my head at the amazing technological discoveries which had been hidden from the world for over half a decade.

Director Arie Rosenberg (Rosenberg) - "May I have your real name, please?"

Amira Abramowitz (Abramowitz) - "My birth name is Amira, my parents died when I was very young, so I have no last name from my youth. My parents gave me the name Amira Abramowitz when I came to Israel. I do not remember my original family, and I consider the Abramowitz family my own. They cared for me, sent me to school, then college, paid for my education, saw to my health and well-being, and asked nothing in return. I ask that they be treated fairly, as they are not in any way to blame for my transgressions."

Rosenberg - "Your parents will not be involved in any conversations we have concerning your—as you call it—transgressions—nor will anyone ever lay any blame at their door. On that, you have my word."

Abramowitz - "Thank you. Your people have already debriefed me; why am I here now?"

Rosenberg - "You're here because we have found that you link back to a gentleman called Al Hemish al-bin Mohammad Karesish. We believe he was responsible for bringing you to Israel, and placing you with your family, some twenty-five to thirty years ago."

Captain Jessica Riley (Riley) - "You may not have been given his name. Can you recall how you got to Israel?"

Abramowitz - "Yes, vividly. In the camp, we were all starving, people were dying all around us, there was shelling going on somewhere close, you could hear the bangs, and the earth shook all the time. Then one evening, a man and a woman came to our tent, grabbed me and one other, put us in an ambulance, and drove us off to a shed. In the shed, we were fed the first meal we had had in three days, given bedding, then allowed to sleep. The only person I ever saw after that was the woman who said she was an aid worker. To me, she was an angel, and the other girls all felt the same way."

Riley - "What happened next?"

Abramowitz - "We were loaded back into the ambulance and drove for about a day. We stopped twice for bathroom breaks and we were offered simple food— rice and flatbread—to eat while in transit. Then we arrived at a village, I don't know its name, but we went into a hostel, where we were put into rooms with other women and girls. We were able to bathe the first time for me in months, given clean clothes, offered a hot meal, then allowed to sleep again. The women looked after us until we were collected again. It was obvious that all the girls had been distressed and rescued from somewhere. No one spoke very much, but you could feel the kindness of the women.

"The next day, a Red Crescent van picked me up, and we drove to a port, where I was put onto a small boat and brought here to Israel. The woman came with me, and my parents met us at the dock.

"It all happened so fast, and they were so welcoming and loving; I never stopped to ask why. I just accepted it as something that happened."

Senior Special Agent Anna Bernstein (Bernstein) - "Did you ever see the woman again?"

Abramowitz - "Yes, on what was celebrated as my fifteenth birthday. I didn't know my birth date, and we assumed I was six years old. We had to guess the date because I had no memory of it. She brought me a present, which I took with me to Technion University because until that time I had never seen a laptop computer."

Bernstein - "Didn't you have computers at school?"

Abramowitz - "Yes, big clunky ones, in a computer lab, and you had to book time in the library if you wanted to use them out of school hours."

Bernstein - "I see. Where is the laptop now?"

Abramowitz - "It was confiscated when I was arrested. I don't know where it is now."

Bernstein - "We know you went to university early—when you were fifteen. We know you excelled at coding and nanotechnology—in fact, some of your published work still stands as the benchmark in those disciplines. Arie said his Agency tried to recruit you when you were just twenty after you finished your doctorate. Why did you not take them up on his offer?"

Abramowitz - "I had a better offer."

Bernstein - "Who from?"

Abramowitz - "Sir, you will keep your promise regarding keeping my family out of any trouble I might bring to them?"

Rosenberg - "Yes. Your family will not be punished for anything you have done as long as you tell us the truth, and we can prove it is true."

Abramowitz - "When I turned twenty, the same woman who had given me the first laptop met with me again. She said her name was Helen, and she worked for an organization vested with the responsibility of ensuring that people like me had all the things they needed to carry out their research. She gave me a new computer, a satellite phone, and access to a group of scientific and military databases focusing on my work. She introduced me to other women working in similar fields around the world, and she helped me format my thesis for my second doctorate. I was attached to a coding and a nanotechnology group and given access to a huge laboratory at the university that I didn't know existed. All she wanted from me was my best work, and she promised me a role in a superlab at a different university when I finished my doctorate, with a stipend that would feed my family and me for life. She swore me to secrecy and left a bag of shekels for incidental expenses—a bag, I might add, that held more than my parents earned in a year. At this time, I didn't see any real harm in it."

Riley - "You finished your second doctorate seven years ago. You hung around the campus for less than a month, then what happened?"

Abramowitz - "You have my passport; the woman I knew as Helen came through. I went to the US on a post-doc scholarship to Harvey Mudd College. As you probably know, it is a world leader in STEM. I worked in the Nano lab and also on coding for three wonderful years. I simply could not imagine life being any better."

Riley - "Did you maintain contact with your parents? "Would you like another soda?"

Abramowitz - "Yes, please. "You asked about my parents... "Excuse me.

"Yes, I spoke to them every week, sometimes twice a week. Why do you ask?"

Riley - "Arie, perhaps you would like to take this?"

Rosenberg - "Amira, we asked you this because we have been unable to find any trace of your communications with your parents since you left Israel. Can you suggest why that is?"

Abramowitz - "I'll tell you, but before I do, I want to explain what happened at Harvey Mudd College.

"Having been brought up in Israel, I was used to a militaristic tension in everything we did in class. After all, we were being attacked almost every day from somewhere. After a while, you get used to it, but the constant threat and tension shapes your behavior and your performance. Then I get to the US, and it's as if I have entered a whole new world, no militarism, no overt censorship, no bombs going off, just wide-open fields of grass and smiling people and even smarter people doing very clever things.

"In the first year, I did more good work and advanced my thinking further than I had at home in the last five years. It was exhilarating. I was suddenly part of a loose cabal of thinkers able to run experiments with very little supervision and an awful lot of help.

"It was heaven, as I told my parents every week. I even sent them progress reports, knowing they would probably not understand half the language. But it was the happiest time of my life. I had several experiments running in three labs and a pile of people wanting to help or observe. Then the Hand of God reached out and made me aware of my true purpose, why I was saved from the camp, and why I had been allowed to learn and prosper all this time.

"To say I was shocked is an understatement. Initially, I was horrified. Then they explained the background and asked me to think about it. No pressure. Just the thought of hundreds of children dying every day in camps all over the world made my skin run cold. And I had been one of those children before I had been saved and brought to my new family. I could be dead.

"They did not put any pressure on me at that time. But I felt it, ever so subtle, under the rhetoric, lying in wait for me to realize I had a debt to pay."

Bernstein - "You said 'the Hand of God.' Did you mean that literally?"

Abramowitz - "It was the woman who called herself Helen, and a young cleric identified himself as Mohammad bin Usha Rashad. He said he was representing the interests of my sponsor, a revered cleric who was now in self-isolation in the desert of his home, praying for our success; bin Usha Rashad was direct and to the point. I owed my success, and my very life, to my sponsor, and I now had a duty to do his bidding.

"I asked what that bidding may be, and he told me that I would be briefed in detail in a day or two once I was able to commit unreservedly to their cause.

"They left me to consider my options, and I must admit I yearned to tell my parents, but they had warned me that I couldn't contact anyone but them—and they gave me a cell phone with which to call them. They left, and I went back to my room."

Bernstein - "What did you do next?"

Abramowitz - "I wrote a detailed summary of the conversation on my laptop, and then I spent all night using the university library to research the current refugee status. You no doubt know what that is today, but it was bad enough five years ago.

"The UN estimated that a child was dying every three minutes in a camp somewhere, and I couldn't turn away from that.

"After all, I had been one of those children. I could have easily been one of the dead.

"I was working in very advanced nanotechnology and had two projects running on a new code algorithm, so at the time, I wasn't sure what they would want of me.

"I called them, and they set up a meeting the next day off-campus in a little coffee shop. They were direct and to the point. I would work with a small group of hand-picked collaborators at the university and manage two projects— one to refine my nano work but specifically in the oil and gas field, and one in coding to create a means of filtering data off the internet and communications satellites undetected. Neither project looked threatening; the oil and gas work was for remediation of mass oil spills, and gas eruptions from fracking operations, or so they said, and the data grab was supposed to enable the group to monitor some of the countries whom they judged to be the creators of the worst of the refugee problems without their knowledge. Again, given who some of those countries are, it seemed to be a reasonable request.

"I chose to believe them, thinking I could always pull back and withdraw my work.

"The next day, I met my cohort and recognized three of the people from my own lab. There was one outlier, a brilliant Chinese post-doc from Tsinghua University, who seemed to know everything going on, and what we had achieved so far. She and I immediately formed a bond; I suspect it was because she had also been rescued from the camps, or so she said, so we had that in common. We started work, and in a very short time, we managed to produce a nano bug that would literally eat its way through the atomic structure of crude oil, leaving only fine semi-carbon-3 dust.

"It passed every test on a small scale, and we sought and gained permission to try it on a large oil spill that had just been reported in the channel between Nova Scotia and New Brunswick. On the world scale of catastrophic environmental damage from oil pollution, it was quite small and had been mostly contained within floating barriers and the application of foam.

"We were flown to Nova Scotia by the Coast Guard, provided every resource by the local technicians, and let loose. Our little bug worked, and within hours the oil spill was a floating mass of little silver carbon3 particles that bobbed around for a while, then sunk to the bottom of the bay to join their ancestors in the slime and muck of the seabed."

Bernstein - "I remember the incident, but I don't remember any report on the solution, other than it was described as a new type of foaming reagent; it gained little attention."

Abramowitz - "Yes, that was the PR that they put out at the time, as Michele, as we knew her, suggested that we needed to keep it quiet until we could file all the necessary patents and get approval from the university. As you know, anything developed at a university lab that goes on to be a commercial success automatically vests a twenty percent return in the IP back to the university.

"At the time, I thought we were doing the correct thing. And I must admit, I was more than just a little enamored with Michele."

Bernstein - "How far did your infatuation go?"

Abramowitz - "We had been very close for nearly two years, and then it just died on the vine, as it were, because the very next day Michele had disappeared, with all my notes, discs, reports, and samples, and we never saw or heard from her again."

Bernstein - "Did you keep backups anywhere?"

Abramowitz - "I may not have done everything right, but if I learned one thing working and learning here in Israel is to always keep a backup of your work somewhere and to keep the location to yourself. And no, it's not on my laptop. I think you will find that it has been compromised by Helen or someone from her organization.

"I suspect there is spyware on it, and I haven't used it since I left the university.

"There was a second major reason I disappeared for a while, then came back home.

"You see, my work on the code was also taken, but not by Michele. Helen came and got that herself. And that was the trigger for my going underground."

Rosenberg - "What are you referring to?

Abramowitz - "The day after Michele disappeared, Helen turned up, asked for my laptop, worked on it for a while, then gave it back to me.

"Then she asked to be taken to the lab and asked for all the code we had generated, all the discs, the backups, and then she wiped the entire system in the lab. Right after, she explained what she wanted me to do."

Riley - "And what was that?"

Abramowitz - "She wanted me to go with her to Turkey to run what she called 'missions.' She pointed out how good everyone had been to me, how they had paid for everything I had achieved, and now they wanted my help righting some wrongs.

"She said I had to pay homage to the children who had gone before me, never having the chance of a real life."

"To be fair, I had expected to be asked to do something from the very first time I had been approached."

Rosenberg - "But you said no, and you ran?"

Abramowitz - "I said okay, but I needed a day to clean up so the university wouldn't come after me for the damage she had done to the lab, and we arranged to meet up the next day at the airport. Then I ran."

Rosenberg - "Why did you decide to attack the country that had adopted you?"

Abramowitz - "It was the only way I knew to get your undivided attention, and then at the very top of the Intelligence tree, with any vestige of credibility. I wanted to demonstrate what I was capable of, so you would believe me. And I wanted a meeting just like this, so you could tell me what they have done, and I can tell you how to fix it."

Rosenberg - "How much do you know of the events of the past four weeks?"

Abramowitz - "Not much. I have been in a small, barred room for the past month or so, with no access to electronics, no visitors, just the scuttlebutt that passes between prisoners. If I have interpreted the gossip I picked up from the guards, you are all in a world of hurt. I can fix some of that."

Riley - "Arie, what would you say to Interpol taking charge of your prisoner, with the guarantee that we will return her in the same condition she is in now, at any time you require it. I would like to get the boys in the backroom on the fact-checking and follow-up, then get our contingent back to Venice—with young Amira here."

Rosenberg - "On two conditions. She wears a security bracelet, and you personally take responsibility for her security. Agreed?"

Riley - "Good at my end. Amira, are you willing to come with me to Venice and work with our people there to rectify some of the damage your work has done?"

Abramowitz - "Providing your earlier promise about keeping my parents out of this is kept, I'm happy to swap a cell for a bracelet.

"And I've never been to Venice."

All this had been set in motion by a single imam pissed off at his family for reasons unknown but easily guessable. A man with untold wealth because, by chance, he had the money, being seventh in line for the Throne of Arabia and one of the many signatories of the Pan Arabia Wealth Fund. He started setting up seemingly legitimate funds in multiple countries, and as we found out—once we had taken down the lead mercenary, a stunningly professional killer known as "Shetani," and analyzed his communications with Al Hemish al-bin Mohammad Karesish, or Mohammad bin Azaria as he had changed his name to—billions and billions of dollars had been secreted in some thirty countries and had fueled the attacks that had crippled the world.

Of course, there was a lot more to this story, as we all found out around twenty years after he had taken the first of the refugee children, when in a series of stunning attacks by unmanned aircraft and other vehicles the Vatican was bombed at the time of the Conclave to elect a new pope, chopping off the head of the Catholic Church in one foul blow; sixty percent of the Dome of the Rock was destroyed, causing both Christians and Muslims to rise up in arms; sections of the Grand Mosque were blown up, further driving nails into the sides of Muslims all over the world; West Point was carpet bombed, killing thousands of cadets as well as the Chief of Staff; the Internet was destroyed, creating havoc in the world's communications, and some said, took everyone back to the nineteen seventies in terms of capability and capacity; the space station was destroyed, and by a fluke of timing, with no loss of life, as the astronauts were practicing an evacuation maneuver at the time of the attack; eighty percent of the world's oil and gas supplies were destroyed or blocked, some of them for hundreds of years, and Lloyds of London, the oldest and most respected insurer and reinsurer, had been crippled by the destruction of their three major data hubs.

The world, literally, was in chaos. Civil war broke out in most countries, with hundreds of thousands killed or displaced. Commerce at any level, local, national, or international, stopped dead in its tracks.

Survivors foraged in garbage dumps or simply killed their neighbors for whatever food they had tucked away.

Anarchy reigned supreme, and in some countries, the situation was so bad it was impossible to see how they could ever recover. The worldwide pandemic of just four years previous had taught a strong lesson about the strength of community, which had promptly been discarded as household fought household, neighbor fought neighbor, and ultimately, county fought country.

And in the post-terrorist attack analysis that I was currently working through, all seven hundred pages of it, the likelihood was it had been masterminded by one man and carried out by less than ten women ex-refugees and around three hundred mercenaries. If I hadn't lived through it all attack by attack and been so closely involved from day one as an investigator for Interpol, I would not have believed it possible that so few people could do such damage on a global scale.

And in such a short amount of time.

It was, undoubtedly, the most sophisticated, technologically orientated attack since the atomic bomb was dropped on Japan.

Less than twenty-three days from the first attack until the mercenaries had been wiped off the face of the earth by a series of coordinated military attacks in sixteen countries instigated by intelligence provided by Interpol.

Interpol had been able to have observers at two of these attacks, up close and personal, thanks to a cadre of military specialists attached to our unit.

Due to the sheer scale of the attacks and their aftermath, we had been forced to consider the possibility that the investigation would have to be conducted in two or three phases—as we had been directly involved in the forceful elimination of the mercenary terrorists in the middle of our investigation into the banker and his refugees after they physically attacked one of our working locations.

The small problem of discovering that every area of interest to the investigators worldwide suffered from some type of electronic masking was just the icing on the cake. We knew exactly where some of the terrorists had been hiding—but all movement in and out of those areas was invisible to us, even before they crashed the internet.

There was some very sophisticated technology being used against us, and it seemed that it had been developed, at least initially, by some of the refugees once they reached the university level of their education. And by people embedded in our systems for perhaps thirty or forty years.

How did we come to this conclusion?

Well, Amira's interrogation pointed to the major bits but left a lot unanswered.

Her sponsor, a woman, called "Helen," had offered Amira a role going forward in the planning and execution of the worldwide attack, and Amira had stalled, hidden, then done a runner and remained invisible to the world for five years.

Subsequently, all her work was stolen by her partner, a Chinese master hacker, and her sponsor, who had effectively mentored her through the various schools and colleges, mostly as a means to keep an eye on her and her work, until the field trial in Nova Scotia.

But Amira's principal work had been in nanotechnology of the oil-eating variety and digitally in the kill-the-image type—we had experienced the bitter end of both developments and struggled to make headway against their impact. She had also worked on computer code, and her work had led directly to the terrorists being able to conceal areas of interest from prying eyes for some years.

Technology at its best and worst again. Not being a geek, I only had a vague understanding of the technical aspects of the black holes, as the Boss had labeled them, but they worked and left us blind to years of information we needed to access to be able to prosecute our case against the refugee women.

We had a line on "Michele," her lover, and even knew a little about "Helen," her recruiter. My musing was suddenly interrupted by the thunderous arrival of my team, obviously somewhat refreshed by the rest we had dictated, except maybe for one of them.

"*Mi scusi, colonnello mio, non vedo una macchina per caffè espresso qui, questo incontro deve essere illegale!*" Indigo shouted, creating a roar of laughter that rippled around the room. Indigo had a fondness for looking after us, and genius-level espresso was one of his tools.

This room, provided by our local Israeli field office inside a secured compound, had no such luxury. Bottled water was the order of the day.

Missing from this meeting was our local agent, Beth Arezzo, Amira, Arie, Anna, General Saunders, and two of the geeks. They were still back in the clandestine HQ of the EDL, working on the "black hole" problem the Boss had tagged. Anna and the general were teleconferencing with the NSA back in the United States, using all the wiles and grunts of the best white-hat hackers available. For once, I was glad they were somewhere else. I had my fill of ones and zeros and looked forward to investigative police work again. After all, I had a seven-hundred-page summary of all the evidence gathered to date to start my musing on!

This was my meeting, so in the absence of coffee, I jumped right in.

"Pete, lead off, please, your opinion on where we are at this point." The lean, lanky, weathered Special Forces master chief, affectionally known as "Black Pete," looked around the team as if seeking inspiration. He wasn't. We all knew him well and were not surprised by his response.

"Captain, with your permission, I'd like to throw that ball to Tom." Tom looked at the Colonel, looked at me, then back at Pete, nodded to himself, then stood, his military bearing unmistakable. As the head of the US Special Forces team, the Boss had requested for the duration; he was no slouch. He had also participated in the raids on Shetani's terrorist cells, so he had a firsthand view of what we had been up against.

"Sir, I am familiar with the military actions we have executed, but I haven't been briefed on the political or social side of your investigation. From that limited perspective and having been on the ground at two of the operations against the mercenaries, I feel comfortable that we have eradicated the majority of Mohammad bin Azaria's troops. Our intelligence, largely due to the internet blackout, is sketchy, but every country to which we gave identifications and locations to has reported successful strikes, with only a very few survivors."

"Are they being interrogated?" I asked.

"Yes, ma'am, that's where the sketchy comes in."

"As in, no one is prepared to share anything they get from the prisoners?"

"Exactly, ma'am. There is so much residual anger at what the mercenaries have done, some countries are finding it difficult to keep their prisoners secure."

"Do we have anything at all from anybody?"

"Yes, ma'am, but frankly, nothing we hadn't already got from our raids and intelligence gathering."

"Okay, thanks, Tom. I want you and your team to transfer to Venice. Pete will give you the coordinates. We need to secure the location and ensure a minimum of ten kilometers of early warning and security. After you complete your recon, put a plan together, and if you need more boots on the ground, contact Colonel Kashasini here," I said, pointing to Indigo slumped in his chair. He had a full no-coffee sulk on. It was wonderful to see under the circumstances.

"One other thing—on your way back, see what we need to transport from our temporary HQ in Milan. You will find some of the Colonel's excellent staff ready to assist you in clearing out the warehouse."

"You want us back with the monks?" the Boss asked, and I just nodded. "We need to work this on at least two fronts—maybe three. It's clearly a geek feast for the next few days, at least; I'm not getting around that, and my suggestion is that we leave Amira here in Israel with Shami and let them put a team together under Arie's watchful eye.

"I need a short conversation with you before we put that in motion. We also want to explore possible contact with Amira's girlfriend, Michele. We go back with Luigi and get assistance from Indigo and maybe even from Lyon if we need it; the monks can help, I'm sure of that, but their capacity might not be so much. Initially, Anna can link up with Frank Reynolds and his resident geeks, and I think we need to consider using General Saunders to provide overall coordination for all three geek teams."

"You're thinking of the politics," the Boss said, his lack of inflection leading me to believe he had gone down this road as well. I nodded, looking around the room, realizing that I was voicing my plan without input from the team. Too late now, so I plowed on.

"I also want to do a very deep dive on the missile site, and I need the US to be fully invested. They shut it down, blew a few things up, and traced the comms cable from the dish to the missile site, so they're feeling good about themselves. I want to look under the dirt, outside the black hole. I want investigative boots on the ground, mine, Anna's, and anyone Roger can spare.

"And I want the best geeks available backing me up."

"When you leave, you'll take Pete with, at a minimum." I nodded again, already part of my plan, but good to have the Boss on my side.

"Your 'black holes,' as you call them, are the result of clever technology, no more, no less, and my feeling is we have all been too hidebound by what we think we know. Time to get back to first principles, put boots on the ground, ask questions, look for clues, you know, what we used to do before the tech revolution." The Boss just nodded, giving nothing away, his slouch, if anything, deepening in his chair.

"What would you like me to do?" he asked casually, fooling no one. The Boss was the Boss for very, very good reasons.

"Get some boots from Arie, get to Libya, Turkey if you have to, start asking questions.

"We need to dig under the surface, understand how they operated, see what they left behind if anything. We have to get into their minds if we are to have any chance of catching them." He nodded, seemed to consider something for a moment, then stood up, unfolding like a wrinkled, rusted erector set. He looked around the room, took everyone in, and noted their tiredness and Indigo's sulk due to his coffee deprivation.

"Listen up, people, we're at a critical stage. You have all done a fantastic job getting us to this point. In standing up the Captain's plan, make sure you get some genuine rest.

"This phase is all about finding patterns, uncovering little mistakes they will have made, and applying your not inconsiderable brainpower to thinking through how they did it and where they are now. We have to find them. Our Client States are relying on us; we have unlimited resources, up to a point, now is the time to really make a difference." No one responded, not even with a smirk or a smile hidden behind a hand. Then Pete broke the silence, and laughter filled the room.

"Boss, sit down for Christo's sake. You're embarrassing us!" And that did it. The room broke up, even Indigo smiled, shook his head, then arms on his hips and a stern look on his face, shouted over the laughter, "*Vi avverto tutti, nessuna macchina expresser dove mai finiamo, e l'Italia ritirerà il loro sostegno!*"

"Sure, Indigo, you'll get your espresso machine. I guarantee it!"

Chapter 2

I sat down with Amira, Indigo, Arie, and the Boss for my second but short planned conversation. The small, tight meeting, the last time I would see Amira and Arie for a time—we were all going our separate ways to run the female terrorists down. But I needed to make a point before Amira and Arie stepped off into the hidden bowels of the Israeli digital technology center and disappeared from sight.

And I needed to let them know about two pieces of information I had received in the last hour, through the nebulous monks and their brilliant communication system—still the only one working in the known world.

"Boss, we have a secret or two not yet shared with the general, and I've got some more data from Venice that I haven't shared yet with the team." He looked at me, his majestic blue-grey eyes sparkling with his normal intensity, so at least one of us was firing on all cylinders.

"I've asked Anna to keep stum for the time being because we need to keep the lid on the fact that Amira and the geeks cracked your 'black hole' wide open, and we have three to four years of data now over our target areas. We need to analyze this data, find the patterns, track the movements of the women, get their faces, then run them down. But's that not the real issue." The Boss just looked at me, face expressionless, as if he was marginally bored with the whole process. But his eyes bored into me in a way that made the skin on the back of my neck tingle. "I worked that out days ago when you and geeks had your shouting fest back at the monks' hideaway." I nodded, not in the least surprised; the Boss hadn't got his role as head of the most agile investigative arm of Interpol because of his good looks.

"Boss, there are potentially other nano products in play; we know their genesis but not their current state. I want you and Arie in the loop in case something pops up unexpectedly. But before I get Amira to run it through for you, we have a bigger problem than we had before."

"If you're referring to the shutting down of the coal plants across the EU, Asia, and the Americas, I got a flash on that from our US friends about ten minutes ago." I looked at him. I should not have been surprised he knew, but I was surprised he hadn't said anything, but I tucked that away for a more private conversation we both would have.

"Okay, Amira, run the nano story through for the colonel, please."

She looked at me, her shoulders tightened, maybe a little guilt creeping in; after all, her nano bug had shut down sixty percent of the world's oil and gas, radioactivity having taken care of another twenty percent for the next one hundred years. No small achievement. "Ah, Colonel, sir," she started, looking directly at Arie, who sat as still as a Buddha, obviously tired from the machinations of the last two days. "Before we closed down our work at Harvey Mudd, we derived a number of different functions that were past the experimental stage, ready for production. I should mention that all this work was done by Helen and, as far as I know, Michele.

"I had it all in a file that I kept on a device I carried on my person. Unfortunately, the day Helen made her move, I'd left the data on my desk in my room." Arie turned to look at the Boss, then looked back at Amira. She nervously pushed her long black hair back from one ear, then flicked her head to straighten it again. I couldn't get over how young she looked.

"Amira, your parents, will not be involved in anything you have done or have yet to do for us. You already have my word on that." She looked a little more at ease, but her body was still full of tension, and she started to wring her hands with a washing motion. I reached over and placed my hand on hers, a silent offer of support. She looked directly at me, and a tiny smile creased her eyes.

"Colonel, sir, the original intent for the nano bug was to provide an environmental solution to oil spills. This, you know. What we did around the time of the live trial up in Nova Scotia was an experiment with some derivatives, using the carbon3 as a base, and we were able to produce small samples of materials that had unique properties, which we took back to the university."

"And they were?" Arie asked, his voice so soft I leaned slightly forward, the better to hear him.

"Well, we worked out how to produce a solar panel that was ninety percent efficient and would have cost just cents per kilowatt to produce. We also managed to capture carbon, CO_2, and radioactive elements and neutralize them. Using the same technology back in the lab, we created a biofuel that has a carbon-neutral footprint. We also developed an anode and cathode alternative for batteries, which improved energy storage by around six hundred percent theoretically."

The room went so quiet I could actually hear us all breathing.

"This was in the laboratory, right?" the Boss asked, suddenly sitting up in his seat. His face hadn't changed, still a neutral expression, but his eyes were alive with interest. Amira nodded, her shoulders relaxing slightly, her hands now still undermined.

"Yes, sir, but the work was at the point that with a laboratory and sophisticated manufacturing and mechanical development tools, I believe we could have produced a working sample of each, at least at scale."

"From what you remember," Arie asked, his voice firming up as the conversation developed, "could you replicate these devices here, now?"

"Yes.

"I know that Helen had a lot of people being trained in electrical engineering, mechanical engineering, adaptive printing, and nanoscience. She referred to them once or twice in our conversations. I'd like to make one comment based on a hunch—if you would forgive me this one time?"

Arie looked at the Boss, and both nodded their heads in agreement. Amira looked at me, turned to look at Indigo, who just offered her a warm smile, then tipped her head to one side, letting her shining hair drift like a small waterfall down one side of her long neck.

"We weren't the only girls taken. My instinct is that there were many, many more taken after me. Just little things Helen said. I don't know who they were or where they are, but I do know that they were refugees just like me, and I got the impression that the plan was to develop and manufacture what we created in the lab at full scale." Again, the silence in the room was palpable. Arie looked at the Boss, the Boss looked at me, and all three of us shrugged our shoulders at the same time. "You must have a fantastic memory," Arie said, scrubbing his face as if to keep himself awake.

"No, sir, I just wrote everything down when I went into hiding and ran a few thought experiments to perfect my thinking. I have everything I just described to you in a notebook. It's in code, I doubt if anyone could crack it, and you confiscated it when you arrested me." Arie laughed, his body losing up just a little, from his previously hard-edged stance. We were all still tired, that showed, but Arie had the added problem of the incessant bombardment of his country by his next-door neighbors and the constant demand on his time and attention twenty-four hours every day. The fact that he was accommodating us at the same time spoke to his incredible resolve and dedication to his country.

"Amira, you can have it back as soon as we return to the data lab." He turned to face me square on, giving nothing away with his body language. "Captain, what would you suggest we do with all this new information?"

"Bury it somewhere safe, out of the way of prying eyes, and concentrate on opening up the black holes and getting under the skin of the female terrorists. Leave the rest to the Colonel and me." To my mind, tracking the women were the first, second, and last priority we had if we ever wanted to approach a normal situation anytime soon. But my mind frizzled with the possibilities Amira had mentioned because just as one set of nanomachines had destroyed our way of life, these other potentially world-changing nano developments could reverse the entire situation.

Maybe.

But first, the girls.

In just a minute.

I looked at the Boss, Indigo, and shook my head. "Have you given any thought as to the consequences of the attack on the world's coal supply?"

"Yes."

"And?"

"Now the manure will really hit the fan. The oil and gas DOS (Denial of service) has created the biggest worldwide social issue in the last three hundred years. It has and will continue to change the balance of power right around the globe for years to come. At least with the availability of coal for things like electricity supply and the provision of heating and other related services, we might have been able to limp through the winter while we developed alternatives."

"And now we can't."

"No.

"And now we can't. Those little nanomachines Amira was talking about might become the most significant opportunity we can point to. But think about this—the atomic bomb started a cold war that split the planet almost in half—in recent times, terrorists and nation-states have developed their own weapons and used them to both terrorize and hold to ransom anyone they had a disagreement with. In the main, sanctions and diplomacy have held the line. Imagine what would happen if suddenly green alternative power technology was weaponized—can you think what that might do to the world?"

"It could turn tree-hugging into a major pastime. But I get what you are saying."

"It's been—what—twenty-four, twenty-five days since the first attack."

"Hundreds of thousands are dead, displaced, or just gone plain crazy. How do you undo that in a similar timeframe?" The Boss looked reflective, Indigo somber, but suddenly started to bounce on the balls of his feet. For a hardwired warrior, he sure had some moves!

"*Speranza!*" he almost shouted, punching the Boss in the arm, bouncing around like a battery bunny. "We give them hope!" I looked at the Boss, a wan smile splitting his face in spite of his best efforts.

"How would that work, Indigo?" he asked, straightening up to his full height, which enabled him to look down on the wiry Italian head of Interpol. Indigo seemed to be thinking, then he spread his hands out like a supplicant before an altar.

"Colonel," his perfect English underlying the seriousness of his answer, "we get Amira and Arie to put a team together to unravel her notebook. Then once we know what the possibilities are, we go from there." The Boss nodded. It made perfect sense; whether or not we had the resources to track down the women and decipher the notebook at the same time was a puzzle better solved by others smarter than me. "Okay, I'll amend my instructions to Arie and leave it to him and his people to work it all out. Now, I'm feeling a little worked up, so I think it's time we had a serious conversation with our prisoners. Who's going to join me?"

They both did, so we worked out a strategy and called the guards to find the Jesuit priest, the prisoners, and three interrogation rooms. Which took the best part of an hour but allowed the Boss, Indigo, and I to work out how to run the interrogations with the imam and his acolytes.

We started low—I took the guard who hadn't been shot and killed in the attack on the imam's hidden bunker, Indigo took the bookkeeper who had been at Mohammad bin Azaria's side when we had captured him in his tent, and the Boss and the general stood outside the small room where the main man himself sat, with the Jesuit priest at his side. They spoke to each other, almost head-to-head, so low that their words were unintelligible. But the idea behind the interrogation technique was simple. Show respect, resist intimidation, and approach the conversations from the point of view we already knew everything we needed, and we're just trying up loose ends. The fact was, the sheer amount of intelligence and data we took of the laptops and computers captured firstly by the Canadians, then during the attack on Shetani's setup in Arabia, and then our own, found when we took the imam down at his campsite, had provided practically everything but the answer to two critical questions.

Why he selected the targets. And how he expected creating worldwide death and destruction could possibly help the refugee cause.

I finished with the guard. Indigo finished with the bookkeeper. We met up outside the small room. The general looked at the Boss, at Indigo, then at me, with a gaze that clearly said, "don't fuck up, or I will kill you with my bare hands." I really didn't know what her agenda was; she had been belligerent back at the team meeting and debrief, and now she was shedding any resemblance of self-control and letting her animosity lance out like puss from an open wound. I stared back, nodded to her, smiled to put her off her game, then opened the door and walked into the room.

"*Signore, la prego di lasciarci ora, devo parlare privatamente con* Mohammad bin Usha Rashad." The Jesuit looked up at me, nodded, made the sign of the cross, kissed his fingers, then placed them on the shoulder of bin Usha Rashad. He looked at me as he rose, curiosity mixed with fear, bobbed his head, then left, closing the door behind him.

"Salam Alaikum."

"Wa Alaykum as-salam." His deep green eyes, ringed with slight golden color, looked up at me, and in a sense, through me, sending shivers up my spine. I had to remember all that this man had done, presumably in the name of his God. Brought the world to its knees, killed hundreds of thousands, probably millions by now, ruined the economy of more countries than I could list, set us back several decades technologically, yet sat now on a silver metal chair as relaxed as someone entertaining a tea party with friends.

Except for that look. I really had to work on reminding myself of our agreed strategy of showing respect to the prisoner when my instinct was to reach forward and snap his neck.

"We will conduct this interrogation in English, as you would understand; it is being recorded, and parts of it may be disseminated to countries affected by your actions, direct or indirect. As you are currently being held under the EU Terrorist Laws as modified in 2022, you are not entitled to legal representation, although we will respect any cultural requirements you may have regarding prayers and meals."

He nodded, not taking his eyes off me for a second.

"Sir," I said, using a formal salutation, "we have evidence going back to your time as a missionary teacher in Baalbek, Lebon, when you were known as Brother Fernández and plotted to take refugee children out of the camps and place them with families in numerous countries.

"We know you financed these activities using funds from the Arabia Sovereign Wealth Fund. We know you hired the mercenary known as 'Shetani' and paid him millions to launch physical attacks on oil, gas, and coal infrastructure worldwide. We also believe he was behind the bombing in Avion and multiple sports stadia in Europe, England, and the United States—" He put his hand up as if stopping traffic.

"You know all this, I know all this, but you can, at the very least, be accurate. We did not just take refugee children out of the camps; we took the smartest of the female children, placed them with good families, and then supported them all the way through their schooling, enabling them to go as far as they were able. How is that act of compassion in any way related to your precious Terrorist Laws as modified in 2022?" The disdain in his voice was a thing to behold. I had not expected righteousness, certainly not a pitch aimed at my emotions. I decided to change my tactics and expand on his diatribe rather than my planned attack.

"How many girls did you relocate? And how many countries did you place them in?" I asked, my voice quiet and encouraging, not taking the bait he had thrown out like someone feeding starving dogs.

He smiled, folded his arms inside his sleeves, sat back, and shook his head. "You haven't found them all. In fact, you probably haven't found any of them," he said, almost laughing. Did I ever tell you I played poker with the toughest faces to read in the world? I looked at him directly, hardened my face, and stared directly into his eyes, subtly sending body signals that I was telling the absolute truth.

"We know you used a woman known as 'Helen,' an imam known as Mohammad bin Usha Rashad, and we know of at least thirty camps you took girls from. In fact, we have traced a number of these girls and are currently observing them as they go about their daily activities. We also know that you used the ancient symbol 'Hamesh Hand'—or the Hand of Fatima—as your method of recognition. We know this without a doubt." I held his stare as his smile faded, replaced by a small grimace. And I waited.

Silence in interrogation was a powerful weapon. He dropped his head, closed his eyes for a minute, then slowly opened them as he looked through me again.

"Why would you pursue innocent women who have done nothing more than escaping an early death or indentured slavery at best because they got out of the camps? What possible harm could they have done to you?" I let the question hang again, holding his eyes with my own. His penetrating gaze still gave me the shivers, and I must admit, I was intrigued by his stance, if not a little puzzled.

"We are not pursuing the women who got out necessarily—but we are pursuing the women who developed the science and the weapons that were used in your attacks."

Now, for the first time, a glimmer of interest flashed across his eyes so fast that if I hadn't been looking so hard at him, I would have missed it. Maybe worth developing a little. I broke the cadence of our conversation and opened my hands to draw his attention away from my eyes.

"Sir, would you care for some water or perhaps tea?" I asked in my best schoolgirl voice. He wasn't fooled for a country minute.

"No, but nice segway. By the way, you did not introduce yourself. Who are you, and whom do you represent?" I considered my options and tilted my head slightly as if thinking through my answer. At this point in the interrogation, I did not want him to be able to anticipate my body language.

"My name is Captain Riley, and I'm with Interpol." I watched carefully for his reaction and saw what I had expected. He knew of our pursuit of him, but he hadn't had my name. Interesting.

"Well, Captain, how about we stop playing around the edges and get down to what you really want to know." He sat back, eyes closed again, head tilted towards the ceiling. Arrogant. Confident.

In control. I smiled to myself. My turn to rock the theoretical conversational boat.

"Sir, we know some of your refugee children grew up to be first-class terrorists. Designed and built nano weapons, digital weapons, and robotic weapons, and killed hundreds of thousands with them, without any regard for innocents or collateral damage. Attacked the world's oil and gas supplies, used radioactive material to deny the use of major oil fields for hundreds of years, and crashed the Internet. We know you used Shetani's mercenaries to launch attacks across the world, using these and other robotic weapons. We have your records and data from twenty-six years of plotting and planning. The proof is incontrovertible, the evidence damming. It's these women we want to find and prosecute, and we will do so. You have my word on it." I paused, hoping to create some tension between us. Then I asked the question we most wanted an answer to. "Why did you pick the targets you so obviously carefully selected?" And watched his reaction.

He turned his head to one side as if looking through the wall. Nodded to himself. Turned to look at me and smiled. I imagined what it would be like to look an alligator in the jaws.

"Captain, you may not believe me, but I have been waiting years for someone to ask me that question. In fact, it's the reason I did not resist when your stormtroopers attacked my camp and killed some of my support staff so unnecessarily." The fact that said support staff had been firing fully automatic assault weapons at us seemed to have slipped his mind. "In fact, I would ask that you share this information with the whole world, unedited, so that you can all see what drove us to take the action we did. I don't expect you or anyone for that matter to condone what we did, but I do expect you to at least acknowledge the truth of what I am about to say."

"No. You can't dictate the terms of your interrogation. But I will give you my word that what my superiors agree to will be released to all vested parties at some time during our investigation. They deserve to know why you so viciously attacked them, threatened their very livelihoods, destroyed five decades of technological progress, and created so much chaos and destruction. Everyone will need to know and understand the 'why' before they can begin to heal." He looked at me with a somewhat bemused expression on his craggy face, one that had been permanently stained brown by the desert sun. He had the look of someone in command, sure of himself, and as I felt that was working for us at the moment, I chose to let him maintain his arrogance.

"Start with the girls. Why did you take them?" He looked a little surprised that I had gone back to the beginning. He shrugged.

"As you, no doubt, found out from the Jesuit, may Allah bless him, at our time at the camp, we had children dying every day, I forget the absolute number, but it was well over a hundred. They died from neglect, malnutrition, disease, and just the plain lack of will to live. When the slave traders didn't take them, negligence and disease did. Several aid agencies would visit, drop off a box of supplies and medicines, and then disappear for months, and the cycle was repeated. In the meantime, more refugees crowded into the camp, more children died, and while we did our best, our best was not enough. So, I decided to do something about it, laid out my plans, recruited the few I needed, and moved out of the camp with the first of the girls. My plan was to settle them into good homes, in a number of countries where they had a chance of a good life and the chance to develop their innate talents."

"How many girls did you take?"

"Initially, in the first few years, we only took ten or eleven at a time. Later, we were able to manage around twenty to twenty-five at one time." This surprised me; we had been working on a much lower number. Suddenly our treasure hunt for the women had become a little more complex.

"Why did you stop after the first few years?"

"It was eleven years, and we wanted to see what we had fostered. What skills the girls had developed, and how we might use them in the future." I nodded, remembering the detail from Amira's interrogation and how Helen had appeared as if by magic at each pivotal development milestone of her career.

"After we restarted the process, we were able to find a permanent solution, and in the last five years, we have been able to place over one hundred girls every year."

"Not associated with you and what you did?" I asked, masking my surprise. "No. Totally independent, fully financed by trusts set up years ago, and sufficient to support the program for years to come."

"Maybe. Don't you think the current situation outside these walls will prevent that from happening?"

"No. They are in no way to blame, have never been involved, and once the world adjusts to the new order, the program will start up again." I let that statement settle for a minute, trying to envisage a world where civilian unrest was at an all-time high, people fought daily for food and drinking water and fled the major cities of the world as if they were avoiding the plague.

Would such a world actively welcome little refugee girls, even if they were financially supported? I was unsure. But I wasn't unsure of my next question, which I fired at him as if from a gun. It had bugged me since we had found out about the girls just a few weeks ago.

"Why girls?" He smiled again, this time to my surprise, with some warmth. "They are smarter, their egos are more contained, they work and study harder, and they are the future of the human race. Little boys like to strut, act out, form gangs and are quick to either sulk or fight. I'm sure we could have found really bright boys in the camps, but the fact remains that the best students we had were little girls, and even if certain sects of my religion do not see the future as I do, not one of the girls we rehomed let themselves or their adopted parents down." I inwardly winced at the "rehomed" comment; they were people, not dogs or cats, but I figured to get more about the "not letting themselves or their parents down" comment. And I decided to stop the pretense of compassion.

"So, the only women who took part in your vicious attack on humanity were the first ones you plucked out of the camps and relocated?" I asked, my voice as sharp as a razor, something he instinctively keyed in on, as his whole body braced as if I was going to strike him. He looked at me with what I chose to interpret as respect but was probably derision. His problem, not mine.

"How many of the girls lived up to your expectation?" I asked, the acid dripping off my voice like butter off hot bread. He smiled again, almost as a challenge, I suspected, but I was on a roll, and I sensed the right question at the right time would unfold a lot of the answers we were looking for.

"I don't know what you mean."

"Really? Remember I mentioned the attacks you launched on an unsuspecting world? Why don't we start at the beginning? The attack on the Holy See, with an air-craft purchased nine years before the attack, stored in Turkey, flown by artificial intelligence in a little black box, and dropping bombs stolen from the United States Air Force back in 2002 or so. Wiped out the entire head of the Catholic Church, tens of thousands of innocent worshippers and bystanders, and reduced the Vatican catacombs to dust, destroying thousands of years of irreplaceable religious history and artifacts." He looked a little surprised at all the detail I had offered, so I pressed my point.

"Now, we do not blame the girls for anything you did before, say 2010, 2011, you might have had some very fast learners, but we'll let that go for the moment. But all those years before, you had help-ers—maybe a nation-state or two really doesn't matter. We will find that out in time. But tell me, if you didn't know what the girls could invent, develop, add to your war chest, when did you first come up with the plan to bomb the Vatican back to the stone age?" The smile was genuine now and almost full-faced.

"I admire what you have been able to discover. But you only know the rim of it. We did not have a specific plan in mind when we started to prepare, but one is always smart to anticipate, particularly when opportunity affords something that otherwise might be denied to you."

"But your girls designed the AI for you, programmed the box, and for all we know, set the aircraft and bombs up for the attack." Again, I made my voice intentionally harsh, sending the message that we were going to prosecute this to the fullest extent. And just like that, he popped up with a statement that I just knew would drive the general madder than she already was.

"No. Listen to me. The girls did not participate in the attacks. Ever. They may have developed some of the technology we used—in fact, I will own up to that. There were several very clever things they did that we later took advantage of. But they did not plan or manage any part of the attacks, other than in a theoretical manner or game playing."

"I don't believe you. I'll explain why, but first, I want your rea-sons for so grievously attacking the Roman Catholic Church." He looked slightly taken aback at my refuting his statement. He would have to get used to that. I decided to stir him up a little more.

"I hope the reason for all that carnage was more than just your Muslim sensitivities getting their panties in a twist?" His face shut down as if I had chopped it in two. He looked through me again, leaned slightly forward, and in an expressionless voice, told me his rationale.

"Forget the Crusades—they were just a well-documented con-flict that had been brewing for hundreds of years. The simple truth is that the Catholic Church, in its many guises, is the most war-mon-gering state in all of history. You cannot find a period in the last three thousand years where the Roman or Catholic Church has not been either the instigator or the perverse middleman in global conflicts that have only benefited the church.

"They raped and pillaged South America, destroyed civilizations all over the globe, and, through the seemingly perpetual rule of old white men, controlled a third of the known world, building the richest treasure chest in history.

"Well, no more. Now they start behind the eight ball, and I pray to Allah that the new cadre of young priests understand that they are in the business of saving souls even though their God is false, not building unimaginable wealth and perpetuating a world order through fear and terror.

"They no longer have the wealth that gave them the base for their power— they no longer have either of their previous historical seats of power—and they are now nothing more than a fragmented but well-distributed religious network in the midst of turbulent civil wars and civil unrest. I wish them success." I sat perfectly still—what he had said was not necessarily untrue, but to hear it all out in one breath, as it were, was mind-blowing.

"You set out to destroy one of the world's biggest religions, one of its oldest, one of its most respected and honored religions, from the top down in one attack?"

"Yes, we did. And we did. You know that yourself. While there are literally thousands of priests and nuns still alive around the world, the hydra that they paid allegiance to is dead—forever purged from our world. It will not rise again in the same form—we have made that certainty with the nature of our other corrections." Inside, my mind filled with anger, and my blood boiled, but I was a professional interrogator, and I owed it to both myself and all those depending on me to get the truth, or at least the truth as this repulsive little man sitting in front of me thought it to be. We hadn't dressed him in the traditional gaol orange, leaving him in a clean set of his desert garbs. I almost wished I could change that, but I didn't want to spoil the arc of his confession.

"How do you justify the attack on the Dome of the Rock? By a UAV, supposedly out of a US base, but proven not to have been, with stolen missiles you obtained some years ago. Your girls were involved in that attack," I stated, all innocence. He bristled at the mention of the girls, so I stowed that away for later. "After all, that specific piece of history is one your religion shared with others, going all the way back to nine hundred CE—as well as being the Mi'rāj, where the Prophet Muhammad ascended into heaven. You wilfully destroyed the most sacred relic in Islamic history; how do you justify that?" He was starting to bristle at my deliberate baiting him about his actions, and I felt a measure of comfort realizing that I could get under his skin. He fired back at me as if I were a paper target and he was a shooter on the pistol range. Both hands held out and pointed at me, no doubt holding an imagined gun of some sort.

To emphasize his words, he leaned slightly forward, underlying the intensity of his response.

"If you know the history of the Dome of the Rock, then you know the accursed Jews took it from us in ancient times, disrespected us in modern times, and have done their very best in recent years to betray our faith by turning it into an amusement park and tourist attraction. And if you look closely at the photos after the attack, what do you see?" he asked, his voice turning harsh from his intensity. I wasn't going to give him the answer he sought.

We had seen the part of the monument that had been untouched by the missile attack; it was one of the first triggers we had that moved us towards suspecting a deliberate Islamic bias in the attacks.

"I see an ancient religious relic destroyed wantonly by a crazy terrorist murderer who is desperately trying to justify his rabid actions. I see a man shrunken by his actions, who has desecrated the very ground on which his so-called God was said to have ascended into heaven from. I see nothing else." He sat back, silent for the moment, his lips compressed, his eyes burning with the desire to reach across the table and throttle me. But he had more to say. I could sense it in him, so I continued to push his buttons to see what would happen.

"Tell me about the attack on the Grand Mosque? How did that play into your plans? Weren't you attacking the very heart of your religion? After all, doesn't every Muslim want to pilgrimage to Mecca?" His face froze over again, and for a second or two, I thought I had gone too far and lost him. Then he relaxed his shoulders, his face as bland as he could make it. But I was getting under his skin, and that gave me hope that I could get to some real answers that we could act on. "Again, if you care to examine the after-attack photos, you will see that it was a directed attack on the infrastructure of the mosque and left the main headquarters and the courtyard where we pray, and the imam's quarters totally unscratched. But after, the attack on Qubbat aṣ-Ṣakhra motivated Muslims all around the world to really consider who their enemy was and do something about it. We have guaranteed a worldwide uprising of every Muslim against the forces of evil that you and those like you have forced on us over the centuries." I sat stunned, the full force of his mad scheme settling in my mind, but outwardly I smiled, sat back in my chair, opened my palms in a gesture of acceptance, and looked him straight in the eye.

"And how do you think it will play in the world media when we show proof that the attacks on two of Islam's most sacred sites were masterminded by you, the seventh—my apology—now the fifth in line for the throne of Arabia, an imam of great stature, who is no more than a narcissist, psychopathic indiscriminate terrorist killer who bombs his own religion into the dust?" And he smiled with such force he almost shook my confidence.

"But I didn't. Israel owned the missiles and the UAV that bombed Miʿrāj. The evidence will prove that mercenary terrorists funded by the French attacked the Mosque; again, that is all the world will see, as well as the thwarted attack on my home country's palace and our king in the failed overthrow attempt. The French are one of the greatest causes of the refugee crisis in middle Europe and Africa. The enemy of the Islamic faith for centuries. Oh, and in case you believe you have a counterstory, we have already uploaded photos and proof of what I have just said, and it is already being distributed to the media as we speak. They may not yet have the ability to disseminate this information as widely as before, but when they do, the story will flood the world with the proof that the forces of evil in the form of two sovereign nations, France and Israel, who throughout history have persecuted us at every opportunity are behind these attacks." I tucked away in my mind, which was now a seething mass of hatred for this little man and his grand plans, the fact that the terrorists had a worldwide distribution ability that we obviously did not know about. I would get our friendly geeks and monks on that as soon as I could if the Boss, who was listening to this interrogation, hadn't already done so.

I let my mind slow down, breathed in through my toes, an old trick I had learned from a black belt Krav Maga Master, and forced my face to reflect calm.

No mean feat at this point.

"How do you explain the attack on West Point? That was perpetrated by one of your refugee women, something that will work against you when the rest of the world finds out about it. You killed thousands of young men and women who were doing nothing more than moving between lecture rooms, sports fields, and barracks, minding their own business. How is this story going to work for your cause, whatever it is?" I couldn't help but let a little sneer into my final question; I wanted to see his reaction. He radiated glee; his face split with a huge smile that reached his eyes, and they literally lit up with the passion reflected in his voice.

"Americans attack America! What could possibly play better on the world stage? A stage where the United States of America has started, participated in, facilitated, supported, or financed over three hundred wars and conflicts just in the last two hundred years. And one of the greatest causes of people being displaced and refugee children being left parentless in known history. Singly the most war-mongering nation of God's earth, may His name be praised, sticking its flawed fingers into every nook and cranny in the endless search for resources and power.

"Driven by white supremacists and bible-bashing religious fanatics who have attempted domination through economic blackmail, political force, and direct military action. Who is the only country to use atomic weapons to attack another country? The USA. Who interferes anywhere in the world where their economic interest may be harmed? The USA.

"The history of the American oil companies in my country is proof enough—and before you ask the obvious, the mercenary terrorists were responsible for using the isotope to poison the oil fields, and won't that shake up the world order?" He was almost laughing, so I decided to wipe the smile off his face permanently.

"Thank you for confirming that attack, and perhaps you would be interested to know that we have tracked, and can prove, that you personally authorized every mercenary attack and paid for them, one at a time, all around the world, from your identified funds transfers, and from the electronic receipts kept by your terrorist friends—and I might add, from the emails we found on your bookkeeper's laptop.

"The link is so solid the World Court had no hesitation in freezing all your accounts, all the way back to the Sovereign Wealth Fund, so your brothers are going to be a little pissed at you as well." I stood up, moved to the door, then turned back to look at him.

"There's no glory in what you have done—just horror, death, and destruction. You might care to think about how this will help your cause while I have a shower and rid myself of the stench of you. Back in an hour." And I opened and closed the door, with a little more force than necessary, looked at the three guards standing at ease in the small corridor, then leaned back on the wall.

"Take him back to his quarters, have him back by thirteen fifteen, give him food and water but don't talk to him." I looked the guards in the eye, sensing their resolve, as no doubt they had been listening in as well. I moved down the corridor to the recreation room, where we had set up a temporary headquarters and where the video and audio from the interrogations were recorded and replayed. Where my team and the general sat around a large table looking at screens. Where a massive coffee machine of some type huffed and puffed at one end, being tendered lovingly by Indigo, who waved me over and handed me a scalding hot mug the size of China with a smile that melted my anger and sorrow.

"*Qui il mio Capitano, il nettare degli Dei!*"

"Thanks, Indigo. I see you got your coffee machine?"

"*Assolutamente! Sto facendo un ordine per avere questo come equipaggiamento obbligatorio ovunque andiamo d'ora in ora in su!*" I smiled at that; the idea of an espresso machine being packed up with weapons, spyware, and computers made me smile at the sheer insanity of it.

Yet it was a known fact that the very first thing that landed in any American ship-borne attack back in the Vietnam days was a Coke machine!

"I'll be back in fifteen," I said to the room, moving through the clutter to the far door. "I was serious about washing him off me." The Boss gave me a hard smile, choosing not to say anything. The general just looked pissed, staring into her empty coffee mug.

At least Indigo beamed at me, boosting my self-image a little. I hit the showers, turned the water up really hot, and, as I scrubbed and washed, started to work out my strategy for round two. We had deliberately used a female interrogator against him, knowing the usual attitude of Muslim males toward their female counterparts. That wasn't working in this case; he seemed to have overcome any reluctance to respect and work with women many years ago. But I was getting under his skin, and I intended to turn what was now just a small incision into a fully-fledged open and bleeding wound before I finished.

Meanwhile, back in the United States, as a direct result of the video conferencing between Anna, the general, and whomever they had engaged on the other end, the president now sat with her CIA, NSA, FBI, and Homeland Security directors, as well as her secretary of state. The mood was somber, but in that strange way of all things political, there was a faint sense of hope, power, and direction. While it was true that every person in power eventually turned on those that had given or granted them that power, in this room, the force emanated from a woman who had well and truly beaten the odds. Originally elected as the vice president to an older, well-worn politician, she had arrived on the scene at a time of constant political upheaval, armed insurrection in the Capitol, a worldwide pandemic nightmare, and an ex-president who still manipulated his party from the background, but in a way that shredded the country's belief in the political system, and consequently their confidence in the people running the country.

And then, just more than a year into their first term, the president had died in his sleep, leaving the job to her. Now, three years later, with another election just a year away, she wondered not for the first time how in the hell she could facilitate an election when the country was up in arms, with multiple cities still burning from angry mobs and mass infrastructures such as transportation, electricity, water, power, health, and food distribution in chaos. Military law had been in force now for nearly a month, and the elected members of Congress and the Senate had been sent back to their electorates to help project calm and show a leadership presence in the midst of the turmoil, with indifferent results.

Some elected members had come to the fore and taken leadership positions, others had played the power game and blamed the other side for everything, and others still had been killed by rioting mobs too worked up to allow a sustained political argument to flourish. But the United States had managed to run elections during the Civil War, the Spanish Flu, and the Great Depression. A mid-term election had never been canceled or moved. Not even World Wars had prevented the democratic process from being implemented. And, in the middle of the greatest disaster ever to hit her country, she needed a strategy to move them all forward.

There had been a normal party process prior to the terrorist attacks; her party had competition in the form of a strong candidate in the governor of Texas, and the polls had shown her to have a slim lead up until the first attack. Then in a matter of days, like a rollercoaster breaking through the rails, the polls went for her, then catastrophically against her, where they presently remained frozen in time. The crash of the Internet changed everything. Now everyone was relying on old-style handphones with wires and even older-style fax machines to get their messages out. The political money train had been cut off mid-stream, as had the messages and pleas for funding to fight the good fight. The only thing that had not happened was that no one was attacking her personally for the chaos and disruption to their way of life.

Yet.

And this was the crux of the matter in her mind—how to man-age the communications around the attacks.

What to say, and how to say it. Who to blame, and the con-sequences of that? With everybody at each other's throats already, inflaming a religious war seemed ludicrous. So far, no one outside a very small and tight group of people knew the background to the attacks. How long she could keep it that way was beyond her, in a world used to three-second sound bites, three clicks, and the answer to every question in the palm of their hands. The one good thing about the crash of the Internet was that it had slowed the business of information dissemination down to a trickle.

To her knowledge, there hadn't been a newspaper or magazine printed since the attacks. That wouldn't last. Local pirate radio stations using old valve equipment were already up and running, feeding battery-powered radios that were being made by teenagers out of electronics, not fried by the crash. The hottest item on the black market was an old valve short wave radio.

Enraged DJs around the country pumped their rhetoric out, sandwiched between music played by record players older than they were, and shouted rhetoric about the civil unrest, the lack of food, water, transportation, and anything else they could fit in. She was reminded of a saying her mentor at college had often said: "You can attack the human spirit, but you can never crush it!"

"Madam President, we have the feed from the first interrogations set up; would you like us to run it?" The marine colonel, resplendent in his "Greens," stood ramrod straight in front of the massive screen that filled one wall. She nodded slowly, her mind still on the problem of what to say and how to say it.

And when to say it.

Maybe she would glean an answer from what she saw. She hoped so. She had never felt so inadequate in her entire life!

I walked back into the recreation room, clean and fresh, and prepared for round two with Mohammad bin Azaria. My team hadn't moved, nor had their dispositions changed very much. Quiet, a little glum, no joy or laughter. Indigo was the only one who showed any energy, playing with his espresso machine. I stopped midway, looked straight at the general, held her eyes, waited until I saw her focus, then held my hand up, making a stop sign with my palm to prevent her from speaking.

"It won't get any better, General, but at least we will have his version to work with." I held her stare, waiting for a reaction. She just nodded, passive-aggressive to the last. I looked at the Boss, who nodded, so I moved back down the corridor to the small room we were using. The guards stood easy outside the door, nodded at my approach, and the one closest to the door reached down and opened it for me.

"Good luck, ma'am," he whispered as I crossed in front of him. The subject of our attention sat slumped in his chair, rolling prayer beads through his fingers, a habit I had not seen previously.

In fact, this was the first time I had seen the beads in his possession. The guard saw my look, placed one hand on my shoulder, and whispered again. "They have been tested, and they're clean." I nodded my thanks, closed the door, and took my seat.

"So, to pick up where we left off, you have admitted to funding the terrorist attacks and having hired the mercenary terrorists. Let's clean up some other things, starting with the attack on Lloyds of London. Why? What harm had they ever done to you and yours?" I had hoped to throw him off his tempo with the question, but he puffed himself up and leaned into me again as if wishing to make a physical impression. I didn't move, letting him think he was cramping my personal space.

"When Edward Lloyd set up his coffee shop in London, back in 1686, the very coffee he made money from was carried halfway around the world by our dowels and sailing ships. When the maritime industry started to insure vessels against the various elements, he and his board refused to provide insurance cover for us on the basis that we were probably pirates, our vessels were unsafe, and therefore uninsurable.

"This drove us to create our own market, and when our Islamic scholars decided that we could not insure because of the element of risk and that the money would be used to support alcohol and other forbidden products, we devised our own scheme for protecting our vessels. Islam has always seen the insurance industry as corrupt and evil, so we simply removed their ability to do business. No one was hurt, but the financial pain is felt worldwide."

"What about the death of the chairman just a day before your attack."

"Pure coincidence. We had nothing to do with that event, even though you will probably lay it at my door."

I decided to move on to the big stuff.

"You said earlier you sponsored the attack on the Arabian oil fields with nuclear materials to deny the world their oil. You know that the radiation spread throughout all the adjoining fields, effectively shutting down sixty percent of the world's oil reserves and killing a few thousand innocent people in the process. Why? What did you hope to achieve?" His smile now was childlike; I had obviously hit a sweet spot in his rhetoric.

"Oil destroyed my country, threatened to destroy our Islamic values, corrupted our people, drew your accursed way of life into our peaceful deserts, and as history will show, the money from those accursed oil fields turned us against ourselves, caused Sharia to war against Sunni, destroyed the simplicity and beauty of our faith by your greed and lust for power. Take away the oil, and you take away the power."

"But your Sovereign Wealth Fund, which you parceled up and sent all over the world to finance your terrorist attacks, was built purely on revenue from your oil reserves. How do you rationalize that?"

"It served its purpose; I have no more to say on that. If my brothers cannot maintain their lifestyle without their evil profits from oil, then they can adjust their lifestyles accordingly. Perhaps they can smash down those atrocious buildings they have erected everywhere, a blight on our skyline." He shrugged his shoulders as if dismissing the most vicious attack on modern civilization as a simple righting of wrongs. I added two more words to my description of him—delusional and maniacal.

"So, you irradiated the oil fields to get back at your brothers and cousins, because they chose the Western way of life," I asked, letting credulity strain my voice. I wanted him to get upset and off-balance because we were getting to the heart of the matter, even though he appeared to be unaware of the arc of my questioning. He just sat with a smug smile on his face, his hands now back inside his sleeves. I held the silence for a full minute, just looking at him, smoothing my inner feelings of rage and temper. I would need another shower quite soon at this rate, but I would not stop now until we finished.

"Your refugee children that you are so proud of grew up to be first-class terrorists, developing sophisticated technology weapons for you, which your mercenary friends used to great effect. There is no getting away from the fact that these women did create the weapons and, as such, aided and abetted terrorist acts. Further, as you provided the funds for these women and the terrorists, we can and will charge you with multiple counts of first-degree murder and terrorist activities. There's a whole basket of charges lining up. And we will hunt down every child and woman and tar them with the same brush. Terrorists. Murders. As I asked before, what did you hope to achieve with these attacks?" For a brief moment, I saw worry flicker across his face, but he regained his composure so fast it was just an impression. But I had seen it. And as we had worked out in our strategy meeting, the girls were his Achilles heel.

"The girls were not involved in any attacks. I told you that before. Some of them might have developed technologies that we later turned into weapons, but none of them had anything to do with the terrorist attacks. Nothing! And it was time for the world to experience the same conditions that refugees live with every day of their miserable lives! And tell me honestly, with little or no fuel, no water or electricity, civil war in nearly every country on the globe, mass migration of whole populations, uncontrolled and unwelcome, do you not think that I will have made my point by the time it settles down if it ever does?"

"Who shot down the International Space Station?" I fired at him. "We know you brought the aircraft from the boneyard; we know your refugee woman pilot flew it out to your nest in the United States, just as we know she set up the aircraft that took out West Point. We have her face, her history. We know everything there is to know about her."

"The women had nothing to do with the attacks!" he shouted at me, little bits of spittle flying out of his mouth like bees escaping from a shaken hive. I just smiled at him, sat back, and let him vent. I had no clear idea how we would manage the women; in fact, I had no idea how we might find them unless we got lucky. We only had the one person we had identified and tracked back to her third grade in primary school. The American pilot. Her adoptive parents had disappeared completely off the grid, and while we had her history in glorious detail, almost day-by-day, we didn't know who she really was or was now posing as, and we didn't know where she was. I decided to hammer the nail in as hard as I could.

"The women will be hunted down like the terrorists they are, and we will prosecute them to the fullest extent of the law. That's if they survive the hunting expedition, and trust me when I say we have skilled hunters ready and willing to go, just itching to make their mark. And as we consider you to have declared war on us, we will shoot these women first and maybe ask a question or two later. You have my word on that."

And I stood up and walked out of the room, leaving him fuming. The guards smiled at me, happy that I had at least scored a point or two with our prisoner. But we had a lot of ground to cover before we really scored any points that mattered.

And we had to find the girls.

I walked back into the recreational room to do a lot of finger-snapping.

"You beast!" Indigo shouted, laughing over the top of his shout. "The look on our terrorist's face when you said we would hunt down and kill the women is the best thing I have seen all this year!" I patted him on the shoulder, happy with his response and mildly surprised to see the general and the Boss snapping their fingers as hard as Indigo.

"Enough! Enough! I'll sign autographs later. Form a line!" I said, melting into Indigo, who now had me in a bear hug. His head, with its wiry crop of jet-black hair, only came up to my chin, so it was a little one-sided. The general put her hand out, so I took it, felt the mild compression as she squeezed my hand, then smiled at me.

"You did it. You found his soft spot; we can work that and maybe get what we need to find the women. Thank you." I waved her thanks away, mindful that we really hadn't got a whole lot more than what we had in the evidence summaries and transcripts.

But she was correct. We now had a lever to work him with. If he wanted to protect his girls from my fabled but mythical hunters, although under the circumstances I had no doubt that the general had teams of them hidden away somewhere, he would have to help us identify and locate them.

Time would tell.

"What next?" the Boss asked. I looked at him, knowing he had the next steps planned to the ninth degree, so I spoke my mind.

"We walk the walk, talk the walk, put boots on the ground, and get inside the minds of these women and we find them. Simple. And I think that in a day or two, we let Arie have a chat with our friend in there, so he can let him know how close we are to locating some of the women, and how happy we are to hunt them down and kill them."

Back in the secured bunker, the president and her intelligence staff finished watching the video of the first interrogation. A moment of dead silence followed the end of the video, and for a change, no one jumped in to fill the silence.

The president broke the ice. "She's good, isn't she?" she commented, not expecting anyone to answer.

"Yes," the FBI director said, standing up, "like her boss, one of the very best."

He should know. He had been friends with PJ Anthony for over thirty years and had survived the shelling, bombings, and getting shot with him over the years before the colonel had been recruited into the special division of Interpol. And he had inwardly cheered when PJ had recruited a fierce warrior who had just shot him repeatedly with a high-caliber weapon outside the gates of an overseas military base. A warrior who had graduated top of her class from the NCIS academy spoke several languages like a native and commanded total and utter respect for the men and women under her.

The captain and her colonel were now leading the charge against the terrorists, and for the first time in twenty-four days, he felt the first ray of hope.

His president didn't, reflecting on the statement that the terrorist leader had made, bold as brass, that the evidence against Israel, France, and the US had been sent around the world, by means unknown, ready to be shared with the general public as soon as the civilian media infrastructure was up and running again.

How to control that? How to mitigate the damming messages? She could only imagine one outcome, and she physically shivered at the thought.

The meeting broke up, leaving the president with her uncomfortable thoughts.

Chapter 3

It was a truism about police work, had been for centuries, and would probably still be in another hundred years. Roger Winslow, somewhat dapper in his Amani suit, sat with his highly polished brogues on his desk, long legs crossed at the ankles, reading the intelligence summary his people had put together in the last ten days, from sheer, hard, consistent, and sometimes dogged work, one-on-one, around the clock and across the still smoking borders of twenty states.

Boots on the ground, get in people's faces, make it personal, and tug the tiniest of threads until it either leads to another thread or unravels. Old-school policing, nothing like it. He still remembered the days when he had been in uniform, required to write his interview summaries on eight-by-six cards and file them in a little metal box. He shook his head at the memory, wondering where all those little ink-stained cards now rested.

Probably in some dusty warehouse. He picked up his phone, at least as old as he was, listened for the mechanical clicks of his connection with the hastily erected switchboard, then, as polite as he could manage under the circumstances, requested he was connected to his opposite number in the NSA.

"Reynolds!"

"Roger. Don't you miss caller ID?"

"Yes. What do you want?"

"Polite, aren't you? What's got your knickers in a twist?"

"The fact that these bloody heathen terrorists have managed to get video and audio messaging around the world, under our bloody noses, and we have no idea how they manage it."

"Well, it's obvious. They're using someone's satellites and ones that were not killed by the crash of the Internet. Work out how that works, and you'll have your culprit." At the other end of the phone, the head of the NSA just grunted.

Typical Winslow, blather on about something he didn't know anything about as if he was an expert!

"Roger, we've already figured out how they avoided crashing the computers and machinery at hospitals; we had that data the day after the Internet went down. And we have enough of our own equipment back up and running to see anything transmitted via satellite. Nothing. And remember, most of our computers are air-gapped, so all we really lost was our outside connectivity."

"Then they're using the undersea cable network."

"You think we haven't got that covered? Roger, we're not stupid."

"Then what could they be using? It had to be in place before the attacks, it had to be relatively bulletproof, and it had to be able to operate in every country. Could they have hacked into the underground cable infrastructure?"

"No. The first place we looked. It seems to me that they have similar technology to the monks that are helping Anthony. Remember, the monks were able to intercept the calls from Mohammad bin Azaria to and from the secretary of state, which we were unable to do even when we had everything working. And before you ask, we don't know how the monks do it; we've done everything but shred the little laptops they have given us, and all we have learned is that a signal, heavily encrypted, goes out somewhere and lands somewhere else. It has to be a satellite somewhere, probably hidden in one of the thousands of commercial constellations that were also killed by the Internet attack. But we can't find it at this point."

"Have you asked them?" The silence that filled the line said it all. Sometimes the simplest solution was the best and only solution, another time-proven parable.

"No. But I will. Why did you call?"

"Have you watched the second conversation with Mohammad bin Azaria?"

"Yes."

"And your opinion?"

"She's found his weak spot. We knew all that other data he confirmed, but we did not know how precious his women were to him. We can use that. But I've got another puzzle for you."

"You have? This should be interesting." To Frank's highly tuned ear, his friend sounded a little sarcastic, but he put it down to the sheer tiredness that had hit everyone working the case for what felt like a year but had only been three and a half weeks.

"The money. It doesn't add up. We have him moving around one hundred and twenty-six billion into thirty-odd accounts over ten years, all legitimate, all managed by qualified and licensed practitioners, all visible. Taxes paid, certified, as clean as a whistle. Then we have the three hundred and seventy million dollars paid to the mercenaries, through several accounts all controlled by Shetani, and that lines up with the number of oil, gas, fracking, and coal sites attacked that we have been able to identify. Add in the drone attacks on the stadia, and it gets close to what we see. It was a simple relationship with the mercenaries, one million a hit, paid within twenty-four hours of proof-of-strike.

"And here's another puzzle. He managed to move the funds into the terrorists' accounts after the Internet went down, in at least twenty-six accounts in twelve countries spread all over the world."

"That will be easy to track. He probably used prepaid transfers where the money was already in the target accounts but only became visible to the account holder when a special code was applied. A typical blockchain strategy."

"We hadn't thought of that; do me a favor and run that down for us, please."

"Done. Now, why I called. Would you be interested in a small factory in New Zealand that seems to be working just fine under the circumstances, don't know what they do yet, but we do know that they were seeded by funds from the Sovereign Wealth account five years ago, to the tune of six billion dollars, again, legitimate transfer, listed as investment/start-up capital, lodged in a trust account, passed all the smell tests, and all audited and taxed as appropriate, and drawn down in a manner that suggests a serious manufacturing endeavor, and it's a pattern we are seeing in quite a few places. All located on the ocean, but the countries are interesting."

"How so?"

"Well, what do you think northwestern USA, Canada, Greenland, Chile, Portugal, Ireland, Denmark, Norway, Finland, Estonia, Sri Lanka, Solomon Islands, New Zealand, Japan, and Iceland have in common?" The director of the NSA went into deep thinking mode and became an innate pattern thinker. He loved a puzzle and quickly dialed up a world map on his screen, then highlighted the countries his FBI friend had listed.

"No idea. That's more your territory, I would have thought."

"Well, the detail is still sketchy at the moment, but it looks the same sort of business model, six billion in an account, all legitimate, then split out to different companies all over the place, and we will have boots on the ground in the next few days, travel as you would imagine is not as easy as it used to be, and the military is hoarding their strategic reserves of fuel like there is no tomorrow. I just thought you might be able to dig something up from the raw data we have compiled and save me some time." The director of the NSA scratched his chin, where he had cut himself earlier in the day, trying to shave with an old disposable razor in his private bathroom off his office. Roger might be FBI, but he had a good head on his shoulders, and his instincts were first class.

"Send it over by courier, safer that way, and I'll see what we can do."

"Thanks. Appreciated." And he hung up the handset, bent over the cradle, grimaced, rubbed at his forehead, rolled his shoulders, then sat back and stared off into space, letting his mind absorb this new information. The FBI had a lot of irons in the fire, but he sensed they were getting close to something tangible.

He just didn't know what that might be.

Chapter 4

The Canadian border fought a constant war with the United States, so far as the little jut of land called Point Roberts was concerned. The borderline chopped left and right carving up the islands to the south but rudely interrupted the jut by chopping off a good third in favor of the US, along the forty-ninth parallel, leaving the rest to the Canadians, who, with their usual good humor, ignored the—to them—hypothetical line in the sand and still behaved as if the locals owed their allegiance to Canada, and to hell with the US! This had proved to be a serious flaw in Canadian/US relations, as people living on one side of the line and needing to work or go to school on the other side had two different sets of rules to live by. The recent pandemic had proved the meat of this discomfort, and more than one family had moved because of it. Not to mention that any Canadian who moved across the line south had only six months less a day before their temporary Visa expired!

It made certain parts of life much harder than they needed to be. And Point Roberts wasn't exactly flush, to begin with.

Sort of the runt of the litter as towns on the jut went, important to everyone who lived and visited there but not much impact on the world scene. And to add to the angst, if you already lived in the US and you wanted to go to Point Roberts, you had to cross the Canadian border twice, something that did not sit well with either side of the argument.

But the residents of Point Roberts had grit—passed down from generations of tough, salt-encrusted families with a moral code so strong that nothing could really destroy the pride in the town that the inhabitants had. And there were smarts there as well, an unknown statistic being that better than half of all the teenagers who left the town for college returned within three years of graduation, simply because nowhere else felt as good as living on the jut. Once back, many of them worked for large corporations remotely, using a massive low-earth-orbit satellite constellation for their high-speed internet.

That model hadn't survived the crash of the Internet, so, temporarily, around a hundred very smart young people were out looking for work.

When an obscure corporation registered in Portland as an environmental scientific organization purchased, quite openly, the small houses and tin sheds along Vscandia Lane, off Boundary Bay Road, and then expanded their interest by buying all the allocated plots along Claire Lane and Apa Road, all the way to the foreshore, no one particularly objected.

The houses in that area had not been occupied for some time, and then by people usually associated with those damn inconvenient Canadians to the North.

The Point Roberts Chamber of Commerce looked at the application to enjoin all the blocks, totaling some thirty acres into one title, looked at the simple plans to build an ecologically friendly series of small sheds and laboratories, install power and waste systems independent of the town, and hire perhaps as many as thirty local and currently unemployed engineers and scientists, not to mention the massive local workforce required to build the infrastructure; they saw no reason not to approve it. The town had been literally broke for nearly half a century, not having moved very far from its origins as a staging point for pirates back in the good old days, or the gold miners of more recent ones. This could be the miracle they had all been waiting for. When the notices went up for public comment, one item on the bottom right under the surveyor's drawings drew particular interest. All the excess power generated by the site would be pumped straight back into the local grid, at no cost to the community, and once established, the company would offer alternative sourced power and storage at a fraction of the usual commercial cost to any resident who wanted to take them up on the offer.

Point Roberts, which boasted a long grass runway at its municipal airpark, and a sizable marina, sadly lacking anything with sails, suddenly saw itself in the twenty-first century, with little or no effort by the city fathers.

This might just give them the revenue they so desperately needed to modernize—perhaps even to pave the runway at the airpark!

And if the revenue started to flow in a predictable and sustainable manner, they would, at last, have something they could hold over their neighbors in Boundary Bay and Tsawwassen to the north, in accursed Canada!

That was three years ago, and today the newly elected mayor stood on a tiny, wooded platform in front of a small crowd excited to be in the spotlight.

The turmoil and chaos that raged through parts of Canada and the United States after the terrorist attacks had mostly left them alone. After all, what was there for others to desire? They were self-sufficient, to an extent; their fishing fleet did good business, and the growing areas across the border supplied most of the products required in the town, and there weren't many empty houses anyway for an influx of migrants.

Those that were looked like they needed a lot of love before they could be occupied again. It was almost as if they were the forgotten part of Washington State, and wasn't that a real blessing in disguise!

The mayor stood up to the microphone, looked at her audience, and for the first time in her life, wished that Point Roberts wasn't such a backwater from a media point of view. The day was cold, wind chills down in the very low single digits, so the only remarkable thing about her dress was the red, white, and blue mayoral sash that crossed her not insignificant chest. Her face was red and blotchy from the cold, but you could see the pride and strength in her if you looked at her blazing green eyes, which shone with such intensity she held everyone's attention.

"Friends, thank y'all for coming. I know it's way far from your usual places, but today is a really important day for us and the whole area that is our very own Point Roberts. Our population is quite small, less than two thousand people at the moment, but with this here wonderful company, from today, we'll be getting a free boost to our local power grid that will give us all the power we need for heating, cooking, and working. It could be called a miracle, but too many of you have worked so hard over the past three years to make this possible. It would be rude to try to make it something it isn't. I've been informed that it might be possible for us to actually send power north to our neighbors, and won't that set them back on their heels! Maybe more. So, without further to-do, let me cut this ribbon here—there we go—and send this mighty power on its way!" Polite muffled applause followed, intermingled with a few encouraging yells until the small crowd started to move away back towards the town and their homes, the promise of electric power for the first time in a month or so its own drawcard. Most walked, some rode bicycles, and a few more of the elderly climbed aboard a school bus that had been electrified some years ago with a rare government grant.

Standing back in the shadows, the engineer and the scientist watched the pantomime, their faces neutral. Neither was dressed in any fashion that was noticeable, both covered from head to toe with standard cold-weather gear, gloved, and watch caps pulled down over their ears.

Their eyes also shone, but with a different passion to that of the mayor.

That they had facilitated a local miracle never crossed their minds; so focused on their project they were, and from their perspective, this was just the first step in delivering hope to a bunch of people who were mostly good at heart and had proven themselves day after day getting the facility up and running. The local workforce had stabilized at just under a hundred, with an average age of around twenty-five years. Another fifty had been trained in the distribution and installation requirements for the power, storage, and generation systems and had been sent off to the small offices up and down the West Coast purchased and opened specifically for them six months ago. Each office had a large garage attached, where a Pantech could easily enter, unload, then return to the highway without effort. The distribution agents, as they were called, had spent their time building up local networks through which they could move the devices once they were unloaded.

"Okay, that's done. Now we need to get the shipping component up and running."

"Have you identified who you'll approach?" the engineer asked, thinking about the logistics of turning a huge barge that would sit off the end of a pier yet to be built into an efficient, self-contained electric vessel that could run between the point where their massive pipes entered the water, and Seattle to the south, and Vancouver to the north, to fill the Pantech's that had been fitted out months ago, and now sat waiting in garages and sheds.

"Yes. One of the boats will come from Portland, the other from Seattle. They are both low, flat, shallow-draft barges; they are perfect for our purpose. They will be here in three days; getting the fuel was the hardest part, but as usual, money talks. I've already recruited twenty of the young graduates from town; they've been training in Lab Three. I could have got a hundred; the Internet crash killed a major contributor to the revenue stream here, and job-sharing is not out of the question. Perhaps you could give some time to thinking about how we might create a small industry up here modifying the barges?"

"How many will we need?" The scientist shrugged her shoulders, waved her arms to warm herself up, and stomped her feet, accidentally drawing the attention of the few remaining spectators. She just smiled and looked down at the ground, not allowing eye contact to be made.

"This and the New Zealand plant will be all we have for the next six months. So, if we say that we limit our supply to West Coast Canada, the US, and South America, maybe ten or even fifteen units at a time; the scalable production rate you designed is perfect for a staged approach, and we really don't want to draw too much attention to it all so early. Just one thing. We will need deep keel boats in New Zealand, so I'm sourcing them from the mainland. You can work out how to do that?"

"Yes. So, start with two here and maybe only the one in New Zealand, then let the natural outside demand force us to expand, make them come to us, as it were?" the engineer asked, not for the first time awed by the massive planning that had gone into this phase of the operation.

It had taken years to put it all together, but she could see it playing out all around her exactly as it had been planned as if the world was responding to the biggest movie script ever written. She remembered the words of an eclectic forensic psychologist she had studied under in the last year of her doctorate, "People are not programmable, like a computer, or necessarily predictable, but they are hostage to their emotional patterns and beliefs. Change their beliefs, and you can change their attitudes, behaviors, and values."

They wanted the world to suffer as their refugee child friends had and still were in their millions, to come to understand that without hope, life was meaningless. Well, they had the hope, but they also had a plan to dribble it out until people changed their beliefs and came to realize what really needed to be fixed in the world order of things. Stop the genocidal and politically motivated wars that blew up the innocent, split families, killed unnecessarily, and achieved, realistically, when you looked back through history, very little other than to create a new wave of refugees to flood an already overcrowded tent city somewhere meaningless.

Well, the whole world now was experiencing what refugees lived with every day of their shortened lives.

No fuel, water, no power, little or no food, and trapped in a location because moving away got you killed by marauders and thieves intent on bettering their lives at your expense. And if you were a child, probably with no parents, no name, and the only support in the form of some random adult that cared and, against the odds, managed to keep you alive, your future was probably no more than living and dying in a refugee camp and achieving in your life nothing more than just adding to the statistics in some educated tome.

No, the world had to change, and the sheer sense of pride that built in the hearts and minds of the scientist and the engineer as they watched the village people fade into the twilight almost became unbearable. With tears in her eyes, the scientist, who could bench press her own weight plus forty kilos, turned and hugged her friend, then carefully steered her away back to the entrance of the facility. It was a good day, and it would get better when they put the next part of their plan to irrevocably change the world into motion.

Halfway around the world, above the beautiful landscape of Great Barrier Island, off the northeastern coast of New Zealand, a micro drone flew a racetrack pattern around the area bound by Okiwi Airfield, Omahungaiti Bay, and Komahunga Bay, with its longest run over the flat grasslands bordering the forests and mountains to the south. The little drone had been offline and broken down for maintenance during the Internet attack, so it was still fully functional; the only modification needed to make it useful again was the addition of a flash storage drive in lieu of the data transmitter that now had no working receiver to transmit its video images to.

The controller sat in a small solar-powered plane on the end of the strip, next to the pilot, who was counting down the minutes before the little air vehicle ran out of power.

"Three minutes," he called, looking up through the windshield to see if he could spot the drone.

"On the way back," the controller said, turning to look out the other side of the plane. A tiny, black dot slowly grew in size until, with a snap and a distinct plop emphasized by the high-pitched buzz of the propellors winding down to a sudden stop, the drone dropped out of the sky beside the aircraft, as if it were exhausted from having run a marathon.

"Got it, hold one," the controller said, stepping out the side door. He picked up the drone, checked to see if the flash storage was intact, then climbed back into the aircraft. The pilot wound up the sixteen small electric engines that made a sound not unlike a squadron of bees out for a pleasurable run to a pollen-enriched flower crop and turned the aircraft into the wind.

"Auckland Control, Mike November Mike Okiwi circuit, request airways clearance, taxing at this time." The very old high-frequency radio transmitter, the size of a bunch of shoeboxes, lashed together, hissed, and squeaked with ionospheric interference, making the pilot sound like he had crackers in his mouth. The controller in faraway Auckland replied, but all the pilot heard was squeaks and buzzes and static intermingled with the odd part of a word. In the absence of other aircraft in visual range, he lined up on the runway, advanced the throttles, the engines revved themselves up into a high-pitched whine, and the aircraft gently moved down the runway until its flimsy Dacron-covered wings generated enough lift to get it in the air.

Far from the days of real powered flight, only a month ago, in reality, the pilot thought, everything had changed. No satellite navigation. No digital radio. The only navigation radio aides that had survived were the really old valve-based radio frequency finders or non-directional beacons, NDBs as they were known in flying circles, and while they were a time-proven aid to navigation, the modern crop of pilots had never trained on them, other than to read about them in their airport maps as a footnote: "in case of loss of signal from DGPS or VOR, resume navigation using NDB and advise bearing and radial data to airways controllers."

And now he was relying on the NDB as his sole electronic means of locating Auckland, some one hundred and twenty kilometers away, over water. Well, that's what he got paid the medium bucks for, so he tuned his primary navigation equipment, his mark#1 eyeballs, checked the map on his lap, then watched the small magnetic compass mounted on the central cockpit windscreen pillar swing and bounce in its spirit bubble until he had his desired heading. He checked his gyro-compass and shrugged his shoulders; they wouldn't get too far off the rhumb line flying at just a little over eighty knots once they climbed to height, and the main island should be visible in half an hour in any case.

And as his father would have said, way back in the days, New Zealand was flying massive Hercules C-130Js, then C-17 Globemasters in support of humanitarian relief missions all over the globe, "piece of cake!"

Chapter 5

The bunker was well equipped. One full wall of screens, now just displaying the logo of the president of the United States. One wall of photos, mostly of military men and women in various groups standing in the open, on rostrums, at airfields, or in front of serious-looking military hardware. A bragging wall of sorts, though I couldn't determine the core of it.

A third wall held art, some modern, some old, very few pieces I recognized from my abandoned studies of the creative world some years ago. The fourth wall held a long bench, on which sat a range of weird-looking instruments and objects, some I recognized, most I didn't.

The middle of the room held a talking circle, in the shape of an open square, made up of three exquisite chesterfield lounges, each capable of seating four people, centered around a massive oak table that sat on squat legs made out of tree trunks. The only thing missing to make this wilderness scene perfect was the lack of a double-headed ax embedded in the table! The open side was interrupted by a single chesterfield, currently occupied by the president of the United States. This eclectic room belonged to someone, and that someone had a sense of humor as far as style went. Didn't matter now, as my focus was on the people sitting on the couches, some relaxed, some tense. Make that very tense.

Anna and the General had flown over with Pete and me in a plane supplied by the United States Military Air Transport Command. The General had sat removed from us, up forward, behind a small screen, which I took to be the navigator's position. This suited me to perfection because I could – and did – sleep most of the way across the Atlantic. I knew Pete had slept 3as he had snored across in the seat from me, twisted and turned in a restless mania, until I had moved to an empty row further back. Anna had kept very much to herself, choosing to sit away from us, and on the other side of the plane. It wasn't personal, she looked as tired as I felt, and we had been living in each other's pockets for weeks.

We may or may not have refueled mid-air, I had slept through it if we had, but I really didn't care. My mind was occupied with how I was going to track down thirty or forty faceless women with no history, no documentation of any sort, who could be living anywhere in the world and probably were. And had, between them, developed the most sophisticated weapons ever unleashed on an unsuspecting world. Interpol had been endorsed in the last twenty-four hours by a brace of African countries who woke up some time to discover all their oil and gas wells and pipelines bore the badge of high tech—the ubiquitous silver clag where oil and gas had once flowed so freely. As many of these countries were, by my light at least, terrorists' states, I didn't really concern myself with the details. It wouldn't change our approach, but I had sent a message to the Boss to see if some of Shetani's people were still at work or if it was simply the lack of communication that had created a time-lapse between attack and report.

We at Interpol had worked out the minimum number of women needed to mount the attacks, given that the mercenary terrorists led by Shetani had done the physical work on the ground. We got between four and six at the minimum. In interrogation, we learned that the mastermind behind all of our troubles had recruited hundreds of girls over the years, with a pause at around year ten or eleven. The first tranche seemed to be no more than fifty-odd. The second more than doubled that amount, but I was discounting them at this time because, by our math, the eldest would have only been mid-teens at the time of the attacks, maybe late teens, but far too young to have participated in the development of the technology weapons. Time would prove that assumption wrong.

But that left fifty-odd women to track, with the starting point of two seriously bombed-out locations, one in Libya, which the Boss would sort out, and one in the midwest of the United States.

My target.

I'd get there eventually, but first, I had to survive this little fireside chat with the president, who had signaled her attitude to us quite clearly in the way we had been met and escorted to the bunker once our plane had landed somewhere.

I wasn't even sure of the location.

Three blacked-out SUVs had pulled up to the steps, the general and Anna had got straight into one and driven off, Pete had been loaded into another, and then I had been invited by a helmeted and well-armed pair of escorts to climb into the back of the third. Why Pete and I had been separated was never made clear.

Not a single word had been spoken. A gloved hand had been held in front of my face until I hand handed over my weapon, then another pair of gloved hands had patted down my legs and ankles, and then we took off at such a fast rate my head hit the back of the seat rest. My little laptop still sat in my pocket, as well as my Interpol credentials.

We arrived in silence. I was escorted into a darkened tunnel, then left to my own devices until I emerged into the annex of the underground bunker, where I was offered a pile of clean clothes, two towels and sneakers, then pointed to a door marked "femmes." I took the hint, showered, perhaps a little longer under the hot water than I should have, took my time drying myself, applied the fairly neutral cosmetics sitting on the mirrored shelf, and brushed my hands through my hair, which was in serious need of mowing, rolled my shoulders, put my clothes in the basket labeled "clothes," the towels in the one marked "towels," wondered for a split second about the obsessive-compulsive mind who had set all this up, then walked out.

To an entirely different atmosphere.

I was handed a mug of steaming coffee by an ensign dressed in navy blues, the creases on her pants capable of slicing bread, offered a plate of sandwiches, and soon spotted Pete digging in with his normal gusto across the small anteroom, his back to the wall, his eyes moving continuously.

Of Anna and the general, there was no sign. I looked over at the hovering ensign, smiled, and cleared my mouth of the excellent sandwich.

"How long do we have?" I asked, noting she did not have the usual name tag on her uniform jacket. She looked at a watch hidden under her jacket sleeve, then looked back at me with a semblance of warmth in her eyes.

"Ma'am, the president will arrive in ten minutes. If you could please finish your meal, then go into the conference room before then, it would be appreciated." I nodded my assent, and looked at Pete, who winked at me, always a reassuring sign from him; it meant he perceived no direct threat and was comfortable abiding by someone else's rules for the time being. The fact that he was enjoying his lunch with a wall at his back, and a view of every exit and the room, in general, did not go unnoticed. We both cleaned up our plates, finished off our coffee, then stood up and wandered into the conference room. The general and Anna entered from the other end, almost simultaneously, suggesting they had us under video surveillance or their timing was just lucky. My paranoia being healthy and in fully heightened awareness mode, chose surveillance.

The general was in her uniform, and like the ensign, the creases so sharp they could inflict serious wounds, her chest resplendent with rows and rows of salad dressing, as we called it, but when I had looked her up the first time I had learned of her, I realized she was a very heavy hitter and had more than likely earned every little colored ribbon the hard way—and twice—once as a woman in a male-dominated environment, and once again as a soldier in real combat.

Anna had slipped something simple on, her usual standard FBI black suit. A crisp white shirt with the requisite black neck scarf completed her innocuous ward-robe. She smiled at me, raising her eyebrows at my matching top and pants, which could only be called classy by a blind person living in a cave.

"Jessica, sorry about the wardrobe, but that is all they had here in your size. Your bags have gone straight to your quarters." Anna smiled, and again I perceived no threat, and thinking it through, they had really done well by us, given how little notice we had provided to them about what we intended to do.

The president arrived, her back straight, but her posture very stiff sat in her chair and looked a little worn around the edges, which I could sympathize with. Directly opposite her, Anna sat with the general, with Pete and me sitting on one of the sides. Then the secretary of state walked in, with an aid of some sort, who carried a large portfolio, and took the remaining couch. I noticed the general sat next to the Secretary but in front of the president, even though all three were on different lounges or seats. Very strategic, and I remembered the general's words to me just a day or two ago, "to get to the Secretary, you'll have to go through the president, and to get to the president, you have to go through me."

Well, I had got my wish because all three were now in range, so I wasted no more time.

"Madam President, thank you for seeing us, and Madam Secretary, thank you also for your time. How would you like me to proceed?" The president, dressed in a smart blue suit, crisp white shirt, her hair pulled back behind her ears with some sort of tie, looked to her Secretary, who was also dressed in a power suit, but this one in light greys, with a light blue shirt.

Her hair was cut very short and obviously styled by a professional because it had that fresh, casual, just out of the salon look, which made me subconsciously run my hands through my own still, slightly wet hair. I couldn't match them with the style and grace of my bland appearance, so I would have to rely on my training and instincts.

There was a critical element to the backstory here, and I fully intended to dig it out.

"Captain Riley, or may I call you Jessica?" the president asked, her tone neutral. I nodded my assent. "Good, that makes it easier. This is your meeting, your agenda, and let me say at the outset, your interrogation of Mohammad bin Azaria was masterful."

"Thank you, Madam President. I appreciate your comments. We would like a full rundown of all the contacts between bin Usha Rashad and the Secretary. And if I may, could we please get either a recorder or someone to take notes?" She looked at me, her face hardening just slightly then looked at the general and gave the slightest of nods. Her hair swept slowly across her face, only to be pushed back with a hand that was not quite still. I understood her pain due to the attacks; her country was in shambles, probably on the verge of a major collapse in some areas, but why was she nervous?

"Everything in this room is being recorded and has been since you arrived," the general said, in her best parade ground voice.

"I hope not in the showers?" Pete asked in an almost humorous manner; that got the attention of everyone in the room. He just sat back and smiled, Pete at his best. "If you did, I'd like a copy." The general looked as if she were about to swallow her tongue, the president looked baffled, as if such a suggestion was beyond her comprehension, and Anna hid a huge smile behind her hand as she bent her head towards her knees.

She had seen Pete up close and personal and knew his extreme sense of humor.

I cut across the confusion and got back to my point.

"Excellent. Then, Madam Secretary, if you would, could you please give us the details of every conversation you had with Mohammad bin Azaria and any you had internally with your own people as a result." The aide opened the portfolio on her lap and passed the first sheets across to the Secretary. The Secretary looked up and stared at me with the look of a haunted person. While she had been cleared by her own president of any complicity in what the terrorists had achieved, the strain of having carried on high-level government-sponsored conversations with the master planner of the attacks for nearly two years had left its stain. And on the president as well, as the Secretary and the president had been friends since prep school, and the old saw about guilt by association was never truer than in the political arena. I had to defuse this quickly before anyone went into CYA mode. "Madam President, Madam Secretary, as the senior investigator for Interpol, now commissioned by some fifty nations to pursue these terrorists, let me say right up front, we are not looking for any material from you to use in any prosecution.

"This is a fact-finding mission, no more and no less.

"Mohammad bin Azaria has made it clear to us in the interview that his passion for the refugee children was his driving motive, and we have evidence that suggests that you may have something to add to that, in that you were in conversation about the refugee situation, and how it might be managed, and we suspect that some of what you talked about maybe put into action by some of the refugee women at some time in the future. And we want to be there when it is.

"We have to find the women who developed the weapons, who programmed the aircraft and drones, who took down the Internet and Space Station and provided the blueprint for the mercenaries on the ground. We must find them, and we must prosecute them before the world court, or we will not have done our job." The president looked down at her lap, smoothed an imaginary crease in her skirt, then looked straight at the general.

"Jessica, how many people know of the women's existence, and the part they may have played in the attacks?" The general turned her steely glare on me, and I swear that if her eyes had been lasers, I'd be toast! But I was starting to see what had driven her defensive and aggressive manner back in Israel.

I looked at Pete and gave him a subtle nod. Two could play the winking game and I settled back to study the three main actors in this fascinating play. The president was talking to me, a direct question, but looking directly at the general, who in turn was using me as a target for her laser eyes. Neither of them would ever successfully face me at a poker table!

"Madam President, Master Chief Pete. Please call me Pete. I have no last name. I am Captain Riley's aide-de-camp, so I'll answer that question for you. We cannot vouch for your team. We don't know all the players other than Senior Special Agent Bernstein here, the general, and your directors of the NSA, CIA, and FBI, and certain computer specialists in their employ. That aside, there are only fourteen people on our side that know of the women, and that includes the Israeli contingent. However, the fact of the mercenary terrorists led by Shetani is widely known, at least by the sixteen countries we contacted directly and took the appropriate military action, and through our secretariat in Lyon, who distributed a worldwide-all-agency warning about the possibility of the terrorists just before the Internet crash.

"Included in our fourteen people is an agnostic monk and two of his people. They were the ones responsible for providing us with the means to communicate with your people immediately after the Internet attack."

"And on our side, General?" The general's face tightened, the import of what she was about to reveal not lost on anyone in the room.

"Probably less than twenty. I'll have to check with the FBI; they have had agents on the ground actively looking for the pilot of the Hog."

"Madam President, if I may offer a comment?" Anna asked, leaning forward in her seat to make her point. The subtle movement took the general by surprise as she reacted by turning her head with a snap at the interruption. The president waved one hand, now a little steadier than before, and Anna looked over to me and smiled.

"Madam President, I've been working with the Interpol team since day two of the attacks, and I can vouch for both their absolute professionalism and their security. I know my director has kept in constant contact with Colonel Anthony, who he has personally known for many decades. I can fully support the captain's estimate of fourteen people; I've been present when almost every single one of them was brought into the investigation." The president sat back in her chesterfield, seemingly a little more relaxed. Anna paused, let the room catch its breath, then continued. "As the senior agent in charge of the investigation by the FBI, I have been made aware of every step taken by the director and any specialists involved here in the United States.

"I think the number may now be a little higher than twenty due to the NSA pursuing the electronic side of the investigation, but certainly no more than thirty or so. Does that help?"

"Yes, it does, and I have a question for the room. Think seriously about your answer. Do you think it's at all possible to blame everything on the mercenaries and leave the girls out altogether?" The room went dead silent, and I looked at Anna, who seemed to be puzzling over the question, then at Pete, who had his famous crocodile smile splitting his face. I knew exactly what he was thinking; it would be the same as me. Politics! Cover your arse and blame everyone else. I waited on the general, wanting her to make the first move. She did the smart thing and looked at all our faces, holding each one of us eyeball to eyeball for a few seconds, but as I had mentioned earlier, Pete got his name "Black Pete" by winning a poker hand while under rocket fire, and I had never been beaten by anyone I had played since graduating from the NCIS academy. So I don't think she got what she was looking for, at least from us.

"If you look at it clinically, the only woman involved somewhat publicly was the pilot of the Hog that took out Westpoint. Everything else discovered about the women has been behind closed doors.

"If we go with 'rogue' pilot and then mercenary terrorists for all the rest, I think we could get away with it in the media, which is in distress in any case. People believe what they want to believe, and if you repeat it enough, the worst lie takes on the persona of the greatest truth. Look at what one of your predecessors was able to achieve for years, just by repeating the same lie over and over." Anna sat quite still, reviewing what she had just said. "Yes," she added, sitting back on her couch, "we might be able to get out in front and spin it that way." I looked at Pete; he maintained his relaxed and casual manner, but his gaze had hardened just a little, as his eyes, always lost in the creases on his face, drew his lids just a little more closed than usual. The Secretary and her aide sat perfectly still; if they were breathing, it was through the soles of their feet. Then the president nodded once, her hair falling over her face again, only to be briskly flicked back by one pale hand. She turned to look at me, and I met her stony look for stony look.

"Madam President, Interpol has no issue with anything you may or may not release to the media. We will pursue our agenda regardless of any direction you take; we cannot and will not support overt lying to the world community, so please don't ask us to. However, I can see no harm in leaving the women out of the equation so long as you understand we will continue to pursue them to the ends of the earth if that is what it takes. That is our mission, and we will not deviate from it one whit."

I paused to let them all digest what I had said, and across from me, Pete's crocodile smile widened, if that was possible, on his scarred face.

"One point of caution," interjected Pete, still more relaxed than anyone I had ever seen in such a high-powered meeting. "If you check the video of the interrogation, you will clearly hear Mohammad bin Azaria claim to have sent media messages all around the world identifying America, France, and Israel as the attackers, and giving his rationale for turning the world upside down." Again, you could hear the veritable pin drop in the room as the president and her general digested that little gem, one which I believe might force them to change their approach. I smiled to myself and thought through the interview I had facilitated with the terrorist.

"It's unlikely that the women will be credited with anything; he was very strong on the idea that the women had nothing to do with the planning and little more than a marginal hand in the development of the weapons. We know firsthand that to not be true, but if he holds that line, your story might hold water. Now, madam secretary, can I please get an answer to my question? Starting from the first contact, please describe everything you talked about."

The Secretary, who had yet to speak, looked at her president, then back at me. "Captain, could I suggest you take these tapes into another room, review them, and then ask me any questions you may have?" Her aid leaned forward and pushed a small cloth sack towards me.

"What a great idea. Pete, with me. Madam President, thank you for your time. No doubt your people will let you know when we are ready to resume."

And with that, I walked out back into the annex, turned to Pete, and whispered to him, "See if you can get Anna away from the general." He nodded and walked back into the auditorium. The ensign came up to me, braced at attention, and all but vibrated.

"Ma'am, your clothes are clean and pressed and ready for you if you wish to change. A viewing room is being set up for you now. Can I get you anything in the meantime?"

I nodded. Coffee would be great, probably not up to Indigo's gold standard, but when in Rome, drink whatever coffee is available!

We reassembled in the anteroom on the other side of the auditorium, the general and the president obvious by their absence, but Anna was there with Pete, now resplendent in his combat trousers and a T-shirt with Pink Floyd all over the front. His combat boots were clean, and he actually looked cheerful. I had a message for the room and also for the hidden recording system that had tracked us since our arrival.

"Before we get started, Anna, I want you to know, and you too, Pete, I believe the women had a significant role in the planning of these attacks. You know we suspect a nation-state as one of the very long-term players, but we are certain that the guts of the attack plan were either drawn up by or driven by the women."

"Why?"

"Because it's so damn smart. When you look at the timing, the simplicity of it, in a sense, the sheer elegance, it's beyond the reach of the traditional terrorist, no matter how clever they might be.

"I'll wear that the theft of the bombs and missiles was long-term planning, but everything from the time of the acquisition of the air-craft was driven by the women or whoever was running them at that time. I think they just took stock of what they had available in some-one's armory and shaped their plan accordingly. And one other thing, Mohammad bin Azaria is in this up to his eyeballs.

"I had Roger do a very deep dive on him, and he has the skills to lay out a plan in broad detail without a doubt," Anna chipped in.

"I don't know where he interacted with the women or when, but I will bet my cat on his involvement and that of the women. I just want to be upfront with you on this, so you don't get blindsided by all the political bullshit."

Anna smiled and moved over to stroke my arm, calming me and making me realize again just how well she had fitted into our team from the get-go. "Let it all out, girl. Nothing changes except we've now got access to the Secretary's conversations." I nodded and moved to the table on which a small laptop had been set up. Pete looked at me, then pushed one of the keys. The Secretary's greeting floated out, followed by the unmistakable tone of Mohammad bin Azaria, drip-ping with charm and as smooth as silk.

We settled down to listen and take notes. Nearly two years of conversations. The things you had to do to hang a crime against humanity on someone these days!

One day later, I was ready. Not much sleep, endless conversa-tions with Anna and Pete. Frequent video chats with the Boss and, on three occasions, Arie.

But we had worked out our approach, and we thought we understood what we had to know. The players were assembled, minus the president and the general, coffee had been served this time, perhaps a recognition that we were not going to blow up the place, but I had to admit I was starting to lust after one of Indigo's superior cappuccinos.

"Madam Secretary, thank you for all that data. We have absorbed it and have a few simple questions for you. We understand you involved Home Affairs, Homeland, Immigration, Attorney General's, and Education and Welfare departments in your frequent conversations with Mohammad bin Azaria." I wasn't going to let her off that hook.

"Yes, Captain."

"On what basis?"

"We had, as you would have heard, constructed a hypothetical, based on how to rehome some ten thousand children, initially unaccompanied, and over a small time period—if memory serves me correctly, around three months." There was that "rehome" word again, and without even thinking about it, the hairs on the back of my neck started to bristle.

"So you were, what, looking at the infrastructure required to support such an effort?"

"Not just the infrastructure. There were cultural and language considerations as well as health and welfare.

"You can't just pluck children out of a camp without some accounting for the action, reporting to responsible authorities, record keeping." Oh yes, you can, I thought to myself. Mohammad bin Azaria had been doing it undetected for twenty-five years at the very least.

"In your scenario, who would the responsible authorities have been?" The Secretary looked blank for a minute, then tilted her head to one side. Today she was wearing a power suit in bold red, with a white chemise covering her chest, and bright blue shoes with needlepoint heels, which must have been killing her feet. And if they weren't, they should be.

"Mohammad bin Azaria represented Red Crescent. We had him checked out, and he had a clean history with them going back decades, mostly through his funding efforts. So we had just one authority, as

Red Crescent oversees many of the camps. "We checked with the UNHCR. They were advised of the conversations, or so I was told by Mohammad bin Azaria, and our delegate to the UN contacted them and gave them a broad outline of our conversations."

"And what were they?" She had the good grace to look a little guilty about what I didn't know, and right now, I didn't care.

"We worked up a model on how the United States could manage such a project, given appropriate funding, which Mohammad bin Azaria assured us he had in hand. He was—or still is, I assume, in line for the throne of Arabia, so that gave us confidence that he could provide the necessary financial support."

"Unfortunately, since the coup in Arabia, sponsored by the French, and given the case we are building against Mohammad bin Azaria, it's unlikely he will ever sit on the throne." Pete's inciteful interjection, spoken with no inflection at all, reset the tone I wanted, so I plowed on.

"How much was he offering?" I asked, homing in on what I suspected was behind the Secretary's real interest in the whole refugee situation. She struck me as a well-rounded, highly educated politician, so grandstanding on the backs of little children who might otherwise be dead made for a great platform on which to run for higher office.

Like the presidency. Not my issue.

"One million per refugee, with an additional one million on graduating college."

"A measly twenty billion dollars. And what, exactly, would that have brought?" I asked, unable to hide my sarcasm. The Secretary heard me clearly, but was either too good at her job or too inured by events to rise to my bait. She arched her back, sitting so straight I thought she may have had a spine seizure. In a tone that left me in no doubt as to what she thought of me, she outlined a plan to move ten thousand abandoned children from camps in Europe and Northern Africa to prepared infrastructure in three cities in the US. Cities that were in the wilderness, far from large population centers, where the minders and carers would have to be relocated from all over America. The mind-boggled, just the language and cultural issues were almost insurmountable at that scale, not to mention trying to manage thousands of parentless children with carers and minders.

Insanity. Impactable. But potentially politically astute.

Not really worth going into. In this respect, Mohammad bin Azaria had a model that worked. Place the children in willing homes, support the parents and support the child's education. Just don't turn them into terrorists!

"Thank you, Madam Secretary, that's all we need for now. We appreciate your candor." I motioned to Pete and Anna to wait, stood when the Secretary and her aide left, looked around the room, shrugged my shoulders, then sat again, a huge feeling of despondency falling over me like a fog.

"Well, the numbers Mohammad bin Azaria transferred into all those accounts now make sense, sort of. But that plan could never have worked." Pete had succinctly hit the nail on the head. "Might have looked good in the media, but sorry, wrong way to go about something like that."

"What was she going to do with all that money?" Anna looked blank, so I gave her my two cents worth.

"Get herself elected president, or maybe get the president re-elected. Doesn't much matter, but I don't see an impact on what we have to do, do you?" I asked them both. They both shook their heads. I was tired; they were looking a little beat, so I decided to pack it in for the day and led my team back out into the low light of a mixed-weather evening. Hard wind chill, no snow, but slippery ice on the pavement. An SUV pulled up, and as I climbed in, my weapon was handed back to me, along with the sheath knife I slipped in my boot on occasion. My little laptop already sat snug in my pants pocket.

I was a cop, an investigator, but just recently, some very nasty people had tried to kill us, and as the news about the oil and gas attacks in Nigeria and other African countries had come in after our search-and-destroy message to the eighteen countries where we had tracked Shetani and his crew too, the bad guys were still out there, and who knew if there were any left in the US. No need to take any chances.

Chapter 6

Malcolm Tannery, a wiry, long-legged, and blond header surfer, just happened to be the preeminent white-hat hacker employed by the NSA to trace and track down electronic and digital enemies of the United States of America. When he wasn't actually surfing, which was most days as the NSA HQ for all things electronic was hidden away under Frontier Mountain in Nebraska, he was talking about it to anyone who'd listen, long arms and fluid hands waving around, blond hair flying with the passion of his speech, his lean body mimicking the subtle balance movements on his imaginary board racing down the face of a thirty-foot break with the grace of a ballet dancer.

On this occasion, he sat mute, still, a dark shadow in an even darker room, lined with acoustic tiles and an inbuilt faraday cage. The images on his multiple screens were all frozen at the same point but showed a different angle or perspective of the same scene. A mix of satellite and land map images of a truck stop on Route 15, just south of Great Falls. Another world-class white hat sat in another dark room mirrored his visual choice on her huge multiple screens, and she too was motionless, frozen in the moment to let her capricious mind filter what she was seeing. The NSA had worked out very early in the digital revolution that two brilliant young minds were better than one, and as these minds tended to be encased in personalities and bodies that were mostly socially inept, working in pairs helped the communication back to normal people when they had unearthed whatever it was they had set out to find. Or do. They, as a stereotype, always seemed to be creating algorithms for this and that, in a bewildering display of genius-level skills that were understood not at all by their superiors.

"What do you see?" Malcolm asked. His workmate bent her head to one side, long, shiny brown hair falling over her face, blotting out one side of her glasses, making her look like a cartoon character.

She shook her head slowly, her hair waving from side to side in a gentle rhythm. She didn't surf, preferring her horse for all things outdoors, and given where they worked, it was a hobby a whole lot more practical than the one that consumed Malcolm.

"It's what I don't see, Mal, and like you, I have run this data six times from Sunday, so there's no mistake."

"No, there isn't. The anomaly is consistent with the black hole data, but nothing changes. Absolutely nothing. Same vehicles in, same vehicles out. And we can track every vehicle to their destination, even the ones that went off-road. Conclusions?"

She looked up into the camera mounted above her screens, dropped her head, wiped the hair out of her eyes, took her glasses off, gave them a quick polish with the bottom of her tee, then looked back up at the camera.

"We have tracked every single vehicle along that route as far back as a hundred miles and back from the epicenter of the old missile site, and there is not a single vehicle that we can identify for the period of the satellite images.

"Either they got there three years ago and never left, or they have a cloaking mechanism that the satellite can't detect. But I ran infrared and heat traces, and they matched exactly to the vehicle count."

"I did the same, and I concur. Somehow, they masked their vehicles from the satellite from wherever they eventuated, at least eighteen months before the strikes. We have all the trucks and equipment vehicles in and out during the rebuild of the missile silo, but from the time of the last truck out, nada. And the report I have here says the FBI had established that there were no persons present anywhere on-site when the contractors finished. The work was signed off by a person in the Helena Council Chambers, accepted, and paid for, and of that person, there is not a single trace. Anywhere."

"What about the helicopter?" she asked, referring to the bombed-out underground helicopter hangar that had been built over an old swimming pool near the very old homestead that was now also a smoldering ruin. It was assumed that the hangar had been used because the burnt-out twisted remains of the Hughes 500 helicopter had been recovered by the FBI investigators.

"Not a single flight in or out of that area back as far as three years from the time of the Special Forces attack. And to make matters worse, every activity by the SF is on the data; in fact, we even have images of birds flying across the target site for the duration of the satellite data. No, they were invisible electronically; I think we have to face that fact. How they did it, I've got no idea. But I think we have to get this analysis to the talking heads soonest."

"I want to do another run, clean data, from the start before I agree to anything," she said stubbornly, sitting as far back in her padded seat as she could.

The whole invisible thing was nagging at her; there had to be a simple explanation; logic and science said so, and so had everything she had read in the classified national reports she read every day. No one in any country had laid claim to creating any invisibility technology.

There had been work done on a reflective shield that bent light waves away from the source and created the illusion of invisibility, but that simply would not work on a fast-moving object like a car or a helicopter. Malcolm studied her determined face on his monitor and nodded his agreement.

"Okay, one last time, with feeling!" As he cleared his screens and dialed up the source code for the satellite data, he wondered how the terrorists had managed it. Blinking rapidly to ease the strain on his eyes, he attacked his keyboards, determined to find something, anything, that might help the investigation. He had liked the look and tone of the lead investigator and wondered how he might make that turn into something wonderful.

Chapter 7

The colonel, the Sgen Aluf (head) of the Israeli 104 commando troop, was slightly unhappy but very motivated. He had successfully led the attack on Shetani and his mercenaries in Arabia, cutting the head of the most dangerous snake to surface in a very long time. And after that, he had led the raid on the terrorists' headquarters in the desert that had resulted in the capture of Mohammad bin Azaria and a veritable treasure trove of intelligence material.

He now sat in a small room, dressed for combat, watching a visual presentation by the man with whom he had made both attacks but had yet to figure out. The head of the Interpol team.

He was tall, well-built, and authoritative but dressed as casually as someone going to the beach. Faded jeans, a loose shirt, also faded, covering a handgun slipped in behind his back, sleeves rolled up to reveal scars on one arm and a tactical watch on the other. Scuffed jump boots completed the ensemble, except on this occasion, his head was wet and messy as if he had just had a shower and forgotten to dry it. An astute observation because that was exactly what had happened. The Sgen Aluf's direct chain of command led back to a brigadier in a hidden Israeli command center, but on this occasion and as had been for the two sorties in the desert, he was seconded to the EDI, the intelligence arm that looked after everything digital and electronic in Israel, overseen by Aire Rosenberg, a legendary figure in the Middle East.

There was more going on here than met the eye, and that was part of the reason the colonel was a little disgruntled.

He had been shut out of briefings and after-action reports and had the distinct feeling important things were being withheld from him.

Not the way to treat someone who had been fighting for his country since he was thirteen when he had foiled a terrorist attack on his village with three other boy soldiers. This got him recognized by the elders, and within months, he had been offered a fast-tracked education at the military academy in Tel Aviv. He couldn't get there fast enough, and over the next three years learned everything anyone was willing to teach him about fighting clean, or preferably dirty, killing, making and planting bombs, blowing stuff up, and generally just having the time of this young life.

He graduated first of his class, and a day after his seventeenth birthday, dressed in his combat fatigues, all crisp and ironed, probably for the last time, was whisked off to another school, this one very secretive, where for the next two years he learned how to think like a terrorist, how to be a spy, and how to be sneaky to the point of discomfort. And to keep his hand in the time-honored military art of killing, he participated in around one hundred attacks and retaliatory actions against his neighbors, for they continued to bomb, attack with rockets, or send suicide squads across the borders aimed at civilian targets day and night.

Such was life growing up in modern Israel.

And now he sat being briefed on what promised to be a seriously dangerous and one-sided mission into Libya and Egypt.

With no squad weapons, no long guns, grenades, flash bombs, or force multiplication weapons of any type, just personal weapons, all of which had to be on open display. Having waited for the room to settle, the Boss started the brief.

"Our mission is simple—we get to this point, where the entrance to the mountain was, and we dig our way in as far as we can, using the equipment the Egyptian government will have at the site. We will be in civilian attire; we can wear sidearms strapped to our thighs or on belt holsters if that is your preference, but this is not—and I emphasize not—a military mission. You will be issued with high-visible gear identifying you as Interpol to any curious onlooker.

"This is an investigation by Interpol, in a friendly country that is a member State of Interpol, to try and establish any data we can concerning the terrorists who once occupied this target area.

"In a strange way, the Egyptians are as interested as we are as to what went on there, right under their noses."

"Sir, how do we get there?" one of the commandos asked, his English heavily accented.

Everyone was taking notes, even the Sgen Aluf, who the Boss had a distinct feeling was not a happy camper.

"We take a boat to Alexandria, then drive down to the target, then tab it across the border into Libya; there's a farmhouse we need to check out, and in the new spirit of friendship, the Libyans are letting us play to our heart's content. We will be on our best behavior; understandably, both countries are nervous about what we will find, and neither wants to be seen to be involved in the terrorist attacks. So we play it low and slow. And as some of you have been there before, you will know what to expect." He looked around the room, thinking that this excursion would be very different from the last one when they had flown in by heavy transport, then crawled and inched their way from country to country like thieves in the night. He noticed Tom sitting off to one side, three of his troop sitting close, heads together, obviously discussing something. He looked at Tom, and raised his eyebrows, got a shake of the head in response, so he continued the briefing.

Maybe when they wrapped it up, he would find Arie and then have a chat with the Sgen Aluf and find out what his beef was.

Maybe.

Chapter 8

The train from Washington, where it turned out we had met the president in the mysterious bunker, to Great Falls in Montana was fast, comfortable, and mostly empty. But what aroused my senses and interest the most was the subtle taste of new leather, not unlike the smell a new car gave off that precious first time you opened its door. And the train, being electric, was the most efficient way to travel given the current situation with oil and gas—as in there wasn't any—and it probably was the safest, as the civil disruption threatening to destroy America from coast to coast had not yet resulted in any attacks on rail infrastructure. The train was armored with a series of UAVs that flew off the roof to provide look-ahead coverage and security and a platoon or two of seemingly regular army troops. One group to the rear, one to the front, leaving us the sole occupants of the middle carriage, which had sweet armchairs for the day part of the trip, giving off that wonderful new-car smell, and private sleeper compartments for the night. Good bathrooms, a little privacy, and the catering was first class.

I had asked Anna where the train came from when we first saw it at the underground station where we had boarded, and she just said it was a backup to Air Force One, the presidential jet. That made me feel special and also made me reappraise the president's attitude and behavior during our recent conversation. I had my very own private train and my team, which had expanded during the three stops we had made so far, with the addition of four FBI agents and three Special Forces troopers. The FBI were all specialists in different forensic skills, and the troopers were for our protection in the field. And as they were part of the team that provided on-the-ground support for the Secret Service and the president, I sincerely doubted they were in any way just "ordinary."

They had all been introduced to me and then immediately split off to be briefed by Anna and Pete. Now they were all back as we approached North Dakota. We had stopped in Minneapolis to take on fresh supplies and some specialized equipment I had requested, which was now loaded in a fourth car just behind us. I looked around the narrow conference facility, made eye contact with everyone, checked Pete's status, Anna, and lastly, the bull of a man who had arrived with the SF team, broad shoulders, and a very tough-looking face, with a scar running down one side from hairline to top cheek. Dressed in mufti, the only giveaway he was military was the buzzcut of his grey hair, his stick-up-the-arse posture, his dead black eyes with their thousand-yard stare, and the sheer physical force he projected with every movement.

But he had passed Pete's smell test and had been introduced to me as "Bob," so I let it go for the moment and saw him settled in one of the comfortable green leather armchairs, drinking a power drink. I rolled my shoulders, a habit I was aware of that had started a good three weeks ago, but I had to get the kinks out somehow, and it seemed to work, so what the hell. I'd just make sure I abandoned it before I played poker again.

"Ladies and gentlemen, if I may call you that, rather than thugs and molls," and I paused to let the laughter wind down, "welcome to our party. This is a police investigation; we are representing Interpol in this little adventure of ours, and yes, we recognize the American component, but all of you, FBI and military, have been TDY'ed to Interpol for the duration, specifically myself as your in-field commander.

"My second-in-command is Master Chief Pete, who you have met, and any legal or operational issue that causes a potential problem will be analyzed by Senior Special Agent Bernstein of the FBI. Does anyone have a problem with that?" I looked around the room and saw only interest, no dissension, so I carried on with the briefing—a briefing that moved the truth over the line but supported the president's stance, which would be public by now. It was a very fine line we would cross, but for reasons of my own, it didn't cause me any real grief, and Anna and Pete had agreed with it wholeheartedly, as had the Boss, as the best way to move everyone forward.

"Our objective is to collect as much data as we can forensically so we can say with some accuracy exactly what the sites were used for, create a timeline, and potentially get a lead on where the terrorists were based. We know the permits were issued by Helena City Hall some four and a half to five years ago for the rebuilding and cleaning out of the missile silo and control room, and a permit was issued for the rebuilding of the swimming pool next to the old homestead. We know that the work finished two years ago, at the very latest, and that sometime around then, all the physical and electronic records were destroyed, lost, or wiped.

"We know that someone dug a three-meter-deep trench from the homestead several miles west to where the satellite uplink was mounted on the ranger and fire station. We have no records of that activity. Nothing on the dish. Our in-house engineers, working only from topographical maps, estimated that trench alone would have taken three months to complete, and the natural grass, trees, and coverage reported by the Special Forces troops that walked the line before blowing it to kingdom come said that the there was nothing to indicate anyone had dug anything up for a very long time.

"So, I'm guessing that the trench was dug at the start of the rebuild, four-plus years ago, and the dark fiber buried soon after. The NSA has no data on the uplink being used before the attacks.

"That may or may not be true. We know that the terrorists have been in our IT systems for twenty-plus years, so I'm not inclined to trust any electronic data at this point. What I do trust is the instincts of the FBI, who have a theory that the terrorists had a base in one or more of these towns—Great Falls, Helena, Butte, Bozeman, or Billings. Why? Because these are the staging points where all the materials and infrastructure were shipped to and then on into the missile silo build site. For two and a half years, trucks can be seen making their way to and from the site, and we estimate that over eleven million dollars' worth of materials were moved during this time, all paid for from legitimate bank accounts in each town.

"Our money people, working with the American IRS, can find no data that is not consistent with a transparent financial operation—taxes paid, IRS data filed, audit reports from the banks perfect, and strangely, none of this data was wiped. The funds were withdrawn using debit cards or bank cheques when the amounts exceeded ten thousand dollars, and the people who used these cards or requested and were issued the cheques were all authorized employees of the same construction company who acted on behalf of an entity we can't trace.

"The FBI has interviewed over seventy people, from the owner of the construction company on down, and they all have the same story. A well-dressed female, in her fifties, with a slight southern accent, named Charline Wordsworth, ostensibly representing a company registered in Texas, Righthand Mining Co. LLC, but originally from Bath, in England, set up the accounts, funneled the funds into the construction company, had a meeting every month for three years to get a report on the progress, then after inspecting the work and signing off acceptance, she simply disappeared. And I mean completely. No Social Security number, no driver's license, no history, all wiped professionally, just like all the other data we seem to have lost."

I paused to catch my breath, felt a little guilty about not revealing her other name and what she might have done or facilitated in Iraq and Egypt, then thought about a little detail I had missed.

"Oh, I just remembered—on the day that our mystery woman disappeared, somehow the terrorists managed to delete all further physical movement in and out of the area, for a hundred miles in every direction. That was eighteen months ago." I could see Pete had a question. I looked straight at him and shook my head so slightly I could have been clearing a kink in my neck, but he got my silent message and relaxed back into his burgundy leather seat. I had to admit, the train carriage was a real luxury for us, the benchmark while we had been in Italy and Israel being a fold-up metal chair three sizes too small for my back!

"And to add insult to injury, when the FBI followed the money trail, it led back to several deposits made by an unidentified company five years prior to the start of the build. It had been washed corporately so many times all we could really trust was that the money movements happened, with full regulatory approval at the time." Anna's soft voice was in direct contrast to mine, which had been edgy from the start. I hated lying to my team, and I had deliberately crossed the line in the sand by describing the mystery woman as someone we had no data on—she had, in fact, been an engineer by trade, or so she said, and the contractors agreed that she had the skills and knowledge of a first-class engineer and had contributed to many discussions on what was to be done, and how it was to be done. I could share the engineer bit, but not the fact that it was someone we knew, probably one of the six who had engineered the whole attack scenario worldwide if our theory was correct. Or maybe one of the real brains of the whole operation.

The president's wishes to have America focus its hate on the mercenary terrorists and leave the refugee women out of it would be respected for as long as we could.

Anna continued in her soft voice, but no one could mistake the steel sitting just a fraction behind her words.

"And we know for a fact that the funds originated from the Sovereign Wealth Fund, under the hand of Mohammad bin Azaria." Anna looked around the rail car as if seeking something from everyone in the briefing. "I see some of you are not familiar with that part of the investigation. Jessica?" she asked, raising one eyebrow to support her question, but I bent my head slightly and indicated she should continue.

"Mohammad bin Azaria is the person we have established, funded the terrorist attacks, hired the mercenaries, masterminded the attack plan, and was captured last week and taken into custody.

"He has been interrogated and, in fact, is still being questioned, but there is no doubt he was the banker. He moved billions all around the world over an eight-year period, all above board and transparent, all supposedly for aid work, all sanctioned by various governments, and no one said a thing when various amounts were moved into secondary accounts, only a fraction of which we have been able to trace."

"Because of the terrorists being inside our IT?" one of the FBI field agents asked. Anna looked pleased with the question and nodded her head.

"Yes. The horrible fact is, they have been inside our systems and computers for twenty-five years at least and may well still be. The NSA says no, but my personal feeling is that they are saying that to give us confidence. I would caution you all to regard anything electronic with suspicion—except for anything you may see on one of these little laptops," she said, holding up the device we had given her from the monks. The FBI agent smiled and asked the expected question.

"Who do I have to kill to get one?" Which, of course, drew laughter from everyone and moved the mood in the carriage down from frosty to slightly warm. Anna laughed with everyone else and pointed to me, so I held my hands up in surrender, which got another laugh.

"Very early in the investigation, we connected with a group of agnostic monks, thanks to the head of Interpol in Italy. Turns out the head monk is his brother. They spend all their time finding, then logging ancient texts and artifacts that support the broad non-secular religious history of the world, have been doing so for decades, and have developed some amazing technology that turned out to be immune to the crash of the Internet. They provided us with these little laptops and managed the system that connects to them wherever we are. I never got the the system that connects to them wherever we are. I never got the chance to ask them how they do it, and even if I had, I probably would not have understood the first word." Another laugh, more gently this time. We were getting into a rhythm. "I would point out that this information is classified Presidential Restricted, and if you do tell anyone, we will kill you." I looked around and saw twinges of smiles but mostly blank, neutral looks. Good. We had to protect the monks at whatever cost.

"How long has Interpol been involved in the investigation?" Bob asked, leaning forward in his seat, the top of his head moving down as his bushy eyebrows moved up to look at me with an intense gaze. There was a slight edge to his voice, but I didn't find it to be overly offensive.

"Since day two of the attacks, when both Italy and Israel asked us to investigate the bombings of the Vatican and the Dome of the Rock.

"Interpol is a worldwide but European-based international police force, with the ability to cross borders freely and at will. We were working on the case when West Point was bombed; the Americans immediately asked us to act on their behalf, and they sent Anna across to us in Italy to act as the FBI liaison. Other countries joined the bandwagon as the subsequent attacks rolled out, and that's why we have the lead in this investigation." He nodded to himself, then looked straight at me with an intensity I was starting to get used to.

"Did Interpol have anything to do with capturing Mohammad bin Azaria?" he asked. I looked back at him as hard as he was looking at me. I didn't know that the news of his capture was out, but nothing surprised me about this case anymore.

"That raid was led by my boss, Colonel Anthony, in partnership with the Israeli commando troop Shayete 104." I held his eyes, waiting for his next question. He had been on the sidelines during all the attacks, and now he had been seconded to a strange international coalition led by a woman, with another woman heading the FBI contingent, and no doubt his information until such time as he got on the train had been no more than "go there, report here, do this," so I didn't blame him for his directness. I decided to give him a little more. I very much needed him and his team on my side.

"I had the pleasure of interrogating Mohammad bin Azaria personally, so I know firsthand exactly what he is all about, what he is trying to achieve, but I don't know his end game yet, and I'm hoping you and your fellow troopers will help us find a clue or two as to what it might be on this operation." He held my stare for a second or two, then nodded.

"Okay, good enough for now, thank you," he said. I looked around the carriage and checked my watch to see what the run time was; we still had a while to go to Great Falls, and I made one of my amazing instinctive social decisions. "Let's take a break for an hour or two. Pete, could I see you and Anna for a minute, please?"

And I stood up, giving the signal to the others to do the same. Bob and his troops moved off to the far end, where the bar had been set up, albeit only with fizzy drinks and juice, no alcohol, and the FBI team moved to the other end, where a large, bronze coffee machine puffed silently, leaving us the middle.

"Pete, you had a question before?" I asked. He sat down next to me and leaned in so only Anna and I could hear him.

"Yes, thanks, Captain. It only occurred to me as you gave us the rundown on the construction company. Is it possible the terrorists actually worked on the build? As subcontractors or maybe even hired-on daily workers?" Once again, Pete's sharp brain belied his physical powers. Why was I surprised?

"It occurred to the Boss when we talked about it before we left Israel. More than likely, what better way to make sure you were getting what you wanted than to be inside, as it were?"

"Good. I'm glad you all got there before I did, but I've got another one for you. If these terrorists have done a runner—and why wouldn't they, given what they have done—how in hell will we track them?"

It was a good question, a great one, in fact, and one that had occupied my mind for the last two weeks at least.

But I had faith in our master planner—Mohammad bin Azaria—he had an end game, and his precious girls were not finished; of that, I was quite certain.

Now I only had to prove it and hope it wasn't as devastating as his opening salvos!

Chapter 9

In the cramped quarters of HiResPhoto Inc. in downtown Auckland, New Zealand, the three resident American Embassy representatives, who of course were FBI, NSA, and CIA undercover agents, not a particularly well-kept secret since the worldwide terrorists' attacks, watched on as the UAV cameraman carefully inserted the flash storage drive into the only working computer in the entire city. Mind-boggling fact, the NSA tech thought to himself; he was just a little under thirty years of age, as he liked to tell all the girls, and didn't know a world without electronic pads, smartphones, dual-screen multi-dimensional video, and instantaneous communication from anywhere on the surface of the earth.

And, of course, the instant answer to any question, non-curated, in the palm of his hand. To say he was struggling with the slow fax machine, a twenty-six baud link that took forever to send and received a message and actually beeped and buzzed as it worked—white text on a black background, no less—and forget anything visual, to scan and send a photo at the lowest resolution took nearly an hour and then you couldn't guarantee that it wouldn't be scrambled at the other end.

He shook his head at the thought of his parents having to deal every day with such archaic technology and understood why they had been so stressed all the time bringing him up.

"Ready?" asked the cameraman. The three agents nodded and spread around the cameraman sitting in his chair. The screen was a sixty-inch 8k HD, but the video was only 4k, so while clear, the images were not as sharp as the agents were used to. The airport floated up central screen, then the image tilted as the UAV headed towards the coast. It took nearly an hour. Then they replayed it, going backward and forwards on some areas, making notes by hand as they worked. One agent was somewhat talented with pen and pencil, and she took it upon herself to draw the various structures and buildings, and the result was just slightly less than that of a photograph. They debated the drawing and the summary notes for another hour, then agreed on what to send through to the FBI Directorate.

Six hours later, Frank Reynolds, the director of the NSA, and Roger Winslow, the head of the FBI, sat huddled around their own big screen, watching Julius Bronstein who ran the CIA, as he moved a small laser pointer around the screen.

"Ten buildings, all the same, apparent size, all approximately thirty meters high, and a hundred meters by fifty meters. It appears that they have some form of panel on the roof, which might be solar, and if so, like nothing we've seen to date anywhere else. There's a satellite uplink dish positioned between these two buildings, there's a five-meter covered walkway linking the buildings, and at the ocean end we have four one-meter-diameter pipes running into the ocean, and our guess at this point is for water supply and cooling.

"This sealed road," he said, pointing to a black linear line in the form of an "H" on the drawing, "runs around the entire complex, with a massive loading dock just here."

"What's our best guess as to the structure near the pipes?" Roger asked. The head of the NSA sat down, scratched at the back of his head, screwed up his face, then shrugged his shoulders.

"We think it's a floating dock. Without satellite coverage or assigning ground assets on a watch-and-see basis, we don't know for sure. But I would point out that everything about this compound is on the up and up. Planning permits from the New Zealand government were inspected at every stage of the build, which took two years and employed forty engineers and scientists, mostly from the mainland. They are billeted here, near the loading dock. According to the papers filed and the news reports in the Auckland press prior to the terrorist attacks, this is an ecologically responsible and government-sanctioned site for the manufacture of alternative energy materials and systems.

"There's even a photo of the New Zealand prime minister opening the site two months ago."

"But it links back to Mohammad bin Azaria's bankroll?" Roger asked. The NSA's head nodded and looked at Julius. "Yes, it does, but these funds were in play five years before the attacks, all processed through the Foreign Investment Review Board, the NZ Tax Department, and while Mohammad bin Azaria was involved in setting up the accounts and transferring the funds, his fingerprints are not on anything that has happened in-country since. The only really interesting thing is the names on the corporate filings, such as CEO, COO, MD, and General Counsel. They are all women, aged thirty-one down to twenty-seven. They are all citizens of either Australia or New Zealand, studied in both countries as well as overseas, and while we did dig deep on that aspect, there's absolutely nothing to link them to the female terrorists except their sex. And one other thing."

"And that won't fly in this day and age."

"No. Very touchy area."

"What's the other thing?"

"They were all refugees, adopted through the Australian Red Cross and an organization called the Salvation Army, and all their documentation from the date of their adoptions is still on file and fully curated. However, we can't track back to where they originally came from, and all their personal and family history has disappeared."

"So what do you think we should do?" Roger asked. As head of the FBI, he had been requested by his peers from the NSA and CIA to find out what the countries of Canada, Greenland, Chile, Portugal, Ireland, Denmark, Norway, Finland, Estonia, Sri Lanka, Solomon Islands, New Zealand, Japan, and Iceland had in common, other than huge sums of petrodollars being shipped to those countries three to five years previously. The NSA had helped with the data from New Zealand; now, perhaps it was his turn, and Canada was a lot closer than New Zealand.

"I'll get a ground team up into Canada as soon as I can. Let's leave this until I get something back."

The meeting broke up, and no one thought to inform Interpol of what they had just discussed.

Outside the one-hundred-mile boundary of the "black hole" that was now being looked at with a vengeance on two continents, the president's train pulled into a private siding in Great Falls, and the Interpol team unloaded through one side straight onto a blacked-out school bus, with a driver wearing camos.

No one said anything, and the twelve and a half miles between the debarking point and Malmstrom Air Force Base seemed to fly by, something I was happy for. I noticed that the troopers all ringed the inside of the bus, having occupied the window seats on both sides and at the rear, and I also noticed that their guns all pointed outwards. I was not aware of any threat, the civil unrest had been short-lived in this neck of the woods, and the lack of traffic on the roads suggested the curfew was still in effect. Pete had cleverly managed to get the seat beside me, one in from a trooper who looked to be about twelve.

"They get younger every year," I commented, shaking my head. Pete just smiled, his head on a swivel, watching everything inside and outside the bus. The Boss would ream him a new one if anything happened to Jessica, and he was here to see that nothing did. To his sharp eye, she looked a little tired, but he figured once they got the briefing on the missile silo, she'd perk up. Apart from the Boss, he didn't know anyone in Interpol who had so much courage, stamina, and the brains to go with it. And she maintained her femininity seemingly without trying, a rare trick in a male-dominated world.

The bus pulled up abruptly, the door snapped open, and a shaved head popped in, looked around, fixated on Jessica, then waved her forward.

"Captain Riley, Master Chief Pete, Senior Special Agent Bernstein, come forward, please. Everyone else, wait for one." He stepped aside to let me climb down the stairs, followed by Pete as if he were attached to me. Anna, more used to the military protocol on heavily secured bases, walked behind us, our footsteps echoing on the icy pavement. Before we could chill down, we were ushered into a corridor, down a flight of stairs, then into an elevator. Armed guards stood on either side of the massive door, and to my eye, the woman looked as big as the male, but both held the at-ease stance, looking straight ahead. The flash of the 341st. Missile Wing rode proudly on one shoulder, and the striking mission patch for the Air Force Global Strike Command filled the upper right-hand side of their uniforms. They both snapped to attention as I walked into the massive elevator and remained that way until Anna had passed them.

The triple armored door slid shut silently, then the lift descended smoothly, the lack of floor numbers leaving us all guessing as to how deep we were going.

"Sir, Master Chief, Special Agent, please wear these at all times; you will not have access to any part of the base without an escort, but with luck, they might prevent you from being shot on sight." His gallows humor was not lost on us and drew a wan smile from me in spite of my best efforts to the contrary, and I fitted the bright yellow lanyard over my head, still encased in my watch cap. I could only imagine the red tape and outright refusals that the president or maybe the general would have had to overcome to get approval for three non-military people to access this hidden base, one of the very few missile bases still active in Montana. But the missile silo that had been refurbished by the terrorists had once been part of this command, so the hope was that we could get good, solid intelligence that we could use to track the refugee women.

The elevator doors opened as silently as they had closed, and we were led by the unidentified airman through a blast door and then into a massive control room where three people sat at a round table in the middle of the room. All were dressed in Air Force camos, their rank on little epaulets that sat in the center of their chests. A full colonel, a "chicken" colonel, and a captain. The walls of screens that ran around the curved surface of the wall were all blank, and neither laptops nor paper and pens were to be seen anywhere.

"Sir, our visitors." And our escort snapped a salute at the colonel, turned on his heel, and marched back out.

The steel door slid into place behind him and left us trapped in the chilled bunker. I moved towards the colonel, who had not stood up at our arrival, so I took control of the meeting, something the Boss told me I did far too often.

I reached out my hand, forcing him to turn in his seat to take mine. I was not in his chain of command, I was not in uniform, and I was simply an investigator for Interpol on the hunt. I carried the credentials to prove it, as well as a letter signed by the president giving me permission to get what I wanted from anyone I needed it from. I also held the rank equivalent of a one-star general, should I need to pull that out of my hat.

I smiled my very best and warmest smile, noticing that both Pete and Anna had arranged themselves on either side of the trio, something that was bound to create tension when the trio worked out that they had been silently flanked.

By civilians!

Curiously, we were still armed, as no one had asked for our weapons. "Colonel, Interpol thanks you for this courtesy," and as he had no nameplate on his uniform, I let it go at that, then walked around the table and sat opposite him.

Silence fell like a ton of bricks, and apart from the three of them looking backward and forwards at each other as if seeking inspiration, the room remained silent. "Colonel, if we could get down to it, please, we need everything you can tell or give us concerning a decommissioned missile silo in Montana; it is the one your Special Forces bombed into oblivion last week."

I watched his face intently, looking for the little tells that would guide me in terms of reading his tonality and posture.

"Captain, as I told the president's military liaison, this unit has had nothing to do with that silo for fifteen years."

"And how did General Saunders respond to that?" I asked, softening my voice just a fraction, which might be taken for as a move towards empathy for his plight. He looked at me with a glare that would have frozen any other soldier in place but just ricocheted off me like so much fluff.

I had played hardball with much more imposing military staff than this group during my career. I understood their discomfort and perhaps even anger at having to share their precious military secrets with foreigners, but we were on the hunt for terrorists that had literally turned their world upside down, not to mention killed hundreds of thousands, perhaps even millions by now, so soft-pedaling it was simply not an option.

"I thought so, and Colonel, if you want confirmation of our status, please pick up your little red phone and ask for the president."

I looked at Pete, who was enjoying the discomfort of the trio, then at Anna, who was maintaining a neutral posture, then delivered my ultimatum.

"Colonel, I'm sorry, but we do not have the time to waste while you play your power games. If you can't—or won't—give us what we need, I'll have you replaced until we find someone who can." The captain almost choked, his face leaching all its natural color to become a pasty caricature that was most unattractive.

"Just who the fuck do you think you are?" he shouted, standing in his seat, meaty knuckles clenched so tight his hands were white. Spittle flew out of his mouth, and I swear his eyes bulged.

The colonel sat back, grabbed his captain by the arm, and pulled him back into his seat.

"Captain, you don't have to threaten us. We have been well briefed on you by our upper command, but I have to emphasize that we haven't had anything to do with that site for fifteen years, and like everyone else on the planet, our internet and satellite communications were crashed by the terrorists, so I'm not even sure we can get archived material for you. What do you need?" The anger in his voice was palpable, but I gave him credit for holding my eyes as he spat out his question. I did not understand his hostility. We came at the behest of his president, with the support of the military liaison to the president, but as I had just told him in no uncertain terms, time was of the essence, so I let it go for now.

"Plans of the installation, details on all communications links, and any data on surrounding infrastructure. We know there was a multistory building at one end of the silo layout; we need to understand what you had underground, ingress, and egress points, how you rotated staff, and where they bunked off duty.

"We're looking for the terrorists that rebuilt the complex and used it for the attacks on America, specifically the attack on West Point, the International Space Station, and all the oil-and-gas infrastructure in Canada and the US." I localized the attacks to make them more important to him and his men. I could literally see the wheels turning behind his eyes as he fought with himself to stall us or help us. There was something else in play here, and remembering the questions Pete had asked me earlier today, I had a flash of insight. I placed my hands flat on the tabletop, pushed my shoulders back slightly, saw Anna and Pete react as they both tensed up, then leaned back and folded my arms.

"How many people from your base worked for the contractor?" It made total sense; who better to help with the rebulbing of a technically orientated site than the people who first built it and controlled every nut and bolt during the Cold War? His face went beet red; he took a huge breath, grabbed the arm of his captain again, then shook his head.

"Our base has undergone six organizational changes in five years. We are now a censor-orientated workforce, and at the start of the process, we lost over one thousand highly trained staff. In the second year, we lost around six hundred technicians and engineers, and we were happy to release some of them to the prime contractor because of their experience. We sought approval from the Pentagon, and they signed off on it. When I took command of the base two years ago, the rebuild was all but finished, and most of the ex-Air Force personnel had been released."

"Do you have the paperwork on the site, the personnel records on your ex-staff, any detail at all about the rebuild?"

"No. And what records were kept here were destroyed during the cyberattack two weeks ago."

"Colonel, you are the wing commander responsible for looking after the condition and readiness of over two hundred intercontinental ballistic missiles. Are you telling me you have lost control of them?" I asked, unable to hide the astonishment in my voice. Again, the silence in the room was deafening.

"What I tell you stays in this room. I acknowledge that by presidential order, I have to fully brief you and help you in any way possible. I do not agree with this order, but I will honor its intent. I repeat, what we discuss stays in this room." I looked at Pete, who gave the slightest of nods, then at Anna, who did likewise, then nodded myself. With one proviso.

"Colonel, we will respect your wishes, but understand that I will fully debrief my Boss, Colonel Anthony. I can't speak for Senior Special Agent Bernstein, but if the FBI is not read in already, I would be very surprised." He gave me a very hard look, one I'm sure would peel the skin off a newbie, but I held his stare and hopefully returned the intensity.

"Yes, the FBI has been read in, but you represent an International civilian and pseudomilitary police force, and I do not know you."

"I do, and my boss will vouch for Interpol. He is responsible for contacting Colonel Anthony and Interpol in the first place." Anna's quiet comment drew his stare, but like me, after the weeks we had just experienced, it was like water off a duck's back.

"I see.

"All right then, to answer your question specifically, no. Not totally lost control. We have no ability to control them electronically other than to fire them manually, and even then, we might or might not be successful because we still don't know the extent of the damage the cyberattack did to the guidance systems of the missiles. We're pretty sure we can't load target data into them at this point, but that issue is being addressed as we speak. The Pentagon has forbidden us to strip down a missile at the moment, they have teams of specialists waiting to get access, and that is the main issue."

"You can't get into the silos?" I asked again, not being able to hide my astonishment.

The look that fleeted across his face reminded me of a whipped dog, but he quickly got his emotions back under control, and for a fleeting minute, I sympathized with him. The master of the destruction of the human race as we know it, and he's locked out of his precious system by triple pressure locks once controlled by computers, but now dead in the water due to the cyberattack.

And deliberately designed to go into a full lockdown in just such an event! Ugly.

"Colonel, I understand your frustration, but to return to what interests me most, can you help us with any data on the decommissioned missile silo?" He dropped his head as if seeking inspiration from the desk.

"No," he said, looking back up. "We can't. And that frustrates me more than you will ever know."

I stood up, nodded to him, then headed out the way we had come in, with Pete and Anna a step or two behind. The door opened, and our surly guard slid into position and marched us back to the elevator and eventually the bus. As the door shut, the driver looked at me with a question in his eyes.

"Back to Great Falls, Electricity Speedway specifically, please."

"Ma'am."

We resumed our seats, but this time the three of us managed to cluster in the center of the bus, almost equidistant to the troopers at the windows. As before, the FBI and Special Forces managed to avoid each other as far as the insides of a school bus allowed, although the stares they were giving us burned with curiosity. They'd have to wait.

"Anna, can you call Roger, get him to organize a group chat with Julius and Frank, and I'll see if I can rope the Boss in. Pete, look over my shoulder, block the view to the rear while you are at it, please." Anna bent to her little laptop, and Pete crouched at my shoulder, creating a physical barrier between my screen and the FBI and troopers at the back of us.

Whatever magic the monks commanded, it worked better than any IT I had ever experienced, and I made a note to get the Boss to put them on permanent contract once things got back to normal.

If ever.

"Jessica, I've got Arie here, and I can see three call signs on a linked call from Washington. Okay, there they are. Jessica, your meeting." The Boss and Arie looked even more tired than I felt, contrasted by the smiling and obviously rested faces of the trio of directors of the FBI, NSA, and CIA. I focused on Julius; the CIA might be able to substantiate the really bad feeling in my gut that had been building in intensity since the wing commander had admitted to having lost control of all his missiles.

"Julius, thanks for taking our call. You are briefed on the situation here in Great Falls?"

He nodded curtly. I chose my next words carefully. We had to assume that the terrorists were still in our IT infrastructure, although I was fairly sure the monks' network had not been breached, but we simply couldn't take that chance.

"Can you confirm that this situation may not be localized?" He nodded again, and my worst fears were realized. In all probability, every intercontinental ballistic missile was locked out of local control in India, Pakistan, China, Russia, Israel, and possibly the Middle East, although I did not know if the relatively primitive guidance system of the Scuds would be affected. On the surface, good news, it meant that maybe, for the foreseeable future, we might not be destroyed in an atomic holocaust.

The bad news was that if our super-intelligent terrorists had managed to maintain control of them by blocking the cyberattack in some way, preserving the chips but shifting the control of the missiles, then we had a new, massive issue to deal with.

"Captain, if I may add to the conversation?" Arie asked, his weary face carrying more lines than I remembered from our last chat just an hour or two ago.

"Yes, Arie, of course. You are secure?" I asked unnecessarily, but this was a critical chat, and I wanted to make sure he understood that.

"We are, thank you, Jessica. We detected this anomaly in our vehicles just after the cyberattack and were able to determine the degree of damage caused. We anticipate it will be a year or more before we have them back online."

I nodded and thought to myself that this was, in a way, good news, but then with a flash of insight, I realized it could be the very worst news possible. I suddenly had another question, this time for the American military. I hung up on everyone other than the Boss and Arie and dialed in General Bridges. Her unhappy face swam into view, and it was obvious she was in some sort of meeting.

"General, privacy, please, immediate." If she thought I was rude, she was probably correct. The image behind her moved in a kaleidoscope of color until I sensed she was in a small room.

"Go."

"Your subs—how many have you lost contact with?"

"Only five, all safe but out of action for a while. And to anticipate your next question, every nuclear submarine has hydraulic manual reversion controls to get them to the surface in case of total systems failure, and apart from every sub we have now sitting on the surface somewhere, giving their locations away to anyone who might have eyes in the sky, we're good there as well. And yes, to your next question." Which would have been about the missiles in the subs being locked down and inert. I sat back against the hard edge of the bus seat, aware that I was starting to smell. The nervous energy that had been driving me for the last hour was also responsible for creating a wet shirt, stinky armpits, and an uncomfortable crutch. I mentally slapped myself for not having got here faster; at the time of the cyberattack, all I had focused on was the loss of our ability to reach around the world with our excellent technology.

The full consequences of the cyberattack had not really sunk in.

Yes, the terrorists had not attacked the chips in medical equipment, and I didn't quite understand that yet, in spite of having it explained to me several times by the geeks. And aircraft had lost their GPS and automated flying systems but still had their inertial gyros and manual controls, so the losses there had been minimal. What was keeping most aircraft grounded was the almost complete lack of aviation fuel.

Thank you, nanomachines.

I canceled the call to the general, looked at the small window where the Boss and Arie were still framed, thought for a minute, then smiled.

"Thank you, Arie. I'll let you and the Boss go; boots on the ground next, good luck." And I hung up. Pete squeezed my shoulder, then took the seat immediately in front of me. Anna pushed her mini laptop back into her pants pocket.

"That was fun. What do you want to do next?"

"Get your FBI friends tracking down any Air Force personnel who worked on that rebuild. Call for more agents if you have to, but in the next twenty-four hours, I want someone to interrogate that site. Can you do that?" She smiled at me; at least I still had one friend. I'm sure the directors and the general would be pissed at me for being so abrupt. But they would have to get used to it because I still felt deep in my gut that the terrorists had an act two, and I didn't have a clue what it might be.

Chapter 10

Colonel Shami Borowitz, at five feet, five inches, and presently dressed in tattered jeans with holes in the knees, a watch cap pulled down to his ears, and his slightly enlarged glasses perched on the top of his nose, looked nothing like a colonel in the Israeli Defense Forces (IDF). He looked more like the computer nerd he really was and nothing like his forty-five years of age. Blessed with youthful genes, he had no problems keeping up with Amira, twenty years his junior. Between them, they snapped at keyboards, slid fingers across smart screens, muttered in six different languages, and occasionally cursed in six more until Luigi and Indigo at the other end of a video link called a halt.

"Guys, it doesn't matter how many ways we cut this. There is simply no data there. None. Zilch. Zero." Indigo's English was impeccable, underlying the stress he felt supporting such a talented team of geeks. "If it's any solace, the monks confirm your findings, and as you know, they have been able to record satellite data through all the attacks, and they have nothing as well."

"But how do you do that, sir? I'm familiar with most systems used for up and downlinks, electronic cameras, and digital visual data capture and storage. If there really is no data, then it had to be a ground-based technology that prevented the images from being recorded."

"Yes. Agreed. We don't know how, but that is our conclusion as well." Across the Mediterranean, Amira dropped her head into her hands, and Shami quickly put his hand on her back and gave her a gentle rub.

"It's not on you, Amira. Someone we don't know developed this technology, just as you did with the nanomachines. We had estimated that Mohammad bin Azaria took at least thirty of you before they paused, and that gave them a very large pool of talent to work with. Also, you have been out of contact with them for nearly five years, and that brings some of the second tranches of refugee girls into the calculation." Amira looked at the video of Indigo, his kind smile lighting up his face, and Amira had no doubt he at least was not blaming her.

"*Forse potremmo considerare la questione in un altro modo?*" Indigo suggested.

Amira immediately perked up, startling Shami for a moment. "What do you mean, look at it another way?" she asked.

"Well, using all our combined thinking power, how would we make something invisible to digital cameras, infrared sensors, lidar, side-scan radar, in fact, invisible right across the spectrum?" he asked. At both ends of the video, silence reigned supreme.

"Can we have access to the laboratory where I worked on the nanotechnology?" she asked, looking at Shami, then quickly turning back to look at Indigo on the screen.

"I'll clear it with Arie," said Shami, "and once we get set up, we'll call you back again." Indigo only had enough time before the connection was broken to nod his agreement and sat back in the ubiquitous folding metal chair. Being a lot shorter than the others, he didn't have an issue with his back! He turned to look at his brother, who had watched the video call from the sidelines, staying out of range of the camera. The monk looked all his years, the past weeks had taken a toll on his inner reserves, but he still managed to look somewhat regal in his long, brown, flowing cassock. He looked thoughtful, was about to launch into a suggestion in Italian, then remembered he had English speakers in the room and did not want to embarrass them.

"Indigo, Tom, Luigi, may I make a suggestion?" he asked, his voice barely above a whisper. All three looked at him, their faces warm but their eyes showing curiosity. "Just as we were able to pluck out of the ether the conversation between the American secretary of state and Al Hemish al-bin Mohammad Karesish, perhaps, if you could give us the exact coordinates of one of your famous 'black holes,' we may be able to find something."

"*Stefarino, fratello mio, per favore, con tutta fretta, questo sta diventando il nostro più grande problema.*" Tom smiled, looked at Indigo.

"Colonel, I assumed you just told your brother to proceed?" he said, his face creased in a grin to deflect any sense of animosity.

He was used to being left out of conversations because his language skills lay elsewhere—as in Arabic, Yiddish, Hebrew, and Russian. And the odd bit of Chinese, all five major dialects.

"*Si*, Mister Tom, yes, that I did. My apologies. I forgot myself in my haste to get my brother looking for us. Perhaps you could give me the exact location where he can start his investigations?"

Tom thought for a minute; he knew exactly where the Boss was, as well as Jessica, and he knew their objectives.

He decided to provide the epicenter of both major "black holes," then changed his mind.

"Latitude 46.771006, Longitude -109.353283."

Stefarino nodded his head; he had guessed the American "black hole" would be the priority, and he gestured to his geeks who had been standing mute along the side of the chamber, hands folded into their cassocks, hoods hiding their faces. They moved as one to a deeper recess in the cavern and faded into the dark.

Chapter 11

The small Coast Guard inflatable—if you called sixty feet of highly engineered go-fast boat small—pulled into the visitors' dock in the Point Roberts marina with the relaxed skill of a highly trained midshipman. He might not look like he was old enough to shave, with his pasty complexion, pimpled face, and distinct, sunburned nose, but his skill belied his age, and he was considered one of the best coxswains on the East Coast. The boat barely bumped after the first feather touch, then two sailors jumped off the fore and aft decks and stabilized the inflatable with a quick crossing of mooring lines. Three FBI agents stepped off, dressed casually, but no one would mistake them for tourists, as each wore the unmistakable dark blue windbreaker with FBI stenciled in yellow across the back made infamous by thousands of TV programs.

They moved with purpose and, as three electric bikes were unloaded behind them, moved into the small tin shed marked with the Harbour Masters sign and logo. The harbormaster, as was his wont on days like this—clear sky, low temperature, little wind—was out fishing in his own twenty-foot fishing boat, so the FBI agents had to put up with a mechanical clock face with red hands set to the four o'clock position and a reversible sign that simply said, "back soon." They turned on their heel, met the bikes halfway, checked their old-style radios, checked the paper map one carried, fitted their safety helmets, then set off, wobbling slightly as they got used to riding again. You might not ever forget how to ride a bike, but when you hadn't ridden one in twenty years, it took a bit of doing to stay in the saddle!

"How far?" Special Agent Vernon asked, almost skidding off the cobbled track. The other two agents avoided contact, barely, then all three steadied down as they got into a pedaling rhythm.

"Four and a half clicks," answered Special Agent RuPaul, the oldest of the trio at thirty. All three worked in the Seattle office, but each had its own territory up and down the coast. There were major aerospace infrastructure companies in the area, and the FBI was charged with vetting all employees, and the companies themselves, in the never-ending battle against cybercrime and other security issues that threatened the homeland. The youngest at just twenty-eight, and only out of the academy for the last four years and already a senior agent, as she was constantly reminded, led the trio, pedaling steadily and with purpose. Point Roberts, with its exacting border require-ments, was in her territory, and she had a file on her computer—make that had a file on her computer—six inches thick on the occupants and behaviors of everyone who called Point Roberts home and a lot of the visitors from the Canadian side of the border.

"There are no signs of civil disturbance," she called back over her shoulder, her short, streaked blond hair just managing to peek out from under her bike helmet. Her long legs flew up and down as she pumped up the small hill. Her two male companions were using their motors, something she tucked away for the next time either one of them took a swipe at her back in the office.

"No one on the roads, but the place looks clean and calm. Hope that lasts." It only took around twenty-five minutes, but in that time, they saw neat, tidy, proud, and undeniably American values in the square, squat houses, manicured lawns and nature strips, and trimmed paddocks, with the occasional resident moving around purposefully outside in the chill. They arrived at the security gate and stood and looked at the camera perched high up on a post, then read the sign on the fence. Normal people would have read the sign first, then looked at the camera, but the FBI was nothing if not observant and paranoid about being, in turn, observed.

A metallic voice rolled across the street, the source hidden from view by tall and lush bushes. "Thank you for calling. The office is not open at this time. Please come back between eight A.M. and four

P.M., Monday through Friday. If you wish to leave a message, press twenty-one hash star on the intercom. Have a lovely day." As this was technically her territory, Special Agent Fay Remer propped her bike against the fence and hit the 21#* buttons.

"This is Special Agents Vernon, RuPaul, and Remer requesting entry. We have a warrant but would prefer someone in authority to meet with us so we can discuss what we came here for." While young, by anyone's standards, her voice had clarity and firmness that belied her years, and the edge she gave to the request left no one in doubt that she meant business. A full minute passed, then a new voice floated across the street.

"This is Farid Tremblay. How can I help you?" Fay searched her eidetic memory, which she sometimes felt was a curse, but since the cyberattack had turned out to be a superpower, in that she remembered everything she had ever read or written in her files and came up with the name of the chief operating officer of the Point Roberts Environmental Development Company, incorporated in Delaware, and as far as she was aware, totally above board in all aspects of their business. And as yet, the FBI had no video recorders that worked; she would rely on her gift to memorize the entire establishment. But first, they had to get in.

"Ms. Tremblay, we would like a face-to-face, please, to outline our intent. Can you let us into the compound and meet with us?" Again, there was a long pause, but at the end, the crack and rumble of the gate unlatching and rolling across the road in its little tracks broke the silence, and having secured the bikes, the three agents moved down the well-marked and lit path. All three thought the same thing at the exact same moment, but being well trained, they kept their own counsel. Someone who had the power to waste on electric gates and rows of high-powered lights which had suddenly turned on along a pathway had the ability to have some form of observation capability. Power was life, and back on the mainland (although Point Roberts was actually part of the mainland of the United States and just felt like an island), there was precious little power—anywhere outside one of the areas with wind or solar generation and the occasional wave-based system. Even then, the distribution was uneven due to the proximity of the users and the location of the generators. Most renewables were fed into the same grid as the coal/gas/oil-fired power plants, and as they were now all offline, the renewables had to do all the work.

The blacktop ran for over a kilometer and a half, then took a sharp left-hand turn. Fay memorized the shape and size of the buildings they passed, all some one hundred meters long and at least thirty meters high, and she guessed the width at around fifty meters because she didn't get a clear view of any building's front or back. They passed six rows, and in the middle of the complex, down a well-lit narrow pathway, a very large satellite dish pointed at the misty sky. Both sides of the blacktop and the pathway were lined with large, very bushy trees and smaller dense shrubs. The brilliant lights seemed to float over their heads with no apparent support. At the end of the turn was a low, single-story building, the front of which was all mirrored glass, and the three agents watched the images of themselves walk up to the full-height double door.

The door opened before they could get to it, and a tall, very fit-looking woman in a bright red pants suit, which dipped slightly between petite breasts, with long, flowing dark hair flecked with highlights, smiled at them as if they were guests of the week.

"Good evening, I'm Farid Tremblay. How may I help you?" Her full-watt smile fired out of her coffee-colored face, and the origins of her mixed-race heritage were unmistakable. The sound of sea breezes and island music flowed through her voice, and for a split second, the three agents were bounced back on their heels. With a strong forward movement, feet planted firmly, Fay reached forward and held out her hand, which was taken unhesitatingly, and the innate warmth of the firm grip sent tingles up her arm all the way to her stomach. At some elemental level, Fay knew this woman, but training had her tuck her personal feelings away as she introduced the agents.

"Ms. Tremblay, this is Special Agents Vernon and RuPaul, and I'm Senior Special Agent Remer. We have a warrant that authorizes us to search your property under the Terrorist Act as amended in 2022." And she passed the folded warrant to the woman, who had not stopped smiling during the introductions.

"Thank you. Please come inside, and I'll get our general counsel to read this and advise me on what I can and can't do. Come this way." And without waiting for an answer, she led the trio into the foyer, then through another floor-to-roof glass door, into a mid-sized conference room that lit up automatically as she walked in. Once again, the three agents reflected on the sheer unfettered use of electricity, something none of them had experienced in a month. As she settled into a seat at the head of a beautiful wooden table, a young man walked in, dressed in a neat, grey suit, his shoes so polished Fay could see her reflection in them, with a floppy head of hair that just made her inner girl smile. "This is Arnon. He will get you anything you need, coffee, tea, or your choice of beverages. Arnon, these are Special Agents Vernon, RuPaul, and Remer. Could you please scan this to our general counsel?" she asked, her melodious musical voice lighting up the room. He literally bobbed his head, almost bowing, as he acknowledged the request. He walked over to a desktop machine and fed the document into it, pressed keys, then handed the document back to Farid Tremblay, who sat as if she had all the time in the world, and the only threat was the remote possibility that she might damage the shiny clear lacquer on her closely cut nails.

The three agents noticed the speed at which the fax had operated, far faster than anything they had seen in use in the last four weeks.

"Coffee, black for me, cream and sugar for Special Agents Vernon and RuPaul. Thank you." Fay was finding it very difficult to maintain a hard edge to her voice; the whole environment shouted money, comfort, calm, style, and massive resources. "Perhaps, Ms. Tremblay, while we wait for your general counsel, you could give us a rundown on what you do here." With her smile fixed on her face, she leaned back in her executive chair, a rich blue leather trimmed with white; the headrest was hidden by her hair, which flowed around her face like soft waves.

"Certainly. As you would have gleaned from our corporate records, we are a privately owned and financed environmental company dedicated to creating the next generation of renewable energy and mass storage devices for both industrial, commercial, and private use. Our plant here has been up and running for just over six months, and our first systems are within a week or two of being ready for delivery." Fay couldn't detect any prevarication in the COO's calm delivery, her melodious voice almost hypnotic. So, she decided to push around the edges and try to break the absolute conviction and calm being projected by the COO.

"Ms. Tremblay, isn't it unusual for the COO to be manning the desk, as it were, on a Friday evening, and what exactly are your systems, how will they be delivered, and who are the buyers?" She smiled as if enjoying some private joke, sat forward in her chair, put her long, manicured hands on the tabletop, and casually linked her fingers together.

"We are a privately financed company, which, again, I am sure you know from your extensive background research. Out initial systems will be delivered to a number of small communities on the West Coast, both here and up in Canada." Her smile deepened, if that was possible, as she continued. "With the tragic terrorist attacks, which we have all suffered from, there are literally thousands of small communities without power, and we hope to address this lack as soon as we can."

"What's stopping you today?" Special Agent RuPaul asked, pleased with his partner's approach to the interrogation and happy for her to run with it. But like the other two agents, he had not fully recovered from the sheer magnificence of the buildings, pathways, roads, and this office—and all the power they used with an almost careless abandon. He sipped his coffee and let the fragrance of the blend circle his palate, yet another sign that this organization had a supply line outside the norm. There hadn't been genuine coffee available in Seattle for over two weeks.

"Well, as you would be aware, just recently we had the ability to send our excess electricity into the town. There was a nice little ceremony to celebrate it, and I understand from the Chamber of Commerce that over ninety percent of the businesses and homes on the peninsular are now getting it direct. We are shipping the energy into the local grid, which is not very efficient, but we work with what we have. We don't have the ability to connect directly to the broader areas of America and Canada, as it were, so we have designed portable units that scale up and down depending on the amount of power required. The smallest system is three meters by two and just as high, weighs in at four hundred kilos, and will power a small factory, or around forty to fifty homes. We have a better long-term solution for private homes, but we thought that getting them power now was more efficient than waiting for supporting infrastructure, which under the present circumstances may be delayed for some time. As to what's stopping us, transportation. We are waiting for two barges to be shipped here, converted to electric power, and then we can ship the systems as fast as we can make them." The three agents sat stunned by this information and the casual way it was conveyed.

"How do you select the areas you will send the power units to?" asked Fay, working overtime in her mind trying to unpick all the data she had accumulated on this organization to see where the potential flaws might be. The truth was, she hadn't been able to find any before they left Seattle, and she couldn't find any now. But she noticed that the beautiful eyes of the COO had suddenly iced up, and while the smile was still on her chiseled face, no one could misinterpret her stare.

"Company proprietary information, and while your warrant might cover access, it will not cover intellectual property or proprietary commercial information, so you will have to limit your questions to your present remit." She held her stare, and Fay was at a loss on how to break the tension that was suddenly in the room. Her older and more experienced partners came to her assistance.

"Ms. Tremblay, our warrant covers a physical inspection of the premise, and the interview of all and any staff on the premise, and then anything else we might think of based on what we see. We are not interested in your commercial propriety data; we will subpoena that when we need it." Special Agent RuPaul's voice was calm, pitched mid-range, and measured, but you could not miss the steel sitting just behind the words. The COO's reaction was anything but expected. She burst out laughing.

"I apologize, but you have to see the funny side," she said, putting one hand over her mouth as if she wanted to be polite. Her head literally shook with mirth, her hair waving as if in a strong breeze. "The world is in total disarray, millions of people are either dead or without food, water, or power, and you want to walk in here and flex your muscles? At a time when what we produce could be the difference between life and death for thousands of people? Outstanding!" She stood suddenly, smoothed some non-existent creases in her pants, then focused her full force on the three agents. "You have interviewed me, so I'll leave you with Arnon; he will take you on your tour, and he is also the only other person on site today. In case you haven't noticed, it's almost the weekend, and we send everyone home for weekends. Have a lovely tour!" And she walked back out the huge glass door and disappeared behind a wall. The three agents looked a little shell-shocked but rose as one to face the smartly dressed assistant. He bobbed his head at them, turned on his heel, and walked back out to the front door, opened it, and held it until the three agents had passed through.

They all exited the building, turned down a small and again well-lit path, and ended up facing a monstrous black wall that shimmered in the light and gave off little sparkles, not unlike those of a firefly.

"It feels slippery. What is it?" Fay asked, reaching forward to run her hand up and down the wall. Arnon, for all his youth and lack of guile, had been trained by the management to be open, honest, and transparent, but to protect their interests the management had also seen to it that he had only ever been exposed to limited data, like the majority of the staff. There were over thirty young, bright engineers from the local town that now worked onsite, and Fay made a mental note to try to interview some of them before they left.

She knew who they were; the FBI had accumulated data on almost the entire town over the past years, just like they had on towns and businesses all up and down the coast.

"It's a new energy-absorbing material that we developed using renewable raw materials. I only work in administration and building three, so I can't tell you much more than that." He looked like a schoolboy answering questions from the headmaster, but the FBI agent knew from his background check that he held double degrees in electrical engineering and plasma physics, so he was no dummy, and she decided to press him to see how far she could go.

"How long have you worked here, and what do you do specifically?" she asked, continuing to run her hand across the building as she walked to one corner. She noticed that the surface was cool but not cold, suggesting that somehow it was warmed. She wondered why and how.

"For two years now, and I report to the production manager of building three. I am responsible for quality control, testing, and fabrication analysis." She turned to look at him, spotlighted by one of the high overhead lights. He looked very young, very neat, and very innocent.

"What do you make in building three?" He gave her a small smile and shook his head.

"I'm sorry, ma'am, I can't tell you that until I have the COO's permission."

"I see. Okay, then, can we go inside this building?" He smiled again, shook his head again, and his shoulders hunched inwards as if he were embarrassed.

"Sorry, ma'am, I only have access to building three, and then only during working hours; all the buildings are hermetically sealed when offline. Everything is running on preprogrammed workflows, readying for the next full workweek." Fay looked at him, seeking any scent of prevarication or outright lying, but her BS detector didn't so much as burp, so she nodded, not accepting the situation, merely acknowledging she had heard what he had said. For a second or two, she was at a loss as to what she should do next, which Special Agent RuPaul solved for her.

"Arnon, what can you show us?" his voice was a little harsh; the FBI had a warrant, and they had every intention of fulfilling its intent. But with all the buildings sealed until Monday, he was trying to work out what to do. It looked like a stalemate—their warrant only gave them physical access to the site, inspect anything they could see, and question the staff. It was the very basic warrant the FBI used on fishing expeditions when they did not know what they were looking for but were sure that they would find something out of whack that would support a fuller search supported by a much more detailed warrant.

"I can walk you around the whole site if you wish, but every building is exactly the same on the outside. Would you like to see them all?" Fay nodded, putting her hands in her pockets, tilting her head to one side, thinking about their options. They had no real grounds to push any harder than they were. At this point, they were not being denied anything in the warrant; they could go back and fully interview the COO, wait for the general counsel to give their opinion on the warrant; they could walk the outsides of the buildings, or they could choose a different option.

"Arnon, thank you, please inform the COO we will be back at oh eight hundred Monday morning, and at that time, we will expect to be able to inspect every building on the premise and interview all staff, without exception. Please ask her to make a room ready in which we can interview the staff in private." And she turned on her heel and started to walk towards the main road they had walked in on. Within a minute, she was flanked by the other two agents, both with wan smiles on their faces.

"I love it when you play hardball, Fay, but what's on that tiny mind of yours?" RuPaul asked. His tonality was inquisitive, not insulting, so she let the quip go. As a very young senior agent and a female, she had learned to pick her battles.

"I suggest you and Vernon go back to Seattle, come back early Monday, and bring more agents. We will have over a hundred people to interview. A few stenographers would not go astray. I'm going to find local accommodation and work the town, find some of the staff here and question them offsite." RuPaul turned his head to look Fay in the eye and rolled his bulky shoulders as if flexing for a fight.

"Not on my watch. You stay. We all stay. And the accommodation is limited to holiday-focused hotels, mainly on the West Coast. As far as I can tell, there is very little in the town." Fay looked at RuPaul, heartened by his response; where usually he was the ringleader in trying to put her down all the time, for the first time, he seemed to be supportive.

She wondered what had caused such a transition in his attitude.

"Fine by me. Find us accommodation." He looked askance and shook his head.

"No internet, no smartphones, remember?" She looked at the older agent and smiled a smile that only a millennial used to digital everything and all the answers to every question in the world just a click or two away could smile. "RuPaul, check your phone. Not only is the mobile phone working here, but we've had access since we landed." He shook his head again, pulled his smartphone out of his jacket pocket, where he had been keeping it largely out of habit, turned it on, and his eyes went as wide as saucers, and the look on his face was one of shock and amazement.

"How do they do that?"

"Excellent question, perhaps the first one we might ask on Monday. Find us somewhere to sleep and eat, please. It's getting really cold."

The three agents climbed onto their bikes and set off back to the township just as a light snowfall laid a carpet of power across the road and the dense foliage. Once out of the heavily wooded area that led back to the plant along Apa Road, it seemed that the entire area was opening its arms to the agents as the gentle spread of houses and buildings revealed itself in the lowering evening. Bright spots of light shone powerfully perched on telegraph poles, creating small pools of illumination highlighting the powdered snow. Once again, all three agents shook their heads in disbelief. They had come from an urban area earlier that day—Seattle— that housed millions and was as black as a coal mine, with the only power in evidence being the red emergency lights that now pointed to hospitals and fire stations. While there were emergency generators in almost every building, certainly the government ones, there was such a fuel shortage that the building managers had been instructed to shut them down.

Yet here they were, in a rural community of fewer than fourteen hundred souls, with seemingly unlimited power up and down every street and obviously in most of the houses that they passed. The lack of vehicles on the road was a surprise until they thought of where people might go on a Friday evening. The majority of the bars and grills were on the western side of the peninsular, and it was both out of the tourist season and post the terrorist attacks, which probably depressed the small market for social outings.

"There's a nice, small hotel down on South Beach Drive. They have three rooms and will fit our meager FBI budget. I've reserved the rooms and asked about food; they haven't replied yet."

"Nice to use your smartphone again?" Fay asked, enjoying the physical demands of the short ride. RuPaul nodded and moved his finger over the screen to take a call. He listened intently, nodded, then hung up.

"They will have dinner ready for us in an hour and will organize breakfast. I suspect the rest will be up to us to manage." They pedaled on in silence, turned into South Beach Drive, and marveled at the sight of the Moon spreading its magic across the ocean in the distance. The lightly falling snow added a surreal element to the vista, and for a brief moment, Fay felt that the whole terrorist thing was just a faint blur at the very back of her memory. But there was one critical issue she would have to run down before they left the peninsular. It was tickling the back of her prodigious memory as well. She knew the COO's face from somewhere back in the day, and she made a decision that flew in the face of proper FBI procedure. "You both go on and get us organized. I want to ride for a while longer, get my thinking straight." The two agents looked surprised but nodded to themselves; she was a fitness nut, by any standard, so they saw no harm in letting her ride off on her own. She backtracked, got back onto Apa Road again, and pedaled back to the production site. Without having to look after the egos of her male counterparts, she made the trip back in six minutes, slammed her bike into the fence, and stared up into the camera lens.

"You know me, I know you. Can we talk, please?" she asked, shaking the snow out of her hair and coat. She looked like a fuzzy, small blizzard for a moment, then the gate slid open, and she walked back down the path, the lights coming on sequentially, making it look like she was being invited deeper and deeper into the dark. She broke into a light jog, not only to quicken her arrival but to relieve some of the chills that had started to invade her bones. She was met just before the turn in the road by the COO, wrapped up in snow gear, a navy watch cap pulled down over her ears.

"Hello Fay, I was wondering if you would make the connection. I recognized you the first minute I saw you on the security system."

"It is you. From the room at the Syrian border. You kept your name."

"Yes. The Tremblay family who adopted me felt it was necessary that I hold onto my roots, no matter how tenuous. I grew up in Canada, not too far from here, so moving to Point Roberts was relatively easy. You didn't keep your birth name?" She looked at the agent as they walked down the road. The creases and lines etched on her pretty face spoke of physical and emotional stress or hardship, and she wondered how her adoptive family had treated her.

"My family was fantastic and supported me as best as they could. They gave me the name 'Fay' when I first arrived, as they couldn't pronounce my given name, and I could hardly speak because I was so scared. But they were wonderful for as long as it lasted."

"As long as it lasted?" The agent seemed to be looking inwardly, reflecting on her memories, and for a fleeting moment, Farid saw a young girl fighting with the memories and emotions from her past.

"There were three other children, all older than me, and the family ran a ranch out in Montana. We were all expected to pitch in and help with the chores and the work around the farm, which I loved. But farming is hard, and by the time I had graduated high school, all that was left of it was an untidy fifty acres, my mother, and one of my sisters. My dad died during a winter blizzard while trying to get the cattle into shelter; my eldest brother left home one second after he turned eighteen, and my eldest sister had died in childbirth. The last few years before I went to college was a depressing time, to say the least." Farid instinctively put her arm around the agent's shoulders, remembering her own time growing up with her adopted family, who had been the greatest parents in the world from her view.

"How did you all manage?" Farid asked, sympathy lacing through her words in genuine concern.

"Mum was getting a monthly stipend from a trust fund my dad set up at the time I was adopted, and basically that paid the bills, fed us, and provided for most of the farm. But my mum was tired of trying to manage things on her own, so she asked me and my sister if we would move with her to Bozeman, where there was a university I could go to, and her son-in-law still lived. We agreed, a little sadly, as I would be leaving my horses behind, but I was able to keep my dogs, so that was something. Mum put the property on the market, and to our surprise, our next-door neighbor offered us more than we thought it was worth almost immediately, so we moved. Mum brought a beautiful house, which we made our home. She is still there, with my sister who runs a restaurant in town. I go back as often as I can, but the job tends to tie me down to Seattle and its surroundings, as you can imagine."

"Yes, I know how that is. I haven't been able to get back home this last year and probably won't for the next if things go the way we plan. Why did you think 'university' when you moved?" she asked, thinking she knew the answer.

"Mum said the people who gave me up for adoption asked my parents, as a condition of the adoption, that they educate me as far as I was able to go. Mum and Dad were only too happy to agree; they wanted all their children to get a college education, and as much as they wanted to keep the farm going, they never tried to shape our interests. And Mum said that they got a huge amount of money to pay for our education—all three of us—and I think that's what Dad started the trust account with. But we were blessed, of that, there is no doubt in my mind."

Farid looked off into the distance, letting her own thoughts about how she had grown up roll around her mind, and smiled to herself. They had indeed been blessed, and in the most beneficial way, but she suspected that the wider world would never see it that way. She shrugged her shoulders; she had a purpose in life, a job to do, and a responsibility to deliver on, so she would keep her thoughts to herself.

"Now that we have had this chat, what will you do about your warrant?" she asked, also thinking she already knew the answer.

"We are staying in a small hotel down on the beach. I'm going to find some of your staff in town and question them over the weekend, then on Monday, as we told your young man, we'll be back at oh eight hundred to inspect the production facilities and interview the rest of the staff." Farid nodded her head, expecting the answer. She wondered just how much the agent didn't know about her sisters-in-arms and what trouble she may cause in the future for the production site. Taking what she judged to be a huge risk, she stopped, turned to face the agent head-on, and fixed her gaze on her with some intensity.

"Can you remember where you originally came from, what the conditions were like, and how many young children just like yourself died every day?" she asked softly as she reached across and grasped both the agent's arms. She held the agent's eyes, looking for any subliminal tell. Fay held her gaze and, if anything, stared a little harder at the question.

"Yes, I can. The tent I slept in lost fifty to sixty children every week, and there were plenty of tents in that camp. Plus, when you add in the people smugglers and all the adults who just wanted free labor, it adds up to a lot. Why do you ask?" Farid pulled back just a little, tightening her grip on Fay's arms, and warmed her smile just a fraction. What she said next would either change the arc of the conversation or create an even bigger problem for her and her mission. She was aware that just a few hundred yards away, the scientist and the engineer were watching through a night vision-equipped camera built into the foliage and knew their view on this subject; they had discussed it at some length after the agents had left just hours ago.

"In times to come, I believe it will be important to remember your roots and the death and destruction you survived due to the fact that you were pulled out of the camps and given a better life. Personally, I celebrate my survival every single day. I came from a camp, unlike yours, and every day I prayed it would be my last. Now, every day I pray I can do my best." Fay held her eyes, noticing that small tears were working their way down her face as if running away from something. She drew in a breath, the air chilling her lungs. She thought for a minute, turned her head to one side, and looked at the lush foliage that was speckled with light, the snow acting as little mirrors. She drew back to the COO.

"Are you doing anything here that is illegal; are we going to find something that causes us to come back with a more specific warrant? Will we have to lock you down?" There was no edge to her voice, but the COO felt the steel behind the questions, and she smiled, the grin spreading all over her face.

"Fay, I give you my word, nothing we do here is illegal; we have permits for everything, we are ecologically responsible, and the devices we are manufacturing are going to change the lives of millions of people up and down the coast in Canada and the US. Time will tell if we will be able to reach further, but we have a plan for that as well. As for closing us down, I sincerely hope not, but who knows what the government will do when they learn of our efforts."

"But you have a plan for that as well?" Fay asked, a small smile splitting her lips in a not unattractive way.

"Of course, girl, of course. Now get back to your FBI playmates, and we'll talk more on Monday. And it would be better if you interviewed all our staff then rather than on the weekend. They're just kids in the main, and most of them lost their jobs in the pandemic, so an interview with the FBI, no matter how righteous, will frighten them unnecessarily."

Fay thought about the last suggestion from the COO all the way back to the hotel as she replayed the entire conversation back over and over, looking for little clues, just like she had been trained to do by the FBI. She had become an agent because of her passion for what she believed was the truth behind the intent of the law. And she had been plucked out of her university six months before she graduated by an FBI recruiter and provided temporary access to the local field office in Bozeman on the weekends to study and watch the agents in action. She was doing a double degree in law and social justice, so this arrangement suited her just fine.

And she remembered her graduation ceremony, her mother and sister standing proudly in the visitor's area, and the tall agent from the FBI office standing next to them as if they were already family. And a week later, she was in Quantico, at the FBI academy, learning how to be a field agent. In truth, it had never occurred to her to be anything else.

She parked her bike, noticed the lights were on in the dining room next to the hotel and went in out of the cold. She shucked her jacket off, her scarf, her hat, and then her jumper, the heat from the wood fire causing her cheeks to flush. The two agents saw her, and RuPaul waved her over.

"We're claiming temporary free time until at least tomorrow morning, so one beer or a glass of wine is fine, and we put your dinner on hold. Where did you go?" he asked, in his very best and sharpest field agent inquisitor's voice. They both looked at her expectantly, having put their knives and forks down from what looked like an appetizing roast. She shrugged, poured a glass of white wine for herself from the bottle on the table, and unconsciously took a step that would have an impact far beyond the dinner and the reason the agents were in Point Roberts in the first place.

"Just rode around, cleared my head, thought about things, no big deal." She signaled to the waiter, waited until he approached, then politely asked for her entrée. The two agents watched in silence, then regained their cutlery and resumed their attacks on their main course.

She was their boss; they trusted her implicitly. If she was keeping something from them, there would be a reason, and no doubt, in time, she would let them in.

Chapter 12

I stood just below the slag heap of twisted and burnt-out metal that had once been an uplink dish for satellite communication. Our security force was around a hundred yards away, arranged in a circle, all looking out for any threat. Bob, the leader of the special forces team, had taken control of the soldiers that had come with us, and in just minutes, had whipped them into a formidable protection force. The FBI agents were busy digging in and around the pile of junk, muttering to themselves as they did so, using scanners and big black boxes with dials and screens pulsing data. Pete stood next to me and Anna next to him, happy to watch this impromptu episode of *Star Wars* versus *Planet of the Apes*. In this case, I felt like an ape because in spite of all my forensic and policing experience, I didn't have a clue what they were looking for.

I decided to take a more personable tack and signaled to Tom, who stood almost on the very top of the technological destruction, moved back and away from the Ranger Station, and found a small mound of unmarked ground to sit on. I looked at Pete and at Anna, let my shoulders slump a little, and ran my hands through my hair. It needed a wash, just like the rest of me.

"We need to think simple fundamentals. Let the boys and girls play with their toys; we need to think like cops. Anna, you've made this point a few times. Why don't you start the conversation?" She looked at me and smiled.

"Yes, I even sprouted off the same mantra to the FBI, NSA, and CIA directors, who took it well, and my boss did something about it. He sent our oldest and most experienced field staff out with pens and paper to conduct face-to-face interviews, which were in progress before I flew back to Israel. But that's not what you mean here, is it?"

"No. Not quite. I'm a great believer in the old saw 'action, reaction.' Take that slightly used satellite dish back there," I said, pointing over my shoulder. "Who did it talk to? How often? What did it say? We know the signals came from the now-demolished missile control center or from that general vicinity. What satellites did it talk to? I remember a comment Mohammad bin Azaria made in the interview about having sent his version of the terrorist attacks around the world waiting to be released. How did he do that? And more to the point, how did they coordinate all the attacks after taking down the Web?"

"They had their own satellite communication," Pete offered.

"Yes. And I believe they still do. Remember, I suspect there is a 'Plan B,' something that follows on from the attacks. So, first question, how do we track and trace satellite transmissions?"

"Here in the USA, the NSA would be all over that. The real issue is what satellites didn't get hammered in the cyberattack. For that matter, think back to the monks. How do they get data around the world? It has to be via satellite." Pete added, mirroring my thoughts.

"Exactly. How did they protect their space assets? I wonder if they'll tell us."

"One way to find out," Anna said, pulling her microcomputer out of her pocket. She dialed up Roger Winslow and got him on her first attempt.

"Are you secure, sir?" she asked. He nodded, his background suggesting he was in a gym. The faint sound of slapping, punching and grunting seeped through the transmission, creating an eerie and surreal backdrop to the stern face of the FBI director.

"Sir, could you reach out to Colonel Anthony and ask him to call us, please?" she asked, knowing that her director would understand the rather convoluted route she had asked for when they both knew she could have dialed Anthony up direct. He nodded sharply and hung up with a snap of the lid of his mini laptop. Twenty seconds later, my mini laptop buzzed, and the Boss's face swam into focus.

The background was moving behind him, so he was obviously going somewhere where he couldn't be overheard.

"You called?" he asked, his voice gruff and demanding, but it was all puff. I knew him too well. He took the job as seriously as anyone I had ever come across, so I waited him out, and once I saw the start of a small smile, I grinned back.

"You remember where we were going on our second stop?" I asked. "Yes, you're there now, according to your computer GPS."

"So ask yourself the question, how is it so? And could that answer in any way help us to establish who else had such services?" I wasn't being oblique, just very careful. I believed this was a critical aspect of tracking down the female terrorists, and I didn't want them to find out about us until I was ready.

"I get your point. I'll get back to you. But if I understand your current establishment, you may well have someone who can help you with that." I thought for a moment, shutting the lid on my mini. I looked at Anna and saw Pete work it out in a flash.

"Anna, one of your FBI suits is a forensic specialist in electronics?"
"Yes."

"Ask him to join us, please." Anna got up and walked back up the gentle slope, covered with tiny shoots of new grass and weeds, with the weeds winning the "this is my turf" battle. She returned with Special Agent Jacob, still holding a large electronic device of some sort, and pointed to me. I stood up, making my inquiry more formal.

"Special Agent, can you tell us what you have found in, let's say, the last ten minutes?" He looked concerned as if he had been asked a question that he didn't want to answer. Anna waved him on, placing one hand on his shoulder.

"Captain Riley is the head of the Interpol investigation unit. We are here at her pleasure; speak freely." He looked at Anna, furrowed his brows, then back at me.

"Ma'am, in the last ten minutes, we have detected both satellite uplink and downlink signals, heavily encrypted, in short bursts. They came from this area, within fifty meters of where we are standing right now, but there is nothing transmitting from the original disk. It is completely destroyed. We may or may not get something from its sonde, as in latent signals, but that will have to be back in our lab at Quantico."

"Can you identify the satellite these bursts were talking to?"

"No, ma'am, not with the equipment we have, but I can give you the technical data, and you can check with the NSA, and they will be able to tell you." I nodded; I had worked that little bit out myself. He had detected our conversations with the FBI and Interpol, and that gave me another idea, and I mentally kicked myself for not thinking of it earlier. I needed a chat with Malcolm Tannery. But not here, and not now.

"Thank you, agent. Please continue with what you were doing." I sat back down on the stubble of the weeds posing as grass and drew in a very large breath. "Do either of you know how many satellites you need to maintain twenty-four-hour connectivity with ground stations?" Anna looked puzzled; Pete just smiled.

"Well, before the crypto attack and back in the old days, it was as simple as six sats in geostationary orbits, four around the equator, and one at each pole.

"When the small-sat business really kicked off, because they had thousands of satellites literally in low earth orbit, you could maintain high bandwidth transmissions anywhere you were, even in the remotest regional area." I smiled, trusting Pete to know the answer to a technical question. He might be muscle, but he had a good head on his shoulders, and I grinned at his knowledge.

"Okay, for first prize in the 'question of the day' competition, do we yet understand how the terrorists infected our IT systems and crashed all the satellites, phones, computers, etc?" Pete laughed, the most pleasant sound I had heard in the last three days.

"Boss, from the briefing we got on the way here, the current thinking is that over two hundred trojan emails distributed a virus simultaneously, which infected and effectively killed all our software, and a burst transmission traveled around the globe thanks to those very small satellites that roam the heavens, trashing every chip in anything that was online at the time, in space or on the ground. Some chipsets were immune; the terrorists obviously selected ones that suited them to remain operational. We know that hospitals, fire service, and some other emergency services were spared from the attack on our chips, so the terrorists had to have exquisite knowledge to achieve that." My time to laugh. I felt nothing like being happy; this case was wearing me down, but I had to enjoy Pete's enthusiastic summary of the technical issues of the cyberattack that had set us all back to the sixties or the seventies, technically speaking.

"One more question. How would you have protected yourself from this attack if you had been forewarned?" It was Anna's turn to laugh as she pushed her hair back from her ears, an almost unconscious action I had started to notice. The stress was getting to us all.

"I can answer that one. Roger and I had a long conversation about that. It appears he had posed the same question to Frank Reynolds at the NSA. Air gapping computers and turning off anything you wanted to preserve. It would not have stopped the destruction of the WIFI networks, routers, dark fiber terminals, or the microwave network. Now ask me what air-gapping means." I laughed again, having only the vaguest notion of how to airgap a computer.

"No, tell me, make my day!" I said, actually enjoying myself for the first time in days.

"Sorry, haven't got a clue!" she said, shaking her head from side to side. "Roger started to explain it to me, and my brain just went to jelly. Pete, can you explain it?" she asked, punching Pete in the arm playfully. He responded by lightly punching me in the arm, which I rubbed in a mock response.

"Well, it's really simple. You disconnect the WIFI, Bluetooth, and ethernet cables, and make sure that you are not connected to any network, or even other computers, or remote power supplies, so nothing transmitted by any means can get to your computer." I looked at Pete with new respect. Back in Venice, Luigi had tried to explain the same thing to me, and I only got half of it. Our light-hearted mood was suddenly shattered by the sound of machine-gun fire, and all three of us rolled onto our stomachs and faced where we thought the shots had come from. I snatched up the small FM handset we were using for short-range communication, such things being below the technical threshold or interest of the terrorists, and clicked the "talk" button.

"Status!" I almost yelled, then held the little transceiver out in front of my head as if to hear it clearer.

"Captain, we are under attack from civilians in mounted vehicles. They fired on us using automatic weapons; we returned fire with one long gun, dropped the shooters, and now they have withdrawn back below the ridgeline."

"Where is Bob?" I asked, my voice now somewhat normal. I had been under direct fire numerous times during my career, but it still caused me to react in an instinctive and tense manner.

"Sir, he is with the unit on our flank. They are not moving at this time until we can establish the intent of the attackers." Because good field discipline was being exhibited by everyone on the net, no one else had yet chipped in.

"Bob, your assessment?"

"Captain, no activity here. I recommend we wait it out."

"Do so. When you are able, shrink your perimeter by half."

"WILCO." His short reply reminded me he and his small team were the best of the best, but then I had a sudden thought, our terrorist friends were in love with technology.

"Bob, get your UAV disruptors up and running." Silence filled the airwaves, then I heard a grunt.

"This is Team One. You have incoming from three-three-niner degrees, one hundred meters, seven unidentified UAVs." Team One was the FBI agents up on the slag heap. The low-level UAV detector was in one of the boxes I had loaded during our stop in Minneapolis. An old battlefield commander back at the NCIS academy had always told us to "wish for the best, plan for the worst," and personally, I thought it was a great mantra.

"We have a visual, ground attack in progress. Stand by." Silence, more silence, then the unmistakable sound of automatic weapons, but the different tones suggested we were in the fight up to our eyeballs, then a series of explosions pulsed in the air over our heads, suggesting a serious airburst. We were only about one hundred yards away from the fighting, which I was reminded of as the air shattered another six times in a rapid-fire rolling explosion that shook my body with the percussion. I opened my mouth and clicked my ears, trying to equalize them so I could hear again. I motioned to Pete, who, as expected, had his weapon drawn and was facing the attack, belly down, but in front of Anna and me. I reached out, tapped him on the foot, grabbed Anna's leg, and gave it a tug.

"Up the hill," I shouted, motioning with my spare hand. Anna started to crawl up towards the FBI agents, all of whom had gone to the ground.

"Squads three and four, close up on Team One!" Don't know who gave the order, but I immediately felt safer knowing we would soon be joined by ten combat-hardened troops led by a special forces grunt. We reached the top of the mound and found our FBI agents formed up in a protective triangle, guns drawn, protecting each other's flanks and backs. They widened their formation to allow us to enter, and we then formed a ring of six; Pete pushed up against my right shoulder, Anna to my left. A team of casually dressed soldiers swarmed our little defensive position, stayed down just below the level of our waists, and formed a slightly bigger circle. One of the Special Forces women, Kate, I think her name was, looked back up at me, her close-quarters combat weapon wrapped around her on a strap, an ugly black barrel pointing towards the direction of the attack.

"Captain, we need to find a better position. Please follow me." And she led us back down to a lower level, walked around the mound, and signaled for one of her team to climb up into the ranger hut, around forty feet in the air. She had a long gun strapped to her back and a CQC automatic weapon across her chest. Overwatch, I thought to myself. Nice. The air had gone still, no noise of gunfire; it was either the lull before the storm or the firefight was all over.

It was the lull.

Without warning, three big vehicles approached us from the west, guns blazing as they bounced over the rough ground. The shots sizzled and whipped above our heads, smacking into the surrounding dirt. We were all flat on our stomachs, guns pointed at the vehicles, when our overwatch fired three well-placed shots, and we could actually see shooters falling off the top of the trucks. Two shots later and windscreens were shattered, with a third shot obviously hitting the driver because that truck suddenly veered off to one side and rolled over. Our handguns were not very effective from this distance, but our protection detail with their CQC weapons had the range and was literally mincing up the remaining trucks with short, disciplined bursts. I held my hand up as high as I could.

"Cease fire!" I shouted, my ears ringing from all the gunfire. The echoing silence still reverberated from the aftershocks of the rounds passing over us, and the ticking of machinery cooling could clearly be heard by some trick of acoustics. I stood up, Pete quickly moving in front of me, Anna behind, and a soldier I did not recognize on one side.

"Pete, we need a prisoner; we need to establish who they are. Bob, status?"

"All good here. We're just mopping up the mess. We have two casualties and no survivors on the other side. Do you want us back to you?" I tapped Pete on the shoulder to stop him in his tracks. He looked a little feral in the late afternoon light, his head swiveling from side to side like a radar dish at a busy airport, his gun held out in front in a typical weaver stance, elbows bent, sights at eye height.

"Captain, we wait until the other teams form up. Bob can get to us when he's ready; there may be more of these bastards," he said, as calm as could be.

I signaled for us to go to the ground, and typical Pete, he was the last man standing until he was sure there was no apparent threat and that we were all flat on our stomachs. He then pointed to two of the team, who rose with him into a crouch and made their way forward to the wrecked truck. One shot was fired, and I recognized it from a pistol, some very low-level muttering floated across the ground, then the three of them made their way back, dragging a body between them by its collar. Pete remained standing, looking down at the sorry mess he had dropped at our noses.

"Dressed like cowboys, their guns were mostly lever action, a couple of AR15s. And the machine guns were from the Vietnam era, GPMG-60s. Haven't seen one of those since I can't remember." I looked at the prisoner, blood staining his checked blue-and-white flannel shirt, one leg twisted at an unnatural angle, the other with a dirty, white bone sticking up through his jeans. I swallowed; it was always uncomfortable looking at the result of weapons fire on the human body, but in this case, his injuries had been exacerbated by the truck rolling over on him.

"Get him into cover; in spite of what just went down, this is still a police action, and I want as much information from him as we can get. Anna, all yours. Pete, we have wounded coming in with Bob. Your recommendation, please." My voice was sharp, direct, and forceful. You learned how to do that under fire eventually, but the old truism of acting like you want people to believe was a truism for a reason. In less than three minutes, Bob's team arrived, carrying two of their team in ponchos, suggesting serious wounds. I looked back at where we had parked our vehicles, thought about how we had been trying to stay under the radar, then looked back at the two wounded being treated by our field medics.

"Tom, call in a medivac, please. From this point on, we go full visual, fully armed, but it is still a police action, so keep that up front. Pete, with the captive, gets as much from him as you can." Pete looked at me, smiled, and shook his head.

"Captain, with respect, we should send one of the Feebies. I can't leave you and Anna; the Boss will ream me another one if I do." I had forgotten the Boss's instruction to Pete in all the excitement of the attack, so I smiled to let him know I had remembered and took no offense at having been corrected in the field by a junior officer. In front of the whole team.

"Sorry, Pete, my bad. Anna, can you select one of your team to accompany the wounded?" I asked. Bob walked over to me, covered in mud and dirt from head to toe. His eyes were huge, round white circles where his goggles had protected him, his pupils as black as night.

"Captain, this group is identified as Montana Freedom Militia. We have some radios and a handbook from one of their specials. Their weapons were AR-15s, old-style GPMG-60s, and their UAVs' civilian models strapped with C4. We got them all." His blunt statement was delivered emotionless, flat, with no emphasis on any particular word, but you could see the heat and fury shimmering off him in spite of the mud and dirt. He was righteously pissed off, and I felt for any other attackers who crossed our path.

145

"Thanks, Bob. Let me have five minutes with the specialists, then we'll move back to the vehicles." I moved to the three FBI agents, and it was enough for me to just look interested in them for them to start talking all at once. Anna waved them down, walked over to me, put a hand on my shoulder, and gently led me off to one side.

"They're a little wound up; they didn't get to fire their weapons during the attack, and they don't want to look like pussies."

"I get that. I didn't fire a shot either, and neither did you, and Pete only fired the one shot when he was at the wrecks of the trucks, so we all maintained under fire, so let them know that when you get a chance. What did they find?" Anna turned to look at me, her light blue eyes steady, her face a mirror of calm, and I viscerally felt her smooth voice work its way into my bones. I took a very deep breath, let it out slowly, nodded to her to continue, and mentally and physically relaxed for the first time since the attack had been identified.

"They've taken the sonde and a few small pieces of the dish; they tracked our transmissions, but you know that, and there's not much else to tell."

"Expected. Okay, we move on to the farmhouse. Get the wounded and the prisoner on the chopper when it arrives. Join us at the vehicles." I moved off, Pete sticking to me like a leach. "If it hadn't been for that overwatch, we might very well have had a different outcome," I said to Pete. He looked over to me as if checking out a prize at a fairground shooting stall and nodded.

"Boss, if you'll forgive me my military roots, we have to go in better prepared next time. This attack was amateurish in the extreme; the next one might not be so fucked up." I nodded. I agreed with him; we might be a police action, but we were not going to be lambs to the slaughter.

"When we get everyone together, gun up, and if you need call in more troops. We still have fifteen back at the station; we can get them flown directly to our next stop." He nodded, no doubt thinking why I had left half of our protection detail behind with the train.

Simple, really, I didn't know who I could trust—still didn't—but losing the train seemed like an easier choice than having us all decimated by free-wheeling militia. Then I had a flash of inspiration, snapped my computer open, and dialed up General Bridges.

"General, good evening. I need a protection detail on the president's train ASAP. Can you assist?"

"Yes."

"Thank you." And I terminated the call. If the president's most senior member of the military couldn't arrange such a small thing, no one could.

Chapter 13

The Boss, Tom, and three of his special forces, the Israeli contingent led by their Sgen Aluf, and an Egyptian soldier of indeterminate rank ranged around the Soviet Hind Helicopter that had flown them in from Libya to the base of the mountain identified as the terrorist base. Surprisingly, the Libyans had been extremely helpful, first at the farmhouse where the mythical "Helen" had run her operations from, then by providing the transport into Egypt. The farmhouse had been a complete bust, having been burnt to the ground so thoroughly that only oily soot remained as a testament to its prior stature. Why the Libyans had been so helpful was easy to guess—they didn't want any possibility of any attribution concerning the terrorist attacks to blowback on them, given their current precarious position in the world of politics.

The Boss wasn't fussed in this case. He hadn't expected to find anything in the wreckage. The women terrorists were too good to have left anything incriminating behind. Not their style. And the helicopter ride had given him extra daylight hours to work the mountain, which he was just about to do. He looked at the Egyptian, no doubt a member of their security forces, and offered his hand.

"مساء الخير أنا العقيد أنتوني مع الإنتربول" the Boss offered, in perfect Egyptian

"Colonel, please speak English. I need to practice! Welcome." He bowed to the Boss. The Boss, slightly at a loss, bowed back, then the Egyptian leaned forward and hugged the Boss and kissed him on both cheeks. "We have a digger here, ready for your command, and if you require anything else, you have only to ask."

"Thank you. We'd like to dig into the old tunnel to get to the cavern if we are able. Can you do that?" The Egyptian looked at the pile of dirt deposited from a serious volume of explosives, then his face lit up with a smile so big his face seemed to split.

"Yes, we can do that. Please stand back." And he walked over to a group of nondescript workers hidden behind a pile of rubble, waved his hands around as if conducting a concert, then marched back to the helicopter.

"Colonel, it will take a few minutes. Please wait in the shade." The Boss nodded, looked over at his teams, gave them the slightest of head nods, then rested against the frame of the enormous helicopter. Originally designed by the Russians, then copied and built by the Chinese, the helicopter could carry thirty fully armed troops some seven hundred kilometers, but in this case, the age of the airframe was apparent by the worn surfaces, bare metal peeking through in various areas, and hopefully, the Boss thought to himself, not in any essential area required for flight! His laptop vibrated against his leg, so he moved away from the group and opened the lid.

"Anthony."

"Colonel, I have the information you requested. Your hunch was correct—the satellites still functioning are all French weather satellites, geostationary orbits, with a coverage of every area you nominated every ninety minutes a lag time of ten to twelve minutes depending on the receiver's latitude. Does that help?" Stefarino asked. The Boss dipped his head in thought, wishing he were anywhere else but here in the boiling sun of the Libyan desert.

"Stefarino, that is excellent work. Thank you again. We are in your debt." As the head monk's face disappeared into the classic blue of a completed transmission, he dialed Jessica's computer.

"Riley."

"Jessica, French weather sats, ninety-minute traverse, ten-to-twelve-minute dwell time, all hit our target areas. We need to talk. How long will you be in-country?" In faraway Montana, Jessica looked up at the frigid blue sky as if seeking inspiration, then looked back down at the camera lens.

"Boss, we just had an encounter with a local militia. We're on the way to waypoint two. I suspect we will be here for a day or two yet, and then there's the pesky problem of the surrounding towns and the workers who rebuilt the missile silo. I could leave that to Anna and her FBI crew; I can't decide on that at this time."

"Casualties?" the Boss snapped out, his first thought being for the wellbeing of his people.

"Two wounded, both ambulatory, being transported back to the hospital as we speak. One prisoner, banged up by bullets and a vehicle crash, also ambulatory, traveling with an FBI agent. Don't expect much data, local militia, and a poorly executed attack. Our teams handled themselves well. But we are gunning up for the next stage, and at present, we are following the trail of the dark fiber." The Boss nodded; he'd have to find a way to get time with Jessica some other way.

"Okay, continue, consider who you might share the sat data with, luck!" And he snapped his computer shut, looked at the diggers and machinery tearing up the floor of the desert, reaching down to what he hoped would be a cavern intact enough for them to gain some appreciation of how this terrorist cell had operated and maybe some actual evidence leading to the identities of the women terrorists.

Bouncing along the scrubby low-rise hills in northeastern Montana, I gave some thought to what the Boss had said. I had already decided I needed a chat with the white-hat hacker that worked for the NSA, as he had already proven his skills in assisting our geeks in Venice and Israel to unpack Amira's hidden data. How much of a risk would it be to share this sat information with him? Only one way to find out. I dialed him up; we had left one of the monks' computers with him on Anna's last visit to Washington.

"Malcolm, hello, not sure of the time where you are; can you spare me a few minutes, please?" His young face, encased in his long blond hair, which by its unruly and tangled appearance suggested had just been asleep, looked at me with a curiosity that was almost instantly replaced with a smile.

"Captain, good to hear from you. How can I help?" he asked, his background strobing as he moved. The image stabilized; he had obviously put the computer down on a bench because a huge green-and-silver coffee machine suddenly appeared in the frame, and for the next minute, I was entertained by his long, slim hands working as he ground, filtered, tapped, prodded, and then encouraged the rich dark brown liquid into a small cup. His face came back into the frame as the cup disappeared out of view.

"Sorry about that, but I'm useless without my drug of choice. How can I help?" he asked for a second time. I had no option but to smile. I knew exactly how he felt. I had been away from Indigo and his belching espresso machine for only about four days, and I was already suffering withdrawal symptoms!

"Not to worry, I totally understand. Malcolm, can I give you some data that you will have to keep secure, even from your own people?" I was aware I was putting him in a difficult position. The NSA collected secrets from all over the globe; they were a well-compartmentalized organization, and very little, if anything, ever leaked from inside their secured walls.

"Will my boss know what's going on?" he asked, his young face looking concerned, furrow lines linking his eyebrows.

"Your director will know I have given you data; he will not know what data, but if he approaches you directly, I expect you to brief him. But no one, and I do mean no one else under any circumstances. I expect you to work on very secure equipment; this data cannot get to the terrorists under any circumstances. Can you agree to all of that?" He looked thoughtful, then slowly nodded.

"I have very secure computers. I can guarantee absolute security within the area of my workspace, so yes, I can meet your specifications. What do you want me to do with the data?"

"I want you to locate any transmission to or from, and if you can catch the transmissions as well, that would be a bonus." He looked at me blankly for a moment, then smiled again, his face morphing in a way that suited his pretty boy looks.

"You've found the satellites the terrorists are using."

"Yes. Here's the data." And I gave him what the monks had given us and crossed my fingers because if the terrorists twigged to the fact that we could now track their transmission, we would have lost a huge advantage. "Just one thing," I added, "you can work with the geeks we have in Venice and Israel if you want to. They are read-in to this. But if you do, use your little microcomputer."

We bounced to a stop to be greeted by the team from the railway station, a helicopter gunship with its rotors winding down, and a sunset that set the edge of the world on fire. Montana was a very beautiful state. I had to remember that; the fact that the terrorists had chosen it to launch their attacks from was a mere accident of geography. Emptiness, sparse population, and a decommissioned missile silo so old it had been almost forgotten by the military.

"Have we got a report on the helicopter hangar?" I asked Anna, looking at the burnt-out wreck of the homestead. It didn't look as trashed as the satellite dish, so maybe we would find something of value here. The FBI agents led off, our protection detail now gunned up with automatic weapons, long guns, and a squad weapon or two spread out around us.

"Yes. There was a Hughes 500 left in the hangar, fake registration, production ID plates removed, and no trace or DNA, and it was only partially destroyed when the boys and girls blew up the farmhouse. We can still get down the stairs, but the tunnel that leads to the silo is blocked all the way. They obviously had it mined."

"Okay, let's do the stairs," I said, following the FBI team into the wreck. After a twist and turn, we reached the long, sloping wall on which were hundreds of photos of little girls, each notated with the date and location of their death, a grim reminder of the story both the Jesuit priest and Mohammad bin Azaria had told us. By my quick count, there were just under a thousand photos, and the dates ranged between 2014 and 2016. Only two camps were named, both in Northern Africa. The photos had been taken with digital cameras, possibly smartphones, and I tucked that little bit of information away for another time.

We hit the blown-out tunnel, and I saw no reason to linger. "Okay, everyone, back up. Anna, get your team to collect those photos, please;

let's move on." We were packed up and moving in less than twenty-five minutes, the entire group solemn and a little depressed by what we had seen. Death did that to you unless you were a borderline narcissistic sociopath or outright psychopath, and in that case, you would never make the ranks of the FBI, Interpol, or Special Forces. Maybe.

We arrived at the bombed-out entrance to the silo and got absolutely nothing there by way of useful evidence. Then I had the vehicles form up into a wagon wheel circle, posted guards, set up a small antipersonnel radar and UAV detector on a collapsible tower, broke out the tents, got a meal going, then called Anna, Pete, the FBI agents, and Bob in for a council of war.

"In spite of what you think, this has not been a waste of time. No, we haven't got any new evidence, but Pete, Anna, and I have now seen firsthand what their setup was. I can even speculate how they used these resources. The helicopter— probably flown by our pilot friend of Hog fame—was used for communication and flying in supplies. They have a one-hundred-mile 'black hole' over this entire site, but I'm willing to bet the helicopter went out further than that. If so, we'll find it, track it, and possibly locate another nest.

"The house was probably their main base up to the time of the major attacks here in the US, after which they probably moved into the silo. Then after they crashed the space station, they probably moved out down the other tunnel that was destroyed and disappeared. We don't know their role in coordinating anything the mercenary terrorists did, but I'm willing to bet my pension that they gave the 'go' for the big attacks on the oil well heads, major pipelines, coal mines, and things like that. Remember, these attacks were coordinated on a global scale, over just a few weeks, start to finish."

"Planning and coordination. Yes, I can see that," Bob offered, and being a Special Forces-trained officer selected for the president's personal traveling guard as a backup to the Secret Service, exquisite planning would be in his wheelhouse.

"Do you think any of the women are still in the area?" he asked.

"Yes, I do. I suspect that they have a civilian base, jobs, and fit into a local community somewhere, and have for several years. Everything about the attacks, from the first breaches of the IT systems way back in 2000, has the hallmarks of sophisticated, long-term planning. The first of the women terrorists could only have graduated sometime after 2015 and been actively recruited in the next five years or so. We know from our interrogation of suspects that the serious weapons were developed after 2020, based on research work completed before that date." I was keeping Amira our little secret, and as only Anna, Pete, and I knew of her existence outside of the Israelis, it wasn't hard to prevaricate about the information she had given us.

"So, a basic plan was in place for, say, fifteen years, during which time the L100 was obtained, the bombs and Hellfires stolen, the F4 acquired, and no doubt the active bases were located and established, with the planners waiting to see what the women would create, then factor in how to use the new weapons to best effect. We don't believe that the nano weapons or the software bugs existed as weapons much before 2020. We know this silo was starting to be rebuilt three to four years ago. We know Mohammad bin Azaria spread six-billion-dollar packets of cash around the world and established legitimate trading facilities that drew no attention until after the attacks, and we only established this after we captured him and Shetani.

"We know the mercenary terrorists went onto Mohammad bin Azaria's payroll two years ago and then took the next eighteen months to distribute their cells worldwide. They had to be coordinated, and again my money is on the women terrorists, the ones here, and the ones in Libya and Egypt. We don't think that more than six or eight women are involved. There might be more. It doesn't really matter. We have primary targets, starting with the pilot of the Hog and the women who worked on this site. And a woman named 'Helen,' somewhere in Libya.

Questions?" Behind us, I could hear the clatter and banging of cooking utensils and the bubbling of a pot. We were out in the open, not trying to hide our intent anymore, and the feeling was that everyone was loosening up a little after the day's firefight. I could imagine the war stories the new members of our protection detail were receiving and felt a little sympathy for them.

"How do you intend to track them from here?" Bob asked, folding his arms across his broad chest. Before I could answer, my laptop did its little buzzing trick.

"Riley."

"Captain, I have a location for you. It has been in our files for some time; we only just discovered it due to the most recent line of questioning from the colonel. He asked that I pass it on to you." The head monk almost looked apologetic at having interrupted me, but the next thing he said literally made my day.

"Latitude 46.5891N, Longitude 112.0391W. We had a burst reception and a burst transmission from that location six days ago." I smiled; for once, technology was working in our favor.

"Thank you, that is simply fantastic. Stefarino, is there any way you could trace any other burst transmissions like these, say, in the past month?" He looked at me from under his white, bushy eyebrows as if about to scold a small child. Then he smiled, and his whole face lit up.

"*Capitano, per lei uccidiamo il toro!*" I thought about that. I had heard the story of the farmer killing the bull for his lover, and I smiled inwardly. He was paying me a compliment, and it felt pretty damn good under the circumstances.

"Bob, you asked how we would trace the women? Well, at first light, we'll call in the cavalry and head into Helena." Anna looked at me in amazement.

"You've found them?" she asked. I thought quickly; we had agreed to keep the monks a secret, one that Anna knew, but no one other than Pete in this group was read in.

"Interpol just got lucky, and our geeks made an intercept we can follow up on." Anna looked a little curious at the source but said nothing.

"There were a series of burst transmissions from Helena six days ago. We have the latitude and longitude; we can't exactly pinpoint it, but we can get to within a mile. This is the first real lead we have had since the Hog pilot disappeared." The group went quiet for a moment, the sounds of cooking permeating the crisp air. A banging sound echoed through the camp, and a very gruff voice yelled, "Come 'n get it!" I looked at Pete, Anna, then Bob, the FBI agents who had remained silent through the briefing, and we all looked a little weary, if not outright tired.

"Let's get some dinner," I said, standing up. The agents and Anna moved off. Bob looked at me out of the corner of one eye, and Pete stood with his hands on his hips. The contrast in their different builds was marked—Bob thickset, burley, broad of chest, long arms and thick wrists; Pete, long and slight, not narrow of chest but certainly not as broad as Bob's. They were different but the same when you looked into their eyes. Hard, unblinking, focused, penetrating, ready to kill.

"There is a lot you are not telling us," he said softly so that no one else could hear. I looked at Pete; he folded his arms across his chest defensively.

"Bob, need to know, no more, no less. We can't tell you anything that is not authorized by the president or her war council. Interpol is the lead agency, as we mentioned previously, but you have heard a lot of stuff tonight you were not aware of, and I'm sure, knowing the captain as I do, there'll be more if it's operationally relevant." I felt for Bob; he and his people were risking their lives protecting us, with only half of the background story. It would piss me off if I were in the same position.

"Bob, I apologize. There's only so much we can share, but trust me, I will not endanger you or your team without giving you every piece of information that's relevant. Is that good enough?" He looked at me with a very hard stare, his eyes shrinking to pinpoints.

"If it has to be this way, we're here at the order of the president, and so far, your briefings have been accurate, relevant, and timely. But I would really like to understand everything that's going on, but I'll hold my curiosity for now. Let's eat."

Chapter 14

The three FBI agents had rested during the weekend and, contrary to their earlier plans, did not set out into the community and try to interview the staff of the plant. Fay had justified this decision by calling the Seattle office and speaking to the director on her smartphone. He had been so surprised by that and the information surrounding its use that he had instructed the team to bike around the whole area and map the connectivity arc. They had done so and been surprised to find that the signal cut out around three miles from the plant, just short of the Canadian border. This meant that the whole town of Point Roberts had mobile phone connectivity, something that could only be explained by resources at the plant. A topic of interest for first thing Monday morning.

There was no WIFI that they could detect, so the phones had to be talking to either a ground station or a satellite. Common wisdom in the FBI was that all the satellites had been neutered in the cyber-attack, so the agents were leaning towards a ground station. What they couldn't figure out was why this service had been provided in the first place. And most smartphones had been crushed by the cyberattack in any case, so if the town had working phones, then they must have been forewarned of the attack. The agents only had working phones because the Seattle office had just ordered two hundred new models, which had been delivered a month ago but had not been turned on or set up at the time of the attack. And Seattle had ground station repeaters popping up all over the city, so limited connectivity was available, but without all the apps everyone was used to. The internet was still down and likely to be so for the foreseeable future.

The agents stood at the massive gates, with an additional four agents who had arrived by fast boat at first light. They packed their bikes against the fence as the gates opened, and Arnon, the COO's assistant, led them off to the office block. Light snow was still falling, as it had done most of the weekend, and once again, the bright over-head lights lit the way. It looked like a fairyland, the trees and shrubs on either side dark and looming, the blacktop white and reflecting little sparkles from the light hitting the snow, and the illusion of a three-dimensional tunnel formed by the falling flakes in the illumi-nated air.

They were ushered into the foyer, then led to an auditorium, which had been set up with ten small desks, each about ten yards apart, with a privacy panel on three sides, creating the illusion of a maze.

"We weren't sure how many agents you would bring, so we catered for ten; there is a noise canceller in each booth, so you will have total privacy, and we have forewarned the staff of your inten-tions, and they will report to you in groups."

"How many staff?" Fay asked, pulling off her jacket, gloves, watch hat, and scarf. She noticed a large bench on one side and placed them on it, not concerned about the water that was already forming on the tabletop. The other agents followed her lead; they had all been briefed on protocol at breakfast back in the hotel. Six of the agents moved off to claim their interrogation space while Fay looked around the auditorium.

"Thirty-eight have reported for work, we have two away on leave, and one called in as sick," Arnon reported. Fay did a quick sum in her head and worked out that each agent would have to interview six or seven suspects. Working on ten to fifteen minutes per interview, two hours should do it timewise. They might get back to Seattle in daylight.

"I'd like to speak to Miss Tremblay again, please, before I start my interviews." Arnon nodded; he had been expecting this. He gestured with one hand, bowed slightly, then led her out and back to the small conference room where they had first met the COO on Friday evening.

Farid Tremblay stood at the end of the boardroom table, smiled warmly, moved slightly to shake the agent's hand, then sat back in her high-backed chair. "I hope you had a comfortable weekend?" she asked, gesturing to the coffee service.

"Yes, thank you, and I'm fine for the moment. I was hoping your chief ex-ecutive officer would be here today?" Fay asked, watching the COO for any sign of prevarication. Her research had indicated that the CEO was a woman named Kathryn Simmons, a graduate of Sandford University, majoring in both physical and computer sci-ences and graduating at the very early age of twenty-two. According to her biography, she had then gone to work for one of the hot tech-nology companies in Silicon Valley and moved into the position here in Point Roberts four years ago, at just twenty-five years of age. There was a pattern here. Fay could sense it because the COO had a very similar path and was also very young for her accomplishments. But you didn't lock up people because they were smart and young, she thought to herself, or she would be in jail as well. She would ask the questions that she had prepared over the weekend and form her con-clusions accordingly.

"Kathryn is away at the moment, visiting one of our other facil-ities. She is aware of your visit, has reviewed your warrant, as has our general counsels, and has briefed me on what I can tell you. So, perhaps you would like to get that out of the way first?" Fay hesitated, having momentarily locked in on "other facilities," but she quickly put her innate curiosity on hold for the moment as a stray thought flashed through her mind. She was very young for her position in the FBI, had left college early by normal standards, and had fast-tracked through both the FBI academy and the FBI hierarchy. The Bureau had recognized a smart and highly talented recruit; she had been spe-cifically told this by her local director at an interview. She had been a refugee child, taken out of the camps and given to a foster family, who had given her an identity and formally adopted her, a genuine family dynamic growing up, and supported her all the way to her present position. She wondered if the CEO had a similar story but recalled there was nothing in her file that suggested anything but a normal upbringing. She asked the question anyway.

"Was your CEO also a refugee?" At the question, the COO sat straight up in her chair, her posture rigid, then in a split second, she relaxed again and smiled.

"You caught me by surprise. Yes, she was, but you will have to get her story from her. It's not my place to comment. Your other questions?" she asked, seemingly relaxed but internally wound up like a spring. She thought back to her conversation on Friday evening with the FBI agent and thought she might yet regret having brought the subject of refugees up. Time will tell. On the other side of the table, Fay watched the COO go through all her physical manifestations and silently admired her self-discipline. But she tucked the performance away to be pursued later.

"Last Friday, you told us that you make transportable power supplies; you described them as being three meters by two, two meters high, and weighing four hundred kilos. Is that correct?"

"Yes."

"And that you would be shipping these units to destinations along the coast, both into Canada and down into the United States."

"Also correct."

"And when I asked you how you would select the destinations, you did not answer excerpt to point out you're needed to protect your intellectual property rights and your proprietary commercial information. You then basically walked out of the interview. Why such a reaction to a simple question?" Fay watched her like a hawk, looking for the micromovements in her face that would signal a lie. The COO sat back and drew in a breath, realizing for the first time that this young FBI agent was going to be as tenacious as a bulldog in spite of their very similar origin stories. She had researched the agent during the weekend and noted her rapid rise through the FBI ranks, having been given her own territory and responsibility at a very early age. And a female to boot! And she was smart, with, according to her college yearbook, an amazing ability to remember everything she read and heard. The fact that their similar refugee backgrounds provided an inexorable emotional link was something she would have to be very careful of.

"I was tired and, to be honest, a little pissed off that the FBI would be calling on me at such a later hour. We are dedicated to providing hope for a very battered world, so being questioned about how we are going about that got my backup. A very normal reaction, wouldn't you agree?" she asked, reaching forward to pour herself a coffee. She looked over at Fay, raised her eyebrows in question, got a sharp nod, and poured a second cup. She slid it across the polished surface of the table, the cup rattling on the saucer as it skidded to a stop just inches from the edge, something that did not go unnoticed by the FBI agent.

"Then I'll ask the question again. How will you—or have you already—determined where to send your power units? And while I'm at it, how come you are providing phone coverage for the peninsular?" Fay watched the COO like a hawk, having thrown in the phone question in an attempt to upset the rhythm of the interrogation. In return, the COO looked at the FBI agent and smiled, and nodded to herself.

"Forgive me, Fay, but I just won a bet with myself. I thought you would be a hard arse, and you have proved me right. Can we drop the formalities and get to the root of all of this, please? I'm tired of all the dancing around." Fay returned her look, straightened her shoulders, and dug in.

"It seems a coincidence to us at the FBI that the world is brought to its knees with the loss of most power-generating raw materials such as oil, gas, and coal, the world wide web crashed, and then as if by magic you have power units ready to distribute big enough to run small factories and tens of houses. Were the terrorist attacks part of your business plan?" The COO's face froze, the unintended truth of the FBI agent's question hitting a nerve. But she had her mission and viewed her role as critical to the survival of the outside world, and after all, she had no direct role in the terrorist attacks and had only a vague awareness of the timing from conversations with her cohorts, the engineer and the scientist, who had helped establish the site in the first place. And both of them had been tight-lipped about the overall plan, choosing to focus on getting the plant up and running. And, she assumed, helping the other plants spread around the world to also get established.

"I find that question insulting in the extreme. This plant was established over three years ago, with full public compliance and governmental approval. You have copies of all our paperwork; our counsel confirmed that late yesterday evening." Fay smiled to herself; she had rattled this beautiful woman, of that she was certain.

"And you just happened to have a spare mobile phone repeater lying around, just in case?" she asked, letting skepticism creep into her voice.

"Yes, as a matter of fact, we did. The reception down here at the end of Ava Road was always spotty, so we put our own repeater in over two years ago. We simply boosted its strength when we connected the town to our surplus power supply as an additional service." Fay took a breath; she had hammered the COO deliberately, trying to get a rise out of her concerning the attacks, but had not got so much as a twitch. What she had got was palpable outrage, something she would expect in an innocent person. Unless.

"You say you were ready to ship around six months ago?" she asked.

"Yes. We have been storing products for weeks, waiting on the barges I mentioned before. Very hard to get ones that can carry a thousand tons or more that can easily be converted to electric power."

Fay goggled at the number, thinking about the space required to store two thousand machines requiring twelve cubic meters of space. Even her prodigious mind had trouble fitting in that quantity of machines into the buildings she had seen outside.

"How do you store them?' she asked, her voice soft and inquisitive rather than harsh and attacking. Intellectually, she was engaged, trying to visualize the equipment required to handle such a massive volume of machines. The change in tonality was not lost on the COO, and taking the second gamble with this FBI agent, she stood up, walked around the table, and headed towards the door.

"Come with me." And she strode out of the room, walked around the wall, and, before Fay could comment, opened a small elevator with her handprint. They both got in; the bronzed door slid closed, her ears popped from the rapid descent, and they slid to a smooth stop. The door hissed open, and her ears popped again, suggesting they had descended quite a way underground. The COO looked down at Fay's feet.

"Good. Sensible heels. We have a bit of a walk ahead of us. You can continue your interrogation again if you wish." Fay was just a little off-balance with the fast-moving COO, but she had been trained well, and her innate sense of fairness gave her poise.

"How many do you produce a day?" she asked. "And where do you get your raw materials?"

"I'll answer the first, but not the second until I get you to sign an NDA."

"The FBI does not sign NDAs, and I can get a specific warrant if we need to get your answer. Your choice." The COO stopped suddenly, almost causing the agent to overshoot her. She pointed one long, manicured finger tipped with glossy red nail polish at Fay's chest.

"What we are doing here will save thousands, maybe millions of lives. Don't you think you should concentrate on that?" she asked in a seriously pissed voice. Fay smiled to herself; she was back in control. The COO was going on the defensive, so she attacked again.

"The reason we came here in the first place is that you are operating against the odds. We have established that this area, along with similar locations in Canada, Greenland, Chile, Portugal, Ireland, Denmark, Norway, Finland, Estonia, Sri Lanka, Solomon Islands, New Zealand, Japan, and Iceland, all received three to six billion euros some four to five years ago. We know those funds came from the Arabian Sovereign Wealth Fund, via the man who masterminded and financed the terrorist attacks-a man known as Al Hemish al-bin Mohammad Karesish-to some as brother Fernández-and more recently, Mohammad bin Azaria.

"From the papers submitted by you—and signed by you as COO—we know you have expended over fourteen hundred million dollars building and equipping this factory. We can't prove that your funds came from the seed funds established by Mohammad bin Azaria, but if they have, we will. You can count on it." The COO's face gave nothing away; her eyes remained focussed on Fay's, the golden ring around her irises not narrowing even a fraction.

"Our funding came from a legitimate source. I can and will give you chapter and verse on that; we have satisfied the Internal Revenue Service and passed a public audit every year we have been in operation. I know you have copies of those documents; our counsel confirmed this just yesterday. Why are you trying to link us to the terrible terrorist attacks?" she asked, with what looked like genuine concern on her beautiful face. It was hard to see a terrorist hiding behind the mask of a concerned COO, but then, Fay thought, the face of the pilot who had flown the Hog and bombed West Point had not looked like that of a terrorist either. She decided, for the moment at least, to park her curiosity and see what the COO wanted to show her.

"Okay, let's put that aside for now; what are you going to show me?" she asked, turning to look at where they were originally going before the sudden stop. The COO looked at the FBI agent, her brow furrowed, and little crinkles appeared radiating out from her eyes. This woman—almost a girl in terms of her appearance—had flustered her with her penetrating interrogation, one who had taken her by surprise. Her team had prepared for the inevitable questions, but the FBI had obtained far more intelligence than they had expected at this point.

"Come with me." And she strode away, forcing the FBI agent to follow in her wake. In less than five minutes, they reached a solid-looking wall with a door, not unlike the ones in submarines. It even had a wheel which the COO spun to open it, and as Fay stepped in over the edge, she saw hundreds of boxes stacked on top of each other, in rows and rows that faded into the dark some distance away. Science fiction-like robots stood idle, huge forks and grippers frozen at odd angles as if they had been partying together and suddenly told to stop. A massive conveyor, not unlike those used to load coal or iron ore onto ships, ran down one side of the stacked boxes, disappearing back into the gloom behind them. Fay was willing to bet her next paycheck that the conveyor led back to the buildings she had seen on the way in. The COO strode forward, pulling the agent with her.

They walked another half a kilometer, by Fay's estimate, and reached a massive door some thirty feet high and as wide. The front row of the boxes was now behind her, but a pair of the red and blue robots with their massive claws and forks stood at attention on either side of yet another submarine door, this one with a porthole in it at eye height. The COO looked through, then spun the wheel to open the door. Fay looked over her shoulder and saw what she assumed was the ocean some ten feet below her feet, currently relatively calm, with just the hint of waves mostly driven by the wind. She climbed through the door and found herself standing on a small wooden balcony with no guard rail.

"You asked me where and how we store our machines and what we use as raw materials. I won't tell you everything, but if you look at those two pipes over there," she said, pointing to a pair of massive black pipes that came out of the base of the building and bent with a purpose as they disappeared into the ocean, "you can see where we get some of our raw materials." Fay looked around her, noticed that she could see the shore and the lights of what she assumed was Blaine in the distance, across the relatively flat waters of Semiahmoo Bay, and mentally put them on the east coast side of the jut, facing east. That meant that the buildings on the surface were behind them but no doubt linked to this stacking area by the conveyor, which, now that she could see it up close, looked like it could handle anything.

"Whose idea was it to use submarine doors?" Fay asked, not really needing an answer but interested in spite of herself. The COO smiled, feeling more comfortable now that she had shared a part of their secret with the agent, albeit only a small part.

"That would have been Kathryn; she served five years in the navy before she left to join us here." Fay nodded; the idea was whimsical but actually suited the whole site. Mysterious buildings made of a material that felt slippery and sparkled in the light, high-tech elevators with no floor buttons, massive robots that looked like they partied, and thousands of boxes stacked in a warehouse completely underground or at least part of it. She'd have to check that in any photos they had of the site, but she did not remember seeing anything in the photos on file.

"I assume you will build a wharf here to land the barges?" she asked, turning to face the COO. In the gloom of the overcast day, the light from inside the storage area projected out of the submarine door like a torch beam, throwing the COO into relief, her face in shadow. Fay noticed that the outside of the warehouse had the same sparkle as the walls of the buildings and moved past the COO to rub her hands across the surface. "This is the same material that you have made the buildings out of?" she asked, feeling the slightly sweaty and fibrous surface that was warm to the touch. She got the faint but distinct smell of seaweed in her nostrils but put it down to the proximity of the water.

"The material we use for all our buildings except for our front office is produced in this plant, absorbs light, and generates power. It is a very sophisticated advanced solar panel that you can build with just like any other fibrous board. Its conversion rate is better than ninety percent, so it will be a game-changer in the renewables market. And yes, we are assembling a small jetty that will replace this one, then we will be able to load a barge in less than an hour."

"How many barges are you getting?" Fay asked out of curiosity. She really didn't need to know the answer, but something inside her was pushing her to learn as much as possible, no matter how irrelevant it might appear.

"Two for the moment; that will allow us to ship over four thousand units at a time." Fay looked back at the COO, who had turned to look at the giant pipes, half her face now lit by the spill from the warehouse. Fay was reminded of a high-class photo or painting, where one side of the subject was dark, the other side light.

"I've asked this question before, but I'll ask it again. How will you—or have you—determined where to send these power plants?" The COO turned to face the FBI agent, her hands clasped in front, seemingly relaxed. She seemed to be considering her answer, tilting her head to one side, causing her long, silky hair to fall like a waterfall over her face. She brushed it back unconsciously, then faced the agent full on.

"I'll give you part of the answer. The rest you will have to work out yourselves. We have trained over two hundred people, men and women, and placed them in small offices attached to warehouses up and down the coast as far down as the Mexican border, from which we can distribute inland. The people we have trained will manage the installation and distribution of the units, based on the local need. We have the same setup in Canada, although on a much smaller scale. We have identified small towns and cities where these units will be perfect until we can start on a permanent solution. A solution, I might say, that will also be a game-changer in renewables," she said with some pride. Fay thought through what she had just heard, letting it settle in the back of her mind. There was an obvious question here, and she wondered if she should ask it. The COO saw the question in her eyes and smiled.

"You want to ask me what happens if the government steps in and takes us over?" she asked, almost laughing. Fay didn't see anything funny about a government takeover of a privately financed and owned business, but she was glad that the COO didn't see it as a threat. "I don't mind if you tell everyone you know— but our power packs are protected; if you break one open, try to pull it apart, or damage it in any way, it will self-destruct. It will not harm anyone in the process, but the puddle of materials left will defy any laboratory analysis beyond the common elements that can be found everywhere— carbon, silica, oxides, various gasses which will have boiled off, and the wooden framework, which has no nails, having been constructed the old-fashioned way, what's called Mortise and Tenon, and Sliding Dovetails. They will get nothing in return for having destroyed an environmentally responsible power source."

"You have carpenters on site?" Fay asked in astonishment. The idea of a woodworker making frames alongside the robots carting the boxes seemed a little far-fetched. The COO broke out into laughter, her eyes shining with tears that ran down her face.

"Fay, the only work people do in our plant is oversee the robotic tasks. We use additive manufacturing and 3D printing, and the only 'hands' that ever touch a product are those of the quality inspection staff, and then only when deemed necessary by one of our technicians." Fay smiled. This was a much better image in her mind rather than the picture of a bent old man chipping away at a plank with a hammer and chisel. The COO paused, suddenly realizing that she was giving away precious detail on their production methods. She decided to move on, hoping the detail would be overlooked in the agent's report.

"If you've seen enough out here, let's go back to the office, and I'll take you through one of our buildings, and you can see for yourself some of what we do." Fay nodded and followed the COO back in through the hatch, which the COO locked with the brass wheel, then led the agent back to the elevator. As they walked back, Fay began to see in her mind's eye the scale of what they were doing here, and it just didn't stack up. They had at least eight thousand boxes in the warehouse, so four loads for the barges and no boxes had arrived during their tour. The COO had claimed that they had been in production for six months, which meant around seventy units every day, based on a five-day working week. That meant a finished product weight of some twenty-eight tons. The raw material requirements would be substantially more than that, so there was more to this site than met the eye.

Much more.

But Fay was starting to think that the fine details around this production site might not be worth the resources that may be needed to thoroughly investigate it. The FBI could seize a box to inspect the contents, but they couldn't pull it apart or deconstruct it because it would self-destruct. And what would it prove in any case? Factory, product, shipping, storage and distribution are all financed by seemingly legitimate sources. A portable power supply that might, as the COO had pointed out, save thousands, if not millions, of lives.

She had been briefed, as had every other agent, that the terrorists were using sophisticated technology weapons in the form of nano-bots and computer software. The nanobots had taken out the oil, gas, and coal sites, the software, the world wide web, and every computer, router, phone, and the digital and electronic device connected at the time of the attack. It was obvious that this plant was utilizing high technology of some sort; the whole area was pristine, no refuse, no slag heaps, no effluent belching out of stained smokestacks, in fact, no evidence of any activity at all above ground.

They entered the bronze lift, and she had a fleeting thought that if there had been three of them, they would have been in sin! Her ears popped again as the door opened, and she followed the COO back to the theatre that had been set up for them to interview the staff. The six agents meet them at the doorway, all holding their wet weather gear.

"You've finished the interviews?" Fay asked RuPaul, mildly surprised. "Yes. We covered off for you. No interview lasted more than five or six minutes; we have all the data here for you." He handed over a small plastic pack in which sat six small recording tapes.

"Thank you. The COO is going to take us to see inside one of the buildings. Are you all ready?" she asked, looking directly at RuPaul. He turned to look at every agent as a small group of staff filed past them and out into the daylight. He nodded.

"Lead on," Fay said, taking her wet weather gear from one of the agents. She put her FBI jacket on, chose to carry the rest, and followed the COO out into the day, which was shaping up to be very cold, even wintery, with the light snow falling in waves, pushed around by the light wind. It was a beautiful sight, and as she took it all in, she wondered exactly what was going on here besides the manufacturing of power supplies!

Chapter 15

The decisions I had to make were essentially easy, but standing in front of my assembled teams was made all the more difficult by the resistance I expected.

It was early morning, the helicopter gunship had already departed, and I was about to send the rest of the teams back to their point of origin, except for a very few.

"Gentle people, for the next step, we have to split up. I want the guard to return to the train and the special forces team as well, but the FBI contingent will stay with me, Pete, and Anna. Bob, when you get to the station, you will find a new guard team provided by General Bridges, take them under your wing and head back to Washington. Make your departure as visible as you can, noisy even, don't be afraid of being seen. Take all the military hardware we have with you; we will keep pistols, tactical knives, and the big box the FBI have stowed their gear in. As I said at the very start, this is a police action, and we now have to go off and be policemen, and as we are going into a very sensitive area, the smaller our force, the better.

"You have all done an incredible job, yesterday, you demonstrated why you are the very best of the best, and I personally thank you for your efforts in keeping my shaggy arse in one piece. Dismissed." Bob gave me a look that said, "no way José," but Pete took him by one arm and walked him away. He was back in a minute, during which time most of the teams had loaded their gear into the ATVs.

"Bob gets it but is not happy; he seems to have a proprietary interest in you, boss. What happens if we get ambushed on our way to Helena?"

"We won't. The gunship is flying high cover for us and will track us all the way to the main road. I've arranged for continuous cover; the general seems very interested in keeping us alive, particularly after yesterday, so I'm not worried about that." He looked at me with his sly grin face, the one I was sure he used in the famous poker games he always boasted about, and I let my shoulders slump, feeling the strain of the last few days.

"Helena is a very small town, less than thirty-five thousand people, although rumor has it, there are thousands more camping to the west, having left the big cities for dead. But they only have the one city hall and records office, so we will be hard-pressed to get what we need and go unnoticed."

"You worried about being attacked by a terrorist cell, specifically the one that used the silo?" I turned to look at him full in the face. It was important for him to hear my truth, and I watched his eyes as I spoke.

"No, I'm worried our presence will send them to the ground." He nodded; he had worked that out for himself.

"So, what's your plan?" He started off as the team's ATVs roared to life and headed off into the early morning mist, fighting each other for pole position.

Boys will be boys, and then I saw the flying blond hair of the leading driver and mentally cheered her on, and I smiled a genuine smile for the first time in days. "Go, girl, go!" I said softly, and Pete smiled in concert with me. I called Anna over with her two FBI specialists. They were covered with the red dust that had conquered this part of Montana probably thousands of years ago, when the faulting and folding had been in full swing, creating the low mountains and multitude of ridgelines that littered the landscape.

"Okay, here's what we are going to do. I will arrange for our accommodation, one area, separate rooms, so we can control the ground tactically if we need to. You," I said, pointing to the FBI agents, "have the ability to track satellite transmissions. And that's exactly what we are going to do. While Anna and one of you formally go into the town center and ask many questions about the silo and the rebuild, the other will man the tracking device twenty-four-seven. We have the latitude and longitude of two burst transmissions some six or seven days ago. I have the data for you, so don't panic about the detail. Yet. But the location has an error circle probable of one mile. I want that down to one yard.

"In this town, a one-mile radius encompasses a lot of houses. My plan is to stir up interest in what the FBI is doing and hide Pete and myself from view so we can explore the neighborhood. We'll do this under the guise of trying to buy a property. Have no idea what that looks like under the current conditions, but we will see what we see. Anna, I want you to play uber bitch FBI very senior pain-in-the-arse special agent, create the impression you are there against your better judgment, it's probably all a great waste of time, and you don't like working with males."

With a flick of her hand through her hair and holding one arm cocked behind her head, the other perched on her hip, she said, "Who said I do?"

That broke the tension that had been building up since we had first gotten out of our sleeping bags, and I was very thankful for it. "Good one, Anna, but the bad news is you will never make it on the catwalk!" We all laughed again, then the two FBI agents got a serious look on their faces as the import of their roles sunk in.

"How long do we play at being FBI agents?" one of the agents asked; I think his name was Roy.

"One or two days until you believe you are getting nowhere with city hall, then I want you to move on the banks. I want your forensic expertise to drill down on any movement of funds bigger than five grand in the last five years from anywhere, to anywhere. I want you to map it. You are looking for seed funding in big chunks, starting at six billion dollars, and work down. We have already tracked the expenditure used to set up the silo and surrounds. What I'm looking for is what doesn't make sense." Anna nodded her head; she had all that information transferred onto her little laptop and what wouldn't fit in the small memory she carried on USB sticks.

"Our earlier research showed a businessman pledged millions of dollars to build the infrastructure for some thousands of houses; this was three or four years ago. As far as we know today, the area was developed to the point of roads, recyclable sewerage, waste management, water supply, a power grid of solar panels, and a wind farm. But not a single house was built for some reason.

"The intelligence I got last night once we identified Helena as a place of interest is that there are now several thousand iterant refugees from the cities camped there, using those facilities and that sometime in the last month or two, the building has commenced along the main road running through the development. The plans lodged with the town building commission are for fifty thousand houses, three very large accommodation blocks for a thousand students each, massive education facilities, and six schools, plus hospitals and shopping centers. That's stage one. Stage two is equally as big." Anna paused as if to let everyone absorb the information. "I might point out that the official population of Helena, according to the last census, is thirty-three thousand, five hundred and sixty people."

Jessica reflected on the conversations with the Americans and the Israelis that had developed as a result of the monks identifying the secretary of state as a possible collaborator with Mohammad bin Azaria some weeks ago, and she remembered the detail of the "grand plan" that had been developed over an eighteen-month period. If she really made an effort, she could make a link between that grand plan and what they now knew about Helena, but it was a thin, tenuous, and thready one that might or might not survive some hard pulling.

And a physical inspection.

"Well, Pete and I will wander that area, a young couple looking for their future home, and in a sense, the migration will give us cover, as it's unlikely there has been a census or a serious headcount yet. Leave that to us. Any questions?" And without further ado, we mounted up our ATV with Pete at the wheel and headed off to find the main highway that would eventually lead us to Helena and, hopefully, the next part of this gigantic puzzle.

Chapter 16

B uilding Three was enormous from the outside and gigantic on the inside and literally took Fay's breath away. The huge space which, she knew to be thirty meters long, was twice that at the very least inside in terms of height and worked this miracle by being at least fifty meters deep under the surface. The conveyor she had seen in the warehouse ran around two sides, and a sister system ran up the walls, moving massive sheets of the same material that the buildings were made of up from the floor and out of the building to somewhere else. Robots were everywhere, and deep down towards the floor, massive dull machines sat in cages, doing who-knew-what but obviously doing it extremely well, and Arnon, the OCC's assistant, moved from walkway to walkway talking into a little device of some sort, and every now and then a red flash of a laser would spurt out and hit one of the cages.

The walkway Fay and the other FBI agents were standing on was, in fact, a long, sinuous cage in that the lattice frame of the floor ran up and across their heads, completely enclosing them. Fay gave the walkway a look that transmitted her lack of comfort, and the COO rubbed her hand down Fay's arm.

"You'll get used to it. We can't afford to lose anyone, so we have the very best safety features for our workforce." They all moved slowly down the walkway, the ground far below lit by eerie blue and green lights, creating dark shadows when the robots stalked across between cages. It was like something out of a sci-fi movie, made all the more dramatic by the clicks and metallic snaps that reverberated and echoed around the massive space as they bounced off the walls.

"No people down there?" Fay observed, more than a little awed by the scale of everything.

"No. The only time we let people down there is during a lull in production, on a strict service and maintenance schedule."

"I still don't see any raw materials sitting around?" Fay asked, thinking she could probably eat her next meal off the floor, which seemed to shine with a life of its own. She would love to have taken a photo of it with her smartphone, but the agents had been stripped of all their metallic hardware before being granted entry to the building. It had been explained that a number of the manufacturing machines were charged, and coming into contact with anything metallic would cause an explosion that would destroy the building. So guns, shields, phones, pocket knives, pens, and, in RuPaul's case, a lightweight leg brace made of Kevlar but with aluminum joints were all left in a big basket outside the entrance.

"Can you explain the process for us, please?" Fay asked, holding the rail and peering over the side, just in time to catch a robot fleeing across the floor with its claws full of...what? She had no idea. But a smaller robot followed the bigger one as if chasing it, carrying dark grey objects that had bright red tips. She shook her head; whatever they were building, they were doing it at a rate that looked very impressive, even to her untrained eye. The COO moved to a dark panel, tapped it, used her palm to open it, then peered into an eye scanner which turned from red to green in a split second.

Dual biometric security, so this was where some of the secrets were kept, Fay thought to herself as the COO's hand scrolled across the huge screen, flicking from diagram to diagram. The intensity of her focus was not lost on the young agent; this was someone who took her job very seriously.

"Here," she said, turning to the agents, who had been forced to spread out into single file by the narrow walkway. "This is a simple flow diagram of what we do. You will see generic descriptors for each process, but you should get some idea. Take as much time as you need." And she stepped away so the agents could scrutinize the screen at their own pace. She was aware of Fay's eidetic memory, so she knew that this diagram would be reproduced faithfully back in Seattle, but it wouldn't be a problem because nothing important was correctly labeled. The COO watched them like a hawk, trusting perhaps the three agents she had first met but suspicious of the rest. She liked Fay and, in fact, did trust her, having shared a similar background. But she wouldn't let emotions cloud her judgment. Her mission was just too important.

What happened next as a result of this visit to the plant by the FBI would be crucial to all their futures. In a sense, Point Roberts was a test case for the entire world's recovery, although only the COO and her cohort knew this.

Hope. The essential ingredient in any form of recovery.

"Can we see another building, please?" Fay asked as the last of the agents filed past the screen. The COO moved back to the screen, flicked the surface, then held her hand to the biometric scanner again, and the screen flicked off, and a thin cover slid out from the sidewall and covered it so completely that unless you knew it was there, you would never suspect it.

"We can get to building six from here. Follow me." And she led the agents along the walkway, across a gantry that led into a pitch-black entryway, which suddenly glowed with the same blue light that floated up from the floor, and then they were in another walkway, this one turning sharply to the left. Again, the massive conveyor ran along one wall, fed into the plant at one point, then rippled out again to run around what Fay guessed was the rear of the building. The sci-fi theme was maintained, but this time by small robots less than two meters tall, who tendered long troughs, moving what looked like big spoons around and around like mix masters. A faint, luminous glow floated above each of the troughs, swirling like smoke with each movement of the robot's stirrer. There was nothing else on the floor that Fay could see other than the troughs and the robots and the conveyor carrying large grey boxes out through the back wall.

"This is one of our additive raw materials plants. As you can see, no people; this one runs twenty-four-seven, is totally robotically operated, and is only shut down for three days a year. This is where our intellectual property rights stem from, rights that are protected worldwide by patents and exclusions recognized by every country in the world." The COO's words were delivered in a blunt tone, almost aggressive, but Fay sensed something deeper under them, and as she turned to ask a question, the COO suddenly waved her hand as if she were swatting at something, and finished the distracting movement by brushing her hair back from her face. "I apologize. I didn't mean to sound so forceful. But this process evolved at the cost of thousands of lives, and I see the faces in my mind's eye every time I come in here. This way, please." And she strode out before any of the agents could comment and lead them back outside to the road that ran through the site.

She turned to Fay. "Are we done?" she asked small tears in her eyes that hadn't yet fallen down her face. Fay looked at her, confused by the woman's statement about the loss of lives, but, sensing that they had got all they would get on this visit, looked at RuPaul for his support, got a sharp nod, then nodded her own head in agreement.

"Thank you, yes. We may need to come back, but I will advise you if it is necessary. Thank you for your help." And it was her turn to lead the agents, this time back to the main entrance where their bikes were waiting.

"Well, that went well," RuPaul commented in a sotto voice. Fay took a long look at him, sensed he was anything but satisfied, and made a mental note to take control of the conversation as soon as they were outside the premises.

She, too, had questions, but her first duty would be to synthesize what the agents had learned from the staff interviews.

The agents were strangely quiet all the way back to the boat harbor, each lost in their own thoughts. For her part, Fay wondered exactly what child refugees from fifteen to twenty years ago had to do with what she had seen and heard at the plant.

Goose Egg

The Boss and Tom were in deep discussion, standing at the bottom of the massive hole the Egyptian digger had created in its attempt to break into the hidden control center used during the terrorist attacks. It was thought that the launch of the L100 with its two massive bombs that were successfully dropped on the Vatican, essentially wiping out three thousand years of Roman history, and, by contrast, the much smaller UAV drone which had fired its Hellfire missiles into the Dome of the Rock and the Western Wailing Wall, setting the Middle Eastern tension flying off the chart, were directed from here.

It was also speculated that the major attacks on the Arabian oil head and the Grand Mosque, the Russian/Chinese gas line, and attendant attacks on fracking sites and oil well heads across the desert had also been coordinated from the hidden control room under the mountain.

Which they couldn't find due to the extensive damage created by virtually the whole base of the mountain being blown up when the terrorists decamped. The Israeli commando contingent was anything but happy, having nothing to do other than stand around looking disinterested, made all the more insulting by the intense heat of the desert. The Boss was pragmatic; Tom was a veteran of the mantra "hurry up and wait," so he and his fellow operatives were at least as calm as the heat would allow, sitting off to one side under their floppy hats, playing poker. Tom gave the "wind it up" signal, and his crew moved back to where the massive Chinese helicopter stood, its cracked and chipped rotors looking like they were exhausted, as they drooped to within feet of the desert floor.

"It's a bust. Get everyone on board, and I'll join you," the Boss said, walking over to where the Egyptian stood, hands on hips, sweat stains under his armpits and the crutch of his trousers, peering into the messy hole. He straightened when the Boss approached.

"Sir, Colonel, I am very sorry we cannot uncover the base you believe to be here." He looked a little scared as if the Boss was going to chew him out for the failure. He just smiled and patted the poor Egyptian on the shoulder, knowing he was probably a member of their Secret Service or some other clandestine arm of their military and likely to get his butt kicked for their lack of success.

"You did your best. My report to your superiors will emphasize that. Thank you, and may Allah be with you." He turned on his heel, noticed the last of the Israelis had loaded, and gave the windup signal to their pilot, of unknown and uncertain origin but probably in the employ of the Libyan military.

Trust was a hard-won virtue in the Middle East, and the standard motto in practically every country was "trust you as far as I can see you." And everybody spied on everybody else all the time!

Chapter 17

Malcolm Tannery was once described as the "greatest white hat" in the cyber hacking world when, at the tender age of twelve, he had called the FBI and informed them that a nation-state—disclosed later in secret papers seen only by the FBI, NSA, and CIA directorate of the day—had launched a denial-of-service attack on the American government and that he, Malcolm, and two of his friends had built a cyber shield that was holding the DOS attack at bay, but would probably break down in an hour or two, so could they please help him?

It took the FBI nearly an hour to confirm what was going on and get a team from the FBI and NSA to his home, where they found Malcolm and his friends kicked back, drinking fizzy drinks, and playing some esoteric online game.

Malcolm's room had been turned into geek central, with computers, screens, hand controllers, and a myriad of random hardware in bits and pieces, literally covering every surface, from floor to roof. It took the NSA technicians forty-four minutes to understand what Malcolm and his friends had done, and then they applied their own brand of magic to build a quick firewall they hoped would give them time to get back to their headquarters and make the temporary fix permanent.

They did, and just three years later, Malcolm and his two friends went to MIT on a full scholarship, from where Malcolm rolled on to Sandford for his post-doc work, his two friends leaving to start up a digital enterprise from which they both made billions. As the NSA had Malcolm in their sights from the day of his timely phone call to the FBI, it was relatively easy to finesse him away from academia and into the agency, where he now ran one of the top digital laboratories in the world. And while he had enjoyed the work he had done at both MIT and Sandford, the agency gave him challenges of such monumental proportions his incredible mind was constantly challenged to the point of bliss. Did he regret that the location he worked in was under a mountain? And that his precious surf was way across the country?

Every day.

But he also appreciated that the director let him use a company jet on his day off so he could fly to wherever the surf was at its best. Although that might be a problem in the future, he thought to himself, given the incredible shortage of fuel and oil. His partner in crime had the day off, no doubt riding one of her beautiful horses somewhere, so he settled himself into his specially built orthopedic chair, sat the minicomputer in front of his keyboards, and, using a physical link, transferred the picture from the small unit to his big screens.

In a matter of minutes, the faces of Arie Rosenberg and his superior IT genius Colonel Shami Borowitz swam into view on one screen, then the images of Luigi, Amira, and Indigo in faraway Venice swam into another screen, then a data box opened up on a third. He didn't waste any time.

"Colonel Rosenberg, thank you for the link-up; if you could give us geeks some space, it would be appreciated." Arie smiled that gentle smile he used whenever he wanted to disarm someone and nodded. His face disappeared from the screen, leaving Shami's face to fill the box.

"Before I start, Captain Riley sends her regards and has specifically ordered me to limit this information to this group, and this group only. You may brief your immediate superiors, but I suggest you do so judiciously, as the good captain made it clear that this information is the most sensitive we have dealt with so far. Clear?" Four heads nodded as one, so Malcolm continued.

"Thanks to your team, we have unpicked the regions where the 'black holes' were used to obscure all activity for the past—in most cases—two years. Thanks to the FBI working with the captain in Montana, and data received from Indigo's team, we have the location of two burst transmissions mapped in a circle error probable of one mile.

"The good captain intends to run this location down and institute a physical search. She has asked me if I can take the data we now have and possibly locate in our files—or yours—similar burst transmissions and intercept them, with a view to decrypting them and learning more about the terrorists. You," he said, pointing to Indigo's screen, "seem to have the ability to review old data and pull signals out of it. We can't do that here because we simply don't have the data in the first place. If we had it, it has been professionally wiped; if we never got it, then the terrorists figured out how to block what they were doing every bit as effectively as their use of the 'black holes.' I'm looking to you for help." Indigo glanced to his side, seeking his brother's attention without letting Malcolm know what he was doing. His brother shook his head, held up five fingers, then folded his arms.

"Malcolm, give us ten minutes, please, so we can discuss this internally, then get back to you," Indigo said, a big smile on his face to dispel any negative thoughts the American may have about being put on hold. On Malcolm's big screens, the two boxes holding the images from Israeli and Venice flicked out, and while Malcolm wasn't necessarily pissed at being put on hold, he did have mild fission of annoyance, not used to being told to wait by anyone in his limited orbit. In Venice, Indigo, Anna, and Luigi were in deep conversation with Stefarino, the head monk, and the sole reason Interpol had got as far as they had broken into the technological swamp that was the terrorists' data mine.

Indigo spoke forcefully, his normal placid nature suddenly gone to be replaced with that of a current senior member of the Italian military. "We must protect Stefarino and his sources at all costs, there can be no debate about this, and we must also protect Amira's data now that we have recovered it. Arie is fully aware of everything we have done and how we have done it, but no one outside our small circle can be brought in. On that, I am firm." In Israel, Shami nodded, having been reconnected to the Venice team the second Malcolm had been disconnected.

"I agree. This is something Arie and I have discussed at length. Working backward, Amira's data must be protected at all costs, and Interpol must take credit for all the breakthroughs we have made and the method by which we now communicate. I trust Malcolm. He is one of us, of that there is no doubt, but if by chance the messages Mohammad bin Azaria says he had posted all around the world surface, the president will look like a liar, and who knows what the Americans will do or who they will sacrifice in order to regain their supremacy." The three faces on his screen looked extremely distressed, Indigo suddenly looking up into the eye of the camera and grimacing.

"This is not how Interpol works—we do not hide information or withhold information from our sponsor states. But at this moment, Shami, I totally agree with you. How can we support Malcolm and preserve what must be protected at all costs?"

"I have an idea on that," Amira said, her voice soft but pointed. "Some time ago, either the captain or the colonel suggested that we send all my data back to Israel for safekeeping. I suggest we do that as a priority. But I also suggest I stay here in Venice to keep working on uncovering the data lost in the black holes." Indigo thought for a minute, nodded, looked up, and focused on Amira.

"That is an excellent idea, but the bigger issue is how do we protect my brother and still help Malcolm identify the burst transmissions?"

"Indigo, as far as the Americans know, Interpol supplied the microcomputers, and your IT geeks, with a little help from us, made inroads into the terrorist codes. Amira has been identified only as an Israeli digital specialist on loan to Interpol. Only the directors of the FBI, NSA, and CIA know Amira's backstory. We can keep it that way for as long as we need to." Stefarino's weathered face slipped into the frame, tilted at an angle.

"Sholom, Shami, thank you for thinking of us; it is a pleasure to work with such fine people. But I have a suggestion, if I may?"

"Sholom, Stefarino, lovely to see you again. Yes, please. Any help you can give us would be truly appreciated. Should I get back Arie?" Stefarino nodded, sensing that, once again, the monks and their incredible technology would sail to the rescue.

"Well, we know what you are looking for. Remember, we found the burst transmission in the first place. So I suggest we find some more, say, going back six months for the time being, and create a master file that we can give Indigo, which he can then share with you.

And then you can both share it with Malcolm." Arie's face popped into the screen and, like Stefarino's, was angled.

"Stefarino, that is a brilliant idea. Can I recruit you full-time for Israeli intelligence?" Everyone on the call, including the head monk, laughed, splitting the tension right down the middle of the screens. "Indigo, I appreciate that Interpol is walking a fine line here, but in my humble opinion, there is nothing to gain but trouble down the road with our American friends if the monks' involvement is made known. On that, I am firm."

"Agreed, we will work on the data at this end, then get it to both you and Malcolm as soon as we can. How long, brother?" he asked, addressing his brother, the head monk, directly. Stefarino stepped away from the camera line, folded his hand inside his cloaked arms, and looked for the moment like a serene religious icon of indeterminate age.

"A day, no more, and we will have your data."

In faraway America, Malcolm got a text message on the bottom of his screen that steadied for thirty seconds, then disappeared.

"Data to you for last six months in twenty-four hours. Let Captain Riley know."

He sat perfectly still for a moment, thought for another minute, then called up his director on the old-style handset. "Sir, I need the company jet. I have an urgent business on the West Coast." He slipped his headphones off, hit the big red button in the middle of his keyboards to shut and lock everything down, picked up his go bag that held his surfing gear, and headed out to the helipad.

He may or may not drop in on the fabulous Captain Riley on his way to the waves, depending on how he felt at the time!

Chapter 18

The town of Helena was laid out like so many towns in the midwest of Montana—the main highway cutting it in half. In this case, Highway 15 raced in from the north, to disappear just as fast to the southeast, and a major rail line knifed from east to west, eventually linking the town to both coasts. The airport fell on one side of the highway, the majority of the houses on the other, and US 287 followed the rail line out of town to the east for ways, then faithfully tracked down through Winston, Townsend, and Toston to the south, finally cutting away and heading off on its own once it crossed US 90 just before Three Forks.

When you looked at the vastness of the surrounding land, the mountains to the southwest, the plains to the east, and thought about the distances involved between population centers, you got a real appreciation for the stamina and determination of the folks who had basically traipsed their way through the area in wagons and on horseback two hundred years previously.

And, Jessica thought to herself, in the "now," you got an appreciation for the efficient manner in which developers packed houses together to save money on services and infrastructure. Her circle error probable of one mile had to contain over six hundred dwellings in the major population area unless you hit the very edge of the circle where the density went down to just thirty-six dwellings, ones that sprawled on quarter-acre blocks. Year-round, there was obviously not a lot of rainfall because the acreage blocks were green in the middle where the houses and sheds sat but fairly barren around the edges, looking like little islands of green in a flat sea of dirty brown.

Jessica and Pete were pouring over old satellite maps of the area, politely provided by the real estate agent they had dropped into, seeking help in choosing an area where they could buy a house. In the town proper, Anna and one of her FBI agents were creating havoc with an official investigation into the silo rebuild, which the town council had approved some four years ago. Jessica thought it was a good diversion, as they already had all the data the town planners had considered, and she hoped it would keep any of the women terrorists, if they were still around, off their scent. The third agent was locked in his room back at the hotel, scanning the device that would detect any further burst transmissions. He was also keeping in contact via the small handheld walkie-talkies they were equipped with.

Pete had insisted that both he and Jessica carried their weapons and wore lightweight body armor under their ski gear. It was a chillingly dry cold, not snowing that happened mostly up in the mountains, but with a bit of wind chill, the current temperature was a measly negative four degrees Fahrenheit, certainly cold enough for them to be covered up from head to toe.

Their choices were limited to very few properties, most of those available having been snapped up as temporary accommodation by the masses that had migrated from both the south and north of the country, fleeing the trouble the terrorists had precipitated. The civil unrest was starting to diminish as the police and the army gradually got control back from the militias, and a number of local radio stations had taken to the air with old-style ham radios powered by valves, which the cyberattack had not affected, to spread the good news.

Of course, the receiving end was problematic in that most radios of the modern era had been killed motherless stone dead, something the youth of Helena complained about day in and day out. However, one of the science teachers at the university had dug out old-fashioned schematics for making crystal sets, and the latest fad was to be seen walking around town with an ugly hearing aid-style earpiece with a colorful wire leading to a pocket, where you might or might not have one playing whatever the radio station could manage from their record collections. The sets themselves were rough, single frequency, and would never replace the Pods, smartphones, or other technologically sophisticated sound equipment, but they worked, and that was all that mattered to the young people of Helena, who personally thought the end of their world had arrived in the form of complete digital silence.

For us, right now, we were down to three properties in eastern Helena, our prime target area, or a new place to the west alongside the main road where "new folk," as they were being delicately called by the locals, had set up their camps and tents. While I wanted to walk that area to see for myself exactly what had been built and then left idle for years, my need to be close to a possible terrorist nest was stronger, so I pointed to a property circled in red by the agent on the sat pic and nudged Pete.

"This one, here on Prairie Nest Drive, can we look at that, please?" he asked, in his best American accent, which today had a distinct Midwestern flair. The agent, all of twelve or maybe thirteen at a stretch, her long golden hair flowing over an oval, innocent face like a cascading waterfall, literally glowed with happiness. I had hated her on sight.

"Oh, well, that place would be just perfect for y'all, right on the road there, twin buildings, one double story with all the bedrooms and a lovely lounging room, three fireplaces, central heating, of course, but y'all can't beat a real fire now, can you?" she prattled, hurting my cynical ears with her melodious twangy pitch. "The kitchen has all those lovely modern appliances. Bless my soul if a good chief could cook up a storm, by golly, if they were so inclined. And the studio and theatre area is just lovely, with great views of the neighborhood. When do you want to see it?" she exclaimed, and I promised you I could actually see the exclamation mark slip out of her pretty lips, dyed as they were with a rich, glossy red lipstick. My real problem with her was that her tight-fitting blue dress, cut to perfection to suit her curvy body, and her rich dark blue shoes, heels to the roof, which probably cost more than I earned in a month, made me feel shabby. In the last thirty hours, I had survived a firefight with a marauding militia, a long, long drive across the dusty dry plains in an open ATV that unerringly hit every pothole without fail, a quick shower in marginally hot water, and then into my unattractive military-style middling snow clothes, which wouldn't impress anyone given they were one up from a supermart rack, with my hair yet to fully dry, no doubt showing some interesting clumps from wearing my hood to the office. Hat hair was a girl's great enemy for a reason.

I held my tongue; I was not here for a fashion contest I had already lost sixteen years ago when I signed up for the navy, and as Pete would say, "Suck it up, Shirley, and get on with it!" So I did, putting my jacket back on and pulling my hood back up to regain a small measure of my dignity. Naturally, the blond was driving the latest big-arsed electric Mercedes, all shiny and sparkling, with seven seats, no waiting, genuine leather, sunroof, and the bit I really liked, seat warmers and dual heaters, which I immediately turned up to their highest setting.

I sat on the right-hand side, Pete on the left, both behind the driver, and I could feel the uncomfortable waves rolling off his snow gear. We were both in the back of an unarmoured civilian vehicle, driven by a female real estate agent who didn't look old enough to hold a license, heading towards a location where we believed some of the most proficient and deadly terrorists on the planet might live, and all we had between us was a couple of handguns, a knife or two, hat hair, and our wits. Not the way we usually went into battle.

"Where did y'all say you were from?" she asked, breaking into my morose thoughts. We were passing some of the denser areas, and the houses had a kind of untidy uniformity, as if little changes had been made to each one to give it its own personality, the result being that while no two houses looked exactly the same, and the whole block looked untidy. I shook my head, knowing I could not exist in such a place without going crazy. Having spent a very large slice of the last twenty years living in military-style barracks, which afforded you a room and shower at best, and communal facilities at worst, the predictability and inherent neatness of my accommodation meant that I could basically ignore them and concentrate on my immediate objective.

And working with Interpol meant that we were either billeted in a hotel or motel or slept on the floor of a temporary operational headquarters, so my experience with actual houses was extremely limited.

Thank God.

"Well, now, we just left the West Coast a few days ago," Pete said in his affected drawl, reaching over to take my hand with a leering smile on his face. I would kick him for it later. I smiled in return, maintaining the charade, and noticed the houses had suddenly become sparse, with dead or dying grass surrounding a plateau of green where buildings were situated. Some looked rustic, some looked like they had been built in the sixties, and very few looked quite modern, the low sun reflecting off large windows and the solar panels on their roofs. We had noticed that every house or building we had seen had panels on their roofs, which tied into our research that showed Helena was one of the most sustainably powered towns in the Midwest. My pocket started to buzz, and I reached in and, pulled out my minicomputer, looked over at Pete, who tapped the estate agent on the shoulder.

"Can you stop here for a minute, please?" he asked, in a tone that suggested an order and not a polite request. Good to see Pete was not being seduced by the curvy agent or the luxurious ride. She pulled over and looked back quizzically.

Before she could ask the obvious question, I climbed out onto the verge and turned my back on the vehicle. Pete joined me, shoulder to shoulder, preventing the driver from seeing any image on the small screen.

"Riley," I answered and saw the Boss's tired and craggy face swim into focus.

I could just make out Tom in the background.

"Hi, Jessica. We need to talk. Can you give me ten minutes, please?" he asked, his voice sounding tired but still full of command. I looked back over my shoulder at the driver, signaled "ten" with one hand, then moved Pete away to the rear of the vehicle, where we leaned back on the smooth curve of the huge door. Mindful of the little reversing camera positioned over my head, I looked up at it, giving Pete a silent instruction. He nodded, slipped a Band-Aid out of his pocket, and in less than a second or two, had the camera effectively blinded.

"Go."

"We have nothing in Libya or Egypt. Clean slate. You said you had nothing in Montana. You're showing now as in Helena. How is that going?"

"Pete and I are on the way out to inspect a property we might buy. Anna and her team are harassing the local authorities. Apart from freezing our butts off, we're fine." The Boss smiled at my comment; I could see the perspiration stains all over his shirt. He smiled, just a hint of mirth, but it reassured me he had not lost his sense of humor in the dry heat of the desert.

"Arie tells me you have Tannery running locations for you based on the 'black hole' work the geeks completed last week. And that Stefarino has pinpointed some burst transmissions for you."

"Yes, that's why we're buying a house. I've also got another idea I'll run past you later. Can you find out who we might have in our Chicago office? I may need one or two of them on the ground."

"We only have the one Interpol agent in Chicago; she sits in the same office as the FBI. Do you want her contact details?" I thought about it for a minute, then shook my head.

"No, maybe I'll let Anna organize it for us. Do you know if she is Section Five approved?"

"No, she isn't. But she has done time at Quantico as part of a shared services development program and has SWAT training courtesy of Chicago PD. Will that be enough?" I thought for a minute again; having qualified both at Quantico and SWAT would give her the weapons confidence we needed. I would have to see her face-to-face to judge if she had the mental horsepower to do what I was starting to see as a parallel investigation and one that could take a lot of time to reach fruition.

I changed my mind about Anna making contact. "Attach her to me, TDY, don't brief her and get her to Helena. Soft clothes, no badge, well and truly under the counter. And she might be here for a while. Any other updates?" I asked, hoping against hope the Boss had something I didn't because I was getting very frustrated being so far behind the terrorists.

"Yes, just one small thing. I'll copy you the statement released by Mohammad bin Azaria; it has gone out to every country and is cued up for sending. We don't know when it will be released, but I'm betting soon, and it won't give the Americans a heart attack, at least not yet." That meant that he had not referenced his highly trained female terrorists in the release.

The pathology that I had observed back in Israel during his interrogation suggested that the terrorist mastermind and banker desperately wanted to protect them from any blowback from the atrocious attacks. In fact, he had made the point, quite passionately, I thought at the time, that the women were not in any way involved with the planning of the attacks, something I found a little hard to believe. The timeline was too long, from way back in 1999/2000 to now, some twenty-five years later.

The development of the high-tech weapons was very late in the plan, and I firmly believed that one or more of the refugee women had taken the opportunity presented by the old-style military hardware that had been stolen, purchased, and hidden away in Egypt and had then blended it with the new technology weapons seamlessly. Maybe Mohammad bin Azaria had linked the timing of the attacks to the conclave at the Vatican, then the attack on the Wailing Wall, and then the Grand Mosque, which made total sense seeing who and what he was. Even the attack on the major wellhead in Arabia with nuclear materials fit his profile.

But the wanton destruction of all the rest of the oil and gas pipelines, and later the fracking sites and coal mines, was clinical and largely bloodless. And exquisitely well planned. Yes, the attacks had been carried out by Shetani's mercenaries, but a younger, more strategic mind had laid out the attack plan, of that I was sure.

I read the release as it scrolled across my screen, being translated from Arabic to English which created a strobing, jerky effect, and I had to blink several times to stop my eyes from blurring. In essence, it didn't say a whole lot more than Mohammad bin Azaria had told us in interrogation. The emphasis was clearly on the plight of the refugee children in the camps, and now the whole world would suffer the very same conditions the children suffered for all of their very short lives. It was a simple, strong message, but I had my doubts it would resonate with most people, especially people who were fighting for food, water, power and trying to keep their families both alive and together on a daily basis.

I snapped the lid closed, tapped Pete on the arm, then climbed back into the gigantic Mercedes. "Sorry about that," I said to the real estate agent. "Home office with an important message. Can we see the property now, please?" She engaged the gear or took her foot off the brake. I was never sure these days with electric vehicles, and, with the satisfying sound of gravel crunching under our tires, we sped off.

Chapter 19

Special Agents Vernon, RuPaul, and Fay Remer, sat in the FBI director's office in Seattle, looking like three older schoolchildren called into the headmaster's office for some infraction. The director, a long, thick-set man of indeterminate age, although the office pool had him in his fifties, sat before a very old-fashioned speakerphone, its triangle of speakers looking very out of place in what was previously a state of the art high technology office just a month before. It, like the bulky handset it was attached to via a thick cable, had been rescued from the telecommunications museum downtown. And at the moment, an old-style fax machine was grinding away, whooshing low-resolution photo after photo to the director of the FBI in Washington, a continent away.

FBI director Roger Winslow and NSA analyst Malcolm Tannery watched the low-resolution images spew out of the industrial-sized fax machine, so old the ink bottles had to be replaced after every fifteenth image. A small man in a perfectly cut Brooks Brothers suit, the trouser creases so sharp they could cut paper, his shoes shined to perfection, but his face bland and blank, stood almost to attention by the machine, a pallet of colored ink containers at his feet. A growing stack of empty bottles caught the light from the overheads, creating the impression of a jumbled kindergarten playpen minus the crawling and shouting toddlers.

Malcolm had been unceremoniously dumped at Regan airport on his return from his day surfing on the West Coast; he had not dropped in on the fabulous Captain Riley, but he had been driven quite quickly from the plane to the headquarters of the FBI almost before he could catch his breath. His longboard shorts, sneakers, and Rolling Stones T-shirt under a yellow-and-red floppy joe were not what he would have chosen for a meeting with the director of the FBI, but he hadn't been given a choice. At least his long, blond surfer hair had dried on the plane, even though little sparkles of salt gave away what he had been doing just hours ago. It was night in Washington, a little chilly compared to where he had been surfing, but the speed with which everything had been happening made his blood run faster, not to mention his heart rate.

And now he was examining some of the strangest photos of machinery he had seen in years. He flicked through the large images, trying to build a picture in his mind, half of it enamored with the robotics, the other half with the FBI agents who had managed to get the pictures in the first place. The images had started out as high-definition digital data but had been converted to low-resolution analog images by the fax machine, so a lot of the detail had been lost. He paused at a photo showing the small robots tending to the long troughs with Mixmaster-like spoons. He grabbed an old-style magnifying glass mounted on a frame and hovered over the image. The mist that formed on top of the troughs made it hard to discern the detail, but a chill started to run up and down his spine. He looked over to where Roger sat, his chin propped on his folded hands, staring off into space.

"This is where they made the nanomachines."

The director nodded his head, dropped his hands onto the table, sat back in his seat, and let out a deep breath. "Maybe. We will never prove it. My experts at MIT tell me that when you use the same base raw materials for the construction of a nano bug, it's the subtle changes to the formula at the end of the process that direct its focus and what it can do. The original field tests up in Nova Scotia on the oil spill created silver sludge that broke up into carbon three or some such thing. The residue of the attacks on the oil and gas wellheads leaves a silvery gritty substance that evaporates into a greasy mist on contact with air or just goes rock hard if you try to chip away at it. The experts tell me that it attacks backward, replicating itself as it flows back through the pipes and into the main reserve."

"It's self-replicating?" Malcolm asked, astonished. This truly was science fiction. Then the full import of what the director had said sunk in, and his shoulders dropped in shock. "We can never get those wells back?" he asked, his voice rising in pitch. The director gave him a morose look, his face showing the strain of the last few weeks.

"No. If the data is correct, and the nerds over at MIT and Cal Tech have modeled the results several times, which the FBI labs agree with, by the way. They all used the samples of the nanomachines we retrieved, thanks to the Canadians, and have all independently concluded that this bug eats its way through carbon-based crude and gas like it's on a mission, expanding all the time until it reaches saturation point when it solidifies. Chip it out, and it evaporates into a greasy mist— and before you ask, no, the mist can't be collected and reversed. We tried that a few dozen times and more ways than I can count."

"What about the coal mines?"

"Same story, different result. The silver flakes or whatever they are dissipate on exposure to air; this time, the mist is dirty and gritty. The bugs eat their way all over the coal and down the conveyors so rapidly some observers thought a metal paint had been sprayed on by protesters. The only difference was the coal mines took days to completely shut down, not just minutes with the oil and gas."

"We've lost almost the entire world's supply of oil, gas, and coal?" Malcolm asked. He just couldn't believe what he was hearing. It beggared belief. The director stood up, rolled his shoulders, and nodded his thanks to his assistant as he dropped another bundle of images on the table, then returned to the now silent fax machine to refill the ink tanks. The director pressed a little switch on his speakerphone, again, something the FBI had recovered from a previously forgotten basement store. Old was the very new "new."

"Agents, can you please describe, from the start of your visit, what you saw, where you saw it, and your impressions?" He sat down again, and Malcolm stared at the photo with an intensity that suggested he would unpick its secrets no matter what.

In the Seattle office, the three agents looked at each other, then, as the senior agent by rank but not age, Fay leaned slightly towards the octopus-like speaker on the table. "Sir, Senior Special Agent Fay

Remer, with Special Agents Vernon and RuPaul. We entered the facility the first time on Friday evening, at sixteen forty hours, and were met by the COO, Farid Tremblay. Later we were introduced to an assistant named 'Arnon.' We handed the warrant to the COO, who passed it to their general counsel. There was a short conversation with the COO, the details are in the report you have a copy of, and by agreement, we established a second time to visit where the staff would be present, and we could tour the plant." Fay paused, thinking about her unreported second visit later that evening, and mentally clinched her leg muscles. If it came to light, she would explain it, but she had a suspicion that the COO would not ever mention the second visit to anyone outside the plant.

"Sir, during our return to the hotel, we observed that our cell phones had connectivity. Our director instructed us to map the area for reception, which we did on Saturday. We returned to the site at oh eight hundred Monday and conducted the interviews with the staff, and took the photos you are seeing now. A detailed report of every interview is also in our report." And she stopped, letting the words sink into the speakerphone, understanding that the questions asked now would be more informative than the report the three agents had submitted together late in the evening the day before on their return to Seattle.

"Agent Vernon, Agent RuPaul, do you have anything to add to Agent Remer's report?"

"No, sir," they said in unison, sitting very still, waiting for the next question. They had agreed to present this way during their preparation for the meeting with the director because the conclusion they had come to is that they had only been partially briefed on the plant, and they were not sure exactly what the directorate wanted from their visit.

"Did any of you draw any conclusions as to what this plant really produces?" Fay waited for a second, then leaned forward slightly towards the black triangle. "Sir, our conclusion, also in our report, is that the plant is a very high-technology production facility for mobile solar-powered batteries; we didn't actually see a physical unit, but we did see drawings of them. We also conclude they are producing some sort of advanced solar panel, which they constructed their buildings with. We did not see any additional solar farms in the area, so we conclude that the buildings themselves are generating enough power for the plant, and as you know, from last week, enough surplus power to supply the entire jut of Point Rogers. Their factory has only forty-odd employees, all young engineers and scientists, most from the immediate area, and hundreds of robots. It was clean to the point of almost being clinical; we saw nothing that aroused our suspicions, and as far as we can tell, they have several thousands of the units ready for shipping."

"Describe a unit for me." Fay took a breath, then offered the director a hand-drawn sketch, which he handed to an assistant who put it through the fax machine. "Sir, a drawing is on its way to you now. The small unit measures three meters by two meters, is two meters high, and weighs four hundred kilos. Or so we were told."

"What about the large unit?" he asked, the gruffness in his voice adding an edge to the question. In faraway Seattle, Fay shrugged her shoulders; she could only tell the truth at this point, just not necessarily the whole truth.

"Sir, we did not see a large unit, and we did not ask that question. But we estimate the boxes we saw ready for transhipping to be nine meters wide and twelve meters deep. The width varied between three and nine meters. So either there are different sized machines or multiples of the smaller unit boxed at the one time." Roger Winslow took this information in as he studied the drawing. Not a bad sketch, he thought, wondering which of the agents had drawn it.

"One last question. How did you photograph everything?" he asked.

"Sir, we had body cameras which we camouflaged in our clothing. We were asked to surrender weapons or phones, anything metallic, so we didn't feel the need to declare the cameras. They were the old style, single frame, one shot every ten seconds, and were sitting in a cupboard during the cyberattack. We downloaded them using one of the laptops we have resurrected in the office and printed them off for you."

"You have the original digital images?" he asked, his heartbeat quickening. "Yes, sir."

"Thank you. Please stand by in the office for further instructions." And he switched off the speakerphone with a deliberate punch with his forefinger.

"What do you think is going on?" he asked Malcolm, who was now sitting back from the magnifier. He had been listening in on the conversation with his interest piqued by the photo with the bubbling silver fluid and the mist. He felt that he had more of the puzzle at his fingertips, but there were still large pieces missing. The director of the FBI was scratching at a yellow legal pad with an old-fashioned fountain pen, the nib expanding minutely every time he pressed it into the paper. "Can I make some wild guesses and not get my head kicked in?" Malcolm asked, thinking it might just be the time for a little extreme thinking. He checked his analog watch. He still had three hours before the team in Venice and Israel would get back to him.

"You're a geek, hacker. Make all the wild guesses you like. Just don't repeat them out of this room," the director said with a smile, relaxing for the first time since the data from Seattle has started to appear. He held up one hand to stop Malcolm from speaking.

"John, thank you, I'll call if I need you again." The assistant nodded, turned, a disappointed look on his face, and left the room, closing the large glass door behind him. He had never heard the director tell anyone to guess before, remembering an old movie he had seen in his youth, where a battered detective had looked at a female client and thrown out "just the facts, ma'am, just the facts," from of the corner of his mouth, over the top of his cigarette.

"Go."

"Well, assuming I know as much as you do, which I probably don't, let's start with the attacks, specifically the high-tech ones. Crashing the web, destroying the chipsets, and using the nanomachines to kill oil, gas, and coal. Okay with you?"

"Yes, make my day!" They both laughed at the worn cliché that had originally been uttered by an incorrigible cowboy figure in a very old black-and-white Western movie.

"We know the terrorists were in our IT systems from as far back as 1999/2000, during the Y2K debacle. We know they stole plutonium, which they dumped in the biggest oil field on the planet. Not easy to make the feed mechanism for the pellets, and it is not easy to make the pellets in the first place from the irradiated rods. But any competent lab that handled radioactive materials could do the job, and there are literally hundreds of them around the globe. No doubt you have someone knocking on their doors?" The director nodded in agreement; indeed, he did, and his agents were halfway through the list without a hit.

Depressing. But so was most of what had happened, he thought to himself, and if there were a common element to everything that had gone down in the last four weeks, it was that one word—depressing.

"Okay, moving on to the attack on the web and the chipsets. They had to have people inside the chip makers, and there is only a handful of those who manufacture ninety-six percent of all chips between them. And you've got people knocking on those doors as well?"

"Yes. One of the first things we did. Hard to trace any specific chip, as they are distributed worldwide, but we can aggregate the attack by identifying specific chip-sets and what they traditionally are used for. We have identified sixty-three chip-sets; we have their frequencies, although I'll be honest with you, Malcolm, we don't know what the next step is." Malcolm smiled. The idea that the mighty FBI was stumped on a technical IT issue warmed his heart.

"Send the data to us at the NSA; we'll sort it out for you."

"Thanks," he said with a dry smile. But he was happy that this good-looking blond-headed surfer sitting opposite him in colorful striped board shorts and a Rolling Stones T-shirt, whom he knew to be one of the smartest and most respected geeks in the government's employ, didn't see an issue with sorting out the chipset puzzle.

"So, back to the attacks. I suspect that this factory or one like it," Malcolm said, holding up a sheaf of printouts, "made the nanomachines. As you say, hard to prove if there is none of that specific bug lying around. And there won't be, they are way too smart for that, and we're dealing with the refugee women here, not the mercenary terrorists. But it does answer one of the big questions Interpol had, and with your permission, I'd like to send this information to them." Roger gave the request some thought, then after wrestling with himself over jurisdiction, and remembering he had been the one to invite Interpol to the table in the first place, thumped the table with his fist.

"Got a better idea. I'll get Interpol the data in Seattle. Keep guessing. What else have you got?"

"Well, this is only a feeling, but I have been looking at all the summaries Interpol has been sending to us, and specifically the ones regarding the number of women who might be involved in all of this. There are a number of components that dictate certain skills—for instance, maintaining the L100 Hercules for years, from the time it was acquired to the time it was used. Airframe mechanics, instrument fitters, and hydraulics are all specialized skills that we take for granted around aircraft. But they had to have them for years. I checked with the DOD; the two bombs they took would require very little maintenance, other than temperature-stable, dry conditions, but both munitions would need a skilled armorer to arm them. And one with both the tools and the skills." He paused to see if the director would react to his summary. All he got was a casual wave, a flick of one wrist, so he continued.

"You only need those skills once, but you do need them. The same person could have fitted out the drone with the Hellfires, and once again, they would need to be armed before take-off."

"Agreed. But it appears that these tasks were completed in Turkey, maybe Egypt, and even Libya. We haven't found where the aircraft and munitions were stored."

"Doesn't really matter. Same applies. Jessica has been continually pointing to the timeline from 1999/2000; she is convinced that there are layers of terrorists, as in some stole the aircraft, different ones the bombs, follow the dots all the way to 2020—when we believe the development work was completed on the nanomachines and the software. The next two or three years for the finishing touches, then a year or two to manufacture and distribute the bugs, and so on. She is also convinced a nation-state was involved all the way from day one. Have you considered that?"

"Yes." The director offered nothing more, just sat staring at the bright geek with a wan smile on his face. He flicked his wrist again, motioning for Malcolm to continue.

"Okay then, to my main guess. Interpol thinks there were no more than six refugee women involved in the attacks. How many are involved in the planning, the designing of the bugs, and the software, no way to know. But they are mostly fixed on six or fewer for the attacks. Now, if I were the mastermind, and I was fixated on seeing my young refugee women turned terrorists get off scot-free, I'd make sure everything is done leading up to the attacks was done by others, without the six being involved in the detail. In point of fact, as Jessica told General Bridges, we may not even be able to prosecute the pilot, even though we have her on the film prior to the attack on West Point. All she has to do is claim duress that she left the cockpit at the armoring point and was taken into custody somewhere. Yes, she can be charged under the Terrorist Laws, but it won't play very well if just one woman is arrested and charged over destroying all the world's fossil fuels and various other heinous acts."

"I get that, we all get that, but what is your big guess?" Malcolm paused, letting his blood cool; he had been getting quite worked up putting his "guesses" before the director of the FBI, not something he would normally choose to do.

"I think that there is a Plan 'A' and a Plan 'B,' just like Jessica has hypothesized. The first plan was the attacks and utter destruction of our way of life—our dependency on oil, gas, coal, and a hit at the major religions that Mohammad bin Azaria blames in part for the refugee crisis in the first place. I also agree with Jessica when she says he was getting back at his family for the way they have destroyed the Shia way of life in Arabia; that rings true for me."

"And Part 'B' is in these factories, the power supplies, and the panels?"

"Yes. Destroy dependency, force massive sociological and environmental change on a world scale, then offer the solution with next-gen or even next-gen-plus environmentally sustainable solutions that can only be accepted for what they are." The director put his chin back on his folded hands, his arms forming a triangle with his elbows resting on the table. His eyes hooded, his default thinking mode.

He looked up at Malcolm, considered his next words, then shrugged his shoulders. Malcolm knew most of it. No reason he couldn't know some more.

"At the request of the CIA and NSA, the FBI started a track-and-trace on money flows to northwestern USA, Canada, Greenland, Chile, Portugal, Ireland, Denmark, Norway, Finland, Estonia, Sri Lanka, Solomon Islands, New Zealand, Japan, and Iceland—six billion euros, three to five years ago years, all legitimate transfers, all declared, all accounted for by the various government treasuries, and all came from the Arabian Sovereign Wealth Fund, but not authored by Mohammad bin Azaria.

"We had a team visit New Zealand; they found a factory, not unlike the one described by our agents in Point Roberts. We only got overheads, but the layout is hauntingly similar, right down to the pipes going into the ocean. If you were to make one of your famous guesses, what would it be now?" The director got up, poured himself a cup of coffee in a large embossed mug, and pulled a pink fizzy out of the bar fridge for Malcolm. He passed the fizzy and raised his eyebrows in question. Malcolm snapped the top of the fizzy, looking deeply into the middle distance.

"My guess would be that we find a factory, at least one, in every country, and that they will be producing some form of environmentally sensitive power system that likely involves some form of nanotechnology. And I'd further guess that their business is legitimate, meets every requirement for fiscal responsibility, and will drive you nuts trying to prove any attachment to terrorists, or for that matter, Mohammad bin Azaria."

"Not bad for a geek and a surfer dude at that. Well, we've yet to explore every country on that list, but we will in time. Meanwhile, you have a choice."

"I have?"

"Yes. Go visit the good captain in Helena, or go back to your mountain hideaway." Malcolm looked at the director, wondering what his game was; he was headed there before he had been shanghaied to Washington, so what was his interest in meeting up with Jessica? The director smiled at the puzzled look on the young geek's face.

"Hey, I'm pulling your chain. I want you to go back to the Captain, keep your aircraft, and when she's ready, fly her and her team to Seattle. Meet with the agents who visited Point Roberts, debrief, see what you think you should do next, then play it by ear. I'll set it up with Frank. And, by the way, go down to our basement and see what clothes fit you. Surfer dude or not, Montana and Seattle are cold at this time of the year."

Burned Finger Tips, Ink Under The Nails

amuel O'Leary was a crusted, bitter old man who had a reputation for never letting go of anything he was passionate about, to the point where everyone around him prayed he would find something else to do. With no hair on his head, a scruffy three-day-old beard, a flannel shirt that had seen better days, and worn work pants stained with years' worth of unidentified smears and blotches, his steel-capped work boots were possibly the best part of his ensemble. But by God, he could still work a cantankerous linotype machine, casting hot metal into rows of type, albeit backward and in fixed character rows, so that when inked on his manual flatbed press and then pressed to the broadsheet paper he had leftover from his glory days, it printed right way up.

It was a bugger of a way to make a newspaper, but it was all he had that actually worked, and then only because he had put the linotype machine and old-fashioned flatbed press on display in his miserable excuse of a foyer as a reminder to everyone of where he had come from, back in the day of real reporters, and real see-feel-touch-smell newspapers made by true newspapermen.

You could wrap your fish and chips in newspaper and eat from on the shore, watching the seagulls bomb the schools of baitfish as the late afternoon sun went down for its nightly rest.

He had the story of his life; there was no doubt in his mind of that; he had pieced it together from old fellow journalists around the world, whom he had once worked with when the *Amalgamated*

World Press still existed, enabling stories to be released simultaneously in every country, stories written by real, boots-on-the-ground, pencil-behind-the-ears reporters, and not by some snotty-nosed juvenile not yet old enough to shave, who thought they owned the world because they had a computer and a blog site.

Well, now they didn't, and he couldn't have been happier!

For days and days after the attacks four weeks ago, he had been accumulating information, rumors, data, stories, and outright lies from anyone who had a short-wave radio or an old-fashioned analog phone. And being a real reporter, if he couldn't confirm the details of something independently at least twice, he discarded it like the crap it probably was.

His headline was simple—"Terrorist Money Man Tells Why," and the story that followed would win him a Pulitzer if there were still such a thing, but frankly, he was so excited to see his skills hadn't rusted like the morals of the modern information world his only focus was the story.

He led with the statement made by the man who called himself Al Hemish al-bin Mohammad Karesish, who claimed to be a member of the Arabian royal family, and then he followed up with the death toll, county by country, and then, as a bonus, listed every refugee camp presently known to the UNHCR, and listed the number of orphaned children, single-parent children, and then all the others under the age of twelve who still had both their parents. And at the very base of that particular table, he listed the current estimate of those under the age of ten who had died in the previous year. He had worked hard to prove the number, as every source counted differently, so he put an asterisk against the number and the words *"estimate only—unable to fully confirm this number from current sources."*

The number he had cast in the molten lead that spat and sparked across his face as he typed was 55,600* and did not count those killed in the terrorist attacks or the civil unrest that had followed. Who knew how to estimate that number.

Like good reporters of old, he drew conclusions and asked questions but did not offer an opinion, simply promising to publish a future update in a week or two once he had received responses from all the governments he had contacted looking for information to support his story.

None of whom, he might mention, was saying diddly squat about anything other than it was a terrible thing the terrorists had done; they would be brought to heel, watch this space. In other words, they had nothing, were spinning their wheels, and didn't have a clue as to who had attacked them or why.

Well, he knew the why, in chapter and verse, the somewhat long-winded story by the master terrorist having been sent to him by hand courier, a story he had confirmed with his remote journalist friends that they, too, had the same story, so he had coordinated all their information for the exposé he was now printing the old-fashioned way.

They had all agreed to use his story as the base for their own articles and had agreed to a timing for the release that would echo around the world in the same hour. The ham radio stations currently being run out of radio station stations would also use his story and release it at the same time worldwide. That was a bit of hyperbole, he thought to himself, as he only had current contacts working with him in the EU, Canada, South America, England, Canada, and America.

But in his bones, he felt that the story would get passed on by other ham enthusiasts, if not by other publishers, as he had an open copyright statement on every page encouraging copying by any who had the desire or the energy, requesting just a simple acknowledgment of his paper as the source.

It took him five more hours to set all the type, let it cool in its form, then ink and print. But at the end of it, a hard but rewarding day, by his lights, he had the story ready to release.

He looked out of a dust-stained window, high up in his shed, and watched the night push the day away, as it always did, as inexorably as the world turned.

Tomorrow the world would know the why and part of the who. But for the life of him, he could not envisage a solution for the poor refugee children dying every day in those miserable camps.

Chapter 20

I sat in my room, reviewing the day. Pete and I had looked at the house and told the agent we were looking at the other side of town and would come back to her in the next day or two. The FBI had not detected any further burst transmissions. We had an Interpol agent who would go undercover in Helena due to arrive in the next six hours, and a message left on my minicomputer from Roger Winslow informed me that Malcolm Tannery would be arriving in an NSA jet in the next three hours and that I should stand by for a briefing as well as prepare to decamp and take the jet to Seattle, timing at my discretion.

I now had more moving parts and less information than I usually liked to deal with, but a sense of excitement had started to build because Roger was no dummy. Malcolm was one of the smartest people I knew, so something was up, and maybe we would make a breakthrough in identifying the terrorists.

With a sharp knock on my door, Pete let himself into my room, closely followed by Anna, carrying takeout bags that hopefully tasted as good as they smelled. Within seconds, a spread of ribs, baked potatoes, hot corn dripping with butter, and salads lay spread out all over my bed, with Pete and Anna munching down on one side, leaving me to fend for myself on the other.

"What are you going to do with your new asset?" Pete asked, pulling a rib apart like a cannibal. We had existed on army rations during our trek around the wilds of Montana, so I understood his glee at having a real BBQ meal. I looked over at him, gravy dripping down his chin, an impossible smile splitting his ugly face, his deep blue eyes sparkling, and imagined him in better days. It was a nice picture to go with the excellent hot food.

"I have a theory."

"Ha!" he retorted. "Not one of those?" He laughed as he spoke, the BBQ rib he had just chewed into, only just surviving. "The Boss warned me about those!" I had no option but to smile as well; it was nice to have a little humor in the room, even if it were at my expense. "To continue," I said, pointing my own destroyed rib bone at him, "if the terrorist cell really is here in Helena, then they may have used the airport."

"So you're putting your asset undercover there?" Anna asked, wiping her mouth politely, in direct contrast to lip-smacking Pete. "Why not one of our FBI guys?" I looked at her, sensing no deeper motive behind her question other than wanting to hear my reasoning.

"They, like us, may have been seen but can't take the risk that they are recognized and scare the women off. Besides, this particular agent will be invisible to everyone, just another backpacker escaping from the turmoil of the cities looking for temporary work." Anna nodded, having worked through the possible scenarios herself, and pleased that Jessica had solved the problem for them. She delicately nibbled her way around a corn cob, mentally thanking Pete for insisting they buy such a mixed bag of food. Little yellow drops of melted butter fell onto the napkin she held under her chin. An observer would see a smartly dressed woman, probably late forties, dressed in relatively plain cold-weather gear, with short hair folding down over her brow, no makeup, and a sprightly look to her. If they looked really close, they would see brilliant green eyes that told of experiences beyond the normal, and if she turned them onto you, you would see the unmistakable focus of a hard-nosed cop.

"What do you plan to do next?" she asked between bites. I wiped my own mouth, looking at the BBQ sauce smears I left. Midwestern USA BBQ was a messy affair!

"Pete and I will go look over the western side of the highway. I want to investigate the whole process that is going on there. Then when Malcolm arrives, you, Pete, and I will take a trip to Seattle—do you have to clear that with Roger?" I asked, suddenly realizing I was giving directions to a very senior special agent of the FBI without so much as a "by-your-leave." She just smiled, put her cob down, and wiped her hands. It was good to see she had also made a mess of eating our meal, so I instantly felt less of a slob!

"We were TDY'ed to you way back, don't sweat it. Now I've made a nuisance of myself in town. I guess I had better keep out of sight." I thought about that for a minute, then shook my head.

"No, let's take it up a notch. Why don't you and one of your boys go visit the airport, ask questions about the helicopter, make a real nuisance of yourselves, and set the stage as it were. Then when Malcolm arrives, meet with him, and bring him here." I visualized the NSA plane landing, then changed my mind. "No, don't bring him here; let's keep him under wraps as well. When the plane arrives, you go onboard, send your agent back here to take turns with the monitoring, and Pete and I will join you under cover of darkness, and we can then all fly to Seattle."

"We've only got the one minicomputer between us," Anna said, reminding me of the pitiful communication resources we really had since the web crash. I reached into my go-bag and pulled out a brand-spanking new one, still in its bubble wrap. I spun it across the bed to her.

"Give them this, brief them on the protocols, and make sure they understand how precious it is."

"Thanks, I was wondering what you had in there," she said, pointing to my go-bag. I just smiled; a girl still had to have her secrets, even if I did score low in the fashion stakes.

Chapter 21

The engineer and the scientist sat at a small table with Kathryn Simmons, the CEO, and Farid Tremblay, the COO of the Point Rogers plant. A small coffee service sat on a lowboy off to one side, and a multi-sided screen formed a square on the table that separated them. They had just watched the FBI agents' tour and final departure from the plant. The screen flickered, then showed the view from a CCTV camera mounted up high on the facade of the harbor Pilots office as the agents climbed on board a very large orange-and-white Coast Guard semi-rigid inflatable. Farid brushed her hair back, and hunched her shoulders.

"I don't know if it's relevant, but the lead agent told me she had also been a refugee. But the worrying aspect is what the FBI does next." The engineer leaned back in her seat, crossing her arms.

"We gamed this exact scenario, we prepared for it, we know they have had a flyover in New Zealand, and we know the money can't be traced back to anyone involved in phase one. Our counsel continues to tell us our industrial IP is safeguarded, and even if they determine we are using nanites in our manufacturing processes, so do hundreds of other companies, so personally, I'm not worried about that. I am concerned about the delay in our shipping schedule." The COO arched her back defensively; while she respected the engineer and all that she had done, she didn't like her manner, never had, but she tucked her personal feelings away and tackled the implied criticism.

"We have ordered the barges; supposedly, they are on their way. We did have some difficulty getting them fuelled under the current circumstances. It costs us ten times what we would normally pay per gallon. The barges, however, were a little cheaper than we anticipated, probably for the same reason. We have the conversion kits at the marina under lock and key, and we have seven trained people ready to do the work the minute they dock."

"I see a bigger problem for us, one we need to address now." It was the first time the CEO had spoken, her responsibilities far beyond this one plant, and in a sense, she was the direct boss of all the women in the room, one of whom she knew resented her position with a vengeance. "I flew back in today, and with the airways system still in disarray, I'm confident no one will be able to track my flight. Our pilot has returned to Helena, and that's the subject of my disquiet."

"Helena?" the engineer said, her tone rising with her temper. "What in the name of hell has Helena got to do with you?" The CEO stared down at the engineer, looked to the scientist for support, saw only a neutral look on her very beautiful face, then looked back at the engineer, once again noticing the best set of toned muscles she had ever seen on a woman.

"In case you have forgotten, I'm in charge of the Americas from Canada down to Terra Del Frago. From memory, correct me if I am wrong. Helena is located in this area." The engineer dropped her head, seemingly acknowledging the CEO's claim. "We have a report here of FBI agents following up on their earlier inquiries about the rebuild of the missile silo. One of the agents just happened to be the same woman who flew to the Middle East three weeks ago to work with Interpol. That would suggest that Helena has become important to both Interpol and the FBI, and I think that should concern us all."

The scientist, used to the moods of the engineer, having worked closely with her for nearly three years, reached across the table and put her hand on the engineer's shoulder. "We are concerned, but there is literally nothing we can do now; there are over forty-nine thousand people camping on the western side, houses are going up as fast as they can be built, and as you know, the infrastructure has been ready for years. What we need to concentrate on, in my opinion, is getting this site moving with deliveries and opening up the site in Canada."

"I don't disagree, but you need to think and think carefully. Have you left anything, anything at all, behind in Helena that could give you away?" The CEO looked at the scientist, held her gaze, saw her shake her head, then nodded to herself.

"Okay, there's an electric car in the garage, a thousand-mile battery, and it's one with universal charging. Consider it yours. Good hunting." Both the women from Helena got up, hugged the COO, then left the room. The CEO pulled coffee service closer, poured a cup for herself, looked at the COO to see if she wanted one, and poured a second cup. "We can't deliver too fast, even though the FBI now has an estimate of how many units we have ready, and they didn't see enough to figure out our production rate. Are our delivery specialists ready?" The COO nodded, her silky hair falling over her face, which she brushed back casually before taking the offered coffee cup.

"Yes, with the vehicles we have prepositioned at the drop-off points, we should be able to have around fifty to sixty units up and running every day. That's not what I'm worried about."

"Helena?"

"Yes. We expected the first investigation but not the follow-up. And I really don't like Interpol sniffing around before we have established the first group of children. In fact, I'm of a mind to hold them back until we are sure that they have lost interest in us there."

"Can you do that?" the COO asked, thinking about the logistics of housing and feeding over a thousand young girls in halfway houses on the other side of the world. The CEO sipped her coffee, thinking for a minute.

"Probably not. But the last group left Coxes Bazar yesterday, and the ship will dock at the South Cove Waterway in Seattle in six weeks. From there to Helena is less than a day, along the I-90 E. We will have the housing ready. We don't know how many families will take us up on our offer, but the indications are we will have enough to cover the first arrivals. The UNHCR and Red Crescent are managing all the paperwork, and I suppose we can slow the ship down if we have to. For that matter, they can continue to live on the ship if we run into difficulties. At least for a week or two. But I'm counting on enough goodwill due to the power packs being in operation to get us over any humps. That and pressure from the government." The COO nodded. They had gone over the plan time and time again, smoothing out any issues they found; the only real unknowable was how many families would adopt a child. Their planning had been aided by a master forensic psychologist, one of their own refugees currently living near Roanoke on the East Coast. A child genius who had modelled the anticipated behavior of different governments and populations hundreds of times and the families they needed to absorb all the refugee children.

They had what she believed to be an excellent motivation for those families that had migrated due to the civil unrest, to willingly adopt one of the children now on their way from one of the worst refugee camps on the planet.

It was a gamble, but when it worked and proved their thinking, the floodgates would open, and they could get on with their real mission.

Chapter 22

"There's no mention of the women in this story," the president commented, having read and reread the article she had been given by her military liaison. "At least we won't be called liars." She put the paper down as if it were alive and stared at the front page of the four-page broadsheet. "And this is now doing the rounds via short-wave radio?"

"Yes, ma'am, for about three hours now, and we are starting to see it being picked up overseas as well." General Saunders held her own copy, which she folded in half and dumped on top of the president's.

"It's a good piece of journalism, in my opinion," offered Frank Reynolds, sitting back relaxed. He had the jump on everyone as he had received the newspaper some hours before when one of his men had dropped it on his desk at the NSA headquarters. The newspaper was being dropped in bundles on every corner in Washington by electric vans just like in the old days before the World Wide Web and digital printing. The one difference being this edition was free. The president fixed her stare on the director of the NSA, wishing she didn't agree with him.

"Right now, that's irrelevant. What do we think the reaction by the public will be?" She looked around the room where every senior person still in Washington sat, most very uncomfortable with the sudden summons to the White House at half-past six in the morning. Most uncomfortable of all was the secretary of state, who was doing her very best to be as invisible as she could under the circumstances.

To the best of her knowledge, only the president, General Saunders, and the directors of the FBI, NSA, and CIA knew of her conversations with Mohammad bin Azaria, but she still felt the eyes of the room on her back.

"In my opinion, Madam President, most people will read or hear this story, shake their heads at the numbers, then get on with their lives. The whole issue is too far away for them to be all that concerned, and research shows that most Americans are firstly concerned with their own safety and comfort and place third-world issues about fifth or sixth on their list of priorities." The head of Immigration Customs Enforcement (ICE) delivered his verdict in a neutral tone that would make any government servant proud, displaying his utter contempt for the whole concept of overseas refugees. He had suffered under a previous government that built part of a wall between America and Mexico at great cost, and to absolutely no real effect other than to piss people off on both sides of the border, and the ramifications of that stupidity still rang through his department. If there were refugees overseas, let them stay there; he had his hands full trying to protect the borders from the incessant flood of immigrants from the north and the south, with a budget that had been cut every year he had been in office.

"Does anyone else have an opinion?" the president asked, choosing not to follow up with her ICE director; in her bones, she suspected he may well be correct, however much that disturbed her. "No, well, go to your offices and keep your ears open. I want to know what ordinary people think about this story and how they react. Thank you. General Saunders, Frank, Roger, Julius, please stay." And her senior people literally flooded out of the room, please to be excused, reminiscent of school children being let out for play lunch.

"Bridget, what is the latest from Interpol?" The general looked up, mildly surprised at the question. She was scheduled to brief the president later in the day.

"Madam President, Interpol has been unable to find any trace of the women in Egypt, Libya, Turkey, or Montana. The technology team has made progress tracking movements to and from the target sites, but the 'black holes' are still defying the analysts. There is an Interpol team with FBI assistance in Montana as we speak, and the

FBI has information regarding the manufacturing plants in both New Zealand and Point Roberts."

"Roger?" the president asked.

"Ma'am, our agents report a high technology facility in Point Roberts producing transportable power packs capable of running small factories, or around forty to fifty homes. They have over six thousand of these units ready to ship and some sort of distribution system in place to get them to where they are needed. We don't know what the status is in New Zealand; we only have the aerial photos to go on at this point."

"Where did the money come from?"

"Originally, the Pan Arabian Wealth Fund, but not by the hand of Mohammad bin Azaria. The funds were sent to these areas—and others—by members of the Royal family or the treasurer, but in every case, with the approval of the banks and countries involved, and all in a two-year period starting five years ago. Our own Internal Revenue Service has audited the funds and the inflow every year without raising any concerns."

"Where has this money been spent?"

"The IRS has identified several companies that have received funds from the primary deposit, transport, builders, and many different providers of renewables. The biggest single transfer has been one point two billion dollars over four years to the plant in Point Roberts. The New Zealand government reports that a similar amount has been transferred over the same period of time to the plant they have there on Great Barrier Island." The head of the FBI handed the president a sheaf of photos of the plant, spreading them out so she could see the progression through the plant. The president picked up the photo taken in building six and studied it intently. She threw it back on the table, where it spun and skidded until it was stopped from falling on the floor by the FBI director.

"You think the nanomachines were made in these factories?" she asked. "Yes, we do, but we can't prove it unless they still have some on the premise, which is extremely unlikely. They are using nanites in their current production, but so are twenty other companies around the country. Companies, by the way, say making the nanomachines that destroyed the oil, gas, and coal is impossible. The first thing we asked them weeks ago." The president nodded. She still faced a bloody mess in her country; while the civil unrest had mostly been contained, the wreckage of weeks of fighting had left many cities in ruin, and the outflow of people to rural areas had taken everyone by surprise. It was estimated that more than sixty million people were now displaced in the greater United States, something unimaginable just a month ago.

"How did the testing of the samples from Canada go?" she asked, running down the list of dot points she had prepared overnight. She met with her senior people as little as possible, letting them deal with their own issues, which were legion.

"Not well. We lost most of the samples just trying to open the containers. When we were successful, no one was able to analyze the samples other than to confirm their effect on oil and gas. The NSA and CIA labs basically got nowhere, and the three commercial labs we engaged did little more than 'ooh' and 'aw' over the technology. Whoever designed these bugs was a genius." She nodded again, looking at her list. Since no one had come to her since the samples had been received from Canada, she had assumed, correctly as it now turned out, that no one had managed to do anything meaningful with the samples.

"What is the latest on our good friends, the senators, congress-men, and women we sent back to their electorates?" she asked, fingers crossed that this action she had taken way back at the start of the internal strife wouldn't come back and bite her on her backside. Roger Wilson looked at Frank Reynolds to see if he would take the ques-tion, but the rather firm look on his face said clearly, "all yours," so he squared his shoulders before answering.

"Ma'am, we know of thirty-seven who have been killed in action. Another twenty-odd are in the hospital recovering from gunshot wounds or trauma; the rest seem to be doing a fair job of getting their districts under control. When I say fair, they are probably doing their best, but as you know, the civil unrest is quieting down right across the country. And that's thanks to the reserve, the army, and the local police forces, more so than the senators and congresspeople." She looked at her FBI director with one of her withering stares, which he absorbed, not having agreed with this particular presidential action at the time, and now even more against it, as a number of the elected representatives had actually led or actively participated with many of militia in the attacks on civilians, troops, and police. He was happy that they had all been accounted for and were now removed from the conflict.

Permanently.

Thank you, SWAT sharpshooters.

But he wouldn't tell the president that. The president looked at her list for a final time, feeling the first pangs of hunger hit her stomach; she had been up since four A.M. and existed until now on coffee.

"One last question for the room. Are we winning?" she asked, watching every face closely for any sign of prevarication. Roger looked at Julius, who looked at Bridget, who was looking at Frank, and almost by accident, they all shook their heads at the same time.

"No better than fifty percent, Madam President, but the good news is that just a week ago, we were at twenty-five." General Saunders delivered this piece of news in a very soft voice, personally ashamed that they could not give the president better news. The president stood, looked at her cadre of commanders, and sensed they were as disquieted as much as she was with the bland statement by the general.

"People, you are the very best of the best, and I know you are personally working beyond the pale to sort all this out, and I thank you for that. Fifty percent is double what it was last week; let's get to next week and see where we are. Thank you." And she turned on her heel and left the Oval Office, the Secret Service opening and closing the door for her.

"What's really going on in Montana, Roger?" Frank Reynolds asked, rolling his shoulders. "I understand you kidnapped my star geek and hijacked our plane?" Roger smiled and opened his palms as if seeking forgiveness.

"I've connected him up with Anna and the good captain, and I've suggested they go to Seattle and follow up on Point Roberts. Should be an interesting visit, and all things being equal, you can have your plane back in a week." He had the good grace to smile, something that was not lost on Frank or Julius.

Chapter 23

P ete and I stood shoulder to shoulder, looking at the wooden framework going up for what would soon be a three-bedroom house of
some twenty squares, excluding the porch and garage. What I
found fascinating is that there were a row of identical frames all being
erected at the same time, as far as the eye could see, in a manner where
no two houses lined up. There were ten work people for each house
and a huge stack of preformed walls, doorways, window sills, and the
typical A-frame for the roof ends. And stacked off to one side was
a mountainous pile of slick-looking greenish-grey-black panels that
seemed to have a life of their own, with little flecks of light popping
out at odd times. Next to this pile was an equally impressive stack of
hard blue foam insulation, and when we looked back, just one house
away, we could see the build method that was being used.

The foam went on the wooden frames, the panels on the foam,
right across the walls and roofs. I moved Pete back three houses to one
that was almost finished and ran my hands over the walls. They looked
slimy but felt warm and dry to the touch, and in the strong sunlight
seemed to change color from green to black as you moved around
them. This house was having its wiring fitted, with two electricians
working on ladders. Most notable was a massive battery mounted on
the end of the house, where I suspected a garage or carport would end
up. It didn't take a brain surgeon to work out that the walls and roofs
were made of some type of solar panel material.

I remembered a short conversation I had with Amira just after
she had managed to unlock her personal cloud store. She had said that

the nanotechnology she had invented could also be used in panels, power supplies, and other environmentally responsible artifacts. I had no doubt in my mind that what I was looking at was a derivation of Amira's early work. Now, carefully, so I didn't spook anyone, I had to find out where the panels came from.

"Pete, watch my back. I need to look at that pile of panels." He just nodded and stuck himself to my shoulder like glue. We walked slowly over to the pile, stopping to look at different materials as if we were considering the prospect of buying into one of the houses. A foreman type, bib overalls, loud flannel shirt, big meaty boots, and bright yellow hardhat holding a clipboard came over to us and, pushing the hat back on his forehead, greeted us with a smile that was a very poor advertisement for dental hygiene.

"Hi, y'all folks, this here is a building site, and y'all need personal protection like gear. Y'all see that sign back there? Can't let you stay here without management approval and safety gear." And he tipped his hat to me, as polite as you like, while spreading his arms out to shepherd us back beyond the building line. I felt Pete tense up, then relax when he read my body language, so we moved with the foreman out of the work zone. I took the opportunity to glance around as if this was my very first visit to a building site.

"What are those amazing panels over there, the ones you are putting up as walls?" I asked, all innocent, the pretty little female in awe of the big burly workman. I heard Pete swallow a chortle, then he leaned over and coughed into his hand. The foreman looked at the pile, then back to a house that had panels on the walls and the roof.

"This here is one of the most environmentally responsible townships in all of America; over ninety percent of all the power used by the town comes from our solar or wind farms, and we have the highest uptake of batteries in our houses probably in all the world." He paused to catch his breath; this speech was probably the longest he had ever made in all of his life!

"The same man that built all our renewables some years ago provided us with the batteries and the panels you see here at no cost to the people who will end up living in these homes. It was explained to me as some sort of bequest to the town where he and his family had lived for over a hundred and fifty years. His name was Howard Westhall, made his fortune out of oil, just like his daddy and his daddy before him." I nodded sagely, absorbing the information. I noticed a woman with plumbing tools attacking a groundwater pipe, and the speed with which she did it indicated that there was some sort of extensive underground plumbing already in the ground. The foreman saw where I was looking and nodded.

"That there is Daisy. She's the head of plumbing services, and along with the land, the panels, and the batteries, this whole area has been plumbed for water, drainage, and sewerage. Rumour has it, mind you, when the man built all of this, he laid it out for one hundred thousand houses. That was his vision, so it's gonna take us a whole while to fill it all up." I had seen this reported somewhere, I forget where, but the one hundred thousand ready-to-use home plots rang a bell. And this in a town whose highest population number had reached the lofty heights of just thirty-three thousand and change only last summer. Someone had planned well and far in advance, and I wondered who could tell me the story behind this very generous person. I couldn't use my minicomputer out in the open without raising questions we didn't want to answer, so I tucked the question away for later.

"But the panels, they look new; where did they come from?" I asked, pointing to the pile sparkling in the afternoon sun. They looked alive, sitting on the frames like they were pulsing with power. Which, come to think about it, they were.

"They were shipped to town over six months ago and stored in a disused hangar at the airport. We believe there's enough to build the first ten thousand houses. The plans we have been provided with include a one-thousand-person dormitory, fifteen schools, three hospitals, shops, three Olympic-size swimming pools, and, of course, parks and gardens."

"And all of this was laid out by the benefactor?" I asked, astonished at the planning that had gone into this. Not to mention the fact that he had foreseen the massive migration to Helena from the bigger towns and cities where fighting had broken out immediately after the terrorist attacks, and ordinary people were killed for no more than walking down a street. Food for thought, and I knew just who to point at this puzzle. It was getting late, and the sun was hovering on the horizon, so I judged it time to move Pete and myself off to the airport.

I thought about the young Interpol agent I had called in from Chicago and worked out her task list. Before she started on the hangar crawl, I would get her to backtrack where the panels had been stored and try to establish when they had first appeared, how they had been transported, and who knew about them besides the builders. And someone in the town council had to be in on it all. It just didn't make sense otherwise. I could feel a chat with my current FBI favorites coming on, but in retrospect, I thought I would leave that to Anna.

Pete and I headed back to our hire car, a lovely little electric thing no bigger than three people could sit in, ultra-light, and I guessed efficient because we had it for two days, and we had yet to charge it. Standing beside it was a backpacker, her world sitting at her feet, her head encased in a red beanie and a hood, her form completely hidden by snow gear that looked new and top-shelf. Obviously, Interpol Chicago had a bigger budget than we did back in Europe!

"Want a lift somewhere?" I asked, playing the game.

"Yes, please, ma'am, to the hostel on Main Street would be nice." Pete smiled to himself, grabbed the piled rucksack and sausage bag off the grass, and stuffed it in the micro boot. Luckily, it just fit. I climbed in the passenger side, the hitchhiker in the back, and Pete eventually into the driver's seat. He turned and leaned over the seat to shake her hand.

"Call me Pete. This is Jessica. Who are you?" he asked. He got a huge smile for his effort, and she took off one mitten to shake Pete's hand.

"Just call me Sally, but call me," she said with a laugh. "I've heard about the famous—or should I say infamous—Black Pete!" I laughed along with the two of them, knowing her life was going to get a whole lot more complicated in a few minutes, so I turned to face her and gave her instructions on what we wanted and handed her a microcomputer, the last one I had stored away in my go-bag.

"Use this sparingly, don't let it out of your sight, and don't let anyone see you using it. We'll drop you off; your only backup is two

FBI agents at the hotel, but you can only call them if you are in dire straits. Got it?" I asked, a little harsher than I intended.

"Yes, ma'am, thank you, I've been briefed by Colonel Anthony. If it's there, I'll find it." The only thing I was really worried about was the distributed nature of my team, with the geeks in Venice or Israel somewhere, FBI agents, and now one from Interpol left in Helena, and Pete, Malcolm, and me on the way to Seattle, then to who knows where. We were literally spread around the globe, and I really hoped we were not chasing our tails.

We had just one objective.

Track and identify the women terrorists.

We had some leads, but I had the feeling that they were so good, and so well prepared, and now possibly so well hidden that we may never find them.

We dropped our agent, and her bags in town, then ran out to Helena Regional Airport. We checked the car in at the desk, then asked for a lift to the far side of the airport where the big Gulfstream 4 sat, resplendent in the colors of the US Air Force, hooked up to a ground power unit that was happily burbling away with that typical diesel chug-chug sound. I wondered how long it would be before it was a super battery on wheels and the diesel engines went the way of the dinosaurs.

We climbed up the stairs to be met by an Air Force pilot dressed to the nines in a light blue shirt, dark blue tie, and dark blue pants with cutting-edge creases. He saluted me, nodded to Pete, then stood back so we could enter. Malcolm was easy to find; he had wound out one of the executive seats into a bed and was fast asleep.

"We'll be wheels up in ten, sir. Please take your seats. Estimated flight time to Seattle is ninety minutes, plus taxi and wait times, so we'll have you there by nineteen hundred hours Pacific time." The pilot had a seriously deep voice, and I imagined him singing in a choir in some beautiful stained-glass church. His skin was as black as the ace of spades, and I mentally chastised myself for my sloppy racism. See a beautiful black man, hear a deep voice, think choir in a church! Stereotypes would be the death of the human race; of that, I was quite sure. To vent my disappointment with myself, I pushed Malcolm's legs off the recliner, pushed past his seat, and settled into the one immediately behind him. Anna took the one next to me, Pete the one in front of her, creating a four-person conversation pit. The door rose up into its seals, and we could hear the whine of the engines starting.

"Anna, before I forget, can you get your agents into Helena and find out everything they can about the town's benefactor, Howard Westhall, several generations, over a hundred and fifty years in the area, made their money from oil. Get them to send it to you securely. Our newest addition to the town is called 'Sally,' don't know if that is her real name, don't particularly care. The Boss has briefed her. I don't know how much she knows. I'll ask the Boss next time I speak to him."

"What's her mission?" Anna asked, pushing her seat back into the reclining position. I wondered what our pilot would think of that, seeing as we were still taxing. Pete had closed his eyes, creating the impression he was sleeping, so when he mumbled, he took us by surprise.

"Find the hangar used to store some sexy new building materials, then lay in wait for the pilot to show. Nothing special." Anna smiled, doubting very much that Sally's tasks were anything but critical to the investigation, but let it go, and Pete to continue pretending to sleep. She turned in her seat to look at me just as Malcolm swung his seat around to face me.

"Jessica, I've got some data for you from NSA and Roger. Can I brief you now?" he asked. I nodded and noticed that suddenly Pete had opened his eyes. Malcolm reached behind his seat and pulled out a portfolio bag. He emptied the contents out on the floor between us, then picked up a bundle of oversized grainy photos. He handed the bundle to me; I started to work through them, passing them to Pete, who then passed them to Anna.

"Roger also asked me to update you on New Zealand. He apologizes. It slipped through the cracks at the time."

"New Zealand?" I felt my eyebrows raise with my question, what in God's name did New Zealand have to do with terrorist attacks?

"Captain, about a week or so ago, the NSA became aware that large quantities of funds had been transferred between three and five years ago out of the Arabian Sovereign Wealth Fund and into accounts held in Northwestern USA, Canada, Greenland, Chile, Portugal, Ireland, Denmark, Norway, Finland, Estonia, Sri Lanka, Solomon Islands, New Zealand, Japan, and Iceland. Frank asked Roger to run the data down, so he authorized an overfly of a site in New Zealand to see what was there. The last photo is an aerial view of the setup we found."

"And these photos of the inside of some sort of plant?" I asked, looking at the photo I would later learn had been taken in building six.

"Exactly the same layout. The funds were not transferred by anyone we know related to the terrorists, have all been tracked, audited, and approved by the various governments, and the common story is that they are for the development of facilities and infrastructure for displaced persons. Vague, I know, but there are no flags on any of the funds, and where they have been drawn down, it has been for legitimate purposes. Point Roberts, where that particular factory is located, has used some one-point-three or four billion since they started up. New Zealand has spent about the same but in NZ dollars." I looked at the photo again, noticing the fog sitting just over a bed of sliver-looking liquid. I felt a chill run up my spine, remembering my first thought when I had been shown a photo of the Alaskan Pipe Line with its claggy, silver nanobots, which had effectively shut it down. As I raised my eyes to ask the question, Malcolm nodded.

"Yes, we think so too. This is where the nanobots came from, or a factory just like it. Hard to prove if there aren't any there now, and plenty of modern factories use nanites in their materials production, so on the surface, this is just a very efficient, high-tech plant-making stuff." I looked at Malcolm again, and he read my eyes. "Solar-powered power packs, multiple sizes, thousands ready to be shipped through a distribution network set up six months ago up and down the west coast of Canada and the US."

And just like that, I had the terrorists' "Plan B." I thought for a moment and looked over at Anna, who was now studying the aerial shot of the New Zealand factory. She tilted her head to one side, considering something.

"Jessica, who's the real expert in nanobots?" she asked, obviously thinking the same thing as I was. I checked my tactical watch, mentally worked out the time in Israel and Venice, grabbed my minicomputer out of the seat pocket, waved for silence, then dialed the Boss. It was going to be four or five o'clock in the morning, so I prepared for grumpy. I got it.

"Buggar off. I'm asleep."

"I love you too, Colonel." I held my breath. The use of his rank should have tipped him off as to the seriousness of the call. The screen showed a kaleidoscope of colors as he obviously moved to a better position, and I had no idea what I had just seen.

"What?" His voice was gruff but neutral; he had gotten the message. "I need you and Amira in Seattle as soon as you can get here."

"Do you?"

"Yes."

"Are you sure? And if the answer's yes, I'll have to check with Arie."

"Yes. I know that. I'll arrange for a package to be sent to you as soon as I can organize the technology. I'm with Malcolm, so he may be able to facilitate that."

"Do it. It's an eight-hour sprint from here. I'll get Arie to provide a ride and will collect Amira on the way. See you for a late breakfast tomorrow. I'll be hungry.

"Very, very hungry." And he snapped his computer shut, cutting off any reply I was going to make. I turned to Malcolm.

"Can you get these photos and a short summary I'll write now to the Boss before he leaves Israel in about an hour?" I asked, having no idea of the technicalities that would be involved in achieving such a thing given our strangled communications facilities. He seemed to think for a minute, nodded, swept the pictures up off the floor, and pointed at me.

"Start writing. Send it to my mini."

Chapter 24

At half-past four in the morning, the Boss was anything but civil, but as he worked through what he had to do in the next hour, his brain slowly kicked into gear, and in the ten minutes it took him to shave and shower and pack a suit and shirts in a go-bag, he had his plan in mind. He waited until the last minute to call Arie, and, no surprise, he found him not only awake but in his office, beavering away on an old-style desktop computer.

"Morning, PJ, what gets you up so early?" he asked, a smile in his voice. The fact that his team of commandos had returned from Turkey empty-handed was not unexpected; he was getting used to chasing his tail as far as the women terrorists were concerned.

"One guess. I need your help. Again. Fast jet to Seattle. I'll fly it, leaving in an hour if you can, stopping to collect Amira in Venice on the way. So I need your approval to take her out of your reach for the duration." The Boss held his breath, knowing he was asking a lot of the retired Intelligence chief, but the trust that had grown between them over the past few years was something neither of them took for granted.

"You want to take her bracelet off?" Arie asked, not really surprised at the request. He no longer felt Amira had anything to do with the attacks, even though it was her work that had provided the base for the nano bug that had killed the oil, gas, and coal mines, as well as the crash of the World Wide Web, and the "black holes" that had been created over the terrorist bases, making it impossible to trace their movements. There were many in his command that wanted to see her in chains, more than a few preferring a bullet in her head. He knew that for a fact, but he also knew the head of Interpol's Section Five would not ask for her if it were not absolutely critical to the investigation.

"Yes, please. I'll monitor her all the way over. Jessica can take over when we land. We will not let her out of our sight." Arie nodded, his glasses slipping down his nose, making him look very studious.

"I'll have a plane ready for you in thirty minutes, with all the flight gear you'll need, and I expect to get our plane back in one piece! I'll arrange refueling for you with the US European Command; it might help if you gave them a call before I do?"

"Agreed. Leave that with me. Thank you, this could give us the break we have been looking for." The Boss hung up and immediately dialed General Saunders, who opened her mini with one hand while drinking scotch from the other. The Boss could hear voices in the background, so he chose his words carefully.

"Bridget, I need fast jet refueling and Israeli ID, but I'll be the pilot from Venice to Seattle, ready in an hour. Arie will be calling your European Command, but thought we should let you know first." She had the good grace to smile, realizing that this was not a request, but she was starting to understand the tempo at which Interpol worked, so she nodded her acceptance.

"I'll have them ready for you. I'll pass the codes to Arie; he can get them to you in the air. Have a safe flight." And his screen went blank again, so he made his final call before heading to Sde Dov airport.

"Indigo, good morning. Can you have Amira packed and ready to travel at the airport in an hour, please, and you can remove her bracelet?"

"*Colonnello, è una notizia fantastica, e sì, avrei Amira pronta per lei all'aeroporto. Posso chiederle dove sta andando?*"

"Seattle. Hooking up with Jessica and Anna."

"Ah, I see the hands of some strong women at work here. Take care," he said, laughter running through his voice like so many air bubbles running up the wall of a brightly lit fish pond.

The Boss, at the back of his mind, wondered what he was running full tilt into, but he knew Jessica would not have called if it were not critical. And besides, a bit of cold might be a welcome relief to the dry heat he had just escaped.

If he could remember how to fly whatever fast jet Arie arranged for him and not crash it into the Atlantic somewhere!

Chapter 25

"Call me Sally" waited at the backpacker hostel until nightfall, then changing into what she perceived to be backpacker chic, she placed her weapon into the small of her back, her credentials in her inside pocket, and a neat folding knife that just squeaked in under the legal length for its double-sided blade next to it. She slipped the minicomputer into a side pocket on her pants, pulled a dark watch cap down over her ears, and headed out. She had phoned the FBI agents earlier and given them her intended itinerary. She had been offered company, but mindful of what the captain had written on her briefing notes, thanked them, then said she would check in later that night. She hauled her snow pants up, slipped a medium-sized Beretta nine millimeter into her boot, covered it up, and considered herself dressed for the mission to the airport.

Hope for the best, and plan for the worst.

She climbed on the new electric bike that she had hired at the hostel and set off. It was cold, not quite freezing but getting that way, and the wind in her face as she rode soon chilled her down. Living and working in Chicago had prepared her for this, but she could feel her face getting tighter and tighter as she rode. No appreciable traffic, and as she alternated between cycling and motoring, she got to the perimeter of the airport in a reasonable time. The FBI was going to find the hangar where the panels had been stored; her mission was to find any trace of the pilot who had been identified at the start of the terrorist attacks—aircraft, hangar, storage, flight plans, anything at all.

Finding details about the Hughes helicopter could also be a possibility, but as a "black hole" had covered the airport, there were at least eighteen months of data missing, so Interpol considered that a long shot.

She headed to the private section of the airport on the far side, where long hangars were surrounded by stained concrete ramps, testimony to years of leaking fuel and oil. The harsh overhead floodlights were at half-power, casting a blueish tinge around the edges of the shadows created by the stubby hangars. She parked her bike against the fence, found a small access gate, fiddled with the lock, sprung it open, then entered the silent, looming row of tall water towers and support infrastructure. She peered into each window, quickly assessing what was stored where, and in less than twenty minutes, had cataloged a shortlist of parked aircraft either being serviced or just stored.

She had the tail numbers of the aircraft and had recorded the names of the service businesses that had been displayed on equipment inside or outside the hangars. She sat on her haunches in the deep shadow of a small hut for a minute, considering her options. She sensed she had nothing of any real value and came to the conclusion she would have to take a different approach to the problem.

She retraced her steps, regained her bike, and headed back to the hostel. When she shucked off her outerwear and made a cup of miserable instant coffee from the meager supplies the hostel provided, she called the FBI agents.

"Hi! Sally here. I need your help. I need a set of creds and a badge, FBI will do, but National Transportation Safety Board would be better. Can you arrange them for me, please? And I'll check in at your hotel first thing in the morning. I'll keep it clear, but will be booked in under Sandra Thomas. Thanks." And she hung up, pulled a sleep shirt over her head, and climbed into bed, with her Beretta under her pillow and her service weapon under the covers pointed at the door.

Just after the sun had fleetingly made an infrequent pale appearance between holes in the overcast, one Sandra Thomas arrived at the hotel, where the reservation she had made the night before was quickly serviced by the concierge and shown to her room. She called the agents.

"Good morning. Whoever is not monitoring the transmissions and will be hunting up the storage hangar, come down and have breakfast with me, please. It's time to go a little public." And she hung up, gunned up, smoothed the creases in her well-cut suit, and brushed imaginary lint off her sleeves. The suit was expensive, made from a material that could be balled up in a rucksack and then hung in a steaming shower to regain its shape and luster, something she found very useful doing as much undercover work as she did. It was a lonely life but rewarding. She hit the breakfast lounge, selected a seat with its back to the wall, walked over, and, smiling at the service staff, sat herself down.

"Morning, ma'am, would y'all like coffee?" The Midwestern accent was pronounced, with a little musical tone to it.

"Thank you." A tall, black-suited, good-looking woman stood in the doorway, scanned the room, and then floated over to where Sandra was seated. Floated was the only way she could describe the way the woman moved, reminiscent of a catwalk model.

"We tossed a coin, and I lost. Gerry Norden," she said, reaching out a hand to shake. Sandra took the hand, felt the callouses, and made it clear the agent was welcome.

"Gerry, you have creds?" she asked, her left hand relaxed under the table, her Beretta resting on her thigh. Gerry reached into her suit pocket and pulled out the standard double-sided FBI identification wallet, flipped it open, watched Sandra's eyes, saw recognition and acceptance, and snapped it shut.

"You can put the gun away now. I'm not going to kill you for blowing my cover," Gerry said laughingly. "We know what you were going to do, and for the life of us couldn't see how it would work. What do you have in mind now?" She signaled to the waitstaff, waited until her coffee cup was filled, then looked up over the rim of the cup at the Interpol agent.

"There's no way I can find my target looking through windows, so I thought I'd try the direct approach. I know one of you is sched-uled to go to the airport today, looking for the storage hangar for the wall material, so I figured if I got a lift with you, it would help estab-lish my authority. How goes it with a set of creds for me?"

"We can make you a set of FBI creds back in our room. You can use Barry's shield for the time being. We can't get NTSB ID for you here in Helena; it would have to come from Seattle, and that's time and distance. Can you work with FBI creds?"

"Yes, thanks. I kind of accepted it would have to be the FBI, so we'll work with that. Once you find the hangar, perhaps you could come back and add weight to whatever I'm doing and wherever I'm doing it?"

"And what exactly will you be doing?" Gerry asked, just a little officially; she had years on the Interpol agent, who looked like a teenager playing at cops and robbers. But she had been briefed by Anna on Sandra's skills and training and was warmed by her confidence and manner.

"Going to check the refueling services all around the airport, as far back as I can, then the tower for ATC movements, and then the flight schools. Between them, someone will have seen something, noticed something, or thought something was out of place or a little strange. That's all it will take." Gerry looked at the agent with new respect; those were all good avenues that no one had yet thought of.

Maybe they would get a thread to tug, and wouldn't that be fun!

Chapter 26

After a good night's sleep in a proper bed, I was up and jonesing for coffee before the sun had even managed to show itself, the air crisp and cold. Anna, Malcolm, and Pete were in adjoining rooms, all booked thanks to the FBI director, who had personally met us at the airport. There hadn't been a lot of chatter on the way in other than to introduce ourselves. With the Boss and Amira due around 0800, I wondered how and when to bring in the three FBI agents who had led the investigation into the plant at Point Roberts. The director had made it clear that the lead agent, Fay Remer, in his opinion, was the agent to talk to, and in a slightly embarrassed manner, had confessed that she "might well be a sensitive," as she had reported details that the other agents had missed. I rolled all this around in my mind as I showered slowly, enjoying the full force of the overhead rainmaker with the heat turned up high.

Our accommodation back in Venice had been nice and comfortable but at the bottom of the luxury scale, as they were mostly wherever we went on a mission. I was being spoiled, and I intended to soak it in for as long as I could. My doorbell rang, so I slipped on the hotel-provided dressing gown, which felt as light as a feather and took the coffee service from the concierge. Under the silver dome, a half dozen triangular slices of toast rested, and I smiled. Pete comes to the rescue again. He was taking the Boss's instructions to heart.

I fired up the minicomputer, eating with one hand and keying with the other, and in minutes I had the daily summary from Lyon, our HQ. Even though they had no reliable way of getting data out other than using ham radios and fax machines, they still posted the summaries on an internal server they had got up and running, which the monks had kindly tapped into for us. We could send and receive secure messages if we chose to. But the Boss and I still thought that we had been penetrated by the terrorists, so we received only leaving any inbound messaging to other means.

The worldwide death toll had crossed the forty-four million mark, making the terrorist attacks the second-biggest loss of life after World War Two. It was estimated another fifty to sixty million people were displaced, and the migration between countries was listed as officially out of control. And the perpetrators of this massive crime against humanity were still at large, and that one statement made my blood run cold. I was supposed to be solving that, and rolling around on a luxurious bed and eating toast and jam in a five-star hotel was not an appropriate response. I stripped off the gown and dressed for the day, choosing my Amani suit and a pair of low-heeled boots. Did minimum makeup, dried my hair, and hated the bags under my eyes that seemed to sink into dark shadows. I wouldn't win any beauty pageant and resigned to what was rather than what might be, I sent a message to Anna, Pete, and Malcolm to meet me downstairs in the breakfast bar in thirty. I wanted time to organize my thoughts, look over the photos again, reread my case notes, and, most of all read the FBI agents' report on the plant visit again.

The director had been right—Senior Special Agent Remer had documented twice the detail in her reports compared to the other agents, little things like how the conveyor ran through all the buildings, how high it was mounted, and the differing depths of the buildings—building three estimated at sixty meters below ground but building six only forty. There was also a direct contrast in her report, as the entire data on the visit to the storage area was condensed and truncated into just six lines.

I wondered what that was about.

Section Five of Interpol had been created specifically to give our agents the right to carry arms, cross international borders carrying those arms, and make arrests under the jurisdiction of any country involved in a case. It had quickly evolved into a paramilitary force due to the nature of the tasks we were given—shut down people traffickers, hunt down drug smugglers, track down any crimes against children and remove the perpetrators from the game board. And having come to Interpol from the NCIS, carrying weapons was second nature to me, but as I strapped on my service weapon and fed my credentials into an inside pocket, I wondered what Pete would be dressed in, given that I had only seen him in various colors of camos and military jackets since the first day we had met. And I had never seen him out of his prized parachute boots, so scarred they hinted at tall tales and wonderful stories every time I saw them.

So the man dressed in an immaculate suit, polished shoes so bright I could see my face reflected in them, knotted tie perfectly formed in the apex of a crisp white shirt with a starched collar, and the fact that Pete's unmistakable scarred face sat on top of all this maleness was the only thing that stopped me from gasping like a girl!

"What have you done with Pete?" I asked, pushing him in the chest. It was a genuine shock, and I shook my head in wonder. Before I could fully recover, Malcolm walked up, as neat as a pin, grey tailored trousers, same shiny shoes as Pete, but this time a royal blue shirt, red-and-blue club tie, and a blazer any ship's captain would be proud to wear. Where in the hell had they got all these fine clothes? Anna lightened the mood, stepping up and taking both Pete and Malcolm by the arms, and, looking over her shoulder, smiled at me.

"Coming to breakfast?" she asked, walking the boys off as if she owned them. I shook my head again, and I wondered who had organized the wardrobe. My minicomputer buzzed in my pocket, so I stopped where I was in the corridor and saw the Boss's tired face swim into focus.

"We're on the ground. There's an FBI vehicle waiting, which I assume is ours.

We both need a shower and a change of clothes."

"Well, don't worry about the clothes. I'm sure that you will find what you need in your rooms. We're going down now, but I won't start the briefing until you get here. Take your time. I need you at full speed." The look he gave me was reminiscent of one you might give a dog when it pooed on the grass, so I shut the little computer and continued on down to the breakfast bar.

We settled in, Anna and Malcolm working their minis, Pete thumbing through the photos and the reports from Point Roberts. It seemed like ten minutes, but it was an hour later when the Boss and Amira walked in and joined us. The Boss was wearing a silky blue suit, looked fabulous except for his well-worn face and scarred hands, and Amira looked like a young girl on a Sunday outing, wearing a light grey pantsuit highlighted by a light pink shirt and multicolored scarf. The Boss downed his first cup of coffee with a purpose, paused only long enough to pour himself a second, took a breath, looked around the table at everyone, and smiled.

"Well, now, not the first thing I would have expected to see in downtown Seattle, but much more comforting. Good to see you all in one piece. Jessica, how are the guys who were wounded in the shootout?" He didn't surprise me; what made him the leader he was always shone through under pressure, and his care for his people was the shiniest light in his toolbox.

"Recovering, both due back with their teams later in the week. I sent them all back to Washington on the train when we headed to Helena." He just nodded and wrapped his hands around his coffee cup, drank deeply, then said something that warmed my heart.

"Where is Indigo and his blessed espresso machine when you need him most?" he said, earning a genuine laugh from everyone around the table. He looked calm, collected, and a little worn around the edges, but then we had been going at this for over a month, non-stop, crossing time zones like they were Lego blocks scattered on the floor, with minimal sleep and, apart from Indigo's magnificent espresso machine, very few home comforts. I wondered how "call me Sally" was faring in the wilds of Montana, then realized if I really wanted an update, all I had to was call her. I didn't get the chance. The director walked in, dressed in a somber FBI neutral black, white shirt, and black tie, and following him was a tallish, exceptionally beautiful woman of mixed-race heritage, coffee-colored skin tucked into a blueish/green pants suit, the cut of which was a little mannish.

"Good morning, all. I took the liberty of picking up the colonel and his passenger, dropped them off here to freshen up, then collected my agent just minutes ago. Please finish your breakfasts; you may not get the chance to eat again today, deciding on your agenda." We took him at his word, and the rich ham, bacon, eggs, and grits whose smell had been tempting us with their enticing smells since they had magically appeared from the kitchen disappeared with a vengeance, and I remembered an old adage I had picked up in the NCIS academy, "never get between a trainee and their food!" and smiled to myself. We were a motley lot, that was for sure, but dressed as if we were in a boardroom somewhere was not out of the question. I looked at the director.

"Sir, thank you for organizing the clothes, food, and collecting the Boss. I don't know what you have been briefed on, for that matter, I don't know what your agent has been briefed on. Perhaps we could start there, please?" Across the table, now resembling a minor battleground, the Boss gave the slightest of nods; we were on the same wavelength, good to know. The director of the Seattle office of the FBI looked at me with a penetrating glare that would put frost on a burning fire.

"Captain, not nearly enough at this point. I don't understand the import of what my agents brought back, and I can only imagine why my city is suddenly full of Interpol agents; however, Agent Bernstein has briefed me overnight about your search through Montana for the terrorists, so I can assume that you think they are somewhere here and that the plant in Point Roberts is connected." His tone said it all; he had held his peace until we were all assembled and had picked his time to perfection. "And one other thing. I was under the impression that Interpol agents did not carry weapons and had no power of arrest outside of local laws and statutes. But I can see clearly that at least two of you are armed and suspect that were I to strip search you, every one of you would be armed to the teeth." The Boss raised his eyebrows, then looked back down at his coffee cup, making it very clear whom he expected to handle the director.

"Sir, my team, most of whom are represented here, along with Senior Special Agent Bernstein, have been trying to locate these terrorists from day two, when Interpol was engaged first by the Italian government, then by the Israelis, and then by your own. We have pursued them halfway across the world but, due to their technological superiority, have had very little success tracking them down. Your agents have brought us our first real lead in a month, and that is why my colonel and my team are here." I paused, letting him absorb that and work through the ramifications for his office.

"As to the weapons the Colonel, Master Chief Pete, and I carry. They are sanctioned under Article Thirty-Four of the Interpol charter, ratified by the United Nations, specifically relating to the rules and regulations as they apply to Section Five of Interpol, of which we are sworn members. The colonel is the head of Section Five, and I am his deputy." He sat still for a brief period, then wriggled in his seat as if the seat of his chair was attacking him.

"But you announced, and I have had it confirmed by official channels, that you took the terrorist leader out in a firefight in Arabia, with the help of the Israelis, and then captured the master planner and money man and have him under lock and key. Why would you think the terrorists are anywhere near Seattle?" And then it hit me: Anna had not shared the fact that we were hunting down the refugee women. I thought hard for a full minute, disguising my puzzlement by drinking from my coffee cup. The head of the FBI, Roger Winslow, knew every detail as did Anna of the attacks, the women, and the interrogation of Mohammad bin Azaria, yet neither of them had briefed the director of the Seattle office. I wondered why and who else did not know this critical piece of information. I was saved from my mulling by Anna.

"Sir, we have been tracking various cells of the terrorists across nine continents, and as you would be aware, the cell that took out the Alaskan pipeline and the fracking sites across northern America was successfully targeted by the Canadians, who recovered samples of the nanomachines that we believe were used in those attacks. When Malcolm Tannery showed the photos to myself and Captain Riley, we both noticed a process in the plant that may be the source of the nanomachines. That's why we are now all in Seattle. May I ask SSA Remer a question?" Anna had taken everyone at the table by surprise, and in a way, I admired her. She was super smart, had worked tirelessly with us to try and find the women, had literally ducked a bullet (or two!) back at the Ranger Hut and was no slacker at holding her own in a room full of ballsy men. The director looked a little uncomfortable, but to his credit, his face lost the angry look he had focused on me, and the tension around the table dissipated a little. He waved Anna on.

"Fay, if I may call you that, we are especially interested in what you saw in building six." The young agent sat straight in her seat, hands folded politely in her lap. Her director had surprised her with the attack on the Interpol agent, but she understood his frustration. Being out of the information loop was a pure bitch, and she detested it as much as the next agent. And this specific case reeked of secrets within secrets and withheld data. Her team had been thinly briefed before setting off to Point Roberts, had to improvise onsite, spend a weekend cooling their heels, then, when they executed their warrant, didn't really understand what they had found. The analysts in the office had poured over the data, pulled every record they could find going back four years, and the conclusion was that not only was the site legitimate but that it may well have the solution to the lack of power and fuel that was choking the country from coast to coast.

"Captain, building six is where they prepare an exotic material they use in the construction of both their solar panels and their batteries. The material has been identified by our technical staff as some form of nanite, and the few experts we contacted yesterday all said they couldn't comment further without a sample. And to be frank, the COO, Ms. Farid Tremblay, was very firm that it forms a part of their intellectual property, and they will not release any details to us. They sought opinions from their general counsels over the weekend and supported the COO in her position."

"You also saw their storage area, didn't you?" I asked, keeping her edited report on this uppermost in my mind. She looked at me, eyes wide, highlighted by a little liner and mascara, all innocence, but didn't fool me for a second. Smart, smart woman, and for a fleeting moment, I wondered how tough she might be.

"Yes, Captain, I did. It's in my report."

"No, it isn't. You edited that report. Why?" She looked at me again, the barest hint of a grin forming before she could answer my challenge. But she still held my eyes, not blinking or looking away.

"I didn't think it all that important; once I established what was in the boxes and approximately how many, it seemed to be of lesser importance than how the factory worked and what they actually made there." She sat quite still as if she was frozen at the moment. I admired her strength. To be so forthright and positive when she was undoubt-edly telling a barefaced lie in front of her director—and Anna, for that matter—took a huge leap of faith and a heap of courage. I decided to let it go for now. I would corner her later at some other time when it was just the two of us.

"I think it would be good if you briefed us, Jessica," the Boss said, sensing we were on the point of forcing some invisible issue, which he obviously didn't want to do now with the director of the FBI Seattle office present. The use of my first name tipped me off. He was on my wavelength as far as Fay was concerned, so I sat back and collected my thoughts. Did I mention my unrequited love for this bear of a man who I had once shot six times in the chest? We read each other's minds, a tactical advantage in any situation. And he enabled me to do my best, which was a rare experience with my former bosses in the navy, who all seemed to hover and probe and poke at you when under pressure. I turned my attention to the table but addressed the director pointedly.

"Sir, we have brought one of the world's experts on nanomate-rials science with us, that is Amira Abramowitz, whom you brought here with the colonel from the airport. Miss Abramowitz is an Israeli nanomaterials scientist who helped us identify the material used in the attacks on the oil, gas, and coal fields. We would like to take her, with your agent, back to the plant to see if we can dig deeper into the nanomaterials they are using. We think it may be possible that this plant, or one just like it, made the nanomachines that have been used to attack us.

"Additionally, if they did not manufacturer those bugs, we may be able to get them to help us work on a solution to counteract the damage the bugs have done." Yes, I shaded the truth, but not by much, but I couldn't reveal our real interest in the plant until their own gov-ernment came clean. The president had released a statement clearly identifying the mercenary terrorists commanded by Shetani as the cause of the world's troubles, so who was I to dispel that statement? The Boss leaned across the table slightly, taking command physically, something he was an expert at.

"Director, as you know from your briefing by your senior agent, materials being built at that plant have appeared in the town of

Helena, Montana, in very large quantities. Your agents, even now, are establishing how they got there and, most importantly, when they got there. We also have an Interpol asset in Helena working with them, as you know. This is the first tangible lead to the terrorists we have uncovered since the photo of the pilot of the aircraft that bombed West Point was circulated. She has not been found and may never be.

"These attacks on us have been with vastly superior, technologically sophisticated weapons, specific to the target, and, with very few exceptions, bloodless. You could argue that the outcome of the attacks has not been so much so, but that is a societal issue of unintended consequences. We believe these attacks were mounted to show the world what living like a refugee is really like on a massive scale. And if you have read or heard the story running around the country at the moment, Mohammad bin Azaria is direct and specific—his children have been mistreated for decades—the world chooses to turn a blind eye, and now we all have no option but to experience firsthand the harsh and terrible conditions the children suffer every day of their short lives and do something about it.

"This was his mission, and he executed it to perfection, without remorse, with a plan that spanned at least twenty-five years. Unfortunately, the mercenary terrorists he chose to implement his plan got out of control, as they often do, and did more damage than was probably intended, but we have no way of knowing that. I'm referencing the regime change in Arabia as an example." The director sat back, his face frozen in a very hard look, one I suspected he usually reserved for some poor criminal he was about to grill.

"Colonel, I get all that, but if you actually think that the world will now suddenly sit up and take notice of the refugee problem, let alone do anything about it, you are sadly mistaken. And is your only link to Point Roberts the panels they make and the fact that they have turned up in Helena?" My turn again, I sensed it as the Boss sat back, removing his imposing presence from the table. It was amazing how well he controlled a room just with his body language.

"Sir, if the plant in Point Roberts made those panels, when? How were they shipped? Why Helena, out of all the towns in the Midwest? How did the people behind this know they would be needed in such large quantities? In fact, one of the questions we want to be answered is why was Helena set up for a one hundred thousand house expansion some four years ago, all the way down to drainage, sewerage, waste disposal, and power supply? There is a link to the terrorists here, of that we are sure, and with your help and that of your office, we will find it." I sat back and let that sink in, noticing that Fay had been studying me intently throughout my speech, with an intensity I found encouraging. Maybe she had seen or sensed something that fed into our suspicions, and what I had just said jogged her memory. I really needed to get her alone to push the point. The director had been nodding during the last part of my diatribe, so at least we were getting through to him, or he was getting bored with the entire exercise.

"Senior Special Agent Bernstein is attached to your unit on temporary duty?" he asked, looking at Anna. She nodded. "So, if I were to attach Agent Remer TDY on the same conditions, would that be of benefit?" Fay's eyes lit up. I promise you, the intensity would have illuminated the room had it not been morning. "I'll provide office space for your team, Colonel, and anything else you need. I ask you to keep me informed of your plans as a courtesy, please." And he stood up, a tall man in a difficult position, but one who had cast his vote and was waiting to see the outcome. The Boss stood up opposite him and reached across the table to shake his hand. They sealed the deal, the director left, and the Boss, true to form, sat down and filled his coffee cup again.

"Jessica, why don't you, Fay, Amira, and Anna talk a walk? The boys and I'll have a chat, and we'll find you when we need to."

"You don't want me with Jessica?" Pete asked, automatically standing and mirroring my movements. The Boss's instructions back in Venice had been specific, "don't let her out of your sight," and he took his orders literally. The Boss looked at me, Anna, then at Fay, and shook his head.

"Between the three of them, they have enough badges and guns to stage a robbery; we'll let them be alone for a while." Pete sat down, helped himself to a glass of juice, and looked at me out of the corner of his eye.

"Take care, now, Captain. I won't be there to pull your shaggy arse out of the fire," he said in a fake Scottish accent. We all shared the joke, me most of all, because I had enjoyed the company of this talented soldier, scarred face and all. Not to mention the fact that his quick action of pushing me to the ground and covering my body with his had saved me from getting shot by the militia. I led Anna and Fay over to a comfortable seating arrangement in a small amphitheater, called for coffee, then sat with my back to the wall again, soon joined by Anna, with Amira taking a seat off to one side, leaving Fay to take the seat directly in front of us. She looked back over her shoulder, judged where she would be the least exposed to anyone wanting to commit suicide by attacking us, and turned her chair slightly side-on to the doorway. Good situational awareness, I thought to myself. Whoever had trained her had trained her well.

"Fay, good to have to aboard. I know you have questions, but we do too, and I'd like to get ours out of the way first." I raised my eyebrow, and she nodded, a little guardedly, I thought. Before I could speak, Anna leaned across the small table that our coffee service sat on and grabbed one of Fay's somewhat delicate-looking hands.

"Fay, Jessica here is the best person I have ever worked with. You can trust her implicitly. I do, and with my life on more than one occasion. If you want to work with us, and both Jessica and I can see that you do, then we need the truth, all of it, and your best thinking." Anna held Fay's hand for a beat longer, then released it. Before I could add anything, Fay flicked her hair out of her eyes, rolled her shoulders, making little ripples and sparkles run up and down her suit, and leaned forward towards us. When she moved, it was with an internalized power and purpose that impressed me.

"The plant is a gigantic factory, super high-tech, only forty employees, all engineers, scientists, and a sprinkling of mathematicians, only one person I would class a 'blue collar,' and he spent his time sitting in a little control box supervising the robots in the loading area. And yes," she said, looking directly at me, "I did leave things out about that area, things that happened there, and things I saw there that needed thinking about, and I wasn't prepared to share until I had worked some of it out. Now, in case you're wondering, I was originally sent to the plant with two other agents, RuPaul and Vernon, both much older than me and more experienced, but neither particularly technically literate. The briefing we received was a joke, and the warrant we executed was the mildest investigative warrant I have ever seen."

"You were set up?" I asked.

"No, I don't believe so. I just don't think anyone in the Seattle office took the whole thing seriously. What could a modern factory up against the Canadian border have to do with sweaty mercenary terrorists roaming around the countryside creating havoc? I'm fairly sure that was the mindset."

"Then how did you get invited to the party?" Anna asked, checking something on her minicomputer.

"I was their team leader. Only one of us has family, so a weekend away would be no real inconvenience." I thought about that for a minute, then reflected on something the Boss had passed onto me about Fay being "sensitive," according to her director. So maybe her choice wasn't as random as it looked. I hoped so because that implied the director was someone we could trust if the s-h-one-t hit the fan, and I was sure it would somewhere, sometime. My musings were rudely interrupted by Anna's melodic voice.

"Sir, I'd like your permission to read in SSA Remer of the Seattle office. She conducted the inspection of the plant in Point Roberts and will need to know what we are really looking for the next time we visit." Looking over Anna's shoulder, I could see Roger Winslow's face on the tiny screen and realized what Anna was doing. "Granted, but keep it out of the office. Understood?" Anna nodded and closed her minicomputer, looking at me as if to say, "what next?" So I answered her silent call. "Fay, what I am about to tell you stays with you; you are not to communicate anything you hear from this point on with your director or anyone in your office. To do so will be a felony punishable by the severest incarceration you can imagine, and this is not an idle threat. Can you agree to this requirement?" The young agent looked at Anna, reminding herself no doubt that there here was a very senior special agent of the FBI, based in Washington, right alongside the director of the FBI, whose voice she had clearly identified on the call.

There was something quite amazing going on here, and she intuitively wanted to be part of it, no matter the consequences. When she had joined the FBI right out of college, she had been bright-eyed and bushy-tailed, as the saying goes. A few years in, several ball-busting cases and three promotions later, the shine had worn off, but not the enthusiasm to make a difference. She had seen up close and personal what a difference good policing could make in a community. Here was her chance, she sensed, more from what had not yet been said, but she trusted her instincts.

"I've just overheard the director of the FBI instruct his senior special agent to inform me, but no one else in the Seattle office. It couldn't be much clearer than that. Yes, I agree. Right up until the time I sense that what is going on is detrimental to the welfare of the agency or the people I stand for. Can you agree to that?" she asked, with just a touch of belligerence. Anna reached out again and took her hand. "Yes, we can agree to that, but you might need to get used to representing a larger slice of the people you stand for because you are now part of a truly international effort to rebalance the world and bring the most successful group of terrorists we have ever hunted to heel, hopefully before the world we all love comes crashing down around our ears." That sobered Fay up, the stakes so high as to be unimaginable. They both looked at me, sitting relaxed as if I didn't have a care in the world. I smiled, then told Fay the strangest story she had probably ever heard. She didn't move a muscle while I told her about the refugee girls, who turned into the smartest terrorists ever known, and the amazing things they had done. I deliberately left out Amira's involvement, simply reinforcing her role as a nano expert.

Fay let me finish, then dropped her bombshell on us, taking us so completely by surprise, for a moment I lost my voice.

"The COO told you what?" I exploded, almost shouting. It was my turn to feel Anna's hand on mine; she was as shocked as I was but was managing to handle the information more calmly.

Wow!

That was all I could think.

Another refugee woman, this one ran a plant that produced remote power supplies, and who knew what else. And Fay, the FBI agent sitting in front of me, the very one I had just shared the most sensitive information on the planet with, admitted to also being a refugee, with a similar background to that of the terrorists. Had I just made the biggest mistake of my life? I looked at her, not sensing any deceit or guile, and wondered how Amira was feeling now, meeting another of Mohammad bin Azaria's "children." I had to ask, I didn't want to, but she had left me no choice.

"How were you recruited, and where from?" And immediately recognized my mistake, recruitment hinted at being part of the terrorist organization, and I rushed to correct that implication. I held up my hand to stop her from answering. "Sorry, my abject apology. Let me reframe the questions again. How were you taken out of the camps, and where was your camp?" It sounded all wrong to my ears. No way to repair it than now, and to my surprise, Fay was actually laughing at my embarrassment.

"Please, Captain, after hearing what you have all endured these past weeks, I take no offense at your use of words." I smiled back and leaped in with both feet. "Call me Jessica when we are in private, and this is Anna and Amira; we only go formal when we think it's necessary." She smiled again, nodded, sat back, relaxed, and told her tale. It wasn't too dissimilar to Amira's. She told us how she had got her name, the way her adoption family struggled on their farm, the death of her adopted father, the funding that was provided for all the children in the family to go to college, setting up the trust funds for the children, the promise her family had made to the people who had put her up for adoption, the move to Bozeman when the farm became too much for the family to manage, her sister running a restaurant, and he brother taking off at eighteen, and her sister dying in childbirth. And of the FBI agent who had mentored her and eased her way into the academy. If you forgot that this person had started life parentless, in a refugee camp, with no future, you could say that she represented a very large slice of normal American families.

But you couldn't forget her roots. We couldn't forget her roots; it was germane to our pursuit of the women terrorists, all of whom had shared a similar life story, at least up to the time of their adoption.

And the most important part of her information was that she had been in a Syrian refugee camp, right near the border, and that she had been taken with eleven other girls all around the same age, and all chosen because they had exhibited intelligence beyond the average at an early age. Maybe our count of the number of girls taken from the camps was underestimated.

"And you say Farid Tremblay was in the camp with you?" I asked.

"No. I saw her once we had been taken to a staging point, a small building across the border where there were many other girls just like me. I recognized her eyes. They are quite distinctive, and the shape of her face. We slept on adjoining mattresses and talked a little to each other. We were both really shy and didn't know what was going to happen to us. She recognized me when she saw me on the security camera, although I don't know how." I thought I did, but I held my peace.

"Do you know the name of the people who pulled you out of the camp?" Anna asked, her tone much more sympathetic than mine. Fay nodded, her face creased in concentration.

"There was a woman; she worked for Red Crescent, she said her name was Marion, and a man, I think he was an imam; he wore a clerical collar, and his name was Mohammad ah Rasher, and he was also a medical doctor. The woman traveled with us all the way to America on a big cargo ship; we lived in containers but were quite well looked after. We each had a bed and books to read, and we were fed hot food twice a day and allowed out on the deck from time to time to play. I remember being awed by the sight of the ocean, the vastness of it, and its moods. I hadn't seen or heard of such things previously, and the image of that voyage is imprinted on my mind forever."

"How many of there were you?" Anna asked.

"I think about forty." Yes, we had badly underestimated the number of girls Mohammad bin Azaria had repatriated from the camps.

"Did you ever see those two people again?"

"No. We were bussed to a hostel somewhere on the coast, I think it was somewhere between Los Angles and San Francisco, and then we were driven individually to our new homes. As I was only six or seven at the time and had never seen cities or buildings like I saw on arrival, it was all a little overwhelming. Even when we arrived at the farm in Montana, it took a while for me to understand where I was. I didn't speak English, and I really didn't speak Arabic very well, which is why my family named me Fay after one of their grand-mothers. They couldn't pronounce my real name, and I couldn't really help them with it."

"Did you ever see any of the other girls other than the COO again?" I asked, trying to refocus the conversation. All this social stuff was interesting, but I was on the hunt for terrorists, and I wanted to remind all four of us that that had to be our priority. And in the back of my mind, I wondered how Amira was talking all this; she hadn't said a word since we had sat down. I glanced over at her, but she appeared to be relaxed and listening intently.

"Amira, do you have anything to add?" I asked, wanting to see what might eventuate. She shook her head, her long hair flying in little circles. She still looked like a teenager to me, but then I was approaching the middle thirties, so I was probably regarded as a grandma by these younger agents!

"No, thank you, Jessica. I found Fay's story very touching. What do you plan to do next?" I looked around the three women and, know-ing I had unimaginable mental horsepower at my disposal, threw the conversation over to solution mode.

"Fay, why don't you guide us in planning our next visit to Point Roberts?" I said, taking her by surprise from the look on her face. Then with a snap, she shifted into full FBI agent mode, leaned for-ward, and looked at me from under her eyebrows.

"Obviously, we need to find any link between Point Roberts and the terrorists. We also need to tie down the movements of both the power supplies and the panels sent to Helena. And you also want to get a definitive answer about the nanites. Does that cover it?"

"Not bad for a start. How do you recommend we do it? Hard, in-your-face approach, or soft and gentle, and try to seduce them."

"Up the guts and take no prisoners. Can Interpol issue warrants that can be served on American companies?"

"Yes, we can. We have been commissioned by the US govern-ment to investigate on its behalf. All or any activities we suspect may be linked to the terrorist attacks. What are you suggesting?"

"Can I assume that the colonel, the IT guy, and your bodyguard will accompany us?"

"The IT guy is one of the smartest white hat hackers on the planet and just happens to be on loan to us from the NSA. My body-guard, as you call him, is a master chief, has served in the SEAL teams, and is one of the smartest asymmetric warfare specialists in the world. So, yes, you can assume they will be with us."

"I can't take anyone from the office; do you anticipate a ground action? Or resistance to serving the warrant?" I looked at her, trying to see beyond the tactically relevant questions. I sensed there was a whole undercurrent of thinking going on here, and I needed to unearth it. I aimed for the heart but pointed at the head.

"Why did you go back to the plant and not tell your partners or your director?" I asked, watching her face for any tell. Surprise was her first reaction, followed by acceptance and then grudging respect. She pointed one manicured finger at me, tipped by pale pink nail polish. If she was going to survive with us, she would have to get rid of the glam; it could get her killed.

"You deduced that from the lack of detail in my report." A state-ment, not a question, and as it turned out, totally true. Sometimes even the smartest people forget that when you read something, you automatically form a pattern from the language—and if you are read-ing about the same thing but told from different points of view, then any discrepancies tend to show out like the proverbial dog thingies.

"Yes. What you told us, what you had in your report, and the reports of the other two agents tell their own stories. Did you have a private and unreported conversation at any other time with the COO?"

"Yes. In the warehouse. She asked me if I remembered my life in the refugee camp and the number of children that died every day. Then she said something I did write down, but I have not shared it." She pulled a little calf-leather notebook out of her pocket, opened to the pages that were split by a pretty blue ribbon bookmark, and read. "I quote, *In times to come, I believe it will be important to remember your roots and the death and destruction you survived due to the fact that you were pulled out of the camps and given a better life. Personally, I celebrate my survival every single day. I came from a camp, not unlike yours, and every day I prayed it would be my last. Now, every day, I pray I can do my best.* Then I asked her, point-blank if she was doing anything illegal, and I quote again, *Fay, I give you my word, nothing we do here is illegal, we have permits for everything, we are ecologically responsible, and the devices we are manufacturing are going to change the lives of millions of people up and down the coast in Canada and the US. Time will tell if we will be able to reach further, but we have a plan for that as well. As for closing us down, I sincerely hope not, but who knows what the government will do when they learn of our efforts.* And I believe her every word. That's why this did not make it into my report.

"From the get-go, I felt we were on a fool's mission. Our briefing was shallow, the warrant was sketchy and thin by any standards, and my overall impression was we were fulfilling some corporate request without any real intent. I still do. And now I know what's at stake; I can confidentially tell you no one in my chain of command has the slightest suspicion about what you are doing." I dropped my head, the better to let what she had said sink in. Someone in the FBI had requested the plant visit. I would need to track that down. And if the COO's words were true, then we might find ourselves on the edge of a razor blade where the wrong move could cause a lot of fatal damage. I need to talk this over with the Boss, Anna, and maybe Pete. Our approach was no longer obvious, and we would need a degree of caution we were not renowned for.

Section Five was Interpol's hammer, so touchy, feelie, "after you, ma'am" was not our strong suit. "Okay, thank you for that. What we need to do now is think about our options, so I need you to get a room here at the hotel, get your go-bag, and dress appropriately. Lose the female touches, don't go pure bitch but imagine yourself walking across Canada for a month, and you'll get the picture. Be back here in two hours, please." Our little conflab broke up, Fay left to reorientate herself, and as I stretched, I wondered how we could balance our approach so as to not spook the natives or give the FBI or any other government agency an excuse to move on the plant before we needed to.

We arrived at the breakfast table, where the Boss and Pete were in the throes of a furious argument. About baseball.

"Okay, boys, we need a catch-up. Interested?" The argument stopped as if I had cut it off with a razor blade. Malcolm pulled his head out of his minicomputer, and I saw him regain his focus on the real world. His eyes literally went from glazed over to sharp as a point in a blink, something I had not seen before. "Amira, why don't you bring us up to date, please?" I asked. We might not be warm and fuzzy, but we believed utterly in inclusion, and getting Amira's take on our meeting would give me an insight into her mental state.

She summarised the meeting, in a smooth and warm voice, with no emphasis on the refugees and their plight, but, to my surprise, added a comment about the pictures from the plant.

"The nanites they are using are a derivation of my original work. If you remember, back in Israel, I mentioned solar panels and batteries? Before we locked my work away again?" The Boss and I nodded, Malcolm had not been part of the conversation, and I didn't remember if Pete had been there or not.

"Yes, I do," I answered, wishing I had paid more attention back then, but I had other more important things on my mind.

"Well, the cinter bath you can see in building six is a standard for the mixing and propagation of nanites, but I have never seen one at that scale before."

"How so?" the Boss asked, reaching for yet another cup of coffee. If he didn't stop soon, he would vibrate from the caffeine!

"Well, to give you some idea of the scale, the bath we used to propagate the nanomachines we used in our experiment at the oil spill had to be viewed with an electron microscope." That stopped me in my tracks because not only had the scientists at the plant—or at the laboratory, they were using that we didn't know about yet—had taken something very, very small and blown it up as if it were feeding on steroids, they had turned it into a robotic production line. I wished I had the science to fully understand it, but for the moment, Amira was our resident expert, and I'd rely on her take.

"How would you have done that?" I asked her.

I genuinely wanted to know because, as an investigator, if you didn't understand everything you were being presented with, you missed the details that could wrap up the case. And we had been behind the women for over a month, make that a year, and the number of moving parts hadn't got any less. Anna's minicomputer buzzing like a trapped bee drew my attention to her, and she opened the lid and saw one of her agents on the screen, with "call me Sally" jammed into the side of the frame.

"Sandra, use your computer, link to 'team,'" I said. Her pretty head disappeared, and then she suddenly shared the same screen with the agent.

"Agent Norden, Agent Thomas, good morning. How can we help you?" While Anna was welcoming them, Malcolm, the Boss, and I all opened our minicomputers and joined the conversation, with Amira and Pete looking over our shoulders. It was not optimal by any means, but it was better than a shared landline.

"We've found your panels, can't really take credit for it. Our young spy here followed a truck that took us straight to it. It was a big electric Pantech, and we estimate they unloaded eight to ten thousand panels, but that is only an estimate looking through binocs from half a mile away. We got the registration of the vehicle, so you may be able to trace it from that data. Now Sandra has something for you."

"Hi, everyone, wish you were here! We've found a Boeing 737EX sitting in a hangar that hasn't been flown for four months, and according to the hangar records, it is owned and operated privately by a company called 'Vision30 Incorporated.' The pilot was described to me as 'young, sexy,' and she had two other women flying with her, one built like a bodybuilder, the other thin and like a model, although, to be honest, the tower guy's tongue was hanging out so far, I couldn't be sure. But I did get ID photos, thanks to the Covid-19 protocols, which required visual ID to enter and use the airport." My blood froze, the Boss's head shot up, and Pete broke into the biggest grin I had ever seen on his craggy face.

"Bingo! Their first real mistake. Never occurred to them that those records would be kept. Thank you, Jesus!" I shared Pete's joy, but my practical mind snapped back to possible intersections where this data might cross with other elements of the case. Amira, Fay, first cabs off the rank. But I already had my first cross because the photo of the pilot was unmistakably the same person who had taken the Hog and bombed West Point. The photo showed her a few years younger, a little thinner, but unmistakably her. I saw recognition in the eyes of both the Boss and Anna, confirming my instincts. I held my hand up to stop the chatter that had suddenly broken out around the table.

"Good work, in fact, excellent work. Okay, new orders. Take the photos into town, and try to establish where they work, if at all, where they live, and what they do. Start with the town records, keep a watch on the burst transmissions, but I would suggest you watch each other's backs because if you get too close, you might stir up a hornets' nest."

"If they are here, we'll find them, but I wouldn't count on it."

The snap of lids closing was the only sound around the table. The Boss was the first to speak, drawing everyone's attention to him like a candle draws moths. "Jessica, how do you want to handle it?" He looked at me like I had all the secrets of the universe, and not for the first time, I felt a little embarrassed. I didn't have all the answers. I didn't have all the questions. But he had just very subtly put me in control of our destiny, so I manned up, looked every member of my team in the eyes, and laughed.

"Bloody hell!" I said, "I know when I'm being set up!" The Boss smiled as well, then waved the back of his hand at me as if he were shooing away a pest.

"Well, we expect the best, even if we do have to work with defectives like Pete here and you." Laughter rang out again, effectively quelling any tension that had built up from the call from Helena.

"The girls and I were just on our way to give you options on how to handle the plant. Now that we have three positive IDs, I'd like to pursue them as far as we can before we go any further. And I want Fay included in the conversation."

"I agree, so we wait." The Boss stood up, stretched like a giant cat, looked around the room, and, seeing no one who could give him more coffee, shrugged his shoulders.

"Let's meet back here in an hour; do me a favor and consider all our options, please. I'll want input from everyone."

Black Hole Theory

The breakthrough came after hours and hours of digital mining, hacking, and inventive language. Only the presence of Stefarino and the other monks had kept the curses muttered and not shouted, but Indigo had seen the little smiles on the faces of the brothers, often enough to know they had perhaps heard some of the more inventive curses. He had done his best, supplying coffee and sandwiches on a frequent basis, calling for short breaks, and even offering a massage or two to the geeks.

Then Shami, the Israeli Colonel who had started life as a white-hat hacker, had yelled across the airwaves and thrown his hands in the air. In seconds, the citadel inside one of the oldest churches in Venice had rung with the shouts of the other geeks, headed by Luigi, who sat back in his orthopedic chair, exhausted.

"Dial up Amira. We have to share this with her." Indigo looked at Luigi, nodded, moved to the console, and dialed into Amira's mini-computer. She answered, but her background was strobing and bobbing around, indicating she was on the move somewhere.

"Amira, good to see you," Luigi said, straightening up in his seat. "Guess what we found?" She looked intense, trying to figure out what they had done.

"The black hole?" she asked finally.

"Yes. We cracked it. Or rather, Shami did, with a little help from us. Want to know how it works?"

"Hold on a minute." Her screen continued to bounce all over the place, then finally settled again, this time two faces centered in it. "Okay, I've got Anna with me, shoot!" Luigi, in faraway Israel, thought of the constant bombardment his area was under and grimaced at Amira's casual use of language. He did as he had learned to do since childhood, he ignored it.

"The monks are to thank, Stefarino in particular. They ran a series of algorithms for us that speeded up the search a thousand times. The terrorists' had the satellites running on loops over a year-long recorded, and we found the data that had been uploaded but screened by the loops. They also used disruptors on the ground, probably vehicle-based, to distort the images. We can't unscramble those, but we can track them. We ran a test on your target area at Helena, and we can now show you every movement in and out for the last three years, provided the satellite provider has saved it and we can access it. No guarantee of that. What do you think?"

"Fantastic, well done. I have a suggestion. Can you take a look at Point Roberts, up against the border with Canada, and see if there is a black hole over there? And if I give you a New Zealand address, can you have a look there as well?" Anna asked before Amira could react.

"Yes, we can. Back to you soonest."

"By the way, we've identified the pilot and at least two others," Anna added.

"You have? Fantastic! Send us the pics. Please," Luigi said.

"On the way."

Amira turned to Anna, flicking her hair out of her eyes. She was glowing at the news. At last, they had undone some of the damage the terrorists caused, even if it might be a little late.

"We have to let Jessica and the Colonel know," she said, turning to stand at the rail that ran along with the outside balcony of her room. "Do you have any idea how we should tackle the plant?" Anna thought she looked incredibly young standing in the wan light from the atrium, and worried about how she was handling everything, having been pulled out of the laboratory in Israel just hours before, flown across the Atlantic ocean at supersonic speeds, then dumped unceremoniously in Seattle. Just the change in humidity and temperature would be having its effect, not to mention the time shift and inevitable jet lag.

"Amira, we have bigger issues now than the plant. We're going to have to pursue the women under the radar. The President has released the summary that claims Shetani and his mercenaries were the perpetrators of all the attacks. We can't now just pop up and say, 'hey, look who we found'." Amira thought about it for a moment, then her eyes clouded over.

"I can see that, but how do you keep something this big a secret?" Anna smiled, grabbed the younger woman by the shoulder, and walked her to her room. "The FBI is really good at finding out about secrets, and that makes us very good at keeping them. Let's rest up and think our approach through, as the Colonel has requested."

Back in Venice and Israel, the geeks looked at the photos of the women as they evolved on the big screens and were immediately hit by their sheer beauty, and not for the first time, wondered how such smart people could wage war on their own world.

Chapter 27

"Roger, how did the trip to Point Roberts come about?" I asked, lying on my bed, shoes off, silky robe replacing my suit, and my hair still wet from my shower. I was having trouble washing the Montana dust out of my system and the disappointment with not finding anything useful for days. But now we had IDs on three women, and the refugee story was starting to make more sense. Multilayered, to be sure, but a consistent line of activity moving through it. We'd need to put some thinking time into all those layers, but that was something Interpol was very good at. I also thought I needed to revisit Mohammad bin Azaria and question him about his 'girls'. But this time, I would take Interpol's smartest forensic psychologist, maybe not in the room with me, but certainly within touching distance, albeit if not behind a window.

"Frank asked us to investigate a bunch of countries, all of whom had received very large sums from the Arabian Sovereign Wealth Fund. Six billion euros, to be precise, all deposited legally some three to five years ago. Northwestern USA, Canada, Greenland, Chile, Portugal, Ireland, Denmark, Norway, Finland, Estonia, Sri Lanka, Solomon Islands, New Zealand, Japan, and Iceland. No trace of Mohammad bin Azaria having his fingers in those pies. All the transfers were approved by the various governments and treasuries. All were open, and above board, so we picked places where we thought we would be mostly invisible, like New Zealand and Point Roberts, and sent in teams. New Zealand only managed a flyover, those are the overheads we sent you, and when we learned that Point Roberts had a company actively using the funds, around one point three billion dollars to date, we sent the team in. You have met."

"So you had no idea what you might be getting into other than they were using funds from the Sovereign Wealth Fund?"

"No. Has it become an issue?" I thought about the local director. I still felt he could be an asset, so I let my disappointment ride, it was easy to second guess, and no one could have predicted what we would find in Point Roberts. The New Zealand aspect was interesting, and I wondered what it might be manufacturing, so they had two factories up and running, and the timing could not be coincidental.

"All good. But I might need your weight here in Seattle. I'll let you know. Are you doing anything more in New Zealand?"

"No. Waiting for you Interpol genius's to tell us what we should be doing and how we should be doing it!" he said, with just a trace of sarcasm in his voice. I let that ride as well.

"Thanks, Frank, appreciated." And I terminated the call. A cranky head of the FBI I didn't need just now. But it was obvious that the FBI had left us out of the loop as far as the deposit sites from the Sovereign Wealth Fund were concerned, and now they were feeling a little guilty about it. And if that was the biggest mistake anyone made, finding the terrorists would be easy! But I started to wonder, how would we go about finding the women who had worked in Libya and Turkey? I wondered where the nearest deposit had been made to their headquarters in Libya and if 'Helen' was still involved.

But there was a common element to all the refugee stories, and that was the Red Crescent, the Muslim version of the International Red Cross. They had been involved in every refugee extraction so far, so maybe they had records of all the girls they had helped. I knew their headquarters were in Geneva, and I knew Pete had been accompanied by a senior member of the organization when he had tried to establish who had been taken out of the camps but to be truthful, we had never really concentrated on them, and now maybe we should. I thought about it, worried myself into a muddle, and couldn't see a clear-cut path to a solution that wouldn't get us noticed by the wrong people. The refugee ranks had swelled significantly since the worldwide attacks, as had the cross-border migration, so I imagined they would have their hands full at the moment.

Then I had an inspiration.

"Boss," I said into my little computer, which I was starting to think of as my pet and my best friend. "You have an upline at the very top of the pile?" I asked, knowing he did because we had shared a one-sided conversation with his Boss two weeks ago.

"Yes, so what?" Was every male in my life going to be grumpy today?

"Can you ask him to contact his counterpart in the International Red Cross— Red Crescent—and see if they have any records of the girls coming out of the refugee camps?" His face gave nothing away, but I could see his thinking going on behind his crystal-clear blue eyes. I rolled my shoulders; I would really have to get over my unrequited love for this man. It was unhealthy!

"Yes, I can do that. Why didn't we think of this before?" And he disconnected, probably kicking himself for not thinking of it earlier. It was easy to see in retrospect—we had been tightly focused on finding the terrorists, not the wider activity of taking the girls out of the camps, except for the possibility of identifying the earlier removed girls. Classic tunnel vision.

Now, what next? I tapped my teeth with my fingertip, another bad habit I had started up again. Next thing you know, I'd be sucking my thumb! A not-so-subtle knock on my door caught my attention, and checking to see I was not showing anything but the regulation amount of skin, I opened the door to the Boss.

"I was just thinking about you." He looked at me critically, from top to toe, as if he were inspecting troops at a passing-out parade.

"Yes, I can see you were." He pushed past me into my room and settled on the small chair at my desk.

"We need to think a little more about these refugee women," he said in his best parade ground voice. I shut the door and sat on a corner of the bed.

"Why?"

"The general just told me that Red Crescent has been taking girls out of the camps since 2002; in the first seven years, they successfully moved forty-one girls into homes all around the world; there was a hiatus for three years; then they took on average thirty girls a year until three years ago when there was another hiatus; then just six months ago, they were asked to find one thousand girls to be shipped to the United States next month. I'm told that they are on the way." I sat, shocked at the number of refugee girls that had been set up for adoption. It was far greater than we had estimated, and the obvious questions came to mind.

"Who paid for all of this? Amira told us her adoptive parents were given a lot of money to support her all the way through college and that they still get some two thousand dollars or so a month." He nodded, his tired eyes looking like hollows in his face.

"We know Mohammad bin Azaria organized the first tranche. Who organized the others, and where did the money come from?"

"And account set up in Switzerland, back in 2001, when one hundred twenty billion euros were transferred into a trust account that has been steadily drawn down in accordance to papers filed that match the movement of the girls. The authorization is via the use of codes, which are changed every year, so we have no way of tracking that. All correspondence leads back to securitized bank boxes. But if you ask me, Mohammad bin Azaria created his version of a business model. It proved successful in the first seven years. He gave it a rest to see what he was getting for his money, liked what he saw, then restarted the program in 2012."

"By then, the eldest of the girls would have been, what, nineteen or twenty?"

"Yes, and remember, Amira was on her way to college at fifteen, so we can assume there were other very clever girls doing similar things during that time. But do you know what stands out to me?" He looked up at the roof as if seeking inspiration.

"The planning for this had to be exceptional, fluid, and inventive. And consistent, coordinated, and tightly held."

"Yes. To go from sneaking a few bombs and aircraft out of the system to stealing plutonium, then developing advanced nano weapons, and having the right people trained at the right time, all over a twenty-five-year span, is an amazing achievement. Do you have any idea how they could do it?" My turn to look at the roof and think outside the box. I looked at him, a thin smile on his lips as he looked back at me. I could almost read his mind, and a frisson of anticipation ran up my spine. Then I got it.

"Game players. Video game players. He grew his own strategists using video games."

"I think so. Yes, that's what makes the most sense to me. Young players are coached by military specialists, special forces experts, and asymmetric warfare experts, then encouraged to play games with all the input and plan a war on the planet. Now, the bigger question is, how do we find such people?" This time I smiled. I just happened to personally know two of the best hackers on the planet. One of them was just a room or two away from us right now!

"Malcolm and our Israeli colonel. If they can't find them, no one can. But before we call them, do you mind if I get dressed first?" He looked at me as if I were speaking Chinese, the bafflement on his face palpable.

"Oh. Yes, of course. I'll just step outside and bang my head on the wall." I shook my head. No wonder my love for him was unrequited; he only saw a soldier when he looked at me, never the woman! I bent to the inevitable, dressed in urban dull, ran my fingers through my hair, and joined him on the balcony. He dialed into Shami's computer. I went and knocked on Malcolm's door and signaled him to join us when he answered.

"Shami, when we're finished. Please brief Arie. I have Malcolm and Jessica here; we'll stay on the one mini for now, but we have something we want to run by your both." In faraway Israel, Shami nodded, his face a little solemn given the excellent news he had given us just an hour ago. Malcolm stood to one side, his long surfer frame dressed in board shorts and a noisy tee once again, his go-to outfit whenever he could manage it. "Jessica and I believe that the battle plan that is being executed and has been in operation now for nearly five weeks was the work of gamers. We want you and Malcolm to find them for us, please." Shami's eyebrows shot up, and the mention of gamers, Malcolm muttered an "I'll be damned" under his breath, and the tableau of the three of us frozen in time for a second or two must have been lost on Fay, as she swung around the corner at a clip and nearly cleaned us all up with her go-bag.

"Oops! Sorry, I'm a little late. Apologies."

"Do you always run like that?" Malcolm asked, mildly interested in the young agent and not just for her innate ability to move fast and dodge even faster. He tried to imagine her on a board, riding a twenty-footer, right-hand break, and thought she would look fabulous sliding down the face of a full-blooded curl. Shami broke the interlude with a crisp reply.

"Colonel, we'll get on it as soon as Malcolm can get to a mainframe. Malcolm?"

"Yes, Shami, give me thirty minutes. I'll have to go into FBI headquarters." He looked at me as if seeking permission. I nodded curtly, at the same time sizing up Fay. Jeans, sneakers but deep-soled ones that you could climb a mountain in, faded blue shirt, hooded jacket, with her military-style rain protector over the top. And the nail polish had gone, leaving a matte clear surface. Much better.

Fay dumped her bag in her room, and we all moved downstairs to a conference room Anna had arranged. The first thing I saw was an industrial-sized coffee machine and a smiling barista, so within minutes we all had excellent refreshments sliding across the table and, soon after, the room to ourselves.

"Who wants to go first?" the Boss asked.

"I will. I've taken the opportunity to speak with our attorney general's office. I spoke to an expert in the Terrorist Laws, and I posed a hypothetical based on what we now think may have happened." Anna spoke firmly, without hesitation, very confident of her facts. "Firstly, the source of the large transfers to the nominated countries was legitimate; every transfer was government-approved, audited, and had no link to the terrorists other than they were also funded by the Sovereign Wealth Fund. As you all know—except for you, Fay—Interpol has placed a Red Notice on the fund and frozen it, which will be challenged in the World Court as soon as things die down and Arabia gets its act together.

"Unless we can prove that the funds taken out three to five years ago have been used for terrorist acts, we can't touch them or any companies that use them. And if those companies are manufacturing power supplies and solar panels, there is little chance we can interfere in any way. And the real question becomes, 'why would we?' given the condition of the country today."

"Do you think Mohammad bin Azaria set this whole thing up so we would close down the Fund and, in effect, punish the Arabians?" Pete asked, adding an insight that came right out of the left field. "I mean, the money being used by the Environmental Development Company and whatever else they call themselves would appear to have nothing to do with the terrorists' attacks. Yes, the timing sucks wide, definitely a connection there, or serious intelligence, or part of the master plan."

"Yes, I do," I said, supporting Pete's supposition. It was one I had come up with myself, especially after interviewing Mohammad bin Azaria. "There were things that stood out in our interrogation—how passionate he became when we accused his girls of being terrorists and the total disdain he had for his royal family. Somehow he got control of the funds, or control of the people who controlled the funds, and made all those deposits. The irony of those funds coming from the very thing they attacked can't be lost on anyone." I thought for a minute. "And as most of you know, I've been in favor of a 'Plan B' since the interrogation. This all makes perfect sense to me. Create a worldwide situation that forces people to think about the refugee experience, open their eyes to the deprivation and disaster that is inherent in most of the camps, let everyone suffer for a while, punish his family for their greed, and turning their back on their religion, then provide a humanitarian solution to get everything moving again."

"He could come out a hero," Pete said between clenched teeth.

"Not while I still draw breath," the Boss offered, digging his head into another cup of coffee. "The real problem will be keeping the politicians out of this mess until we can find and arrest the women. That's still our core focus, so thanks, Anna, for the update. Now, who has any idea about how we should further investigate the plant in Point Roberts?"

"What is our objective this time?" Fay asked.

"Step one is, did they make the nanomachines that were used in the attacks?"

"And step two would be, what are they doing now, and how are they doing it?" Anna added.

"And step three would be, can they identify the IDs we have from Helena?" Pete threw in, just to remind us he was still there.

"Yes, and I'm really interested in their timing, specifically how they knew a situation would arise that would demand such a large stock of panels and power packs. To me, it's the timing that is their real weakness. They've been in operation for three years, and we know they have supplied thousands of panels to Helena, but we don't know over what period of time."

"I can fix that." Fay turned from a young good-looking agent to a hardboiled experienced FBI field agent in a heartbeat. She punched a number into an old-style handset that had been provided by the hotel.

"Andrew, hello, yes, thank you, all okay. I need you to find some data for me, please, priority one. Contact the border control on the Canadian border at Peach Arch Border Crossing and Boundary Bay Border Crossing. You are looking for Pantechs, originating from Point Roberts, and track them onto Route Five, to Route Ninety, then Fifteen, and into Helena. Use the toll trackers, please, and go back three years. If they complain about lost data or hardware, tell them we know they back everything up on analog equipment and mechanical counters, and I think you'll find no more than four or five different vehicles, so once you get a license plate, it should be easy. Please send data to this phone number, and I needed it yesterday." She listed for a minute, then hung up. "That was Agent RuPaul. He and his partner, who was with me in Point Roberts, will get that information as soon as they can. The beauty of the toll system is that they track traffic for both flow and maintenance reasons, and Route Ninety is a toll road in enough places to give us an accurate reading."

And right here, you had the reason why Interpol relied so heavily on local input as often as we could. I didn't know Route 90 was a toll road. Simple, brilliant thinking by Fay, no wonder she had risen through the ranks of the FBI so quickly. Before I could thank her, Anna did it for me.

"Good thinking, Fay. That will helps us answer one of our questions. Colonel, I'd like to make a suggestion regarding the visit back to the plant." The Boss just opened one hand and waved his go-ahead. "I'd like to suggest that we don't go in with Interpol and the FBI, for starters." The Boss raised his eyebrows.

"Why?"

"We have the tactical advantage at present. We arranged an FBI ID for Sandra in Helena, and so far, at least on this segment of our investigation, Interpol has been pretty much in the background. We go back with Fay in the lead. They will be used to that. We bring a couple of technical experts, which will be expected. We keep our warrant to building and systems search and request a reinterview with the staff, show the photos of the three women, and try to tie them into the plant. That gives us a link to the terrorists." The Boss considered Anna's suggestion carefully, looking for what they might lose by way of leverage by not having an Interpol presence.

"Would you take the same agents you sent last time?" he asked.

"No. Fay's team, yes, but Pete, you, and I can substitute for the other agents. There were only forty-one staff members, even with the ones missing on the day, and we were all expert interrogators. And I know you and Jessica want to see the plant firsthand, and I know you won't let Jessica go without Pete." He nodded at this; he had given Pete explicit instructions back in Israel about looking after Jessica, and he expected his request to be carried out to the letter.

"Okay, listen up for a minute. Fay perceived no threat at the plant; her instinct is that they desperately want to be able to continue to produce and deliver their panels and power supplies, so, in my humble opinion, armed conflict is out of the question."

"So, are you going anywhere without Pete?" Said with such finality, I just let it rest.

"So the bigger question is if we go in as FBI, we wear suits; is that the story?"

"You going to make me change again?" Fay asked, the picture of innocence.

She got a laugh; she was slipping into the team like a pro.

"I think suits and ties, and maybe we get a helicopter in this time, rather than the Coast Guard. That should make a statement all by itself."

"Do we take Malcolm?"

"Yes. I want his take on technology. We won't leave until tomorrow morning, first light; it's a short flight, up and back on the same day. I'll call Bridget and organize transport." The Boss calling the general by her first name suggested a familiarity or a casualness I had not experienced before, and I wondered what might be behind it. I looked around the table and didn't see any further questions, so I broke the meeting up. As we walked back to our rooms, I pulled Anna aside.

"No issue with the FBI creds?" She looked at me and smiled.

"None. Means I'll outrank you at last." My turn to smile. We had come a long way together since the first time she had dropped in on us in the monks' lair; it seemed like years ago, but it was only weeks. I wondered if she was as pissed as I was that the FBI didn't let us into the information on the funds' transfer and plants in New Zealand and Point Roberts, but when I thought about it every now and then, I'm not sure that we would have done anything differently.

Maybe it was time to let that go as well.

Anna peeled off into her room, and almost apologetically, Amira, who had said little to nothing during our two briefing meetings, sidled up to me.

"Jessica, can I have a moment, please?" she asked, her voice so soft I had to lean toward her to hear her. She gently steered me towards her room, and out of the corner of my eye, I saw Pete brace and go on alert, just like a highly trained Alsatian. I shook my head, followed her into her room, and heard Pete take up the post outside the door. Amira looked very uncomfortable, so I sat her down on the bed and took the chair from her desk, turned it around, and sat to face her at eye level.

"What's the problem?" I asked, in my smoothest voice, which wasn't an act. I genuinely liked her and admired her for how she had managed her life to get to us.

"It's about your earlier conversation about video gamers. I couldn't help but overhear what you and the Boss were discussing. I think I may know one of the people you might like to talk to."

"Was she a refugee?"

"Yes."

"From the same camp?"

"Yes."

"Why do you think she can help us?"

"Because the day we were taken, she took with her a video game that had been given to her a month before by one of the Red Crescent people. She was specifically asked to learn it, and she did. She did not go with me to Isreal, she went to Pakistan, and I didn't see her again until I went to Harvey Mudd. She was already there and had been for two years, studying computer science, game theory, and artificial intelligence. She had a similar cadre of docs and postdocs working with her as I did on my work. We talked a little, but we were both too busy with our work to find much time to spend together. If what you say is true, then I could easily see her constructing a game that would match what has been done to us so far." I sat gobsmacked again. We had such tunnel vision. We had never asked the simplest and most obvious of questions. Again, I forgave myself; at the time, we were trying to prevent the world from melting down.

"Do you know her name and where to find her?"

"She called herself Reve Anaisha. Her family gave her their name when she was adopted; her parents were very successful people living in Karachi, her father a doctor, and her mother an industrialist. She had a sister who came from another camp. Her name was Nazreen; she came from a camp in Libya, and she, too, was into games. She wasn't at Harvey Mudd; she went to MIT. I met her once during summer break; she was a lovely person but very smart."

"Do you know where they are now?" Amira looked a little embarrassed, but I pushed as hard as I could. This could open up an investigation.

"I know Reve works for some government organization. I don't know which, but they were paying for some of her development work in AI modeling. I don't know where Nazreen went." I leaned back, mindful that I had been creeping forward the whole time Amira was speaking. I had another thought.

"Will you be able to tell us what they are doing with the cinter bath and the plant and the nanites?" She looked at me with her big, beautiful eyes that seemed to have sparkles in the corners; beautiful mixed-race young woman who had guilelessly created the most dev-astating weapon probably in history, one that had literally taken out all the oil, gas, and coal production on the planet, seamlessly, and with practically no casualties, and wondered not for the first time how she would live with that knowledge.

"The real work on the nanites will be being done in the labora-tories; if we can get into one, I will be able to tell you most of what is going on. But just looking at the center bath from the gantry, I won't be able to tell you much more than you know now."

"We're not really interested in what they are doing now; we want to establish if they could have produced the nanomachines used in the attacks."

"That I will be able to tell you if we get into a laboratory."

"Good. Now all I have to do is work out how to get you into one." I stood, returned the chair to its former position, and turned to leave.

"Get some rest." I shut her door behind me, tapped Pete on the shoulder as I walked down the corridor, mouthed "Anna, Boss" and left him to find them. I dialed Malcolm up on his mini and told him to stop; more to follow.

Chapter 28

S amuel O'Leary's "Terrorist Money Man Tells Why" story had far and wide unforeseen repercussions. One of which was a small cell of Shetani's mercenary terrorists, fresh off successful attacks on seven fracking sites in the Midwest of the USA, was now sitting down in a diner in the small town of Park City, Montana. Their immediate concern, getting paid for their attacks, had just been solved when the use of their encrypted code had released six million dollars into a series of overseas accounts that they controlled individually. It had been explained to them at the very start that once the major attacks were underway, local communications would be difficult, if not impossible, so, like smart people everywhere, they had set up their anonymous accounts two years ago in countries with little or no regard for tax laws or financial reporting.

The six of them, four men and two women, were all now millionaires, several times over. All they had to do was survive long enough to be able to collect their hard-earned bounty. Unlike their terrorist brethren, they didn't wear camouflage, visibly carry automatic weapons, or act stupidly. In fact, when you looked at them, what you saw was a work crew, tough, tanned, polite, but obviously tight with each other. Their leader, a small woman of just five feet six, perfectly dressed for a school mum but noticeable only for her pure white hair, which ran down the sides of her tough face like cascading water over rocks. Her boots were well worn but normal for the assumption that onlookers made about her. Her innate toughness came through her voice, which was raspy from a packet-a-day habit that was now forty years in the making.

Their four-wheel-drive crew/cab truck with its ladders, poles and work paraphernalia on top of a boxy cargo container reeked of one of the electrical service companies that floated around the area from time to time fixing overhead wires and power poles. The six workers dressed appropriately in tough outer gear and hi-vis vests looked and played the part. Over their sausage, bacon, eggs over easy, pancakes, toast and jam, and a large pot of coffee, the six talked among themselves as they passed a copy of the paper they had picked up off the server bench when they had arrived. They also passed around a little note, which was of more interest in that it offered another three million for the removal of an unknown number of FBI agents in a place called Helena. A road map of the area lay on the table, with Helena circled in pencil.

Their plan was simple. Finish breakfast, drive the six or seven miles to Helena, scope out the area, locate the FBI agents, kill them, then collect their money on the way out of town to their next stop. What could be easier?

In Helena, tucked away at the back of the hotel, the FBI agent who had been monitoring the burst transmission detector went on alert as the device warbled at him. He looked at the coordinates, checked his field map, furrowed his brow, checked the calculations for a second time, then nodding to himself over said furrowed eyebrows at the information, picked up his FM handset, and called his partner, Special Agent Gerry Norden, who was at that exact moment holding a fascinating conversation with the owner of a local gym. When her FM handset squawked at her, she excused herself and moved away.

"Norden."

"Terry. I've just triangulated a burst transmission on the frequencies we were given, but it didn't come from this area. According to the map, it came from a town called Park City, which is approximately eight miles to our southwest. It was encrypted. I'm running it through the program now. Stand by." Gerry thought for a minute, flicked the frequency button on her handset, and called Interpol agent

Sandra Thomas, who was presently out at the airport, tracking the delivery of the panels.

"Sandra heads up, burst transmission eight miles southwest, being decrypted now; you might want to watch your back or just get back here. Your call."

"Thanks, Gerry, appreciated. Stand by." She put the small transmitter back in her pocket, thought through the options, pulled a map of the area up on her mini-computer, and not for the first time wished the satellites were all still working, but there were still options, and she exercised one as she called up the colonel.

"Sir, we have contact with an unknown force eight miles to our southwest, burst transmission being decrypted as we speak. My intention is to ride to the junction of the inbound road from Park City and observe."

"Keep us updated." And the Boss hung up and looked at me with a somewhat stern look on his face.

"'Call me Sally' might be in contact with the enemy; burst transmission from a town called Park City just detected. What resources do we have in that area other than the two FBI agents?"

"Only one of the agents has been visible, plus Sandra, who has FBI ID and creds. The local police seemed okay when we went through Helena if not a little overwhelmed by the influx of transients due to the attacks and civil unrest. I sent the train with the troops and special forces back to Washington; they should be at least to Chicago by now." The Boss sat and put his thinking face on, a scowl that would surely scare little children, and tapped his fingers on the table rapidly.

"We don't know if this is signaling an attack, and if so, on what or whom, or just check-in with home base. If it's a terrorist cell, it's one we missed, but traffic will be very light between those two towns, and according to my map, the main road is called Grizzley Gulch Drive. How can we get surveillance on it?"

"We have no air assets on hand, no satellite coverage that I know of. What did Sandra suggest we do?"

"Didn't suggest anything. Just said she was going to sit at the junction of the inbound road and observe."

"Sounds like the best we can do. Can I call her?"

"Go for it." I dialed up her minicomputer, and her face swam into view with a rapidly moving background strobing across the screen. The picture jumped and shook, so I guessed she was riding her bike and holding the mini in one hand as she did so. "Sandra, go invisible. Ditch anything that says FBI. Do it now." The screen tilted, then pointed at the ground, which was part tarmac and part dirt. A long shadow worked its way across the image, then cleared, and her pretty face came back into focus.

"Okay, I'm now dressed just like everyone else; I've ditched the FBI windbreaker. I should be at the main intersection within ten minutes. Call you then." And I was left looking at the typical blue screen of a disconnected computer.

"Where were we?" I asked, momentarily confused. Just minutes ago, we were working out how to approach Point Roberts with maximum effect. Now we were sweating on information about a possible attack by terrorists who had proven themselves to be well-equipped and well-trained.

"We were discussing how to get into a laboratory." Pete had that look in his eye, the one that said, "why am I here talking when there's the possibility of a firefight outside?" Always the warrior, no doubt he was lamenting our inability to get to Helena and help them out.

"My agent in Helena had decrypted the transmission. The message is as follows: Payment of three million dollars for the removal of all FBI agents in Helena, Montana, within the next forty-eight hours. One identified as female, name of Sandra, Thomas, one female, Gerry Norden, maybe more you will need to check. Payment is for full removal, not partial. Usual codes apply." Anna closed her mini, folded her hands on the tabletop, and dropped her shoulders. "There was a full physical description of both Sandra and Gerry attached to that communication." I snapped mine open and dialed Sandra.

"You are all compromised. Assume your descriptions and IDs are known in full, change your appearance asap, and go to ground."

"Yes, ma'am. WILCO."

Now the fun would begin. But the bigger question was why someone had launched an attack on the FBI in Helena? Why draw attention to that town if it were your base of operations? It didn't make sense. And the intelligence had to come from someone in Helena, someone who had seen both Sandra and Gerry. But there has been no burst transmission from Helena, so it had to have been transmitted either by phone or fax. So they had observers in Helena, but the command center was somewhere else. And if we didn't know all that we did about Helena, would we notice an attack on FBI agents necessarily? Couldn't it just be the terrorists hitting out at a visible target? What was there in Helena that we hadn't found yet? Pete and I had been crawling through the town, but we weren't on the hit list. So that meant it was from a very recent contact with Sandra and Gerry.

"Sir, our agents in Helena, are under imminent threat. Their descriptions have been passed to parties unknown who have been offered three million dollars for their removal. The attack is FBI-specific. Can we get them assistance from the local office?" Anna asked FBI director Roger Winslow. Roger, who was enjoying the first day off in five weeks, put his beer down and reclined back in his sun lounge.

"From memory, we have one assistant field agent and one office staff. And both of them will be well known to the townsfolk. We can ask the police for backup, keep the office covered, or even closed, but I can't think of much else we can do. Where are our other agents?"

"Sir, the two of them are located in a hotel on the edge of town. They can move,. That's not an issue. There is also an Interpol agent involved; she has been identified as a target. Sir, I don't think three agents armed with handguns are a match for terrorists armed with who knows what. And if the terrorists go for the office or the hotel, the possibility of civilian casualties is high."

"Anna, there is a National Guard unit in Helena. We can call them out for you.

Where do you want them located?"

"No, sir, thank you, not a good solution. I think we simply disappear into the woodwork. Nothing to be gained by taking them head-on, but if you want the guard to deal with them separately, then that's fine by us. Thank you." She hung up on the director and dialed Sandra again. Looked at me for approval, and I nodded. I was ahead of her for once and could see where she was going.

"Sandra, I'm with the captain; your orders are to disappear, get out of Helena immediately, and get to us here with your two partners. Do it!"

In Helena, Sandra turned around on her bike and headed for the hotel. She called the agents on the move; they had their car packed and ready to go when she arrived, and within twenty minutes, the three of them were headed out of Helena via Route 15. She was wearing a huge blond wig and sunglasses, the two agents' baseball caps and sunglasses, and all three were feeling very happy with themselves.

Back in Park City, breakfast having been comfortably finished, the terrorist hit team moved back to their truck, which had been recharging on the solar panel station, and headed off leisurely to their targets.

In faraway Washington, in the head office of the FBI, the duty officer took a call from her director, acknowledged the order, and immediately arranged for the call out of the National Guard in Helena via the governor of Montana, to intercept any vehicle entering from the south, and if necessary restrain and incarcerate anyone who looked suspicious. They were also told that they were "weapons free" in the case of any doubt; the temperature in halls of power was such that just the idea of terrorists still roaming around the state was an obnoxious insult to be dealt with terminally.

"Well, that was exciting," I said, mainly to break the ice. The idea of our people being targets of opportunity created a sour taste in my mouth. Anna looked a little more relaxed than she did just minutes ago, having received a message from Sandra that the three were on the move and safely out of Helena. What struck me about all of this was the seamless way Interpol and the FBI had worked together, a testament to the Boss's management style. "Okay, where were we? Oh yes, getting into the laboratory. Why do we want to do it? To prove a connection between the plant and the attacks. What can we do if we manage that? Shut them down under the Terrorist Laws. The FBI can't do that, but Interpol can. We might have to change our identities mid stream. What might that achieve? We cut off a guaranteed supply of panels and power supplies that we desperately need right now and possibly far into the future."

"And if you look at that clinically and cynically, that is a master-piece of planning just in itself."

"Yes, I agree. Maybe we can separate the people from the problem, go after whoever was around, say, eighteen months ago, compared to now, or say, just six months ago. But that becomes very messy."

"Well, I can promise you one thing, the president is not going to accept a partial solution, so we need to think this through."

"I agree. I need to make a call to Malcolm and brief him on Amira's information. Maybe you three can solve this by yourself?" I asked hopefully, knowing I would not be let off the hook. Then I had a flash of inspiration. "Wait a minute, when did the plant start hiring local engineers and scientists?" I asked. Anna started flicking through a written summary that had been prepared for us by the Seattle office of the FBI.

"First local staff hired three years ago were builders, carpenters, electricians, and plumbers. All are released by the end of the first year. Then a hiatus for six months. First, scientists and engineers were hired mid-year two, then the main group at the start of this year. We need to ask Amira how many people are needed to make the nano-machines, how long it takes, and what sort of equipment you need. Anna, can you please do that while I brief Malcolm on the game players?" She nodded, stood up, and walked out to Anna's room.

I got Malcolm on the mini. "Malcolm, I've got a starting point for you in your search for the game players. Names of Reve and Nazreen Anaisha, Pakistan nationality. Reve went to Harvey Mudd same time as Amira; Nazreen was at MIT two years before and during Amira's time at Harvey Mudd. Amira's comment was that both these girls were recruited because of their absolute command of the games they played, and both were streamed into computer science, game theory, and arti-ficial intelligence. You might start with the Anaisha family in Karachi, doctor, and industrialist, but keep it to electronic records initially. I'll get our local agent to interview both the parents and get the data to you asap." The whole time I spoke, he stared at me with a wistful look, no doubt thinking of all the surfing he was missing. I smiled my goodbye and hung up, switching my attention back to the meeting.

"Amira says initially two people, and then depending on what volume of nanomachines you want—or is that how many?—one person can manage the process once it is started. As for machinery, she only ever worked with laboratory equipment, so she can't even guess what production at scale might look like."

"I'm sensing a theme here, and it goes back to the way the terrorists prepared everything before the attacks. The trucks and their drone bombs specifically, and the fact that we know Shetani was moving his people around the world at least twelve months before the attacks, and that they had the nanomachines delivered to them six months before the attacks. Can you guess what I'm thinking?" Pete clapped his hands as if congratulating me.

"You clever popsie, you. And I'm not being sexist!" he yelled across the table. "You think there is a central manufacturing plant somewhere that prefabricates all the equipment and hardware needed to make the bugs, then the pieces are simply shipped around the world, bolted together, then brought to life by mad scientists!" Everyone laughed at Pete's enthusiastic summary, which wasn't far from what I had concluded in my own mind. Except for the mad scientist bit.

"Yes. I think we'll find—or might find if we're lucky—that no equipment manufacturing was actually done in Point Roberts, just bits and pieces shipped in and assembled. That makes the most sense to me. But someone somewhere was making all the machinery that is being used now."

"How do we find the main factory?" Anna asked. "It's bound to be under one of your famous 'black holes,' and in all likelihood, was closed down before the attacks."

"Not necessarily," Pete said, pointing to the sheet we had hung up on the wall with the countries on it that had received billions of euros in seed funding.

Northwestern USA, Canada, Greenland, Chile, Portugal, Ireland, Denmark, Norway, Finland, Estonia, Sri Lanka, Solomon Islands, New Zealand, Japan, and Iceland. We knew there was a factory in New Zealand and Point Roberts, but not the other countries just yet. And we only knew this because the seed funds had been drawn on, and that had been traceable firstly by the NSA and then the FBI.

"So you've got a couple of issues here—firstly, how do you ship parts of machinery around the world given the present circumstances? Secondly, how do you establish one of these factories in public view now we know what they are doing?"

The huge phone, by today's standards at least, shrilled on the corner of the table. I started to move towards it, but Anna beat me to it. She listened intently, thanked whoever was on the other end, then hung the massive handset up. She looked thoughtful for a moment, then raised her head and looked around the table.

"That was the local police chief in Helena. His people, backed by the local guard from the 307th brigade, stopped and searched an electrical repair vehicle inbound to Helena and were fired upon; they returned fire, seven dead on our side, eight wounded, six dead on the other, and the vehicle had a hidden refrigerated compartment with eleven sealed containers that are now in police custody. I need to make a call."

She reached for her mini and dialed her director. It was a short conversation, and towards the end, we heard her mutter "yes, sir" several times, then she closed the lid. "Well, nice to know, but he was royally pissed at us being flushed out of Helena and very upset by the dead police and Guard soldiers, happy about capturing what is assumed to be more nanobot samples, and made me promise that I won't go into harm's way. Of course, I lied about that." We all laughed at her comment. We knew we were all constantly on the edge of a threat with this case. We had gotten used to it, which probably contributed to the stress and tiredness we all exhibited.

"I want one of those canisters." Every head turned to look at me, and I just smiled and repeated my statement. "I want to put one down in front of those people in Point Roberts and see how they react." The Boss was the first one to smile, soon followed by Fay and the rest. The problem would be how to get it to us in Seattle. "Can we use the jet we flew here in?" Fay asked, reminding us we had the NSA G4 sitting at King Country International Airport-Boeing Field that

281

had brought Malcolm and Fay to Seattle. We still had FBI assets in Helena in the local office, and I was sure I could charm use of the jet out of Frank Reynolds.

We put it into motion and decided we needed a break and a meal, so we broke up again to go our separate ways.

"I'm going to get some fresh air," I said casually, starting for the massive double doors to the conference room we had taken over as our temporary HQ. Pete was beside me in a flash, all smiles, and happiness.

We walked out together into a frosty day with small clouds chasing themselves across the sky, which had retreated to a very pale white-blue color, reminding me it was still winter.

He was a great companion, leaving me to my thoughts while his head never stopped turning for a second. I patted him on the shoulder in thanks, worrying about what would happen next.

Chapter 29

The home of the Anaisha family was not small but was not garish or over the top—at least in the opinion of Drishya Singh, an Indian by birth but a Pakistani by adoption, in that she had been moved from the Interpol office in New Deli to the one in Islamabad, as a sign of the necessity for Pakistan and India to agree on something, even if it were only stopping people smugglers and drug mules. At just under six feet in height and with a slender build, she was often taken for a "soft" woman with her fair skin and dark black eyes. She was anything but, as her partner, Tanvir Zahid could attest. At just five foot six, even with his boxer build and wrestler's shoulders, and possibly as much as thirty pounds of body weight in his favor, he had yet to best her in the hand-to-hand they practiced every week back at the office, which they shared with the local police.

She towered over him, moved like a snake, and had been taught the Israeli self-defense style of Krav Maga, considered to be the most deadly of the martial arts, by her boyfriend, who worked at the Israeli Trade Commission. He professed to be a trade specialist, but both Interpol agents knew the smell of a spy, and they had quietly agreed on him being Mossad or maybe Sin Bet. It didn't really matter; she loved him, he loved her, and she could see them merging together at some point to make a family.

At the request of the Interpol head office for the region, they had boarded a small electric-powered plane flown by a Pakistani Air Force officer and flown to Karachi in just over five hours. At the airport, they were transferred to a long black SUV, this time driven by a silent, very big, well-dressed person who literally bulged out of his well-cut suit. He was accompanied by a local member of the Pakistani Inter-Service Intelligence (ISI) agency, who carried a modern HK semiautomatic strapped across his chest and spent his entire time looking furtively from side to side as if expecting to be attacked at any moment.

Far from reassuring the two Interpol agents, it worried at the edges of their nerves, creating a sense of tension inside the vehicle that quickly became uncomfortable. It only took three blocks of fighting the motorcycles, small electric vehicles, pushbikes, buses, and three-wheeled trikes for the tension to explain itself, especially when a small vehicle attempted to ram them off the road and into a ditch. The ISI agent simply lowered his window and fired a burst into the cab of the offending vehicle, rolled the window back up, and carried on as if nothing untoward had happened.

"This happens regularly," he casually threw back over his shoulder, "and if we had stopped, we would have been beaten and robbed, killed, and then the car would have been burnt out. We do not have control of our cities since the terrorist attacks; it is literally every man and woman for themselves." His voice was sing-song like so many on the subcontinent and a little high-pitched. The agents were aware of the situation in Karachi; it was a little better in Islamabad, but not by much. The biggest problem was that delivery of fuel had been made two weeks after the attacks, and it had been radioactive, which had not been detected until people started dying from radioactive poisoning after pumping it into their vehicles. In what would later be described as a fluke of timing, the tanker was loading from a downstream platform, and no one had yet worked out that the radioactive elements had worked their way through the substrata linking many of the oil fields and poisoning them on the way. The mastery of this attack had been the simple fact that from just the one drop site, where the nuclear matériel had been pumped into the well under pressure, the radioactivity had spread like fast-moving cancer to irradiate every oil field for thousands of kilometers in every direction.

The carnage that had resulted from this "fluke of timing" was catastrophic. Vehicles abandoned where they lay, creating blockages that ran for miles, spot fires intermingled with dead bodies left in the street to rot or be eaten by the flies, and armed marauders killing anything that moved in fear of being contaminated. It had taken three weeks of intense fighting by the military to slow things down to a mere slaughter, and at the time they had left the heavily guarded airport, the death toll in just Islamabad itself topped seven hundred thousand. And there were still people dying of radiation poisoning every day to add to that total.

The British and the Americans, who had drilled the first wells nearly a hundred years ago in Arabia, had known the vast oil fields beneath the unforgiving desert linked and joined up like a series of lakes, but that simple fact had been lost in the flow of time, and the greed of the moment.

They arrived at the Anaisha residence, climbed out of the SUV, and were immediately surrounded by home guards wearing white linen pants and shirts with the traditional black waistcoat. And they all carried modern submachine guns. The ISI agent fired a string of Urdu at them, they fired one back, then snapped to attention and saluted. Drishya walked between them and up the steps without acknowledgment, followed closely by Tanvir. The ISI agent stayed below the steps, resting his back against the vehicle. The driver had remained immobile through all the pantomime, but Drishya noted his eyes never left the ISI agent, and his hand had crept into the inside of his jacket.

He was left-handed, which is good to know.

The door opened, and a butler or manservant dressed in the traditional black London professional aide three-piece suit, starched shirt, and tie bowed, hands by his sides, and in perfect Oxford English welcomed them inside.

"Madam and sir will be with you shortly. Can I provide anything for you in the meantime?" he asked, unbowing with such rigidity Drishya thought he might be a robot.

"Thank you, water will be fine," she answered, moving to one side so her partner could join her. The room they were in reeked of old money, the Raj, of times far past the present, with rich red and gold hanging curtains, billowing silks of different colors, and a carpet that was worn with age hinted at exotic times past but still looked luxurious. There were generations of antiques, all maintained exquisitely and fitting the persona of the room to perfection, unlike the duo who calmly appeared from beyond a small alcove, hand in hand.

Modern Pakistan personified. Pinstriped Savile Row suit, highly polished brogues, crystal white shirt, club tie, and a matching Burberry suit cut to perfection to suit a strong, shapely body with glittering diamond earrings and a bracelet Drishya estimated would cost six or seven times her yearly salary. The pair looked rich, prosperous, comfortable in their skins, and relaxed, as if they had Interpol agents dropping in for tea every day.

"Please sit," Hugh Anaisha offered, pointing to a slim lounger that was covered in silk throws and colorful cushions. He and his wife sat opposite the agents; he crossed his legs and sat back as relaxed as Drishya had ever seen anyone in her entire life. The butler reappeared with two tall glasses of water, topped by slices of lime, with condensation dripping down the sides.

"Thank you. Sir, madam, I am Agent Singh, and this is Agent Zahid, and as this is an official inquiry, may we have your permission to record the conversation?" Hugh nodded sharply. Tanvir placed a small cassette recorder on the magnificent glass table between them, one that had legs of scrolled gold and silver that literally sparkled in the light.

"We have been informed by your superiors that you wish to talk to us about our girls—is that correct?"

"Yes, sir. We are interested in both Reve and Nazreen, how you came to adopt them, what they did in school, what they are doing now, and where we might find them." Hugh held up one hand in an unmistakable signal—stop, halt, pay attention to me.

"Firstly, we have not yet called our barrister but will do so the moment we believe we need to protect the interest of our girls."

"Sir," Drishya said, almost in a conciliatory tone. The last thing they needed was solicitors or barristers getting in the way of them finding out what they needed to know, "we only want to establish how you found the girls, why you adopted them, how their schooling went; we know, for example, one went to Harvey Mudd, the other MIT, and that suggests two very bright, intelligent girls." Hugh looked at the two agents as if trying to see inside their heads and seemed to make his mind up about something.

"My wife is an extraordinarily talented industrialist; she owns and runs the biggest technology company on the subcontinent and has done for many years. I am a practicing surgeon-a specialist, and some consider me to be at the very top of the list if you are interested in that." Not said boastfully, just delivered, as a matter of fact, Drishya thought, as she started to form an opinion of him. "We were both working very hard and long hours, but had been unable to conceive children, no matter hard we tried, so we decided to adopt. We let some friends know and were approached by a member of the Red Crescent, an organization our family has supported for generations." He drew in a breath; this was obviously still an emotional issue for him, and she wondered why.

"We were initially offered a beautiful little girl from a refugee camp here in Karachi, one who had no parents; they had been both killed in an uprising on the border. She was smart, and we fell in love with her from the first. We agreed to adopt her, and just as we were about to drive to the camp and collect her, we were again contacted and offered another little girl, this one from a camp in Libya. It was a case of the left hand not knowing what the right hand was doing, a paperwork mistake, no more. We were unsure if we could adopt two little girls at the one time, but this was sorted out by Red Crescent on our behalf, so the next day, we brought home Reve, and two weeks later, we brought home Nazreen and made them our own."

"Did you receive any financial support for the girls from Red Crescent?" Tanvir asked in his most sympathetic voice. Far from looking shocked or indignant, Hugh looked surprised, his green eyes sparkling with secret thoughts.

"Yes, we were offered a stipend, enough to get the girls through college and to university in any country of their choice. But my wife and I politely refused. We were financially secure, so we asked that the money be used for other refugees, which we know it was."

"Did you ever see a representative of Red Crescent after the girls were adopted?" Drishya asked, wondering if this break in the pattern had affected how the girls were managed remotely by the terrorist planners. Hugh looked at her suspiciously, his face scrunched up in concentration.

"Why do you ask that?"

"We have been following other refugee placements, and many of them had visits by their sponsors for a number of years." His face didn't lose its suspicious look, but the scrunching became a little less, and he looked all the more handsome for it.

"Well, then, yes, the key member of Red Crescent who initially helped us visited both girls on their fifteenth birthdays and gave them each a laptop computer. The girls both already had one, as well as a desktop and other ancillary equipment; as I mentioned, my wife owns and manages the largest technology company in the subcontinent, so electronics were free-flowing and plentiful."

"What did the girls do with them?" Tanvir asked as casually as he could. This time Hugh looked puzzled, as if the question was something he could not relate to.

"I don't know. You would have to ask them."

"Did the girls go to Harvey Mudd and MIT on scholarships?" Drishya asked, largely to see the reaction, as she had already divined that the story for the girls was going to be very different from that of the report from Interpol on other refugees. She suspected that if they had been recruited into the ranks of the terrorists, it had happened at the university. But it had happened; she was sure of that, her skin buzzing with anticipation as she watched the reactions of the parents to the questions.

Still, she pursued their main focus, again with a soft voice and relaxed body language. "Were they both into gaming when you adopted them?" she asked.

"In a small way. They both came to us with handheld game platforms they had been given in the refugee camps, so seeing their interest, my wife took them both to one of her plants and introduced them to big console gaming. They both excelled and constantly competed against other online players all around the world." He smiled at some inner memory, and his face lit up. "In fact, they became so good, Nazreen set up her own website and ran competitions using software my wife was developing and games that were developed by her company. They both became unofficial testers for all the new games and, just before they left for university, were writing a lot of the code that went into the games."

"Who went off to college first?"

"Nazreen. She was, we think, two years older than Reve, and although it made no difference to them or what they could do, she got a full ride to MIT. They came here and offered it to her personally, so she left first."

"Did MIT offer the same to Reve?"

"No. She had her heart set on Harvey Mudd from the time she beat their reigning champion in an online game fest when she was twelve. They put her up on their website as the person to beat, and no one ever did, so when she applied, they jumped at her full scholarship and, again, an in-person approach. We were very proud."

"Where are the girls now?" Tanvir asked.

"Reve is in Japan, working for my wife's company as a developer and tester. She will take that office over in another year or two. Nazreen is in New Zealand, working for an environmental technology company that develops high-tech power solutions. They are just at the testing stage, but the promise of their technology is so good, my wife's company has obtained the rights to distribute their products throughout the Asia pacific basin."

Bingo! Japan and New Zealand had both been on the watch-list issued by the FBI just a week ago, and she knew that at least two strange manufacturing plants had been linked to the distribution of funds from the Sovereign Wealth Fund. The beauty of the FBI working so closely with Interpol on the terrorist case was that they shared information rapidly, and the briefing notes were excellent in their detail. Was it possible that this wealthy, immaculately dressed industrialist, as she described herself, was involved with the terrorists? Might her factories be involved in some way? Her train of thought was broken by her partner's next question.

"Madam, specifically, what does your business focus on?" he asked, still playing the role of a low-key subservient government employee, just asking the questions he had been given almost by the route. His antenna, too, had been sparked by the answers the regal-looking doctor had given them. But what had really interested him was that the woman hadn't said a word so far. Not even hello. At his question, her first instinct was to look at her husband as if seeking permission to speak. He gave nothing away with his facial expressions, just looked at her as if waiting for an answer.

"Agent Zahid, you can find all the details you need on our website... Oh! Forgive me, but the web has been crashed." She reached into a hidden pocket, pulled out what looked like a thin, silver card, spoke into it silently, replaced the card, then looked at the agent with such intensity he felt like he was being stripped bare. He could feel the hairs on his arms stand up; the feeling was so visceral. "I've asked my assistant to print off our most recent brochure for you." And she refolded her hands in her lap and sat back in her seat. This time Drishya cut into his reflection.

"Madam, thank you, that will help us considerably. We were unable to do our normal background research before we arrived," she said, only telling a small white lie. A detailed background had been provided as part of their brief, "but for the record, could you summarise your main focus for us, please?" The look she got would have frozen a less experienced agent in her seat, but before the woman could speak, the butler walked in and handed a brilliant royal purple folder to her, which she placed delicately on the table and slid over to Tanvir with a flick of her extraordinary long fingers, tipped with bright red nail polish. As all these observations flashed through his mind, Tanvir reached forward and picked up the folder.

"I think that concludes our business here, Agents. Fredrick will show you out." And the royal-looking couple stood gracefully and exited the room the way they had come in. Left with no polite option, the agents stood and followed the butler to the magnificent entrance. He opened the door for them, bowed, then closed it gently behind them. They stood on the steps for a minute, taking in the view of the almost ceremonial formation of the home guards, saw the ISI agent brace, then walked down the stairs and into the SUV.

As they settled, Drishya put her fingers on her lips and shook her head. She did not want a discussion in front of the ISI agent and his minder. As they sped back to the airport, she wondered just how deep the Anaisha family was involved in the terrorist attacks and what the next steps might be.

Chapter 30

The beauty of being able to command national assets as and when required had made the business of getting a nano bug cylinder identical to those captured in Canada back to Seattle in a matter of hours. And because we were smart, "just call me Sally", and her two FBI companions were also with us, sitting around our makeshift boardroom table. Getting them here was as simple as telling them to turn around, drive back to Helena, get to the airport, and wait for the G4.

I now had my entire American team in front of me, rested, fuelled up, and briefed on current events. We had just received the long fax from Islamabad, so now we had another string to pull on the investigation. But our primary focus was the original refugee terrorists, the ones that had made the initial attacks, the ones that had shattered the modern world possibly for decades to come.

The room was a little full for its size, as we had been joined by the director of the Seattle office, as Anna had received permission to read him into the current situation. Fay's initial team was also present on the basis we were going back to Point Roberts in some form and at some point in the next two days. But first, we had to get to know each other, something I had learned back in NCIS investigator's school. It was called "forming a relational circle"; it took a little time but saved hours down the track because it accelerated the generation of trust, and people always seemed to speak more freely once you had opened up the floor, as it were. So I started the ball rolling.

"I want everyone to introduce themselves and give a one-minute summary of what you have done most recently on this investigation. I'll start, and Director, if you wouldn't mind, please go last so you have the whole story in front of you." He nodded a little tersely; he was obviously uncomfortable not knowing what his own people had been doing for the past days.

"My name is Jessica Riley. I am the lead Interpol investigator on this case. I've been on it since day two of the terrorist attacks, when Interpol was invited to the party by firstly the Italian government, then by the Israelis. I hold the equivalent rank of captain in the US Navy or a one-star general if you are a ground pounder, and I welcome you all to this briefing." I saw the surprise on the faces of the FBI agents; they probably hadn't expected me to be so highly ranked in military terms. I looked to my immediate left, where Pete sat in his classic passive-aggressive pose, seemingly relaxed but eyes scanning everything and everyone.

"I'm Master Chief Pete, attached to Section Five, not much more than a hired gun, but happy to be here. As for where I have been, I was present at the capture of Mohammad bin Azaria, and most recently have helped track the terrorists across Montana via their base in the United States." Anna was next to Pete, and I wondered how she would introduce herself, given that she knew more than her director and probably would for as long as the case was active.

"I'm Anna Bernstein, Senior Special Agent FBI. I've been seconded to Interpol representing America's interest since the first week of the attacks, and like Pete, I have followed the trail of the terrorists across the Midwest. I report specifically to the director of the FBI, and I am assisting Jessica here in liaising with FBI assets around the world." I watched the Seattle director's face; he absorbed Anna's statement, his eyes giving nothing away, and, if anything, sat a little straighter in his seat.

"I'm Amira Abramowitz. I'm an Israeli technical specialist on loan to Interpol. Mostly I've been working with the Italian and Israeli scientists working on the World Wide Web crash and the technology used in shutting down the oil, gas, and coal supplies." The director's eyes popped at this, and he leaned forward in his seat.

"Do you mean you know what was used to shut us down?" he asked, aggravation running through his voice like out-of-control floodwaters over a dam wall. Amira, Anna, the Boss, and I had worked with Amira on her story, mostly to protect her but also to give her credibility with the team.

"Yes, sir. The team I have been working with is aware of what was done, and we are close to understanding how it was done." And she autonomically brushed her hair back from her face and looked impossibly young in the harsh overhead lighting to be one of, if not the, leading expert on nanotechnology in the world.

But we were keeping that little titbit to ourselves. He didn't relax; if anything, he tensed up, so I crossed my fingers that bringing him in on the details of the investigation would not turn out to be a mistake. Theoretically, both the Boss and I outranked him, and for practical purposes, Anna did as well, but none of us wanted to throw our weight around, given the excellent cooperation the American government was giving us on so many fronts.

"Special Agent John Vernon, working with agents Remer and RuPaul, out of the Seattle office, part of the team that went to Point Roberts last week." His partner was the next to speak.

"SA Andrew RuPaul. I was on the Point Roberts team, based here in Seattle." He turned to look at his immediate supervisor, several years his junior, with a warm smile that was almost paternal.

"Senior Special Agent Fay Remer. I led the team into Point Roberts, I'm also based here in Seattle, and as of two days ago, I have also been seconded to this Interpol team." I knew the local director had been asked to make this move by Roger Winslow and that he had not been particularly happy about it, but we saw it as gaining a valuable and highly intelligent asset in the hunt for the women.

"Agent Sandra Thomas, Chicago Interpol office, and my most recent adventure has been fleeing a murderous group of mercenary terrorists and bringing back a sample of the nanomachines they have been using to kill our oil, gas, and coal supplies." She paused, her huge smile decreased a fraction, probably her go-to "I'm being serious now" face. She was absolutely the happiest person I had ever come across, and you couldn't be around her and not feel lighter. "Just prior to being scheduled to be killed, I assisted these two well-behaved FBI agents in an investigation into the terrorist activities in Helena." As she spoke, she reached out and tapped Gerry Norden on the shoulder and pointed to Frank Wiltshire, who sat next to him. They both acknowledged the recognition with a nod of their heads, then Frank gave his side of the story.

"Although, to be truthful, I spent the entire time in Helena in my room monitoring burst transmissions, and Gerry got out to make a nuisance of herself around the town while Sandra here did all the heavy lifting. It was she who spotted the Pantech with the panels on board, which led us to the hangar storage, and she pried the IDs of the three women who are our prime suspects out of the airport staff."

"Yes, but he intercepted the transmission and decoded our death sentence, which is why we three are here today. Don't forget that." Frank Wiltshire blushed, a strange reaction for a seasoned FBI agent. Not unlike the FBI agent whom I had enjoyed being under fire with from local militia marauders out in wild, wild west Montana. His work had been outstanding in that he had detected our local transmissions, then worked out the probable frequency the terrorists were using, which had unearthed the transmission from Shetani's men prior to the electrical service vehicle rolling into the trap we had prepared in Helena.

And instead of two dead FBI agents and one from Interpol posing as an FBI agent, we had recovered eight pristine nano bug canisters and an equal number of not-so-pristine dead terrorists.

"I guess that means we don't have to introduce ourselves," Gerry said into the quiet that had resulted, "but so you don't get confused, I'm Gerry, the good-looking one, and he's just Frank," she said with a smile in her voice, pointing to her partner.

"And it's my fault they were both targets. I recruited their team led by Fay from my office in Washington to help with the investigation." Anna's crisp voice cut across the low rumble of chatter that had started to break out, bringing everyone's attention back to our agenda.

"I'm PJ Anthony, and I head up Section Five of Interpol, and I am running interference between the various countries that have a stake in this. I also had the pleasure of being present when we brought

Mohammad bin Azaria to heel. And I'd like to add another bit to Pete's CV if I may—he was also active during the takedown of Shetani and his headquarters in Arabia." All eyes shifted to Pete, whose turn it was to blush. He didn't really, but I'm sure he would have if he could have moved his scared face the right way!

"And for those of you that might have noticed, Pete is acting as my aid-de-camp while we are out of our normal working zone." I let that sit for a moment; my people knew the Boss had sic'd Pete on me to keep me out of trouble, but I didn't see the need for anyone outside our primary team to know that. "There's one other expert we have on hand; he's at the FBI office at present, tracking down some other suspects we may have unearthed. His name is Malcolm Tannery, and he is an analyst with the NSA. He will be joining whomever we decide will go back to Point Roberts." No need to mention that he was king of the white hat hackers and a keen surfer, but I was giving some considerable thought to how we would disguise him at Point Roberts.

"Does anyone have any questions?"

"Yes, I've got one," the director said, linking his hands on the table and leaning forward on his elbows. If he felt outgunned, he didn't show it, and to his credit, he had remained mostly passive through the introductions. Was he comfortable with what he was hearing? I really didn't think so. He knew about the Point Roberts trip, but at that time, it was a low-interest follow-up request from someone in the FBI headquarters team. That had turned out to become a critical part of the investigation into the terrorists, although we had yet to openly discuss the link between building six and the nanomachines.

Further, he had a combined FBI and Interpol team racing around Montana, no notification or permissions asked, and a serious couple of issues unearthed in Helena, not to mention the recently dispatched mercenary terrorist group and their electrical contractor vehicle and their canisters of nanomachines. Before"call me Sally" had revealed the existence of the canister she had brought back from Helena, no one in the USA other than the president and her most senior intelligence and security heads had known about them. And then only because we had retrieved some from the Canadians.

It had to rankle that so much was going on right under his nose and on his turf, all sanctioned at the highest level of government, without his knowledge. But he seemed to be coping, or he was another I would avoid at the poker table!

"How do you intend to take all these people to Point Roberts and make any sense out of what you find?" He looked around at the expectant faces, and to my surprise, Fay stepped into the metaphorical breach.

"Sir, Captain, if I may?" she asked, standing and addressing the director. "The primary reason for this briefing is that the colonel wanted our suggestions on how to tackle another visit to Point Roberts without tipping our hand. I have given it considerable thought, and my team has come up with a suggestion." Both RuPaul and Vernon didn't react, so either she had talked it over with them, or they were backing her instincts. The Boss nodded his assent, sitting slightly forward in his seat.

"We had seven agents on Monday when we conducted the interviews, so a similar number of agents will not be out of scale. They really didn't like the idea that we would get a warrant to open them up, as it were, so I'm going to suggest that we don't do that this time but rather encourage them to both invite us back and show us everything we want to see." The room was quiet as everyone digested the consequences of "invitations" and "no warrants."

"My—sorry, our—thinking is this. I call the COO, with whom I connected at some level, and explain that my boss—sorry, sir—is unhappy with our report and has demanded we reinterview key staff, whom we nominate and physically view every building, in order to complete a more formal report for Washington. But it's a request from me, a low-level agent, of no particular consequence in the grand scheme of things, and to further deescalate potential trouble, we go in as FBI, or perhaps with civilian contractors, once again lowering the expectation of skills and abilities. My fear is that if we walk in with two or three senior members of Interpol, an expert from the NSA, and then a bunch of agents, they will shut up shop."

She was smart, her idea was excellent, and I could see instantly that the director hated it. So before he could attack the plan and, by proxy, his own agents, I stepped into the same breech as Fay had done.

"Fay, excellent thinking. I particularly want myself, Anna, Amira, and Malcolm to be present, and of course yourself, so if you bring Agents RuPaul and Vernon, we'll have the same number as before, but perhaps more specialized. How does that sit with you, sir?" He looked baffled at how fast I had accepted his agent's suggestion, but before he could respond, Pete mumbled his usual mantra, "where you go, I go," and I grimaced and nodded, and before the director could get a word in, Sandra had her hand up as if she were at school, asking permission to leave the room.

"Yes, Sandra?"

"I want in. I've spent a lot of time over the last three years in Chicago studying exotic weaponry. I'm happy to go in as anyone you want, but I want in." I looked at the Boss, and I could see he was thinking the same thing I was. The difference between seven and eight was not a deal-breaker, and we could civilianize Pete, Malcolm, myself, Sandra, and Amira without too much effort. Then the back of my mind sent me a message, and I shook my head in frustration.

"We don't need so many people. Sorry John, Andrew, Frank, and Gerry. I think we need to limit the number of FBI as well as Interpol. Our objective is to gauge a reaction to the photos of the three women from Helena; have they been seen at the plant, and does anyone know them, as well as trying to establish their level of technology and their possible relationship to the original nanomachines. We have a timeline of sorts, so we can dig into that as well. Fay, you've got a good idea. How do you feel about asking the COO to arrange a meeting of herself, her CEO, and all building heads/managers, people similar to Arnon from building three? I will also want to talk to anyone who was on site two years ago, just after the hiatus. Can you manage that, please?" She had been taking notes on an electronic pad, and she nodded vigorously.

"So the team will be Jessica, Pete, Anna, Amira, Fay, Sandra, and Malcolm?" the Boss asked. "How do you want to introduce Amira, Sandra, and Malcolm?" I thought for a minute, looked at Sandra, thought *FBI*, thought about Malcolm, our lean surfer dude, and thought *university*, then looked at Amira, who had the most pronounced accent, and was the most critical member of the team.

"FBI for Sandra. Malcolm can come from some university or other. Better make that local given the transport difficulties we have, although he could have come up here by rail from Los Angles—he can be a scientist from Cal Tech; maybe Amira can be an exchange student and Malcolm's partner?" Anna nodded; it was obvious she had been thinking about the same thing I had. We had to protect Amira at all costs. "And, Pete, sorry, I haven't got a clue where you come from. I might have to make you FBI as well." I got a grin out of that. "Our order of battle then will be paired; Fay is the SSA and will lead the group; Pete and I will be mid-level FBI agents; Anna and Amira, FBI and university scientists; Sandra and Malcolm, FBI and university scientists. Our scientists will not carry weapons; everyone else will carry standard FBI issue equipment. I want us all hardwired for video and audio, and I'll arrange for us to be flown in by military helicopter. Fay, did you get a good look outside the main gate?"

"Yes. There is a paddock on the right-hand side where the trees and foliage have been trimmed. I suspect it has been used as a helipad previously. I would judge it to be safe for something like a UH-60 Blackhawk. I'll have that checked out locally."

"Why do you want to arrive by helicopter?" the director asked. "You are de-identifying yourselves to lower the perception of the interrogation; won't a military helicopter create too much notice?"

"Sir, you are right. It will get noticed, but I also suspect that these are all very smart women, and I expect they will see 'military' before they see 'science smarts.' Amira and Malcolm are our key elements in this visit, and your agents' summary report mentioned that there was some anticipation the government might want to take the plant over, so heightening that fear, I think, will also blind them a little to the abilities of our scientists. Cal Tech has a fantastic reputation in the STEM world, having born over a hundred Nobel Prize and National Medal of Science or Technology winners in the last one hundred years. It's high enough on the STEM food chain to gain respect, but compared to the geniuses the terrorists have been producing, probably not so much a perceived threat."

"So each 'pair' will have, in essence, an armed bodyguard; you will need an extraction plan, just in case." The Boss's quick read of the way I had set up the "pairs" was reassuring, and the newest member of the protection squad, Sandra, had proved she was a quick and agile thinker back in Helena, so I trusted her to keep Malcolm in one piece.

"Yes, sir." I went formal to emphasize to the director my chain of command because, in essence, we were creating a battle plan right in front of him without asking for his input. His next statement abused me of any idea that he was just sitting still and letting it all happen around him.

"I see several issues here you might care to think about. Many of the employees of the plant may have, in fact, attended Cal Tech. If you posit your people as having attended that school, why wouldn't they be recognizable as fellow students or lecturers? Secondly, without a deep cover background being inserted into the university's records, even the simplest of searches will expose your agents. And Cal Tech is very high profile, maybe too high for your expectation management." He made a good point and reminded me the FBI did not promote dull people to the position of director of a major office of the FBI on a whim.

"Sir, you make a good point. What would you suggest?"

"We have the names of the staff at the plant. Fay's team can check to see how many went to Washington University here in Seattle, and because it's local, we can insert any relevant backgrounds we need to support your people. If you plan your interviews accordingly, and I sense your ID check will be a separate process from your scientific explorations, you should not have any great risk of being discovered. Have I got that right?"

"Yes, sir, you have. My plan would be to get Amira and Malcolm into every building while Fay and I interrogate the COO, CEO, and senior staff. And no one will know their backgrounds necessarily, we won't make it an issue, but we will need them if they do a deep search later."

"And they will," the Boss added, thinking through the issue. It was a mix of providing backgrounds that would stand scrutiny, contained as much of the truth as they could manage, and wouldn't collapse under forensic examination.

"Colonel," I started, "there is no evidence that the women have ever used small arms for defense or attack. In fact, according to the

FBI's assessment, Point Roberts was brightly lit, quite open in terms of infrastructure, and appeared to be what it purported to be: a very high-tech production facility for, at this juncture, panels and power packs."

"Someone called in an attack on the FBI in Helena, in broad daylight, with the expectation of solving a problem, without regard for how we might react." It was a flat statement, but I could see that it jolted everyone in the room as the import of what the Boss had said sunk in. And there was another aspect to that statement we hadn't talked about yet—how many more of Shetani's terrorist teams were still undetected? The Boss didn't let up.

"And I'd remind us all that this case started with an attack on the Vatican, where better than ninety percent of the cardinals and leaders of the Catholic Church were massacred and thousands of years of religious history destroyed. Several thousand innocent spectators were killed in that action as collateral damage, and the pain of that attack has rippled around the world like a tsunami. Then you add the wanton destruction of the Dome of the Rock, the Wailing Wall, and the Grand Mosque, and you have a religious fervor rising up that will take decades, maybe centuries, to quell. Add to that the attack on West Point, the thousands of young lives lost, and all the other atrocities these terrorists have inflicted on us all, and you have a tinder box with the fuse lit and no certainty as to how it will all end. We must never, never lose sight of that, simply because we are trying to run down a group of refugee children, grown into women who have been shaped into the most terrifying and talented terrorists ever to have plagued the planet."

And just like that, the Boss had brought us all back into focus, and I could feel our resolve hardening and our hearts beating just a little bit faster.

Boat People

The neat, flat-sided vessel that had seen out most of its life as a floating holiday palace prior to the worldwide pandemic shutting down international cruising literally overnight was originally set up to carry five and a half thousand passengers and around fifteen hundred crew. When it had been beached, its owners, hoping to recover some of its cost by way of selling the carcass for the value of the metals, furniture, and fittings, had not hesitated to take the offer made to them by purportedly one of the worlds largest aid agencies. The offer had been approximately three times what the owners had hoped to recover from scrapping the vessel, and the only hardship from the owners' position was that they were required to deliver the vessel to a small shipyard in Somalia.

Given that the ship would be essentially empty, the threat of pirates in that part of the world would be negligible, and the skeleton crew of one hundred sailors, cooks, and cleaners had been guaranteed their safety. The ship had been gutted above the waterline, the five thousand cabins and staterooms turned into large open areas, some fitted out for recreation, some for sleeping and ablutions, and all in such a way as to provide a comforting, spacious environment that catered for the soul as much as the physical body. A fully equipped hospital was located on the lower deck, as were a series of play areas, all designed to stimulate young minds and foster confidence and trust.

The ship had been renamed *Amal*, with the Arabic "أمل" inscribed alongside the bow in an imposing script. Literally translated, it meant

"Hope." And for the past year, it had been sailing the Mediterranean Sea, then down the Suez Canal, around the coasts of both the Gulf of Eden and Oman and now it was headed across the broad Pacific Ocean all the way to the west coast of America. Onboard were eleven hundred and six young girls, the youngest six, the eldest twelve, all collected from refugee camps where they had been singled out for their innate intelligence. The process had taken a year because the planners wanted a sample from as many camps as they could manage because this was a mass demonstration designed to prove to the world that there was a solution to the refugee problem if the world would only pay attention.

The support staff was one-fifth of the children in numbers, and from the first day a child was brought aboard, after a health check, each child has nominated a female carer who spoke their language, who then basically looked after five or six children on the long voyage, acting as a surrogate mother and a teacher. As several of the staff were trained psychologists, it was hoped that from this initial voyage, the best management practices would be learned, allowing much larger numbers of rescued girls to be carried on subsequent voyages. The carers had also been recruited from the camps, as single, talented women littered the camps like so much flotsam and jetsam that scurried out of the way of the ship's massive bow wave. They had been promised nothing but health, support, a small stipend, and relocation to any country of their choice after completing the voyage. If they wished to apply for refugee status in the US or another country, it would be supported with no guarantee of success.

If they wanted to stay with their children, then that would also be arranged.

But the plan was to offer the children and their carers an immediate solution to the management of the children once they made their landfall. And negotiations had already started months ago, albeit under the guise of a different resettlement model, but an in-principle agreement had already been reached. What no one on the planning side had anticipated was the sheer outrage the Americans had demonstrated over the discussions that had been held between Mohammad bin Azaria and the secretary of state. They had been discussing a long-term plan that had many aspects, one of which had been the resettlement of refugees in large numbers, but totally provided for, right up until they left for university, and even then, beyond if it were needed.

If someone from outside the program came aboard, their initial reaction would probably be "an intensive, immersive English language environment aimed at young girls, with a huge selection of books, cartoons, and videos!" They would not be wrong. There were six theatres with ice cream and popcorn that ran every children's movie ever made as well as musicals, dancing and singing films, and educational videos that concentrated on language, maths, communication, and behavior. The objective was simple—to give the girls the best possible chance of fitting into their new homes, with as little disruption as possible.

One little girl, her name was Olga, she was six as far as her skimpy records were concerned, and she had been pulled out of the worst camp at Coxes Bazar, where the death toll prior to the terrorist attacks had been a staggering 209 children on average, every day. While she had been in the rusty old bus, with an empty belly, tears in her eyes, and confusion written all over her face, she had seen one of the other girls playing with a brightly colored block. She watched intently, her stomach rumbling, then, after a long, long while, tentatively held her hand out to the girl seeking the block. It had been reluctantly handed to her, and in seconds, she had rearranged the sides so that all the colors lined up.

She did not know what she had done; it just made sense to her that the sides should all be the same red, blue, yellow, white, black, and green. And she did not know the name of the colors, just that they looked better her way.

Little had she known it. She had set a new world record for her age by sorting out a Rubik's Cube in under three minutes. And looking at it completed, she handed it back to the little girl who had so unselfishly given it to her, not knowing what to do with it now that it looked like it should. Of course, not to be outdone by her opposite number, the little girl deliberately wrecked the symmetry of the cube, mixed up the squares with fast and vigorous twists, then, with a cheeky grin, gave it back to Olga. This time it only took two minutes and forty-six seconds, and as quickly as that, a new game was started, which lasted its way all across the Pacific Ocean.

By the time the boat eventually docked, Olga was the undefeated champion of the whole ship's company, crew included, and the navigator, who had a small old-style camera, had made a video of Olga's last attempt, which ran just under a minute thirty. He thought he might send it to the Guinness Book of Records if there was still one.

Chapter 31

"**C**oleen, there were people here yesterday looking for you," Fred called across the pile of refuse from the building he was presently sheeting with the amazing, sparkling solar panels. The engineer stood stock still, her silky muscles bunched, the hairs on her arms and neck on full alert, a wan smile fighting a frown on her face for space. She knew Fred slightly—his son worked in the same garage as she did. He had just recently passed his apprenticeship and had brought his father to the garage a few times to show off where he worked. As casually as she could, she asked the one question, the answer to which could end her time here in Helena.

"Who were they?" He threw his shoulders back as he lifted another sheet into position. The beauty of this new building material was the simplicity of joining a sheet to its neighbor and the way they looked alive and felt so warm to the touch. The current batch was a light blue in color, in contrast to the house next door that had been built using the pale green hue. If you looked up and down the row of finished houses, you got the impression of a happy, bright, colorful place, no two houses exactly the same but sharing sufficient commonality to allow them to be constructed quickly and efficiently.

Already over two hundred had been completed, and to be honest, he had his eye on the little blue number that butted into a new park that had just been built. He didn't know who was selling them, but he'd heard rumors that the workers and the transients would be given the first option and that there was a kicker in the contract, something to do with children. Well, he had two of his own and loved them to death, so he hoped he would fit the profile. And he knew the price would be right, because that same rumor suggested that the cost of the sheeting, roofing, walls, and floors would be zero-summed, again, if certain conditions were met environmentally. Well, he put all his hard rubbish stuff in the yellow top, and all the recyclables in the blue bin, didn't he? So, again, he hoped that his old habits would stand him in good stead to get him into the house he had picked out. Coleen's question echoed in his mind, so he lowered the sheet he was holding and rested on it.

"There was a woman around here, who didn't say who she was, spoke with a Chicago accent, had three photos, and was trying to find out where you all might be. I heard one of the boys tell her you worked at the garage, and one of your friends worked at the university, and that was that. She didn't seem to have much luck otherwise.

"Did she ask for me by name?"

"Yes, that she did. And she mentioned the names of the other two women in the photos, but I don't know who they are."

"Thanks, Fred. I'll ask around and see if I can find her." She walked off down the row of half-finished houses, thinking furiously. There had been a woman mentioned with the FBI agents, and she knew that a male and a female had walked the building site just last week, although they asked no questions other than about the building materials and seemed to have been shopping for a house. Maybe she was sprung, maybe not, but the fact that someone they didn't know had photos and names of the three of them was inherently suspicious and potentially dangerous. And she remembered an old saw that had been drummed into her before the project had started by an ex-army ranger who had been hired to polish off the edges of the three of them: "If there is doubt, there is no doubt."

She climbed into her vehicle and, during the short ride home, considered her options. The build was going extremely well; they would be able to release the first hundred or so houses next week once the various certificates were obtained. They needed eleven hundred places available within five weeks, and at the current build rate, they would meet that quota easily. What was still unknown was the reaction of the American government and their ability to find parents who would be willing to adopt. Her role was to facilitate the local scene here in Helena, but if she had been identified, and linked back to the attacks, then she needed to get out of Dodge double-quick smart.

But she needed to ensure that their plan would go ahead, come what may. She mentally brought the home of Howard Westhall into her mind and thought about the two young women that now lived there, waiting patiently for her call. It might come much sooner than any of them expected, but she knew in her heart that when she did make it, the project would be secured. The girls—even though they were both in their late teens and well-developed—were still just young girls to Coleen, who, at the ripe old age of thirty-one, viewed herself as grown-up and experienced.

As she drove down her street, her sharp eyes saw the black SUV parked at her front gate, so she just continued on down the road, turning back towards the main highway that would take her around the bottom end of West Helena. She considered her options, steadied her speed to just below the limit, and concentrated on her driving. To be picked up now by the local police would be insulting, and she would never live it down with her sisters. She thought about using the in-car satellite transmitter, then rejected it. If it were the FBI poking around, they only had two people locally; she knew the others had left by car some time ago, but she started to worry about her friend, the pilot, who was due back in town the next day. For the first time since she had arrived in Helena over two years ago now, she felt out of control.

She arrived at the old Howard Westhall home, a beautiful 160-year-old mansion that had been preserved and restored continually over the years and was now heritage listed by the American Preservation Society. The original family line had died out when Howard was put in the ground, but the property had been gifted to a well-known charity and its future secured with a trust fund that had been topped up some years ago by a generous unnamed donor. When Howard had come up with his "one hundred thousand homes" idea, the town had two predictable reactions—half the people laughed at the stupidity of the idea, seeing that the entire population of Helena had never crossed thirty-odd thousand, and the second was one of wonder. A wonder that expanded into amazement as the very modern solar farm went up, trenches dug for underground power, water, waste management, and services, and the massive area he had purchased was surveyed and marked off into building blocks.

And then the project had just sat fallow for years, regularly maintained by workers who came and mowed, weeded, swept the roads, and trimmed the trees every month.

And now, in just weeks, homes were sprouting up like colorful fresh garden flowers at a rate that staggered the mind. Tents, caravans, SUVs, trailer homes, and all manner of transportable living spaces littered the countryside along the highway as families from the north, south, east, and west fled the civil unrest and devastation caused by the terrorist attacks. But it was almost as if the town council had anticipated both the attacks and the resultant flood of humanity because the town had managed to absorb approximately the same number of transients as made up the population of the town in no time at all. And when the ads for workers appeared, the flood of workers was enormous, and even a blind man could see the enormous progress being made.

Howard's family had made all their money out of oil in Texas and gold in California but had rooted in Helena for reasons unknown. The family had always been held in high regard, had always played a major role in community events, and had a library, a park, and a major street named after them as well as perpetual scholarships at the university. One of which, by a strange coincidence, had supported the salary of a part-time maths teacher for the past two and a half years.

A maths teacher currently on leave, as she had been for the past few weeks, as the initial reaction of the university was to close its doors after the attacks started, the classic "wait and see" philosophy of tenured academics. But now, with all the bustling around the massive building site, which was quite visible from the university grounds, the flood of new people into the town, and the palpable excitement in the city streets, they were ready to reopen their doors. Of course, a cynic would say that they had noticed the plans for several new schools, and a large university posted on the community notice board along with the copies of the building approvals and sensed they may soon have competition for students.

They would have been correct. But the issue of communication rose large with the internet crash, and the town now relied on old-fashioned analog telephones, most of which had not yet found their way into every home, so paper notices were posted, and messengers sent out on bikes to contact all the faculty staff. It was a slow and tedious business, but one by one, the staff reported back to their faculties, and the university planned its reopening date, class programs, and academic lists. As far as the board of governors could see, the new university would not be finished this side of Christmas, although the bottom floors of the accommodation wings were nearing completion, as were the four junior and middle schools. They scratched their heads, and a quick survey of the itinerants just last week showed around two thousand children of middle school age, less than one hundred of university age, but quite a lot of pre and junior-school age.

Even factoring all that data in, they could not immediately see the need for the sheer volume of new facilities. But department by department, working at a feverish pace, the university rose back to its stately heights, ready for a commencement ceremony. The mayor was hyped, and the board of governors was hyped, for the word on the grapevine was that they would be one of the very first universities in the whole country to resume normal classes.

Coleen knocked on the massive wooden door, carved with symbols of the old world, and was let into a huge spacious foyer with majestic staircases rising up from the left and the right, as far as the eye could see. A sparkling waterfall roared down between the stairs, seemingly falling down from the roof, which was hard to see as the light flared on the dome that covered the atrium-like room. The pool that caught the cascading sheets of water was blue, large, and dominated by massive orange fish that swam around as if they were demented. To finish the experience, the walls on either side of the atrium were covered with massive hand-made rugs, at least one hundred years old but still holding their shine from the silk embroidering.

It was a clash of styles, the old and the new, and against this backdrop, the two young women dressed in jeans, matching tee shirts, and bold-colored hightops looked completely out of place.

"Hi, Coleen. We were expecting to see you soon. How are you?" Moya, the younger of the two by mere months, asked, slipping her dainty hands into the back pockets of her jeans. The elder of the two leaned forward and embraced Coleen in a bear hug, made all the more potent by her five feet ten-inch frame. Coleen could look after herself, having taken a few self-defense courses and studied a little judo, but the leverage the younger girl exercised almost pushed her off her balance.

"Hey, easy there, girl. You've grown another inch since I saw you last!" she said, ducking to escape the petite arms. They all laughed and, linking arms, walked past the stairway into a more formal and normally decorated lounging room. They sprawled on crinkled leather couches, so old that the faded patches that got direct sunlight three times a day from the huge overhead skylights looked like dirt stains. Coleen looked closely at the two girls, remembering their training and their heritage. Both had been pulled out of the same refugee camp in Libya less than twelve years ago; both had been moved to Ireland, where they had been adopted by loving families; and then both had excelled in mechanical and electrical engineering, graduating early, and both had readily volunteered for this part of the plan and moved to America, sponsored by the trust that maintained the grand old house.

Officially, they were there as a writer and a painter, brought in to document the history of the family and, by virtue of its proximity, Helena. Both had been welcomed by the town council and the various members of the arts community and had settled in quickly. Elizabeth had established herself at the building site by plunking down a folding chair and umbrella every day to record the progress of the build. She was so well known onsite that she had been given a high visibility vest and a hard hat with her name on it. The matter of how she would take over management of the project was yet to be worked out, but the companies and the proxies had been set up years ago, so the legal and formal framework was in place; it just needed gentle hands to caress the controls every now and then to ensure that their objective was achieved.

"I got some bad news, I'm afraid. It seems that the three of us have been identified. I don't know how that happened, but it has. As you know, the FBI was here in force last week, so it may be a result of that. They were parked outside our front gate just now. That's why I'm here." The girls looked shellshocked; it was one thing to learn stuff and computer model things yet to be done, but it was quite another to actually have to do them! And do them well.

"Ah, I don't suppose there's any chance you are wrong?" Moya curled her legs up under her, a feat that created the impression of a boa constrictor wrapping itself around a tree. Elizabeth looked pale as the realization of what they would have to achieve sunk in. While the three older women were around, managing things, giving encouragement, and helping with the planning, the strategy they needed to embrace, the responsibility had been at arm's length; now it would become theirs. Elizabeth smoothed imaginary creases in her faded jeans, her hands moving up and down the invisible seams quite rapidly.

"How much time do we have?" Her expectant look would melt the heart of any other woman except Coleen, who had lived with the terror, guilt, and wonder of what they had been able to achieve, but she forced her warmest look onto her face and took Elizabeth's small coffee-colored hand.

"We have to act as if we have been busted. I need one of you to intercept Rosie tomorrow at the airport if the FBI doesn't get there first. I'm heading out now to our safe house; keep a lookout for me every three cycles, starting at seven hundred tomorrow."

"What do you want us to do with Rosie?"

"I'm going to try to get her a message while she's in the air and divert her. If I can't, then you have to get her here as quickly and as quietly as you can, then let her make her way to me."

"Where is Iona?" Coleen looked at Moya and thought about the need to know and all the other concerns she now had, but trust between the sisters was absolute and not to be demeaned under any circumstances.

"She's now safely in New Zealand, ramping up the local plant. That's what Rosie has been doing. She took the little five-seater, used the biofuel dumps we set up, and mirrored legitimate flights as far as she could, then under her 'cloud' when she couldn't."

"Okay, we'll figure something out. How are you feeling?" Coleen looked at Moya with a wan smile; she felt dirty and had for weeks, but she didn't let this little nymph see her troubles. They had a righteous job in front of them, helping to make the world sing again, while she had actively helped bring it to its collective knees. She shrugged her shoulders, stood, embraced both girls, then left the way she had come. They both stood at the door, watching her leave, their hearts heavy with a sense of loss but also alive with the fission of anticipation. They would be part of the team that turned the lights back on, as it were, gave people hope, and showed the way to the future. And in the process, they would welcome thousands of their sisters from refugee camps all over the globe to not only a new, bright world with hope but one that really cared.

Chapter 32

Sideways-flying sleet and low, angry clouds filled the windscreen, and the howl of the wind almost overpowered that of the twin engines roaring over our heads. Even the headsets we were issued failed to keep the banshee-like noise out, and the buffeting from side to side, frequent sudden drops, and then uplifts just as violent reinforced my total dislike of flying in helicopters. In contrast, Pete sat almost hanging out the open side door, eyes bright, tongue licking his lips, looking like a big, hairless dog enjoying the slipstream in a car. To no one's surprise, the Boss had snagged the copilot's seat and, dressed in the army equivalent of a camouflaged flight suit, looked the part. It didn't go unnoticed that we were accompanied by two gunships, which the Boss had informed us would be rotating in and out as their fuel allowed providing high cover.

This had become an expensive exercise, but the general had made no apology when she had given me her terms—yes, we could have a Blackhawk, but the air cover went with it. And yes, sorry about that, but a Coast Guard cutter would be just off the coast of Point Roberts, with a full complement of navy SEALs aboard, ready and willing to get into the fight.

A fight I was determined not to have. Somehow. But General Saunders had taken personally the aborted attack planned on the FBI in Helena, not to mention the militia attack on us a few days prior, and she said she wasn't taking any more chances with civilians. My skin had bristled at being called a "civilian," but from her perspective, I had crossed to the dark side by transferring from NCIS to Interpol, and I know the military never really considered the FBI to be battle-hardened, so I swallowed my pride and got on with the mission. But I did secretly admit I would have been much more comfortable having Tom and his team around, or even Bob and his. I wondered how Bob and his train were going; they must be back in Washington by now, as I had just turned them around before we left Seattle.

We bashed and shuddered through the air and through the broken cloud, which by now was skimming the tops of the whippy standing waves, wind against tide. It was a classic for a reason, the fringes of the forest that presaged the plant flittered into view. We sunk, rose, twisted, then shuddered into a freefall, arrested at the last minute by a heavy thud, then we were down, I think, and the rotors started to spin down in ground idle. Through the open side door, I could see two golf carts lined up by the side of the grassy area we had selected as our landing zone. To my surprise, the COO stood out in the rain, holding her broad-rimmed rain hat on her head, fighting the downwash from the slowly decelerating rotor blades.

Not the reception I expected. I looked over at Fay, sitting in front of me but to the side. I keyed my mike.

"Fay, all yours, remember you are in command. Sell it." Her eyes hardened, and at that moment, I lost my concern that she would not manage whatever situation she found herself in.

"Yes, ma'am." And she jumped out of the helicopter into the whirling devilish created by the storm and the rotor wash. Pete followed, then stopped dead at the doorway, looked at me, and smiled. He held out his hand, which I ignored, and jumped down. He would pay for that, but much later when we were back home. The others quickly deplaned and, heads bowed and bodies bent against the wash of the rotors and the fury of the storm, headed to the golf buggies. I ended up sitting next to Malcolm, with Anna, Pete, and Amira for company, and with a jerk, the little cart sped off down the entrance road. We sped past the buildings; they all looked the same, huge black blocks of sparky material that glistened in the sheeting rain, but Pete had a little detector in his palm, and he grinned at me in such a way I intuited we were being monitored.

We pulled up at the entrance to the main building, stood for a second or two, shook off the excess water like wet dogs, then took our ponchos off and handed them to a waiting young man who looked familiar. Fay's staff photos of one of the local men hired by the plant a year ago. Arnon, I think his name was, had led Fay's team through some of the buildings on the last visit. He collected the ponchos and put them on pegs. I found this a little anal, but from what Fay and her team had reported, we were in for much more of that before we were finished. I stood still, waiting for Fay's orders. I was merely a mid-level SA FBI agent, just one of the boys, supporting Fay as the SSA. To her credit, Fay was quick off the mark.

"Ms. Tremblay, thank you for meeting us. We are organized in two teams, as I said on the phone, one to check physically every building and the warehouse, the second to requestion some of your staff, and hopefully have a conversation with your CEO."

"Agent Remer, welcome. We have organized a tour for your team; if they would go with Arnon here, and if the others would come with me, we can get started." Anna, Amira, Sandra, and Malcolm immediately peeled off and followed Arnon into a dark hallway and disappeared into the gloom. I watched them with some trepidation; if we were to be ambushed, I had just lost more than half of my team, but before I could develop this fear further, the COO ushered us inside a brightly lit foyer, off which three separate well-lit areas flowed. She took us into the middle one, which turned out to be a medium-sized boardroom with a long, polished wooden table running down the center. It looked like a massive jigsaw puzzle, and as I reached down to run my hand over the surface, a tough, raw edge voice echoed around the room.

"That table is handmade, out of one thousand eight hundred different pieces of teak, all from sailing ships that used to ply this area. If you look underneath," and the voice lowered as a head of reddish-gold hair filled my vision, and I bent to look under the table, "you can see how each individual piece was assembled." It was a huge jigsaw puzzle, I was right, but it was also a remarkable testament to the craftspeople who had painstakingly assembled it. The undersurface was rough, discolored, and uneven, with some pieces so dark you could almost smell the saltwater. I stood up, looked at the woman who had provided the commentary, and smiled my acknowledgment.

"Special Agent Riley, nice to meet you, and yes, this is exquisite craftsmanship."

"Kathryn Simmons, I'm the chief executive officer. Welcome to our little facility," she said, reaching out and shaking my hand.

"This is Senior Special Agent Remer," I said, turning to introduce Fay, "and Special Agent Pete." They shook hands with the CEO, then Fay subtly took control in a manner that made me proud.

"Ms. Simmons, thank you for your welcome. My agents and I would like to have a conversation with you both before we requestion some of your senior staff. Is that okay with you?" Her body language telegraphed that she was serious, and the way she positioned herself at the door suggested no one was leaving before we had our little chat. The CEO nodded and sat at the head of the table. Her COO sat on one side, and not wasting an opportunity, I sat directly opposite. Fay effectively hemmed the COO in, and Pete sat opposite me. The home team had the positional advantage, but we had managed to surround them in the politest manner possible.

I scored that a nil—all draw. Fay started the ball rolling.

"During my last visit, I had the pleasure of seeing building three and building six, and, thanks to Ms. Tremblay, the warehouse and docking area. Of specific interest is building six, where we saw what looked like molten mercury flowing in some sort of bath, with the big—may I say, very big—additive 3D printers on each end. Our analysts believe you are using nanotechnology; can you confirm that, please?" And not pausing for a second, she fanned out the three ID photos of the women from Helena like a Las Vegas card sharp, "And can you confirm these three people work here?" Both women were caught off guard, and both let it show in their eyes before both faces hardened, then slipped back to warm and conversational. It was as if two minds had acted in concert and spoke to the extensive training both had. But Pete, Fay, and I had clearly seen the shock and surprise on their faces, and now I had a new problem to deal with.

I rested my hand on the table and looked at Fay; she saw what was in my eyes, nodded minutely as if giving me permission, and at the subtle byplay, Pete stood up and filled the doorway, standing sideways, so he had a view of the boardroom, and the outside corridor. I took a deep breath. I didn't know where this was going to go, but deep in my gut, I knew it would go somewhere and fast. I really wished I had Bob or Tom and their teams here hidden under the table, but I pressed the little button on my watch strap and remembered that there came a time in every agent's life when you just had to bite the bullet and take the consequences.

"Ms. Simmons, Ms. Trembley, my name is Jessica Riley, and I am the senior investigating agent for Interpol, and unless you both can convince me otherwise, I will be taking you both, and possibly a large number of your staff, into custody under the Terrorist Act as modified in 2022. Initially, the arrests will be made by the FBI, but the overarching warrant will be issued by the World Court in the Hague." Neither woman spoke. They didn't look at each other, their eyes remained locked on mine, and a deathly hush descended on the room like a wet fog. Then the CEO brushed her hair back from her ears in a typical female gesture, the reddish-gold hair fanning attractively, and smiled.

"Captain Riley, or may I call you Jessica? Never mind, we were aware of you and your pursuit a month ago; we have followed your progress with interest. We expected you would get here eventually, but not perhaps so soon. As Farid told Senior Special Agent Remer here on her last visit, everything we do here is legitimate, above board, well documented, audited by several government agencies, and will stand any test you care to make. We are the solution, not the problem, as you will no doubt find out."

"The Terrorism Laws provide for aiding and abetting, assisting, enabling, moral or physical support, and or ideology aligned with any specific terrorist attack. Do you deny that you assisted, in any way, the terrorist attacks of five weeks ago that claimed the lives directly and indirectly of some fifty-five million people worldwide to date?" I let a very hard edge slip into my voice, but I kept my voice low, the better to emphasize my controlled anger. I was looking forward to their explanation, but first, I had to hit them with a few inalienable facts to see how they reacted. Technology would give us some answers, the timeline some others, and the staff would undoubtedly, unintentionally identify some or all of the women from Helena, which would give us a direct link, but we had already seen confirmation of the three women being involved in the plant in their reactions.

But the hardcore proof was going to be very hard to come by. The only person we had on camera committing a terrorist act was the pilot, and then all she had to do was claim "coercion," and she might get off the hook, although I didn't really think so. All we really had after five weeks of hard slog were strong suspicions of involvement, linked by very tenuous information.

"You began shipping solar panels to Helena some six months ago in the thousands, long before any need became apparent. Who ordered them from you, and how did they pay for them? And why were they stored at the airport and not taken directly to a building site?"

"And when did you manufacturer the nanomachines that destroyed the oil, gas, and coal sites?" the Boss asked as he stalked across the room in his soaked flight suit, leaving a muddy trail from his flight boots. He swung into a chair, turned it around so he faced the two women, and the look he gave them would have melted steel. "We know you made them; we suspect your New Zealand factory also made those bugs, and in the current political climate, suspicion is all we are going to need to shut you down and wrap you all up for about, oh, I don't know, how about a thousand years?" Pete and I looked at each other and inwardly smiled; this was the Boss at his finest and not totally unexpected.

"And, by the way, just in case you still have a few of your mercenary terrorists lying around somewhere, we have a SEAL team with us, and they are just looking for a fight, something about the rough voyage they had getting here upsetting their equilibrium." I watched the faces of the two women as the Boss hammered home his points, and to their credit, neither flinched or gave any sign of discomfort. In fact, if anything, the CEO's face had hardened, her green eyes flashing sparks at his words. She held up one immaculate manicured hand, the clear lacquer on her fingernails flashing briefly in the light, and she tilted her head to one side.

"Colonel, welcome. We were expecting you at some time. Nice to meet you in the flesh. Can we offer you coffee, tea, something else to drink?" At the mention of coffee, the Boss's eyes glazed over, and his craggy face split into a smile.

"Thank you, you know me too well, but it had better be an exceptional cup of coffee for us not to take you away in chains." The CEO smiled, a tight-lipped mimic of the Boss's, but the tension in the room lowered just a fraction, so I decided to pull the attention back to me.

"Ms. Simmons, our technical experts are now examining your plant, and they are able to inform us of your capacity and capability for producing the nanomachines. We only need one piece of hard evidence to shut you down, close you down permanently, and cart you away—as the Colonel said—in chains.

"Jessica, if I may call you that, we know your technical expert, Miss Amira Abramowitz. We studied her work some years ago. And your NSA expert, a world-class white-hat hacker before he was reformed, I believe, is also not totally unexpected. But I am surprised by your insistence that we, or our sister company, made the nanomachines that destroyed the oil, gas, and coal sites."

"The nanites you are using in your current production are close enough to the ones used to destroy the oil, gas, and coal sites," I challenged, knowing I was on very thin legal grounds. She looked directly at me and smiled as she might at a poor child begging in the street, full of condescending concern.

"Jessica, like is not the same as exact. To prove we did what you have accused us of, you would have to either produce the formula from our systems or samples of our work that match exactly the microstructure at the nanoscale of the nanites you are referring to. This means you will need the ability to define the nanostructure of both nanites and prove their exactness. I've no doubt that Miss Abramowitz could manage such a thing in her laboratory in Israel. Or even the one she used at Harvey Mudd, but the key here is proving that your bug came from our plants." She flicked her hair again, this time, I think, with just the hint of a little anger behind it. "Good luck with that."

I looked at her steadily; was I surprised by her knowledge of Amira and Malcolm? No, not really. We knew the terrorists had been inside our IT infrastructure for years, possibly decades, so it was to be expected that they knew all about Interpol and our pursuit of them, as well as Amira and Malcolm's professional backgrounds and histories. I had a sudden thought, looked over at Pete, still guarding the door, and he shook his head. He was tuned into the tactical channel our people in the buildings were used, as well as the SEALs.

"No, Jessica, we are not attacking your people. We are, in fact, showing them everything they want to see; you are not in any danger here." She had read my mind. "It is imperative for the recovering world for us to continue our current production activities, and I'll tell you anything you need to know to achieve that." No small agenda here, but a little gloss over the boasting got my attention—"recovering world" not only sounded pompous, but it also sounded downright autocratic. "Then start with the three women whose photos we showed you. When were they here, and what did they do? And start with this one," I snapped, pushing the photo of the pilot across the table. She looked at it, picked it up, and then, with her face perfectly bland, placed it back on the table.

"I don't know this woman." I spun another at her. She picked it up, and a little smile crossed her eyes for a flicker of a second. "Yes, I know Coleen; she is an impressive person. Irish has an infectious smile and is one of the most brilliant engineers I have ever had the pleasure to meet."

"What did she do for you, and when did she do it?" I couldn't help snapping, the tension in me had me wired like an overwound clock spring.

"She helped us set up all our additive 3D printing and manufacturing machines, tuned them, so to speak, then helped build and program our robots. She was here some time ago. I would have to check our records to be sure." I bet she did. I spun the last photo over, looked for the tell, saw it, and smiled to myself. She was clever, undoubtedly highly intelligent. It seemed to be the default position of these women, but I had years of experience interrogating some of the nastiest and, in their own way, smartest and cleverest of the bad guys and girls, so while I might be handicapped on the IQ side, I was well ahead on the interrogation smarts side.

"Iona is a scientist; she, too, is a lovely person. Kind in nature and is a very hard worker. She's one of those rare breeds of scientists who can cross over different disciplines—metallurgy, chemistry, nanotechnology, quantum physics, plasmas, that sort of thing. She was here from day one, helping to set up the equipment, then she went overseas for a while and came back only last year. She hasn't been here for some time. I would have to check our records to know exactly when." She was lying, there was no doubt about that, but she was mixing enough of the truth in to make it hard to divine the lies. I tried a different tack.

"When you say you are familiar with Miss Abramowitz's work, what exactly are you referring to?" For the first time, when she shifted her attention to me, I saw a hardness in her eyes that caused a chill to run down my spine. She was a woman full of anger, I could see that, and I needed to work out what her trigger was.

"From memory. When Amira was at Harvey Mudd, she led a team of scientists and engineers that conducted a live test of nanomachines on an oil spill. I forget where, somewhere up near the Canadian border, I seem to recall, and at that time, there were papers being published that described what the expectation was, and that triggered our professional interest." I noted the use of Amira's first name and tucked it away, leaned across the table, hands folded into a V, linked fists pointed directly at her for emphasis.

"And what company were you working for at that specific time?" I asked, catching her by surprise. She hid it well, that hair flick and hand brush again, but I was not a susceptible male with raging hormones. She stared at me, eyes hot with the challenge, and even the COO looked a little uncomfortable. Interesting, this was a line we had not tugged previously. I had made the question up simply to get a reaction, but I had accidentally hit gold. There was something in the past that would point to the future, and I thought back to the timeline we had constructed from Amira's briefings—or, more correctly, interrogations because, at the time, she had been under military arrest as a suspected hacker.

"I'll be specific—where were you working in 1999, 2000, and what were you doing?" The frosted look she gave me this time made me smile; we had hit a nerve, and I was going to hammer it until I got an answer. She had folded her hands, sat very upright, and almost spat at me.

"From this point, our lawyers will handle any questions you may have. I can have them here in an hour."

"No, you won't. I'm placing you all under arrest, under the Terrorist Laws, for aiding and abetting terrorist activities, which will be specified in your warrant and made public. I'm also closing this site effective immediately. A Red Notice will be issued by Interpol to cover it; everyone on the premises will be taken into custody by the FBI and held under guard until we get the answers we need. And just to remind you about the Terrorist Laws, they give us the right to hold you without access to counsel for ninety-six hours, during which time we will search this plant and pull it literally to bits." And I sat back and watched her face cloud over as she fought an internal battle of some kind, and if the pink flush that was building on her cheeks and throat was any indication, tearing me to bits with her own hands was high on her agenda.

"Ms. Simmons, you have no rights. This is not a civilian arrest; although it will be carried out by the FBI, it is a military one, as Section Five of Interpol has military status granted to it by the United Nations, which is why so many of us carry military ranks or equivalents. We will execute this immediately unless you tell us what we want to know. Let me list some facts for you. You have knowingly associated with at least two of the women terrorists who launched the attacks on the Vatican, the Dome of the Rock, the Grand Mosque, West Point, Lloyds of London, the space station, numerous sports arenas, I might have missed one or two of your targets, but the cruncher is the destruction of our oil and gas fields and our coal mines; you might not feel the same way, but crippling the world's energy supplies is proba-bly the one thing that will get you burnt at the stake." He still lounged in his seat casually, one long leg crossed over the other, and his voice was low, slow, and almost emotionless. The Boss brushed the back of his neck and rolled his shoulders, an amazingly relaxed look for a self-confessed executioner. Where had he got the "burnt at the stake" line from? Must be reading books again.

"Master Chief, call the SEALs in, please." I stood to emphasize the finality of what the Boss and I had just said. We were not bluffing, but the thought of cuffing thirty or forty people, most of whom were simply working to support their families and probably had stars in their eyes about the panels and batteries they were making in an effort to relieve the pressure on other ordinary families who were just trying to stay alive and turned my stomach. Then to my amazement and pride, Fay scooted around the table and cuffed the CEO in a movement so fluid I thought she could have been a ballet dancer. In a mirror of her movement, Pete had left his post by the door and had slipped plasticuffs on the COO, and the surprise on her face was wonderful to see, as was the outrage on the CEO's. Maybe now we would get somewhere.

"We had nothing, absolutely nothing, to do with those terrorist attacks. In fact, we are the exact opposite of those attacks. We exist solely to bring hope to the world by providing low-cost renewable power to every household that needs it. How is that a terrorist act?" the CEO practically screamed across the room, spittle flinging itself across the surface of the table. If her hands weren't cuffed and being held by an FBI agent, I could imagine them pounding on my face until I was a bloody mess!

"Then explain how you were so ready to provide help when it is needed most. Explain how you had a warehouse full of panels in Helena six months before any known terrorist attack. You had to have been warned, you had to know in advance when and where the terrorists would attack. And that makes you part of it." I didn't shout, but the image of my smashed face at the hands of the CEO did put an edge to my voice, and my heart was beating twice as fast as it usually did. I was pissed, I was angry with the professional facade we were facing down, but I sensed by the amount of anger and fury in the face of the CEO we just might be getting closer to answers.

"A trustee managing the assets of the Westhall family contacted us late last year and ordered enough panels for fifty thousand new houses to be built on an estate that Westhall Senior had set up prior to his death. I can show you the order. As part of our charter, as set by those that funded us, is to provide these renewable services to any who asked, at a discounted cost; we quoted the work, received payment in advance, and started shipping them as requested." She still shouted but a little softer, but the fire remained in her eyes, and I would still fear for my face if Fay loosened her grip any.

"And who exactly are your funders? And before you lie and really piss me off, we found you by following a money trail that started with the Arabian Sovereign Wealth Fund, to banks in this area and in Seattle, for six billion euros. And we know from the bank transfers that your company has drawn some point three billion dollars down just in the last two years. And do you know what else? This is the same pot of money the terrorists used to build their hideouts and their weapons, and used to attack us. How do you answer that?" I stared across the short distance at the CEO, chest pushed out by the firm grip Fay had on her handcuffs behind her back. I was about to throw Mohammad bin Azaria's name into the mix when the COO, Farid Tremblay, spoke for the very first time since she had welcomed us to the plant.

"Why would you attack us at this time? As Kathryn said, we have nothing to do with the attacks. For the last three years, we have been working around the clock to get this plant up and running so we can provide hope for all those most disadvantaged by the attacks. We have been preparing for this for years, and at the time of the greatest need, you threaten to shut us down and throw us in chains?" She shook her head, her long hair moving in gentle waves, and with Pete standing behind her holding her cuffs behind her back, I marveled at how calm she was. I changed tack.

"Farid, if I may call you that, how long have you been at this plant?"

"I came here for the first time seven months before we broke ground. I was assigned by the auditors for the firm that manages the trust that provided our funding. I have been here since we started the build, and before you ask, I lived in the town for the first few months, then moved into an apartment here soon after. And if you are trying to pin me as part of the terrorist attacks, I will refer you to my direct employers in Seattle, who are one of the most respected firms in the country. And they will sue your backsides off just for pleasure."

Okay, no pushover, but more information. A respected firm in Seattle looking after the six billion euros. I could imagine the pleasure they would have had receiving the funds, seeing them multiply exponentially as the euros were changed to USD, then also seeing the huge interest they would receive on the funds over time. Even at a shitty rate, they would be banking millions and millions of dollars for very little work. Good business if you could get it. And they had the money for at least five years, according to the FBI.

"So you are responsible for the funding and how the money is spent?" I asked. "No, I am responsible for the funding, and I audit the expenditure of the funds.

"The CEO has sole authorization on how the funds are allocated."

"But you are involved in the decision-making process at some stage?" This got me a glare as she tried to work out if I was asking a legitimate question or baiting her. Pride in her work overrode her reluctance to tell me.

"As a courtesy, the CEO has involved me in most of the big decisions, and yes, I have the power of veto, which I am proud to say that in the three and a half years on this project, I have not had to invoke once."

"So the profit your firm makes is solely from the interest on the principle?" The Boss was still hyper-relaxed, almost sprawling, and I could see he was jonesing for coffee, which he literally lived on. We were getting somewhere, so I decided to take a risk. I pointed at Fay, then Pete, flicking my fingers.

"We will take the cuffs off, for now at least, but please don't forget anything the colonel or I have said previously. We can put them back on and lock this place up in a heartbeat." The CEO rubbed her wrists, which showed a little inflamed circle, no doubt from her fighting the restraints. The COO just looked depressed, and her shoulders sunk as she put her hands on her lap.

"Haven't you asked yourselves how and why we are now providing free electricity to Point Roberts? And a free phone service for those that still have working smartphones." Her voice was almost plaintive, and the look on her face was one of hurt. I thought about that and reflected on the private conversation she had had with Fay about the refugee girls in the camps and her shared history. And I started to wonder if this was not the model we had hypothesized in action. The early tranche of refugee children, in the first seven years, were encouraged to study, then molded into the terrorists that had launched the attacks; the second tranche, and possibly all that followed after the hiatus in recruitment, educated and offered honest roles in the rehabilitation of the planet, post the attacks. Separated by years, distance, recruiters, and ideology. And if that were the case, we would have a very hard time proving the latter refugees were anything else but caring, helpful people doing their professional best to provide hope. And at a time when it was desperately needed.

And hadn't Mohammad bin Azaria hinted at that very same thing during interrogation? Once again, Fay threw herself into the silence. I was getting to really like her style.

"Farid, when we met last, you shared your background with me, so I wonder if you would mind telling us how you got to work for the firm in Seattle?" The CEO was still rubbing her wrists, making a point of her displeasure, and the Boss suddenly had had enough.

"You offered coffee some time ago; any chance of getting some now? Please?" The COO stood and looked at Pete, who smiled at her, something akin to a shark smiling at a fish it was about to consume, and motioned to her to follow him out. As he turned to leave, he flicked a quick look at the Boss, as if seeking permission to leave me, and I shook my head in mild frustration. I was a big girl. I could look after myself. And, after all, wasn't I the one who had shot him six times in the chest? We waited patiently, then they returned with a tray, six cups, and a huge pot. Without ceremony, the Boss filled his own cup, pushed the pot down the table, and was drinking it before the CEO could stop the pot from sliding off the tabletop.

"Now, Farid, where were we?" he asked, as cool as a cucumber. He had all but gulped his first cup and was accepting a second from Pete, who had rescued the sailing pot, and who knew the Boss's caffeine habit well. Farid looked into her cup, seeking inspiration.

"I loved numbers. So, without much effort, I slipped into economics and accounting. My family supported me totally, I graduated reasonably early, only by a year, and I won a scholarship to go to the

University of Western Ontario, where I fell in love with auditing. I mastered it, and during my final year, I was recruited by the firm. This was four years ago, and my first big account was the trust fund for this plant. Because of the speed with which Kathryn wanted to move, it was decided that I should move here, which I did, and the rest, you know."

"But you remain independent?" I asked, looking directly at her. Her face colored a little. It might be an embarrassment, might be temper, I would soon find out. "Yes, of course. I submit my monthly reports to the board of trustees and a weekly report to the office. Why would you ask?"

"Because you were in control of the plant the weekend we visited," Fay interjected, putting her cup down with a 'click.' Farid looked a little sheepish, probably wondering how to separate herself from the plant when it was clear she had managerial duties as well as those of auditor. She flicked a hasty look at the CEO, got absolutely no response at all, rolled her head to one side, and sought inspiration in her coffee cup again.

"I was invited to assist Kathryn as a member of the senior management team back last year when it became necessary for her to leave the plant for periods of time. As I was usually a part of the day-to-day decision-making process, I knew what was going on in the buildings, so it didn't take a lot of effort to maintain coordination and oversee the work. It was no more than a caretaker's role, I can assure you. After all, we are mostly automatic; the robots look after themselves, and our staff mostly just watch the progress from the balconies and check the boxing and shipping arrangements. We don't have anyone who actually touches the manufacturing processes."

"But you do stop for scheduled maintenance?"

"Yes, of course, but only for a few days every year."

"I see." And I did, and I'd bet my next skinny paycheck that this was when the engineer and maybe even the scientist came to visit. I would have to establish when the last shutdown was.

"When did you start to manufacture the power packs?" the Boss asked, on his third cup of coffee in as many minutes. We had only ever seen the drawing Fay's team had made, and I decided to change that immediately, following the Boss's lead.

"And talking about the power packs, can we see one, please?"

"Now?" the CEO asked, her voice shrill.

"Yes, right now." I kept my eyes on her; she didn't wilt, but a smirk started to build at the side of her mouth.

"Come with me." And she stood so fast and was out the door before Pete or Fay could corral her. Her high heels clip-clopped down the highly polished wooden corridor, with us trailing in her wake. I had to admire her choice of suit; it was pure linen in a warm pale blue color, which fitted her to perfection. Against my Armani, which had been cut and shaped to allow my weapon to be concealed, she looked stylish. I looked like a bag woman. I was really starting to have clothes envy in this case; I think I needed a vacation. She ground to a sudden halt at a large screened window, pushed a button, and the screen silently retracted up into the roof, revealing a moving conveyor on which sat huge, spider-like apparitions, all dark shadows and hidden corners, which revealed themselves to be folded up machinery of some sort when she turned on an overhead floodlight. She pressed another button on a small computer pad built into the wall, and the conveyor stopped so smoothly it must have some sort of compensating suspension. She pulled the pad off the wall, tapped a series of keys, and the apparition directly in front of us on the other side of the glass started to unfold like a bear coming out of hibernation and stretching in the moonlight.

With a slow dignity, what I assumed were solar panels opened like the petals on a wildflower, one by one, sliding into position with a click I couldn't hear, only imagine. It was as graceful a mechanical ballet as I had ever seen. As each panel settled, less and less of the box supporting the panels were visible, but it was square, grey in color, and a series of open plug holes ran down the side. Little wheels were sunk into its bottom, and I could imagine it being moved from place to place as it was needed. Fay had told us it weighed four hundred kilos—a quick conversion gave me eight hundred and eighty-one pounds imperial, so it was not light by any means.

"How much power does it produce?" Pete asked. We all had our noses pressed to the window like kids at a lolly shop.

"Each panel produces over three thousand watts, the battery can store up to eighty thousand watts, and the panels produce power in rain, hail, fog, even on some moonlit nights. They are super efficient, have a one-hundred-year life, and we are producing them at the rate of three hundred an hour." The CEO's voice was filled with pride, and if we weren't investigating her possible role in the terror attacks and the death of fifty-five-odd million people, I would have shared her satisfaction.

"So to run a small factory, you'd run them in series?" Pete asked.

"No, in parallel. We've demonstrated that ten of these units can run a factory of five thousand square feet and the machinery in it. If you use our panels on the roof and on just the sunny side of the building, you get as much power as you need. In a housing estate of one hundred houses, we can run them with just six units. Of course, if the house is built out of our new panels, like the ones we have shipped to Helena, only a smallish battery is required in the basement as a buffer, and each house can export sufficient power to run five more houses. Our plan in Helena is to provide excess electricity at no cost back to the town grid, which I'm sure you already know is ninety-five percent renewable in any case."

"Who helped you to develop this plan?" I asked, bringing us all back to the reality of millions dead and dying and the planet effectively without fossil fuels. The CEO stood back from the window, pressed some keys on the pad, and behind the window, the articulate machine folded itself up like a massive spider retracting into its web. As the final panels slipped into place, the conveyor started up again, as smooth as silk. The lights faded, and the screen ran down, creating the impression of a show finishing to an appreciative audience. I admit, I was impressed, but I couldn't lose sight that we were hunting down terrorists that had done such incalculable damage to the world as to defy description. I suspected that one of the two beautiful women currently in my view was part of the main group of terrorists, the other just an innocent bystander caught up in the web of treachery and deceit— but a knowing one, nevertheless.

And I had to work out a way to separate the two without bloodshed or risking the productivity of the factory. And I had the whole metaphorical world looking over my shoulder. The Boss could read the conflict on my face, he was good at that, and he stepped up to the CEO.

"I have a suggestion the captain might like to entertain. We'll leave the plant running, for the foreseeable future, under the guidance of your COO, who is, by your own measure, competent. We will take you with us back to Seattle, where we can question you further and either prove or disprove your involvement in the terrorist attacks. We will leave some people behind, just as a precaution, but at this point, this is the best you can hope for. Captain?" It only took me a minute to process what the Boss was doing; it was an excellent ploy, seemingly a compromise, one that didn't leave us exposed that I could see, and one that would give me the opportunity to really hone in on the CEO and her history. But it was a ploy designed to change the rhythm of the interrogation once again, as I had by requesting the inspection of the power packs.

As we walked back to the boardroom, I asked what I considered to be a casual question laced with a landmine. "How do you communicate, plant to plant?" And without thinking, the COO answered, and we had another part of the puzzle answered.

"We use satellite automated transmissions, computer to computer, to enable the time zone differences to be minimized. Why do you ask?" I smiled, but carefully. I didn't want it to show.

"No real reason. The usual satellite services were crashed with the World Wide Web and cyberattack that took out our phones and computers, so you must have your own satellites?" She turned to me, confusion filling her eyes as the mistake she had made hit home. So they were part of the terrorist plan, they did know the timing, and now I was royally pissed off at having had one single good thought about them and their bloody machines. The Boss read my eyes again, and the look he gave me was one of great sympathy.

"I've changed my mind. You will both come with us. You are under arrest, as previously advised. Colonel, please call the SEALs in and clear out the plant. Fay, call your office, please, and have them send sufficient people to secure this location for the foreseeable future. Pete, call our people in, please. We'll take over the conference room, escort the prisoners to the helicopter, get them back to Seattle, then bring back the FBI continent. Everybody clear?" I almost barked the instructions, so irritated I was almost being sucked in. There were layers of that, I was sure, but the fact remained that even if an innocent person knew of the attacks prior to them occurring and did not inform the authorities, they were as guilty as the terrorists who mounted the attack.

That's what the Terrorist Laws were all about and had been since the tragedy of 9/11.

Pete and Fay marched the two women towards the helicopter; the SEAL team ran down the road and out of the tunnel; Anna and Amira popped, looking happy and contented, followed by Sandra and Malcolm, who looked as if he had just been let loose in the best toy shop in the world. I would soon wipe that smile off their faces, but before I could damage the egos of my team, the Boss pulled me to one side.

"Jessica, let it go. They were never going to fool you, and besides, look at what we now have to play with!" The excitement in him was palatable, and I struggled to think why, and as he rubbed some of the tension out of my shoulders with his large, strong hands, and I actually thought about purring, he told me why.

"Fay's team told us they have the distribution organized up and down the coast; the machinery is automatic, and if the engineer was here in the last few weeks as we both suspect, then the annual maintenance has been concluded, and I can't believe that between Amira and Malcolm we can't keep the factory running until we find some help. We need to get all the workers together and make an assessment of who can stay and who has to go home. Who do you want to start with?" He made a good point. I moved to Amira, took her aside, and noticed Anna moved like her shadow; she was picking up bad habits from Pete!

"Amira, can you run the nanite production you saw here?" The honest shock on her face was wonderful to see after the confusion and deceit we had looked at all morning. "I don't mean physically run it, but can you keep the plant running as it is now?" She stared at me, looked at Anna, and looked back at me.

"Why?"

"We've taken the CEO and COO into custody. There are humanitarian reasons for keeping the plant running; if you tell us what you need, we will find the right people. Or Anna will. I suspect that the American government will want to have a say in this." Anna nodded; she could virtually hear the bellows from Washington as she stood in the rain. I looked at the Boss.

"There are a million things we have to follow up on—do the trustees know anything? Where do their instructions come from?"

"Slow down, Jessica. You have just captured the first of the women we are after, and she wasn't even on our radar until today. The FBI will take over a lot of the detailed follow-up. That's what they are good at. You need to keep your focus on the main game."

"Where are the other three women. But we need to get a team back into Helena and straighten out everything there."

"Yes, we do, but don't forget we now have people who have been there once, people who dug out our terrorists' faces in the first place. There should be no threat to the FBI now, but we can send in some protection with them just by getting your train back."

"Already done. I sent a message to Bob; he turned the train around a few hours ago and will be in Helena at midday tomorrow. He has his special forces team and twenty army regulars, the ones that provide the guard for the train under normal circumstances, and they are not dummies."

"Do you want some here?" I looked around in the rain; the staff was slowly filtering into the conference room, looking upset at the armed SEALs and confused with their instructions. We would have to sort them out quickly. The helicopter would be back in an hour or so, so I needed to have everything done by then.

"It would be comforting, but I suspect if we leave it as an FBI role, we'll probably get less pressure to turn it over to the feds before we're ready. I want to trace their satellite. I want to know who is in that communication loop. I want to establish if this plant made the original nanomachines. There are a lot of questions to be answered here; all we need is security and time." He nodded, gave my back one last rub, and led me into the conference room. His voice bellowed around as if he was on a parade ground.

"Settle down, everyone. Listen up. Managers and supervisors down this end, everyone else over here, do it now, and do it quietly."

He looked around as people moved into roughly two groups. "Thank you." Fay and Pete were back from depositing the two women at the helicopter and were acknowledged with a nod of his head. Pete took up his normal position by my side, and Fay wandered over to Anna. This could turn into a clusterfuck in a heartbeat, the SEALs in their combat camos, armed to the teeth, helmets dripping cameras, comm gear, high-intensity lights, goggles, and snap holders for night vision binoculars, apart from looking like people with bugs on their heads, they had managed to terrify the workers, something I felt good about. I was really pissed as to how I had started to go a little soft on the CEO and COO, and I had to shake that off.

"Listen up," I shouted over the rumble of complaining people, "if you have worked here for longer than two years, come with me. Everyone else, shut it down, or we'll arrest you for pissing us off." And I gathered a small group of eleven young men and women and took them into the room that had been intended for our reinterviews.

"Sit down, shut up, or I'll have one of these fine SEALs restrain you," I said, pointing to the two SEALs filling the doorway. Anna and Fay walked in, Anna with a pleasant smile; she had more practice at being nice than I had, and Fay walked in with a little jaunt. "Call me Sally" strolled in, her happiness infectious until you looked into her eyes, which shouted, "don't fuck with me" in every language in the world.

"What do you need, Captain?" she asked, scanning the room with an intensity I liked.

"Did you get any recognition from the staff when you showed the IDs around?"

"Yes, two of the women have been here regularly, as recently as last week." I started to fume again. That prick of a CEO dragged the truth unnecessarily; she had obviously not thought we would ask her people, something that was so basic in law enforcement as to be mind-boggling.

Arrogance, pure and simple, and guile, stupidity, and genius-level arrogance.

There, I had vented, and I needed to pull my emotions in to brief my people. "Sandra, Fay, I'm looking for a timeline. I want to tie in the presence of the other women, when they were here, what they did, that sort of thing."

"Pete." I turned to my shadow. "Please get the canister we brought with us." He nodded and looked at Anna, who moved to take his place at my shoulder; what was it with all this protection today? I would have fumed, but I judged it a waste of time. "Anna, since you're here, I want to tie this to a specific time period. I'm guessing it started eighteen months ago, certainly as long as a year ago at the latest. We will use this data to prove the bugs were made here. Questions?"

"No, Jessica, I was wondering when you would bring it into play. I thought you might have revealed it to the CEO and her partner."

"Didn't need to," offered Fay. "They cracked like an eggshell under her interrogation. Masterful." And she moved away to start questioning the staff.

"You've got a fan," Anna whispered in my ear as Pete came back with a small canvas bag. Now we would see what we would see.

"Who are your scientists?" I scanned the room, picked out the guiltiest-looking people, and moved toward them, Anna and Pete in my wake. "Think carefully. In the mood I'm in, you lie, you're out of here with a SEAL up your arse, cuffed, and arrested under the Terrorist Laws, and this will be the very last you see of daylight for centuries." I looked at the small group and read the fear on their faces. Good, we were getting somewhere at last. "Be very careful what you say next." I pulled the canister out of its bag and held it up.

It was unmistakable, a silver canister, a red-and-yellow band around the cap, a sealed lid, and a mid-brown line running down one side. They didn't know it was empty, the sample having been taken to the FBI labs back in Seattle, but I had arranged for a small block of dry ice to be placed under the container, so a convincing puff of chilled air followed the canister out of the bag. Of the four so-called scientists, two immediately gave themselves away, their eyes opening wide and their mouths forming a question. They didn't get a chance to ask it. I pulled one towards Anna, took the other myself, and forced marched him out of the room. I headed for the small office I had seen on the way in and pushed my scientist down into a chair, and Anna did the same to her scientist.

I put the canister in the middle of the desk and leaned over my victim, and spoke right into his little, pink ear.

"When did you make these, how many, when did you ship them, and who did you ship them to?" My voice was humming with anticipation, my pulse elevated, and if I didn't watch it, I would start bouncing on the balls of my feet. Anna's victim spoke first, and really, really fast, so much so that I had to ask him to repeat what he said. He looked at me with genuine fear in his eyes; Anna patted him on the shoulder to calm him down, and he tried again.

"We shipped batches of nanites in containers like those; they were samples for the labs and were never meant to be used here. I don't know how many in absolute terms, but we were producing samples for at least three months before the chief scientist was happy with the result. When they left, they were in refrigerated boxes two hundred at a time."

"Let me get this straight. You made the nanites that went into containers like this for over three months?" A fast nod from both of them. "Then shipped them two hundred at a time?" Another fast pair of nods. "When?"

"Just eighteen months ago, the last refrigerated box left, and it was addressed to a lab up in Canada. I recognized its name. From that time on, we were told that our production nanites were stable, and we started the production of the panels, batteries, and biofuel." The first time the second scientist had opened his mouth other than to gasp, but pure gold if he was telling us the truth. And biofuel? There was an investigation all unto itself, but I'd let the FBI handle that unless it crossed with our three missing women. "Name of the lab?"

"Reynold's Scientific, in Prince George." *Mounties, here we come,* I thought to myself. But now I had proof that this plant had produced the nanomachines that had destroyed our oil, gas, and coal. I was willing to bet that we would find the same timeline at the New Zealand plant or close to it and at any other plant we were yet to uncover. Now I needed to document everything; the World Court was a pure bastard when it came to detail and evidence. I looked at Anna, and she nodded. Good, the Feebies would take care of that for us. What next? I had an odd thought. I turned to Anna as Pete walked out with the two scientists in cuffs. At this rate, we'd have to get a bigger helicopter!

"It took them more than three years to bastardize Amira's work. We'll have to ask her why that is; it might be the key." She nodded, reaching for her mini, snapped it open, and dialed her boss. No formality this time, I noticed, just a person-to-person data dump. She rattled off what we had found and the actions we had taken and nodded at his only comment.

"Roger wants us to wait for thirty, then dial the general. He'll have Frank and Julius present and wants our forward plan."

"Of course he does. If only we had one." She smiled at my gallows' sarcasm and turned to the remaining group, who was shuffling around nervously, most scared out of their minds. Good. It was about time people paid attention to what we were trying to do. I flexed my shoulders, walked outside to cool off, was met with a chilling rain that had turned into a downpour, and let the water run down my face, neck, and back. I swear I could hear the "sisssss" of the water evaporating from my body heat. Pete tapped me on the shoulder just as the Boss and Sandra walked up.

"The FBI team that conducted the first interviews has just arrived. They will take over the questioning of the staff, and Fay will lead that. What do you want to do next?"

"I want Amira, Malcolm, and Sandra to quickly sit down with Anna and give her their impressions about the plant. Just the basics, something we can explain to the general and the boys in Washington. I want to sit down with you and Pete and plan our next steps. I want a shower, a long bath, a warm meal, and a little puppy to play with. Did I miss anything?" Pete looked baffled. He had never heard me ramble on like this ever before, but the Boss had, and he read the signs all too well.

"Good. You're working off your mad. Let's go inside, find somewhere secure. The FBI guy with the burst detector is here; we can get him to scan the room we find to make sure we aren't being bugged."

"Good move, Boss. You know we were under video surveillance both outside and inside the plant?"

"Yes, I saw the cameras. If we can find the recorders, we will have a great record of what went down here in the last hour or so."

"Get someone on that pronto." The Boss walked us into what was probably the CEO's office, all high tech, silver, and white, wood everywhere, a very modern style that reminded me of a Swedish furniture store.

"Coffee." The demand was forceful, and as I shook my head to clear the water from my ears, I wondered what Indigo and his merry geeks were up to. There were FBI agents wearing suits running around the place like they had taken over, and I guess, in reality, they had, as far as the day-to-day policing work was concerned. My immediate problem was how to keep the Americans out of this plant long enough for Amira and Malcolm to find out how it worked and give us an appreciation of how to manage it so we could continue both the manufacturing and delivery of the power units. That was my hope.

"Boss, what can we do to secure this plant under Interpol jurisdiction?" He put down his coffee, looked at me from under his eyebrows, connected the dots, and nodded.

"I can have Lyon issue a Red Notice, seizing it as evidence in our case, which would require a United Nations peacekeeping force, but I have a better idea. Why don't we ask Arie who he can send over to run the place technically? The Americans will like the fact that they are being distanced from the production of the bugs, and then they can come in and take it over when things have cooled down and claim all the credit for the environmental panels and batteries that will be going out every day." I held my head in my hand; I had just remembered something Fay had told us in her debriefing back in Seattle.

"We missed something. Fay said that the plant had ordered two barges, which were due for delivery just about now, to move the boxed power packs in the warehouse up and down the coast. Why now? Why not months ago? I don't think the CEO actually knew the date of the attack before it happened."

"Doesn't matter. She may not have known the exact date, but she knew something was going down. She supervised the manufacture of the bugs, shipped thousands of panels to Helena, and had trucks on the road as recently as last week; we don't have to prove she had the final dates and targets, just that she was complicit in the overall attacks, which she most certainly was."

"Will you take them into custody?" Anna looked at me, smiled, and shook her head. "No. They are yours. I'll argue that until the cows come home. We might hold one or two of the scientists and engineers who participated, but even then, when you look at what we need to move all the politicians in every country forward, we need Interpol to be seen to be doing its job. The core organizing police force that is bringing it all together with the help of local enforcement."

"We need to find all the other plants. We know New Zealand is up and running, but we don't know anything about the other countries. And then there's that Pakistani family we need to pursue, and the gamers, Japan, New Zealand. Boss, we're spread too thin. We need to be able to send teams into all these places now before anyone can rabbit. What we have done here will get out, too many people involved, and we can't shut the locals up for long, no matter what we threaten."

"We need a credible story to give us time."

"It might not be as big a problem as you think. Remember, no web, no cell service."

"Not true here. The factory provided cell service to all of Point Roberts, all the way to the border." Anna stood to go and get Amira and Malcolm's report, "Fay mentioned it in her notes. Her team mapped the coverage the weekend they were here."

"Won't matter. If the COO was not lying, there are automated satellite transmissions going out of here in any case, and when they are interrupted, the other side will know we're around. We know the engineer was here a week or so ago; where did she go then? Where is the scientist? My bet is New Zealand or one of the other countries that had seed capital from the Wealth Fund. And the pilot. Where is she?"

And in a strange twist of fate and timing, at that exact moment, the pilot was being whisked away from Helena Regional Airport, hidden in the back seat of a nondescript city car by an anxious but excited Moya headed for the statuesque home of the late Howard Westhall. Several cars back, a small nondescript vehicle shadowed them as unobtrusively as possible.

Anna came back into the office with Amira and Malcolm in tow, pulled chairs out, and immediately helped herself to coffee. "It's like a bloody science fiction movie," she said, gulping the coffee in a very unladylike manner. "I recorded the information, but don't expect me to explain it to you. I'll leave that to these two brainiacs." The Boss smiled; this was very unlike Anna, whom we had come to love, respect, and depend on as the solid, balanced, thinking heart of our investigation. But it was nice to know she could get off the straight and narrow when needed.

"Pete, are we secure in here?" He looked around and signaled to two of the SEALs standing guard outside, who immediately stood shoulder to shoulder outside our door. Pete waved his little detector around and nodded.

"Good to go, Captain." I signaled to the Boss and Anna; we opened our minis and connected to Roger. The faces of the general, Julius, and Frank swam into focus, splitting the screen into four. We each had a little box down the bottom, with Pete looking in over my shoulder.

"Gentlemen, General, good afternoon. Nice to see you all again. We have something to share." I watched the faces to see who was going to take the point and won an internal bet as the general pushed her face further into the camera.

"We've picked up a little bit, SSA Bernstein to Roger. Plus, we've got the Interpol report from Pakistan and a summary of your resource use so far today, SEALs, and all. I take it no one has tried to kill you yet?"

"No, but it's still early in the day. Thanks for all your support, General. It made the difference."

"Good to know. Now, spill."

"We've arrested one of the main players in the attacks, responsible for the manufacturer of the nanomachines. We have confirmed the identities of the three women from Helena, the women we believe managed the attacks here in the US and possibly the drone and UAV attacks in Italy and Israel. We have some of their movements and a possible location for one of them." I left it at that, largely to see what the general's reaction would be. She sat back so far her face shrunk to half its normal screen size. Then she leaned forward again, and all was right with the video world.

"What location?"

"New Zealand."

"I've seen a CIA/NSA report on a plant over there, is this connected?"

"We believe so, yes." The general looked like she was considering her options, then just as obviously, seemed to have reached a decision.

"I'll send you the details, and I will brief the New Zealand Special Air Service commander on a takedown plan. I assume you want the plant intact?"

"Yes. You need an investigator as part of the takedown team, preferably someone who has seen this plant. Can your takedown wait twenty-four hours?"

"Yes, but I'll have the plant isolated and surrounded within the hour and wait for your investigator. Who do you think you will find at this site."

"A woman called Iona Boyle, mid-thirties, very smart and multi-skilled in science, maybe one of the creators of the bug, the timing fits, according to her workmates, she set up the factory here and probably set up the New Zealand one as well. A second woman, Coleen Fergusson, is the engineer who set the plant up. She was here recently and has now gone to ground somewhere. The pilot, Elizabeth Kane, who was originally identified on the CCTV from the Hog attack on West Point, we are currently tracking in Helena. She just got back from a long trip somewhere, and our best guess is delivering the scientist to New Zealand. We have established a link between Helena and the terrorists, but we need to do more work there to unravel everything that is in play."

"You've been busy."

"We have, yes, but I'd point out the help we have had from the FBI, and the NSA has made the difference. Giving me Anna as early in the case as you did has enabled us to move very quickly in a number of different areas, so thank you, Roger, for that."

"Our pleasure. And Anna tells me we will be hosting a number of suspects in Seattle, with the possibility of a PR bonus sometime down the track?"

"Yes, to both. But I need you all to keep your grubby hands in your pockets as far as this plant is concerned and trust Interpol to manage the situation going forward. There is a lot you don't know yet, Anna is having it all transcribed for you, but in the meantime, we have terrorists still to catch." General Saunders gave me one of her famous hard looks, but next to the ones that the Boss sent my way on a regular basis, it paled into insignificance.

"So what do you suggest we tell the president?" she asked, her voice edged with that sharp bark people in command seemed to cultivate. My turn for a crocodile smile.

"As little as possible right now; we are on the hunt, we are very close, and we are cleaning up everything as we go. No need for her to worry just yet." I was watching the Boss out of the corner of my eye, and this statement even took him by surprise.

"Keep in contact," and she disconnected with a snap. Back in her office, she reflected on the conversation and mentally congratulated the Interpol and FBI teams; they were making excellent progress, but nothing they were doing would necessarily embarrass the president. People disappeared into the system all the time, and the circle that actually knew about the women terrorists was extremely small. Who's to say their capture ever had to be made public?

Chapter 33

The G4 streaked across the Pacific at just below the speed of sound, carrying Fay, Agents RuPaul and Vernon, and Sandra, who Jessica had nominated to head up the team. They knew what Interpol was looking for, more proof that the nano bug had been produced in the plant, they knew with intimate detail what we had done and decided in Point Roberts, and Sandra had been pivotal in identifying the three women in Helena. General Saunders had the plant locked down, every movement in and out being recorded and tracked, and traced. While the New Zealand Special Air Service troops covered every exit and scanned the buildings with infrared, optical, and ultrasound devices, such were their exceptional skills, not one soldier was detected during the sixteen hours of their initial deployment. The SAS was regarded as one of the finest fighting special services units in the world, and while they regarded this as essentially "guard duty," their pride in their training and their craft kept them focused.

Besides, the briefing had described one of the occupants of the plant as the most wanted terrorist in the world and described her as a stunningly beautiful woman, and there was a pool running as to who would spot her first. A copy of her ID was in every pocket, and not a few of the troopers imagined themselves in love with her.

The G4 landed on Okiwi Station Airfield, legally too short a runway for the G4, but it squeaked in any way, the main wheels hitting the very edge of the tarmac and the jet decelerating under reverse thrust all the way to the other end. It was met by a military jeep, and without any fuss, the team deplaned. They had worked out their strategy on the plane; they had a warrant to search and seize issued by the World Court; they also had as a backup a search warrant issued by the New Zealand government, who had been mortified to learn that their lovely islands might be harboring the world's most wanted terrorist.

No one had seen it fit to brief them on the possibility that the plant might be involved in the manufacturing of the nanites that had shut down the world's oil, gas and coal supplies.

"Ma'am, what are your orders?" the sergeant asked, dressed in jeans and a light blue hoodie. The only giveaway was his well-worn combat boots and the bulge in the middle of his back where his weapon sat. And his eyes. They were dead, little black pinpoints of intensity that killed the warmth of his welcoming smile. Sandra, dressed in a tailored light grey suit in contrast to the black FBI-suited agents, handed a small carryall to the driver, watched him place it reverently between the front seats, then motioned the agents into the vehicle.

"To your operational commander, please." And she sat back to enjoy the view, never having been out of the northern hemisphere before, but having seen the movie about short, stumpy men with huge feet and magic that had made the islands famous. It was a short drive, and within minutes they were behind a strand of dense, tall trees that effectively cut out the sunlight. At the base of the trees, three people huddled, looking at black-surrounded screens arranged on top of big bulky green boxes. Two were women, and one was a dark-skinned male, a Māori Sandra assumed, a descendant of the indigenous natives that had first settled in New Zealand hundreds of years ago.

The Māori walked over to the vehicle, and on his chest in a faint grey/green sleeve, she could see the pips and crown that indicated the rank of colonel.

"Welcome to Great Barrier Island. I'm Colonel Tāne. How do you want to play this?"

"Sir, I'm Agent Thomas; these are SSA Remer and SA's RuPaul and Vernon. We want to walk up to the front door, announce ourselves, request an inspection, and interviews, see how we go, then take over the plant. I imagine you have enough troops to achieve that?" The SAS commander looked at Sandra; she looked trim, fit, and a fraction on the small size compared to his troopers, but he saw the total focus in her eyes and went with his instincts.

"I assume you are armed. Use this com device, and we'll listen in to your conversations. You'll need a code word, and what is your policy regarding the use of weapons in the first place?" He had been thoroughly briefed; he had expected tough guys from the United States, but he did not see that in this quartet and wondered at their ability to handle a serious firefight. Sandra disabused him of his doubts with a style he appreciated.

"Colonel, we are all armed, and just so far this week, we have escaped an ambush by mercenary terrorists sent to kill us, taken into custody one of the originators and planners of the terrorist attacks, and taken over a plant just like this one, in about four hours I think it was, without a shot being fired, and we expect you to be weapons-free if needed, but frankly, we would prefer to achieve our objective in as peaceful a manner as possible." She paused to give him time to take in everything she had said, then, like a magician, pulled out the photo of the scientist. "Have you seen this woman?" He looked at the photo and shook his head.

"No, Ma'am, not since we arrived. But the airport reported an aircraft landed late yesterday and that one person, a female, was picked up and delivered to the plant. We have no CCTV at the airport; it is a very small regional one, as you probably noticed on your arrival."

"Okay, Colonel, can you get your driver to take us to the gate, please? Let's see what the reaction is. One last thing—we need the woman alive, so be careful, please." And she led her team back into the jeep, which drove away back onto the dirt road that had led from the airport boundary. They were soon engulfed in the dense forest, the sunlight flickering through the canopies like little flashes of stars. It was really quite magical, but the thought of what might come tapered their enthusiasm for anything but the practical.

"Fay, you take a point, please. An FBI presence will be sufficient, I think, but I'm willing to bet that all our IDs have been sent to them, not to mention a summary of what we did back at Point Roberts."

"Maybe not everything. Once the SEALs moved in, and Malcolm took over the communications room, nothing went out,"

RuPaul said, turning his head to look at the ocean, which pounded its way across a golden stretch of sand. The roar completely muffled the engine noises and had an intensity they could feel on their skin. "Malcolm would love this," Vernon said, referring to the NSA analyst's passion for surfing. Sandra smiled. It was nice to know her team didn't differentiate between jurisdictions, and not for the first time, she mentally saluted Jessica for building a truly integrated team across all the agencies working the case. Right across the world, for that matter, she added as an afterthought.

"Okay, here we go. Assume we are being recorded." She stepped out, deferring to Fay, who approached the access panel at the massive front gate.

"Good morning, I'm Senior Special Agent Remer of the FBI, and I have a warrant to inspect this facility and interview all persons on the premise." Behind her, Sandra recovered the canvas bag the driver had secreted over the gearbox and discretely pulled the cigarette lighter cable out of its socket.

"Please come to the foyer. It is approximately two kilometers down the road. You will be met." And the huge gates swung open with a ponderous groan and screech as the little wheels on the bottom ground their way along the sunken track. Fay led her team along the road, mentally comparing it to the one at Point Roberts, noticed the same number of buildings, all built out of the same material, the sparkling panels, and even noticed that the satellite uplink dish was in the exact same location. And she saw one of the tiny CCTV cameras glinting in the sunlight, hidden amongst the foliage of the trees.

It was a longish walk, but the walkways and road were pristine. A lot of effort obviously went into maintenance. They arrived at the office block, a mirror of the one in Point Roberts, and were met by two stunningly beautiful women dressed in contrasting designer skirts and jackets, one bright red, the other a deep, rich green. Sandra just had time to think that Jessica would have clothes envy again when the woman in green moved forward and held out her hand.

"I'm Wendy Sommers, I'm the CEO here, and this is my partner Arshia Spicatas, who looks after the finance. Please come in." They followed the two into a boardroom, again, identical to the one in Point Roberts, the only difference being the boardroom table, while wooden, looked like it had been hewed out of one massive log and not a jigsaw puzzle.

"Please sit. We have been warned of your visit. Which one of you is the Interpol agent?" She looked at the team with keen green eyes tinged with gold, her mixed-raced heritage obvious from the coffee color of her silky skin. She could have graced the front cover of any high fashion magazine, Sandra thought to herself.

"What, exactly, have you been warned about? I'm Agent Thomas, Interpol; these are my team, SSA Fay Remer, and SA's RuPaul and Vernon." The CEO looked guileless, as if she hadn't a single problem in the world, so all four agents watched closely as she answered Sandra's question.

"Our head office in Point Roberts warned us that we could expect a visit from Interpol and the FBI a week ago and told us to show you everything you wanted to see and question anyone you needed to." Fay spun the photo of the scientist across the polished surface and noticed it was trapped by manicured nails with a glossy finish before it could slide off the table.

"Do you know this person?" she snapped, hoping to shake the CEO's apparent calm. Apart from raised eyebrows, and a shake of her head, setting bronzed red hair flying, there was no other response. The CEO turned the photo so the accountant could see it, and she inadvertently gave herself away with the briefest flick of her eyes, which were jet-black circles under heavily made-up eyelashes. Her Middle Eastern heritage was obvious from her skin color and the shape of her head, which was quite regal with its slightly down-turned nose. "I see that you do, Ms. Spicatas. Where do you know her from?" The accountant looked embarrassed and flustered, her hands twisting and turning in her lap.

"Ah, I don't remember. It was a long time ago."

"A long time, like just yesterday?" Sandra snapped, standing to face the two women. "You now have but one choice—you ask Ms. Boyle to join us now, or I'll call in the troopers we have surrounding this plant, and we'll pull this place apart nanite by nanite." Both women looked shocked and looked at each other as if what they heard was an impossibility. Sandra slid the Interpol warrant across the table, where it sat lopsided while both women stared at it. "Too late." And she sat down again to wait for the SAS, and signaled to Fay and RuPaul, who stood rapidly and cuffed the two women in a blink of an eye, then stood behind them motionlessly, holding the cuffs up behind their backs.

They would do it the hard way, Sandra thought, and to a certain extent, it gave her a visceral pleasure to flex her muscles a little because the brilliantly maintained plant and its perfect, fashion-conscious women were setting her nerves on edge. It took six minutes of silence, a silence that you could have cleaved with a carving knife, before the SAS arrived in force. All dressed in jeans and hoodies, weapons strapped across their backs and chests, floppy hats and baseball caps of odd shapes, colors, and sizes, almost made Sandra laugh at the thought of these very fit-looking men and women hiding in the tree line with their mismatched hats and caps, as she had seen them just a while ago.

"Colonel, thank you for coming. Could you please clear out the buildings, get everyone into the larger conference room you will find to the right as you exit, and would you provide two guards for these women? I am placing them under arrest under the Terrorist Laws. You may have as many as ten prisoners when we are finished interviewing; we will take the main prisoners with us, but the rest will have to be secured locally." And if the colonel had any doubts about this team going in, he certainly had none now; the sharp edge of authority in the voice of the pretty Interpol agent and the sight of the two FBI agents standing behind the cuffed CEO and her accountant left him in no doubt that the tough guys he had expected had, in fact, turned up, but disguised as two beautiful women and a pair of regulation black FBI suits.

"Fay, when you are ready, I want you and I to interview these two, and John and Andrew can start on the staff. Same profile as before, separate out the long-term employees, and the scientists and the engineers." She threw the canvas bag to Agent Vernon almost casually. "And, John, same strategy. We need to confirm the timeline and the presence of the bugs." He nodded, having seen the video of how the canister had been used in the earlier interrogation in Point Roberts to confirm the manufacture of the original nanomachines. The SAS, except for two burly Maoris, went on their way with the two FBI agents. Fay took a seat next to the accountant, Sandra stayed where she was, and the colonel chose to sit two seats away as if fearing contamination.

"Now, here's how it's going to play out. Fay and I will ask some questions, and you will answer them truthfully. And I caution you, this is a military arrest; the warrant has been issued by Interpol, and our friends here, as you can see, are SAS. You have no rights, none at all. We know exactly what you have done, almost down to the day. Ah! I thought we might have a visitor. Come in, Ms. Boyle. Welcome to our little party." Another really beautiful woman, dressed immaculately, Sandra thought; she was starting to understand Jessica's clothes envy. The SAS soldier who was holding the plasticuffs halfway up her back looked to his colonel for guidance, then forcibly pushed the restrained woman into the chair next to Fay.

"Well now, that's two for two, or four for four, depending on how you count. I wonder how our counterparts are going back home?" The feral look Sandra gave the scientist had her blood running cold; she had expected that at some time she would face questions, but she had imagined it would be a polite, if not reserved process, due to the wonderful work they were all doing to restore hope to the planet. What she saw in front of her now was someone who looked as if they wanted to physically tear her limb from limb and would enjoy every minute of the process. Fay looked at Sandra and made her mind up on the spot. When she got back, she would immediately petition Jessica to be attached to Interpol. In fact, if she could transfer full-time, she would do so in a heartbeat. These agents were a huge cut above the rest, and she knew she would learn things from them that would change her life. Still smiling at the thought, she started the conversation, remembering how Jessica had tied the CEO and COO up in knots with her discordant interrogation style, soft, hard, soft, then totally bad-arse.

"Ms. Sommers, we know this plant produced the original nanites that were used to attack the oil, gas, and coal sites around the world."

And in a flash, she switched her attention to the scientist. "And we know that you started the nano process at Point Roberts, perfected it, and then flew here to set this plant up." Then facing the accountant, hammered her with what they had gleaned so far. "And you, Ms. Spicatas, have managed the funds drawn down from the Arabian Sovereign Wealth Fund in the amount of—how much was it again, Sandra?" She used her first name to emphasize how tight her team was and how insulting she could be to the terrorists. Sandra got the message and made a pretense of looking up at the roof as if she was calculating something.

"I think it was two billion one hundred thousand New Zealand dollars, but that could be out by a few thousand or so." The accountant looked shocked, not at the knowledge Fay and Sandra exhibited but at the casual relationship between the two. Where was the respect? She had worked twenty hours a day for over three years helping to get this plant, literally in the middle of nowhere, up and running; she had forgone a social life, friends, family, and the comforts of her home in far-away Wellington to take this role, on the promise that what they were doing would change the future for thousands of families; and now she was being treated like a common criminal. No, worse. Like a terrorist. It had to stop.

"I want to say something." Her petite chin jutted up and out, her shoulders squared, and a flame started to burn behind her eyes. "I know nothing about terrorists, terrorist acts, or anything other than the management of the trust that provided the funds for what this plant produces."

"Were you here three years ago?"

"Yes."

"Were you here eighteen months ago?" This got a cautious look from her, and she seemed to be considering her options. Her eyes slid to the side as if seeking direction from the CEO, who now sat transfixed and immobile at the head of the table, a burly Maori SAS trooper standing behind her.

"Yes, I was, but I don't see what that has to do with anything." Sandra grinned and relaxed back into her seat, crossing her arms.

"That's the beauty of the Terrorist Laws. You don't really have to know what is going on, but if you are present during the preparation or implementation of a terrorist act, you are judged to be guilty of terrorist activities. You were at this plant when it was shipping nano-machines that destroyed the oil, gas, and coal supplies around the world; you may not have the technical knowledge. We will establish that later, but you were here."

"Eighteen months ago, we were doing nothing more than shipping nanites to different laboratories for quality control prior to setting up the production runs. I don't know what you are talking about." And said with such finality, she probably believed it. Both Fay and Sandra shook their heads in concert. Made no difference to them; they just gathered the evidence, arrested the suspects, and left it up to the courts to decide the rest. And for their money, they had now captured three more of the terrorists, one of whom was on the very, very most wanted list.

"Take them to the plane, please. Fay and I will come with you; we'll leave Andrew and John to conduct the staff interviews. As to whether or not we shut you down, that's a question for another day, but for the foreseeable future, you're officially out of business. Colonel, thank you, we'll leave this in your capable hands. I'm sure your government will want a piece of this, but you may not hear from them for a day or two."

"What do you want to do with the staff?"

"See what our agents pull out in interrogation; they will tell you who's who, some you might get to send home, some you will have to detain. This plant only has twenty-six employees, so it shouldn't be a problem. Just one thing—from this moment on, this plant is subject to an Interpol Red Notice, no one in, no one out, and that includes any politicians or media. I suggest you move your HQ here inside this building and set your guards accordingly. You have permission to shoot anyone on sight that trespasses, and I'll check in with you every four hours." She passed him one of the monks' minicomputers.

"Use this exclusively when you want to talk to us; the others on the end of the line are the commanding general of the joint chiefs, the heads of the FBI, NSA, FBI, Sin Bet, Interpol Section Five, and a few lowly people like myself and Fay. Don't lose it." And she smiled at the colonel, who was now handling the mini as if it were alive in his hands. But one thing he was absolutely sure of was the two women who he had just seen take a terrorist cell apart at the seams in just minutes were anything but lowly people!

"We'll wait at the plane for our agents to finish; we're looking for a Pakistani woman, last name Anaisha. She will be late teens or early twenties. We want her with us as well. Thank you." Fay and Sandra walked out of the room, taking the three terrorists with them, surrounded by six SAS, a comforting feeling. They got to the jeep, locked the terrorists to their seats with additional cuffs, then, with two of the SAS hanging off the sides, drove back to the airport.

The G4 pilot had, optimistically, lined his aircraft up at the exact end of the strip, there being less than an inch of grass between his main undercarriage and the edge of the tarmac. The airport had provided a ground cart for him, which now huffed and chuffed at the front, and while he had been waiting, he had paced off the remaining length of the runway three times, and no matter how small he made his paces, he couldn't get it longer than just shy of three thousand feet. His balanced field length was two thousand feet longer than his nominal landing distance, which he had abused severely on this trip by landing short, and applying reverse thrust before touchdown, then braking like a mad bastard at a car rally so as to not run off the tarmac. He was lightly loaded, having burnt off a good amount of fuel coming across the Pacific. He intended to fly to Auckland and refuel there for the trip back.

But a balanced field length was computed to get him over the proverbial fifty-foot high obstacle with an engine failure on takeoff, and looking down the runway, it was plain to see where the airport had been carved out of the dense forest that surrounded it. Using his fingers and his thumbs, he had estimated the highest trees in his way to be somewhere between thirty and forty feet in height. The odds were stacking up. But he would get out; the only question in his mind was how much foliage would be caught up in his undercarriage!

The jeep pulled up alongside the plane, and the SAS escorted the three women inside and secured them to the seats in the rear. They gave the interior a longing look. The best they ever got flying around with their SAS brothers was red webbing seats and noisy open back doors of lumbering cargo aircraft! Fay and Sandra both shook their hands, thanked the driver, and stood with the pilot in front of the wing as the jeep went back for the next load.

"How many more pax?" he asked, and Sandra, being a highly qualified pilot herself, noticed the position of the plane, did a quick mental calculation, and shook her head.

"Allow six hundred pounds for the four of us, three hundred and fifty for our guests, and possibly another one hundred and twenty for late arrival. Can you handle that?"

"So, all up one thousand and seventy pounds. It'll be an interesting takeoff." His smile was infectious, and Sandra felt his confidence. Any pilot flying for the NSA was ex-military, likely still serving in the Reserve and no slouch on the controls.

"If it's any help, I can sit up the front with you and hold your hand," she said playfully and with just enough tease in her voice to have him consider it.

"Better not. You might want to hijack me to Australia," he said. She looked at him, but before she could think of a clever answer, Fay cut in.

"Now there's a thought. Where in Australia do you want us to hijack you to?" he laughed, enjoying the moment, very much aware of what the two women had done and the instructions he had received after his flight briefing from Captain Riley, who looked like she chewed rocks for breakfast. His instructions were clear. *Take the agents to New Zealand, bring them back in the same condition they left in, or I'll have your guts for gaiters.*

The jeep sped down the runway, the airport having been closed until the G4 could make its getaway. The two FBI agents climbed out, with the women shackled with handcuffs and zip ties. One of them was unmistakably from the subcontinent, and again the two SAS troopers escorted the prisoners into the aircraft.

"Better add another one hundred and fifty pounds to the load," Sandra said, turning to look at the pilot. She didn't sense any tension, so she relaxed.

"All aboard, I think, unless you have more to join us?

"No, this is it. Let's go."

It was what was described in the flight manual as a short field takeoff, and the pilot executed it to perfection. Both feet on the brakes, flaps set, engines up to one hundred and ten percent, let the airframe shake a little, like a terrier trying to get off a leash, release the brakes, hold the centerline, rotate at minimum stall speed, hold it in ground effect, snap the wheels up, build airspeed, then at the last moment back on the controls and over the trees. The SAS watching from the side of the runway recognized one of their own and roared off back to the plant.

All in all, a good day's work.

Chapter 34

The Mounties reported that Reynold's Scientific Laboratories had been shuttered for over a year. No surprise there. The president's train had arrived back in Helena, and I had issued Bob his instructions, which were simplicity itself. Find the Westhall property, liaise with the FBI agents on site, then arrest anyone inside on suspicion of aiding and abetting a terrorist act. The G4 would go and collect the prisoners, thought to be three in number, one of whom would be the pilot of the Hog that had bombed West Point. The young assistant special agent that manned the Helena office and his assistant had done a fabulous job there, identifying the inbound flight and tracking the pilot to the vehicle that had then taken her to the Westhall property unseen and hidden in the back seat or so they thought.

The FBI agents had also already located the house where the three women had lived for over two years, and a forensic team was literally tearing it apart. DNA would prove conclusively that the three women had been there, and interviews with the neighbors would give us a picture of their movements.

We had at least one of the gamers, the Anaisha girl who had been swept up in New Zealand. We would have to show cause to get to the other sister in Japan, but I wanted to play that cool, as I suspected that the technology business that the wife of Hugh Anaisha ran was complicit in the software hacks and web attacks, but I had yet to prove it. It made sense that the terrorists had strong support from sympathizers, and for some reason, according to Drishya Singh, our Interpol agent in Pakistan, the wife reeked of an equal measure of guilt and disdain. And I trusted her instincts. An Indian posted to the Pakistan office spoke volumes for her skills and talents in a country ready to go to war with its neighbor for little more than who drew a chalk line in some rocky pass.

Thanks to Malcolm's work in Point Roberts, we had the frequency of the satellite transmissions the terrorists had been using, and that would allow us to track and locate the other terrorists who had been working out of Libya and Turkey. I had passed that little task onto the NSA and informed Arie that we were on the hunt in his neighborhood again. He had sounded relaxed on the call, something about not being bombed or shelled for a whole day, a bit of a record from what I knew of the tensions in the middle east.

The only problem I had was terrorists in chains in Israel, terrorists in chains on a plane, and terrorists in chains in Seattle, and I wanted to play them off against each other at some time during their interrogations, and I had yet to work out how to do that. One thing I did know, from checking in with the general, is that there would be no resistance from the Americans in taking all the women out of the USA, and as fast as I could manage it, was the unspoken message. The president and her cabinet were happy having publicly claimed success against the mercenary terrorists, and she saw no benefit from involving the women in the story.

Didn't worry me or the Boss, we were doing what we had been commissioned to do, and Interpol had the legal resources to keep it all under a security rug for as long as we liked.

There were outstanding issues—what to do with the power packs at both plants; distribute them as planned by the terrorists? Keep the plants running for as long as necessary? And what was the grand plan in Helena with the small city being constructed at such a frantic rate? Houses were going up like Poptarts out of a toaster, so we were going to have to understand what was going on, if only to justify our future actions in the town. This whole complicated ball of wax was still an official Interpol investigation, and the Americans were giving us a lot of leeway, but they would want their country back sooner rather than later, so I had to factor that in as well.

And our fabulous geeks back in Venice and Israel were now feeding us information almost hourly from having solved the Boss's "black hole" problem, and we were getting hard data on the movements in and out of our areas of interest that would have to be prosecuted. And I was really missing Indigo and his beautiful espresso machine. The Americans could make coffee, no doubt about that, but no one could match the artistry and magic Indigo got into every cup.

We were two days into our ninety-six hours where we could hold a suspect without legal representation or official charge, and I fully intended to run the clock down a little more until we got everyone back to Seattle. It would do the women well to sweat a little, be locked in concrete cells and monitored twenty-four-seven by big, ugly, and very visible cameras, and even bigger, beefy, and more visible army guards marching up and down the corridors.

And I still had to sort out the layers of participants in the attacks—did we just charge everyone with the same crimes, or could we differentiate between prime participant and onlooker? It was obvious that the refugee girls had been recruited and managed in tranches and that the primary damage had been done by some of those recruited in the first seven years. Obviously, there were a number of girls who had grown up in Mohammad bin Azaria's system who had not participated in any terrorist act. Quite the opposite, in fact, look at what Amira had done and Fay, the super-smart FBI agent. And there would be more scattered around the world doing all sorts of normal things that had nothing to do with the terrorists.

So there was the distinct possibility of creating a stigma attached to the refugee girls and their histories if we weren't careful, and I was determined not to allow that to happen. But to a certain extent, whatever Mohammad bin Azaria's "Plan B" was might have an impact on that. And at the root of it all now was Helena, a small town by American standards on the edge of a famous park, named after two of the explorers that had opened up the west, Lewis and Clark, population normally around thirty-three thousand, and now going on fifty thousand, thanks to the migration of scared families running from the bigger cities where civil unrest had killed off a big chunk of the American dream with the ripple of automatic gunfire.

"Have you finished dreaming yet?" The gruff voice of the Boss snapped me out of my mental meanderings, and Anna looked as startled as I did. She had also been in the deep-thinking mode, which had been a luxury up until now because of the pace of the investigation and the sheer planet-wide breadth of it.

"Who do you think we will get to run the plant?"

"I've been giving that a lot of thought. At first, I thought we'd hand it to Arie, but there's no direct benefit there. Amira and Malcolm have found out as much as we need to know about how it runs and where the raw materials come from, and we have the complete shipping list for the first five thousand power units.

"The FBI has established the distributors are small business people, recruited specifically for the task of installation, and yes, they were trained in Point Roberts but only in the last six months, and, yes, again, they are funded by the trust, but none of them show any sign of having a relationship with anyone from the plant other than on a commercial basis."

"So your idea is?"

"When Amira gives us the go-ahead, we turn it over to the government and let them manage it."

"I don't like that solution one little bit."

"Why?"

"It gives the Americans an advantage economically and politically, and if you think it through, the unequal distribution of resources is at the root of this entire catfight."

"And, guys, just to remind you, all three of us carry American passports, even though you two turncoats don't live here anymore." Anna's voice was soft, warm, and enticing, and I wondered how she pulled it off after the week we had just had.

"Well, Interpol's charter doesn't allow us any leeway here, national interest, national solution. If the trust fund is paying for the manufacturer and distribution, I can't see why the government can't just keep the status quo. And between Amira and Malcolm, we have enough technical knowledge to duplicate the production process anywhere we want to."

"Provided we have the funding."

"Yes, and I've been thinking about that. What about all the countries that have already been seeded with funds from the Sovereign Fund?"

"Canada, Greenland, Chile, Portugal, Ireland, Denmark, Norway, Finland, Estonia, Sri Lanka, Solomon Islands, Japan, and Iceland. The US and New Zealand are already in play."

"Yes. To my simple mind, the plan all along was to open plants in these countries and set up distribution systems to serve the immediate areas. We know they need seawater and sand in large volumes, so the location has to be coastal, but what interests me is what these countries have in common."

"Stop right there. You just answered a question I have had kicking around in my mind since this all started. How many women terrorists?"

"What do you mean?"

"What Jessica is hinting at is the fact that these other countries do not have operating plants, and might mean that the terrorists are resource limited." Suddenly, Anna came alive, leaning across the table towards the Boss.

"Not by money."

"No, not by money. By experienced people who are able to set up a plant from scratch. Jessica raised that thought with me in Point Roberts. Maybe that's where the engineer and the scientist come in. We know the engineer visited both sites, and we know the scientist did likewise. Maybe, just maybe, there are only two women who have the skills to set the plants up."

"Where's Amira now?"

"Still back in Point Roberts, reverse engineering the nano bug that took out the oil and gas."

"Why is she doing that?" It was my turn to soothe the Boss, and I just knew he would kick my backside in the process.

"I swapped Pete for Anna; she's my shadow now. Pete is looking after Amira. And the reason she's doing what she's doing is she feels guilty for having created the nanotechnology in the first place." He looked at me as if I had just come down from the Moon, then his rough face split with a grin.

"Pete called me before he swapped out as your guard, and why the hell would Amira feel responsible? She was part of a team. She told us that herself."

"Yes, maybe, but from all the reports I read, she was the driver, the one person that kept it all in place and had the motivation to drive the team to success. The fact that it took the terrorists three years to modify her original nanite says it all. This is not an easy process, and even with all the answers, unless you are brilliant like Amira, you won't make it work. What do your FBI labs say, Anna?" She shuffled her hands a little as if needing to apologize for something.

"They have had no success at all. They can't duplicate it, control it, or stop it from self-destructing. And they tell me that the other labs in Canada and Israel have had similar results. And Arie pulled in some of Amira's original team from years ago, and they had no success either."

"Have we tried to use a sample from the plant?"

"Yes. Amira provided three that our labs have been playing with it, and they have Amira's original work to compare them against, and as they tell it, Amira's original bug has a self-destruct capability that the terrorists have not been able to turn off in either of the bugs they developed. Amira designed it that way so that once the nanite finished its work eating the oil, breaking it up into its organic components, it would automatically break up and dissipate into the ocean, leaving no trace or residue. Whatever that self-destruct mechanism is, no one can defeat it."

"That would explain the behavior of the bugs that attacked the oil and gas— they dissipate when exposed to air, feed on themselves inside the pipes and wells, and solidify. The coal experience is slightly different, but from the pictures I have seen, it's a very similar process." The Boss rested his chin on one meaty hand, then moved it to scratch his face.

"Get Amira back here. Leave the plant shuttered under the SEALs and the FBI. We've already got it secure under a Red Notice as evidence in the terrorist attacks. Let's just wait a while before we play any more with it. Did we get any DNA from the missile silo?"

"No, the fire destroyed everything; it was a very thorough exit strategy." I nodded at this, the facts were that we only had the pilot on camera prior to the Hog attack on West Point, and the other two women were only associated by proximity in that they had apparently lived together and probably worked together in the silo, but that would be very hard to prove. But we had them dead to rights on the manufacture of the nanites, and that would be enough to send them to cells for the rest of their lives. Then I thought of something else.

"The FBI tells us that the two barges they ordered have been delivered to the shipyard at Tsawwassen terminal in Delta, British Columbia, just to the northwest of Point Roberts. I wonder how they would react if we told them that the coal terminal that now looks like a snow-bound playground was the result of nanites produced at the plant?"

"What's the story?"

"According to Fay, the COO told her the barges were to be used for shipping the crates up and down the coast to Canada and the US, a thousand at a time. They are to be converted to electric motors, and they have staff at the harbor to do that work."

"Clear it with the Mounties, get some FBI suits over there, tell them to be polite, let them finish the conversion, and then we will see what the future holds. They would need a large jetty somewhere; I didn't see any in the aerial shots." The Boss had a point, and I scratched my memory, trying to remember if Fay had mentioned that.

"They were building a wooden one when the FBI team went in the first time, so it's probably finished by now. I'll ask one of the agents to scoot through the warehouse and see." My mini buzzed loudly, as did the Boss's and Anna's, and we open them almost in lockstep.

"Ahh, Captain, Agent Bernstein, my apologies. I only meant to dial one of you up, haven't got used to this computer yet."

"Report, major, this is Colonel Anthony." The Boss used his command voice, and Bob's face froze up.

"Sir, again, my apologies for bothering you. We have secured the Westhall premises, shut down the satellite transmitter that was secreted in a walled-off area, and taken three prisoners. Two young Irish women named Moya O'Halloran and Elizabeth Cane, whose IDs describe them as a writer and a painter, sponsored by the trust that supports the house, and one other woman we recognize from the

IDs you provided us, confirmed as Rosalind Sanchez." The Boss's face creased into a huge smile as he thumped the table.

"Major, you have just captured the number-one terrorist on the planet. Well done. Confirm the details with the captain." And he snapped his computer shut with a bang, nearly breaking the little device. Anna smiled and kept hers open. I had the floor, thank you, Boss, but on this occasion, I was as happy as them both.

"Well done, Bob. No casualties?" He shook his head. "No, ma'am, very peaceful and a lot of surprises."

"Thank you again. There'll be a G4 with you sometime this afternoon; when you load the prisoners on, make sure they are shackled securely. Set up your bivouac at the house, and keep it secure; you may get some interference from the local council, stall them, and wave the Red Notice we sent you if you have to, but we will have a team of investigators for you as soon as we can. Keep the troops on the train. Keep them out of the way if you can; we may well need them before this is over. Well done."

"Well," Anna said as she stood up and stretched, "now we have two of the three and a whole cluster of bit players. I'm looking forward to how you manage them all."

"You're looking forward?" I laughed at the thought. I still didn't have a clue how I was going to manage the interrogations, but now I had something to look forward to. Then I smiled, stood, and stretched.

"Two questions for you, Anna, put your mighty FBI mind to this—we have the Hog pilot; we have the scientist who probably made the nanites. Then we have a whole bunch of women with their knickers in a twist about us arresting them and throwing them in cells when all they did was stand around and let the bullets fly. How would you tackle them?" She looked thoughtful, and for once, her mild, warm, motherly facade turned into that of a hardened, fierce, and determined-looking investigator, her eyes sparking with anger, her fists curled as if she wanted to strike something or someone.

"Same answer. Find the deepest pit on the planet and throw them all into it and fill it in with concrete, and then forget where the pit is." I smiled at her response and determined never to get on the wrong side of Senior Supervising Special Agent Anna Bernstein!

Waves Of Hope

The ship cut through the Pacific Ocean as it was designed to, rising and falling gently with the wave motion, cleaving a straight path towards its destination, still three weeks away. The girls had settled into a routine that the carers had worked hard to establish, the biggest single problem being that there were some forty different nationalities on board, most of whom did not speak the same language, or any for that matter, and the English classes were moving slower than expected, and not for the lack of interest. These were very young minds, conditioned by their past experiences and environments, all of which had been horrific by any modern standard.

Most had not eaten more than three or four times a week. Clean clothes are a rarity. The battle for survival was something that required adaption to the circumstances and a keen vision of what you needed to make it to the next day. So the uptake in classes, social integration, and language was slow, hesitant, and lacking the normal drive found in children with a humane and positive upbringing. The carers worked very hard to imbue a sense of purpose and fun into everything they did, and ever so slowly, the children responded. Their common attribute was that they were all very bright and had demonstrated an ability to learn something quickly once it took their interest.

The biggest issue on board had been the food. Given that most of the girls had never had any sort of stable or balanced diet, it had taken weeks before even the most basic meal of naan bread, rice, and chicken could be consumed and then not regurgitated by sensitive stomachs. But once the girls had got used to eating three times a day, their appetites became voracious, and the hoarding of food that had been a hallmark of the early voyage soon dissipated as they learned that there was no need to hide food away. And the transition to a more Western style of diet was something still in their future when the ship crossed the equator, and a massive party was held, with fun, music, noise, party food, and with some of the ship's crew dressing up as the fabled Neptune and his mermen helpers who gave out little colorful packets of cake and sweets.

The girls had no idea of how to process so much unstructured activity, and it took nearly three hours for the carers to get them all out on the deck where they could join in the fun. Many hid behind furniture, thinking they might be thrown overboard, and many huddled in groups, watching the wild goings-on with wide eyes and frightened faces. And it was at that point the carer responsible for the management of the children realized that they would have to amend their classes so that the children lost their fear of being outside on the deck.

They were on a ship, a ship that had been rebuilt into huge open spaces with small private sleeping quarters for four to six children at a time, but almost everything they did was below decks except for the physical exercise classes held in the former pool and entertainment area. Classes were poorly supported, as the concept of exercising was so foreign to the children as to be unattractive. The carers were learning as well; many never having been on a ship before, and while they had received specific training from the Red Crescent and Médecins Sans Frontières, whose doctors were amongst the carers on the voyage, this was the first time anyone had tried a mass migration like this. If it worked, then the process would be duplicated many times over to destinations far and wide around the world.

There were several enticing learning structures scattered around the central lounging area, and where once-grand chandeliers and pianos had enthralled paying passengers, small groups of girls flicked and puzzled over how to make different wooden machines work. It was the brainchild of one of the nurses, who had worked in a military repatriation hospital where soldiers severely wounded were making their recovery. There were a number of machines designed to develop fine motor skills, things like long, bent wires with little wooden balls on them, where you had to move the ball without touching the wire. So she had the ship's crew construct a version of this device, paint them bright primary colors, and attach a gumball machine to the end of the wires so that a successful movement of the ball dropped a gumball into the hand of the child.

Chaos had reigned supreme at first, the children never having seen a gumball before, simply either letting them drop where they fell or throwing them away. But once the first wrapper had been pulled off and the word got around in that mysterious way all good rumors traveled, the machines were never without players and an audience. The crew was now racking their collective brains to see what they could come up with next, and the competition to produce the next learning toy was fierce.

But the most visited place on the ship was the platform built into the bow, where the girls could congregate and watch the waves being split open by the sharp edge of the bow and the porpoises diving and playing around the ship's wake. None of the girls had ever seen the ocean before, and the sheer sense of freedom and joy they gained from just being out in the open air, with the smell of the sea and wash from the occasional spray from the top of a cresting wave created memories that would never fade with time.

The girls did not yet know where they were going. All they knew was that their lives had changed in a remarkable and impossible way; they now had food, shelter, and people looking after them. If there was fear of the unknown, it was swamped by the feeling of freedom and possibility, even though none could foresee the truly amazing future that awaited them.

But they all felt free, and with differing levels of anticipation, all had hope.

Chapter 35

The primary interrogation room was set up in the Seattle FBI office like many others all over the world, a featureless rectangular box that would fit four people, with the fifth being in sin. One wall is mirrored, visible video camera, and usually a desk bolted to the floor with a restraint bar running down the middle. The COVID-19 pandemic had required subtle changes, which were surprisingly still in place. A long, clear screen neatly divided the desk into two halves. I had agonized over the interrogation lineup right up until the Boss received permission to ship everyone out of the country as soon as we liked. That changed everything. I was only interested in one thing—finding the engineer, the third woman we believed was responsible for the primary terrorist attacks.

We had the pilot, and we had the scientist. All the other players were important for building the open-and-shut case that would see them locked away from the rest of their lives. But we had a lot of bit players who had been swept up with the major stars, and I was still trying to decide how to handle them equitably. With Fay, her two fellow FBI agents, Sandra, and the two FBI agents she had with her in Helena, and the Boss watching from behind the glass, Anna and I faced off against the pilot, who we had the strongest case against, as she had been captured on film preparing the Hog, then taxiing it out to the armaments bunker.

"Ms. Sanchez, have you been told what you are to be charged with?" A stoic look was her only response. "For the record, then, you are charged with actively participating in a terrorist act, in that you did knowingly take an aircraft known as an A-10 Warthog and did then attack the West Point Military Academy, where some three thousand seven hundred and six persons lost their lives." Same response, so I continued in my best parade ground voice.

"The detail of these charges specifically cover that action on that day but will be extended to include the control of a drone wherein you did mastermind an attack on the Dome of the Rock, destroying one of the most significant religious artifacts in known history as well as the loss of over five thousand civilian lives."

I might as well have been talking to a concrete wall. "Further, we will charge you with the acquisition under false papers of an FA-4 Phantom aircraft and the shooting down of the International Space Station." This, at least, got a wry smile, and I wondered why. So I drove home a few more nails to try and shake her confidence.

"We have your DNA from the house you occupied for some two and a half years in Helena. We have that of your companions, Ms. Iona Boyle, a scientist, and Ms. Coleen Fergusson, the engineer. We also have you flying Ms. Boyle to New Zealand just in the last week. There may be other charges against you at a later date; we will keep you informed." Back to the stoic look. I looked at Anna as if to see if she had anything to add, but it was just playacting; we had agreed going in how we would handle the two prime suspects. She shook her head on cue, stood, called "On the door," and stood back as two guards took the pilot out, and then brought a shackled Iona Boyle in and secured her to the steel bar on the table.

"Ms. Boyle, you are charged with the design, testing, manu-facture, and distribution of a weapon of mass destruction, under the Terrorist Laws as modified in 2022, and other sundry charges. We have your pilot, we have your compatriots from the plants in New Zealand and Point Roberts, and we have you on camera at both plants; is there anything you would like to say to us?" Not stoic, but not blubbering either, and considering the seriousness of the charges, I would have expected some reaction, even if it was just pissed off. She really was a beautiful woman, her coffee-colored skin shone in spite of her incarceration, but her hair looked a little dull in the harsh overhead light. Supervised showers and small hard bars of soap would do that to you. She looked up and, if anything, looked a little sad.

"My sisters and I accepted that at some point we would be asked to explain ourselves, and we agreed then that there would be little point in trying to change your minds. So I won't waste my time. All I will say is that the children of God have spoken, and they have truly shed tears of blood, and we only hope that the world has got the message." And she linked her hands together within the limits of the cuffs on her wrists and sat as still as a statue.

"Did Ms. Sanchez fly the Hercules to Turkey?" Her eyes flicked, and she looked a little shocked. Bullseye. "Good, that will give us another charge to bring against you— aiding and abetting the attack on the Vatican. You will never see the light of day again." I folded my hands this time and looked over at Anna; she was working very hard to hide a grin. She stood, called "On the door" again, and this time when the pilot was removed, the CEO—correction, make that late CEO— of the Point Roberts plant was marched in and given the impossible clash between the color of her hair and the orange prison suit, my clothes envy was retired for good, as least as far as she was concerned.

"Ms. Simmons, thank you for your patience. Are you aware of the charges against you?" She wriggled and squirmed in her chains, confirming my guess about how she would react. "To summarise, then, you are charged with the design, testing, manufacture, and distribution of a weapon of mass destruction under the terrorist Laws as amended in 2022. We now have video evidence from your own files of your attendance at the plant when canisters of a nanite code name 'D1' were packed and distributed, for some three months. We have you handling the canisters, placing one in a shipping crate, and having a laugh with your scientist, Ms. Boyle, whom, by the way, we also have arrested." She looked furious, and I sensed I could tip her over the edge with little effort.

"We have also taken into custody Ms. Spicatas and Ms. Sommers from your New Zealand plant, your pilot, and Ms. Kane and Ms. O'Halloran from Helena." I watched her face; her eyes were furious, with little tears leaking as if they were trying to escape. So I threw in a random comment to see if I could get her on tilt. "And we've confiscated the two barges you ordered; they'll make a nice acquisition to the Coast Guard fleet." She banged the table with her fists repeatedly, and it was Anna and my turn to be stoic.

"You stupid people, don't you know the damage you have done? Do you want more people to die? Our power packs are their only hope. You have to let me go back to the plant. And you have to let my people go!"

"No, we don't. Where's the engineer?" She looked at me as if I was stupid. "Why would I tell an arsehole like you anything?"

"Well, it might make the difference between her being shot on sight or taken alive; the choice is yours." And I let the threat hang. We had not expected to get any real information out of the key people, but for form's sake and the evidential requirements of the world court, we had to go through the process of interview and statement of charge. Anna, Fay, and I believed we would strike gold with the COO and the accountant and perhaps the young Irish girls from Helena.

"You'll never find her, and everything that happens from now on is on your head!" said with such fury I winced, as if being struck. Anna laughed outright, unable to help herself. I pointed to the door, and we swapped a spitting, fuming ex-CEO ex-clothes horse for a very subdued COO. And Fay, who had moved her seat, so she was sitting at the end of the table. She had established a report with the COO on her first visit, and I was hoping to work on that.

"Ms. Tremblay, apologies for keeping you waiting. We're having a full day. Are you familiar with the charges against you?" Her pleading look right from the get-go gave me hope. This was not a toughened terrorist; this was someone who had been swept up in the drama and excitement of the day and hadn't thought through the consequences of her actions—or in this case, inaction.

"As I said before, I know nothing about any attacks. I was at the plant on behalf of the trustees to oversee the expenditure. I was never involved in any technical discussion other than signing off on requests for materials, hardware, and software. I really don't see how you can hold me?" The hopeful look in her eyes reminded me of a cocker spaniel looking for a handout at the family BBQ. I tapped the table as if considering her statement. It was a signal to Fay to start the interrogation proper, which she did with all her empathy showing.

"Farid, I know your background. You know mine. We both have a lot to be thankful for, given our beginnings. Under the Terrorist Laws, all that is necessary to prove aiding and abetting is a physical presence during the planning or execution of a terrorist act. You were present, by your own admission and by video evidence we have from the plant, when the nano bug we call 'D1' was designed, tested, then shipped around the country. That bug has since been classified as a weapon of mass destruction. It's really difficult for us to see that you were not involved, especially since you confessed earlier that you were a member of the senior management team, making up for when the CEO, Ms. Simmons, was absent from the plant. In fact, you were in charge of the plant the first day we arrived to talk to you." The room took on a palpable silence as this young ex-refugee woman absorbed all that Fay had said.

She sat back as far as her chains would allow, a thoughtful look on her face. "What can I say or do to convince you I had no knowledge of the technicalities of what the plant was producing, almost up until I saw the first power pack being assembled?"

"Let's go back in time. Your plant was obviously prepared for a worldwide catastrophe well in advance of what occurred. What was your thinking then?" She looked at Fay, almost as if seeking some semblance of sympathy for her position. "The first we knew of the attacks was the media reports from Rome and Europe. If I was honest, I guess I would say that Kathryn's reaction was a little one of satisfaction, but like all of us at the plant, it took us by surprise. We watched every newscast every day until the web went down, and some of our computers crashed. We were all shocked and, quite frankly, more than a little scared, and then the only news that got through was via a ham radio one of the techs had at his home, and we even lost that just after the attack on the Grand Mosque."

"When did you learn of the attacks on the oil, gas, and coal infrastructure?" She tilted her head as if she was hearing this for the first time.

"What attacks?" Anna gripped my thigh, so I relaxed and let her have her head. The intensity with which Fay was watching the COO could have burned a hole in the wall. Anna placed her hands on the table, nice and relaxed.

"Farid, you were never aware that almost the entire supply of oil, gas, and coal was taken down by the use of a nano bug?" She went white; literally, all the blood drained out of her face. She shook her head violently from side to side, sending her fair hair flying uncontrollably.

"No. When did that happen?" she asked, shock and horror in her voice. If it was an act, it was a first-class one, Oscar-worthy probably, but my sense was she really didn't know. If the ham radio was the only outside means of communication, and it had been taken down by some form of jamming, and I was willing to bet it that it had something to do with the sudden provision of phone service by the plant, then there was the possibility that she may not have known about the attacks. Then I thought of something else. We had never identified the methodology by which the terrorists had attacked the oil, gas, and coal infrastructure—we had only described it as a "terrorist attack," and we had never allowed a description of the physical damage to leak out into the media.

"What was the story behind providing all the panels for Helena months in advance and the full-on production of the power packs?" She looked a little calmer, as if she had just skated to the edge of a cliff and been pulled back at the last minute.

"We received an order from the trustee of the Westhall trust instructing us to deliver the panels to Helena, and as far as we were concerned, it was a legitimate request. We all knew about the one hundred-thousand-plot housing estate he had planned before his death; it made all the papers up here for weeks. Most thought him mad, and no one took much notice until we received the order."

"Has anyone you know been out to the coal depot at the Tsawwassen Terminal recently?"

"No, why?" I let it go; it was time to switch tacks.

"Where is the engineer who was at the plant last week?" She looked confused, not sure how to relate a conversation about coal terminals with the location of a person.

"She left to go back to Helena; she was to inspect some of the early installations to ensure that the build quality was as it should be."

"What was she driving, and what else was she going to do?"

"She drove a little grey electric SUV, and I have no idea; she is not someone I chose to associate with. All those bulging muscles, definitely not my type." And as if to underline her feelings, she gave a little shiver, which made her chains rattle. I looked at Fay, saw the concern on her face, decided to call a break, pointed to the door, and, as Anna stood up, told her to hold the next person. The door shut, and I signaled to the mirror that I wanted drinks. Within a minute, the Boss walked in with a coffee pot in one hand and three mugs in the other. He poured for us all, then sat where the COO had just vacated.

"You're thinking we might not be able to charge any of them if they were not actively involved in the technology?" I nodded, too busy with my head in the mug to answer. I almost slurped down the last drip.

"If you think about it, with the restricted media since the web crash, how would you know any of the technicalities about the attacks? We didn't release any, and all the reports I saw simply described silver crud blocking the pipes. The only real description was of the radiation poisoning from the isotope contamination of the Arabian oil field. It is possible that the CEO, the scientist, and the engineer kept the lid on. We'll test that theory next when we chat with the New Zealand accountant. You should stay for that as well, Fay; she already had the hots for you."

"As in, she would like to see me boiled alive?" Fay asked, refilling both her and my mugs. We laughed, a nice counterpoint to destroying people's lives.

Arshia Spicatas's story was scarily similar to Farad Tremblay's; she denied all knowledge of anything technical, acting only on the advice of the trustee, and also claimed to not have known about the attacks on the petrochemical infrastructure.

And when I looked at it like a dummy, which in the case of nano-anything, I absolutely was, and if I imagined myself at the plant in the early days when they produced the "D1" version, and I was told that it was being sent off for testing, then when the production run started, all I saw from fifty feet up on the gantry was the silver material flowing between additive 3D printers; how would I know the difference?

Did that mean that all the staff was, essentially, never in the loop regarding the development of "D1"? Could we return them to the plants and let the process flow again? I would have to think about that. In the meantime, I had an APB out on the engineer's vehicle and another CEO to interrogate.

Wendy Sommers walked in and hobbled, just like her counterparts, but still managed to look regal. I admired that in a woman, even a class-one terrorist. I was out of patience, just a little tired, and out of coffee!

"Ms. Sommers, your fellow conspirators have confessed everything. Your accountant felt no need to protect you or the plant. She preferred to protect herself, so let's get down to it, shall we? SSA Remer, read out the charges please." And in her quiet but unmistakably "fuck you" voice, she did, laying it out like a well-worn carpet.

"So, you see, Ms. Sommers, we have the video evidence, we have the statements by your own people, your accountant, and surprisingly statements by your counterparts in Point Roberts. Before we lock you up and throw away the key, do you have anything to say for yourself?" She had sat motionless through the reading of the charges, didn't even twitch at the mention of "weapons of mass destruction," in fact, was the calmest of them all. So when she did speak, it was a surprise. "Captain, all I will say is that if you had ever been to a refugee camp and seen the conditions the children have to endure every single day just to survive, I think you would have a better appreciation for what we have achieved. I don't condone the damage we have done; if you look at it clinically, the nanites we produced took almost no lives. It was a bloodless event, one that may save not only refugee children but the planet. I am not responsible for what the mercenaries did. I had no control over them, nor did anyone else, I suspect. But I do believe utterly in forcing the world at large to examine the refugee issue and the bigger opportunity of ridding ourselves once and for all of the petrochemical smog that is choking our planet.

"Tell me, please, how have your actions helped the refugees?" She smiled the smile of the one with the secret, and for a moment, I thought she was going to keep it to herself.

"The planners have built-in a cost for being saved—look at it this way, perhaps a child's life is worth a solar panel that will power a home? Maybe a power pack such as we are manufacturing is worth twenty, perhaps even as many as fifty lives? There's no such thing as a free lunch. You, of all people, should know that." And she folded her hands within her shackles and sat back in her seat. Now I was beginning to see what Helena might be really all about, but I would keep it to myself for the moment.

"Where in New Zealand have you been shipping panels?" She looked at me and smiled, her eyes lighting up with an intensity that had been missing so far. Here was a true "believer," no doubt about that, and I suspected a die-hard environmentalist to boot.

"Good guess, Captain. You will find it in our records, so there is no need to play games. We have a site down on the Wairoa River at a place called Dargaville. A benefactor laid in multiple plots for five hundred homes, some schools, a university, a hospital, and shops. All manner of things. The population is around five thousand, and we will grow that considerably over the coming months. It will be a lovely place to visit." I would let that sit, someone else's problem unless, our engineer was on her way there. I pointed at the door, Anna did her thing, and Reve Anaisha entered, looked around the room as if in a daze, then seated herself across from Anna and me. She had not been shackled, only handcuffed, as I still had not worked out the level of culpability she had earned. And I had deep suspicions about her mother's company, which I would also pursue.

"Reve, thank you for joining us. I'm Captain Riley with Interpol, and this is Senior Supervisory Special Agent Bernstein of the FBI. You have not, as yet, been charged with anything, but I must warn you that we are acting under the Terrorist Laws as modified in 2022, and as such, you have no rights at this time to an attorney—or lawyer, perhaps in your country. Do you understand this?" At roughly six feet tall, well proportioned, with a head of jet black hair and a thin face that had yet to see its twentieth birthday, she looked young and vulnerable.

Not like the master planner of world-shaking terrorist attacks.

"I don't understand. What could I possibly have done for you to say all those things?" Then look on her face was pure confusion, and it seemed genuine.

"Reve, we have information that you and your sister, Nazreen, possibly working with others, did create a game, or the code for a game, that involved various attacks on popular icons and that this game, or the code for this game, was used by terrorists to plan a real attack, such as we witnessed some six weeks ago—attacks on the Vatican, the Dome of the Rock, the Grand Mosque, West Point, just to name a few, as well as the denial of oil, gas, and coal infrastructure worldwide." The stunned look on her face was real. I had no doubt about that, so knowing what I knew, I wondered how her mother had compartmentalized the planning so that Reve had not connected the dots.

"None of that's true. Yes, I was commissioned to create games, but nothing like you have described, and Nazreen and I worked separately, as did the other gamers."

"Who were the other gamers?"

"I don't know. We used numbers, I was number five, Nazreen number nine, and the way we worked was that we were passed sections of code to test and improve, but we only saw small pieces of the finished game. I worked on the part of the game that involved a high-energy weapon being used in space, as well as working out how to cover multiple targets in different countries—the timelines, resource needs, and communication requirements. Nazreen worked on other components, but we never discussed what. We were required to sign non-disclosure agreements, but last Christmas, when we were both home at the same time, she jokingly told me she had invented a way of getting money out of a bank account just by using a simple mathematical key."

"When did you start all this work?" She looked at me, eyes wide open, her cheeks pinked by emotion I had no doubt she was telling me the truth, and I wondered how a mother could justify letting her children design war games and sleep at night. Then I remembered our agent Drishya Singh's comments about the mother's poise during the interview and the fact that both children had been adopted. Perhaps the mother-child familial relationship had never developed. And we knew that the mercenary terrorists had been drawing down funds using one-time codes; we had the records from what we had seized when we captured Mohammad bin Azaria and his bookkeeper.

"About five years ago, when Nazreen was at MIT, and I was just finishing at Harvey Mudd before going to work for the Pakistani government."

"Did you ever do any work on AI?" That big, open-eyed look again, the innocence of children should never be overlooked, but I had a job to do, no matter the bitter taste that was building in my mouth. And at my question, her eyes had come alive.

"Yes, it was my specialty. The last game I wrote used AI to work out how to program flying machines to sail through hills and valleys and all sorts of obstacles automatically. The game was fantastic to play; you could choose any environment or any city anywhere in the world, then get the robot to work out how to fly a specific route and do specific things." Like flying a drone across the Middle East, changing altitude, mimicking a legitimately registered flight, then attacking the Dome of the Rock with Hellfire missiles. Or program a Hercules L100 to attack the Vatican. She may have been designing a game, but someone had taken that code and adapted it to reality.

"What else did you design?" She looked at me as if I had asked a hard question, her brows furrowed, then she smiled.

"Right at the beginning, we were all asked to think about how we could hide what was happening in our game from a spy, and we were given free rein to think of anything we thought might work. That went on for about five months, then we were moved on to the more specific game playing. I know Nazreen was very good at that; she boasted about it at Christmas time. She called it her 'secret cloud' and claimed she could hide anything that happened on the surface of the earth from satellite observation." So the gamers had developed the "black hole" that had so devilled us for the first month of the investigation. Good to know. But while I was getting information, I really wasn't getting anywhere from the investigative point of view.

The girls may have designed the games, written the code, and created all the scenarios you could think of, but someone, or multiple someone's, had stitched it all together into a cohesive battle plan that had, against all the normal odds, survived the first shot. I was starting to get an itch. My imagination was working overtime as I was starting to see the picture of how it had all been put together. I ran the now vast and growing cast of characters through my mind, one by one, going all the way back to the first person the investigation had crossed, looking for a likely suspect.

Helen.

We knew she was involved in the early recruitment. We knew she visited, at the very least, Amira three times during a twelve-year period. We knew she nearly recruited Amira from Harvey Mudd after the successful trials of the nano bug. We knew from the burst transmissions we had tracked back in Libya and Egypt that she had worked out of a house in Libya and probably managed the underground team in Egypt. And maybe the base where the aircraft, bombs, and rockets had been secreted somewhere in Turkey, which we still had not found. Maybe it was time to look to the Middle East again. I would have to give that serious thought. I pointed at the door, then signaled Anna to sit before she could usher in the next contestant in "tell me another lie," with the first prize being we would lock you up for life somewhere dark, cold, and miserable.

And forget about you. She sat down, the door opened, and the Boss, Sandra, and Fay strolled in and stood with their backs to the wall.

"Well?" the Boss's question hung in the air. I looked at him and turned to Anna. "Jessica feels as if we are not getting anything that will help us find the engineer or any of the other main players. I agree. We can take over the questioning locally, with any that Jessica decides she doesn't want to haul before the World Court." Anna was spot on—we had been commissioned by multiple countries to run down the terrorists who had created all the damage, not to mop up the detritus of the investigation. The FBI and others could play that game to their heart's content.

We knew where the nanomachines had been developed, tested, manufactured, and distributed. We knew both of the main players and two others involved at a very high level. And we had all four in custody. We knew who had bombed West Point, flown the Hercules at one time, and the FA-4 that had shot down the Inter-national Space

Station. And maybe guided the drone attack on Israel. And we had her in custody. We now knew how the planners had stitched together a twenty-five-year plan with analog and digital components, thanks to the game players. And we had one of them in custody and would arrange for her sister to be collected by the local authorities in Japan.

We suspected a larger role had been played by their mother and her technology company, but as yet, had no proof. Back to Japan.

We had hypothesized that six to ten women had managed the staging of the attacks other than those mounted by the mercenaries, and it looked very much like that number would stand the test of time. If you counted the engineer, then we had four prime movers here in the United States, and so far, only the one in New Zealand that had managed the majority of the work. If you added in Helen, wherever she may be, and then perhaps another scientist and engineer, you had the making of a basic crew that had destroyed the world as we knew it, all the time helped by children developing and playing games!

"Where did you come up with the idea that anyone had classified the nanomachines as 'weapons of mass destruction'?" the Boss asked, taking me by surprise.

"Oh, that's just something Anna and I cooked up to make it all sound very serious." He shook his head as everyone laughed, then led them all out of the room. We followed; we were having a tea break, need it or not.

Chapter 36

When you took out all the oil, gas, and coal-fired power stations, apart from crippling the majority of the industry, you slowed everything else down. People couldn't just go to the airport and fly where they wanted to when they wanted to. Cars and buses were soon abandoned by the side of the road wherever they ran out of gas, and electric vehicles seemed the obvious answer until you had to recharge them, and unless you had a renewable energy supply, they, too, became victims of the attacks.

There was a power grid of sorts, mostly maintained by the military so they could move troops and supplies around as needed, but the big winners in the current climate were all the small towns dotted around the vast landscape of America that had converted to renewable years before the attacks. And those towns became the natural destination for most of the migrants from the big cities, where very little worked and armed gangs wantonly killed any who crossed their path for no reason at all.

The Reserve, Regular Army, and police had regained control over most of the insurrection, with only small pockets of militia still viable after week six. The president's strategy of sending all the men and women representatives and their fellow senators back to their constituents had mostly worked but had cost the lives of some eighty-odd members of Congress, who would no longer warm their backsides in Washington.

But the real issue was that the fabric of government was broken, and that wonderful wheel of peddled influence, pork barrelling, and essentially buying the type and level of power you wanted was trashed. The lower level of the machine, the lobbyists, had suffered the worst, as their money had dried up overnight as companies fought firstly for survival, then position on a stage where there was no Master of Ceremonies or willing audience. Those states with the biggest influence, those driven by the sheer power of oil, gas, and strategic industries, died overnight. The coal peddlers lasted a week longer, then they, too, had to pack their political bags and go home.

The middle level, the members of Congress ready to sell their collective souls for another four years in office, were spread around the country and too busy trying to stay alive, let alone listen to some lobbyist pleading a case for this or that.

The upper level of the machine, the all-powerful House Committee on Appropriations, and all the other special interest groups where the real power of government resided were fractured and spread across the country with no reliable means of communication. And since the first attack, there hadn't been a single bill presented or passed other than the state of emergency declared unilaterally by the president, and so far contested by no one.

She sat in her office, feeling anything but presidential, at the two-hundred-year-old desk and surrounded by flags that carried the history of the country on their banners, wondering what in the hell would go wrong next and how she could get the country going again. The country needed power—not just for light and heat but work. Machines had to make things, and people had to make the machines that make things, earn some money, then go spend it in the shops to get the economic ball rolling again. It wasn't so much as the economy of the country had tubed. It was simply that right now, there was no economy at all.

And the United States was not alone. Any country that previously had relied on oil, gas, or coal was literally out of business. For that matter, any company— and there were thousands around the world—that relied on oil, gas, or coal for the electricity or trade that powered their profit was out of business. The old saying that "you never knew what you missed until you didn't have it" rang true around the world as people groped blindly for a way out.

Communication was slowly returning to some sort of stabilized activity, thanks to landlines, undersea cables, old-style phones and faxes, and even teletype machines in some places. Newspapers were being printed on really old flatbed letterpress machines, but slowly, ever so slowly, the word was getting around from place to place, and it wasn't a pretty picture by any means.

In that way of the natural world, the small countries, the island nations, those separated by distance or oceans from the upheaval of the masses in the northern hemisphere had survived the best. But the international political scene was fraught with danger. Russia and China were still looking for a target for their nuclear bombs, the death of their joint gas pipeline, and the destruction of their other oil and gas infrastructure a painful blow that could not be easily sheeted at any other country's door. And the wealth that these assets had provided the very few had dried up overnight and exposed both national resource management systems as ones of corruption, greed, and an abuse of power.

The Russian oligarchy and the Chinese Peoples' Congress were hanging onto power by a thread, but to be honest, had there been the usual foreign media scrutiny in either country, it would have been reported that the majority of the leaders of both countries had fled very early during the attacks, mostly to islands in the South Pacific, where many were now stranded due to the lack of aviation fuel, a lack that the nations concerned were determined to maintain. They had the people with the gold, soft captives, but nevertheless, not going anywhere unless things changed dramatically, and no one without a functioning crystal ball could see the future, given the dreadful state of the world's economic health.

The president closed the summary report that had been prepared for her and called her military liaison in. The White House was still functioning, the generators deep in the basement using gallons and gallons of the strategic reserve every hour, even with two-thirds of the building shut down. But while she still drew breath, she would keep the White House running and the illusion of government and control, for to project any sign of weakness could effectively lead to the end of American democracy as they knew it.

"General, thank you for being available; we need to talk."

"Certainly, Madam President, I serve at your pleasure, as you know." The smile the general gave the president took the sting out of the formality of her words, and she arranged herself in the chair across from the president.

"I bet you do. What's the latest from Interpol?" The general opened her mini laptop, punched some buttons, reached across the president's desk, fiddled around with a controller, and a huge screen rose out of the sideboard, and Anna's face in faraway Seattle swam into view.

"Anna, how are you?" the president asked. She hadn't heard from her favorite FBI agent for over a week.

"Fine, thank you, Madam President, for now getting my wind back as we have been in one place for nearly three whole days."

"Sitrep, please, SSA," the general demanded.

"Yes, general. We have isolated whom we believe to be the prime leader in the attacks, and Interpol will take them into custody and out of the country and stand them before the World Court. The FBI will process the rest locally, and we are currently determining which of the secondary level of leadership can be returned to their communities."

"Can the attack on the oil, gas, and coal infrastructure be reversed?" the president asked, her voice firm and strong, the exact opposite of what she felt at the moment.

"No, Madam President, it cannot. The specialists we have had working on the problem in the laboratories in Point Roberts tell us that the nanites are designed in such a way that once they are activated, they can't be reprogrammed. So, for the foreseeable future, we have lost all our petrochemical resources other than those stored in strategic reserves." The president visibly blanched and rubbed her forehead. This was so much worse than she had hoped for.

"There is some good news, Madam President. There are thousands of renewable power packs ready to ship in Point Roberts and New Zealand, and if we maintain the production rate, we can supply a large percentage of the country with power and light, and that includes factories and industrial sites. Also, the terrorists have developed a new solar panel that is amazingly efficient and can be produced quickly, and if we can get these out into the towns and cities, we can get the country moving again. It will be different, there will have to be major changes to the way we do things, but we can recover." Now the president looked up, the first glimmer of hope removing some of the frown lines from her face.

"What do you need to make that happen?"

"Well, we're thinking through that issue at the moment. If we let the two terrorist plants run and deliver to the schedule that they had previously established, there are distribution and installation points already set up to move the power packs. We're thinking of letting that ride, and then set up additional production plants and force multiply the supply. We're looking very closely at how to do that right now."

"This is all going to take time."

"No way around that, Madam President. The technology is relatively simple once it is established but highly complex going in. The terrorists only had, it seems, two people trained in all aspects of setting a plant up, and that would have been out of perhaps hundreds of candidates. We also know that their plan was to establish plants in several other countries, where billions of dollars of capital funds had been located several years ago, and there are indications that there are civilian companies involved at some level; we are running that down as we speak." The president rested her chin on one hand, thinking through how she could use this news to get the government and the country going again.

"Is Colonel Anthony there?"

"Yes, ma'am." And Anna's head was replaced with the Colonel's. "Colonel, how far are you into shutting down the terrorist leadership?"

"About halfway, we estimate, and that's thanks mainly to your excellent people at the NSA and FBI. When we move from here, it will be to where we believe the others are operating from."

"So I can, metaphorically at least, have my country back again?" The colonel smiled; he hadn't realized the Washington view was Interpol had taken over!

"Yes, Madam President. We will have to make a stop or two on our way out, but you have excellent people in charge here; they are fully briefed, and we are satisfied we have the core of the terrorists, at least here in the United States, in custody." The president nodded, seeing a glimmer of hope on the horizon, and wondered how to frame her next question. She looked at her general and was reassured by her strong, solid bearing, so she dived in.

"Colonel, from our perspective, there is no need to name or identify the terrorist leadership; we would be happy for them to be tried and incarcerated out of the country. Do you understand where I am coming from?"

"Yes, Madam President, we were made aware of your position and that of your government earlier and have no issue with it. The only area where you may be exposed is the video of the A-10 pilot doing the pre-flight and taxing out to the bunker." The president nodded, accepting that risk, having already had the videos and CCTV footage seized and the few personnel involved on the day contacted by the FBI and placed under a total media black-out and an injunction issued by the Department of Justice on the threat that they would be prosecuted under the Terrorist Laws as accomplices. That had not gone down well with the military staff, but as there were less than twenty airmen and specialists involved, plus the tower staff, she believed it could be contained.

"Thank you, Colonel. I'll let you get back to it." The president made the "cut" sign with her hand slicing across her throat and sat back in her chair as the big screen slid back into its hidden recess.

"What do you think?" She looked at her general, the one person she relied on the most, particularly when it came to matters of the military. The general schooled her face, adopting a placid, relaxed countenance, all the more to give her answer credibility. She knew the president was skittish, she knew her cabinet, for what it was, was divided and confused, and she knew the pressure she was getting from the members of Congress that had been sent out into the wide, wide world of reality, was intense, as they jockeyed once again for the power that had been stripped from them so unmercifully. There was an election in just sixteen months, and the general, ever the practical voice in the room, had, literally, no idea how the country would manage that most fundamental of democratic processes.

"I have the advantage of all the background information, detailed briefings by everyone concerned, both here and overseas, and I think the colonel has not only done a good job, I think he has given us an exit strategy that will not only work for you politically but the country practically. And we have the FBI plugged in at every level. Interpol had been totally inclusive at every step, so we have the corporate memory working for us for once. And along the way, the military specialists they have worked with have all reported clean contacts, so there is no mess we usually have to clean up. All in all, I think we have reached a turning point." The president nodded, knowing that the country needed a turning point, but couldn't yet see it in her mind's eye.

"Thanks, Bridget. I appreciate your insights and your honesty. Better let me get back to worrying."

In Seattle, the local director of the FBI, Anna, the Boss, Fay, Sandra, Pete, Amira, Malcolm, and I sat around the table, having watched and listened in to the short and sharp conversation with the president. The room was silent as we each processed what we had heard for ourselves, something I was getting used to now that I had a cast of thousands to work with. I broke the silence; it was time we got down to the next steps, steps that would no doubt cause concern both in Washington and here in Seattle.

"Sir, we would like to keep SSA Remer, SA RuPaul, and Vernon with us for the short term; we have work we need them to do in Helena." He looked at me, then at the colonel, then at his SAA, and nodded.

"I understand you have a military force waiting in Helena?" His face was neutral, but his eyes gave his interest away, no doubt having between impressed with the casual relationship between the colonel and the president, and Anna and the general. Anyone with any brains could see the mutual respect and trust, which in government circles usually came very hard-won.

"Yes, sir, we have the presidential guard that normally rides the train and a small group of special forces; they are the ones who captured the pilot. With your approval, I'd like to send the three agents back to Helena to find out what is really happening there now that we have secured the location. And I'll be sending Agent Thomas to represent Interpol's interest." He looked directly at me, no doubt understanding that I was subtly not asking for his permission but only his approval. He didn't seem to mind the slight, which was not meant in any case, but it was my decision to make, not his, and I did need his agents for the sake of continuity with the investigation if nothing else. Sometimes the politics of getting the simplest things done made my head ache!

"I've been instructed to give you whatever resources and help you need for the duration, so you have my approval. What do you intend to do with Point Roberts?" I looked at Amira and Malcolm. I needed her back in Israel; Malcolm's boss wanted him back in his mountain hideaway, but for now, I needed them both back in Point Roberts to work out how to duplicate the plant if they hadn't already done so. Anna and I had some ideas on that, but we would leave it for another conversation. I nodded in the Boss's direction, and he picked up the ball.

"Mr. Director, the FBI has just concluded a successful interdiction in a major terrorist location and taken into custody several players who will be reviled by the general public if they become known. So they won't.

"We believe the majority of the workers at Point Roberts were never aware of the development of the first nano weapon and believe they work for an environmentally responsible company dedicated to providing affordable renewable energy sources, power packs, panels, and biofuel. We would not choose to dispel that belief but rather support it. And, sir, this could become a major PR coup for the FBI if it were seen that the continuation of this plant led to the solution of the almost total lack of power in parts of America."

The director looked at the Boss, a new respect in his eyes; he had expected this overseas contingent of international cops to walk all over him and his office, and yet here they were, giving him the prime position in getting the country going again, providing hope for millions of ordinary people currently scrabbling for survival. With no mention of Interpol's involvement. His boss in Washington had told him that Anthony was a solid cop, had a brilliant team, and that had more than once been demonstrated over the past weeks.

"We can do that, with our thanks. How do you want to play it?" The Boss pointed to Amira.

"Have you worked out how to build and run a plant like the one in Point Roberts?" Amira still looked impossibly young to my eye, but the last few weeks of stress had hardened her outer shell, and I noticed a few lines on her face that hadn't been there when we had first met.

"No, but there are four staffs we interviewed who know how to build them; they had nothing to do with the nanites, and Malcolm and I can stand in for the engineer and the scientist, with a little help from the locals. The plants have to be on the ocean. There's no getting away from that."

"Will it take three years to build them?"

"No. In the beginning, they were developing the nanite that was used to attack the oil, gas, and coal infrastructure. Then when they switched to developing the nanite used in the panels and the power packs, which took another six months or so. In the early days, they built with sheet wood, then replaced the sheets with panels as they produced them. Using panels they have already made, we can have a plant up and running in three to six months, provided we can get the additive 3D machinery and the robots, which are also proprietary and were all manufactured offsite somewhere. Find those factories, and we will be in business. We can take seed nanites from the plant and use them to start the next plant, and so on."

"Are you saying these nanites are self-replicating?"

"Yes. That was in my original design; the nanites replicate until they lack the raw materials to keep building. In the case of our nanites, that was an oil slick— once the slick is consumed, the nanites dissolve and fall to the ocean floor, where they are absorbed by natural organic processes. The nanites—the ones you dubbed 'D1'—work exactly the same way, replicating through the oil, gas, or coal until they run out of material to convert, then they just cease to function, mostly dissipating into the air or solidifying. The ones in the factory are used for the panels and power packs, and the biofuel use themselves and the raw materials they are fed on to replicate. If you want to stop it, you just stop feeding them."

The Boss shook his head in amazement; it sounded so simple, yet he knew it had taken this young refugee genius and her teams six years of hard work to create the first sample, then the terrorists another three years to bend the nanites to their will, and so far no lab on the planet that had received samples from either the Canadians or from the Point Roberts plant could keep them alive, let alone use them. It might be science and not magic, but it was the closest he had ever gotten to it in his life so far.

"How many power units can you build a day?"

"The way the plant is set up, they are producing five thousand panels and five hundred power units every day. The plant needs to shut down for three days a year, and we will need to duplicate the engineer's skills there, but it can be done. We need some smart people if we are going to duplicate this process successfully."

"Where would you build the next plant?"

"Do I have all the money I need?" The Boss looked at me. I shrugged my shoulders before answering.

"There are around fourteen or so deposits of six billion dollars each, or there-abouts, locked up in trust funds in Canada, Greenland, Chile, Portugal, Ireland, Denmark, Norway, Finland, Estonia, Sri Lanka, Solomon Islands, New Zealand, Japan, and Iceland. We have cut off the Arabian Sovereign Wealth Fund, and we know that this is where all these deposits originated, although not through any agency of Mohammad bin Azaria as far as we can tell. I think we could talk those governments into freeing up those trusts on the basis that we will build a plant for them sometime in the future. We can get a Red Notice issued by Lyon and start the process. But let's be serious, according to the FBI, there are at least four billion dollars left in Point Roberts, as yet unallocated."

"So we have the funding."

"Yes."

"I thought that Interpol did not have powers of arrest and could not dictate the restitution of funds between countries, other than through the World Court?" the director said, confusion written all over his face.

The Boss stood up, rolled his shoulders, then sat again. "Section Five has both judiciary powers, arrest powers, and we carry weapons, all sanctioned by the United Nations, but you are correct; as far as the rest of the world is concerned, we act in concert with local law enforcement agencies around the world, not under our own auspices. So if there is any dirty work to be done, you, sir, and the FBI will have to do it."

"But because we were invited to this party by Italy, then Israel, the United States, and other countries, we have cross-jurisdiction authority to prosecute our case from country to country," I added the last to remind everyone that we, Interpol, were the big dog in the room, and not to get too fancy with local or parochial thinking. I decided to move the party along; we were wasting too much time debating what had already been decided.

"Susan, please take Fay and her team back to Helena, establish yourselves in full visibility of the local law enforcement, use the FBI office as a base, and sort Helena out once and for all. Watch out for any burst transmissions, and let us know if you detect any, and pass the data along to Malcolm, wherever he may be. You have the troop train and its complement as backup, and you'll find Bob and his troop at the Westhall house. And if you can dig up the engineer, all the better." Sandra and Fay stood, nodded to the director, and left.

"Amira, Malcolm, you still have not answered the Boss's question. Where would you build the next plant?" Amira frowned, caught off guard by my sharp tone. But showing the steel backbone she had, immediately flipped her lovely hair as if flicking away irritation and looked me straight in the eyes.

"Next door to the existing plant. There's plenty of room. Malcolm and I estimated we could duplicate the entire site perhaps ten or eleven times before we ran out of room." I snapped open my mini, dialed the general, and obviously caught her as she was eating a sandwich at her desk.

"General, sorry to bother you. I need a detachment of the Army Corps of Engineers here in Seattle, ready to move to Point Roberts immediately. Can you help?" She put her sandwich down, looked down the lens, frowned, then picked the sandwich up again.

"You'll have them within the hour. Who do they report to?" I looked at the director; he was as surprised as Pete and the Boss were, but he just nodded his head anyway.

"The local director of the FBI here in Seattle; will have to bivouac onsite at Point Roberts until accommodation can be found, but if you want your country up and running again, the faster we do this, the faster you will have as much power as you need." I snapped the lid shut, stood, rolled my shoulders, then walked out of the room, hoping Anna and Pete and maybe the Boss would follow me.

Back in the room, the director looked a little uncomfortable. "Does she always move so fast?" he asked no one in particular.

"Pretty much," Pete answered, standing to follow Jessica. The Boss joined him at the door, leaving Anna and the director alone.

"Boss, we need Malcolm back in his office. Then I want a word with the president in private, just you and I, then I want us all back in Venice, maybe Israel. We need a chat with Arie, and I'd like it to be face to face." He gave me that look that said, "better know what you are doing," then nodded sharply just once. As Anna came out of the room, he gestured to her, tapped Pete on the shoulder, grabbed Malcolm's arm, then pulled them into a little three-way conversation.

"Jessica and I are flying to Washington. Malcolm, take Anna, Amira, and Pete in the G4 and drop them off in Washington; Anna, get Roger to organize a plane for you all to get to Venice as soon as possible. We'll meet you all there." I wondered how we were getting to Washington, then I remembered he had flown over here with Amira in the backseat of an Israeli FA-18.

And so ended our little vacation on the West Coast of the US.

In Helena, the building teams at the site celebrated a milestone, having just finished the five hundredth home. A ragged tree that had seen the best of its days had been proudly mounted on the roof in the time-honored tradition to let everyone know. The school was more than half completed, the shopping center was taking shape, and a football field and a large park were being planted by the local nursery. There were now over two thousand workers on the site, mostly made up of people who had fled the larger cities and the civil unrest that swept America after the terrorist attacks. And they were spending what they were paid in the local shops, and the whole town of Helena was suddenly alive and prospering in a way that it had back in the early days of the gold rush.

Helena was almost untouched by the civil unrest, as the town fathers had the foresight to invest in renewable power resources many years before, so when the national grid went down, the town lost less than ten percent of its electric generation capacity, which was soon filled by clever switching and battery management. Not to mention all the surplus power the new houses were now pumping into the grid from their multicolored sparkling solar panel walls and roofs.

The build rate was now better than fifty houses every day, and the constant flow of electric trucks with materials and prefabricated framing tied up the highways in both directions. A number of retailers visited the site, trying to estimate what would be needed to fit every house out with furniture, conveniences, and all the usual paraphernalia people stuffed into their homes, and warehouses up and down Route 90 were frantically trying to grow their stock-on-hand, but their usual suppliers had the same problem as everyone else. No power to run their machines. But little cottage industries started to dot the horizon, and wooden furniture and shelving, bed frames, and bike holders started to accumulate in previously empty sheds and garages.

And business in the appliance market that had built up stocks of electric stoves, refrigerators, coffee machines, garbage disposal systems, and the like, suddenly found the demand for their products soon stripped the shelves of their warehouses, starting yet another panic as they could not get the products they sold replaced.

The one thing Americans had been good at since the first invasion by the Spanish nearly five hundred years previously was innovation, and Helena sat in the middle of a huge national park network covered with forests of really big trees. Trees that could be felled with hand-swung axes and electric saws. It might seem that the building industry has gone back to its beginnings, but the woodworking skills have not been lost, just devalued by technology and time. And the wooden frames that supported the new style homes became the new standard overnight, as did the sparkling panels that were still being shipped from Point Roberts.

There was one little issue that had everyone stumped. The land had been donated to the town council prior to Howard Westhall's death, and the houses were being built with funding from the trust he had set up years previously. So who owned the homes that were being built, and who had control of the sale of them? The town council claimed that they did, as they had control over the land. But the

fly-spec bold conditions scrawled on the bottom of Howard's will dictated that the land could never be sold or leased, only lent at the cost
of five dollars per year, on rolling ninety-nine-year agreements, on the
proviso that whoever used the land agreed to maintain it and the services that supplied it. So, in theory, as argued by lawyers, the Westhall
trust controlled the buildings and their future, and therefore the own-
ership and transfer of title where and when appropriate. And again,
scrawled on the back of Howard's will, in an almost illegible scribble,
he had stated that the houses, if passed on to willing third parties,
would transfer for the cost of framing plus one dollar, and on certain
additional conditions being met. Conditions would be revealed by his
lawyers once the first one thousand homes had been completed, along
with a minimum of two schools, one hospital, three shopping centers,
and various parks and gardens.

And those conditions were sealed away in a bank box, and the
trustees refused point-blank to even entertain the idea of opening
them until the building met the terms of the agreement. After all,
they were being paid out of the interest on the capital deposited in the
trust several years previously, and that amounted to millions and millions of dollars every year, for very little work other than the monthly
meeting to review the account, so, in their minds at least, the longer
the whole process took, the better for the firm and the partners, who
had selflessly given themselves a substantial raise every year in line
with the profit generated by the compounding interest.

Hidden away in a nondescript vehicle that she had hired the day
before down in Bolder using a false ID, the engineer watched the progress with pride. Their plan would work; all she had to do was stay out
of sight for another week or two, and she'd be free. But first, she had to
enable the contracts for the houses, and she would have to do it through
a proxy because she knew the authorities had her photo by now and a
good description of her. What the trustees didn't know is that when
they opened the bank box, there was an instruction that a code had to
be obtained from a representative of the trust to enable the opening of
the final set of conditions. Coleen had that code, and her task was that

once she could confirm that the terms and conditions of the initial build had been met, she would give the code to the trustees.

Now she couldn't give it to them in person, and the two Irish girls had been taken away by the FBI. So she would sit and wait and work out how to complete her part of the mission.

And while she could change the color and shape of her hair and build up her shoes to add another two or three inches to her already tall five feet ten, she couldn't hide the color of her skin or her Asian roots. She felt a burka might be in her future but worried about the natural prejudice that might rear its ugly head in a small midwestern town if she did.

She would solve that problem when she came to it, as she and her sisters had solved every other problem these past three years. She had hoped, at one time, that when it was all over, she could resume working in the garage, doing what she loved best. Working on and fixing cars and broken machinery. But that was not to be, thanks to the efficiency and speed with which Interpol and the FBI had pulled their network apart. She looked over at the small satellite burst transmitter sitting on the seat beside her and considered her options, and decided to wait.

There was nothing she or anyone else could do until the conditions of the trust could be implemented.

Chapter 37

By the time the Boss and I had got to Washington, the G4 had deposited Sandra, Fay, and her two agents in Helena, then taken off to follow us with the rest of our team. I slept all the way across the United States, the Boss choosing to let me be for the two-and-a-half hours it took. I assumed we refueled, and when we landed, we were both met with a military escort and clothes bags, so we went straight to the base officers' quarters, showered, changed, and put on our best smiles and behavior.

Then we were whisked to the White House and dumped inside the recently fortified walls, straight into a plethora of Secret Service agents, who never stopped talking into their cuffs. We entered the Oval Office and were politely greeted by General Saunders, in full military blues, a chest full of ribbons and badges, the yellow stripes running down her dress pants legs, making her look tall and slim. I wondered what the occasion was but instantly forgot my curiosity when I saw the president. In the three weeks since I had seen her, she had aged twenty years and looked haggard and incredibly weary.

Your country being killed by technology and terrorists while you sit safely in the White House would do that to you. I just wanted to ease her pain, and I hoped what I was going to tell her would lift both her spirits and her morale.

"Madam President, General, thank you for seeing us on such short notice." Both of them looked at the Boss and I with bland faces; we had not telegraphed our intentions before the meeting had been set up. I started our conversation.

"Madam President, I want you to know exactly where we are up to and what the future holds for you and your country. To be perfectly honest, I don't usually get involved in the politics of a case. I leave it up to the colonel here; he is much better at it than I am. But as the lead investigator, this time, I believe that you need to hear the story from the horse's mouth, as it were." The president smiled; no doubt she had been well briefed on my behavior by the general.

"We have two of the three prime suspects in custody, one of whom is the pilot that bombed West Point and probably piloted the drone that took out the Wailing Wall and the F-4 that shot down the International Space Station. The second is the scientist who developed the nanite that took out our oil, gas, and coal infrastructure, and we also have in custody the two women who managed the infrastructure for making the nanites. There are other sundry players in custody, but their roles were relatively minor compared to the others." She nodded as if she was confirming what she had been told previously.

Good. The "no surprise" rule was in force, which would make it easier for me to tell her what she had to do next.

"Madam President, the plant we raided in Point Roberts is making an advanced solar panel power pack and biofuel using a derivation of the nanite that was used in the infrastructure attacks. We suggest that, officially, you never mention that. Keep the technology out of the media, out of all conversations. You need that plant to be as productive as it can be and maximize its production potential." She looked startled for a moment; the idea of an investigator telling the president of the United States what to do was not something she had ever considered. The general certainly hadn't; she started to bristle.

"And before you attack me, General, let me explain why." She sat back, her face still fierce, her posture still very aggressive. Against this, the Boss, sitting placidly in his borrowed suit, sipping delicately on a Wedgewood teacup filled with coffee, made quite the contrast. But his eyes were telling, tight pinpricks of black in a sea of deep blue focused on the president with an intensity she must have felt, for she slid her backside around on her seat as if uncomfortable.

"The psychology is simple. I spoke to one of our forensic behavior experts about this. No one really knows what was done or who

it was done by. You successfully sold the idea that it was the mercenary terrorists that delivered all the attacks. That was both smart
and timely. We have eliminated most, if not all, of those terrorists;
the last cell we are aware of was taken out in Helena just in the last
week. If you let the conversation move into the technology arena, our
experts believe that there will be such residual emotion leftover from
the attacks and the civil insurrection, that any solution that has anything to do with nanite technology will be openly attacked. And I'll be
frank, that is the very last thing you want at this juncture."

"Why?" The general managed to get all her anger into this one
word, a skill I admired.

"Because the hope you can give your country right now, today,
in fact, is that the renewable power sources the Point Roberts and
New Zealand plants are producing will enable you to, literally, turn
the lights back on, restart industry, and get America back again." The
president did her resting her head on her hand thing again; it seemed
to be her default position for thinking through difficult decisions.

"What did you do with the army engineers we sent you?" the
general asked, a little of the anger dissipated.

"Under instructions from the local engineers and technicians,
all of whom we have cleared to continue work at the plant; they will
duplicate the buildings and force multiply the production rate. The
FBI will supervise everything; their people are well briefed and experienced. We estimate that within three to six months you will have
more than ten thousand businesses back up and running, and after
that, you should manage thousands every month."

"West Coast?"

"Yes, initially, but once you have built one plant, you can duplicate them here on the East Coast as fast as you like. The FBI has
the data on where the seed capital is located, and Interpol will help
you get hold of those funds. You will have to trade with the various
countries concerned, but there should be little or no resistance there if
you do the right thing. If you keep the nanotechnology under wraps,
you will manage to get a good solution in the shortest period of time."

"What is the right thing?" the general demanded in her best
parade ground voice.

"This is a solution for the whole world, not just America, so be willing to share and help, not limit and try to control. If you want to avoid an all-out war, make sure you share the solution as widely as possible, and in the best possible manner. It's already in New Zealand; help them spread the solution in the southern hemisphere. Keeping politics out of it will be impossible, of course, but feed the need for hope; power brings light, light brings work, and work brings economic recovery. Keep it about economic recovery, not just survival. Petrochemical smog has driven the greed of too many countries for centuries; now you have a new, renewable source of power, and I mean that in the best possible way."

"But the recovery will be different—we will have to adapt to the new technology and work out other ways of coping?" It was almost a plaintive question, but at least the president had her head up and some light in her eyes.

"Yes, it will be different, and we still have to unravel Mohammad bin Azaria's 'Plan B.' We have a suspicion, but no real data, so we'll get back to you on that."

"Then there are the commercial entities who supplied the terrorists with their infrastructure; we need to uncover them as well. If for no other reason than we need their equipment for every new plant." The Boss had put his delicate teacup down before speaking and leaned forward in his chair. "We think we have a line on one major supplier of robotics and software development; we will pursue that to the fullest extent when we get back to Venice."

"Why are you going back to Venice when there are still issues here to resolve?" The general's animosity had lessened, but there was still a bite to her words.

"The FBI has it under control, and we have Interpol agents in place to monitor and help if needed. We need to uncover the other women who actively helped launch the attacks. We'll run them down from Venice; it's closer to where they operated from. And it seems a small thing, but Arie wants his jet back." The Boss smiled at the thought, the general grimaced, and the president just looked blank. Obviously out of the loop as far as our transport was concerned.

"I'll walk you out," the general said, standing. Indicating the meeting was over.

I wondered if the president had got my message. Time will tell.

"Madam President," I said, which was echoed by the Boss. Out in the corridor, the general buttonholed us both before the Secret Service could take over.

"Anna has requested fast jet transport for your people, and Malcolm will be back in the mountain in five hours. I smell something cooking that you're not talking about. Care to share?" The look in her eyes was intense, and the Boss just smiled.

"Bridgett, why don't you come with us and see for yourself?" She looked startled at the suggestion, started to shake her head, then gave it another run through her thought processes.

"Who will look out for Point Roberts?"

"The local FBI director has that well under control, and your army engineers will have all the experience needed to build plants wherever you want them."

"Helena?"

"We have one of our best agents there, backed up with the president's guard on the train, the special forces group you lent to us, and three excellent FBI agents who have been working in and out of that area since day one."

"Where is the third woman? The one they call the engineer?"

"Good question. We'll tell you once we know." The Boss moved towards the massive double doors and was immediately surrounded by whispering Secret Service agents, and I tried to settle the general down one last time.

"He knows what he is doing. Think about joining us for this next part of the hunt. It could be fun." And I slipped into the Secret Service cordon and followed the Boss.

We got Arie's plane back to Israel. He was up north somewhere fighting the good fight, so after a faster and more terrifying ride than usual on the cigarette boat, we found ourselves back in Venice. The team would arrive later that night, and Pete had let us know the general hadn't come with but might follow at some point.

Chapter 38

Nazreen Anaisha was, at twenty-four, the youngest vice president of any serious multinational Japanese electronics company and had more than made her mark with innovative thinking and skill with software and hardware design to die for. In just five years, she had invented over sixty technologically brilliant devices, all of which had found their way onto her mother's factory floors from Karachi to Los Angles. The fact that she and her sister had worked on the gaming software for a wonderful woman by the name of "Helen," and been paid handsomely for it, had just added icing on the corporate cake and, in a strange way, kicked started her real interest in robotics.

She had been a refugee, plucked out of the camps, and had been placed with the Anaisha family almost by accident—they had already taken one refugee girl into their home, but a simple clerical error in the Red Crescent office had given her a chance she would never regret, and from the moment she saw the gaming consoles in her new home, she knew she was in heaven. And her adoptive mother had seen her talent very early on and provided a fast pathway for her to learn the craft of code writing, robotics, artificial intelligence, and software development.

When the factory she played in during meetings and executive responsibilities received an order for five hundred specifically designed robots and a plan for a self-contained and automated factory, she immediately looked at the puzzle—like she would any new game console. She had a full-scale model of the intended plant constructed, imported the additive 3D printers from an American supplier, and then worked for two straight years getting the kinks out.

She personally wrote the code that ran the robots, designed the AI that ran the machines and flow systems that linked the printers, and even dummied up the nanite and the additive raw material baths, which used colored water to simulate flow. Two impressive women had visited the mock-up three years ago, and apart from also being refugees, each one introduced themselves to her, and only her, as the CEO of a new plant to be, and immediately ordered everything Nazreen and her staff had designed and built, in a ship lot of twenty sets. The destinations were varied, from the United States all the way to New Zealand, so for the next year, the factory worked twenty-four hours a day to meet the order.

The genius of the design was that every component snapped together like a giant Lego kit, so the build time was minimized. The initial ship sets were delivered, and then a strange order was received. The client wanted a ship set packed and dispatched every month, which was achieved, and the ship sets now sat in boxes in Canada, Greenland, Chile, Portugal, Ireland, Denmark, Norway, Finland, Estonia, Sri Lanka, Solomon Islands, Japan, and Iceland. The ship sets were sent to America, and New Zealand was turned into working factories, proving all the amazing work that Nazreen had done at the Japanese plant.

She had even managed a short visit to Point Roberts in the last year to see for herself the remarkable system she had designed. At that time, the two women present were introduced as only our "engineer" and our "scientist." And when she had been flown as a guest to New Zealand, the engineer had gone with her, introduced herself as "Coleen," and once again, she saw for herself how wonderful her robots and AI functioned as the plant rolled out sheet after sheet, power plant after power plant. She had flown home to Karachi to tell her mother of their great success. Her father had been a little stoic but had nevertheless joined in the family celebration.

Nokomoto Senji, at six foot three inches, with pure white hair cut short in an almost crew-cut fashion but with one long side of silvery-white hair flopping down over his ear and a great knee-length coat hiding a light blue skinsuit looked anything but a seasoned Interpol agent. He had worked the docks, sweeping up smugglers of all types, and had actively worked in the anti-yakuza division of the Toyoko police force for seven years before being recruited to lead the head office for Interpol in Asia. He had also worked in offices throughout the Pacific region, in Indonesia, the Philippines, Australia, and New Zealand, just to get a "feel" for the area and its problems.

As he flicked through the thick brief he had been sent over a military-secured network he didn't know Interpol had, he formed an opinion of what was at stake, both in Japan and other countries. He had decided on a soft approach, no lights, no sirens, no uniformed police, just himself and his assistant, a mixed-race woman three years his junior and ten times tougher than he was, as she liked to remind him every day. They were an odd pair, one tall and fine-boned, the other a little short and squat; one with a sense of refinement in his speech and manners, the other a little rough around the edges, a persona she put on and off as often as she refreshed her lipstick, which today was a violet purple.

It matched her boots, Nokomoto thought to himself as they approached the security desk in the massive silver-and-black towering building, one of just many that ran the length of Nuebenu Road. They presented their IDs and requested directions to Innomatchi, which they knew from their research was on the thirty-fifth floor. The security guard bowed, and led them to a rich, bronzed elevator, ushered them in, then used his key to select the floor, then bowed his way out. The lift flew up the risers, stopping with such a smooth push of air the movement was almost imperceptible. The door opened, revealing a lush but very high-tech reception area manned by five women, all dressed in modern, well-cut suits, all the same silver color.

"おはようございます、情報へようこそ," the woman in the middle cried out, standing and bowing. Nokomoto and his partner both bowed respectfully, then stood straight.

"We wish to see Ms. Anaisha, please, on a matter of urgency," he said, holding his ID out for the women to inspect. His partner mirrored his movements. The woman looked flustered for a moment, then bent to a hidden keyboard, seemed to relax a little, then finally stood tall again and bowed.

"Ms. Anaisha will see you. Please take a seat until her assistant can come and escort you," she said, pointing to a series of lounge chairs that sat in a semicircle around a massive tinted window that opened out onto a view of the rivers and rail yards. The agents both moved toward the chairs but stood almost shoulder to shoulder. Under the cover of pointing to something outside, Nokomoto used a tap code on the shoulder of his partner—*under obs, vid, and aud.* His partner just nodded, pointing outside to carry the charade. Both had turned on their miniature video recorders long before entering the building, both had the suspicion that there would be electronic interference at some point, and both were sufficiently confident enough to know that what they saw and heard could faithfully be reproduced when they got back to their HQ. The instruction from Captain Riley had been specific and succinct.

The person they were about to interview was deeply involved in the terrorist attacks, and they should not be distracted by either her youth or her physical appearance. And she was to be taken into custody no matter what resistance might be offered. A long-legged brunette in an immaculate pinstriped suit with amazing bright blue high heels glided in and bowed in the traditional Japanese manner.

"If you would both follow me, please," she said, in a high sing-song voice that did not go with the suit, as she led them into a plush corridor lined with electronic photos that slid into each other.

Game on, Nokomoto thought to himself, positioning himself just slightly forward of his partner. They didn't expect armed resistance but were taking no chances. The death toll in Japan from the civil insurrection that followed the attacks had only claimed around seven hundred thousand lives, but the images of the shredded and ruined bodies had formed an image in his mind that haunted him every day. He would not let one of the instigators of the worldwide attacks through his fingers, and he knew from experience that his partner, who had visibly tensed her shoulders, would back him up no matter what.

Chapter 39

Our headquarters in Venice hadn't really changed much since we left it for the monks' brilliant technology cave, but we saw immediately the improvements Indigo and his brother had made in our absence. For starters, there were now two massive espresso machines huffing and puffing like demented steam trains, one in each corner. And the computers, screens, and telecommunications had been seriously upgraded, and three of the monks were visible, putting the finishing touches on the wall-to-wall screens.

As I looked around the room, I could see Amira engrossed with Anna, and Indigo just as busy with Tom, now dressed for the street, in that if you didn't look at his boots, you would think "classic American tourist." His entire team lay sprawled asleep around the walls, gear packs and weapons tumbled together as if having been thrown out of a washing machine. Now that we had a totally secure link with Israel, the US, and our Interpol offices in the Asia-Pacific region, specifically Japan and Australia, I was starting to feel a little more in control.

By agreement with the Israeli government, all our prisoners, including the scientist and the pilot, were housed in a special facility outside Tel Aviv. They were being held in isolation but very comfortable quarters for terrorists and were under a twenty-four-hour physical and electronic guard. I had a million questions, but for now, we had to stay focused on finding the other women and the engineer. And work out what Mohammad bin Azaria's "Plan B" was.

I had a strong feeling we had seen some of it for ourselves—as in Point Roberts and Helena. And just as I was developing this idea, one of my favorite agents blipped into existence on our massive central screen, a smile so wide it was infectious.

"Just call me Sally!" the smile said, then the camera zoomed out to reveal Agent Sandra Thomas, dressed in a lightweight silvery-dark suit with a bright blue blouse tucked under wide lapels. She might have been working the Chicago scene for the last two years, but she was literally bubbling in her new role managing twenty troops from the president's train guard, three FBI agents, and a brace of special services people whose leader Bob looked like he chewed nails three times a day.

"Hi, boss, I hope I'm not interrupting anything, but a little bird told me you were back home, drinking excellent espresso." I wasn't, and then I was, as Indigo placed a steaming mug with a handle carved like the bow of a gondola into my hands.

"I wonder who the little bird was?" I asked Indigo innocently and got another twenty-megawatt smile for my effort.

"*Il Mio Capitano, le mie ali sono ritagliate!*" he replied, hugging his elbows into his sides, then making a flapping motion with them as he moved out of camera range.

"Sandra, how goes it?"

"Excellent. All the boys and girls are here, doing what they need to do. Bob is being the perfect gentleman, and Fay is her usual super-smart self. We have the new build site under constant surveillance, and the reason for this call is that the FBI boys have detected a burst transmission from up the road toward Mid Canon. After the initial transmission, a second one was detected, this time a receiving stamp—so we are speculating the conversation was two-way. The frequency and content have been sent to Malcolm, Luigi, and Shami, as per your instructions." I looked at the relaxed, smiling features of the young agent and tried very hard to remember myself at that age, but the picture was blurred.

Had I ever had such intensity and confidence? I didn't think so.

"Excellent. In terms of the buildings, how are they progressing?"

"Another Pantech arrived at the airport last night, one truck loaded with panels, the other with batteries. As for the building site, there was a tree flying proudly on a roof a day ago; Bob tells me that is the builders' sign that they have reached a milestone, but short of going out and physically counting all the houses, we don't know how many are completed. There is a school, university, hospital, and shopping center being erected, but none of us are builders, so we don't know the actual state of construction." I thought for a minute.

"Get Bob here, please." The frame went to a bland background somewhere in the house, then the meaty face of the commander of the special forces swam into focus.

"Bob, pick one of your troops, get them dressed in civies, no weapons, no ID other than a driving license, and see if you can get them taken on as casual labor at the building site. Then get us as much intel as you can, as fast as you can. Please." I tacked on the "please" because, while I was in a hurry, there was no need to panic my team by barking out orders. He just nodded, then moved out of the frame to be replaced by Sandra.

"Are you keeping an eye on Point Roberts?"

"Yes. Fay has direct contact with the FBI team there; we are getting eight hourly reports. The engineers have started the layout for the foundations for two more plants, but that's all they can do for now until you send the machinery, equipment, and robots. According to the plant engineers, the entire plant arrived in boxes, and they built the frame out of timber until they could make the panels. So somewhere, there is a factory or two that makes all the guts. Have you found one yet?"

"Yes, we think so. Your situation is priority number one, so just be a little patient. Please."

"Please" was added for the same reason I added one for Bob. Then a stray thought slipped into my mind, and I looked at Sandra from under my eyebrows.

"Is there any movement on selling those houses?"

"We have our eyes on three realtors, all of whom claim to be able to negotiate a sale, but they claim they are waiting for the terms and conditions to be released by the trust set up by Howard Westhall. The trustees claim they are waiting for a code phrase from someone unidentified before they can release the documents the realtors need. It all seems a bit circuitous to me, but if you think about the timing, he built up the infrastructure five years ago, funded the trust, and three years ago, when he passed away, the trustees took over the management of the estate. So he was either complicit in the master plan or a very important part of it at some stage." I thought about that. The scenarios we had built around the timing of the attacks from the Y2K debacle on.

"Okay, keep at it, tell everyone good work, and chat to you again later."

"Boss," I called, looking for his unmistakable shape in the gloom of the back areas of our working space. He walked out of the gloom, holding one of Indigo's boat-inspired expressos.

"You shrieked?" I nodded, my mind too full of questions to hear his sarcasm. "What did that Red Crescent report say about the thousand-plus girls that were taken two months ago or so?" He looked at me with a funny look, started to put the dots together, smiled, dropped his head, then looked up at me with an evil smile.

"Good one. You've put it together. I shouldn't have been so slow. You think they are on a boat somewhere, headed for somewhere, and this is part of Mohammad bin Azaria's famous 'Plan B'?" I nodded, only just having seen the possibility for myself.

"Why build hundreds of houses, now, for migrants who have come with their own mobile accommodation and really don't need immediate attention?"

"We need to talk to the Red Crescent people again. Can you arrange that, please, Indigo?"

"*Certamente il mio, colonnello, subito!*" And Indigo turned and fired instructions to one of the monks, who immediately attacked a keyboard as if he were mining it for diamonds.

I looked at the Boss; he looked at me, and Anna, who had drifted over during my chat with Sandra, had a look on her face that said, "surprise! surprise!"

"What's the fastest way to get a government to change its mind?" I asked them both. The Boss grinned, no doubt thinking about "shock and awe" and the immediate effect of a bullet in the brain, the old "one in the heart, one in the head" mantra. Anna tilted her head, thinking about the question. From her perspective, rules and regulations, statutes and laws and precedents made her world turn. And it turned slowly, at the best of times, ruled by cognitive and discretionary beliefs and attitudes, usually based on some form of bias. Compared to a bullet, the law was slow, cumbersome, and very much subject to political will, bastardization, bribery and corruption, and just plain bullshit.

"Embarrassment."

"Yes. Embarrass a country before the rest of the civilized world, and you stain the entire population, whether or not that is your intention. And talking that thinking a little further, under the current circumstances, given that social order had broken down in so many ways and that most governments are holding on by the thinnest of threads, what do you think the likely response would be to a boatload of refugee children landing on your shores?"

"Fully funded, all paid for in advance, no cost to anyone other than a little care and attention?"

"Yes." You could hear a pin drop in the cavern, and it seemed for a moment that even the expresso machines had stopped puffing.

"Who do we tell?"

"No one. It is just a good guess right now; we need more facts to support our supposition before we scare the bejesus out of anyone. Agreed?" I looked at them, both trying to process what we had just discussed from a risk management perspective. Anna owed her allegiance to the US, the Boss, and me to the World Court and the 194 countries we represented. And no one, Russia or China included, ever wanted to hear speculative news that could upset the political balance within their borders.

But it did beg the question of how the terrorists intended to pull it off, and I would give that some serious thought. Indigo came back with a little electronic notepad in one hand. He seemed excited, bouncing around on the balls of his feet.

"My captain, my colonel, princess Anna, I have the latest news from Red Crescent and Red Cross for you. He slid a finger over his screen, and the data magically appeared on the big screen that now filled one wall. "Princess" Anna? Was there something going on between Indigo and Anna I had missed? Or was he just being his joyful, happy self? Questions for a later time.

"Look at those numbers at the bottom. Two lots of one thousand plus, then over one hundred thousand in five thousand lots, and that is repeated ten times. Indigo, what exactly is this please?"

"Captain, these are the numbers of little girls that have been collected in the last three months and the plan for the next six months. Staging centers have been specially set up in fifteen countries, all paid for by volunteer funding and labor, and all sanctioned by the UNHCR, and according to a footnote, also agreed by the secretary of state of the USA—in principle. The countries are USA, Canada, Greenland, Chile, Portugal, Ireland, Denmark, Norway, Finland, Estonia, Sri Lanka, Solomon Islands, New Zealand, Japan, and Iceland."

"The same countries that got six billion euros five or six years ago."

"Yes. I wonder if this is a one, two, three punch to the gut of those countries?"

"As in?" the Boss asked, drawing Indigo into the conversation as I had failed to do. No excuse, my manners were bad at the best of times, and this was turning out to be anything but. We all sat, following the Boss and Indigo's lead.

"Punch one, six billion to play with. Punch two, we will build you an ecologically sound plant that will give you cheap power wherever you need it and encourage you to consume your renewable resources that will be so plentiful you will never know the difference."

"And punch three, here are all these little girl refugees, and we will pay you for taking them in and giving them homes."

"Stop! Just stop!" I held my hands out flat and in their faces, and my tonality was not polite. "Personally, I have a problem with using children as bargaining chips at the best of times, but if what you are suggesting is correct, this will be human trafficking on a scale we have never imagined previously." Anna leaned forward and ran her hand up and down my arm, calming me.

"Whoa, Jessica, that might be a step too far. Child trafficking? I don't see it." I dropped my head, the images from our last big case rippling through my mind like a hurricane. Children as young as two years were being enslaved and eventually sold for their body parts, and fat profiteers laughed over their whiskies while it was all going down. We had killed most of the perpetrators deliberately and with malice and aforethought, although I would take that statement to my grave before I admitted it to anyone outside the recovery team. The Boss was watching me carefully, and I sensed he knew exactly what I was thinking about. Like me, his hand had also been on the trigger.

"Anna, Jessica has a point. If the children are being taken without their permission and then transported across international or state lines, you need to be careful how you describe the process, or you cross too many predetermined mandates which can come back and bite us in the backside." Anna looked uncomfortable as if she had crossed some Rubicon. She seemed to pull something into herself and rubbed my arm faster.

"Colonel, Jessica, I see what you are saying, but there is a larger question that needs to be examined. How do we explain the mass movement of refugee children to anyone, given the current conditions? Remember, we have not yet released anything about Mohammad bin Azaria or his girls—make that women now. The only thing saving us at this point is the lack of worldwide communication, but that will not last much longer." Then a voice spoke up and startled me because, in all the fuss, I had completely forgotten my shadow, Pete, who stood behind me, and I had no idea where he had been for the last twenty minutes. And he was one of the team I would protect to my grave, so he also probably knew what was going through my mind. And just to be very clear, I had pulled the trigger as dispassionately as the rest of the team at the time, and I had yet to lose any sleep over it.

"Jessica here is reflecting back on an op we ran last year, sufficient to say it was not the best reference for managing children refugees. But I'm with her. We really do have to consider the legality of what Mohammad bin Azaria has done and is still doing, albeit via surrogates because someone with a pointy head will ask that question, and not having an answer could trip up everything we need to do." There was that giant mind inside the lithe body of a trained killer again, an attribute I kept forgetting.

"Pete's right. Apologies for my overreaction, no excuses. I can't promise I won't do it again, so let's move on. Our role is to corral the terrorists. We need to focus on that. We have an engineer to capture an unknown quantity of women terrorists working out of the sandy countries. We now have a few leads; can we focus on them, please?" The Boss looked calm but serious; he and I would talk this out later. The legal ramifications of what Mohammad bin Azaria had done and was still doing now via his surrogates was a legal quagmire, but Anna was correct. It wasn't for us to take sides, just prosecute the terrorists.

And then later, if some country wanted to involve us on the basis of people trafficking, then that would be a separate issue.

Having finally got my head straight, I started to continue the discussion but was rudely interrupted by the big screen again, this time with signaling chirps and beeps. I waved at one of the monks, who immediately turned the noise off. The young, elongated face of our man in Japan swam into focus next to his partner, who could only be described as "rugged," featuring bright purple lips, dyed black eye sockets, and a piercing in her nose. Whatever her looks, her record as an investigator would embarrass all but the very best in the world.

"*Konichiwa*, Nokomoto-san, lovely to see you both." His smile lit up the screen, and they both bowed, causing their heads to move in and out of focus.

"Captain, please excuse our call, but we have some information for you that may be time-sensitive." I nodded my acceptance, but before I could answer him, Aikido spoke. "Captain, Nokomoto and I have just finished our preliminary interview with Nazreen Anaisha and another called Maiko Satsuma, who is the president of the corporation. They were very forthcoming, appeared to hold nothing back, and provided us with all the data we requested, going back seven years."

"That's good. But what do you have that is so time-sensitive?"

"Well, Captain, in your brief to us, you mentioned that you had instructed the army engineers to duplicate the Point Roberts plant, and we have data here that shows twenty ship sets of complete factories minus the nanomaterial and panels were transported eighteen months ago. There is one complete ship set in each of the fifteen countries you listed, plus five stored in the US—two sets in San Diego and three in Charleston. To further confuse the issue, just a year ago, another twenty ship sets were ordered and paid for and are currently sitting on the docks here in Toyoko waiting for dispatch details."

"Just for the fun of it, do you have any idea how much a ship set costs?" The grin the young agent gave us was almost feral, and she nodded so violently that her long dreads flipped over her face a couple of times.

"A complete factory, sans the nanomaterial and panels, ships out the door for six hundred million and change. According to Ms.

Anaisha, they can be assembled and up and running in three months, provided the panels are shipped in from one of the other plants and the nanomaterial is seeded. She did mention that both Point Roberts and the New Zealand plant had been producing panels for the last eighteen months and felt that there would be sufficient for at least fifteen factories from the get-go."

"Did she have a view of how the nanomaterial could be 'seeded' as you mentioned?"

"Yes. Very simple, according to her, and supported by her company president, both existing plants know the process and are set up for it." I let the silence hang for a moment, collecting my thoughts. Anna looked at me, so I nodded.

"Agents, what is your level of confidence in the information you have obtained?" she asked, no doubt seeing a potential win for the US if they could get an additional five plants up in double-quick time.

"One hundred percent. Everything we are telling you is documented, and we have schematics, plans, drawings, timelines, and on another subject, that of gamers designing the attack plan, we know how that was achieved as well." My ears pricked up at that, so I looked up at the cameras expectantly.

"Nazreen and her sister, through her mother's company, Innomatchi, in concert with groups of gamers from all over the world, entered a competition to design and build a new series of games six years ago. The prize was one hundred thousand US dollars and IP rights to the game. The girls won the competition, and their mother's company built and released the game. You will not believe how the terrorists did it; it is so simple it is terrifying."

"Simple?"

"Yes. The gamers were given scenarios, and chapters, if they liked, and tasked with working out how to maximize the use of the different resources provided for each chapter. No one gamer had access to more than one or two chapters and was eliminated progressively. From the outside, we believe the competition was rigged, the objective being to get the girls and their mother involved in both the planning, albeit in nonconnected sections, as well as in designing and building the plants. Ms. Anaisha admits freely to having designed and built all the machines and robots that make up a plant and then took us to a 3D scale model she had built to explain to us how they worked."

"All open, volunteered, no hesitation, no prevarication?"

"No. None. It was as if they were waiting for us to arrive."

"I bet. Thank you both. That is excellent work. Please send all the data through, and stand by for more instructions." We disconnected and sat in silence for another moment, considering the implications of what we had just heard.

"Major Japanese corporation, worldwide reach, a leader in robotics, coding, and AI, plugged into every military establishment on the planet, probably has more corporate power than the Pentagon. Every order they will have received will have been vetted, audited at the highest level, and legally bulletproofed. And they got paid some, what, fourteen billion dollars—no, scratch that—there are ship sets sitting on the docks already paid for, so that number is probably more like thirty billion dollars. Wow! Who said crime doesn't pay?"

"No. Not crime. Terrorism. But we will never be able to prosecute them or anyone associated with them." I brought our focus back to our main task.

"All very well and good. Now we know how the planners worked, but I want the engineer in chains, this 'Helen' woman, and whoever worked the desert headquarters for the attacks. Until that is done, we don't stop or get distracted by the pretty baubles being thrown our way.

"We need to put it all together and go talk to Mohammad bin Azaria again."

"Yes, good call, Jessica. Anna, could I suggest you get the US data to the general, so she can get the army engineers up to speed; in fact, just limit the information to the five ship sets in the US, please; keep the rest to ourselves for the immediate future." She looked at the Boss, thinking through the consequences of not fully informing the general of all that they knew, but trusted the Boss to know exactly what he was doing, so she nodded in agreement. The Boss had his mini out and was tapping furiously, then flicked the image up to the big screen. It was filled with the faces of Shami and Malcolm.

"Afternoon, lads. Good to see you got home in one piece. Malcolm, I'm going to hand you over to Luigi, who has a problem for you all to solve. Luigi?" And the Italian geek took over the Boss's mini and, sitting cross-legged on a chair, started that wonderful, unintelligible geek babble with his counterparts, their faces all lit up like it was Christmas. Anna moved off to talk to the general, who had come in from the outside unannounced, leaving Pete, Amira, and the Boss with me, so we moved to a quiet area to consider our options.

"The geeks will get us the locations of the burst transmissions, and that will pinpoint where Helen may be, or at least some of her crew. The transmission from near Helena is being tracked now, and that may or may not give us the missing engineer. Amira, I have to ask you some tough questions—I hope you don't mind, but someone will ask them at some point, and I want to get ahead of that if I can so we can concentrate on the terrorists." She looked so impossibly young to be one of the world's leading geniuses on nanotechnology and computer coding, but with a fast whip of her hair back behind her ear, she nodded her agreement. Out of the corner of my eye, I saw Anna drifting back towards us, so I waited until she took her seat next to Amira.

"Amira, I only partially understand the whole nano-thing, so I may ask the wrong question the wrong way, so please forgive me if I do." She looked serious, her face tightening a little, but her eyes never left mine. "For the sake of simplicity, let's do this—nano number one was the bug you originally developed to eat oil spills. Okay?" She nodded, a small smile forming as she had no doubts and considered all her hard work being boiled down to a dot point. "Nano number two will be the bug used to kill the oil, gas, and coal infrastructure. And that took another three years of development by the terrorists, we believe." Another nod. "Then we have the nano bug they are using in the plants to build the panels and power supplies— we'll call that nano number three. But here's my first question—you stated quite emphatically back a week or so ago that you could not reverse the process at the oil, gas, and coal infrastructure because, if I remember your words correctly, you couldn't reprogram the nanomachines." She nodded again, then her face softened, and she looked all of fifteen or sixteen, an amazing transition.

"Do you know how a nanomachine works?" she asked, looking from me to Anna, to Pete, and then to the Boss. Almost in unison, we all shook our heads. She brushed her hair back behind her ears again and rolled her head from side to side, obviously working out how to describe one of the greatest inventions of the twentyfirst century to us mere mortals.

"Okay, all this happens at the molecular level, but imagine for a moment that a nanomachine is a matchbox with a brain. I program that brain to ignite all the matches on command, the matchbox burns, and all that is left is ash. With me so far?" As if we were all attached to each other, again, all four of us nodded in sync. "Good. Now, with my nano number one, as you labeled it, I designed it to break up the oil into its chemical component parts, destroy the nasty bits, then create a neutral substance called carbon3, which sank to the bottom of the sea bed and became no more than part of the majestic chemistry set that is the ocean. The power for the transformation process came from the seawater, a relatively simple process."

"So you are saying that in the case of nano number one, it self-destructed during the process of cleaning up the oil spill."

"Yes. Exactly. So, onto nano number two. As you speculated, it took another three years to develop it, but this time it was programmed to solidify in its own chemistry or evaporate if exposed to air. The net result is the same—once triggered, it can't be reprogrammed. And because it literally eats and grows on its own waste, the damage is not just to the pipes and pumps but to the underground deposits as well."

"Are you saying that the oil and gas, and coal for that matter, is destroyed forever?" the Boss asked, the tension in his voice palpable. She nodded this time, looking quite pleased with the Boss's question.

"Yes. The 'gunk', as you called it, will be all the way down into the rock strata, and the nanomachines will have followed the oil and gas to the ultimate point of origin, like a giant snake eating its own tail. Not so much the coal."

"Why not the coal?" My turn to ask a question, the Boss, Anna and Pete were shocked by the knowledge that the oil and gas deposits were gone forever. Somwhere at the back of all our minds, for no reason other than not being able to imagine a world without oil and gas, I suspect we had deluded ourselves that the damage was a surface thing and that we could recover from it.

Not to be. Amira waited until we settled down, then held her palm out in a little cup.

"Coal is a solid form of chemical soup, made up of carbon, hydrogen, oxygen, nitrogen, and sulfur, and was originally formed from plant decomposition and pressure. Oil is another form of coal, with different ratios but essentially the same, in liquid form. While we used the chemistry of the ocean to generate the power the nanomachines needed to work with nano number one, what the terrorists have done with their version of my nanomachine is get the power from the consumption of the carbon, changing the residual nature of the waste. The waste is what you call 'gunk,' which is inert, chemically stable, and either solidifies or evaporates, as I explained before. Because coal is a solid, once you break it down into its chemical constituents, you destroy its molecular structure, forever changing its nature. It just becomes a primordial soup of chemicals, all of which are altered at the molecular level by the nanomachine."

"So, no more coal?"

"No. Now, if we look at nano number three, we see the real smarts of what they have done. They have taken my formula, one which I had constructed as part of our original project but not built a nanomachine from, and reversed the carbon three process so that the ocean supplies all the raw materials needed to build the panels and the power supplies. Essentially, they are taking sand—full of quartz, silica, or silicon dioxide as it is more commonly known, rutile, zircon, monazite, and ilmenite. You would know that glass is often made from sand. Then you take the ocean—full of bicarbonate, sulfate, chloride, nitrate, calcium, magnesium, sodium, potassium, iron, and again, silica, and you have all that you need for their panels and power packs. And I might add, we had speculated on manufacturing a biofuel using the same technology, but again, we had not yet gone there in the development phase."

"You had all this worked out at the time of the trial you ran in Nova Scotia?"

"Yes, except for nano number two—we had no interest in killing oil, gas, or coal."

"You have all of this documented and could produce it to a court if we have to?"

"Yes, I told you all this when I was questioned by you and Anna in Israel. At that time, we couldn't get to the data in the cloud, but thanks to Luigi, Shami, Malcolm, and Indigo, we've got access to all my notes from the very first time I started work on the project in Israel. And as with all original research material, it is time and date stamped and version controlled, with all attributions to the various authors."

"Could you make nano number three?" I asked, curious to see what the possibilities were.

"Yes, but no need to; the nanomachines feed on themselves, share energy, and only need the raw ingredients to sustain themselves, which they already get from the ocean."

"So you could literally start a new plant from scratch, using the 'seed stock' from either Point Roberts or New Zealand." She considered my question, her eyes furrowed slightly, and she looked quizzically off to one side.

"I think so. I would have to run tests; it might take a little time, but I see no reason why we couldn't do that. If your information is correct, and the entire plant is available in a ship set, then all you would need is the nanomachines to complete the process." Huh! And then, a question so obvious popped into my mind, and I vaguely remembered having asked the same one a long time ago.

"Who else, besides yourself, could work this magic?" She smiled at my use of the word "magic," but then, to be honest, everything she had described to us seemed to be one of the most magical stories I had ever heard.

"Michele, and one engineer we worked with, you have her photo from my files. Her name is Coleen. She is Irish, was a refugee child, just like I was, but her adoption family was in Ireland, and she has the most amusing accent when she chooses to use it." I signaled to Indigo; he fired up one of the computers that littered the floor, accessed Amira's files, then popped the photo of Coleen onto a side screen. Red hair, cut into a bob, strong face, good bones, bright green eyes, tallish. I would estimate around five-ten, maybe eleven, not a bodybuilder's form, but certainly fit and looked after herself. And her smile was pixie-like, enchanting, with just a hint of mischief.

"Only the three of you could do this?" I asked, needing to make certain I had all our ducks in a row. She nodded, looking at the photo of the engineer with a wistful look on her face.

"Yes, we had other engineers and scientists working with us, but none of them actually got the essence of what we were doing. Some got the math but not the chemistry; some got the chemistry but not the math. Michele got it almost as soon as I did, and Coleen was probably only a few months behind us. But she was brilliant in her own way and a lovely, caring person." I nodded. As loving and caring as she may have been, Michele disqualifying herself by what she had been doing in the freelance hacking world left Coleen as the instigator of the nanomachines and probably the same person we were still chasing in Helena.

I wondered why she was lingering around.

"Amira, when all this is over, what do you think you want to do?" Anna asked, and I looked at her in surprise, as that was the last question I would have thought to ask. Amira looked up at the roof of the cavern, the muted hidden lighting throwing up weird shadows and bright spots.

"I don't know. Can this ever all be over?" she asked, looking like a lost child seeking her parent's approval. My heart bled for her. Here was a master genius, lightyears ahead of her contemporaries, has created a fantastic solution to massive environmental issues and developed ideas around a whole slew of wonderful solutions to the world's energy problems, only to have them hijacked by a group of terrorists and used against the very people she had been trying to help. Not to mention the first seven or eight years of her life surviving in a refugee camp against all the odds. Sometimes life kicked you in the guts, but what I saw in front of me now was someone who cared, with a spine made of steel, who would continue to work as hard as it took to get her world back in balance.

Time to move on.

Roadside Stop

Coleen had no choice. The building site now had over one thousand homes ready for occupancy, the schools were a week away from being finished, the hospital another two weeks, and by the end of the month, they would be approaching fifteen hundred homes, with a second school completed. The building was going at a frantic rate as more and more temporary residents of Helena, all of whom had called different towns and cities home up until five or six weeks ago, worked as hard as they could, the prize being they could move out of the tents or caravans they and their families were living in temporarily, and into a really decent home, one that promised a level of comfort many had not imagined possible under the prevailing circumstances. In fact, a level of comfort many had not yet experienced in their lives so far, no matter where they had come from.

And the rumors circulating the building site were that the cost of a home would only be around the fifty thousand mark! A clever person could immediately compute that was the raw cost of labor, and they would be eighty percent correct. But there were also rumors that purchasing or even renting a home came with conditions, and no one, from the project manager down, had any clue what those conditions might be.

The three realtors who had indicated that they would be the sales agents for the houses were tight-lipped about the conditions and, in truth, had absolutely no idea what they may be, as the trustee had indicated that the conditions would be released when they were satisfied that the terms of trust had been met.

That's where Coleen came in. It was to have been the Irish girls living in the Westhall house, Elizabeth and Moya, who would unlock the conditions, but they had been taken in by the FBI for reasons unknown to her. So Coleen had pulled to the roadside, midway between Helena and Cascade to the north, and sent an encrypted message to Helen. Helen had then sent the coded data back, and that was the burst transmission that had been detected by the FBI Team in Helena, the intelligence services in Israel, and monks in Venice.

Coleen sat by the roadside, thinking through how to contact the trustee, prove her credentials, and then pass the codes on. It was a real problem because she was sure that there was an Interpol Red notice out on her, and that would undoubtedly throw the trustees into a legal spin. As she was thinking about how to circumvent creating a problem, a shadow fell over her windscreen, and a helicopter gunship lowered until it was at road level, skids just a foot off the road surface, facing her car head-on. The multiple barrels of the twenty-millimeter Gatling gun under the nose looked huge, even at a distance of fifteen feet, and the gunner's helmeted head with the face shield down reflected back the image of her sitting in her vehicle. She smiled to herself; perhaps this would solve her problem, perhaps it would make it worse.

A small-town car pulled up behind her, and two jacketed FBI agents stepped out and approached either side of her car. A third person followed, a woman wearing a combination of clothes Coleen could not associate with law enforcement, and she shook her head at this cogitative dissonance, trying to clear her mind for the ordeal to come.

"Out of the car, please, Coleen. You are under arrest for aiding and abetting terrorist acts under the Terrorist Laws as modified in 2022; more charges will be specified at your booking." Susan stood back, letting the FBI agents manage to get the terrorist out of the car. Her orange jacket rolled up to a couple of folds above her delicate wrists, sat on top of a very light blue shirt, collar up, and was completed by long, silky black pants and shiny boots. If she had emerged from a catwalk, Coleen would not have been surprised in the slightest. She was even more surprised to see that this really beautiful woman was holding Interpol's credentials out for her scrutiny.

"Who, specifically, is arresting me?" Coleen asked, her voice quiet, as she had her hands cuffed behind her back. SA RuPaul reached inside the car and retrieved the burst transmitter, which looked like a small black radio with a few big knobs. Unless you knew what to look for, you would not recognize it. SSA Remer pulled the boot open and found a treasure trove of intelligence, one of which she recognized from the briefing back in Seattle, where a photo of the "magic" artificial intelligence controller used in the aircraft and truck attacks had been shown.

"Well, look what we have here. Sandra, how do you want to move this?" she asked, holding up two canvas bags full of electronic equipment. "Just call me Sally," literally beamed, her chiseled face splitting into a wide grin.

"Well, the day just keeps getting better and better. Fay, you okay to drive this back into Helena?"

"Absolutely. Keep Andrew with our guest," she said, waving the helicopter off, which immediately rose, creating a shattering dust storm with the shriek of turbine engines, the beat of the rotors drowning out further conversation. SA RuPaul put Coleen into the back seat of the town car, Susan got in the front seat, tapped the driver on the shoulder, and the two-car procession executed a U-turn and headed back to the FBI office in Helena. The gunship positioned itself overhead, sitting at five hundred feet, the wash from the rotors beating on the roofs of the vehicles.

"Noisy bastards, but you can't help but love that nose gun!" Sandra yelled, waving out her side window at the gunship, as happy as she had ever been.

Chapter 40

The general's face looked calm, but beneath the surface, she was anything but. Looking at the faces of Arie, Jessica, Anna, Pete, Amira, Luigi, Shami, Indigo, Malcolm, PJ, Roger, Julius, and Frank, not for the first time, she wondered when the team had grown so large. She thought about Jessica's last report, shook her head, and decided to challenge it. Not out of stubbornness but because she believed that this elite team, at least the Interpol part, would be denied to her from this point on.

"Captain, as you said, you now have the engineer and are on the way out of the country. But with all the other goings-on in Helena, Point Roberts, the plant ship sets, and the like, why are you saying that you have completed your responsibilities to the United States?" She would need a solid answer because this was the first question she would be asked by the president. She'd bet her pristine uniform on it.

"General, we have the banker and planners in custody, along with the three women who managed and mounted the attacks on the US, as well as several ancillary persons, all of whom attributed aid and support to the terrorists in some form. It will take us considerable time to prepare the warrants against them and present them to the World Court. Your FBI is well and truly in the loop, your army engineers are on top of the plants, and we now need to focus our attention on locating and arresting the other women involved in the attacks on Italy, Israel, the UAE, and Europe. Do you want Anna back?"

"No. Keep her as long as you need her." Roger cut across the general; keeping Anna with the Interpol team ensured that he, at least, would be kept in the loop on the investigation. The general looked anything but happy at the interruption but finally nodded her agreement.

"Will you still need the assistance of the NSA?" she asked, knowing the answer in advance.

"With your permission, we'd like to keep Malcolm and his team until we have concluded the mission. He has proved invaluable, and working with our geeks has given us a significant resource." In one of the picture squares, the image of Frank Reynolds nodded; he had the exact same thought that Roger had had—keeping Malcolm embedded gave him first-class and immediate access to what Interpol was doing.

"Well, on behalf of the American government, thank you for everything. We trust you will at least keep us informed?" Everyone from the Boss on down on the Interpol side nodded, and with wan smiles, the feed was cut, leaving Frank, Roger, Julius, and the general looking at each other.

"General, they are not being rude or playing games; their mandate is very clear, and while they got involved in Point Roberts and Helena, it was in pursuit of the main terrorists. I had a long chat with Anthony a few hours ago, and he was very clear. Their focus will now be on the Middle East and cleaning up the international supply chain for the plants. He will keep us in the loop and will advise us on the logistics of enabling the plants to start production once the engineers have erected the basic structures. He suggests we get panels from Point Roberts to complete the build." The general acknowledged Frank's comments, then smiled a wicked smile.

"Have we got back our SR-71?"

"Last I heard, it was parked in Washington. So I guess that's a yes."

"Keep me apprised, specifically of any movement in Helena and anything to do with those plants." The general clicked off, mindful of the fact that the US was now very much on its own as far as the terrorist attacks and the aftermath were concerned. Little did she know of what was to come, and it was this very subject that the Interpol team was running down with Arie.

"From what you tell me, there could be several thousand children on their way from refugee camps in Somalia, Libya, Algeria, Myanmar, Sudan, Mozambique, Yugoslavia, China, Syria, Russia, Bangladesh, India, Pakistan, Venezuela, Afghanistan, Iraq, Iran, and who knows where else. The Red Crescent admits that they have had the children in special camps they set up, but as of today, they have only released two thousand odd to the carers who had been living with them. They are on boats; we don't know how many or where, but that thought alone scares the hell out of me."

"No one is reporting any mass movement of refugees, other than the flood of people still moving across Europe and the Asian continent due to the terrorist attacks. How do you move two thousand children and their carers? The Red Crescent must know where they are; why aren't they telling us?" I was a little upset by the image of children drowning in the ocean and falling out of small, ill-equipped boats, as had happened on many occasions in the Mediterranean, but Anna's assessment of the situation was accurate.

"They told us, in no uncertain terms, that a 'sponsor' had paid them to select the children, paid for the temporary accommodation, and was providing the transportation. The funds were paid out of an UN-sanctioned account three years ago, and a deal struck that benefits everybody—or so they say. I'm willing to bet that if we dig deep enough, we will find another billion-dollar slush fund that originated in Arabia. They claim that the funding is dependent on them never releasing the name of the sponsor, but assure us they are cleared by the UN and possibly some of the major countries around the world. The timing is too coincidental for my liking, but what better way to move people than in the middle of worldwide chaos."

"Is this really something we need to focus on?" the Boss asked, "Unless you see this as part of Mohammad bin Azaria's 'Plan B'?"

"It is. I bet my next paycheck on it. What I can't deduce is how he will manage to resettle them anywhere where the after-effects of the terror attacks have hit hard; the public sympathy surely will be against any plan he may have?"

"That may well be, but there are always other pressures you can bring to bear. Why not let it sit for a day or two, and we can revisit it after we have a plan for capturing the other women." The Boss's tone indicated he had made up his mind, and not having a good counter-argument, I let it go. For now. But I sensed a call to the US secretary of state was in my future. In her briefing notes from the president via the general, some weeks ago, she had mentioned that the funding for their "Project Apollos," which was contained in the October 14 briefing to the president, which strangely had never arrived at the White House, was fully funded. By whom? When? And how much? And what was Apollos?

"Jessica, I can see you thinking evil thoughts again. Spit it out!" I considered the Boss's comment, then decided to put it away for a day or two. We had far more important things to do with our time.

"Okay, pay attention. Questions will be asked." Anna punched Pete in the arm as if to get his attention; he just laughed and lightened the mood of us all. It was an interesting dynamic in our relationship; if one of us was in a bad mood, it infected the whole room.

"The engineer will be here in a few hours. Indigo, I'd like you to take your people and secure her from the aircraft. There may or may not be some FBI with her; if so, bring them all back here. Have the aircrew looked after and ask them to wait for our instructions. I will want them to take the engineer to Israel, to join her friends in hard lockdown, but I want her here first to check a few things out."

"*Sì, capitano, sarà un piacere portarla qui per lei. Prevedi un ETD per lì aereo?*" I looked at the Boss.

"Four hours should do it. Get them off in six-max?" He raised his eyebrows, thinking through the timing and that maybe four hours was a long time to interrogate anyone, let alone one of the smartest terrorists to ever attack the planet.

"By the time they get here, it will almost be dark. Keep them all overnight, wheels up at first light." I nodded. Indigo did his little bow thing to the Boss, then looked at me with a huge smile.

"Captain, it will be my pleasure to watch you interrogate this person. I will see to the conference room immediately!" His perfect English did not go unnoticed; Indigo was on a high, and it lifted us all. I motioned to Anna, and she and Pete, and I moved to a quiet corner.

"Anna, I want you in with me and maybe Amira at some stage. Everyone else, outside. Indigo will set the room, we can count on that, but I want you to think of the questions I might forget to ask."

"Unlikely, but okay. What will your main line of questioning be?"

"I want an outline of who did what on both sides of the Atlantic. We got very little from the pilot other than her admission she had delivered the Hercules. She did not tell us where and, in fact, did not deny anything we accused her of, but she didn't tell us anything, either. Arie's report on his interrogation of the scientist was similar—she admits to nothing other than helping to set up the plants in Point Roberts and New Zealand. So, in reality, the only way we can tie them to the attacks is through the pilot being positively identified on video, and the other two women living with her for three years in Helena, and a track of their comings and goings."

"Don't forget the burst transmissions." I nodded. I had, and it was a strong link to the terrorists.

"How would you frame the prosecution if it were only an FBI case?" There were a few differences between what Interpol could do and the FBI, but I hoped to learn something from Anna's approach.

"Firstly, as you have done, aiding and abetting a terrorist act under the Terrorist Laws. That is broad enough to get a conviction in any court, and we can prove their involvement at multiple levels, so to my mind, that is a lock-up. We—that's the US—have already claimed the mercenary terrorists were the prime attackers, so there's no joy for us in suddenly revealing the involvement of the women. But as the FBI, I would be pressuring them as hard as the law allows to get a description of every event because I would want that on record in case their involvement ever came back to bite us on our backsides. Secrets leak, and even though you are prosecuting them in the World Court, and I assume under seal, it will leak. Some countries will use the information to try and position themselves as a bigger victim than anyone else and seek a bigger slice of the restitution pie—whatever that might turn out to be."

"And the slush funds sitting in all those trust accounts have got to be a prime target." Pete had hit the nail on the head. We—actually, the US—were using some of those funds to set up additional plants, and there were fourteen other countries whose realistic expectation would be to directly benefit from the billions stacked away by the planners five or six years previously. And not just with a plant running and producing on their soil, as they already had the ship sets stored somewhere. We needed to coordinate that very quickly before it could get out of hand.

And then I had a sudden inspiration. No plant would work without the seeded nanomachines. And there were only a handful of people who knew their secrets. And one of them was in the same room as I was. I held my hand up to get everyone's attention, looked at the Boss, saw his wicked smile, and enjoyed a laugh as he took the piss out of me.

"Listen up, everyone. Jessica has had an idea!" The room didn't roar with laughter, but it did resonate a little, telling me the joke had been enjoyed and not seen as sarcastic.

"Shami, please connect the big screen to Arie wherever he is." He bent his head in acknowledgment, and his fingers flew across the keyboard, and Arie's tired and worn face filled the screen, several times the size of real life.

"Shalom, Arie, can we have five minutes, please?" I asked in my most polite voice. We couldn't see anyone else, but they easily could have been out of camera range. He waved to someone behind him; the background moved, strobing as the camera tried unsuccessfully to keep up with the action.

"Jessica, how can I help?" Every head in our office was turned towards me, not looking at the screen where Arie's face eventually stabilized.

"Arie, Amira is a Jewish citizen?"

"Yes."

"And as such, is a citizen of Israel?"

"Yes."

"And when we interviewed her, did she not hand over documents and files for all her work in both Israel and at Harvey Mudd?"

"Yes, again, and I understand the geeks have opened those files?"

"Yes, they have. Arie, I need you, on behalf of Israel, to own and control everything in Amira's files, with her permission, of course, and I want an announcement ready to be made to nineteen countries. You already have the list, claiming Jewish proprietorship over every nanomachine invention, worldwide IP rights, and claim to be the only source of being able to initiate the nanomachine process at any plant that is successfully erected from the ship sets. Without mentioning nanomachines."

Stunned silence reigned between the two countries as what I had said sunk in. "Further, I want our geeks to hijack every slush fund except for Point Roberts, Helena, and New Zealand and move them into accounts controlled by you." Now the silence was deafening. "And if you could, make it appear that the entire restitution of the terrorist attacks is an invention by an Israeli citizen, and willingly and openly shared with the world for humanitarian reasons by Israel."

"Why not take the funds in the US and NZ?" Anna asked, her voice as soft as rose petals falling in a summer breeze. She had folded her arms in a semi-defensive pose, but her body language and face read calm, collected, and marginally on my side of the conversation.

"I want to see how Mohammad bin Azaria's 'Plan B' plays out. We might be able to use it in some way down the track."

"Got that, okay." I got a considered nod; she relaxed back into her seat. The Boss was looking at me with one of his "I'll kill you as soon as I can" look, but I could see him thinking behind his scowl. Pete had a small smile on his face as if he got it as well, and I was sure he did because of smarts; he was the finest of muscles but had an excellent mind, which he tended to hide. Amira was shocked, to say the least; she kept switching her focus between Arie's image on the big screen and me, sitting calmly in my seat ten meters away.

"Do we tell the Americans?" Arie asked finally, breaking the silence.

"Yes, we do, and I believe they will play along with us because, in a sense, you and I have all the cards." Arie looked at me critically, thinking through the entire scenario, no doubt from a very different perspective than I had. But then he was responsible for a whole country's security, and I was just a lowly Interpol investigator.

"It would mean that we would have to agree to freeing Ms. Abramowitz and creating a story to background her work at Harvey

Mudd, as well as expunge her record as far as the attacks she mounted on our systems."

"All that and more. I want you to induct her into one of your security services, then permanently attach her to Interpol as a technical liaison, reporting to Section Five. She, and only she, will become the face of the recovery in so much as she will be the visible engineer who jump-starts each plant as they can come online." He started to nod as he worked through the logistics.

"How far back would you want us to go?"

"How about from the first time you tried to recruit her?"

"Brilliant!" The Boss had not said a word until now, but his one word made my heart sing. We could turn the entire story around in such a way that the women could be shown to be a part of the mercenary terrorist organization and not a separate cell working in parallel. That would muddy the waters enough for us to get as many countries as possible back up and running, and I had an idea for financing the hundreds of plants we would need to make my idea viable. We already had nineteen sites with funding distributed around the world, funding that we had access to, another twenty plants on the dock, just waiting for a delivery address, and two plants in full production. We could pull this off with a little finesse.

"Amira, what do you say to all of this?" Arie asked, sounding like a grandfather asking a granddaughter about her hopes for the prom.

"Before you answer, Arie, Amira, I have a question for you." She turned to look at me, giving me her full attention.

"Why did you turn down Arie's offer just before you went to Harvey Mudd?"

"Simple, as I told you both during the interview. I had a better offer."

"From the woman known as 'Helen'?"

"Yes. And as it turned out, the offer was amazing. My own lab, technicians, and engineers working with me, no limits on my experiments, and look at what we produced." Her eyes clouded over, and she hung her head at that, no doubt thinking about what the terrorists had done with her work. "When the trial in Nova Scotia worked, I could see a bright future for renewables and our ability to deal with environmental disasters that previously had been a stain on technology. If I had agreed to work with the Israeli Security Services before I went to Harvey Mudd, none of that work would have been possible."

It was my turn to nod; it not only made sense, but it was also probably very true.

A security service had a very different agenda from that of an open university. "Okay, thank you, now answer Arie." She looked at me again as if trying to divine what I might want her to say. It wasn't up to me, it was her life, and she needed to live it her way, for her reasons, with her purpose fully in mind. And somehow, she had to put what the terrorists had done with her work behind her and concentrate on all the good her work could now deliver to a broken world. She looked back up at the screen.

"I would be proud to serve you, Mr. Rosenberg, and I enjoy working with the Interpol people, so if you can continue to guarantee that nothing I have done, or will yet do, will come back on my family, tell me what you need me to do now." She didn't look happy, didn't look sad, just somewhere in between. I decided to give her a boost.

"Geeks of the world unite, get us those slush funds, leave a billion in each account to build their plant with, and seed their first year or two. Arie, we will need a master account set up at your end and the authority to use the funds as we see fit. Does anyone have any questions?"

"Captain, yes, I have one. Can Italy put her hand up for a plant or two?" Indigo asked in his best Oxford-accented English. I smiled; the avalanche had started, which is why I wanted the Israelis involved. They could take over the management of everything to do with the plants, and we would "lend" them Amira whenever a plant was ready to be seeded.

Now I had three agendas—find the women who launched the attacks on Italy, Israel, the UAE, and Europe; find out what Mohammad bin Azaria's "Plan B" was; interrogate a bunch of women terrorists and their supporters and work out how to contain them and keep what they had done from the world at large. And I couldn't forget the engineer and her role.

As a pilot friend of mine used to say, "piece of cake!"

Chapter 41

Aleena Anaisha, as the absolute head of Innomatchi, headquartered in Toyoko but with branches all over Southeast Asia, was an imperious woman who openly flaunted her personal bias— men were weak, women were the future, and her two daughters were the smartest people in her company, possibly the whole world. The fact that both daughters had been swept up by Interpol, and no one now knew their current location, angered her to the point of visible fury. Sitting in her office in Karachi, which looked more like a royal palace than a workspace, she glowered at the Interpol agents sitting in front of her.

She had agreed to this meeting in her Pakistan office simply to see what her enemy might do now that they had taken her adopted daughters into custody.

Dressed in a twenty-thousand-dollar suit of grey-green, which effectively brought out the emerald green of her eyes, with a pair of ten-thousand-dollar shoes that literally shone on her feet, Nokomoto Senji, in his less than five-hundred-dollar grey suit straight off the rack from a discount store didn't in the least feel disenfranchised or embarrassed. Aikido Namoki, his partner, dressed today in pure goth from laced-up-to-the-hip purple boots all the way to her heavily blackened eyelids, did all she could to not laugh. Nokomoto gave her a lot of leeway in her dress because that's what good partners did, but there were some things he would never forgive, such as dismissing the high-priced fancy apparition in front of them with a sneer or a giggle.

So, in the Japanese way, she hid her derision behind one delicate black laced hand and made sure her eyes never met the CEO's. There were nine impeccably dressed suits in attendance, sitting on either side of the woman, none of whom had been introduced, but all of whom had the tell-tale look of either security or lawyers.

This was a corporation that had sucked at least thirty-two billion USD through their doors while the world was being terrorized by the attacks launched by the women, the planning for which had been traced directly to her two children. And the ship sets for the environmental plants had been designed, built, and shipped from her Tokyo factory, and the fact that she and her factories had started on this work some three to four years ago meant that she had been aware of what was going to happen long before the first bomb had been dropped on the Vatican. She was in it up to her over-decorated throat, even though Nokomoto thought that the sparkles given off by the exquisite and obviously expensive necklace was a nice touch.

"Agent Nokomoto, I speak for Madam Anaisha, and her corporation and I have here warrants issued by both the High Courts of Japan and Pakistan for the immediate release of two persons, namely Nazreen Anaisha and Reve Anaisha, both employees of Innomatchi Southeast Asia Corporation. They are to be released immediately and returned to Toyoko." The suit was sitting on the right-hand side of the CEO, who looked to be about forty, clean-shaven, with short cut hair and thick glasses tinted with a blue wash that made his eyes seem even blacker than they were.

"Do you have a name?" Aikido asked, looking the suit straight in the eyes, or in this case, where his eyes should be, as they were very hard to actually see through the coloration of his thick-framed glasses. Aikido picked him as a member of the Yakuza, probably a middle boss, with his big boss sitting somewhere in the group, watching intently as his subordinate worked. She also had no doubt that every male in the room was armed, not only with guns but with a tantō, the favored short sword of the clans that provided personal protection for high-order Oyabun. The question of why one of the most powerful industrialists in Southeast Asia had aligned herself with a noted and ancient criminal organization was moot.

A stare was all she got as her answer, as the inscrutable face of the suit remained passivate and emotionless. He flicked two folios wrapped with light pink ribbon across the ornate table, which slid to a stop just short of falling off the edge. Neither Interpol agent made any move to pick them up. Aikido bowed her head towards the suit, smiled, and muttered, "*Domo arigato gozaimasu*," just loud enough for him to hear her. If the insult hit home, he did not show it. The room descended into an uncomfortable silence, one which Nokomoto was happy to let develop. If the impressive line of suits thought they were dominating his partner, then they were sadly mistaken. She was one of the toughest, smartest agents he had ever had the privilege to serve with, and while he wasn't sure he agreed all the way with her baiting the suits, he could appreciate the strategy. He decided to break the stalemate.

"Madam Anaisha, we have here warrants issued by the World Court for you and your corporation, and all senior members of said organization, for your immediate arrest for aiding and abetting terrorists, terrorist acts, and for the engaging, planning, and implementation and the execution of terrorist acts, in accordance with the Terrorist Laws as amended in 2022." Contrary to what the suit had done, Nokomoto stood, bowed respectfully, then handed the warrants to the suit sitting next to the one who had slid the folios across the table. He looked the CEO straight in the eyes to convey the seriousness of what he had said.

"Further, this building is surrounded by troops of the Pakistani SGG and will move in on my request to take you into custody. Your assistants here will also be retained until their role in the aforesaid actions has been clarified. Do you understand all that I have just said?" Again, the silence was deafening until the suit with attitude held his hand up as if to stop traffic.

"Madam Anaisha will not leave this building with you or any of your heathen soldiers. You will immediately hand over the two girls and return them to Tokyo!" Spittle flew out of his mouth as he stood violently and waved a pudgy hand at the agents, who through the tirade, and seemingly outnumbered and considerably outgunned, continued to sit placidly as if nothing was troubling them, and the angry, gesturing little Japanese Yakuza was of mere entertainment value. Nokomoto flicked his forefinger against his thumb, and within seconds, the sounds of boots could be heard coming down the corridor in a rush. In the deep background, sounds of spasmodic gunfire could be heard, and as the sounds reached the luxurious office, all nine of the Japanese suits stood and drew handguns from under their armpits.

Nokomoto flung himself sideways, crashing into Aikido and flattening her against the floor. Over their heads, an ear-bursting firefight rang out, short, sharp, and over in just seconds, as a flood of camouflaged troops massed into the office, and surrounded the bodies that now mostly lay across the table at odd angles, blood staining the ancient and no doubt expensive carpet. The CEO had not moved during the firefight, still looked imperious, if not just a little shocked if you caught the horror in the corner of her eyes, and owed her life to the fact that hidden in Aikido's black lace bodice had been a pair of miniature cameras, clearly showing the location of everyone on the other side of the table.

The SGG, one of the world's foremost special services groups, had used the videos to position their shooters, and in the furious exchange that followed, not one outward flying bullet had hit any-thing more meaningful than a wall, ceiling, doorway, or objet d'art, where in contrast, every suit had at least nine or ten bleeding holes in them, mostly grouped into a tight circle about an inch in diameter. Several handguns lay scattered across the table, one or two still slowly spinning, creating their own gruesome tessellation.

"Sorry, Aikido, I've ruined your hairdo," Nokomoto said, almost laughing at the expression on his partner's face as her hands tore and pulled at her now messy hair. She looked up at him from the floor, smiled, then put her hand out so he could pull her to her feet.

"Just this once, I'll forgive you, but you're buying lunch!"

The engineer, now dressed in a plain blue overall, soft shoes, and a snazzy pair of handcuffs linked to an equally snazzy chain-link belt, accompanied by Agent Sandra (just call me Sally) Thomas and SSA Fay Remer, was collected with some ceremony by Indigo and his four prized Italian police guards from the American jet parked at the far end of the strip at Marco Polo International Airport. A secondary ring of guards, their carbines pointing inwards, mirrored their movements. Indigo had requested the plane stay overnight and had arranged for the crew to be lodged in the military barracks on the other side of the terminal. Maintaining silence, the group moved to the edge of the runway, then stepped down to a wooden jetty, where the ubiquitous red cigarette boat bobbed to a hidden beat.

"*Signore, signora, per favore salite a bordo della mia umile barca.*" Indigo got in last, tapped the mad driver on the shoulder, then sat heavily as the boat reared up and spun around, all in one motion.

"Well, I guess this is one way to see Venice!" Sandra's words were lost in the roar of the engines, and Fay was trying to catch some of the wash from the bow with her hands and having some success as the spray rose up and over the stern of the boat. It thundered down the canal, its blue-and-red flashing lights rotating on the masthead, creating a colorful pall inside the cockpit. Indigo turned to look at their prisoner, who also appeared to be enjoying the experience. He wondered how long that would last once they got to Interpol's head-quarters. A second, smaller boat followed in their wake, carrying the four guards, and it bounced up and over the cigarette boat's wake like a flying fish, its bow swerving from side to side.

Our strategy was simple. To date, we have not interviewed any of the women we had collected from the various locations. This was deliberate, as, in truth, we had enough evidence to convict every person we had arrested so far ten times over.

More than enough.

But we had short-sheeted ourselves to a point because by sweeping up the CEOs of the only two operating plants in the world and now the head of Innomatchi, we may have seriously affected the production and future supply of both raw machinery and finished product. We were still waiting on a report from the Army Corps of Engineers on that point. The bigger one was what our agent from Toyoko had reported—that a 3D mock-up of a plant and all the equipment needed to build one-came from just the one factory in Japan and that it was undoubtedly under Yakuza control, based on what had happened in Karachi.

We had the ship sets, and we were confident—or at least Amira was—that we could seed the plants with the nanomachines that made the whole thing work, but that had yet to be proven under combat conditions.

Pete and I watched the frantic approach of the cigarette boat as it hopped over its own wash; it reversed course, bouncing in the air, engines overrevving with a scream, then pulled up to our jetty as softly as the touch of a feather on your arm. The maniac was talented, there was no doubt about that, but I was very pleased that others had been the victims of his full-out driving style and not me this time.

We stood by silently as the four emerged from the boat, the second vessel with the guards sweeping in more modestly, and watched as Indigo directed everyone to our trunnel-like entrance. The guards disembarked without any fanfare, and one of them walked over to me, saluted, and handed me a canvas holdall, with a huge smile.

"*Capitano, il mio colonnello mi ha chiesto di farle i complimenti a Wirth, è stato recuperato con la persona che le abbiamo appena consegnato.*"

"*Grazie, apprezzato. Potete tutti timbrare l'orologio fino alle 06:00 di domani.*" A snappy salute was my only reply, and the four swaggered off for what passed as downtime in Venice. Before I could heft the bag, Pete took it out of my hands, gave me one of his "poor, weak female" looks, then led me into our headquarters. If I didn't like him so much, that alone would have earned him a combat knife in his ribs!

The Boss waited for us against the small, oval table he had positioned off to one side of the big screen, but in full view of the rest of the room, where geeks beavered away and screens flickered with data, images, maps, and all sorts of confusing information. Front and center, on a small screen mounted just off the floor, the pictures of the pilot pre-flighting the Hog ran, and next to it, a lot of DNA and forensic data flowed slowly, so it was clear to read. The engineer had been positioned on the side of the table where she could see everything we were processing, some for the show and some as part of what we needed to do to find the other women. Indigo stood relaxed in full "blues" uniform off to one side, but clearly in her eyeline. On a screen next to the one holding the image of the engineer, photos of all the women we had collected so far, as well as Mohammad bin Azaria's mug shot, silently scrolled through, each one holding for around five seconds.

I took up my seat opposite her, the Boss to my right, Anna to the left, then Sandra and Fay around one end. Then Amira came in and sat at the other end, and I watched the engineer's eyes light up with both surprise and warmth. As we had guessed, the terrorists knew her or of her.

"Miss Ferguson, I'm Captain Riley. This is Colonel Anthony, both from Interpol, Supervisory Special Agent Anna Bernstein, FBI; Agent Sandra Thomas, Interpol; Senior Special Agent Fay Remer, FBI; and Agent Abramowitz, Interpol; and standing behind me pretending to be invisible is Master Chief Pete. We have enough evidence to commit you to trial at the World Court and will do so once this conversation is concluded. As to your possible sentencing, which may require several concurrent life sentences in a very hard environment, we may be able to mitigate some of the harshness if you are able to give us certain information. Do you understand all that I have just said?" While I had been talking, she had been looking at everyone around the table, no doubt trying to find a possible chink. She would be surprised, but I was happy to let her have her fantasies for a while longer. It would help if we could get some hard data from her, so I needed her engaged and relaxed.

Then she did the most extraordinary thing.

"Senior Special Agent Remer was one of the first FBI agents to visit Point Roberts. I remember seeing her on the CCTV feed. And, of course, both she and Agent Thomas took me into custody just outside Helena. And I know Agent Abramowitz, or at least I did when she was just plain Amira, back at Harvey Mudd. Her work was the foundation for everything we have achieved." Amira hung her head, obviously upset with both the recognition and the accolade, but without any effort on our part, the prisoner had clearly attached herself to the terrorists without a single visible qualm. The fact we had her DNA from the forensic sweep back at the house the three women had lived in was something I had been going to hold in reserve, but that was now moot.

"Do you admit to living and working with Kathryn Boyle and Rosalind Sanchez in Helena for at least the past three years?"

"I take it that asking for legal representation is a waste of time?"

"With the Terrorist Laws under which you have been charged, legal representation is not legally required at any time during your interrogation and will only be provided one week prior to your trial, and then only as appointed by the court."

"So I take it that is a no?"

"Correct."

"Then what exactly are you offering me, and what is it you want to know?" I found it curious that this woman, who I judged to be in her early thirties, was tall and well-balanced, looked fit, if not a little lithe, and had a head of flaming red hair, which, as far as I could tell was natural, was so relaxed given her present circumstances.

"At this point, when you are sentenced, you will be facing multiple life sentences, no parole option, hard labor, and the hole they will put you in will be, at best, a concrete cage, and as for the conditions, I'll let your imagination do the rest. You will have a very long life in that cage, no privacy, no physical contact with anyone, ever, no privileges, and very little daylight." She looked at me with a slight smile, and I wondered if she was actually taking all this in.

"Against that, if you assist us in locating the others involved in your plan, we will see that your conditions are at least less harsh, and your cage less restrictive." She nodded; maybe she was considering our offer, or maybe she was just acknowledging what I had said. She sat in her chair, hands locked in place on her lap, the chains that bound her glinting in the overhead light.

"I have to admit, I was expecting more from you, Captain. It seems you have yet to fully understand what we did and why we did it. That's a pity because we were counting on you—that is, Interpol—to give the world a better picture of our actions than you seem to have so far. I am a simple mechanic. If you followed my path in Helena, you would have found I worked in a garage, went canoeing on the local lakes whenever I could, and camped out in the state forest. I hurt no one and helped as many as I could." This time I put my hand up to stop her mid-thought.

"You also oversaw the construction of a decommissioned missile silo and worked with the two women I have listed to launch attacks on Italy, Israel, the UAE, the UK, the EU, and America, the result of which was massive social disruption to transport, infrastructure, food delivery, and last but not the least has resulted in several million deaths so far. Deaths of ordinary people, doing no more than trying to live good lives, who did nothing to you or your fellow terrorists. So you may be just a mechanic, but you are also a terrorist, of that we have no doubt."

"As you no doubt know, I spent my early years in a refugee camp, then by the hand of God, I was taken into a family and given a real-life—one with hope and a future. In the camp I was taken from, children died at the rate of one every twelve minutes. When you took back the silo, you would have found some of their pictures on the walls. We left them for you to remind you of their existence, as, in fact, they may as well have never existed because there is no record of them, no memory of them, and no one but us grieving for them.

"Originally, two years ago, the plan was not to create as much chaos. But we had to change what we did in accordance with what was happening in the US, and in a different form, all over the world. The former president of the United States lost the election, clearly, yet by simply repeating the mantra 'the election was stolen,' at the end of the first year, some forty percent of the population actually believed and were invested in that lie.

"Around the world, the anti-vaxxers' campaign to deny the efficacy of the various vaccines for COVID-19 created a schism that lives to this day—better than thirty-five percent of the globe will not get vaccinated at any cost. No evidence was ever offered; it was simply repeated over and over the same message. It was a replica of the big lie—never any proof, never any facts, just the same diatribe repeated over and over again.

"This is why we decided to hit so hard, so broadly, and so completely. Deny everyone everything that was dear to them, making them experience firsthand the same conditions the refugees suffer every day of their short lives. And then the belief structure would shake and finally crumble under the undeniable truth of the appalling conditions of no internet, no fuel, no power, no food, no security, and no hope creates.

"When I was asked to use my skills to help change their circumstances, I looked back at where I had been and where I had been allowed to be, and I agreed wholeheartedly. Do you know what it is to be invisible? To go hungry for weeks on end? The be beaten for no reason other than you exist? To not be given a name because you have no parents to claim you, hold you, love you, and support you as you grow up? There are at least twelve million refugee children in the world as we speak, and at least a third of them could be dead within two years.

"The people smugglers will take the lucky ones, live well for a few months, be given medicine if they need it, fed well, kept clean, and then butchered for their body parts. At least they will have lived well for a few months. Others will have simply been sold into slavery, or child sex rings, or become a resource to trade across borders, and who knows what their future might be? This is happening every single day in the so-called civilized world, and precious little is ever done about it. Do you deny this?" Her upturned face reflected the light from the roof and looked pained, and I felt for her, but I could not let that sway me. She had planned and executed several attacks on the world that had created chaos, killed millions, either directly or as collateral damage, and while I fully understood the terrible conditions she was describing for the children in the refugee camps, I could not let that soften my approach to her.

Less than two years ago, I had worked with my team to put down a vicious international child trafficking ring, which was taking refugee children and selling them into sex rings or to body-part farms, and I had reveled in my ability to personally kill a large number of the perpetrators who decided to fight instead of surrender. I knew these camps; I had walked inside their ramshackle tents and humpies and been sickened at the festering conditions. I knew these children; I had held their tiny, dirt-encrusted hands as they cried on my shoulder. And I could never forget the smell of the burning pyres of dead bodies, looking like little discarded rag dolls. But I could not condone throwing the entire world into chaos and killing millions as a means of solving their dilemma.

"What we need is information on where the other members of your female group are located. We know about 'Helen,' if that is, in fact, her name, and we want to find the women who manned the underground bunker in Turkey." She looked at me with derision in her eyes, and she didn't exactly sneer but got close to it.

"I will not give you any information about anyone. Or anywhere, for that matter. I will negotiate with you for my release on the basis that I hold the key to solving a major problem you will have shortly, one that will further embarrass the American government and quite possibly cost the American president her job." If I looked astonished, then the Boss looked gobsmacked, and Anna looked incredulous. Curiously, neither Sandra nor Fay looked surprised, which took me by surprise! I turned to my young agent, raising my eyebrows.

"Sandra, you know something I don't?" My voice was low, calm, and pitched as softly as I could. She turned to look at me, looked at her neighbor, then turned back to look at me.

"From everything we have learned at Point Roberts, Seattle, and Helena, and based on your suspicions of a terrorist 'Plan B,' Fay and I have speculated that the bones of their plan might be rolled up into their planned delivery of the power packs up and down the West Coast and the provision of the panels and power packs to Helena. We can't figure out the what or why of it, but it all looks very connected to us." Next to her, Fay nodded in agreement.

"I concur. The barges arrived just before we closed the plant down, and the COO was quite clear about their delivery schedule and claimed to have trained staff and agents in place to receive the power packs and install them. Exactly where was never spelled out, but we have FBI agents running that down at the moment."

"Yes, I saw that in your report. Describe exactly what is going on in Helena."

"Some years ago, probably five or six, a very wealthy benefactor by the name of Westhall who lived in Helena vested several billion dollars to a trust, currently managed by one of the accounting firms in the town, and then built infrastructure for one hundred thousand houses. Remember, the population of Helena has never exceeded the thirty-three thousand mark, so it was by anybody's light a very significant project. He died before the development was completed, and the land lay fallow until the current influx of temporary migrants from other cities started to flood into the town after the terrorist attacks. You and Pete walked the site, you saw the development, and you saw the migrants and their temporary shelters.

"Almost overnight, they started building houses on the estate and found that water, sewerage, waste management, and power had already been laid to every site, and that's when we came in, tracking the panels from Point Roberts to the airport. Every house is made of panels produced in Point Roberts, roof included, and the technicians onsite tell us that every house produces enough power to run several houses if necessary, and that's without using the existing renewable grid that was already in the ground.

"As of yesterday, when we left the States, there were over twelve hundred houses completed, along with two schools, a hospital, and other infrastructure. But the realtors were still not able to sell any of the properties because the trustees will not release the conditions for purchase or rent."

"We don't know why," added Fay, "I had a chat with them with RuPaul and Vernon in tow and got absolutely nowhere. They claim that the conditions of the trust must be met before they can act, and they will not release the conditions even with a court order, which we obtained. We were going to let them sit in cells for a while to see if it would loosen their tongues, but after talking it over with Sandra, we backed off to see what might happen."

"Good call." Both the Boss and I had been watching our prisoner quite closely while our agents had reported and had seen the tells on her face, so a picture was starting to build in my mind as to what her bargaining chip might be. I looked at the Boss; he gave the slightest of nods, so I turned to my mini, opened the lid, hit some keys, and brought up a current drone image of the Helena build site. The drone was flying about fifty feet above the sawtooth layout of the roofs, with a slightly forward view. The color mix was bright and spectacular, creating a very summery feeling, and I had no doubt that whoever got to live in this "instant" village would enjoy themselves.

"Who's flying the drone?" I asked, staring at the screen. The sheer wall of a very large building swam into view, and the drone climbed up and up until it was looking down onto the roof of what I assumed was a hospital or school building of some sort. Hard to tell from the drone photos, but it looked like a fifteen or maybe twenty-story building, with every floor covered in a different-colored panel, creating a rainbow effect. Pretty. A word that I usually didn't associate with terrorism.

"The young assistant agent from the Helena FBI office. Seems he has a talent for it." My attention switched back to the woman sitting in chains, and my female instincts got the better of me.

"Miss Ferguson, would you like some water?" She nodded, still holding her almost jovial look. We were amusing her, or at least she thought so, and I started to wonder what she might know that was so bracing from her point of view. Then I signaled to Indigo, who had been standing stoically in the background looking important in his dress blues, and within minutes, we had steaming mugs of coffee made exactly to everyone's liking sitting in front of us. The prisoner had a glass of water and was bending her head into her lap to drink it, and for a split second, I registered surprise and perhaps even envy in her eyes as Indigo delivered our drug of choice. The exotic smell of the espresso was palpable, and if my instincts were right, she was responding to it.

"Miss Ferguson, do you have the codes that the trustees require to release the conditions for purchase or rent in Helena?" She looked straight at me, her face suddenly bland and giving nothing away.

"As I see it, Captain, you have a choice. Let me go, and I'll give you the code and procedure for the trustees, or don't and suffer the consequences." A very ballsy statement from someone in chains, surrounded by Interpol and the Italian military three deep. At the back of my mind, a thought was fighting to get through, something the secretary of state had said in her deposition. It was just a vague thought, but I knew who could untangle it.

"Anna, give me a minute, please. Colonel, excuse us." And I stood up, followed by Anna, as we walked into a small anteroom at the corner of geek heaven. I pulled the door shut behind us, turned to face her, ran my hands through my hair, rolled my shoulders, then gave her a hard study. She wasn't looking tired or fatigued; in fact, she looked quite rested, and I wondered how she managed that.

"Anna, think back to the deposition given to us by the US secretary of state. She mentioned something about a project called Apollo, or Apollos, something like that, in a US town. Can you remember the details?" She bent to her mini, hit the keyboard several times, ran her eyes up and down the small screen, nodded to herself, then looked up at me.

"Originally was going to be located in Nevada, but that changed. The small town in the Mideast, Roanoke, established back in the fifteen hundreds by the English, primarily as a base from which to fight off the Spanish, grew up slowly, has a first-class university, with around three hundred thousand residents, was reasonably stable during our most recent riots and civil unrest. It's not the town that was first nominated in the Secretary's report but was added as the principal location in an edited update due to the transfer of billions of dollars into a city trust fund. This deposit was made between the time the report was first mooted and January of the next year.

"Work on renewable power farms, and underground infrastructure was commenced just two months before the terrorist attacks, then halted for obvious reasons. This entire project was to be approved by the government and managed by a local committee of citizens from the area.

"It was listed as an official university research project, sanctioned by the UNHCR, and co-sponsored by the Red Cross and Médecins Sans Frontières. The kicker here is that the 'test,' as it was being called, involved the migration of ten thousand refugees, all children, all under the age of ten years, and all to be homed within six months of completion of the infrastructure."

"Another Helena?" She looked at me as she considered my question. "Probably, but this one involved the government, not a bequest by a benefactor."

"If that is what Helena really was."

"Yes. Good point."

"Do we have any hard evidence that civilians are involved in these terror attacks?"

"Apart from the Anaisha family?"

"Yes. Might Westhall also be a contributor?"

"To answer that, we would have to dig deep into his finances, the trust setup, but that is something the FBI can do. Can you start that process? And should we be looking for other contributors, say, in those countries that got the slush funds and where plants were to be set up?"

"Without a doubt. There are twenty ship sets on the docks, all addressed, just waiting for someone to move them. We have the key players from Innomatchi, so perhaps we should invite them to a conversation."

"Where are they?"

"Tucked away in Israel. Arie has given us our own building, fully secured. It can hold up to one hundred prisoners and is extremely well-guarded. Ms. Ferguson out there," I said, pointing back into the room, "is headed there after we finish with her." Anna nodded, thinking about something. She looked back up at me, her eyes sparkling.

"You've made a fan out of SSA Remer; she wants to transfer over to Interpol. How do you feel about that?" I laughed. I had already seen the glee in Fay's eyes when she briefed us, and the way she and Sandra got along, I suspected something was cooking.

"Now is probably not the right time, but it will be fine with me, and I'll run it past the Boss."

"You're stealing all my best people." I just smiled and opened the door, and looked to where the collective was sitting around the table and talking amongst themselves, completely ignoring the star of the show, much to her obvious discomfort. Time to hit her hard.

I sat.

I stared.

I looked at everyone slowly, and they immediately quieted down, focusing their attention back on me.

"To continue. Ms. Ferguson, you obviously have the codes for the trustees in Helena. Where are the women associated with 'Helen'?" She gave herself away on the code point, but her eyes tightened up again with the mention of the women. I didn't really expect to get anything from her, but I had to try. So I fired my biggest shot and watched her reaction.

"What you don't know is that we tracked and found you via your burst transmissions. In fact, we have been tracking you since you left the silo. And thanks to our really geeky geeks, we have pinpointed the earth station that downloaded your sent messages. We know the frequency you were using, the transmission period, and even the individual satellite's ID. So, back to you. The codes. What are they, and how do we get them to the trustees."

She looked shocked. Having destroyed the Internet and killed most of every computer chip on the planet, she no doubt thought that what they had been doing would not be able to be traced. Certainly not as far back as the silo. So I stretched the truth a little? Hey, this was an interrogation of one of the terrorists that had tried to destroy civilization as we knew it. And in truth, we had discovered the burst transmission process at the destroyed uplink at the ranger station, so I wasn't stretching it too far.

"One last time. What are the codes, and how do we get them to the trustees?" She looked uncomfortable, as if she was having an internal debate. This time the silence was not absolute; keys were being tapped, low conversations could just be heard, and the room seemed to be on the edge of worry. Indigo moved from his position near the screens, stood behind me, looked at the Boss, then gave just the slightest of bows. He tapped me on the shoulder, indicating I should go with him.

I did.

He whispered in my ear, and the both of us turned away from the table.

"Colonel, if you will forgive me, perhaps this good person in front of us doesn't know how to behave under these circumstances?" His perfect English indicated he was deadly serious. The little bow meant he was being respectful, but what he had said made sense to me. Not trained. Not professional. Limited exposure to social and military environments, tunnel vision as far as her mission had been concerned, and totally convinced she and her partners were in the right. Maybe I had been looking at this the wrong way. How did you manage a religious zealot? Or a messiah visionary? Or, for that matter, a suicide bomber in the last few minutes of the soon-to-fail negotiation?

I looked back at the table.

"Colonel, could I suggest a ten-minute break, and Anna, Amira, join us, please?"

The Boss, Anna, and Amira all followed us back into the little ante-room, where we would now surely be in sin, cramped as we would be.

"Boss, Indigo has just made a very critical observation. He believes that our prisoner has no life experience beyond her mission, and that may be why she is not reacting to our offer of leniency."

"I think Colonel Kashasini is correct. If you take me as an example, I only learned skills unrelated to my work when I ran away to Australia. I had never been exposed to what you would call normal people before, ones with differing attitudes to all sorts of things, and it took me the first two years to gain enough confidence to open my mouth. Even on something as simple as the weather." I looked at Amira, and in her, I could see the very young woman struggling to make sense of the wider world from her very limited experience in the laboratories of her universities. Genius came at a price, and social skills were usually part of that personal cost.

"I also think we may have our approach wrong." They all looked at me expectantly as if I held the holy grail. "How do you approach a jihadist? A religious zealot?" The Boss started to nod, no doubt thinking through many of the interrogations we had managed over the past year with some of the most devoted shit-heads in the known universe.

"You're saying we should align ourselves with her version of the truth and see if that shifts her willingness to trade." I looked at the Boss; he had nailed it on the head.

"Yes, and I think all the male members of this inquisition should fade away somewhere and leave it as an all-girl chat." He looked at me quizzically, probably not sure of how removing himself, Pete, and Indigo could affect the outcome. But he trusted my instincts.

"Okay. Pete, Indigo, let's go for a walk." And the three of them trooped out, hit the long entrance hallway, and disappeared into the gloom. We girls walked back to the table and arranged ourselves to be a little less threatening.

"May I call you Coleen?" She looked at me in surprise. Nodded sharply, realized what she might be transmitting subvocally, then smiled to soften the edge. "Good. Coleen, we understand your passion for helping refugee children. We do. As you have pointed out, Amira, who now works for us, was a refugee herself, and to hear stories of the camps, the death of all the children, and the appalling conditions break our hearts. And something you might not know, but some of us around this table played a very large role in shutting down a child trafficking ring just a year or so ago, so we have firsthand experience of the conditions in the camps."

"Do you really? Do you know the current conditions in Libya just now? Do you know how many of us died just yesterday?" The passion in her eyes lit up her whole face and gave her a whole different personality. Here was someone who deeply believed in her cause, and I think we had finally tapped into her consciousness.

"Yes. Yesterday, in six camps in Libya, two hundred and three children died, and another two hundred and six died next door in Algeria, and nearly four hundred in Chad. Coleen, how can we help you help these children?" She looked at me with some suspicion, checked out Anna, Fay, and Sandra, saw nothing but empathy in their eyes, looked around at Amira, who had tears in hers, and dropped her head, so her chin rested on her chest. She looked up at last, tears streaking her pretty face.

"That's all we are trying to do. That's all we have ever tried to do. Our spiritual leader believes, as do I that only by showing the world what the real conditions are in the camps and letting them experience them for themselves will anyone actually pay attention and do something to stop it. That's what we are trying to achieve. And unlike the camps, where there is no hope, we set up environmentally responsible plants to manufacture power packs that will turn the lights back on for everyone but force them to change their beliefs and attitudes. They will have to learn how to share, how to help and support each other, how to stop all the internecine warfare that never seems to stop." The passion she was exhibiting was real; this was a deeply seated and held belief of hers, as serious as it gets.

Now I had something to work with.

"When you say that, it is hard to reconcile the absolute chaos your attacks caused and the fact that millions more people, many of them children, have been displaced." She looked a little shaken, then threw it off, moving her shoulders back square, and sitting up in her seat—or at least sitting up as far as her chains allowed her to.

"To change someone's belief structure, you have to be able to prove what you are offering. You have to make the truth inescapable, undeniable. You have to shake the belief structure right down to its foundations. You don't change attitudes unless you first change beliefs. We made it so everyone would experience the same conditions in the camps, with one exception. In the end, we are offering hope. Why is that so hard for you to understand?"

"Why did you destroy the space station?" She looked perplexed, her mind trying to catch up with the shift in the direction of the questioning. She just shook her head in frustration and said nothing. I let the silence hang. I tried another tactic.

"How can we help you help the refugees?" This time she looked straight at me with a glare that would cut through glass.

"Take me back to Helena; let me do my job."

"And what would that job be?"

"Giving the trustees the codes they need to unlock the terms and conditions for purchase and rent of the new homes."

"And after that?"

"Throw me in the deepest hole you have, I won't care, and our plan will have worked." I looked over at Indigo, hiding behind a stack of screens, only visible because of his twin yellow stripes that ran down his dress blues.

"*Indaco, riportala nella sua cella per favore, toglile le catene, vedi che è nutrita. Allora torna e congiunti con noi.*"

"*Sì, capitano, in una sola volta.*" He marched over with Pete, and they took our guest back out to the small cell we had set up for just such an occasion. As requested, he and Pete were back inside a minute or two, during which no one around the table spoke. The Boss came back and sat heavily in his seat, his face neutral.

"You're putting things together. I can see it in your eyes." I looked at him, relaxed as ever, mindful I now had a superior brain's trust to engage with, so I didn't need to work through all that I suspected alone. As if by magic, steaming cups of espresso appeared, and the two guards who brought them bowed theatrically, then stepped away back into their area. The geeks kept working on whatever they were currently focused on; the screens flashed and burped data and streams of information, and if you didn't know better, it could be just a normal day at the office.

"Colonel, I sense a theme here. The Red Crescent has confirmed that a significant number of girls are on the move somewhere, in the thousands, maybe even more. We have Helena turning out houses and schools like they were on a production line, and New Zealand has reported a sister development on the Wairoa River at a place called Dargaville. Their capacity at the moment is two and a half thousand homes, but apparently could easily double or triple that in time. Both plants started to supply panels and power supplies to each area over a year ago, and both areas were funded four to five years ago, both from the same source. The Point Roberts people tell us that they have thousands of power supplies, each one capable of running up to thirty or forty homes or a small factory, with agents set up right along the coast from Canada to Mexico.

"Now we have the engineer who undoubtedly participated in the terrorist attacks, wanting to go back to Helena and give a code to the trustees to release the conditions for sale or occupancy. I have one question at this point."

"And that would be?" The Boss looked smug, no doubt drawing the line between the dots I was throwing out so casually.

"Do we have satellite coverage of the Pacific and Atlantic oceans?"

"Why ask me? Indigo, can you please ask your geeks the question?"

"*Certo, colonnello.*" He got out of his seat, walked to where Luigi was working, bent his head to maintain privacy, listened, then turned on his heel and walked back. "*Lo facciamo, colonnello, cosa vorresti trovare?*"

451

"Some big boats. Big enough to hold a couple of thousand people. One heading for the US West Coast, one heading for New Zealand. Probably two to three weeks to landfall." Indigo nodded and turned towards Luigi, who also nodded and bent back to his keyboard. I joined the nodding brigade; we all looked like those little toys with their bobbing heads you put on the instrument panel of your car.

"What the lovely Jessica is alluding to, for those of you who have yet to work it out, Helena and the New Zealand sites are being prepared to take refugees. They are coming in by boat, a few thousand, she believes, and they are a couple of weeks from landfall. And there is a distinct possibility that thousands more are hot on their heels."

"And the site in Roanoke?" Fay asked.

"Same story, different plot. This one was supposedly sanctioned by the US government as part of an experiment run by the university, funds provided by—let's cut to the chase—our friendly Sovereign Wealth Fund. That's why the secretary of state said that Mohammad bin Azaria alluded to there being no issue with funding the 'trial.' That was, from memory, a ten-thousand-refugee migration plan."

"But it never reached the president's office for approval."

"Obviously, that memo didn't get to the right people. The 'trial' started the build and only stopped when the terrorists hit. I wonder what its status is now?" All around the table looked engaged but concerned. Of us all, the Boss, as far as I knew, was the only one of us experienced with the political side of life, and he was terrible at it. Maybe Anna had a better touch; I wouldn't be surprised. While I was rolling this around in my mind, Luigi signaled to Indigo, who immediately got up and went over to his workstation. The sound of a printer spitting out real paper, something that was a bit of an anomaly in today's digital age, echoed around the office. Indigo came back with a handful of color prints as big as the old broadsheet newspapers we used to have years ago. He slipped them onto the table and unfolded the sheets. He pulled a huge red marker pen out of his pocket and quickly circled seven blotches on the paper.

"Four of these are electric container ships. That leaves just these three. At first glance, they look like the type of ship used for tourist cruises. These ships used to come to Venice before the ban, and they could hold up to five thousand passengers and a crew of fifteen hundred or so. No way to tell how many are on them here. The angle is all wrong."

"So, how do we find out who is on those ships?" I wasn't being pedantic; I just wanted hard evidence before we stirred the politician's pot and had the angry bees swarming all over our investigation. The Boss sensed my boiling point was getting close and took over the meeting.

"People, let's put this aside for the moment. Comments, please, on how to manage the lovely Coleen?"

"You mean apart from finding that deep, dark hole to put her in?" Sandra offered, breaking the tension I had unconsciously built. Fay playfully punched her on the arm, and they both giggled, another sound we didn't hear very often in our office.

"I believe we should take her back to Helena, get her to release the codes, then take her to Israel." Everyone turned to look at Amira, not expecting this from her. The day was turning out to be one of the surprising sounds and even more surprising suggestions! Take her back? You're kidding! She obviously saw what was in my eyes and reached out to hold my arm. "Jessica, if this creates a situation where refugee children can get homes, even though we may fight the circumstances, we shouldn't punish innocent children for the appalling behavior of a few adults. Adults, I may add, that we now have in custody."

"Not all of them, and I want to address that next." I spat the words out, realized I was being bitchy for no real reason, and held my hands up in surrender. "Okay, okay, I apologize. No need to get irritable. Who votes for sending Ferguson back to Helena?" Everyone nodded, and that surprised me. Maybe I was letting the whole situation cloud my judgment.

"Right, Sandra, Fay, as soon as she is fed and watered, pack her up, take two guards with you, and get her back to Helena. Get the codes to the trustees, then Fay, you stay and manage our interests until we can clearly see what is happening. You still have your team there?" She nodded. "Good. Warn them what we are going to do. Anna, you have a choice, as far as I can see, but before you answer, I think we really might need you when we talk to the Americans. It would be lovely to have you in the same room as the general and the president when that happens." She nodded; she had probably worked that bit out for herself.

"I'll go and pack my bag."

"Good. Sandra, we will see you in Israel as soon as you can get there. Fay, I have a book you need to read to keep you out of trouble on the flight over. Anyone, any questions?" No one had, so I stood and walked over to my little office desk and pulled a copy of *Procedures, Laws, and Regulations for Interpol Officers* out of my file, and threw it to Fay, who caught it deftly. The Boss came over and stood by my side.

"Going hunting?" he asked in a soft voice. Next to him, Pete visibly shined, and Indigo was not far from the mark, bouncing up and down on the balls of his feet.

"We go hunting, yes?" he asked, a smile as big as it could get on his craggy face, his accent flavoring his question in that unique Italian manner.

"We are going hunting, yes," I responded, feeling lighter just for saying the words. When would we talk to the Americans? I figured fourteen hours before our people could get to Helena, allow another six for stuffing around on the ground, releasing the codes, then getting back on the plane, and another fourteen hours to Israel, so the answer to my own question was sometime in the next day we would face down the bear that was sure to be the American government when they learned they were about to receive, ready or not, several thousand refugee children, courtesy of Mohammad bin Azaria's "Plan B."

"Sandra," I called over my shoulder, "make sure you have sufficient detail on Helena before you go wheels-up so you can brief the president and her cabinet." Anna hid a small smile; I had no doubt she would get a version of the message to all interested parties without giving away any detail long before we made our call, and I trusted her to pave the way for what we might choose to do about it. As for what I had just asked Sandra to do, well, we all had to get our fun where we could!

Chapter 42

We sat in a long room, heavily fortified against the constant rocket attacks from across the border, but the air inside the room was calm and controlled. As far as I could see, there were three things happening simultaneously.

One team of geeks and uniformed soldiers was managing some sort of battle, with images of explosions and point-of-view bodycam footage flickering on a group of screens, of which I had no idea. The second group of suited workers, both male and female, looking like an executive team at a board meeting, were having a furious argument over another set of screens, voices raising in pitch as one shouted over the other. No idea what that was about. And there was the constant panning video of our prisoners, flickering from cell to cell, and it gave me no joy to see the lost expressions on the faces of the women.

Each cell was large enough for a bed, toilet, small table, and one chair, plus a walking area twice the area of the bed. It was sterile, and I could only imagine the sense of loneliness and despair that would permeate through the block over time. Everyone wore the same dull blue overalls and sneakers without shoelaces, and most just sat at their desks, staring off into the wall or lying on their beds, staring at the roof.

The CEO of Point Roberts, Kathryn Simmons, looked nothing like the runway model of just a few weeks ago, and she had visibly aged. In the next cell, her COO, Farid Tremblay, looked like a lost soul, seemingly collapsed in on herself. The two young gamers, Reve and Nazreen Anaisha, just looked small and lost, whereas their mother still looked regal, make that regally pissed off. The New

Zealand woman, Wendy Sommers, and Arshia Spicatas, and the girls from the Westall property, Elizabeth Kane and Moya O'Halloran, didn't fare much better. They seemed insulted that they had been incarcerated.

The pilot, Rosalind Sanchez, of all of them, actually looked at peace, lying on her bed with her hands behind her head, eyes closed, and a small smile on her face. Her scientist friend and co-conspirator Kathryn Boyle looked amused until you really looked into her eyes, which were black holes in a once pretty face. I could imagine a lot of anger hiding in there, and we would find out soon enough.

Coleen Ferguson would be back in a matter of hours, so I had time to prepare my interrogation strategy. We really only needed the answer to one question— where were the infamous "Helen" and her cohorts. And to be realistic, I didn't think I would get it. Apart from the militias who had attacked us in Montana, the mercenary terrorists who attacked our temporary headquarters in Venice, and those who were heading into Helena to kill us all, not a shot had been fired in taking the women terrorists and their cohort into custody.

I didn't count the short firefight bringing in Mohammad bin Azaria—that had been reactionary. Now I had to sort through them and ascertain who we kept and who we let loose. But before I could do that, the president and her chief of staff had to be brought up to speed. I held a hand up to the geek manning the console that we were using, the images of the prisoners disappeared, and slowly, the faces of Aire, the president, General Saunders, and the usual suspects from the FBI, CIA, and NSA swam into focus.

The Boss was at his formal best.

"Madam President, General, Frank, Roger, Julius, Arie, thanks for joining us. Is Anna with you, General?" Her image on the big screen nodded, and the focus pulled back slowly to reveal Anna sitting between the heads of the CIA and the NSA. "Thank you. Has Anna briefed you on where we are up to?"

"Colonel, we are up to date in so much as we are waiting for a briefing on the current state in Helena and someplace called Dargaville in New Zealand."

"General, I need to call in another party. Agent Thomas, please connect now." And like magic, "just call me Sally's" bright, young face swam into view in its own little box that seemed to float between the heads of the American team. "Madam President, may I introduce Agent Thomas, our Interpol presence in the Midwest and the leader of the team that captured the pilot, the scientist, and the engineer." The president seemed to be staring at Sandra, then she sat back in her seat, pulling the focus with her, and an awkward silence ensued. The Boss broke it.

"Agent Thomas, report, please." Sandra smiled and bent her head as if she had notes, which of course, she didn't, but it added a nice touch. We could just see some fluffy clouds reflected in her image, probably bouncing off the windows of the G4 as she flew back to Venice.

"Madam President, the FBI team I have with me just accompanied the engineer, Collen Ferguson, to a meeting with the trustees for the Westall estate, where she produced a code that unlocked the terms and conditions for the sale of the properties being built in Helena. Before we discuss these terms and conditions, I believe Captain Riley has a more detailed brief for you."

"Thank you, Sandra. Yes, I have. Madam President, as you would be aware from other briefings Interpol has provided, Helena has been a point of interest to us because of the intersection of the data concerning the decommissioned missile silo, the materials from the plant in Point Roberts, and the fact that three of the female terrorists lived there for the last three years or so. As you know, two of the three were taken into custody there in the last two weeks.

"We have other data from the International Red Cross and Red Crescent that they were commissioned to locate and prepare thousands of refugee children, starting over a year ago, for transportation to other countries. The data indicated that there are three groups—two of approximately twelve to fifteen hundred children and a larger group of some ten thousand or so. We do not yet know where the larger group is being assembled, but we suspect that the two smaller groups are currently on large ocean liners in the Pacific and Atlantic oceans. We have put geo markers on both ships and will continue to track them." The president's face and those of the heads of the FBI, NSA, and CIA reflected surprise and some measure of concern. Once again, the biggest and supposedly best intelligence agencies in the free world had been blindsided and in no small manner.

Julius Bronstein, as the head of the CIA, viscerally felt a cold freeze run up his back, and as he looked at the director of the NSA, Frank Reynolds, he saw a similar reaction. How had their agencies missed all this data for so long? And then he thought about the compromised information technology systems and the hackers who had been in every government database since the Y2K debacle, and he understood just how thoroughly they had been sandbagged.

The morbid mood was broken by Roger Winslow, who, with Anna—his best SSSA—embedded in Interpol, had a more tangible understanding of what Interpol was now saying.

"Captain, are these ships headed towards us?"

"One is. The other, we believe, is headed to New Zealand."

"What do they intend to do?" the president asked, completely unsure of what she was hearing. Under the present chaotic conditions within her country, she could see no benefit in shipping anyone in for any reason. Particularly a child that may require more care and attention than anyone was able to provide.

"Sandra, back to you."

"Thank you, Captain. Madam President, under the terms and conditions for the purchase of a property in Helena, any purchaser must agree to house one refugee child, female, through to the conclusion of their education. An allowance per child of fifty thousand dollars per annum will be provided, plus all school and university costs. If the purchaser takes an additional child, the same support will be provided, but the cost of the initial purchase will be reduced by fifty percent."

You could have tried to cut the still air between the countries involved in the conference call with a sword, and it would have bounced off the chill.

"What is the initial purchase price?" Roger asked, beating others to the question by a hair's breadth.

"One hundred and fifty thousand dollars for a four-bedroom home, down to one hundred and twenty thousand for a three-bedder. There is one little catch in all of this."

"You can't buy a house without agreeing to take a refugee."

"Correct."

"Anything else we should know at this point?"

"Yes, Captain. The conditions provide free education for any natural children the purchasers have, all the way through to college, and free medical and dental care for everyone for as long as they live in the homes, parents included."

"Over ten years, you're talking five to six hundred million dollars just for the refugee children. Where is the money coming from?" Frank's voice was incredulous; the scope of Mohammad bin Azaria's "Plan B" was beyond reason. But then bombing and poisoning the world back half a century was also beyond most people's comprehension, so maybe this plan would have legs.

"Sir, the trustees would not release any financial information, but by our estimates, they have had six billion dollars for some four or five years; the interest alone on that sum would pay for a lot of children, and the conditions require the purchasers to sell the homes back to the trust for the same figure they pay for them. This is a long-term plan, Director, and well thought out." Julius broke the tension again with a question that had been on my mind for a while.

"Agent Thomas, is the situation the same for New Zealand?" he asked.

"It would appear so. That location is being managed by the FBI and CIA, with help from the New Zealand SAS."

"Then how do you know they are duplicating the Helena project?" Sharp edge to his voice, he was pissed and professionally embarrassed.

Sandra was no slouch, which is why she worked for us, and with just the faintest hint of a sly grin, looking straight down the barrel of the camera of her mini.

"Sir, I also led the FBI team in New Zealand, where we captured one of the gamers and the scientist. We also took three others into custody at that time, and we had the opportunity to have a chat with them."

"I see. You have been busy."

"Yes, sir, we have. But the real credit should go to your FBI team led by SSA Fay Remer; they did the real work." I smiled to myself. Sandra has just put the whole ball of wax back in the hands of the Americans and, by default, made the FBI out to be the hero. Clever, very clever. And possibly give Fay a boost that might see her on her way to us full-time. My turn to stir the pot.

"We do not know what the conditions of sale might be in New Zealand, but we suspect they will be similar if not exactly the same. The real issue for you is Project Apollos and the missing white paper from your secretary of state." Again, the silence was so absolute you could imagine no one breathing or daring to move.

"Why is that?" the president asked, the ice in her voice palpable.

"Madam President, as I mentioned earlier, some ten thousand children are— or have been—prepared to be moved to occupy a test site under university supervision in Roanoke. Originally, it was planned to be established in Nevada, but for some reason, that was changed in just the last few months. There are, we believe, as many as one hundred thousand children also being prepared to be settled in Canada, Greenland, Chile, Portugal, Ireland, Denmark, Norway, Finland, Estonia, Sri Lanka, Solomon Islands, Japan, and Iceland. We do not know the distribution plans, but these are the same countries that were gifted six billion dollars each five years ago, and also the countries that were—or still are at this time—the destination for the completed ship sets. There are also additional ship sets sitting on the dock at Tokyo."

"So the deal is you get a plant that can produce the panels and the power supplies, and then you get a bunch of refugee children. Someone planned all this exquisitely well. But you arrested the gamers, didn't you?" I nodded.

"Yes, Madam President, we did. But like so much of Mohammad bin Azaria's planning, there were more people involved; over a twenty-five to thirty-year time span, the girls were only used to suggest strategies to bring all the elements together in the last three years. And we seriously doubt that they had any idea of the consequences of their work."

"Can you prove that?"

"We're working on it. It's low on our priority list at the moment, but I have a team in Venice working on the problem." The president sat back again, then a thought occurred to her. I could see it literally cross behind her eyes.

"How are we going to manage whatever is planned for Roanoke?"

"The FBI will manage that, Madam President," Anna said. "We have all the data, and we have a copy of the Apollos plan. The UNHCR had a copy. We can share it with you if you wish."

"I very much wish, and gentlemen, put your minds to how a document as important as this simply disappears on its way from the secretary of defence's office to the Oval Office. I really want to know how that was done and by whom."

"Yes, Madam President," all three directors muttered in unison, probably finally seeing their careers, such as they were at this point, being flushed down the proverbial toilet.

"Is there anything else we need to know at the moment?" Anna asked, seeing that all but the president had retreated inside themselves.

"No, Anna, we'll keep you in the loop; our next step is to interrogate the prisoners, and find 'Helen' and her cohorts. We'll transfer the shipping data to you, so you can keep a watch on that yourselves."

"Just one thing you can clear up for us," the president said, leaning forward in her seat again and filling the screen. "When I read the report on the plants and how you—or we, now—intend to open new ones, I see a reference to seeding them with the nanomachines, but I don't see how or who. Why is that?" I looked over at the Boss, sitting next to the screen image of Arie, and he gave me a clear signal that this question was mine to answer. After all, I had created the situation in the first place, so I guess him putting me at the pointy end was only fair.

"Madam President, the original nanomachines were invented and produced by an Israeli scientist; the IP and all manufacturing rights to the nanomachines are owned and controlled by Israel, so at the appropriate time, Israel will arrange for the seeding to be completed. However, we have also requested the Israeli government to oversee the building of any plants from the plans and schematics we recovered from Innomatchi. Quality control is critical, as is setting up the robotics. Do you have a problem with that?" It was a direct challenge, and if we were going to have issues, better to get it out now rather than later. For the third time, absolute silence reigned between the countries, as no doubt the political implications of what I had just said filtered through the minds of all the players.

"Madam President, if I could make a comment, please?" Arie broke the silence. All he got was a go-ahead hand gesture from the president, who looked perplexed. On the one hand, she had her Army Corps of Engineers building a shadow plant up in Point Roberts, and no doubt they had failed to mention the nanomachines. By now, they had to have come to realize that they needed a ship set to enable the machines and robots to be installed, and probably had that element under control. There were at least five ship sets floating around some-where. I forget where, but I knew that they existed.

"You have my word and that of my government that there will be no politicking or party favorites with the seeding or enabling of any plants, wherever in the world they are located. We see this as a necessity for getting the world back into some sort of balance, and national, secular, religious, political, or other bias will not be allowed at the table." She nodded, seemingly happy with the situation. But how could we tell?

"Thank you, General Rosenberg, that is appreciated. I think we are done." And the feed from America winked out, leaving Sandra and our team in Israel. I thought for a moment and turned my head to one side to release a crick in my neck. I audibly heard the "snip" as I moved my head. Did it a second time, this one to the left. Another "snip."

"Okay, team, Sandra, get your good selves here. Well done with the president, very well done. See you soon." And I cut her feed off. Looked at the Boss. Looked at Arie. I could feel their tension, I had some myself, but I needed to focus.

Question time at the zoo was just around the corner, and I needed to prepare.

The president sat perfectly still, the directors of the CIA, FBI, and NSA also still; the only person moving was Anna, pouring a cup of coffee from the silver service. She was a little tense; the Israeli position had thrown them all, she felt, as it had initially done when she had first heard the instructions issued by Jessica. After she had the time to absorb what Jessica had done, she realized that not only was it clever, brilliant even, but the right thing to do. The solution had to be one of a humanitarian focus, not for political, commercial, or profit reasons. And it had been an Israeli who had invented the nanomachines, even though the final work had been performed at an American university.

"What is your view on this, Agent Bernstein?" The president's face gave nothing away, but her tonality suggested she was anything but happy. Anna looked at her boss for guidance, but Roger Winslow, the director of the FBI, sat mute, giving nothing away. Anna shrugged her shoulders, pulled herself straighter in her chair, and looked the President straight in the eyes.

"Madam President, we can still take the high ground. The nanomachines are just a step in the process; the plants will be the focus and what they produce. And the hope they give. You will be seen as having run off the terrorists and then provided a way out for not only America but possibly most of the free world."

"Particularly if you send army engineering teams to every country that has a ship set and facilitates the build." Julius recognized his precarious position; as the director of the CIA, his organization had been completely blindsided by the terror attacks and everything that had happened subsequently.

"Do we have control of the Japanese company at the heart of this situation?" Every head shifted towards the president again; this time, Anna shut up and let her boss take the question.

"Interpol had the organization locked down, with the full support of the Japanese Ground Support Unit. At this time, Interpol is still questioning everyone and has all the senior staff in isolation and under guard. Their factories have over eleven thousand workers, and I believe they are halfway through interviewing them. The agent in charge is Nokomoto Senji, and he has taken the owner and chief executive officer into custody."

"So the answer to that is no." The three directors nodded, Anna maintained her silence, and the general leaned forward in her seat.

"Madam President, there are multiple moving parts to this puzzle, and every day we uncover new elements that must be addressed.

In my view, Interpol has done an excellent job, continues to lead from the front, and is moving extremely fast under the circumstances." The president had the good grace to smile; it didn't reach her eyes, but the tension went out of the room.

"Thank you, General. I appreciate that. It is just very hard to sit where I am and, on the other hand, watch my country disintegrate, and on the other, watch as people out of my control run around the world making executive decisions that affect our very survival."

"You're upset because Interpol has given the Israelis the nano-machine technology."

"No. It is clear that they already had it. And we can trust them to do the right thing. It just would have been nice for someone to ask us what we thought about it before they did it." The room went silent again, and Anna started to wonder how this meeting would end. She didn't have to wait long. Her pocket buzzed at her. She looked at the president, held the mini in her hand, got a positive nod, stood, opened the mini, and moved to a corner of the room.

"Anna, how did the president take the news about Israel?" She looked a little worn on the screen; the tension could do that to you.

"Not well, Jessica, but she seems to have settled with it. The information about the boats and Roanoke seems to have thrown her off her game."

"Yes," I said, "I saw that. Perhaps you can tell her that Malcolm and the geeks here have pinpointed the location of all the satellite downloads, and we're organizing to get additional electronic coverage on them as soon as we can. What do you think her response would be if we asked for you to come back here to Israel to help with the inter-rogations?" The image pulled back, revealing more of her shoulders, and the camera lost its focus for a second.

"It shouldn't be a problem. I'll ask Roger." She put the mini down, walked to her director, and whispered in his ear; he gave her a hard look from under his eyebrows, then nodded sharply. She returned to the corner and picked up the mini.

"Roger's fine with that. I'll ask the president and let you know." By the time she regained her seat, the five others in the room were all staring at her.

"Madam President, Interpol has located the downlink for the terrorists' satellite transmission and is digging deeper on that as we speak. Captain Riley has requested I return to Israel to assist with the interrogation of the terrorist prisoners."

"Do you have Helena under control?" Sharp, pointed, but not harsh, Anna thought to herself; maybe the president was thawing a little.

"Yes, ma'am, with your train contingent as backup, Agent Remer and her team have the Westall property secured and as much local support as she needs for now."

"Roanoke?"

"No, Madam President, we will stand up a team as soon as this meeting is concluded."

"Then go. General, can you arrange transport?" the president asked. The general nodded. The president stood and walked stiffly out of the room.

"Why does Jessica want you back?" Roger asked, also standing.

"I think she sees the value of indirect representation. If I'm on the same ground as Interpol, we will know everything they know as they know it." Roger nodded; he had the same thought. "What are we going to do about Roanoke?" He looked at his watch, a slim, expensive piece of jewelry that usually hid behind his tailored cuffs.

"Leave that to me. I'll stand up a team and send you the details." And with that, he walked out of the room with the others, leaving Anna by herself. With no other choice, she stood, took one last look around the gloomy room, then walked out. A thought kept flitting through her mind. She didn't understand how a document—a white paper as it was called—a major policy document, could just up and disappear. She'd give that some thought on the plane trip to Israel if she could.

Chapter 43

Arie, the Boss, the Sgen Aluf in charge of the Israeli 104 commando troop, Tom, and Pete sat around a small glass table next to Arie's office. It was gloomy, like most high-tech rooms, where preference for lighting and air conditioning was given to rows and rows of blinking boxes and miles and miles of wall screens. Consequently, it was a little chilly as well as gloomy, a fitting environment, Pete thought, for the topic under consideration. Projected onto the table was a detailed map of the areas surrounding the long border between Libya and Egypt. Arie was using a grease pencil to make little circles, which in an accidental manner matched the crop circles made by the irrigation sprays.

"We've been in this area before; we crawled the dark fiber line between the uplink in Libya and the underground bunker in Egypt. We also looked at the farmhouse to the north, and it was empty. Now, according to our geek geniuses, the satellite downloads are all hitting these three areas to the south of the farmhouse. Here are the photos from the reconnaissance aircraft we put up, one-meter resolution."

A series of high-resolution photos popped onto the table, showing a series of small buildings in the shape of a star, all linked by covered walkways, with a large, metal-roofed building in the center. Several semitransparent roof panels were spotted over the entire star structure, and it was these that drew the attention of everyone around the table. Shami tapped one of the roof panels with his forefinger, the nail chewed down to the quick.

"This is where the majority of the transmissions emanate—they are on a ninety-minute cycle, with a four to five-minute window. The downlinks are here," he said, pointing to the next roof panel, "and here." He pointed to three more, and Arie crossed them with his red grease pen.

"With the roof covering, it will be hard to get a people count, and no hope of facial recognition. Shami measured this site at four hundred meters square, and the road that enters here," he said, pointing to a black line that entered the complex from the east, "has what look like speed bumps on it, but I would suggest they are hydraulic tank traps."

"I agree. And I wouldn't mind betting that they have all sorts of electronic disruptors and shade-throwers and plenty of automatic weapons." Tom looked at the pictures and tried to visualize how he would defend them. "You know, this could be a 'last stand' type of thing. Except for the mercenaries, no armed resistance had been offered at any other location except for Innomatchi, and they were Yakuza and a private guard."

"Why do you say that?" Arie was curious; the more he learned about the Boss's people, the more he came to understand the great intelligence and thinking capacity they brought to the table. Tom looked up from his study of the photos.

"They haven't moved very far from where we detected them the last time. Either they think they're protected at the political level, or they're very sure of themselves." Arie nodded; he had a similar thought. But now it was different. Their oil production had been successfully shut down, as had the wells all over the Middle East, and while they had escaped the radioactivity that spewed from the Arabian fields, the mercenaries had applied equal measure in the form of the nanomachines polluting every wellhead in Libya and the surrounding areas. No income from oil, and you got a very nervous government hanging on by a thread.

"Pretend you have unlimited resources. How would you attack this site?" the Boss asked, lounging around in his chair as if he didn't have a single care in the world. The Sgen Aluf put his hand up as if asking permission; the Boss just nodded, respecting the Israeli commando's manners.

467

"Sirs, the battle plan we used to take down the Devil was extremely effective. No one got away, and we had zero injuries. However, I acknowledge that Libya is a different battleground to Arabia." The Boss nodded; his first thought was to use the same tactics, but his instinct told him he had to find a more politically acceptable way. He looked over at Arie.

"Anyway we can liberate one of those ship sets and use it as a bribe?" Arie looked amused, not having gotten this far in his own thinking. He turned his head to one side and seemed to contemplate something, then a thin smile cracked his lips, and his eyes actually sparkled!

"PJ, you are, as always, a surprise. What a wonderful thought. Seeing that Israel now controls the production and distribution of nanomachines, this could be a wonderful solution. However, we promised not to let politics influence our humanitarian dictates, so how would you rationalize that? And I'm thinking specifically of your Jessica's reaction." The Boss bent his head, locked his lips together, and thought hard and fast. He could see the trade-off, the value in getting Libya's willing participation in the attack and capture of the terrorists, but on the other hand, he could see Jessica's scowl as she reviewed the plan.

"Jessica will be okay with it, so long as we deliver the terrorists. She wants 'Helen' most of all, and she wants everyone still in play from thirty years ago."

"In other words, she wants to clean the slate of the terrorists once and for all."

"Yes. Can't blame her. Emotionally, she empathizes with the refugee issue, and as we have seen, not all the girls taken became terrorists. SSA Remer is just one example, Amira another." Arie nodded his agreement; he had seen firsthand what the opportunity provided by Mohammad bin Azaria could produce, and while he could not condone what had been done subsequently, he could actively support some form of refugee reformation going forward.

"There's another wrinkle in that plan you haven't thought of." Pete sat somewhat stoically, his back straight, his long legs crossed at the ankles.

"And that would be?"

"If you look at the list of countries that are considered primary creators of refugees, guess who is at the top?"

"Libya."

"Libya."

"So you're saying, no way can we help them get out of the bog they are in, having lost all their oil and close to losing their country into the bargain?"

"Not saying anything. Just pointing out a conflict that our good captain is sure to raise."

"How would you talk her around?" Pete looked gobsmacked; the idea of anyone talking the good Captain Riley around on anything was so far from the possibility that it was, literally, beyond his comprehension. The Boss smiled at Pete's uncomfortableness; he shared the same feeling for his titular number two—but number one as far as the investigation went. He grimaced, mindful that he did not transmit negativity to anyone else in the room.

"I think I have a solution." He opened his mini, punched up Anna's address, and smiled when her face swam into focus. The conversation was brief and to the point, and he was not surprised at the outcome. "Anna says no, the political impact of a decision like that could undo all the trust we have generated in Interpol with the Americans, and that's without looking at who else might get their panties in a twist. Okay, bad idea. What else do we have to bargain with?" The small room fell silent; even the technicians over the far side at the big screens seemed to be holding their breath.

"What does Libya need most of all right now?" The question from Luigi was unexpected; he usually only commented on technical issues. The Boss gave him a hard look, impressed again at the smart thinking of the geek.

"Food, water, probably that would top the list."

"Okay, then how about we do the same thing as we did with the refugee camps?" Tom offered, having been amused at how quickly the mere thought of a political shitstorm had brought down what he had felt was an excellent idea.

"What was that, exactly?"

"Containers full of food, water, supplies, we have some stacked in Tunisia ready to reload what we didn't get to use yet."

"Would they go for that? And who had the creds to ask the question in the first place?"

"Are we agreed that we want to move on the compound soonest?" Everybody held up their hand, giving the Boss the confidence he needed for his next move. "Arie, who is the most politically astute person you know?" Arie held the Boss's eyes as he thought through the problem. He needed permission to launch a full-scale firefight on the sovereign ground, using a mix of nationalities, to wipe out a compound where there would be an unknown number of collateral deaths and possible property damage as well, at a time when the Libyan government was hanging on by a thread.

"The most persuasive approach would be one that came from the president of the United States. Pitched as a clean-up of the terrorists, done in such a way that the government is hailed as heroes and not devil-worshipping heathens letting the infidels take over. We would need to use some of their troops and resources; who has any idea of what that might look like?" The Boss scratched his chin, then looked up suddenly.

"Tom, who was it we worked with last year during that child-smuggling-ring case?"

"No one from in-country. We decided we couldn't trust them. We used the French as intermediaries, and to be brutally honest, that didn't work out so well either."

"What was our solution?"

"Pete took five of my boys and girls and eliminated the problem firsthand, in and out without any fuss, and we picked up the convoy on its way out, and Indigo's boys and girls took over from there, removed the traffickers, and repatriated the children, unfortunately as it turned out, back to Coxes Bazar. We did not know at that time what a first-class shithole it would become in the next year." The Boss went into thinking mode again.

"If we could jam everything electronically, smother the area with suppression munitions but in a tactical manner, so we left at least one way in and out, would it be possible to hit them, close them down, and get out again without creating a fuss?" Tom looked at Pete, then both turned to look at the Israeli commando, who in turn looked at Arie. You could literally hear their minds working overtime on the tactical problems.

"Wait until the satellite passes, drop an EMP on them, followed by full-scale electronic all-frequency suppression, mine the area to prevent ingress or egress, small team, HALO"—High Altitude, Low Opening—"jump, fast chopper out, on the clock, then a cruise missile or drone attack as we exit; there will be a lot of noise, disruption, no way to guess casualties, but if we target the roof, get to the main building, it might be possible. But we need to know where the prime targets are. How can we do that?" It was Arie's turn to look uncomfortable, something that did not go unnoticed.

"We have a deep-cover operative in that area. Let me have a day or two, and I'll see what we can find out." The Boss looked at Arie, understanding the sacrifice he was making. Israel's survival depended on knowing what the crazies were doing before they could do it, and this mission would possibly burn an asset, leaving a blind spot in their intelligence network. He'd have to find a way to repay the tough little Israeli spy, whom he was thoroughly fond of.

"Good solution. Anyone any further points or questions?" Every head shook in the negative; they were all a quick study, at the top of their game, and possibly the most experienced terrorist hunters on the planet.

They got it.

And so, in a day or two, would the terrorists.

Chapter 45

nna and I sat on one side of the table; the prisoners, one by one, would sit on the other. We had positioned it so that they would be facing the one-way glass mirror, providing the best view for anyone wanting to observe the interrogations. I had arranged for a bulky red folder to be provided for each of us, with all the known data on each prisoner stacked in the order we intended to see them. We had agreed on our strategy: I would go in hard and fast, push until I got resistance; Anna would offer a softer, more empathetic approach, and between us, we would decide the fate of everyone we had behind bars.

But we only wanted one question answered. Where were "Helen" and her cohort?

I signaled to the guard behind the mirror, and Reve Anaisha was marched in. She had been collected from the raid at Innomatchi. She had been a refugee pulled out of the camps, given to the Anaisha family, cared for, educated, and focused on game design, was an acknowledged computer code expert at seventeen years of age, and had briefly shared a spot at Harvey Mudd University when Amira had been there working on the nano bugs that would eventually rid the world of all oil, gas, and coal—whether or not we wanted it. I had a little surprise for all the prisoners. As she sat, I pointed to a screen next to the glass, and a pair of faces swam into focus.

"Agents Senji-san, Namoki-san, thank you for joining us. Can you confirm that this is the person you took into custody when you raided Innomatchi in Toyoko?" Senji seemed to be staring deep into the lens, but this was all play-acting; we had spoken to everyone concerned long before we started the interrogations.

'Yes, Captain, she is identified as Reve Anaisha."

"Thank you, agents." And their faces went black.

"Ms. Anaisha, you are charged with assisting in the planning of terror attacks on the Vatican, Dome of the Rock, Grand Mosque, West Point, International Space Station, and other locations that will be listed in your charge documents. Do you understand the charges against you?" While I had been listing the terror sites, she had slowly been going red in the face, a neat trick as her skin was already a beautiful coffee color thanks to her parents, whomever they may have been. I snapped at her to increase her stress. "Do you understand the charges?" She shook her head so violently that her hair flew all around her face.

"No, I don't!" she yelled at me. "I did not plan those attacks. I built a computer game, one that you can play on any computer; it's been available for at least two years. A computer game!"

"Tell me how you did that. Exactly." If her voice was shrill with emotion, mine was so cold it would cut steel.

"Some years ago, my mother was approached to offer myself and my sister an opportunity to write code for a new series of games. We were each given a list of materials and a background on how they might work, and we were asked to design a game that incorporated all the different weapons in a logical and productive manner. I was given the bombs and aircraft, I created a fictional battleground, then worked out how to best use the bombs in attacking my fictional targets. My sister was challenged with a high-tech weapon; it was just called 'the stuff,' and her task was to design a program that would attack every oil, gas, and coal production facility worldwide—again, in my fictional battleground.

"Then, once we had designed the games, we were asked to combine them and plan an attack that would take approximately one month, start to finish, and create a resource plan to carry out the attacks. We were given different scenarios where a different number of people could be used; we designed it so the gameplayer could choose the order of battle and the number of people involved, the end game being all the resources had to be returned to the starting point.

"I even wrote code to program remote vehicles, and the game-player had to either earn points to buy resources or come up with ways to minimize their resource needs, and the objective was to attack the maximum number of targets with the minimum number of resources. My sister designed the targets, and the gameplayer got to choose which targets they would attack and in what order.

"Once you selected your targets and your weapons, you had to take the code packs in the game to make the weapons work the way you wanted them to. You could automate a car, truck, UAV, or even an aircraft. You could plan the navigation using the game-world map; it is really easy to program, and anyone can do it. It was all up to the game player.

"You can buy the game anywhere. It's been out for over a year; it's called *Battle Front-Infinity Earth*. The final version starts off with you selecting the targets you want; each has a value, then the weapons, they cost you, and then you set the time, and you can compete online or play by yourself. My sister and I were paid for the work, and our mother's company released the game." Anna broke the thrall that had been created by letting the young woman ramble on as if she had to cleanse her soul. And if she had come to realize that the game she had created with her sister was the platform the terrorists had used to plan their attacks, then I could understand her need.

"When did you become aware that the terrorists were using your game in real life?" The wide-eyed, innocent look the woman gave Anna was a masterpiece, and if I were not hardened by my life experience chasing the worst kind of terrorists all over the planet, I would have bought it. No one was that innocent, and before us sat a very smart young woman, and if she was anything like Amira, with an IQ off the scale. I flashed the photo of "Helen" up on the screen before she could answer Anna's question.

"Where is this woman now?" I asked, my voice deliberately harsh and edgy.

I pointed to the screen, waiting for her answer.

"That's the woman who briefed us on the game requirements. We never met her; it was always by video conference. I don't know where she is; we only heard from her every month or so during development." And there was the lie I suspected, because I knew she had met "Helen" at Harvey Mudd, at the same time "Helen" had called on Amira. Not the same hour, not even the same day, but during that time, she had been on campus. I smiled to myself, waved to the guards in the control room, and sat back while she was taken away and replaced with her sister. This time I used a video of Sandra, who was watching the interrogation from another room, confirmed the identity of the sister and the fact that she had been swept up in New Zealand, but after less than twenty minutes, we got the exact same result.

Nada.

Anna stood up, stretched, and rolled her shoulders. "You know, a good lawyer could get them off as minor accessories, not really aware of the consequences of their actions, and their youth would play into that as well."

"Just as well they're not getting good lawyers, then." Anna looked at me and smiled, then sat down again.

"Even you are not that hard." I let her comment sit; was I or wasn't I? If push came to shove, then yes, I was that hard. Unapologetically so. I asked the geeks to find a copy of the game for us so we could analyze it in detail.

The next prisoner on our list entered, then sat with a determined look on her face that said, "ask what you like; I'm not saying anything." I smiled to myself; these types of people were the easiest to crack, so confident were they in their own abilities. One good shake and their confidence flew out the window like so much hot air.

"Arshia Spicatas, you are charged with aiding and abetting terrorist acts, specifically the bombing of the Vatican, Dome of the Rock, Grand Mosque, West Point, the destruction of the International Space Station, and other attacks at specific locations that will be listed in your charge documents. Do you understand these charges?" I matched her tough look with a tough look, and already I could see the cracks appearing in her facade. As an accountant used to sitting on the sidelines of most big organizations, being seen as a perpetrator would be a far stretch for her usual job description. Eventually, as I held my silence, she spluttered.

"No, no, no, no. I had nothing to do with any of those horrible things. Nothing. I was in New Zealand all the time, working twenty-hour days, helping to get the plant online; we make environmentally sensitive and sustainable solar panels and batteries, and power supplies. I had nothing to do with anything that happened halfway around the world." Her screech was like that of a little girl having her hair pulled.

"Ms. Spicatas, under the Terrorist Laws, as modified in 2022, aiding and abetting is defined as any activity that helps, enables, informs, contributes to, assists with, or supports a specific act of terror, the planning of any such action, the implementation of any such act, or the foreknowledge of any such action, and/or the benefitting from any such act, directly or indirectly. Your entire business at that plant, which you acknowledge you were a very senior manager of, was founded on the certainty and tragedy of those terrorist acts, and you deliberately and maliciously withheld such information as may have prevented those acts from taking place." She fell forward in her seat, her head buried in her long hair, her hands visibly shaking. And she cried. I sat back and let her go. She was the weak sister. I had picked that up from Sandra's notes of the takedown and a subsequent conversation she had heard between Spicatas and Wendy Summers, the CEO, on the G4 on their way here.

What conversation on a government aircraft is supposed to be private? What world do you live in? And I had the tape if I needed it.

"Ms. Spicatas, we have your timeline, we have all the data from your plant, and we know how and when you distributed the nanomachines and to whom; the fact remains there is no doubt you are culpable, but perhaps we can help you if you help us." She looked up at Anna, hope in her eyes, tears running down her face as if in a race to get somewhere fast.

"What? What do you want?" Anna smiled as she would at anyone needing her help, playing the good cop to perfection.

"We need the whereabouts of this woman. Her name is 'Helen,'" and her photo flashed up on the big screen.

"She came to New Zealand last year to check our progress. She stayed three days, then left with our pilot. I don't know where she went to or where she came from. It was never discussed." New information! I almost let out a whoop but managed to maintain my bitch face. If she got around with the pilot, we had a chance. When first captured, she had inadvertently confirmed that she had flown the C130 Hercules from storage to the Middle East some years ago. Maybe we could get her to tell us where "Helen" was. I waved Spicatas away and waited patiently for our next customer.

Another accountant, this time from Point Roberts, another strong denial of anything to do with the terrorists; at least they were consistent.

The two CEOs were just righteously pissed, played the lawyer card, and then just shut up when they were told there was no such person named "lawyer" in their future. I sensed real anger in Kathryn Simmons; she was so furious I felt that with a little push, she might burst, but to be honest, these interrogations were more for form than information. None of the women we had collected were weak-minded. All had fabulously high IQs and were smart, well-educated, and well-skilled in what they did. Strangely, none of them played the refugee card, and apart from the mention by Reve Anaisha, there had been no further reference.

I considered having a go at our banker and his accountant, then put it aside. We had them, and they would not tell us anything we needed to know, but for a fleeting second, I wondered what Mohammad bin Azaria might say if we told him what we were going to do with "his" girls. I let that idea cook as we prepared for the grand finale.

Mrs. Aleena Anaisha, CEO and president of Innomatchi Southeast Asia, is a woman who has not said a single word from the time we arrested her to now.

I read the charges against her, added on what we were going to charge her daughters with, and throughout the entire indictment, she never moved a muscle. Her face remained frozen in a rictus of disdain, almost as if we were beneath her.

Not a word.

I gestured to the guards, and they entered and left with her, and it was as if she had never been in the room.

"What do you make of that?" Anna looked as puzzled as I did.

"Don't know. Under different circumstances, I would be expecting a phone call from someone high up the political or legal ladder demanding an immediate release. It can't be a secret we have her; the shoot-out in Karachi killed seventeen, all but three of them Yakuza. The local police swarmed the building after the primary attack had finished, arrested another twenty or so, mostly released by now, but our man in Toyoko sent us the local press that described the scene in fairly graphic detail."

"Has anyone in your chain of command been contacted?"

"Not to my knowledge, and the Boss wouldn't send us in here without that information." Anna continued to look puzzled and shrugged her shoulders; she would check her sources, but if there was going to be a move on the Innomatchi CEO, it would have to be very soon because the next step is that they would "disappear" the prisoners to the Netherlands so they could stand trial in camera before the World Court at the Peace Palace in the Hague. Then suddenly, she had a question.

"Is Mohammad bin Azaria and his accountant being sent to the Hague?"

"No. They'll be held here in Israel and tried in absentia. Can't blame the Israelis.

They are really pissed off about their Rock." Anna nodded; she knew how they felt, being of Jewish descent herself. So that just left the women. And just as she seemed to develop a question, I cut across her thoughts like a knife through butter.

"You're starting to speculate that there might be a breakout of some type or attempted en route?"

"Yes. That amount of arrogance suggests something going on in the background."

"Who would have the interest or the balls to attempt that?"

"Who had the balls to send the mercenaries after the FBI in broad daylight in Helena?"

"Good question. So who haven't we rounded up yet?"

"Helen and her cohort."

"Exactly. Maybe it's time to just get on with it and find her." I dialed Arie on my minicomputer, mindful that we were both still in the interrogation room and under video and audio surveillance. Not exactly the place to conduct a secret conversation.

"Arie, any news on our location?"

"Yes. Outside, let's meet."

In the back of my mind, I had a couple of questions starting to form, one concerning ground stations or satellite uplinks on or near the Anaisha home in Karachi and their office, the other the same question but on the Innomatchi building in Toyoko, and a third concerning the pilot. Could she tell us where she had flown "Helen" to? Perhaps a better question is, would she?

Probably not. I decided to keep her in reserve but confirm my suspicions about the satellite dishes. I sent a quick text to our agents, who were now back in Tokyo.

Arie was in his little anteroom, just shy of his small office, which looked like it had been plucked out of a museum and frozen in time. A beautiful old Chesterfield desk was parked in one corner, and a pair of colorful Tiffany lamps stood guard over the scarred leather surface. The only object which shattered the illusion of old-world calm and style was the modern ergonomic chair with its red-and-blue racing stripes.

"Jessica, Anna, I have news for us all; perhaps we could all be seated?" As he spoke, the photo spun up on the glass table again, this time in two sections—a small overhead plan view and a 3D cutaway view that offered navigation via buttons on the map. "We have an asset inside this structure. He has been there for over seven months. He runs the main kitchen and is French, but he is also deep-cover, so I don't want this data spread outside this room. Clear?" Everyone from the Boss on down nodded. Deep cover operatives were the shining star in "HUMINT"—the human intelligence world—and more precious than gold.

"I won't give you his name, but I will give you a code to send before you attack so he can absent himself from the battlefield." Every head nodded again, the assumption that we would attack strengthening the supposition that Arie knew the location of "Helen" and her cohort. I held my hand up to stop Arie from continuing.

"Arie, during the interrogations, Anna had an idea, and I think you should consider it before you brief us." He still looked like everyone's favorite uncle, but when you looked into his eyes, the depth and seriousness there shifted from friendly "uncle" to hard-ass spy. He gestured to Anna.

"When we questioned the CEO and president of Innomatchi, who didn't answer a single question, we got the feeling that she was waiting for something. When you put it alongside the planned mercenary attack on the FBI in Helena, in daylight, it occurred to us she may be waiting to be broken out of custody." By the angle of his head, tilted to one side as it was, Arie seemed to be considering Anna's comment.

"We keep thinking all the mercenaries have been swept up, and maybe that is a wrong assumption. What do you suggest?" I butted in, not to cut Anna off again, but to focus everyone on our next steps.

"Set a trap for them. Make it real and deadly, and send an unmistakable message. But do it while we are attacking the compound because my strong feeling is that 'Helen' is the ring leader here, and there will be a certain symmetry to taking her down while her mercs are getting slapped around." Every face in the room lit up at the thought of the double whammy, so I turned the meeting back over to Arie.

"Okay, Jessica, we'll put that on your schedule. Now, here is where the one called 'Helen' is, and here is where her fellow women work and sleep. There are nine of them in total; they don't go around the compound armed but gun up if they move outside any distance from the compound. They have a small private guard of ex-East German Stasi troops, who, while they are now a little long in the tooth, can be expected to defend to the death."

"That looks to me as if the women are all contained in one arm of the building, with the primary work area in the center hub. And look here, the airfield could easily handle mid-size jets, and those hangars are easily big enough to hide a C-130 and drones. Where is that exactly?"

"Al Kutrah Airport, not registered in any directory, has a nice, long but bent in the middle eight-thousand-foot main strip, 02/20, the original strip alongside is defaced beyond safe use, a victim of shoddy construction and intense heat. No one claims it, but the satellite photos show burn marks in the concrete apron reminiscent of low-to-the-ground attack jets—probably old Russian Mig-21s."

"It really annoys me we were so focused on those satellite dishes we didn't look deeper while we were there the last time. Talk about blinded by what you think you know." Pete was pissed, but it was not his fault. The briefing and the mission had been very specific. Find the dark fiber, and track it to its source.

"We're there now. Let's concentrate on the data and plan how to root these people out of their lair."

"Did your asset say anything about support for the women?"

"Yes. Apart from the private guard, internal and external patrols, around thirty automatic weapons, heavy machine guns outside, all mobile, they rotate in six-hour shifts. The word is that they are disciplined and well trained."

"Then we will need a distraction or two to draw them out. This surrounding area is desert, yes?" Pete was now being a little persistent, his anger at not having gone the extra mile on the first visit to this area getting in the way of his normal subdued nature. I decided to let him run; his thoughts on tactics would be invaluable.

"That's a good idea. Any suggestion on how we do that?" He looked directly at me as if surprised I hadn't shut him down yet.

"Yes. When we took out the Devil, he did the hard work for us, sending the bulk of his troops back to the palace. But it left us in a position where we could apply maximum force with minimum exposure. If we can create legitimate firefighting here, and here," he said, pointing to the arms of the star on the northern side, "draw the troops outside to one, the inside troops to the other, then take the center from the top, then work inwards along the arm where the women are, we could probably eliminate most of their shooters before we have to deal with the women."

"How do we get them out safely?"

"We'll need some form of fast transport, which will be hard if we HALO in."

"No, not necessarily." The Boss leaned into the table, pointing at the center of the compound. "We will not need to worry about local troops; whoever gets us permission to attack can make sure the locals are warned off. And yes, I know that might give our targets a warning as well. But Arie has some new automatic drone toys in his playpen, and I'm sure we could get a few if we asked nicely?" Arie grinned. The idea of the Boss ever asking nicely for anything, including his drug of choice, coffee, was so remote as to be laughable.

"What are you talking about?" Pete asked, his interest piqued.

"Aire has three types of mobile, air portable, automated weapons that could be dropped in just before we jump that can be programmed to attack a specific location on command, and can also be controlled remotely from the ground if we need them. And the good thing is, they self-destruct when they are finished, so they can't come back at us with the bad guys."

"How accurate can you drop them, from what altitude, and once they are feet dry, how long before they are operational?" Now Pete was literally vibrating with enthusiasm, the idea of dropping automatic killing machines on top of the terrorists warming his heart. The Boss just smiled at Pete's enthusiasm and waved his hand around a little.

"Classified, no doubt, but I'm sure if you asked the right question, Aire would give you an answer." Pete went into his thinking mode, his face void of any expression, his eyebrows knitted together. He slowly started to shake his head, pointing to the photo of the compound. Then he ran one hand in from one side, mimicking what an aircraft might do.

"Okay, Arie, I need a quiet approach, so above twenty-five thousand feet. Can you do that?"

"Yes." Pete nodded to himself. His hand was still flying over the target area. "Steerable chutes?"

"Yes, to an electronic transmitter, accurate to one meter, or to a GPS coordinate accurate to three meters."

"Target vision, infrared, all-terrain, plenty of ammo?"

"If you choose the smaller version, 7.62mm squad weapons, times four, one thousand rounds per gun. If you choose the bigger one, 20mm Gatling guns times two, fifteen hundred rounds per gun. And before you ask, you can mix in the armorpiercing, tracer, and antipersonnel rounds into the belts."

"Range?"

"Minimum three kilometers, maximum depends on surface conditions."

"Could you fit one with mortar tubes?" Arie smiled again; Pete's enthusiasm was infectious.

"Yes, we can do that. And we can give you remote viewing and manual override controls if you want that as well. But you need to be within five kilometers for them to work."

"Okay, thanks. Can you give me a minute, please?" Pete asked as he walked away from the group around the table. He signaled to the Israeli commando and the Boss, and the three of them huddled in one corner. I stood up and slowly drifted over to them to stand on the Boss's shoulder.

"Gentlemen, it's rude to ignore your host. What could you possibly need to discuss that you couldn't reveal to Arie?" Pete looked a little miffed, turned to the Israeli commando colonel, and spoke rapidly in Hebrew; the colonel answered just as quickly, nodded positively, then the group broke up.

"Jessica, Pete needed to understand the limits that might be put on the Israeli commandos. And he didn't want to embarrass Arie." I nodded tactfully, but I knew Arie, and I'm sure he wouldn't have been offended. We all sat down again, and I took the lead again.

"Arie, apologies. The boys needed to check out the rules of combat and didn't want to put you on the spot."

"Yes, I thought that might be the issue here. How do Israeli commandos participate in an attack on a Libyan target? Simple answer, we just do the same thing we did with the last intrusion—we go in unidentified but under the Interpol umbrella."

"Arie, this time, there will be people killed, collateral damage, infrastructure destroyed, and probably a lot of visible evidence once we are finished. It will be very hard to hide the results from any interested party."

"Gentle people, the Israeli government, has very credible top-level contacts in Libya, plus the thought that they have been harboring the main terrorist cell for years, if released to the world, would doom them to eternity, something I'm sure they will not want. I could even see the United Nations making a case to take over the country, and

PJ, perhaps you could at least start that process from your end?" The Boss smiled his best crocodile smile, obviously liking Arie's thinking. It was a good strategy.

"Can do, Arie. In fact, we can have a Red Notice ready to go that you can use as part of your conversation. Now, what really interests me is our timing. How long to prepare, where do we get more troops from, how do we stage the removal of the women to the Hague, bring all these excellent ideas together?"

"Unless you and Pete and the Sgen Aluf disagree, I'd like to draw up the order of battle, so maybe you can give Anna and me an hour?" Arie nodded his agreement; the boss nodded; Pete just put his best stoic face on and leaned back in his seat.

"A woman's work is never done!" he quipped, causing everyone to laugh, breaking the tension as effectively as if he had thrown a hand grenade onto the table. I smiled to myself; he knew exactly what I was doing and why. It was one of Section Five's little secrets, a secret that had allowed us to be very successful whenever the s-h-one-t hit the fan. I opened my minicomputer, and dialed up Indigo; it was a short conversation that ended with "*Sí, mi capitán, lo organizaré y estaremos con ustedes en cuatro horas.*"

Four hours was plenty of time for what Anna and I had to do.

Anna and I went into a small room that had beautiful trees in pots covering all four walls and a huge skylight shaped in the form of a dome with ridges running down from the middle. I was fooled for a minute until I realized it was a three-dimensional projection. Whatever happened to real? I shook my head, pulling some leaves off one of the bushy trees to help center myself. At least the trees were real, something to hold onto for the next few days.

Chapter 45

O nce the terms and conditions were released in Helena, the entire
town seemed to take a deep breath. The realtors had stacks of
contracts ready and were eagerly waiting for the rush of buyers. It
was now six hours since they had posted the availability of the homes,
one hundred and fifty thousand dollars for a four-bedroom home, one
hundred and twenty thousand for a three bedder, and a fifty percent
cut in that purchase price if the buyer agreed to take two refugee children. You had to take at least one child, and for that, you would be
paid fifty thousand dollars a year until college graduation, as well as
having your own children educated for free and health benefits for the
whole family for life.

Groups of itinerant migrants from the big cities sat around
campfires in front of their temporary shelters-tents, caravans, four-
wheel drives, and military-style hoochies, debating the terms and conditions. Where were these refugee children? Where were they coming
from? When would they arrive? Did anyone get to choose their child,
or was that going to be done for them? And the T&Cs required that
the houses be sold back to the trust, so what happens to the refugee
children if an owner sells and moves back to, say, Billings? Do the
buyers keep all the benefits? Or are they tied to Helena forever?

Arguments broke out, even the occasional fistfight, and while
FBI agents Remer, RuPaul, and Vernon, dressed in low visibility
cold-weather gear, mingled with the crowds, it didn't take long for
someone to work out that more information was needed, and a march
on city hall organized. The agents faded into the disbursing crowd

and headed for their vehicle, calling their presidentially provided guard at the railway station and holding down the Westall house to warn them.

"No contact, keep out of it completely, let the locals manage whatever develops," Fay said into her minicomputer, hoping against hope that Bob and his troops were not going stir crazy with the lack of action since they had put down the mercenary terrorists. Bob's face was grim, but he nodded his agreement. Fay snapped the little computer shut and climbed into the car.

"I think we just tag along at the tail of the crowd. I can't believe that this hasn't been thought out; it will be interesting to see how it all works out." Andrew RuPaul, as the oldest of the three, married and with three children all still at school felt obliged to point out the family ramifications of the T&Cs that had been released. "If you've already got kids, slotting in another can be a very hard thing to do.

"Now, in this case, the bribe is huge—the money, education, and health benefits, not to mention the crazy purchase price of the homes. It would be very tempting for a lot of those good people out there, having left the chaos and destruction in the bigger cities behind. But I don't know if I could do it. I really don't."

"Me either," John said from the back seat. He was just married, had no kids yet, but some planned, and his family was living in a condo. "Maybe I could be motivated to move here, but from what I saw of the local FBI office, there probably wouldn't be a posting at my level." Fay looked in the rear vision mirror and saw John wipe his meaty hands through his hair, which badly needed a cut. She was mindful that they had all been going twenty-four-seven for nearly six weeks, with very little downtime, something she would have to provide before very much longer.

"If you are seriously considering it, I will make it happen for you. We only have an assistant junior agent here and civilian support, but this area will become a focus for us for a long time to come, so think it through, John. Under the present circumstances, I can have your orders cut within the next twenty-four hours."

"Are you serious?" He looked straight at her reflected in the mirror, her face showing the strain of the last few days, and to his mind, not diminishing her natural beauty in the slightest. She was junior in age to him but senior in rank, and he had been very impressed with her performance to date, particularly her habit of consulting them on every move she intended to make.

"Totally. Just say the word." They drove in silence and parked about half a mile from the town hall, and patiently waited for the bulk of the people to stream by. They eventually tagged onto the tail of the crowd and were dragged along until the street swelled with so many people forward progress was impossible. On the steps of the town hall, the three realtors and two accountants from the trustee's office stood, relaxed but flanked by local police. Fay wondered what was going through their minds, facing down a crowd that now numbered in the hundreds but was surprisingly quiet and well-behaved.

"My name is Ned Johnson, and I'd like more details about this deal you are offering. Can't speak for everyone here, but most folks need more information before they can make up their minds one way or the other." The solitary man stood just proud of the front edge of the crowd; there was no indication of anything other than curiosity as they waited for one of the spokespeople to respond. One of the trustees stepped forward, holding a huge sheaf of papers in his hands. He held a hand up as to stop anyone else from speaking, cleared his throat, then looked down at the hundreds of upturned faces, smiled, and did his best.

It took nearly an hour, but he managed to answer every question in his soft, educated voice and even offered to meet one-on-one with anyone that still had questions. Indeed, it had been well thought out, and John now had a smile on his face.

"You know," he said, turning to address Fay and Andrew, "this could work." The crowd slowly broke up around them, and waiting patiently until the majority had dispersed, they took their time to make it to the steps of the town hall.

"John, you take the lead, you have an obvious and honest interest, and you know what we need to find out. We'll stay in the background." With that, Fay took Andrew's arm and moved away to the fringe of the remaining people. She was starting to develop a plan in her mind and having John located here permanently fitted perfectly into it. She had her own personal plans, and they involved more study of the manual Captain Jessica Riley had thrown at her when she had delivered the engineer to Interpol.

Before she could develop her thinking further, her minicomputer buzzed in her pocket; she turned so that Andrew could shield it from public view and pulled it out, and snapped it open.

"Fay, quick question, do you think Bob and his team will be needed with you much longer?"

"Hello to you too. And yes, things are breaking here. I'd like to keep them for at least another week."

"Okay, thanks. Speak later." And Jessica disappeared from the screen. Fay looked up at the grey sky with its blue-green hue, wondering why Jessica wanted to know about the president's train guard. It was really cold in Helena, and the wind chill made it worse. What was Jessica planning? And could she get an invitation to play? She had seen Jessica work up close and personal and thought she was one of the best interrogators she had ever seen. And commanded enormous respect from those she worked with. Her musings were interrupted by the return of Andrew, blowing into his mittens to warm his hands.

"I've reserved a four-bedder. We need to send a deposit in twenty-four hours. I've put my hand up for two refugees, and once they have our deposit, we'll get data on how to connect with our children. One thing they did confirm—all the children are girls, and their ages range from eight to eleven years. And they will be here in around three weeks." Fay looked at her agent, astonished that he had moved so fast and so positively.

"Have you spoken to your wife?" she asked. He just laughed, nodded, and bounced up and down on his toes.

"Yes. A quick chat, more to follow, but can we please get back to our vehicle? My bloody toes are falling off!"

"You told her about the refugees?"

"No, not yet. Just that you are moving me here to the office."

He seemed to think for a moment, then, with a huge grin, finished his thought. "And we'll have a lovely home with a front and back garden, right next to a park, and we can actually afford to own it right now. That is if the FBI doesn't step in and buy it as an intellectual exercise."

"Oh, well, that makes all the difference. I suppose you will think this through before you become irrevocably committed?"

"Of course I will boss. Of course I will. Anyway, if I need any help on how to bring up a couple of girls, I can always tap Andrew!"

Their laughter filled the small car, and Fay wondered if anyone else who purchased one of the homes would get as much enjoyment out of it as John appeared to. And she really wondered how anyone expected a mass migration of refugees from the third world mixed with a mass migration of displaced people from first-world cities to blend into a cohesive society.

Chapter 46

"Helen," as she had been known for at least three decades, real name Natasha Trotsky, did not look in the slightest like the world's most wanted terrorist. She looked like a grandmother, her silver-white hair bundled up on top of her head, tied today with a yellow ribbon. Her starched white shirt had small collars, and a set of twin pearls floated along in the crease to end up in a simple, looped figure—eight knot in the center of her breasts. Her greenish dress, something that might have come from the finest of BOHO shops anywhere in the world, flowed from a trim waist and ended in a pretty lace footing. Silver pumps with deadly needle heels help create the impression of relaxed elegance.

A survivor of the nineties mishmash of Russian and American geopolitics, a Stasi-trained operative of international reputation, it wasn't until she met a strange, calm man in Budapest that she found her real calling. Having also been a graduate of the fake American town of Vinnytsia in Ukraine, run by the KGB, she had all the attributes Al Hemish al-bin Mohammad Karesish—brother Fernández to his refugee friends—was looking for. A well-trained network of spies embedded in American companies and government departments, not to mention a complete network of embedded spies in the UK and Europe, a hunger for money, and a hunger for a survivable cause.

And a passion for refugee children.

And so had begun a thirty-seven-year partnership that had led to the hobbling of the modern world, the crushing of capitalism, and the disruption of life as it had never been disrupted since the age of the dinosaurs.

Opposite her, sitting on a creased and scarred leather lounge, holding a cut crystal glass of the finest whisky, Saleem bin Mohammad bin Urals in his desertstained kaftan and dirty boots, presented the exact opposite image. Rough, crude, and possibly indifferent to the finer niceties of modern society. The huge crystal chandelier that flowed overhead like a hovering waterfall of tiny led lights threw minute sparkles all over the roof as the air conditioning struggled to move the air around the oblong-shaped room. The mood was probably more spoiled by the dried blood that ran down one side of the terrorist's arms and legs.

"So, Saleem, once again, you have used excessive force. How long do you think the locals will continue to leave us alone if you keep dropping shattered bodies on their stoops?"

"Madam, I only used as much force as was necessary. Don't forget you live here, safe and secure, at my pleasure, and I hardly think you, of all people, could chastise me for being proactive." His thin, cultured voice, reminiscent of Oxford, cut through the room like a sheet of glass, and the tonality was not unlike that of a chalkboard being scratched. Totally unpleasant to listen to, Helen thought to herself, and not for the first time. He may have been well-educated and from a royal bloodline stained by desert sand, but he was in every way no more than human garbage.

"Saleem, your funds have been cut off, and you now rely on us—specifically me—to keep you and your tribe in drugs and alcohol and sex. And it isn't being proactive to attack a small village in the dead of night and rape and kill everyone just because you felt like it."

"My men were getting restless; they needed something to sharpen their skills. I expect full payment as agreed, and I want it transferred to my account today." He looked at his polished nails, blew on one hand, then rubbed the nails on his dirty shirt. *Disdain, rude, indifferent, a bore, dangerous*, all these descriptors applied to him, Helen thought to herself, and she wondered how she could replace him without his troops turning on her.

"Not only will you not get paid, but you will spend the rest of the week camped outside the perimeter of the compound. It's time you learned who has control here. And to ensure your obedience, I'll be sending Wolfgang with you to keep you in line." Now he started to vibrate with anger, his face flushed, his whisky slopping from side to side. Helen was used to this reaction; it was just another fault she found in this most distasteful of mercenaries. Why the Devil had allocated him to her in the first place would remain a mystery, given the Devil's current situation.

As in several thousand pieces of human tissue fused permanently into the Arabian desert sands.

She could honestly say she was pleased with this thought, although it had brought her plans to a sudden stop. Up until that attack by the Israelis, the Devil and his motley men and women had created the havoc she wanted while eliminating most of the world's supply of oil, gas, and coal. Then Interpol—or the accursed Americans—had cut the money chain by freezing the Sovereign Wealth Fund, and the mercenaries everywhere had arced up and become unpredictable once their locally available funds had dried up.

Even that had its benefits, but after a while, very little was being achieved against her master plan. And the most frustrating thing was she was still in limbo, unable to mount a cohesive offensive due to an almost complete lack of resources—and money. She knew some of her women had been arrested, and she knew some of the plants had been attacked and either taken over or shut down. And most worrying of all, she had not had a transmission from Helena for nearly two days. She knew what was going on there because she was still getting the satellite photos of the build area every ninety minutes and could tell that the progress was excellent. But with no reports from her people on the ground, she had to hope the schedule was still being maintained.

The first boat would arrive in just two weeks, and America would be faced with one thousand three hundred and nine young refugees, all English speaking, at least somewhat, all dressed cleanly, all looking forlorn and longing, and all very smart. And their support staff, some two hundred and fifty of them, teachers, medics, engineers, scientists, everyone needed to run a school, a hospital, and a university.

And all with perfect passports and entry visas, all fully documented and previously lodged with the Department of State and Immigration, Customs, and Enforcement (ICE). And all the adults were correctly accredited with their respective departments of Education, Medicine, Social Services, and Child Welfare, so in a sense, they were ready to engage from the moment they arrived.

Perfect. She smiled to herself; she had seen Margarete, a petite French refugee who was staying with her in the compound, hack into the American computers with such ease and firstly create, then enter the data with such fluidity and skill the hair on her arms had stood up. She had pulled young Margarete out of the camps personally, put her with an Egyptian family sympathetic to their cause, and now here she was, just twelve years later, creating the future for her sisters without a care in the world. She looked at her irritating guest, mentally shrugged her shoulders, came to a decision, and held a finger up to draw his attention. He was completely unaware that this was also a signal to Wolfgang, who slid up behind him and slipped a stiletto into the top of his spine, severing his spinal cord with one fluid movement.

"Thank you, Wolfgang. Dispose of the body and send in his number two. Bring two of your men as well, please." Wolfgang merely nodded, picked the now lifeless mercenary up by the shoulders, and physically pulled him backward out of his seat with the ease of a powerlifter. The only sound was the scraping noise made by the terrorist's combat boots dragging on the highly polished Egyptian marble floor.

Salad Oman was an Afghani mercenary, a survivor of first the Soviet and then the American invasion of his country, and at just five feet tall, he often created the impression of being childlike. He was anything but, and as he entered the oval room surrounded by six-foot-two German guards, his lack of stature was almost comical. He came to a stop just off to the side of the leather lounge, now carrying a new bloodstain, noticed the smear marks on the floor that spoke of bloody body disposal, the smashed glass of lack of control, shrugged his shoulders, and looked Helen straight in the eyes.

"Madam, I can see you have had some difficulty here. Is there anything I can do to help?"

"Mister Oman, you are now the temporary force commander. There will be no more raping and pillaging until I say so, and I need you to take all your men out to the farthest perimeter and set up camp for the next week. Consider this a small punishment for your transgression. Complete this mission successfully, and I will not only confirm your appointment but have you paid the standard rate for a successful attack. Is that clear?"

Salad Oman was not especially quick, but he was smart enough to realize an opportunity when he saw one and giving the bloodstains on the couch one last look, he nodded.

"Yes, madam, I will do as you instruct." And with what passed for him as a formal bow but, in reality, was little more than a bob of his bald head, he turned on his heels and walked out, his impressive guards matching him stride for stride.

Wolfgang stood at ease and gestured to three women who had been waiting nervously off to one side, who immediately moved in and started cleaning the bloodstains off the couch and the floor.

"So much blood from such a little prick," Helen said, standing. "Let's go and see what our good girls have for us." She strode off, heading for the annex in the opposite direction to that taken by the mercenary. She wondered how she would maintain discipline with the mercenaries when they learned that she would soon be short of funds, not today, but certainly within the month.

She would have to apply her considerable skills to that problem, and as a matter of priority. She reached an area that was glassed off, the walls a light blue translucent color, reaching all the way from the roof to the floor, some twenty feet below. Inside, it looked like any modern computer lab, with big screens, messy desktops, and people littered all over the place in various stages of sugar highs. The one difference is that every technician was a woman, relatively young, but perhaps old as geeks generally went, beautiful, well-dressed, and sparklingly happy.

Helen stood outside the double doors, watching for a moment. This was her greatest achievement. In all her years as a spy, a recruiter, and more recently, a terrorist, this little collection of intellect was as close to perfection as she ever thought a human being might achieve. Six technical geniuses providing identification and formal documents for thousands of refugees from every camp on the planet, all sequenced to perfection and all seemingly authorized by various governments and departments.

There had never been anything like it anywhere in the world.

The first three thousand refugees were already in transit, just weeks away from arrival at their destinations. Another ten thousand girls had been identified, selected, collected, and placed in temporary accommodation, where their education would commence with language classes specific to where they were to be moved. Over the next six months, ships would take them in their thousands to a better life, where food and water were plentiful, and caring adults were available to look after and nurture them. And once their temporary camp was emptied, it would be refilled with the next ten thousand, and so on it would go until the camps were empty of children. And hopefully, somewhere along that long line of activity, the world would wake up and cease the useless conflicts that filled the camps every day, and in time there would be no refugee problem because there would be no refugees.

Her smile died on her face; she knew deep down in her gut it would never be so. The world was too selfish, too enamored with power, position, wealth, instant gratification, quick riches, and me-be-for-you behavior. Centuries of ingrained selfishness supported at the highest levels of power, politics, and religion would win out, but they would suffer first. Her girls would be given a chance and, with some luck, might well have a say in the design of the future for all mankind.

Look what a simple girl from a refugee camp had achieved with nanotechnology. And wasn't that a miracle? One of her personally chosen girls had risen to the magical call of technology and created something that had literally changed the direction of the world overnight.

True, Amira may not have envisaged the final outcome of her genius, but the work had been done, and the final iteration of her brilliant work was now producing solar panels so efficient they were delivering almost a one-to-one electrical output, and the power packs were so efficient that just one of them could run a small factory or fifty homes. Oil, gas, and coal were dead. That, in itself, would force change. *Was forcing change*, she thought to herself; the change was happening all over the world.

The killing of the internet had been another game-changer, but time would tell if it had the effect they had planned. And it wouldn't matter in the long run, as they had the ability to kill it over and over again until everyone got bored with the process. Another gift from a brilliant refugee, this one saved by the roadside in Afghanistan from where she had run away.

And her almost twins—her two girls from Karachi—look at what they had created. A simple video game in 3D that could be used to plan and execute the most complex military strategy ever envisioned. And anyone could purchase the game for less than fifty dollars American! And if they were smart, they could download the code and program any computer-enhanced vehicle to be automated, with full navigation, in four dimensions.

Not bad for fifty bucks!

She opened the doors, ignored the laughter and music that flowed out, and went straight to the command seat in the middle of the displays. This is where the action was and would continue to be for the foreseeable future.

She felt the power of it in her aging bones.

This well might be her last hurrah, but on the scale of things she measured, it would be her finest achievement, not bad for a girl raped at twelve, then press-ganged into the military and given no real choice in her destiny until she had cut herself free from her brutal masters in a series of orchestrated assassinations that had made headlines around the world.

That was how the imam had found her in Budapest—he had placed a small ad in the personals section of the classified section of the *London Times* and, three days later, sat down with the one person in the world who could make his dreams come true.

Chapter 47

Deep in the mountain originally built as a nuclear bomb-proof control center for the American military, in a well-airconditioned room remarkable only for the surfboard camped in one corner and a pile of dirty clothes left against the door, Malcolm did what he loved best. Hunted the electronic world for intelligence and information that would help his friends unpack some of the chaos and destruction that had accumulated since the terrorist attacks four weeks ago.

It had only been a month, but to him, it had felt like six months. So much had been packed into those four short weeks. Trips across the Atlantic Ocean to Israel and Italy, over to the West Coast to Seattle and Point Roberts, middle America in the form of Helena, Washington, then back to his mountain.

The high point in all this travel had been the surfing he had been able to sneak in on the West Coast. That had been simply magnificent. Big waves, few surfers, low, rumbling clouds that didn't shed their anger while he had been working a cutback; all in all, when you added in the comfort and luxury of the G4, he had made most of his trips across countries and oceans in; it had been a rad time.

But now he was back on the hunt, nose to the grindstone, finger on the mouse, relaxed and ready to do battle with the forces of evil. His assistant had run the full analysis of the game they had been sent, and he recognized the signs of genius in both the coding and the construction. It looked innocuous and ordinary, just a good high-quality game from the Innomatchi stable, one of the great game labels on the planet. But underneath the cool design of the artwork? A terrorist's wet dream. And a very clever one at that. He put it aside and concentrated on the report his new best friends in Europe had sent him. Luigi and Shami, coupled with Indigo, the head of Interpol in Italy, had compiled an amazing list of hacks that had been made on both the European and American government databases outside the Y2K ones they had first seen and corrected.

And they had sent pages and pages of code of current transmissions between a hidden source and those databases. He loaded up the data and fed it into his encryption decoder, made a note of his start time, then sat back and reflected on what he had just seen. A magic game that empowered terrorists that had been invented by two young girls, both refugees who had been abandoned, then given to a family in Karachi. The Anaisha family—coincidentally the owners of Innomatchi, one of the giants of robotics, games, and all things electronic. Not a coincidence, not by a long way.

As always, serious planning, long term, decades in the making. How the hell could they find the mastermind? Did they even need to?

He worried about that question for an hour, then his alarm rang, and he pulled up the decoder on his main screen.

And swore.

He scrolled through the pages and pages of data, started a cross-reference file, opened multiple screens in the process, then wrote a quick algorithm to make the sorting and analysis easier.

He had to call his boss, but he needed to check and analyze every byte of data before he did. And he needed it checked. He flicked open his minicomputer.

"Luigi, *Hola, coma estas*, I need your help."

"What do you need?"

"The data stack you sent me, I've unpicked it, and I need an outside summary of it before I speak to anyone. If I send the decoded data back to you, could you and your crew analyze it and let me know the outcome, please?"

"*Sí, no hay problemas. Envíenoslo, y haré que Estefarino también participe*." Malcolm thought rapidly.

"Thank you, yes, that's good, use Stefarino, Indigo, or any of your geek squad.

"I suspect this will be a real problem for us all. *Si!* Thank you in advance."

"*No te preocupes, amigo mío. Adiós por ahora.*"

"Cheers."

The link closed, the little screen went black, and Malcolm went back to worrying about his question concerning the mastermind. Maybe they did need to nail his or her arse to the wall.

Time would tell.

Chapter 48

The team assembled to take down "Helen" and her cohorts had been in the air for nearly twenty minutes when the message from Arie popped up on Jessica's minicomputer.

Main force now redeployed to area six, bivouac, single palace guard in attendance, remaining three at home base.

She immediately pulled out the map they had generated of the target area and called the Boss, Indigo, Pete, the Israeli commando chief, and Tom over to her red webbing seat on the side of the giant C-17. Below them, just visible through the small window that sat perched on top of the massive wheel wells, the moonlight reflecting off the surface of the Mediterranean Sea sparkled and fled as if trying to beat the aircraft to landfall.

They were entering via Mersa Matruh in Egypt, with government permission, well above thirty thousand feet, using radar spoilers and electronic fog to keep their exact position and height a secret. When they hit Latitude 22.242207, Longitude 25.317264 in New Valley, at the end of the "Junior Empty Quarter", as it was ubiquitously known; they would turn due west, then once they were over their target, turn north, and eventually start their jumps, with the aircraft turning back to the east and the relative safety of the Egyptian border. The intended route was drawn on the map in blue ink, with time-between points listed.

There were only two copies of the map outside the cockpit, and the Boss had the other.

"People, the latest intel from the target has the main force now camped here," she said, pointing to the sector that had been cross-hatched onto the map, dividing the entire area up into squares with numbers. "One of the guards is with them, so we need to change our tactics." She let that hang in the air, letting her commanders think through the problem for themselves. Usually, going into combat, the Boss would have taken the lead, but on this occasion, he had nominated Jessica as mission commander and himself as the leader of a small section made up of two of Tom's troopers and a section of the Italian commandoes Indigo had provided.

"Comments?" The Boss looked around at the faces lit by the red lamp on the side of the aircraft, the dark black and grey shadows making it hard to see facial expressions. He let the silence run its course. What counted most now was that every commander could adjust their tactics to the new information, and then I could coordinate their input into a cohesive plan.

The Israeli Sgen Aluf was the first to break the silence.

"I would suggest that we now drop the automatic UAVs between the compound and the camp, move them slowly forward, but do not engage until they make the first move." I nodded my agreement, watching the Boss's face as closely as I could.

No reaction, tick one!

"I think we now jump in from three points, one at this end of the compound," Pete offered, pointing to the eastern extremity of the wing the women were thought to be occupying. "One on the side here"—he pointed to the southern side of the same wing, around mid-point—"and one in the center of the complex, as originally planned. I would suggest the captain, myself, and Agent Thomas enter at the endpoint, Tom and two of his team in the middle, and Indigo and two of his team in the center. The Boss, Indigo's remaining troop, the Israelis, and their colonel could then jump in behind the bivouac and push them towards the UAVs." The Boss held his hand out, palm down, to stop any further comment.

"Good plan, Pete. Could I suggest a small alteration?" He looked at the faces of his people, fully engaged in the conversation, possibly just thirty minutes away from certain death, and not for the first time marveled at the courage of every soldier he had even gone to war with. "Let the Israelis jump in behind the enemy camp. I will take the Italian troop in with me here," he said, pointing to a spot half-way between the compound and the drop point for the UAVs, "just as a backup in case any manage to get through." Every head nodded, seeing the logic of backing up the machines; after all, they were machines, and like all soldiers everywhere, they intuitively distrusted anything "automatic" and "machine," even though they used and abused them every day of their service lives.

"I would like to also change the time hacks." Every head turned towards me, creating the specter of helmeted and night vision-equipped green lenses surrounding inscrutable grey faces looking like monstrous insects about to attack. "My reasoning is that we don't need to attack the bivouac until we need to, and if we can get in and get the woman, then exfil to this point here, get collected by the 'van,' before we attack the mercenaries, we might have a cleaner mission all around." The "van" in this case was a silenced armored personal carrier that even as we were flying in was slowly creeping into the area via Egypt, and would sprint into the rendezvous point on command.

The big unknown was the fighting capacity of the Egyptian troops manning the "van," but as the soldier in change had been with the team at the cave at the base of the mountain, Pete had high hopes. He knew his captain would carry her own weight, and more, he suspected the newest member of their team, the lovely, bright "Just call me Sally," had performed well back at the barracks in the simulated attack, and he knew Tom and Indigo's troopers would more than cover their backs, but that initially left just the three of them to manage potentially as many as nine women on a dangerous extraction where the participants may not be willing. He had a thought and didn't hesitate to bring it out to the group.

"I've been thinking of the exfil, and I'd like to suggest Indigo doesn't hit the center of the target, as I just suggested, but the other side of the arm, opposite where Tom will breach. They can fight back if they have to, and if they don't have to, it gives us more force to concentrate on the women." The Boss nodded; he had a similar thought. Indigo looked intrigued, then saw the logic and smiled, and Tom just made a fist and punched it at the head of Interpol (Italy), who responded in kind and set off a chain of laughter as their gloved fists collided.

"Tom, *mi amigo, te olvidas de que te supero!*"

"You might outrank me, but I've got the prettiest face!"

"Yeah, that's for sure. Have you seen yourself in a mirror lately?" Pete's voice was husky, but his meaning was clear. Tom, with camouflage makeup all over his normally ugly face, looked scary enough to frighten little children. We all laughed; I took the lack of protest about my changing the time hacks as acceptance of the need to change them, worked them out, hand-printed them on the map, then held them up for all to see.

"Agreed?" Every head nodded in sequence, so I folded the map and stuffed it in my pants pocket. The Boss pulled his copy out, and shredded it into a burn bag, then handed the bag to the loadmaster who had been hovering during our briefing. She had her face shield down and a full-face oxygen mask in place, so the only giveaway as to her gender was a wisp of long, blond hair that ran out from the back of her helmet. She had a big role to play; she had to get three very large armored vehicles out the back while managing our HALO jumps from the side doors, all timed to the second. Did I mention that once she dropped the rear door, the inside temperature would drop to minus thirty-five degrees in a heartbeat?

It was why we were dressed in heavy padded over suits, thick gloves, full face masks, and balaclavas and carried small oxygen bottles strapped to our hips. We looked like moon people, waddled like pregnant ducks, and the moment we hit the ground, we would have to shed around eighty pounds of equipment just to be able to move. The one good thing is that with the changed drop plan, we would use both sides of the aircraft simultaneously to drop from, and the rear door wouldn't be a factor for us.

Unless she opened it in preparation, just to be ornery.

And with that happy thought, I waved the troops back to their seats to get what little rest I could before freezing my butt off and jumping out of a perfectly intact, fully operational airplane.

The next thing I knew, the jumpmaster, disguised as a Martian, was belting me on my shoulder, making all sorts of hand gestures in my face. Luckily, I spoke mad jumpmaster, so I slipped my oxygen mask on, fitted the straps, pulled them as tight as I could, reached around and turned the oxygen on, then held up my thumb in the universal language of "okay." She didn't trust me, reaching around my shoulder to check for herself. Then I got her thumb up in my face, and she moved on to her next victim.

Pete was already standing by the door, Sandra crushed into his side by Tom and his troop, which in turn were being crushed by Indigo and his team. The Israelis would go out last, so they and the Boss and his team of Italian commandos were lined up on the opposite side of the aircraft, ready to jump. Above them, a big domed light radiated red and started flickering yellow; the door slid open, and all the air in the cargo compartment rushed out like a mini-tornado; our door slid open, the light flicked green, and without thinking about it, we all went into the dark of the night.

Assume the open body falling position, stabilize, check the GPS on my wrist for positioning, and look for the tell-tale red pulsing lights of my companions, which showed up as green blinks in my night-vision gear. I counted eight lights, all good, but I felt my hands, exposed pieces of my face, and feet start to snap and freeze, just like we had been warned, but falling as we were in the spread body position, we were traveling down towards the black ink of the desert floor at or near our terminal velocity, around one hundred and twenty miles per hour, so the faster we got lower, the warmer we would get. And with luck, no one would know we were on the way.

Freefalling was one of the few things I actually enjoyed about parachuting, the relative silence, the illusion of freedom, of flying, the world spread out below you like a giant three-dimensional map. But at night, relatively moonless, and over the desert, the only sensation apart from the chilling wind as it streamed past was a sense of having jumped into a big, very black hole, one with no frame of reference to judge movement, or how close to the ground we were, and even the little blinking green lights provided little spatial reference, distorted as they were by the night vision goggles.

My automated drogue chute deployed, helping to both stabilize me and slow me down a fraction. My wrist unit said three thousand feet, and just in front of me, six small black chutes popped out in sympathy, and I started to breathe a little easier, but there was still no ground reference available, so we were well off course unless there were no lights on in the compound.

One thousand feet and my main steerable chute streamed out, jerking me to a sudden stop, still no visual reference. Then as I completed my first circuit, out of the dark, the silhouette of the arm of the compound emerged, gaining in detail the closer I swung to it. Good reference now, pull on the guide riders, stop my circling from getting a straight-in approach, and then as light as a feather, my feet touched the sand. I ran a little, slowly stopping, punching my chute harness off, then kneeling to take a good look around. One black body to my left, one to my right, little green blobs on their heads, all good, time to get to work.

We straightened at the same time, creating the impression we were joined at the hips, but that was just training. We hit the side of the building, and while Sandra used her handheld thermite lance to create a doorway, Pete guarded our backs, then with a deadened "thump," a hole appeared in the building, and in less time than it took to think about it, all three of us were inside, flat on our stomachs, scanning for hostiles.

Nothing.

The only light was the reflections off the doorframes and windowsills and a faint hint of more down the corridor. We moved forward slowly and could clearly see the rooms to the right, and up ahead some fifty meters, the dull light fighting its way out of a large glass wall, which must have been tinted because the light came in waves as if it was underwater. Just as I started to crawl again, a flashing green blob caught my attention as it emerged from the wall on our left, about as far away from the light source as we were.

Tom and his team.

Then just a fraction further away again, another flashing green blob. Indigo and his team.

Good, now we can get on with it. We rose slowly, keeping our focus on the wavy light, and I clicked my comms button twice, telling Indigo to hold, then once, telling Tom to move forward. His group of blinking green blobs moved across the corridor, then aligned themselves so that we could see the three helmet lights individually. I clicked again, telling them to hold. Sandra opened the first door; I looked in and saw a body in a nice bed and comfortable surroundings. I tapped Sandra on the boot; she crawled in, and then I heard the unmistakable sound of a dart being fired.

Silence.

We moved to the next door and repeated the performance. Still silence.

We repeated the process four more times, by which time we had reached the very edge of the waving light. I removed my NVGs, stole a look around the corner of the wall, and saw an oldish woman bent over a keyboard, her silver hair tied up in a bun by a yellow ribbon, her pretty dress hiding the chair she was sitting on. I couldn't guess her age, but she presented as older rather than younger. Was this the elusive "Helen"? The room was partitioned by computer boxes, in stacks of three, rows of three, and from my time with our geeks, I recognized the fact that the computers were all air-gapped. Luckily, the Boss had the forethought to consider the hardware side of this operation, so we were equipped to strip them down and take them with us.

I clicked three times, and the green blobs disappeared, and three bulky figures rose up in synchronization with us and approached the door as silently as we did.

I motioned Sandra and her air gun forward; she paused at the door. Tom reached one side and suddenly swung it open, and like a wraith, Sandra slid in, went down on her knees, and fired her dart all in one smooth motion, then stood and fired again. I followed her in, checked the pulse of the woman, nodded to Sandra, then turned to face Tom. I hand signaled towards the rooms we had previously visited, rolled my fingers over, and he and his men disappeared as quickly as they had arrived, to move the bodies out of the building.

The darts—a beautiful way to take an enemy down—fast, silent, and a guaranteed three hours out, or maybe a heart attack if they were weak to start with, made for quiet attacks and high levels of confidence. I did my hand-rolling thing to Sandra; she nodded, cuffed the old woman's hands behind her back, threw her over her shoulder as if she weighed nothing, waited a few seconds while I photographed the woman's face, then moved off to follow Tom and his men. I heard one click followed by a fast double, pointed to Pete, and we both raced outside straight into a burst of automatic fire. Pete went down; I felt my left shoulder explode with pain, and I followed him to the floor. The next sound I heard was three sets of automatic fire, tight, controlled bursts, coming from where Indigo and his team were hugging the floor. A massive flash filled the corridor, then silence, except my ears were ringing so badly from the gunfire I couldn't be sure. Someone moved towards me, and as I pulled my gun up, I recognized one of Indigo's troops. She slid over to Pete, who had rolled onto his back, and also had his gun up, ready to shoot.

"Captain, we have cleared the corridor, five people. They shot over our heads at you because I think they did not see us at first. The colonel is checking, but they are accounted for. Can you get up?" I had lost the use of my left arm completely; it felt like it was on fire, but the rest of me seemed to be in one piece. Instead of answering, I pulled my knees up, then slowly stood. Just as I managed to get mostly erect, she slid a compression bandage on my shoulder, and I nearly fell down with the sudden pain.

"Jesus, Captain, you're bleeding all over me!" Pete's voice was not a whisper, was not really more than just a hint of a voice, but I heard the humor in it and was reassured. He would live. Then I heard the dreaded words over my radio I had hoped to not hear on this mission.

"Contact front!"

The Israelis were in action, hopefully pushing the mercenaries toward the UAVs and their impressive firepower.

It was the longest three and half minutes I think I had ever experienced, full of the unmistakable sounds of automatic gunfire; then another voice came through my headset, this one I recognized.

"All good, most tangos down, UAVs intact, team four moving to you, minor injuries, we'll be a little behind them, just cleaning up."

"Indigo, watch our backs. Friendly incoming may or may not be clear."

Three clicks. My ears still rang, but I could hear the silence over them. I looked up and down the corridor, made a snap decision, and moved toward the far end from where the aggressive gunfire had come from. Passed Indigo and his team, and kept walking, only to have Sandra suddenly appear next to me. She simply held up her thumb, and we moved forward together, me holding my left arm flat against my side, still hurting like a bitch, my right locking the short-barrelled weapon into my side, still able to cover both sides of the corridor.

We reached the middle, walked over four bodies, all torn by high caliber bullets, blood staining the floor, and I noticed three of them were dressed in black burkas, the fourth jeans, and a blood-stained T-shirt. It might be the fabled ex-Stasi bodyguards. The room was an oval shape, with what looked like slate or marble floors, with a massive chandelier hanging from the roof. A pair of old, scarred leather lounges and a single royal blue TV chair formed a conversation circle, and a decanter of amber liquid stood on a small table with one cut crystal glass.

I'm sure there was a story there, but I didn't have time for it, but the overall feeling was that this place was sterile—no personal touches, no emotional attachment, and, as we had seen in the individual rooms, the women slept in, no sense of gender or attachment.

The silence shattered as the Israelis ran into the room from the side, six carrying three, with blood and guts dripping off the wounded quite freely. I held my hand up.

"Stop. Tend to your wounded. Now." The man in front, a sergeant by his chevrons pasted to the center of his combat vest, looked at me as if I was speaking in tongues, noticed that my weapon was pointed at his center of mass, then all the fire went out of him, and he shouted instructions in Hebrew; the wounded were lowered, and I noticed one of the wounded was the Israeli colonel. Unconscious, bleeding from a least three wounds, two in the legs, one in the upper chest, just above the line of his combat vest. Massive loss of blood might not make it.

"Sandra, the Boss is still somewhere out there. The UAVs have not self-destructed, ahhhhhhh..." was all I managed before the sound of gunfire rippled through the room. The Israelis who were not wounded immediately took up a guard position around their fellow soldiers, Sandra went on alert like a wolfhound pointing at a fox, and I was tempted to turn, but I knew the Boss, and he would have warned me if we were to be penetrated.

"Stand down. That's just team five cleaning up." Three massage explosions ripped through the air, and the roof literally shook, the little lights making up the chandelier bouncing around and making tinkling sounds as they crashed together, some shedding themselves in anger and sprinkling us with tiny shards of colored glass. I looked down until the shower had stopped. Sandra, her head also turned down, shards of glass glittering as they ran off her helmet like a small waterfall and just as pretty, looked at me from under her eyelashes, mouthed "UAVs." I nodded, thinking about what to do next.

I wanted all the computers and their hard drives. I had the women. I think I had the terrorists and the guards. Was it worth the time to search through the rest of the compound to see if we had missed anything? I looked at the young, smiling face of Sandra, tried to imagine how I had felt on an operation at her age, and shook my head in frustration.

Be real. Stay in the now. I called Indigo to me. He arrived in double-quick time. "Indigo, go mine all the compound, leave the arm we came in last, use thermite and phosphor, and pay special attention to the computer lab once we have cleared it out. Sandra and I will check out this other arm for anything of interest."

"*Ciertamente, mi capitán, estás herido, ¿puedo hacer algo por ti?*" I smiled at his offer.

"Thanks, but unless you've got one of your espresso machines handy, I'll wait until we get home." He laughed, patted me on my good shoulder, concern filling his eyes, bobbed his head, and ran off with his men to mine the compound. Sandra and I walked through the carnage, broken glass now mixed with body parts and blood, moved into the long, dark arm, and were quickly outside a large room with the door closed. She kicked it in with a smooth, fast ninja move, and I poked my weapon in and scanned the room, my tactical light cutting through the gloom.

Empty, but obviously the bedroom of one of the bosses. Had a slight sense of female about it, some makeup scattered on a small side table set in front of a long mirror. Again, nothing personal to shout about, no pictures, no flowers, no hint of the person to whom it had belonged. But a battered, thick leather book sat on the table, partially hidden by a blue scarf. I picked it up, opened it up to a random page, and couldn't help myself.

"Sandra or Sally, if you'd prefer, we just hit the mother lode." My grin was large and evil, and if it wasn't for the intense pain running down my left arm, I'd be really happy about finding the journal of our head terrorist—"Helen"—neatly annotated page after page in stylish handwriting, all in German. And the first page was dated November 15, 1996! I handed the journal to Sandra, who tucked it into the side of her combat vest. I was feeling dizzy, entirely not my usual self, probably from the blood loss from my wound, which was really starting to arc up and hurt like a bastard. One of Indigo's troops ran by, pulling a small sled packed to the roof with explosives. I got the message.

Time to go.

We'd been airborne ten minutes before the Boss got around to where I was sitting, opposite our prisoners securely strapped into their webbing seats, Tom at one end, Sandra at the other, neither taking their eyes off the women for a second, in spite of the entire row still being unconscious. Our wounded were all wrapped up, bandaged, and, where necessary, as in the case of the Israeli colonel, being treated continuously by the airborne medics. The Boss's team had escaped any injuries, and after looking at my shoulder, the medic had declared a "through and through, shoulder's busted up a bit, we'll fix it on the ground," which just left me onehanded, pissed, and seriously in pain. I had refused any meds; they made my mind go to mush, and I wanted to keep what was left of my faculties until we were safely back on the ground.

Pete was my main concern; he had been badly injured, taking at least three bullets, and was now lying at my feet on a stretcher in an induced coma, tubes running out from all over him, and bottles of plasma and blood hitched to little racks that shot up from his stretcher like bony arms on a scarecrow. A medic was taking his vital signs every five minutes, and I could tell from the look on her face he wasn't improving but probably wasn't getting any worse. The mood was a little grim, the usual post-fight adrenaline rush moderated by the number and severity of our wounded. And then, to my absolute delight, a miracle happened.

"*Discúlpame capitán, ¿te importaría un espresso?*" And to my utter astonishment, Indigo leaned over the inert form of Pete and handed me a mug carrying the crest of the Israeli Mobility Command, threatening to overflow from the turbulence throwing the aircraft around, full of steaming coffee!

"*Coronel, voy a llorar a tus pies, tener a tus bebés,* ¡debes *casarte conmigo!*"

"He's already spoken for, Jessica, just settle for the coffee." The Boss sat down next to me, holding his own mug.

"*Gracias, Indigo, esto significa más de lo que alguna vez te darás cuenta. Apreciado.*"

He beamed at me, and not for the first time, I marveled that this smallish, rarely serious soldier who ran Interpol in Italy to perfection always made time to look after us. As the coffee went down, my brain started to work again, and I mentally thanked the Lord, whoever she may be, for God's gift of caffeine.

"Jessica, if you're up for it, I can brief you on the firefight." The Boss gave me a searching look and drank his coffee, probably in fear that I'd rip his mug off him and drink it myself. I sipped my own, closed my eyes to better enjoy the experience, and nodded.

"The Israelis were in position around one hundred meters behind the mercenaries. We set up a hundred meters from the compound; the UAVs were fifty meters in front of us. The bivouac was set up in two sections, a collection of hootchies and a small tent to one side. We believe that's where the guard was before the firefight broke out." I nodded, keeping my primary focus on the coffee, building a picture of the battlefield in my mind's eye. In effect, we had the terrorists in a pincer movement, and if you discounted the possibility of being shot by your own side because you were facing each other, albeit three or four hundred meters apart, it was a classic formation successfully used for hundreds of years to take out an enemy.

"A mercenary walked out of the camp, stopped a few meters from the Israelis, and emptied his bladder. He must have sensed something because he zipped up, turned around, unhooked his Kalashnikov from his chest, then fell to the ground and started shooting. Details are sketchy after that, except the Israelis pushed the surviving mercenaries back toward the UAVs; they sensed the targets and opened fire. The Israelis had all gone to ground, and just as well as only three mercs managed to reach our line, where we put them down with little fuss. Just as we were doing that, the UAVs self-destructed."

"Yeah, we felt that inside; how many mercs do you think were involved?"

"The Israelis counted thirty-five bodies. We shot three, but that might be a little bloated given the damage the UAVs did."

"We got three of her guards and an unidentified KIA; did you or the Israelis get a guard in their count?"

"Yes, he was in a black combat outfit. He led the charge on us. I accounted for him personally." I nodded again. That tally given one or two roughly lined up with the intelligence Arie had given us. I just hoped that his inside man had gotten out before we blew up the compound. For that matter, I hoped that any innocents who were there had gotten out, but I couldn't worry about that. We had "Helen," and we had her cohorts; we didn't know what role each had played and may never know unless it was in her journal. I sat and thought for a moment, let all the buzz die down, started circular breathing to lower my heart rate, and put myself into a relaxed posture, but—buggar it!—my shoulder cut through my calm, reminding me it needed tending, so I settled for the middle ground of slightly calm and seriously hurting.

"Did you get a list of the electronics?"

"Yes. Three burst transmitters. That will link them to the American cell, all their computers, and all their communications equipment. When we get back, we'll give the comms gear to Luigi and let him see if he can catch any strays."

"So we have enough proof to put them before the World Court?" He gave me a quizzical look, probably wondering why I had gone all lawyer on him.

"Yes. Unquestionably. Why?"

"I promised General Saunders I would report when we had a satisfactory outcome. I don't expect the Americans to worry much about 'Helen' and her crew, but I do want them to know we did our job from start to finish." He nodded, took my mug from my one working hand, and passed it to a crewmember who was walking the floor cleaning up the debris before we landed. The floor was littered with bloody swabs, sodden bandages and a lot of stuff I didn't want to know about. I looked over at Sandra, caught her eye, and smiled; she returned it, then went back to staring at the women.

I had a sudden thought. Pulled my mini out and dialed up Anna. She listened while I outlined a partially formed plan; she filled in some gaps, but we were essentially on the same page, so I closed the lid and went back to my musings.

The crewman held up five fingers, then pointed down, so I shut out everything but the roar of the engines overlayed with the rattling sounds of the airframe from the turbulence, closed my eyes, and pretended to sleep.

The next thing I knew was being shaken awake by the Boss, looking across an empty cargo hold, then out the open rear door at the streaming rain, slanting sideways from the wind.

"Pete?"

"Moved to the base hospital with the other wounded. The Sgen Aluf didn't make it. Sandra and Tom took the women, and they were transferred to our holding facility. They were starting to regain consciousness, but Tom and Indigo spread their people around one-on-one, so there were no problems there. Arie is waiting to see us if you feel up to it." I imagined I looked like a wreck. My shoulder was a constant throb and scream, but I had nothing better to do, so I nodded, stood a little unsteadily, and walked out of the plane, into the rain, and then into a Humvee, wishing my miracle worker, Indigo, could find a coffee for me before I fell over.

The ride was mercifully short, and I stumbled out back into the rain, stood unbalanced, leaned against the side of the vehicle, turned my face up to the rain, and let it cool me for a moment.

"Sir, we are ready for you." The young face of the staff sergeant dressed in ironed camos stood at attention, saluting me, so I had no choice but to nod in recognition of his courtesy and walk into the building. The whole time the Boss had stood patiently just slightly behind, hadn't grabbed my arm to steady me, done nothing to ease my way in or out of the Humvee, hadn't said a word. Just silently supported me in making my own way in my own time. And you wonder why I loved the man, unrequited as it may be.

We reached Arie's anteroom. I sat down on the first available seat and had a mug of steaming coffee placed in front of me by my favorite Italian.

"*Gracias*, Indigo, *apreciado*." The Boss sat on my left, Tom took the next seat, Indigo the one on the right, the Israeli sergeant on his right, and to my surprise, Sandra took the remaining place. Then I remembered we had entrusted the prisoners to her, and it made sense.

"The wounded are being treated, and your master chief is recovering, but it will be a while before he is ready to fight again and the prisoners are secured.

"Jessica, you need medical attention, and I expect you to get it the moment this briefing is concluded." Aire had a firm tone in his voice that hinted at unassailable authority, so I just nodded and hoped my head didn't fall off. I liked him better in his kindly grandfather mode.

"Here are the aerial views are taken ten minutes ago." We all turned to look at the big screen where the feature was a massive burnt-out area of desert roughly in the shape of the compound. The sand had turned to uneven dirty patches of muddy brown glass in several places, a testament to the effectiveness of the thermite bombs. I felt a small measure of pride in this vision of destruction, and I pointed to Indigo.

"Well done, Indigo, good job." He just beamed at me while he opened his arms to say, "who? me?" and looked really, really happy. Maybe this would help him recover a little from the wanton destruction of his beloved church. I turned back to Arie.

"Did your man get out?" He nodded.

"Yes, thank you. Well clear with the rest of the kitchen staff. I expect they will all be employed again in the next few days. Now, I need the details on how our men got wounded and a decision on what we say and to whom we say it." Bloody politics again, I couldn't live without them, sure couldn't live with them, but this time I had a vote on what we said and to whom, and I had a lovely idea in mind I had yet to explore with the Boss. I looked around and then at him; he just gave me his blankest "who are you again?" stare, and if I had the energy, I would have punched him. So I just took control of the room and knew he would support me even if I got it wrong.

"Arie, the Americans have made a big deal about the taking down of the mercenary terrorists; they do not want any hint of the women's involvement, and I think that suits us very well. The report should state that we had support from the Libyans and that this was a deeply embedded mercenary cell left over from the earlier attacks. We keep the women under wraps, we interrogate them for whatever we can get, and I want another run at Mohammad bin Azaria once we have identified everyone and their roles. Did you set a trap for the Innomatchi CEO?" The image on the big screen started to revolve slowly as the drone or aircraft turned to keep the epicenter of the destruction in the frame. Looking at it made me dizzy, so I looked down at the desktop and noticed my hand was visibly shaking. I remember pulling it down onto my lap, then nothing.

Chapter 49

I came to in a hospital bed, the ubiquitous metal-framed sides up, beeping machines, a strong smell of antiseptic, blue-white lights, far too bright, and a sense of having been removed from my body. I floated around the ceiling of the room, looking for some way back, when a military nurse walked in, looked up at me, smiled, then waved me down. The bastards had tranquilized me, something that always made me feel vague and discombobulated. I started to sit up but couldn't; then the smiling face of a medic was in mine, pulling my head up slightly and moving something behind my head. I had no pain, and I quickly looked to my left to see if they had cut off my arm, only to see a massive pressure bandage that had my whole arm strapped down and then folded at the elbow, where I eventually found my hand, hooked up to some finger-gripping device.

"What did you do to me?" I croaked, not sounding like I remembered.

"You had a smashed shoulder as well as a bullet wound. We put it all back together as it was meant, patched you up, and here you are." Evil man, full of smiles and calm. I hated him on principle. But I had no pain.

"Can you turn the meds down?" He looked at me with mild concern, seemed to consider my request, then walked around the bed and fiddled with a hanging bottle of something, looking at me the whole time.

"I was warned you would want that. Something about your reaction to pain killers?"

"I just don't like them. Now, if you please, find my boss." A little more command in my voice, and I was starting to feel my shoulder, and that was a good sign. He smiled at me. Boy, would he pay for that when I got out, then left the room.

The Boss sauntered in, as casual as you like, obviously enjoying the sight of his number two tied to a bed being fed drugs! He was dressed in casual khakis, neatly pressed, his beloved Sig-Saur hanging in a shoulder rig. Apart from his scarred face, which was normal, he looked fit, rested, and a little perky. I hated him on principle. Then before I could get myself worked up to insult him, Indigo bounced in, all smiles, and with a huge mug in his hands, so I closed my eyes, shut out the vision of the Boss, and let the delicious smell of coffee wash over me.

"I meant what I said on the plane, Indigo. Marry me, have babies with me, tell your wife I'm prepared to share." He just laughed, pulled a metal table on squeaky wheels over, and sat the mug on it. He then pulled a small yellow flower out from behind his back like a magician, pulled a glass that was waiting for my attention over, and plopped it into it. My mind ripped me back a few years, to the time I had first met Indigo when he had presented me with a small possie.

They had been little yellow flowers as well.

I fought back the tears, tried to regain my posture as a hard-arse member of Section Five, nearly made it, and finally gave in and drank the coffee. Nothing had ever tasted better. I looked at the Boss, who had pulled up a chair and was now sitting backward on it. Indigo had produced another mug, which the Boss was quietly demolishing.

"While you were lying around in bed, we've had a little bit of action." His face gave nothing away, but I could tell from his body language he was wrapped up very tight about whatever it was that had happened.

"An attempt to get the CEO out?"

"No. An attempt on her life. Not just hers but the entire group of women. Six ninjas, all with top-level clearance, entered the secured area and blasted their way along the cells, killing everyone in them, then shot out the cameras and tried to escape in an armored vehicle." Obviously, our prisoners were still alive, so I wondered who had been killed in their place. I was about to ask when Indigo leaned over and refilled my mug from a little silver jug he had by his side.

"Captain, these ninjas were carrying perfect identification showing them to be members of Commando 233, all women, all Arabs, and while we are now checking their backgrounds in detail as far as we can, we believe they were smuggled across the border some months ago and embedded. Arie is very concerned, and not just for the obvious reasons." I bet this was first direct action on the ground by the women that we knew of, the command had to have come from somewhere, and the real immediate threat was how many more there were and what were they planning next? And were these women just another version of the mercenary terrorists the Devil had put together?

"Did we ever get the number of women taken out of the camps up until eight years ago?"

"Estimate only. We think thirty or forty in the first tranche, then possibly as many as a hundred in the second. If we go by age, Amira's class, as we'll call it, accounted for the main players now in their thirties. They were the major actors in the attacks and setting up of the plants. The engineer, scientist, pilot, CEO, and COO. The gamers are only in their early twenties, so let's call them 'class three.' We only have a handful of them, six coming in the last batch from the compound, plus the two we swept up at Innomatchi and in New Zealand and the two we took in Helena."

"You have two elderly women from the compound?"

"Yes."

"So you're saying that there could be as many as a hundred women still out there, possibly just waiting to be activated."

"It's possible, yes," the Boss said, holding his mug out to Indigo for a refill. "Where did the orders and the plans for the attack eventuate?"

"We have no idea at this point. Maybe we'll find something in the electronics we took from the compound, but the really worrying aspect of this is that they wanted to eliminate the prisoners, not release them."

"Huh!" I thought about that. We took Mohammad bin Azaria and his accountant down more than three weeks ago, and they had been isolated since then. And the attack on the FBI in Helena, which had only occurred in the last ten days. So maybe someone was hijacking the master plan for their own ends and had a far deadlier view of the world than their predecessors. But the question remained, why kill the women? What did they know or could tell us that was so important?

"Have we been able to identify 'Helen'?"

"Yes. I spoke to Black Bear, my counterpart in Russia, and his records go back eighty years, they are paper, not affected by the technology hacks, and her photo came up circa the mid-seventies, East German Stasi originally, then recruited into the KGB, went to USA Town in Ukraine, graduated, then went into the air, setting up networks of sleepers in the EU and the USA. Disappeared off the Russian's radar scope in the late nineteen nineties. I've asked for her full file and those of her known associates, but whether or not we get that is a moot point."

"Any early indication of what the women were doing in the tech lab?"

"Yes. Very early, but it seems they were jacking into government databases in the UK, USA, and EU creating passports, licenses, and other documents for refugees. We have confirmation of that from Malcolm; his team is tracking hacks from different locations, or were until the raid." I wasn't feeling much better, but at least I still felt that I was connected to the case, and I let this latest information rattle around with all the other data I had accumulated. A stray thought tugged at the back of my mind.

"Fay's team reported that Point Roberts had depots all along the coast, ready to receive the power plants. Is it possible that the missing women are part of that story?"

"Yes. The FBI is following the first delivery, some two thousand power packs, which are being distributed now. They are identifying everyone they come across. The data is being accumulated back in Seattle; we can pull a report anytime you need one."

"What I need now is to get out of here and start chatting to Helen—What did you say her name was?"

"I didn't." The Boss had his "don't fuck with me" face on, his totality unmistakable in its dripping negativity. "And as for you getting out over my dead body."

"Okay, Indigo, shoot the colonel, please, or give me your gun so I can."

Indigo just laughed, and the Boss scowled, but I could move, think, talk, and I had no doubt with Pete on the injured list, someone would be allocated to me as a bodyguard, or shadow, call it what you will; that was just what the Boss did.

"Her name?"

"Natasha Trotsky.

"How old?"

"According to her records, which, as you can imagine, have been seriously redacted, she was born in Gorky, now known as Nizhny Novgorod, USSR, in January of 1946, the bleeding edge of the Baby Boomers. Went into the army at sixteen, went straight to East Germany, did her Stasi bit, was very good at her job from all reports, then went back home to learn how to be an American. We can only hypothesize that she linked up with Mohammad bin Azaria sometime in the mid-nineties.

There is no record of the meeting, and for that matter, there is no record of her after that period."

"Someone deleted her from the records. So that's how they got into the IT systems. They already had people embedded before the Y2K debacle. It also explains how the weapons were taken in 2002 and 2006; probably no actual plan at that time, but they were acquisitions of opportunity. Mohammad bin Azaria provided the money, and the high-level strategic vision, created the mantra about the refugee children, and Trotsky provided the field muscle, using her embedded agents. I wonder why he wound the girls into the plot?"

"*Mi capitán, toda revolución requiere una causa, los niños pequeños arrojados a los campamentos es una imagen muy emotiva y poderosa desde la que lanzar su revolución.*"

I looked at Indigo; he was right. You did need powerful symbols to start a revolution, and what better one than little children refugees? I began to wonder if they were just a symbol or if he did have a strong belief in what he had done—was still doing if the Point Roberts story held water.

"Okay, Boss, back to get me out of here. Can you arrange it, please? I need to have a chat with a few dedicated women terrorists." He gave me a really hard look, seemed to lose an internal battle, and gave a weary sigh.

"I'll get you out on three conditions. You listen to the doctors as to how much you can and can't do. You take whatever meds they prescribe without a fight. And the moment you need a rest, you let us know and back off."

"Agreed two out of the three. You know I hate the meds."

"Yes, we all know, but you have a shattered shoulder just put back together. You lost a lot of blood by stalling the medics as long as you did. Be reasonable." My shoulders slumped in defeat. I hated when he was reasonable. How could you fight that?

"I want to see Pete." He nodded, pulled the side of my bed down, then stood back.

"And if I have one of those hospital gowns with the split up the arse, I'll kill you both." Indigo offered me a lightweight coat, which I half got on, only to have the Boss pull the other half around my shattered shoulder. He pushed the drip around the bed on its trolly, and then the three of us managed to escape the room before any medic could stop us.

It took nearly four hours, but I had seen Pete, inert and in an induced coma, checked on the other wounded, got rid of the trolley and its plastic bag of crap, managed a shower with a plastic wrap covering my bandages, got dressed with the help of Sandra, who was now my shadow according to her, and to prove the point, she snapped a lightweight holster on my hip with a lovely modern Glock 17 in it. She slipped a double magazine pouch on my right side, opposite my restrained arm, but I could get a mag out with my hand with a bit of practice. My entire left arm was strapped to my body down to the elbow, but I could articulate my arm and use my hand somewhat awkwardly.

She slipped my credentials into my belt, no doubt sure the accessories would be noticed by our prisoners. What made me feel really good about her is that she never said a word about my injury, my state, my wan pallor, or the tiredness that flowed out of me like an early morning mist in the forest.

Finally, she draped my suit coat over my shoulders, adding a touch of elegance I normally lacked. As it was my one Armani suit, this was the best I was ever going to look.

"Let's go kick some terrorist butt." She simply nodded, pulled her own weapons around, so they were covered by her jacket, did a quick sweep of the corridor, then led me out. We were in the inter-rogation area before anyone took much notice of us, for which I was extremely grateful. Just the short walk was tiring me out; I had to get my balance back before I faced a terrorist or two. I ran through the list in my mind and decided to stay with my original thoughts, Trotsky first, followed by Mohammad bin Azaria for our big reveal.

What did we need to know? We had all the evidence needed for the World Court; we now knew what was intended for Helena, Dargaville, and Roanoke; we had a fair idea about the plans for Canada, Greenland, Chile, Portugal, Ireland, Denmark, Norway, Finland, Estonia, Sri Lanka, Solomon Islands, and Japan; but to be honest, they were no longer our responsibility.

We would turn everything we knew over to the various govern-ments and let them decide what to do about the planned refugee migra-tion. I needed to talk to the US president before we did that; it was more than just a matter of courtesy. The US had supported us at every step, hadn't interfered, which must have been brutal for the general, and had lent us some excellent people in the process, one of whom I intended to steal. I couldn't have the excellent Anna, her boss would never let her go, but I could have the next best thing—Fay Remer, ace FBI SSA, currently in Helena, keeping us informed of the progress.

The one thing I did know was I needed to chew the whole ball game over with Arie and the Boss. Indigo would give me his perspec-tive from the Italian government's point of view. We could lay it out for the Americans; the Israelis were well and truly in the loop. All we needed was a signoff at some point because the way I was starting to see it was we had fulfilled our original mission—identify and shut down the terrorists who had launched the attacks that had crippled the world. What I was looking for was any sign of a follow-up plan for further attacks, more hidden cells of terrorists like the ninjas who had attacked the prison cells and who had given the orders to the mercenaries to attack the FBI in Helena and the prisoners in Israel.

I walked into the room, selected my seat, arranged my left hand so it rested on the tabletop, had an open portfolio as my prop, and, thanks to somebody who knew my weakness, a steaming cup of coffee. Sandra stood at my shoulder, scanned the room, then took the seat next to me. The guards brought Trotsky in, dressed in a dark blue overall, dreadful cut, no style whatsoever, her hair was matted and unruly, and with no makeup, her face looked washed-out, drawn, and old. I guessed mid-seventies, and that would match the data we had on her.

The look she gave was not one of defeat, or even that of a guilty person, more a partially interested, marginally engaged spectator sitting on the sidelines, waiting for a clue as to what was going on.

"Natasha Trotsky, my name is Captain Riley. This is Agent Thomas. We are with Interpol, and you are charged under the Terrorist Laws as modified in 2022 of aiding and abetting, planning, and executing plans and acts of a terrorist nature, the specifics of which will be given to you prior to your trial. Do you understand the charges against you?" Now she looked more engaged as the hammer dropped for her because she had been brought to the cells unconscious, stripped, dressed, isolated, and we were the very first people to talk to her. Her last waking memory was probably working at her computer in the lab in the compound. Now she was here, facing us and charged with the most heinous crimes imaginable.

"Captain, I have no idea about anything you just said. As a registered diplomat of the Libyan government, I immediately request an embassy representative, and I will not speak again until one is provided." Now the look she gave us was a stubborn, fuck-you-and-all-like-you one, and she relaxed back as far as her chains allowed. I smiled. This was going to be fun. I tapped Sandra on the shoulder, picked up my coffee, and enjoyed a long taste while she laid it out for us.

"Ms. Trotsky, your diplomatic status has been revoked and wouldn't matter in any case. You are charged with planning and executing attacks on the Vatican, the Dome of the Rock, the Grand Mosque, Westpoint, and oil, gas, and coal sites too numerous to mention. We will also throw in the destruction of several sports stadia, as well as the International Space Station, the destruction of Lloyd's of London data centers, and the Internet. Those last two changes may sound minor to you, but trust us, to the world in general, just that last one would have you hung, drawn, and quartered in any country you care to name." She closed the folder and linked her hands on top of it as if putting a final stamp on the entire tragic liturgy of death and destruction.

"And we have your journal, and we have copies of all your transmissions for the last five years or so, linking you irrevocably to the terrorists in the United States, Europe and the mercenaries you employed to do your dirty work worldwide."

"The French were initially happy you didn't crash their weather satellites right up to the time we showed them that you were using them to bounce your burst transmissions. Funny thing, no one knew it, but those satellites store everything on a hard drive and send the data to an earth station every forty-eight hours, and the French literally tripped over themselves to provide us copies of everything you ever said for as far back as they have the data."

"Which is a really long, long time. Helen." Now she just looked furious, her emotions getting the better of her. She looked from me to Sandra and back as if seeking something, staring so hard that under any other circumstances, I might have been intimidated.

"So, as I was saying, you will be taken before the World Court, tried in-camera, then thrown down the deepest hole we can find. Anything you would like to say?" And I smiled at her, gave it all I had to make my point. It must have looked wrong because Sandra turned to look at me with a curious look on her face.

"Haven't seen you so happy in weeks," she said, smiling herself.

"It was the thought of the hole that did it for me. Deep, dark, featureless, made of concrete, no daylight, ever, fed through a slot, shit, and piss in a stainless-steel toilet bolted to the floor. It should be a fun experience. For as long as she lives." If I sounded cruel, imagine your feelings facing the mastermind of the greatest terrorist attacks ever seen on the planet, ones that so disrupted life that the whole world was thrown back fifty years in terms of resources and technology. Millions were killed needlessly, anarchy and chaos the new "normal," and families displaced so fast that no one had yet managed to catch up with it all, nearly six weeks after the first bomb had been dropped on the Vatican.

"What do you want to know, and what can you give me in exchange?" Helen asked, her voice pitched just above a whisper and in perfect English. I had expected extreme language and insults but not a plea for clemency. What could I give in reality? Actually, quite a lot, right up until court time.

"What is it you think you have to bargain with, and what do you expect in return? We have all the evidence, we have all your women, we have all your manufacturing plants, key staff, and everything produced in the last three years, and we've had Mohammad bin Azaria and his bookkeeper in chains for nearly a month." I let the question sit, interested in what she responded with. I didn't know her trigger point; she had been trained by the best security, intelligence, and terrorist masters on the planet, the Stasi and the KGB, and she had survived them both to take up her role with Mohammad bin Azaria.

And then she had worked that role for at least thirty years in partnership, undetected, in every major country in the world while building up the most successful network of terrorists ever to blight the earth. Looking at her, I saw an old woman, not particularly pretty, not really ugly, but somewhere in between. The clothing she had been arrested in was colorful but not particularly stylish, a little old-fashioned, in fact. Maybe that was it. She was who and what she looked like, with no pretense, no false face. I wondered where the women sat with her and whether or not they were as important to her as to her master.

"You say you have all the evidence, but do you really? Do you have any idea of our reach, things, and people you have yet to uncover? Do you have any idea of how entrenched we are in your systems? And I'm not just talking about IT; I'm talking about health, education, and government? I was trained to create agents within operating politically aware systems, and I've been at it for over fifty years. Do you understand what that means in the new world of today?" I didn't attempt to stare her down. I just smiled again, trying to create the impression we weren't interested. Sandra jumped in, and I was immediately reminded of what had drawn me to her from our first meeting. Her sharp intellect and her amazing ability to bubble over like a boiling kettle. She all but bounced in her seat.

"If you are talking about the two boats heading towards the US and New Zealand, we have them under twenty-four-hour observation. And as for the other ten thousand refugees you have stashed away in your temporary camp in Libya, we have that covered as well. Oh! And if you were thinking we hadn't found your hackers creating false identifications for your refugees, that would be a mistake. We've been tracking all your hacks for the past three weeks and have traced all the hacks before that." I could feel her energy, and I was sure she was bouncing up and down on her seat, but I didn't want to take my eyes off 'Helen' because her face was telling me a story.

"Why would you punish young girls whose only crime is to have lost their parents and been abandoned in refugee camps?" she shouted, fury written all over her face. And I had my answer; she was as invested in the refugees as much as Mohammad bin Azaria was, and maybe we could work with that. I needed to get some input on that idea, so I called for someone on the door and waited patiently until the guards had carried her out, shouting and fuming in Russian and German. I signaled to the booth behind the glass, and the Boss and Arie came in, sat down, and gave me a very hard look. Then Indigo burst in with a tray of coffee mugs.

"*Capitán, aquí, para sostenerte un poco más.*"

"Thanks, Indigo, you are a legend!" I turned to Arie and the Boss.

"I want to call the president and General Saunders and run an idea I've had. I need you both to let me know if I am out of order. Indigo, I need your opinion as well."

"You are going to bargain using the refugees as collateral?" Arie asked. "Yes." The Boss looked at me. He slowly nodded; I hoped he saw the same opportunity I did because my instincts were that 'Helen' had answers to questions we hadn't asked and didn't know to ask, and if we wanted to seriously close out this case, we needed to be sure we were not leaving a powder keg behind that would blow up in the faces of the countries that had called on us in the first place. He pulled his computer out of his pocket, dialed up the general, spoke quietly for around ten seconds, then snapped it shut.

"Arie, can we get a big screen in here, please? Need to connect this to it, and maybe a big camera as well?" He nodded, waved to the window, and before you could take a deep breath, two soldiers raced in, set up the screen on its wheeled legs, took the Boss's mini, fiddled with it for a second or two, then the logo of the president of the United States dissolved into focus on the screen. Down the bottom, you could see all of us sitting around the table in miniature. Couldn't do anything about it. I looked like something the cat had dragged in after a hard night on the tiles.

The president and General Saunders swam into focus, with Frank, Roger, and Julius in the background.

"A bonus. Good to see you, Madam President. I hope you are well." the Boss said, taking control from the get-go.

"Thank you, yes, as good as can be expected under the circumstances." The look in her eyes was one of suspicion; her general looked like someone about to pounce on a mouse. In contrast, the heads of her FBI, NSA, and CIA looked relatively calm. I could only imagine what the conversation we had interrupted might have been about.

"Madam President, Captain Riley has something she wants to run by you. We are all in agreement here, but the final decision is up to you. May she brief you?" The president made a point of looking straight down the barrel of the lens, leaned forward, and created the appearance she was looking straight into my tired eyes.

"Captain, I was told you were hurt in Libya. How are you?" Genuine concern filled her face, and I suddenly had a feeling that what I wanted to do might fly. She was the president, and she and her country had been badly hurt, but under all that, she was a woman of compassion.

"Madam President, thank you, I'm fine. We'd like your approval to negotiate with one of the terrorists in an attempt to ensure that they are not leaving anything behind that will attack us in the future or take us by surprise. We believe this will ultimately work in your favor, both at the country level and the political level. May I continue?" I watched her face; it was clear she had no idea of the road I was running down. She indicated to continue by waving at me with an open palm.

"Madam President, as you would have been briefed, we have taken into custody 'Helen,' real name Natasha Trotsky, ex-Stasi and KGB, a graduate of the 'Town America' program, and one who we believe has been working with Mohammad bin Azaria for at least thirty years. To cut a long story short, no one knows more about the terrorists' plans than she does, from start to finish, and we believe we can get her full confession if we are prepared to trade her something."

"And what would that be?" the president asked, visibly arcing up. What I expected, didn't expect less first up, internally I had the exact same reaction when I had first considered the idea.

"As you know, the town of Helena has had a massive building program in the works for the last month, and we believe some thirteen hundred very young girls are headed there for resettlement, starting sometime in the next two to three weeks.

"We know, and your NSA has confirmed that the terrorists have created passports, entry documents, work permits, and professional certification documents for all those aboard the ship that they are on. We believe the plan is to spread the refugees out amongst the displaced people who fled to Helena when the fighting broke out in the cities, people who are buying the houses that are being built as we speak."

"I'm aware of what is going down in Helena, thanks to the FBI, and I am aware of the hacking into our systems to create the documentation. We were, as a matter of fact, just talking about all that when you called."

"Good. Then this is what we are going to recommend to you. Let the refugees in, celebrate it as an American initiative, and hold it up to the world as a bright, shining star in these tempestuous times; we will get the New Zealand government to agree to the same, and as a further step, we suggest you allow Project Apollos to go ahead at full pace." She looked shocked, tried to mask it, failed, leaned back, and looked at me with incredulity all over her face.

"You can't be serious!"

"Absolutely. It will serve no purpose to let anyone know how badly the terrorists penetrated your government infrastructure; on the contrary, this will give you a visual victory that shows strong leadership and a road to recovery. People will gain hope from the fact that at the worst time in their lives, their government is responding to the world crisis in a positive and humanitarian manner. I might also mention that between your Army Corps of Engineers and Arie's technical staff, you have control over the future destiny of the rest of the world as far as sustainable power goes."

"You're talking about all the countries that were scheduled to get the environmental plants like the one at Point Roberts?"

"Yes, Madam President, they already have the money in the bank, as it were. The plants are in boxes sitting somewhere in each country, and once again, America can come to the fore by providing what they need to set up its own infrastructure. You set the example for the world, control the outcome, and take the credit for giving the world direction and hope." She sat perfectly; still, eyes fixed on mine. I returned the favor, fixed my eyes on hers. There was an old saying in police work, "he who speaks first loses." I could hear the Boss holding his breath, and next to me, Sandra was a bundle of vibrating sunshine. I wished I could steal some of her bounce. My shoulder was now screaming at me non-stop and threatening to distract me. I would have to call time. No other way to manage it.

"Madam President, could we leave this with you overnight, please, and seek your decision first thing tomorrow?"

"That's the most sensible thing you have said all day!" and the picture went to black. The Boss reached across the table and put one meaty hand on my one good one.

"How are you holding up?" I looked straight at him and held nothing back. "Need a break." He nodded, looked at Sandra, and stood up. She followed, and always fleet of foot, Indigo was behind me, pulling out my chair.

We had reached the antechamber next to Arie's office before we were stopped.

The guard was overly polite but very firm.

"Captain, you are required in the infirmary. Please follow me." The Boss patted me on my good shoulder and waved me away. Sandra followed, and that was that.

Hooked up to the bag of meds, flat on my back, immobilized as two medtechs stripped off my bandages and poked and prodded at my shoulder. Sandra, absolutely no help at all in preventing these sadistic bastards from torturing me, just sat playing with her minicomputer, an earbud preventing anyone from hearing the conversation. From time to time, she gave me a glance, but her face was neutral, so while I was proud of her on one level and I was really pissed on another. She was supposed to be protecting me. Why hadn't she killed these sadistic bastards from the get-go?

"Captain, we are going to immobilize your left side down to the elbow. This time it will be a semipermanent bandage. You may not have much use of your left hand as you did previously." Fine, if you call a hand flopping around like a beached fish 'use,' make my day! But the meds were working wonders, and I floated away somewhere until I was roughly woken.

"Captain, wake up, please. Time to get moving again." I looked groggily at Sandra, now dressed in ironed camos, wearing her weapon in a shoulder rig, her credentials split open on her belt. Her combat boots were clean but not polished, so we were still thinking in terms of taking fire from someone. I sat up, looked at the meds bag on its wiry support, saw it was empty, tried to roll my shoulder, and failed, mostly due to the strapping and bandaging, and this time not the pain.

"What time is it?"

"One o'clock. We connect to the Americans at oh eight hundred their time. We have an hour for you to get yourself together."

"I've been out for over a day?" I asked, really confused. I had never slept for twenty hours or more at one time in my life. She didn't react, just pulled the bedside down, grabbed my working arm, and pulled me out of bed.

"Shower, dress, food, questions later. Move it." So I did what my bubbly young shadow demanded, and when I got to the dressing part saw that she had laid out combat fatigues for me, with a jacket that had the left arm cut out. As she tied my combat boots, I wondered how hard it had been for her to go from an operational agent in the thick of it one minute to nursemaid the next, then shook my head.

Stupid thought. In this organization, you did what you had to do, then moved on to do the next thing on the list.

"Have we been under attack?"

"Yes. A bunch of crazies from across the way launched a raid on the gaol and the hospice at the same time. They got nowhere; we had no injuries; they lost around thirty troops. No rhyme or reason. Arie is having a conversation with his opposite number across the border to try and straighten things out."

"Arie has friends in low places; if anyone can do it, he can."

"What is the status of our guests?" I asked, referring to our prisoners, who had now, by all accounts, been the target of an assassination squad twice in as many days. Someone wanted them dead, and I wondered why.

"All good. Trotsky is ready for round two. First, we talk to the Americans, then you can have all the time you can handle with her and any of the other prisoners." I stood, this time a little more steadily than the day before, rolled my good shoulder, and followed her out to where a meal had been laid out. For four, I saw, and before I could ask the question, the Boss, Indigo, and Arie walked in, sat down, and patiently waited for me to do the same.

"You're looking much better." The Boss was digging into his eggs and bacon with a relish, which suggested he hadn't had a meal for some time. Arie picked at his, and Indigo ate with the same gusto we were used to. Sandra stood behind me, leaning up against the wall. I looked over at her; she shook her head.

"Got a meal before I roused you." I bent back to my breakfast/lunch, suddenly realizing that I was hungry and that the food tasted magnificent. Arie looked up at me, his kind grandfather face on, and put his utensils down.

"Jessica, your position with the refugees and the Americans is an excellent strategic move, and the word from inside the Pentagon is you not only caught them off guard, you completely surprised them. What do you hope to get from the terrorists in return?" My turn to down tools, and I sat back slightly, thinking through my answer.

"Arie, they had a 'Plan B'; the evidence of that is well documented now. What I am most worried about is a 'Plan C, D, E,' or

531

even 'F.' Why is someone trying to kill the prisoners? What do they know someone doesn't want us to know?" His kindly face morphed into one of anger and pain, and he wiped his brow with his hand.

"It's not anyone we know, and the second attack was quite amateurish."

"How is that?"

"Two teams, not coordinated, and they attacked the same cells the ninjas did the day before. They were empty this time around, and every attacker was dead before they got in the main door. The second team tried for you and the medical center but obviously forgot we live in a permanent state of readiness, and they were mostly held at the fence line; a few got inside the center, and your agent and the med techs took care of them. Thank you, Agent Thomas. Your fine work is appreciated." I felt Sandra come to attention and had the sudden realization that both my shadows had come under fire, so maybe being attached to me was not so good for their health!

"I'll add my thanks to Arie's. First time I have slept through a firefight. It must have been fun. Now, as for what I will bargain for, I believe Trotsky will give us chapter and verse on what they have planned because the refugees are as important to her as they are to Mohammad bin Azaria. We'll dole it out slowly. It's going to depend on how far the Americans will go. But from where I'm sitting, it's nothing but a win for them; it will put them back in control of the world again without firing a shot." Laughter rippled around the team, relieving the tension that had steadily built since I sat down.

"*Potrebbero controllare il mondo, ma Arie controlerà gli americani!*" We all laughed again. Indigo was right. Arie would control the Americans; he had the key to making the environmental plants work-Amira and her nanomachines.

"If that's all, I need to get ready for our next chat. Give me ten, please, and I'll see you in the interrogation room." And I stood, turned, and walked out as smoothly as I could, my bladder literally busting at the seams.

Question. How did I get my pants down and back up so I could pee?

Answer. With great difficulty and with a little help from my new best friend. We washed our hands and looked in the mirror to check how we looked. I resisted the temptation to do anything, for today, at least, what you saw was what you got.

We found the team in the interrogation room, the big screen all set up, and when the Boss walked in, the first thing he did was walk over to me, crouch down so he could look me straight in the eyes, and ask the obvious question.

"Holding up, sitting down, enjoying Indigo's coffee, ready to rock again." Sandra punched me lightly on my good shoulder. Arie walked over, the Boss joined him, and, trailed by Indigo, sat down in their seats. The seal of the president of the United States filled the screen, and when it resolved itself into images, we could see all the usual suspects as well as the secretary of state. A tingle started to run up and down my spine; if she was here, then we might just get what we wanted.

"Good morning Madam President, Madam Secretary, General, gentlemen. Good to see you all. I'll hand over to the captain, if I may?" The president just nodded, looking relaxed and in control, something she had not been able to pull off yesterday.

"Madam President, good morning. Have you had sufficient time to consider our conversation of yesterday?" The general leaned forward, taking control of the frame.

"We have. We have also had the opportunity to look closely at Project Apollos, something we were not able to do previously. We have considered your conversation in detail, and we have a number of questions."

"Go ahead, General."

"Why do you think we need to trade anything with the terrorists?" Her face said it all; governments do not negotiate with terrorists, ever, and the US had been reasonably rigid in holding this line.

Until it suited their purpose not to.

"General, in the last two days, insurgents—terrorists—call them what you may, have attacked the cell block in which we hold the prisoners; the first attempted to kill everyone we had; the second tried again for the prisoners, and also tried for the medical center where our wounded from the operation in Libya is being tendered. Who gave them their orders? How many more groups like this are attached to the terrorist campaign? We need to know those answers."

The general paused, obviously unaware of the two attacks, and she pulled back in the frame, which showed more of the attendees at their end of the video call, all looking as curious as the general.

"Was anyone injured in these attacks?"

"No, General, only the terrorists. Israel lives in a constant state of alert; even though we didn't know them, we were ready for them or anyone else who decided to have a go at us that day." Arie was relaxed, a rare state for him. He almost has his grandfatherly look on.

"Attacking your wounded doesn't make sense—unless it was target-specific." The general's voice had all the edges of command laced with puzzlement. Then she suddenly turned to look down the barrel of the camera again. "Who was the senior member of your team wounded?" Our side held their tongues; we all just stared at the camera. At the other end, she nodded to herself. "I see. Okay then, back to the question—what else do you expect to find out?"

"General, we have yet to determine their order of battle. We have taken all the women involved in the planning and execution of the attacks into custody, even the CEO of Innomatchi and the CEO and COO of the two operating plants. But the discovery of 'Helen' and her cohort leads us to believe that there may be a large number of embedded terrorists we have yet to account for. That, after all, was one of Trotsky's great skills, and she had been at it for decades before she hooked up with Mohammad bin Azaria and then three decades with him as her partner and banker. This network could be extensive and may have been left with orders to strike if she were taken." The general looked thoughtful as she turned to the head of the NSA.

"Hi, Jessica, PJ, Indigo, Arie, and Agent Thomas. We have been watching the work Luigi and Shami have been doing and getting reports from Malcolm as well. It seems we have somewhere in the vicinity of one hundred and thirteen thousand false IDs created and another five hundred and ninety false sets of professional documents for teachers, engineers, doctors, and even a few scientists. At the time of your attack, some five thousand were still to be uploaded into our systems, which of course, didn't happen because of your attack. Are you suggesting that we go ahead and authorize those five thousand false IDs?" We could see the president tensing up; even the head of the FBI tightened his shoulders. The secretary of state, who had remained on the sidelines so far, started to show her nerves and her mettle.

"Project Apollos planned for the arrival of ten thousand refugee girls, all sponsored by Red Crescent and others, in a sanctioned immigration over six months to a purpose-built facility in Nevada. Between the time the white paper left my office and didn't arrive in the president's, Nevada had been replaced with Roanoke. And while the paper was still unaccounted for, building on specific sites commenced, and was only halted when then terrorists struck."

"Have you found out how the white paper went missing?" She looked crest-fallen, embarrassed, and a little out of sorts. As the president's lifelong best friend, she had accidentally placed the entire government in a very embarrassing position.

"Yes. Thanks to the FBI—Roger here—we found the three staff members who took the paper out of circulation. They were deep-cover sleepers, all refugees, and I am ashamed to say one had reached the rank of assistant director in my legal office."

"And there's my point, Madam President. We need to root out any others in your government, and other governments if that is applicable, to give you the best chance of long-term success." Both ends of the conversation went quiet, then Roger spoke up.

"Where's Anna?"

"She is interrogating the gamers, the CEOs, and COOs, putting together an accurate timeline for us."

"Does she agree with your proposal?"

"I'd prefer you asked her that question yourself. But we did discuss it in detail, and I believe she and I are on the same page." He nodded as if he expected nothing less, and in a sense, he was correct because Anna was one of the most senior and brilliant investigators the FBI had, and to ignore her input on any aspect of this case would have been foolhardy.

"Let me make this clear. America is not negotiating this deal. Interpol is, and your reasons are for you to tell at the appropriate time. We will require a formal proposal to us stating exactly what you expect us to do within the limits of what we have discussed previously, and you must make it very clear that we are being instructed to respond, in the interests of moving the world forward. When we have that document and we are satisfied with it, we will announce our support of an immigration program to help ease the suffering around the world, but little more than that in terms of detail. Clear?"

"Yes, Madam President."

"We have a permanent FBI presence in Point Roberts and in Helena and will soon have one in Roanoke. We will negotiate with the other seventeen countries one by one, provide them with the ship sets, help them turn them into plants based on Interpol's specific direction, and we expect the unreserved cooperation of Israel with the technical issues surrounding making the plants work. It will be up to each country as to how they manage any refugee migration, although I suspect you will have a view on that as well?"

"No, Madam President, we don't, not at this time, but I suspect that the Red Crescent will have that data, and we will, of course, keep you in the loop. And I can't speak for Israel, but as they were consulted before we raised this issue with you, I don't see any problems there." In the background, Arie nodded his agreement.

"One final thing, Madam President. What will you do if we don't get the intelligence we seek?" A long pause; no one moved at either end, and no one made a sound, but the president's body language relaxed, telling me all I needed to know. "Thank you, Madam President. We will be in touch." And the screen went to black, and everyone in the room turned to look at me.

"What? Have I suddenly grown horns?" The laughter was genuine, and only my bandaged shoulder saved me from a series of fist punches. The Boss was beaming at me, Indigo's face was split in a huge grin, and even Arie seemed to get the humor of the moment.

"You just got the President of the United States to agree to a win-lose situation, which has the same outcome for us. Incredible!" I looked around to find the bubbly voice full of sunshine and only just avoided a slap on my shoulder.

"Oi! I'm wounded here. Take it easy. Go get me a terrorist or two." Sandra moved to the door, still radiating joy; it might not have been particularly professional, but it lightened my spirits for the first time in two days. She hesitated before stepping out, but the Boss gave her the go-ahead.

"That was a masterful negotiation. Well done. I felt for some time that the girls could be a problem for us, but you have turned them into our greatest strength, and that takes real skill. Why don't you wait until Sandra gets back, then go and see Pete, bring him up to speed, then tackle Trotsky. I'll keep everyone out of your hair." He thumped me on my good shoulder, then stood in the doorway until Sandra came back.

"We're going for a walk." I pointed to the door. Sandra turned and went back out, and I followed. I needed a break, but more, I needed reassurance that Pete was recovering. He had been protecting me, and it still weighed heavily on me. The last time I had been conscious, he had been in an induced coma, so I was hoping he was now awake and alert.

It didn't go unnoticed that we were shadowed by a squad of Israeli soldiers on each side of the corridor.

We reached Pete and ran into a wall of the military, who all looked familiar. Tom and his team. The Israelis faded back into the corridor, and Tom opened the door to the ward with a flourish, his team standing by with weapons at the ready, eyes never stopping on one area for longer than a second or two, obviously on high alert. I wondered what role they had played in the defense of the facility, then let the question slip out of my mind when I saw Pete, tubes and machines in abundance, propped up by huge pillows, half of him bandaged, the other half resting on the counterpane with an ugly, black automatic weapon lying across his bed.

"Captain, welcome to Pete's pity party. Everyone welcome!" The croak was weak, but the intent was clear. He wasn't a victim. He was a warrior, and he might be on his back, but he wasn't out of the fight. His face brightened momentarily. "Jessica, good to see you. How's the shoulder?"

"Fine, can't feel a thing with all the crap they've fed into me. Did you get to use that recently?" I asked, pointing to the submachine gun.

"No, Tom and his team spoiled all my fun, chased them away, whoever they were. I've got this instead of a teddy bear!" I laughed and noticed Sandra had now filled the doorway with Tom, and both had turned their backs to us to give us some privacy.

"Took me by surprise. Shot right over Indigo and his team. It's a wonder Tom and his boys and girls didn't get hit in the spray. How are the Israelis doing?"

"Except for their colonel, all recovering as you would expect. They are burying him later today in his village; we have not been invited. I suspect Arie considers us too great a security risk. We might be able to get the Boss down there; it's under consideration." He looked white as a sheet, with small beads of perspiration spotting his forehead. By my estimation, he was out of action for the foreseeable future, and that might give me a manpower problem if the intelligence we gathered indicated we would have to do some heavy digging.

I'd have to give that some thought.

"We've contacted your partner. She sends her love, so that's one thing you don't have to worry about. I've got to go and squeeze some terrorists by the balls; is there anything I can do for you?" I put my best smile behind my question, leaned over and gripped his hand, and squeezed. He smiled back, but it was obviously forced, so I just punched him in the shoulder, patted him a couple of times, then walked out and pushed my way through Tom and Sandra. I stopped just out of hearing distance of the room and looked at Tom.

"If they decided to move him, it doesn't matter where, have him covered, even if they send him back home."

"Yes, Captain, we will. He'll have a minimum of four of us at all times, and they will have a mini, so you can contact them wherever they are." I nodded, shook my good shoulder, and rested my good hand on my weapon.

"How close did the tangos get yesterday?" He pointed to a blood smear around twenty meters down the corridor. "That close?" He just nodded. The proximity to Pete's room, and then Arie's working space, and our interrogation area was no accident. Arie had a mole or two somewhere, leaking very accurate information to whoever it was that wanted to end us. About time I got back to it and found out who.

I slapped Tom on the shoulder and strode off down the corridor, and in seconds we were being shadowed by the Israeli guards again.

Indigo was waiting at the door to the interrogation room with a huge mug of coffee for each of us. I bowed my head and sat down. Sandra sat on my right and magically produced our dummy red folder.

The guards returned with 'Helen,' sat her down without ceremony, and I started in on what I hoped would be her weak spot.

"Ms. Trotsky, we need information on your network. Who, where, what their orders are, timing, in fact, everything you can give us that will enable us to shut this down once and for all. I have already spelled out what happens to you next— deep, dark, and probably rank black hole made of concrete, no daylight, no contact, and you get to eat, shit, and piss in the same eight-by-eight cage for the rest of your life. Now, I acknowledge you are a highly trained professional, with your Stasi and KGB backgrounds, and the fact that you have operated for nearly fifty years and never so much as raised anyone's eyebrows suggests you were at the very top of your trade, so I won't insult your intelligence with false promises. I will, however, outline your options and our possible actions and see if we can't meet in the middle somewhere. Are you willing to trade?"

"I will listen to you, but I promise you nothing." I nodded. Sandra opened the dummy file and slid it to me. I looked at it, then snapped it shut. I wanted to watch Trotsky's face and body language. I had already got a solid baseline the day before, and I always liked to know what was hitting home and what was missing the mark in an interrogation. And today, I only had a dull ache reminding me my shoulder was still out of action. Time to push.

"We know you have two ships on their way to the USA and New Zealand, with approximately thirteen hundred young refugee girls and support staff on board each boat. We know you have forged IDs and visas and passports for them, work permits, and professional qualifications, and we entered this false data into the systems in each country. We have a choice. Are you paying attention?" She looked at me with such a feral look I was glad she was chained to the floor.

"Choice one, the one I personally voted for, contact our submarines that are following your ships and authorize them to sink both ships immediately and not stop for any survivors." I let that gruesome picture land and watched her face go from fury to emotional overload, then settle somewhere between the two.

"You wouldn't have the guts to do that." Emphatic, positive, thrown at me with a side of venom. I just stared at her, unblinking, with the hardest look I could manage. I looked at Sandra.

"Agent, would I have the guts to do that?" She looked at me with the sternest look she could manage and nodded.

"Yes, Captain, sadly, you would."

"Yes, I would. You and your terrorist friends have set the world back fifty years or so technologically, been directly responsible for the deaths of millions, killed the economy of the world stone dead, and let's not forget the pain, desperation, and agony you have caused millions of people from the major religions. Do you really think anyone will care about an accident at sea that might kill a few unknown refugees? And that's if they ever found out about it, given that you have crashed the internet and most computers on the planet." I could see the wheels turning behind her eyes. It was fascinating to watch. Then she leaned forward in her seat, tried to get her chained wrists onto the tabletop, failed, then threw her hands back down in disgust.

"You do not have the balls to do that. None of you do. You're weak, feeble, barely surviving just because we took away some of your toys."

"Yet you, your women friends, and the key players in your little game are the ones in chains, heading for a deep, dark hole." I sat back, grinned, stood up, and moved to the door. "I'll leave you to think on that for a minute." And walked out and ran into the Boss.

"What are you doing?"

"I need Indigo to chase some data for me and feed it to my mini." He gave me a hard look and nodded once. "Find out if there have been any other burst transmissions and where they originate." He nodded again, then turned me around and gently pushed me back into the room. I knew what was going through his mind, and I saw a reflection on Sandra's pretty face as I took my seat. If I moved, Sandra would moved with me. Full stop.

"Thank you for being patient. Have you considered option one?" I asked in my silkiest voice. She looked stressed. I suspect she was coming around to the view that I meant what I had said. I let the silence hang and held her eyes, forcing her to look away. She dropped her head slightly, then, with a voice that was pitched one octave below a scream, asked me the pivotal question—from our point of view.

"What is option two?"

"You tell us who is ordering the hits on our people here and give us the name of every embedded terrorist you have or have worked with as far back as you go. And we let the girls and their support crew enter the US and New Zealand as legal migrants and make sure everyone knows that they are legitimate refugees being settled in this time of crisis for humanitarian reasons." Her face told the story in spite of her strong will to not tell us anything that gave us an advantage. This was what she wanted—at least part of it.

"I will not give you any information on my people before I partnered with Al Hemish al-bin Mohammad Karesish."

"Not acceptable. We want the names of your agents who penetrated the information technology systems and hacked the government databases back in 1999. We want to know who concealed the theft of major weapons in 2002 and 2006. We want the names of everybody involved in what you have done, or we sink your ships." I said the last with such finality I almost believed myself. She attempted to stare me down, but she didn't know my stare had been perfected over quasi-illegal poker games all over the world with people who killed for a living and enjoyed it. She looked down, seemed to come to a decision, then looked back up with that feral grin she had perfected.

"I will give you the name of the commander who now issues instructions. I will give you the location of our reserves, all mercenary troops, and all previously part of the Devil's network. May he rot in hell. But you will give me more." I just smiled and shook my head.

"Agent, bring up the USPACOM (United States Pacific Command). Please, send the ready signal." Sandra opened her mini, hit a bunch of keys, watched her little screen intently, then turned to look at me.

"Captain, you are connected. USPACOM waiting for your instructions." I nodded the tension building to the point where I could physically feel it, even with only the three of us in the room. She was an intelligence professional trained by some of the very best experts in the world at the time. She had lasted five decades and never blipped on anyone's radar; she would not break easily. Then to my surprise, she held up her manacled hands in the time-honored gesture of "stop."

"Do you have my computer from the compound?"

"Yes."

"You will find an encrypted file under the heading '*Gartenp-flanzungen*.' The passwords for each level are '*Deutsche Distel*,' '*Mine-bot catcus*,' and '*Tränen des Blutes*.' In it, you will find a list of all my operatives; sections one and two have not been updated since 1996, but the third section lists all the little girls we recruited and placed in good homes. There is a fourth section, and the password there is '*Kinder Gottes*.'"

"Not all the girls rallied to your cause," I said, looking towards the one-way window. Someone there would give Luigi and Shami the nod, and they would start the search.

"No, but then we did not invite everyone we had taken. And no one on the fourth list has ever been involved in anything we have done."

"Who is giving the orders now?" She looked at me with that feral look she had perfected, and her eyes sparkled.

"Me."

"You?"

"Yes, me. And the only way you can stop the attacks is for me to tell everyone to stand down." Not going to happen in my lifetime unless I can find a safe way to facilitate it. More thinking time is required.

"On the door!" The guards returned, picked her up as if she weighed nothing, and the Boss, Arie, and Indigo, followed by Anna, crowded in. The only good thing about this was the hot cup of coffee Sandra and I got, so I ignored the bustling stares and the concerned looks and drank heavily.

"Who did you dial up on your mini?" Sandra paused, drinking her coffee long enough to answer me, then just buried her head back in her mug.

"Weather Service." I nodded and smiled. She hadn't even hesitated at my request; she was going to be a real asset to our team.

"Report coming on the burst transmissions; the geeks say they need an hour or two before they have confirmation of the data. What do you want to do next?" The Boss looked mildly happy, which was a real victory for me, as he usually never got really happy unless someone was getting shot or threatened, or yelled at.

"Can you work out how we can let her make a broadcast but contain her so she can't make matters worse?" He smiled again, treachery and deceit two weapons he was a master of.

"Yes. Simple. But do you believe her?"

"Not yet."

"So, I'll ask again, what do you want to do next?"

"Let me talk to Anna, have an hour's break, then we start again."

"Done." And he turned on his heel, followed by Indigo and Arie. Anna grabbed her own mug before Indigo could escape and sat where the terrorist had. I put a fake stern face on and pointed at her.

"You are under surveillance. Anything you say can and will—"

"Jessica, good to see you too. How's the shoulder holding up?" She looked at me over her mug, her eyes crystal clear, her hair finely combed as if she had just come from a salon. In fact, the whole of her looked warm, female, comfortable, and considered. And she had just spent hours interrogating terrorists.

I wondered how she managed to look like she did and manage all that as well when I knew I looked like a well-used dish rag.

"It's good. We're making progress here with 'Helen.' How did you go with the others?"

"Got you a timeline from two years before Amira got to Harvey Mudd. They had someone on her the whole time, even here in Israel. I've got all the details if you are interested, but the main thing is we now know who did what and when. They only started planning the real attacks after the nanomachine trial in Nova Scotia. And the planning only went as far as needing to identify coders who could write war game programs, which they did, and the ball started rolling downhill for real only four years ago. There were several prominent and very wealthy families involved, you know, two of them—the Westall and the Anaisha families; there are more, but they are not yet in play.

"The network they have set up for the implementation of the power plants and panels is extensive, and they have fifty-seven women trained and waiting in purpose-built warehouses up and down the West Coast from Canada to Mexico. These women only know about the power supplies, nothing about the attacks, the terrorists, or the infrastructure. I've passed everything I recorded onto Roger, and he is holding it until you decide how you want it managed." I was momentarily taken aback; why was it my decision? My shock must have shown on my face.

"You're surprised? You shouldn't be. The president wants instructions, clear cut and unambiguous, from you, Interpol, the agency responsible for solving the terrorist problem, and everything that follows. Look at it this way, it goes well, and you'll never hear about it. It goes tits up. They can blame you forever." But she said all this with a smile, so I took it for what it was—a succinct summary of the current political situation in her country.

"We'll see about that. Burst transmissions?"

"Yes, the geeks have mapped them, twenty-two in all, all sending 'Charlie Kilo,' CK, once a day, no answer. Can you guess the seventeen locations?"

"Bank accounts and ship set destinations. Innomatchi. New Zealand. Roanoke. What have we done about Innomatchi?" And I wondered if the seventeen nations lined up for the plants was a CIA or Interpol opportunity. Have to give that some thought.

"Again, your agents and the Public Intelligence Security Agency, the Japanese equivalent of the FBI, have taken it over but frozen all activity until you give the word. In this case, as you, your Agent Nokomoto Senji, and his partner Aikido Anaisha were insistent, they won't let anyone near anything without your approval. You command loyalty as I've never seen before in a distributed, authoritative organization. You'll have to tell me how you do that one day."

"It's easy. I just smile a lot." She laughed a pure, rich sound that made me feel good. "Anything I can use on 'Helen'?"

She went serious for a moment, then shook her head.

"No, you've got the best handle on that. I need to review all the data the geeks are unraveling, so I'll let you get back to it." She picked her mug up, gave us a final smile, then left. The room felt bigger, but some of the happiness and joy had gone. I looked at Sandra, sitting comfortably, hands folded over her mini, her empty mug off to one side.

"How are you holding up?" She looked at me, her face lit up with a smile so powerful I felt it reenergizing me.

"Fine. Learning a lot about how we work, the real difference between us and the other agencies." She made a good point, and I wasn't so sure we hadn't crossed the line somewhere, given all the people who were now waiting on our determinations.

"Get 'Helen' back in, please."

"What happened to the hour break?"

"I lied." She called the door with a wistful look on her face, and we started in afresh. Maybe she needed the break, but I was afraid if I stopped, I'd fall over.

"Ms. Trotsky, we are processing your data, so I've put a temporary hold on sinking your ships. No idea how long it will take our people to make sense of everything, but your ships are prime targets, and we can always turn them around if we need to. Now, about telling all your people to stand down. Who are all your people?" She glared at me, probably an instinctive reaction to anyone who got on her goat.

"I took option two. I have fulfilled my side of the bargain. I can call them off, I've told you that, and I'll tell you no more." I smiled, mindful of the fact that I couldn't appear too happy or I'd lose her connection. At the moment, it was hard arse to hard arse, just how I liked it, so I spun the web a little wider and at the center a little tighter.

"We know the Red Crescent, funded by you, has gathered up some ten thousand additional children and currently have them in a preparatory center in Libya, ready to be moved to the United States. We know you have negotiated a building site in Roanoke, where you hoped to move them to. You think you have the approval of the secretary of state. You think you have forged IDs, passports, visas, entry permits, and work permits for their support teams. I've some bad news for you." She stared at me with horror in her eyes, and for the first time, I saw the woman beneath the intelligence agent.

Any doubt I had about her not being totally invested in the outcome for the children dissolved in a puff of satisfaction. Now I could be confident we would get what we needed and clean up all the terrorists in the process.

"And the bad news is, I can stop the entire migration with one finger."

I held my forefinger up, wriggled it around, and looked at Sandra. She opened her mini and placed it in front of me. I looked 'Helen' in the eyes, saw fear there for the first time, and drove the nail into her confidence.

"You want to say something?" I wriggled my finger some more and bent it toward the keyboard. The silence hung in the room like a bad smell, or maybe it was me. I needed a shower. I could feel the grit on my skin.

"What do you want?" Her hoarse voice reached across the table like a plea from a homeless person looking for a few dollars.

"I want the names and locations of every terrorist you have on your payroll, I want the command structure, and I want any attacks you have planned called off permanently. I want it all to stop here and now. Do I hit that key, or don't I?"

She looked at me, and I felt for her; she had given her life to her craft, and it was about to count for naught. She dropped her head.

"In my journal, in the back is an electronic storage device. The password is '*Speer Gottes, Ruf der Winkel,*' entered three times, with the German numeral added after each. You'll find the ID and location of everyone still on the payroll, and you can call off the attacks by broadcasting '*Wir sind fertig, komm nach Hause, meine Kinder.' Das ist Helen.'*"

"We'll take a break now and follow up on your information. On the door!"

She was bundled out. Sandra and I were left in that happy vacuum where you had a sense of achievement but couldn't quite celebrate for fear that it might all come apart at the seams. I patted her on the shoulder.

"Well done, little cricket, you played the loyal and obedient slave girl to perfection." She laughed as we walked out. This time there was no one to greet us; everyone would be following the data and planning clean-up operations.

"Shower, a few hours down to let everyone catch up. You good with that?" She nodded, her infectious smile lighting up the corridor.

"You played her like a violin. It was masterful. You just got everything we wanted, possibly more, and you gave away nothing. Nothing!" I thought about that; it might have been nothing in terms of a negotiation, but the consequences of it going wrong were too terrible to contemplate.

Now we need the time to clean up whatever she had set in motion before I had my final chat with the mastermind.

Money Games

L uigi, Shami, Indigo, Malcolm, and Stefarino, the head monk who had taken Interpol into his cavern at the time of most need, were sharing a secure encrypted video link that had originated in Venice. The reason for the high level of security was that now some countries had rudimentary local area networks back up and running, and Interpol could not guarantee that there were no terrorists inside those LANs. And that was the very subject being debated by the geeks. Indigo, as the head of Interpol in Italy, was facilitating the meeting of some of the smartest technology focussed minds on the planet, and he was almost bursting with pride just by being able to participate.

"Malcolm, *si!* You are correct. These are the codes the terrorists were issued to enable them to draw down funds. We can assume that these have not yet been issued, but the path is clear for those that have been. We can check against the reported terrorist deaths the various countries have claimed against, as see if there are any not accounted for."

"Does Interpol still have the Red Notice on the Sovereign Wealth Fund?"

"Yes. Those funds are frozen until either the colonel or the captain agrees to release them."

"But the system worked on the basis that a large deposit was made to a bank that the terrorists could draw down from, once they got the code. Have we traced those initial deposits?"

"No. Malcolm, you are a genius. We compare the notes we took off the bookkeeper, with the access codes, we track the banks, we can see what's left."

"Do it. I have another question, one for you Stefarino."

"Go ahead."

"Are you convinced that no one other than us can ever track you back to your headquarters in Venice?"

"I am now, yes. Why do you ask?"

"The data 'Helen' had on her computers shows a large number of embedded people in the IT sections of multiple countries, including Italy, going back twenty to thirty years. We now know who they are, but we do not know if they are active or not. One of the real issues we will have going forward."

"What do you mean?"

"Not every refugee has been turned into a terrorist. I worked with one such person, an SSA with the FBI, and she is the smartest agent I have ever worked with except for one—and we all know who that is. Additionally, Colonel Anthony has sent us the IDs of the women who have set up the transport hubs on the West Coast, and as far as the FBI can ascertain, having now interviewed a number of them, they knew nothing about the terrorist attacks; the timing of their work was solely commercial."

"You're worried some of the embedded women will be innocent?"

"Yes. And I'm not sure how we handle that."

"It will be the families," Stefarino interjected, cutting across the conversation.

Indigo was the first to respond. "What do you mean, brother?"

"Every family that the terrorists came from has been deleted, hidden, all records removed for as far back as their births. If you can find the family, the chances are they are not part of the terrorist plot." Malcolm nodded, his head bobbing up and down with some force.

"I can confirm that, Stefarino; that has been true in every case."

"Then we start with that. Send me the list of embedded women in Europe, and I will find their families—or not."

"I'll do the same for the Americas."

"I've got Asia," called Luigi.

"I'll take Africa." Shami's voice was unmistakable. "Leave the Pacific basin to me," Indigo called.

"That just leaves finding the unused money for the terrorists."

"Why don't you let me put my people on that?" Stefarino asked, already thinking of who he could assign to the task. Since his brother had approached him just six or seven weeks ago to work with Interpol, he had never felt so alive and engaged. It was a feeling he wanted to keep for as long as he could. And working so closely with his brother was an added bonus.

Chapter 50

Arie's anteroom was almost full of bodies. The feeling in the room was buoyant; obviously, the geeks had made progress during my time down, and I felt good for it. The med techs had limited their evil practices to a single needle, the size of which reminded me of horses. And this time, when I dressed, no suit, just loose pants tied at the waist, sneakers, and a tee, brightly colored, with a lightweight coat thrown casually over my shoulders. Sandra had given me a light-weight pouch to sling around my waist, reminiscent of the famous kangaroo pouches from the eighties. Except this one held my weapon and my credentials. Before I could ask the question, Sandra pointed to her belt where two extra magazines would fit my Glock rode. I spun the pouch to one side, practiced opening it and drawing my gun, and found it relatively easy to do. There hadn't been an attack today, and I took some comfort in that.

Maybe the burst transmissions had worked.

"Gentle people, please take the seat nearest to you. We have quite a lot to report." Arie remained standing, a massive screen at his back, on which the images of Malcolm, Luigi, and Shami floated in little boxes.

"We have issued the 'cease activity' message, opened all the files 'Helen' pointed us to, and the geeks are compiling a list of embedded agents and matching them against her journal. Interpol in Venice is running down the outstanding women and their families, and we now have a complete picture of the bank accounts the mercenary terrorists were drawing down from. We also have the access codes to those accounts."

"Do you have a list of embedded agents in the US?"

"Yes, Jessica, that has been compiled and passed through Anna to the FBI. She has instructed them to wait on your command and are not involving the general or the president at this point."

"Do you have the companies complicit in the organization of the terrorists in each of the seventeen countries that have received funding and had a ship set addressed to them?"

"My captain, we have the list. Many of the businesses of families who were the original sponsors are either closed or dead, and every country has a trust set up exactly the same as Helena." Indigo's English was precise and fully articulated, a sure sign he wanted a literal understanding of his report. I looked at him. He had lost a little of his bounce. I suspected he had not stopped working for a day or longer. I looked around at all the other faces in the anteroom and saw similar signs of fatigue.

"Arie, do you believe we have stopped any further attacks on us here?" He gave me his warrior look, his eyes scrunched up slightly, his bushy eyebrows firming.

"It's possible. Not knowing what they had planned, we can only wait to see what happens. But we have identified a number of sleeper agents in our infrastructure, and they are being neutralized as we speak." I nodded, holding his gaze. "Then you won't have any objection to me calling a halt for twelve hours so everyone can catch their breath?" Now the warrior look morphed into the kindly grandfather, and his face split with a great smile. His turn to nod in agreement. "Jessica, now I realize why PJ here placed you in command. Excellent idea.

"There is background work that will continue without us, but in the main, rest will do us all the world of good."

"Excellent. Boss, Anna, Indigo, please stay. Everyone else, see you in twelve hours for an update." The room cleared, and I noticed that a small squad of Israeli soldiers remained spread out around the wall. So Arie thought we had stopped the attacks but was taking no chances, and I couldn't disagree with his caution.

"What's on your mind?" the Boss asked, sitting back down on his chair but this time backward, a habit of his when he was in the mood to be difficult. Look relaxed, fire at will!

"I've been thinking about our mandate, and I want to be clear as to what we will be responsible for and what we will pass back to our sponsors. If you look at the big picture, the terrorists' Plan 'B' is now being managed up to a point. I suggest we get the UN to take over the management of the countries that have ship sets in their future and the UNHCR to manage the migration of any further children or even adults. They will need to coordinate with Red Crescent; to make sure they understand what has already been put into motion. Does anyone disagree?" I looked at the tired faces and decided to hurry up my summary.

"And I've been thinking about our prisoners and what we still don't know. I want to take 'Helen' and Mohammad bin Azaria back to Venice and spend some quality time with them. We have the data, it will take a few days to analyze it all, and any clean-up will be up to the different countries involved. Cleaning out embedded agents is not our remit."

"You want to get away from here?"

"Absolutely. If we are the targets, then by going home, we reduce the necessity for the terrorists to keep attacking Israel. And we have some lovely, old, moldy, smelly cells on the island, and we can work at our own pace."

"Agreed. Indigo, Anna, any objections?" They both shook their heads.

"One other thing. I want Pete flown home with protection until he is fit and well again. I've spoken to Tom; he will send four of his team at the minimum."

"Good idea, but let me arrange the protection. We might need Tom and his crew in Venice. In fact, have you given any thought to how we will protect ourselves back home?"

"Yes. Indigo's team is first class; they know the neighborhood backward. Tom is almost as familiar with Venice as we are, and I have an idea where we might camp." He looked at me, his eyes clear, his face passive, nodding slowly.

"When do you want to leave?"

"Now."

"Now."

"Yes." He nodded and looked at Indigo; they shared a silent message, then the Boss turned back to me.

"Get dressed, camos, gun up, and be ready to pull up stumps in one hour."

"Yes, Boss." Arie came in at that exact moment, saw the body language, and nodded.

"Thought you might want to go home. Don't blame you. I'll arrange transport."

"Aire, we want to take two prisoners with us." He gave the Boss a hard look, then nodded again as he thought it through.

"Of course you do. Shami is already here; will you take Luigi with you?"

"Yes, the geeks don't seem to mind where they work, and I have some specific tasks in mind for him and Indigo." Arie looked at me and turned his head to one side. "Are you going to update the president?"

"Not yet. You'll be on the call. I need to work through some operational issues before we bring her up to speed. Anna has already briefed the FBI, but Roger will hold the data until we release it." He nodded again, held out one wrinkled and scarred hand, took my good one, and squeezed.

"You have done a remarkable job under very difficult circumstances. Your whole team needs to be congratulated."

"We could not have done it without your unwavering support, Arie. It's been a real team effort, and in turn, we thank you and your troops. We are very sorry about your colonel. He was a fine soldier and a fine man." He just looked at me and, with a gentle smile, let my hand go, shook the Boss's hand, then Anna's, and lastly Indigo's. Then he walked out the way he had walked in, unbowed and still totally in control.

Sandra was getting used to dressing me, so we were out the back in the holding area waiting for our prisoners to be delivered in less than the hour we had stipulated. An armored vehicle clanked up, puffing dense black diesel smoke, stopped, the back doors split open, and two Israeli soldiers dismounted and pointed to the inside. I took it as a sign we were to get in, so we all clambered into the dark cabin to see "Helen" and Mohammad bin Azaria with their heads bagged, in chains, locked behind a steel lattice door.

There were no windows in the cabin, so from the bumps and grinding, I suspected we were being loaded into an aircraft, and sure enough, a few minutes later, the whine of turbine engines started, and the movement became more stilted and jerky.

Arie's plan was to fly us to Venice and drive us to a secured location where we could transfer to a boat or barge. It took a little under two hours to cross the Mediterranean, Ionian, and Adriatic seas and the traditional flare, thump, and roar as the engines went into reverse pitch announced our arrival. The floor tilted down, then stabilized; we backed out into what I did not know, but I noticed Indigo was using a little handheld transmitter. Then we were moving again, a short, rough trip, lots of bumps and grinding sounds from the engine, then the floor tilted again, and then we were stopped, rocking slowly from side to side.

Barge. At least it wouldn't be driven by my favorite maniac cigarette boat driver. We rolled and rocked our way to our headquarters, and the sudden stop was followed by the rear doors flying open into a corridor of the heavily armed Italian police. We dismounted, collected our small bags, and with a smart salute, Indigo led us into our Venice headquarters.

Home. At least for a while. The doors on the van snapped shut, and the barge pulled out into the canal, heading for a small island cemetery, under which were some really old gaol cells, the perfect place for our prisoners.

"What do you want to do next?" the Boss asked, turning to look at Indigo, who was cranking up one of our monstrous espresso machines.

"Tom and his team will be here in four hours. I want them to coordinate with Indigo and set a perimeter here and on the island. If they attack, I'm happy for them to get to us, but I don't want anyone leaving. A quick shower, then I want the Americans, full cast, including Malcolm, up on the big screen, with Indigo, you, Anna, Luigi, and myself at this end, and Arie and Shami in a little box. I want the geeks' summary ready, and I want coffee, and I'm happy to wait for it if it takes some time to set it all up."

"You don't want much. Indigo tells me the geeks have broken their analysis up for you; you'll have what they have when you're ready. Go clean up." And he said it so dismissively I actually bent my head to smell my armpit and realized I was well and truly on the nose. Needed the bandage changed and re-strapped, and I'd be like new.

"Sandra, I need a med tech to change my bandage and fix me up so I don't look like the company shrew." She nodded and guided me out to our accommodation area.

The med tech stood in the shower with me, peeled the old bandage off, and cleaned up the dried blood and yellow antiseptic stuff while Sandra stood on the other side of me, pulling a compression bandage strapped across my chest to keep my arm immobilized. They were both dressed, soaking wet. I was naked, also soaking wet, and I wondered if a photo could be used as a recruitment poster for Interpol!

"You have to keep the arm immobilized under all circumstances, Captain, no exceptions." She distracted me with one hand, using the other to plunge a needle into my shoulder. Not as big as the horse needle they used in Israel, but it wasn't the smallest needle I have ever seen either.

"How long do I have to keep it strapped?"

"A week, maybe two. Depends on how you heal. I'll check in on you daily." And with that, she departed, leaving a wet trail behind her. Sandra helped me out, helped me dry myself, then sat me down on a small bench and handed me a hairdryer.

"Here, use this while I clean up."

She showered, dressed, this time in jeans and a colorful collared shirt, and pulled a lightweight jacket over it all to hide her weapon. She dressed me in a loose pair of green pants, fitted rubber-soled boots to my feet, a nice matching shirt, then a matching jacket thrown over my shoulders. I was starting to feel like a runway model. I had never taken much interest in what I wore; as an agent equally as likely to be stomping on a terrorist head as walking through their blood, the practical always seemed the best solution. She fitted my weapon, magazines, and credentials, patted me on my good shoulder, and led me out to our main office.

Indigo had my coffee in my hand at the speed of light.

Luigi had the big screen fired up, and a clock was counting down from twenty-three minutes. Anna wasn't to be seen, but on a small screen off to one side, I could clearly see both our prisoners, now unbagged, sitting in their gloomy cells. I smiled. I sincerely hoped there were bugs, spiders, and cockroaches galore running rampant all over them. The Boss called me over, sat me down, and asked Sandra to give us the room. He looked clean and neat and relaxed. He was more relaxed than I had seen him since I had hijacked him at his beach resort. Was it only six weeks ago? Amazing how time flew by when you were hunting terrorists.

"Jessica, you have run a remarkable, well-balanced, and thoughtful operation. Your ability to work across countries, cultures, and agencies seamlessly has been outstanding. Yes, you've had a lot of help from your team in every country, but the leadership has been yours, and yours alone." I was stunned. I couldn't remember the last time the Boss had congratulated me. Sure, there had been the occasional "good one" here and there, but him stringing actual sentences together had me gobsmacked.

"Boss, are you feeling okay?" He just smiled and stood up.

"Never felt better. Just think about this—you have identified, tracked, and arrested the main players in the worst terror event ever recorded. And you've done it on three continents in less than six weeks from the first bomb being dropped. The fact that the world now has hope and a way forward is due to your incredible insight and persistence. You've done an excellent job, and you have made me proud." He smiled and faded into the dark of the geek's domain, leaving me speechless. A silent shadow appeared on my shoulder, and a warm hand rested on it.

"I didn't hear all of that, but I got enough to know that what PJ just said is the absolute truth." Anna took her hand back and sat and faced me. "I'd like to add my thanks for the inclusion and the support you have given me and the brilliant way you have led this team." I just sat amazed; two of the people I respected the most had just given me the sort of boost you could wait a lifetime for, so I did the only thing possible. I laughed.

"You won't thank me when I tell you I'm going to recruit one of your best agents!" She laughed with me and shook her head.

"Fay has got one of her team on the inside of the Helena operation, she has others from the Seattle office actively tracking the deliveries, and she told me you had given her the Interpol playbook the last time we spoke."

"So, can I have her?"

"My boss will bitch about it, her boss in Seattle will bitch about it, but yes, I'll speak to Roger and smooth it out."

"I tried for you, but Roger told me to go to hell." She laughed again and folded her hands in her lap. Today she was dressed in charcoal, stylish suit pants topped with a tailored jacket over a pure white shirt, with the collar turned up. But her boots were practical and could handle anything from a swamp to the pitching deck of a boat. Gone were the days of the FBI wearing institutional black.

"What do you want me to do?" she asked, looking around the room. People were starting to filter back in, and the clock on the screen was now counting down from one minute. An Italian dressed in an immaculate suit approached, bowed, and handed me a thin file in a red cover.

"*Grazie.*"

"*È un piacere, capitano.*" It was the summary for the Americans and gave me what I needed to keep faith with them. Anna turned her seat around to face the screen; Sandra sat beside me like a breath of fresh air. I promise you her happiness was infectious! Indigo came in with Luigi, the room darkened except for the lights that illuminated us sitting before the screen, and the presidential seal swam into focus. Malcolm appeared in a little box, Arie and Shami in another, our Venice team streamed across the bottom, and then the screen filled with the conference room below the Oval Office. The Boss took control, as he tended to do, and, surprising me and probably everyone else in the room, stood up.

"Madam President, thank you for your time. Captain Riley has a report for you, and the instruction set you requested will be sent to you following this conversation. May we proceed?"

"Good afternoon, Colonel. Yes, please proceed."

"Madam President, we are transmitting to your directorate the data I have here in this folder, but I'd like to summarise it for you in the interest of time." I paused, looking at the screen, saw no one objecting, then following the Boss's example, stood up.

"Madam President, included in this data is a list of every embedded agent placed in the USA by Natasha Trotsky, aka 'Helen,' going back to 1980. There is also a list of the women brought to your country by her network as part of the migration of young girls. You will also find a list of their parents, and our belief is that where you find open data on parents and adopted children, you have exactly that—an innocent child taken out of a refugee camp and placed with a willing family. However, we will leave it up to you to confirm each person's status." She looked at me with a semi-relaxed smile, no doubt wondering how much more I would leave to her own people to sort out. My next statement made that very clear. "Interpol now has a clean-up job to do with respect to the prisoners we have collected during this operation, so for all intents and purposes, we believe we have fulfilled our commitment to you and your government with regard to the terrorists that attacked your country and others.

"We have laid out our recommendations for managing the ship sets, managing the seventeen countries those ship sets were destined for through the auspices of the UN, and future migration of the children through the Red Crescent; there is also a recommendation on how to manage the relationship with Israel regarding the technology you will need to enable the plants once they are built.

"We have people in place in Toyoko, and they will ensure the continuity of the production of the ship sets as and when you decide you need them.

"The terrorists will be tried by the World Court in camera, and no distinction will be made between the mercenary terrorist and the women we hold. We are also requesting a meeting with the new King of Arabia and will release the funds in the Sovereign Account on certain conditions, which you will be made aware of at the appropriate time.

"Madam President, it has been a pleasure working with your people. Needless to say, we could not have conducted this investigation successfully without your resources and support, for which

Interpol thanks you. Do you have any questions?" She looked at each of her people, all sitting straight as if in school, the general being the only one to slouch a little, obviously thinking through everything before she let us off the hook.

"Yes. When can I have Anna back?"

I smiled. I had been anticipating this question, but from Roger, her boss, not the general.

"As soon as she has completed the interrogation of the terrorists." She nodded, probably expecting that answer.

"Does Malcolm keep working with your geek squad?"

"Yes, General, for as long as you will allow it." She nodded again, obviously happy that she would still have direct access to whatever we were doing. She looked directly at the camera.

"Do you want anything else from us?"

"Yes. The NSA G4 would be useful, particularly for the next few weeks." She nodded again, more access for her people; I could see the way her mind was working.

"Thank you, we're good, and please thank all the members of your team for a job well done." And she made the cutting-throat motion to someone off-camera, and the screen went blank, except for Malcolm's little box and Aire and Shami's. I sat down as Arie leaned into the camera.

"You didn't tell them everything?"

"No. Until we clean up the funding issues, consolidate the bank accounts, and work out how much we are going to ask Arabia in repatriations, there is nothing to be gained with another voice in the mix. And if we need to get a message to them, we've got Malcolm and Anna." Arie seemed thoughtful, nodded, then thought of something.

"Have you given any thought to Amira's position?"

"Yes. She's been working with the geeks, doing a fantastic job, and we will return her to your lab in the next week or so to get her working on a few ideas we've had, and no doubt she will be busy starting all those ship sets up once they turn into plants, and I want to make sure the stipend her parents get every month is taken care of." He nodded again, seemingly happy with what I said.

"Thank you, and let me mirror what the Americans said. You have done a masterful, wonderful job. Thanks to all your team."

"Appreciated, Arie. Thank you for all your great support. You are looking after the colonel's family?" He smiled, nodded, then cut the feed. No matter how hard this job got, no matter how vicious, mean, and just flat-out fucked up things were, the hearts and souls of every successful operation were ordinary people doing an extraordinary job.

People. And I had a few of my own to tend to. And a couple of terrorists to pay my respects to. Huh! I had an idea, rolled it around in my mind for a second or two, called the Boss, Anna, and Indigo over, and shooed everyone else away. Sandra ignored me, glued to my side like clingfilm.

"Indigo, I'm going to have a final chat with our two terrorist friends on the island. I'll need security, transport, and minimum fuss. Can you arrange for that, please?"

"*Certamente, capitano, sarà fatto immediatamente.*" He hurried off to set it up for us.

"Anna, I need you to be incommunicado for the next few hours." She looked at me with a strange twist to her mouth, as if trying to work out what I was up to, but nodded and walked off.

"Boss, we need to ensure there can be no collateral damage should the cells be attacked by terrorists. Can you arrange that, please?" He gave me a really hard look, almost grinned, then he shook his head with a wry grin. That just left Sandra.

When we were alone. I turned to her, took her by the shoulder, and made sure we were eye to eye. "We need vests for the visit, and you can sit this out if you wish. I can take Indigo's men with me." She gave me a strange look, almost a mirror of Anna's, then she tilted her head to one side.

"Thanks, but I have my instructions, and where you go, I go." Her look was calming, direct, and focused. I knew what I was going to do, and I suspected that somewhere deep in her soul, she did as well. We'd see.

"Okay, go get our vests. Let's get to it."

Island Of Blood

The Island of San Michele is storied with fables, great gardens, relics, and works dating from ancient Egypt, and the central villa sits on a ledge on top of the Phoenician Steps. It is a beautiful sight for any visitor, of whom in normal times there were thousands from all over the world.

These were not normal times.

And in the very heart of the island, burial sites for Greek Orthodox and Christians going back to the 1800s lay in boxed rows, tended as if the very bodies they stored were still present in some form.

And under one such plot, someone had dug a series of cells into the bedrock that stopped the island from slipping into the Laguna Veneta. Twelve in all, a number that rang through history in every religion; they were wet, musty, dirty, smelly, and extremely uncomfortable.

There were only two occupants, one at each end of the row, and the single guard was rotated every twelve hours. The food for the prisoners came with each guard on the police boat, and the empty containers were collected on the return trip. Cameras embedded into every corner of each eight-by-eight-foot concrete by ten-foot-high enclosure had only harsh overheads light and a single stainless-steel toilet bowl.

A lightweight, single-camp stretcher and two grey institutional blankets made up the entire list of disposable assets.

It was not a pleasant experience. It was not meant to be. And as I arrived at the small dock reserved for officials and government employees on the island, I could not help but notice the Italian police guards, in their splendid uniforms, all blue-and-red stripes, flowing capes, designed by Valentino and George Armani. They were conspicuous, they were meant to be too, and they were all posted exactly where I needed them.

"Thanks, Indigo, perfect. Stay with the boat, and lock the door after, please."

"*Certamente, capitano, sarà il mio piacere.*" I turned to Sandra.

"Good time for you to catch some sun." She looked at me with a tight smile and shook her head.

"You know the rules, Captain." I shrugged my good shoulder; so be it. We met the guard at the bottom of the steps, and he saluted. I saluted him back in acknowledgment.

"*Sei licenziato, riferisci al colonnello* Kashasini."

"*Subito capitano.*" He marched back up the steps. I waited until Indigo had closed the gate, then headed down the dank corridor. We reached the furthest cell and were welcomed by the sight of Mohammad bin Azaria sitting cross-legged in the far corner, facing where I suspected he thought Mecca might be.

"Al Hemish al-bin Mohammad Karesish-brother Fernández-Mohammad bin Azaria, I have here a summary judgment from the World Court, you have been tried in-camera, and found guilty of multiple acts of terror under the Terrorist Laws as modified in 2022, and you have been sentenced to death. Do you wish to say anything at this time?" He rose slowly and stood in the middle of his cell, his blue overalls stained black and brown by the fungus and dirt in the cell. He looked nothing like the imperious imam who had brought the world to its knees through the callous agency of little refugee girls. He just stared at me, his eyes with two deep black holes in his bearded face.

I waited for three beats, threw the judgment onto the floor, pulled my weapon, pushed it through the bars, and shot him twice, once in the head and once in the heart. He rolled down rather than fell, the impact of the first shot throwing his head back at an impossible angle. Next to me, Sandra stood mute, almost stoic, then turned to me with a neutral look on her face. She held out her left hand. I stared at her for a full minute. There was no going back from executing an unarmed human being; it would live with her for the rest of her life.

I gave her the second judgment and followed her to the final cell. I repeated the same mantra to "Helen," the most successful deep-cover agent expert in known history. Sandra threw the judgment on the floor of the cell and shot her as I had done.

We stood in the echoing quiet, looking at her lifeless body, each lost in our own thoughts. I held her shoulder gave it a squeeze.

"Pick the judgments up. Keep them, please, for our files." She did, and we walked out back into the brilliant sunshine. Somehow, where there was sunshine, there was hope. Indigo opened the gate, and I motioned him to leave it open. We got back into the police boat and headed back to our headquarters.

Sometimes it felt good finishing an operation. Sometimes you just felt tired and worn down.

This was one of those times.

> Somewhere in a refugee camp one child under
> 10 years of age dies every eight minutes.

Read about how it all started

The Tears Of Hope - Book I

"Somewhere in a refugee camp one child under
10 years of age dies every eight minutes.

The Mentor

"We had a plan, a good plan, but like all plans, once we wargamed it, we discovered it would not have survived the first few minutes of battle. So now we have created several plans and strategies, you might call them, one for each force element. You will be self-tasked, under your own command and control, on your own timetable. You will have just one primary target, with a secondary only if the primary becomes compromised, and you will be expected to work from our data and fit into our overall timing schedule, but the logistics, personnel, weapons, delivery systems, and exit strategy are for you to create. And only for you to know. It's your backside, and we trust you to keep it in one piece out of self-preservation if nothing else." The two people, one at the penultimate stage of a brilliant career, the other still radiating the bloom of the fast-tracked youth, sat opposite each other, the late afternoon sun creating interesting shadows across their faces.

"Imagine you committed an atrocity—an act of terrorism so vile that literally, half the world would be trying to either kill you on sight or incarcerate you forever in a hole so deep you would never see natural light again. Imagine that others, like you, committed this heinous act in parallel to you another five or even six times in the same seventy-two-hour period. Thousands, possibly tens of thousands, dead or worse, broken, maimed, or damaged and mentally scarred for the rest of their lives. Predominantly collateral damage, civilians, real innocents of the finest type, with a small mix of real targets, but sadly in the minority. Where would you hide, for the rest of your days, assuming that you were still alive at the end of it all? Where?" The general's piercing green eyes bored into the young woman, looking for the faintest sign of discomfort. The woman smiled back, completely at ease, confident, and even comfortable with the concepts being discussed. After all, war was just politics and the projection of power by other means, however, and wherever politicians might apply it.

Their cause was just—possibly the most just cause ever underpinning a war-like action.

And the woman was a warrior.

Trained from an early age to instinctively follow the Code of the Warrior to the point of death.

"Sir, the only place that would be safe."

"And where would that be?" the general asked, somewhat amused by the sense of calm that seemed to exist between the two of them, given the nature of the discussion and the difference in their experience, rank, and age. The woman smiled again, twisting a small gold band over and over between one thumb and forefinger.

"Sir, the only place where people like us could survive. In plain sight."

The Tears Of Joy -
Book 3 In The Tears Of Hope Trilogy

Chapter 1

We had chased terrorists together from continent to continent. We had escaped certain death together more than once.

And then we had personally executed unarmed, confined prisoners together, shot them in the head and in the heart, and left their bodies to rot in a three-hundred-year-old subterranean prison underneath a beautiful Island in Venice, where thousands of tourists once walked in the evanescent sunshine.

But the world had changed, thanks to a cadre of women terrorists who had started their lives as abandoned, parentless refugees on the world's scrapheap. No oil, no gas, no coal, but unlimited power from the sun, had literally changed the face of the earth in less than six months.

No internet, few computers, or anything electronic that worked, changed the way we communicated, reminiscent of what we did as a species back in the 1950s and '60s.

Local, very much not global, except for certain military and private networks that had been protected at the time of the worldwide hack.

And millions upon millions of innocent people were killed by panic, chaos, and home grown militia that forced migration around the world on a scale never before seen. But thanks to the invention of a nanomachine by a brilliant young Israeli genius, herself a refugee, the world was slowly regaining hope as devices able to convert the sun's power more efficiently than ever thought possible popped up around the country.

That was the good news.

The better news was that Sandra *'just call me Sally'*, my partner in crime and the bubbliest person I had ever had the privilege to be around, and I were now enjoying the tropical sun together, sipping cold drinks in long glasses with little umbrellas in them, the images of the executions and what followed now just a dim memory.

"Did you get the banks to release the funds from the terrorists' accounts?" The Boss, lying flat on his stomach, his lounge chair buckling from his weight, squeaked as he moved his head to look at me. Behind him, Pete, recovering from three bad bullet wounds, was asleep on his back, snoring slightly, while his inamorata, a world-class cellist, slept beside him. If you didn't know, you would only see a group of friends relaxing around the pool without a care in the world.

If you tried to come over and be our friends, large well-dressed people would politely stop you, throw a million words at you in Italian so fast your head would ring, then turn you around to where you had started. If there was one thing other than his monstrous expresso machine that Indigo guarded with his life was us, which was stupendous because it allowed us to act like normal people when we were anything but.

"Yes. We had to threaten them with Red Notices, but Sandra got the last of the funds early this morning, and the monks now have several billion to play with. I have given them a list of what we need funds for and requested another fifty minicomputers. Stefarino was very happy, a lot of his private funding dried up because of the terrorist attacks, and he is linking our Italian headquarters to his cavern. He sends his regards and wants to have a conversation with you at some time." I received a grunt for my trouble and decided to drink more of the wonderful green thing that sloshed around in my glass. It tasted like a tropical fruit bomb, but had a sensitive kick on the palate that was unmistakably a high-quality rum base of some sort.

I looked up as Indigo returned, accompanied by a beautiful woman, who I recognized as Fay Remer, our latest recruit from the FBI. Like Sandra, she was positively glowing, having just completed the Interpol boot camp, which had the driest international legal subject matter in the known universe. She had then completed the physical training for attachment to Section Five, and that was obviously what had put the color in her cheeks. The fact that she was dressed in the skimpiest bikini with a flowing silk thing over her shoulders didn't fool me for a second.

"Commander, great to see you. At last, thanks for the invite." A guard hastily set up another sun lounge, and she plopped a handbag big enough to hold a child, a towel, a smaller bag which I assumed held her weapon and credentials, then a huge floppy straw hat.

"Intend on staying long?" Sandra asked, mumbling over her drink as she shielded her face from the sun with one delicate hand as she looked up at Fay. Fay just laughed, plonked down on the lounge, and pointed to my drink.

'I'll have one of those, thanks, Indigo." He beamed at her. I promise you, his whole face lit up.

"*Sarà un piacere per me, e scusa questo maleducato qui, la farò rimuovere se lo desideri!*"

"Yeah, you can try!" Sandra didn't exactly mumble, but the humor came through, and obviously, Indigo's invitation to throw her out of the pool area hadn't concerned her in the least. Indigo took the cowards way out when faced with determined women and left to organize Fay's drink.

"How was the training?"

"Excellent. The HALO (High Altitude, Low Opening) jumps were the best, and the one we did in daylight was over Sardinia, and that's a sight I won't forget in a hurry."

"What about the weapons training? Learn anything new?" Sandra was getting into the swing of it now, sitting up next to Fay, looking like a supermodel in her multi-colored top, baseball cap, and aviator glasses. Between her and Fay, I would forever look like the ugly sister.

"Yes. How much the modern squad weapons weigh, and how loud a flashbang is without ear protection!" They both laughed. In my day, the big event was surviving the gas chamber without a mask, but that test now seemed old school.

I let them bubble on and turned back to the Boss.

"Have you spoken to Roger lately?" Roger was the head of the FBI and a lifelong friend of the Boss's, and had been one of the instigators in involving Interpol in solving the terrorist attacks. He looked at me with one eye open, the other shut, and it squeezed his face into an even more distorted look than his usual scarred appearance.

"Earlier today. All good on his end, they have three plants up and running, and they are happy to maintain the status quo for the time being." I gave him my hardest look over the top of my sunglasses, but half-naked, with a silly drink in my hand, it was difficult to pull off bad arse. He just closed his open eye and shrugged, causing the lounge to squeak again.

"What do you mean 'for the time being'?"

"You don't goad the bear in his own cave and expect to come out unscratched." I settled back. To a certain extent, I had anticipated what the Americans might do by placing the UN in charge of the international distribution and installation of the ecological plants that had been designed and built by the terrorists. And left the nanomachines firmly in the hands of Israel and Amira, who was now one of our agents attached to the Israeli Security Service. Or, in truth, was an Israeli agent attached to Interpol.

"I had hoped that they would at least play the gracious savior for a while longer." He turned to face me, both eyes open this time, his serious look anchored between his scars.

"They took a huge hit-the Catholic and Jewish, and for that matter, Muslim communities in the States are quite large, West Point was an attack on their very militaristic soul, and the smart way the terrorists pushed the immigration of thousands of refugees on them still rankles." I nodded, put my drink aside, and considered my next move. I pulled my towel off my lap and dived into the pool.

The water was crystal clear, comfortably cool, and invigorating. I lazily swam a few laps, letting my muscles warm up, testing my recovering shoulder a little, wishing this quiet time could last a little longer. But the Boss had been pulling in information from all over the world, and all his nefarious contacts in the deepest and darkest places on the planet said the same thing.

In the vacuum created by the terrorist attacks, the lack of fuel, water, and food, and an almost complete lack of international will, was driving the creation of a whole new subset of bad behaviors.

And there was a new actor on the block with the resources and the skills to cause several of our supporting member countries to become very nervous.

I smelt a hard stop to our little vacation down the road.

And in countries where camels, horses, and donkeys were viewed as state-of-the-art transportation, and hard men and women made their living off the land, the balance of power had once again shifted away from technology and civilization to campfires and word of mouth. And no intelligence agency in the world had ever been particularly good at intercepting the spoken word, often in dialects unknown outside of tribal boundaries, without their agents literally losing their heads in the process.

Afghanistan was the center of it all. In the half-decade since the American withdrawal, it seemed that an endless series of new versions of ISIS had erupted, spewed their venom and hatred on anyone in their sights, mostly unarmed and innocent civilians, then self-destructed like one of their suicide bombers. But there were rumors emerging of a newly formed group, disciplined, as yet unnamed, and unidentified, working with some sophisticated weaponry. Didn't know what that was all about and didn't want to until it was on our radar.

We had just spent shy of two months fighting to save the planet, literally, and we needed to decompress, heal our wounds, find our centers as people, not puppets, and regain our balance. When you killed a person one-on-one, no matter the circumstances or how righteous that kill was, it affected you deeply, and you couldn't just shrug it off and pretend nothing had changed.

Unless you were a narcist and a sociopath. And if you were, you would not be working for the world's preeminent anticriminal and antiterrorist organization, Interpol.

I let the water flow over me like a liquid blanket, upped my tempo, pleased with the lack of any twinges or discomfort in my shoulder. The doctors had done a good job, and the physiotherapist that had been assigned to me, straight out of an East German gulag, I swear, had worked me to the bone, cheerfully destroying any excuse I came up with to evade her massive hands. The only good thing I had to hang onto was Pete telling me his recovery from his wounds had been worse than mine. But he didn't have that haunted look he had just a month ago, so he must be close to fully recovered.

The next thing I knew, I was sinking to the bottom of the pool, the sound of crashing water filled my ears, and the rolled-up body of Pete was sitting on my back. We both bobbed back up to the surface, spluttering and laughing like loons, most unladylike and certainly not the done thing in a prestigious military organization. I funneled water into my hands and pushed it into his face, having the time of my life. His laughter lifted my spirits. I had been worried about him, he had been shot three times while protecting me, and while I was not the cause, I always felt I was the root. Being around me could be a very hazardous occupation.

"Children, children, play fair. No hurting each other unless you mean it!" Pete ignored the Boss, and reached over and dunked me again. Now I had options. I could punch him in his manhood, pull him under and drown him, or just let him have his way with me.

Seeing his live-in partner of some fifteen years looking at us over her blue-tinted glasses, with a smirk on her face, lying back and talking it seemed the best option. He let me up, still laughing like a loon but staring to look like the shooter I had entrusted my life to on more than one occasion. The new scars were only obvious from the old ones because they still looked like painted-on pale, puckered healing holes on his otherwise suntanned skin, and his ropy chest muscles flexed and rippled in a very nice manner.

It was hard to believe that it was less than a month ago that I had helped load him onto an Israeli C-17 with blood running freely down his chest from three bullet holes that clustered just below his collarbone. And I had been shot as well, but that seemed trivial at the time. And for the life of me, I couldn't remember why.

I drifted to the side of the pool, completely relaxed for the first time in days. "You look relaxed."

"I am. How're the wounds?"

"Getting me plenty of sympathy, Jenny and I are off back home tomorrow. The Boss has made it clear I'm off call for at least the next six weeks."

"You'll go stark raving mad," I said, climbing out of the pool. He grabbed the side of the pool and levered himself up and out with a nimble twist of his lean body that had more scares than I remembered. But then, I hadn't seen him naked for quite a while.

"Has Jenny got any concerts planned?" He looked over at his life partner, smiled when she grinned at him and turned back to look at me.

"Yes, one in New Zealand, a benefit for their recovery program. They have resettled nearly two thousand children in the site they built on the Wairoa River at Dargaville. The New Zealand government has approved the construction of ten more townships spread across the country, and that means that another twenty thousand girls will be taken in. There are families putting their hands up from as far away as Samoa."

"Chalk one up to Mohammad bin Azaria and 'Helen'." I didn't let the bitterness creep into my voice, but it took all my effort not to. He gave me a hard look, but I suspect he saw what was under my less-than-warm response. He just nodded and walked back to Jenny. I reached for a towel and sat back on my couch. The Boss had one eye open again, a sure sign I was going to get blitzed.

Not quite.

"One thing I picked up from Arie this morning, you might find interesting. Just as the French promised the world that they would remove the radioactivity from the Arabian oil fields, persons unknown clagged up the wellheads all the way across the desert and shut it down permanently." I sat up, this was news, and it might mean that we had missed one of the mercenary terrorist groups.

"Do we know who did it?"

"No. And the French, as you can imagine, are seriously pissed about it."

"Why? Surely the radioactivity was enough. Those fields were out of action for thousands of years."

"Seems like the tech heads got it wrong. They changed their forecast to less than thirty years, and within a week of that being made public, the well heads and pipelines were attacked with the nanomachines, and that ended that."

"Who had that capacity? That would have taken five or six simultaneous attacks across different countries, those fields were the biggest in the world."

"Maybe, but out of play since yesterday. Think about who had the nano technology-the canisters from Canada, the ones we collected. Amira estimates that it only needed around four to do the job. And no, before you ask, she hasn't been cooking up nano bugs out the back of Mossad, and she assures me that the nanomachines in use in the plants would have a different effect on raw oil. No, this was someone left over from the original attacks, someone we missed, being very selective and very, very fast." I thought about it and couldn't see how it could have been done without state-level resources and, most of all, a supply of nanomachines. Who? How? Did it matter? There weren't any oil or gas pipes or coal fields anywhere as far as I knew that hadn't already been attacked, so was this a once-off?

"Arie's view is that the 'shut it down' message that Trotsky had us broadcast was incomplete. No way to prove it, one way or the other, and Arabia and the French are pursuing it themselves, don't want anyone else involved."

"Do you think there are mercenary terrorists connected to 'Helen' still out there?"

"Don't know. There is no movement in the bank accounts that we tracked, according to the geeks. We have one hundred percent of them locked away, matched by the data from the accountant and from Trotsky's own files. It is possible that there are some stragglers out there, but unless we get asked by one of our member nations, we're out of it for the time being." I thought about that, let it roll around my mind for a bit, then just nodded. Yes, we were out of it, but Interpol, in the main, would remain connected to the data and keep us informed of anything that looked like we should get on our bikes again.

Interpol was a huge international coordinating intelligence and data gathering agency, with one hundred and ninety-four member nations, and the agents neither had the power of arrest nor carried guns. That's why Section Five was created, providing a military-trained and well-equipped group that was working with a sponsor country and backed by the Intelligence from Interpol, could arrest and carry weapons and use them with deadly force on those occasions that demanded it.

A shadow fell over me, and I looked up to see Indigo standing at ease, smiling, but with two of his burly guards flanking him.

"Commander, you have a call in the conference room, if you please?" I stood, causing Sandra to stir on her couch, then she was up like a cat. Her energy really was incredible.

"Hi, Indigo, where are we going?" she asked in her bubbly voice as she wrapped a lightweight gown over her bikini.

"*Tenente, il Comandante ha una chiamata sicura nella sala conferenze. Possiamo accompagnarla se preferisci stare al sole?*"

"*Grazie, Indigo non vale l'ira del Boss per lasciarla andare a giocare da sola!*" I just laughed. Arguing about who would escort me was a battle I would never win, so I walked with Indigo and was shadowed by Sandra. She had also been promoted within the tight ranks of Section Five the moment she had qualified some two weeks ago. Fay still had the nominal rank of Senior Special Agent (SSA-FBI), but that would change as her training caught up to her. The ranks were equivalents, simply so other military forces could see where we fit. In our system, a Colonel was the equivalent of a two-star general and a Commander a one-star.

Indigo was the odd man out, still holding his rank in the Italian Carabinieri Special Intervention Group (CSIG), as well as being our head of operations in Italy. But what mattered the most in Section Five was how well you could think under pressure and how well you could shoot. Yes, we were the police force, but one structured to work on any continent or in any jurisdiction, cross any border, and deal with anything that our member nations needed help with.

We went into the smallish conference room and found Malcolm's cheery face center screen, with Luigi and Shami in little boxes underneath.

"Sorry to spoil your holiday, Commander, but what would you interpret this as meaning?" A line of Irish floated into the center of the screen, with Malcolm a faded shadow behind.

"*Éiríonn fir na bhFiníní arís*" I looked at it very hard, racking my brain. The Finnians had been the center of the Irish rebellion for tens of years, an organized terrorist group that had been very hard to put down, but in my mind, there hadn't been any mention of them for some time. The IRA had well and truly taken over their bailiwick and then, in turn, been beaten down to just the occasional flicker of annoyance.

"The Fenian men rise again," I translated, looked at the screen, dialed up some data on my minicomputer, and read it with interest.

In 1858 the Fenian League of Irish was formed in the United States, dedicated to promoting revolution and the overthrow of the English Government in Ireland. They raised money and even a small army of expatriates, who were to sail to the SireLand around 1862-3 and wage war. This rag-tag army was also called 'The Fianna'. They were not successful.

"The Fianna Fail party of Eanmon de Valera was elected to the Dail Eiream in 1927. They are still a predominant Party in the Irish Parliament. Fianna Fail means 'The Armed Men of Ireland.'

I flicked the data up onto the big screen and gave everyone on the call enough time to read it and absorb it.

"Why do you bring it to our attention?"

"We found this posted on an old bulletin board that survived the Internet hack, and on it was a picture of a training camp. We'd been tracking training camps in Afghanistan for some time, just a satellite flyover every now and then, no schedule they could prepare for, then a year ago, it just disappeared. Exactly the same as your 'black holes' we solved recently. So we applied the same technology, and guess what?"

"You found the camp again."

"Yes. That's not the real concern here."

"What is then?"

"Who's in that camp."

"Malcolm, don't play games, please; I was enjoying the sun and a lovely tall drink with an umbrella in it." The words disappeared from the screen, replaced by three facial recognition photos with their distinctive yellow grid lines. My heart skipped a beat, and I felt Indigo stiffen.

"Al Bar al Shirak. They blew up the shopping centers in Israel, linked to our mercenary terrorists, but used the remote control devices developed by the women to drive the vehicles. That's Amir Abbas, one of Hamas's top leaders, and Malik Badawi, he's a Bedouin thought to be one of the leaders of this group. Who's the woman? And has Arie seen these?"

Shami's head grew in size until he filled half the screen. He looked stressed, tired, and in need of some comfort.

"Commander, yes, Arie has seen these pictures. He's the one who told us to contact you. The woman is Irish, or so her passport says. She is suspected of being one of the very heavy hitters in the Republican movement. She was on every watchlist but slipped through with this identification which somehow managed to be inserted in every system across Europe. Sound familiar? And she fits the profile we built for you three months ago when we were chasing the original women terrorists."

"So she could be a refugee pulled out of the camps and placed with an Irish family?"

"Yes."

"Didn't we arrest two Irish women in Helena?"

"Yes, both very young, but they came from Ireland-Elizabeth Kane, Moya O'Halloran-one, a writer, the other a painter, supposedly to write the history of the Westhall property, and there's no proof of their families, which again, fits the profile of the women terrorists."

"Where's the money?" Sandra had remained quiet until now, but I could feel her vibrating beside me.

"Good question. No data on it, not from Mohammad bin Azaria's files or the accountant, Shetani's files, or Trotsky's."

"It could be in Ireland, Afghanistan, or any damn where, and based on our experience so far, it will be a lot of money they have to play with."

"Wait! Ireland was one of the countries that were designated for an environmental plant and migration of children. Where was their funding lodged?" Shami's face reduced in size again, to be replaced by Luigi's.

"A trust account set up six years ago in the family name of Charles Stewart Parnell the Third, and if that isn't a clue, I don't know what is."

"Parnell. That name rings a bell all the way back to the eighteen hundreds and the 'Home Rule' movement. And the Fenians tried to usurp British rule in Ireland with a serious uprising during the first World War."

"Okay, enough already. Who has control of the trust?" Silence was the answer for around three minutes. Then Luigi held his hand up as if to stop traffic.

"A firm of Accountants, name of Reganit and Sons, Belfast. Who the beneficiaries are is under seal."

"Break it." Then I thought how rude that sounded. "Please." My holiday in the tropics had not really improved my humor, and I could tell I was anything but centered and in balance. I started to wonder what might change that.

Then I had a brilliant idea.

"Sandra, get the G4 ready. We're going to Chicago." She looked at me with surprise all over her face but nodded and reached for her minicomputer.

"Thanks, everyone. Follow up and keep me posted. I'll be available via my mini for the next three days." And I walked out of the room, leaving a few startled faces on the screen and one or two in the room.

I mentally composed a text to the Boss-*'running away for three days, taking the jet, let me know where to come back to.'*

Packed in record time, met Sandra at the portico where a black-windowed limo waited, handed my bag to the Italian guard, who practically fell over trying to bow and collect my luggage in the same movement and climbed into the cool of the limo. "Chicago's your home base?" I looked at Sandra, dressed as usual, like a runway model, all flowing curves and exotic colors. How anyone could ever mistake her for an Interpol agent was beyond me, but she cheered me up, and right now that was the most important thing on my mind.

"No, not really. It's where I was posted early last year. I was in Ukraine chasing some of the stragglers from your people smuggling op. Just as a matter of interest, how many of us are there in Section Five?"

"Not as many as we would like. We have pairs here, and there-Japan, the UK, and a few spots in the EU backed up by single agents who are ostensibly Interpol but trained by us; we call on them as needed. The original concept was a hard-core team of five or so; that could collect assets as needed, but that didn't last very long due to the caseload. So the answer is today, including Fay, our most recent recruit, probably twelve full-time, and another six on the fringe." Sandra's reaction was not what I expected. She smiled and bounced around on her seat.

"Fantastic! So I got a guernsey because of my cross-training with the FBI counter-terrorist group and SWAT in Chicago." I couldn't help but smile back. Her energy was infectious.

"That's the direct result of the Boss being able to negotiate with military and law enforcement seemingly everywhere. I don't know how he made all his contacts, but his system works. And we steal the best of the best from everyone, but only a little at a time, so no one gets pissed at us."

"Like Fay." We both paused our conversation and swapped the limo for our jet, settled in, then picked up where we had left off as the roar of the engines took us to another world.

"Exactly like Fay. She managed her team exquisitely well in Point Roberts, then again in Seattle, and Helena, took on everything thrown at her, and in case you didn't know, she is only twenty-eight, and was already a Senior Special Agent with the FBI. That takes some balls." Sandra nodded, thinking to herself.

"And for full disclosure, she is a refugee just like the women we chased down, so she and Amira have a lot in common." When she turned to look at me, it was with her deep blue eyes wide open as if I had zapped her with a Taser.

"So where does Pete come into it? I get Tom and his crew, even Bob and his, but as I understand it Pete joined you and the Boss right at the very start. How does a retired Master Chief get called up by Section Five?"

"Easy. Pete worked with the Boss in a former life in the Teams. When Section Five was formed, the Boss recruited Pete to devise the training program, and run it for the first year, which he did, then retired back to his home in northern Australia. The Boss calls him in from time to time when we need a hard-core shooter, which on this operation, we thought we would." She nodded to herself again, fitting the pieces of the Section Five puzzle together.

"Indigo runs Interpol Italy?"

"Yes, and more besides, he manages Interpol resources across six or seven countries as well as Italy."

"And he's a member of Section Five?"

"One of the very first the Boss recruited. He also makes the best expresso in the known world, and I'd have him on my team just for that alone."

"So the Section Five 'outliers' as I'll call them, work for Interpol in the usual manner, until we call them up, yes?"

"Yes. An example is our Interpol agent in Islamabad-Drishya Singh. She moved there from New Delhi, runs the office out of the barracks of the Pakistani SSG (Special Forces), nothing unusual until we knock on her door, she guns up, changes her credentials, and goes to war for us. Exactly the same as Nokomoto Senji and Aikido Namoki in our Tokyo office, although they spend most of their time working for us because of the large volume of criminal activity in that region."

"They are the ones that broke up the Innomatchi operation."

"Yes. Took some of Tokyo's finest in with them, killed around twenty heavily armed yakuza and a few private guards, and took the head of that organization into custody, located the ship sets, then shut the company down. The way they tell it, they didn't even get a bruise in the gunfight." Again, Sandra smiled, her face lighting up.

"I'd like to meet them." I looked at her and tilted my head to one side.

"Be careful what you wish for." I closed my eyes, parked my head on the side wall, and let myself go.

www.ingramcontent.com/pod-product-compliance
Lightning Source LLC
Chambersburg PA
CBHW020427130626
46549CB00001B/12